Understanding a Child's World

READINGS IN INFANCY THROUGH ADOLESCENCE

Pamela Cantor

Boston University

McGraw-Hill Book Company

*New York   St. Louis   San Francisco   Auckland   Bogotá   Düsseldorf
Johannesburg   London   Madrid   Mexico   Montreal   New Delhi
Panama   Paris   São Paulo   Singapore   Sydney   Tokyo   Toronto*

This book was set in Times Roman by Black Dot, Inc.
The editors were Richard R. Wright and Barry Benjamin;
the cover was designed by Judith Michael;
the production supervisor was Robert C. Pedersen.
The drawings were done by Scalor Publications, Inc.
R. R. Donnelley & Sons Company was printer and binder.

UNDERSTANDING A CHILD'S WORLD: Readings in Infancy through Adolescence

1 2 3 4 5 6 7 8 9 0 D O D O 7 8 3 2 1 0 9 8 7

Photo on opposite page by permission of
Sissy Krook, photographer.

Library of Congress Cataloging in Publication Data

Main entry under title:

Understanding a child's world.
    1. Child psychology. I. Cantor, Pamela.
BF721.U567   155.4   76-54174
ISBN 0-07-009766-6

Dedication

To my mother, for her constant urging to get things done and her pride in my accomplishments; to my father, for his confidence in all that I do and his unconditional love regardless of what I do; to both my mother and my father, for the happiness I live every day but can never repay; to my brother, for sharing all my tribulations and providing continuous support and humor; to my husband, for enduring the deprivations caused by a professional wife and for providing love and support, advice and patience; and most of all to Lauren, who has taught me all that I know and how much I do not know about the most valuable experience in life—giving life and love to a child. Of her I beg forgiveness for all the hours this project took from our time together and I thank her for all the happiness she gives to me in the time we have.

To my family—

My thanks and my love.

Contents

Preface   **xii**

PART ONE   THE PRENATAL PERIOD

Chapter 1   Conception and Birth   **3**

The Prenatal Environment
   John Paul Scott
   "The Prenatal Development of Behavior"   **3**
   from *Early Experience and the Organization of Behavior*

Chapter 2   Heredity and Environment   **15**

Interaction between "Nature" and "Nurture"
   Peter Wolfe
   "Heredity or Environment"   **15**
   from *Pregnancy, Birth and the Newborn Baby*

PART TWO   BIRTH TO AGE THREE

Chapter 3   Birth   **29**

The Birth Process
   Doris Haire
   "The Cultural Warping of Childbirth"   **29**
   from *International Childbirth Education Association News*

   Frederick Leboyer
   "Part One"   **44**
   from *Birth without Violence*

Reflex Behaviors
  T. Berry Brazelton
  "The Newborn's Equipment"   **54**
  from *Infants and Mothers: Individual Differences in Development*

Sensory Capacities of the Infant in the First Few Weeks of Life
  Jerome Kagan
  "The Determinants of Attention in the Infant"   **61**
  from *American Scientist*

Important Issues Concerning the Neonate
  Marvin S. Eiger and Sally Wendkos Olds
  "Should You or Shouldn't You?"   **72**
  from *The Complete Book of Breastfeeding*

  David B. Lynn
  "Father's Child-rearing Approach"   **83**
  from *The Father: His Role in Child Development*

Chapter 4   Physical Development   **99**

Motor Development or What the Baby Does
  Nathan H. Azrin and Richard M. Foxx
  "Mrs. James Potty-Trains Mickey"   **99**
  from *Toilet Training in Less than a Day*

Chapter 5   Mental Development   **109**

Learning the Language
  Courtney B. Cazden
  "Suggestions from Studies of Early Language Acquisition"   **109**
  from *Language in Early Childhood Education*

Measuring Infant Intelligence
  Burton White
  "From Eight to Fourteen Months of Age"   **115**
  from *The First Three Years of Life*

Chapter 6   Personality Development   **125**

What Emotions Do Babies Have?
  Selma Fraiberg
  "How a Baby Learns to Love"   **125**
  from *Redbook*

The Infant in the Family
  Susan Goldberg and Michael Lewis
  "Play Behavior in the Year-old Infant: Early Sex Differences"   **133**
  from *Child Development*

Harry Harlow
"The Nature of Love"   **142**
from *American Psychologist*

Melford E. Spiro
"Infancy"   **152**
from *Children of the Kibbutz*

PART THREE   THE PRESCHOOL YEARS

Chapter 7   Physical Development   **167**

Abused and Neglected Children
   David G. Gil
   "Violence against Children"   **167**
   from *Journal of Marriage and the Family*

Chapter 8   Mental Development   **182**

Cognitive Concepts of the Preschool Child
   David Elkind
   "Giant in the Nursery"   **182**
   from *New York Times Magazine*
   "What Does Piaget Say to the Teacher?"   **194**
   from *Today's Education*

Learning in Preschoolers
   Bettye M. Caldwell, Charlene M. Wright, Alice S. Honig,
   and Jordan Tannenbaum
   "Infant Day Care and Attachment"   **197**
   from *American Journal of Orthopyschiatry*

Play in the Life of the Preschool Child
   Brian Sutton-Smith
   "Children at Play"   **213**
   from *Natural History Magazine*

Chapter 9   Personality Development   **221**

Sex Typing
   Phyllis Taube Greenleaf
   "Liberating Young Children from Sex Roles"   **221**
   from *Liberating Young Children from Sex Roles:*
   Experience in Day Care Centers, Play Groups, and Free Schools

Children's Fears
   Robert Kastenbaum

"The Kingdom Where Nobody Dies"   **232**
from *Saturday Review*

How Child-rearing Techniques Affect Personality Development
Robert M. Liebert, John M. Neale, and Emily S. Davidson
"Congressional Inquiries into T.V. Violence"   **243**
from *The Early Window: Effects of Television on Children and Youth*

Diane Baumrind
"Parental Control and Parental Love"   **252**
from *Children*

PART FOUR   THE MIDDLE YEARS

Chapter 10   Physical Development   **263**

Health Problems of Children
Robert Coles
"Hidden Children"   **263**
from *Migrants, Sharecroppers, Mountaineers,* Vol. II of *Children of Crisis*
"Vitality and Violence, Life and Death"   **267**
from *The South Goes North,* Vol. III of *Children of Crisis*

Chapter 11   Mental Development   **274**

Moral Development in the School-age Child
Lawrence Kohlberg
"The Child as a Moral Philosopher"   **274**
from *Psychology Today*

The Child in School
Paul Goodman
"The Present Moment in Education"   **284**
from *New York Review of Books*

A. S. Neill
"The Idea of Summerhill"   **298**
from *Summerhill*

Chapter 12   Personality Development

Theoretical Perspectives on Personality Development
Arnold Gesell and Francis Ilg
"Seven Years Old"   **305**
from *The Child from Five to Ten*

The Society of Childhood
William Golding

"The Sound of the Shell"   **314**
from *Lord of the Flies*

The Child in the Family
J. Louise Despert
"When Children Experience Divorce"   **328**
from *Children of Divorce*

Lois Wladis Hoffman
"The Effects of Maternal Employment on the Child—
A Review of the Research"   **339**
from *Developmental Psychology*

PART FIVE   ADOLESCENCE

Chapter 13   Physical and Mental Development   **365**

What Is Adolescence?
Group for the Advancement of Psychiatry
"Cultural Factors in Adolescence"   **365**
from *Normal Adolescence*

Physiological Changes of Adolescence
Judith M. Bardwick
"Psychological Conflict and the Reproductive System"   **378**
from *Feminine Personality and Conflict*

Nora Ephron
"A Few Words about Breasts"   **392**
from *Crazy Salad: Some Things about Women*

Chapter 14   Personality Development   **400**

The Search for Identity
Erik H. Erikson
"Womanhood and the Inner Space"   **400**
from *Identity, Youth and Crisis*

In the Home
Bruno Bettelheim
"The Roots of Radicalism"   **405**
from *Playboy*

Teen Culture: Relations with Peers
Anonymous
"The Adolescent"   **414**
from *American Journal of Psychoanalysis*

Problems of Adolescence
    Alvin E. Strack
    "Drug Use and Abuse among Youth"   **418**
    from *Journal of Health, Physical Education and Recreation*

    Susan M. Fisher
    "Life in a Children's Detention Center: Strategies of Survival"   **426**
    from *American Journal of Orthopsychiatry*

    Pamela C. Cantor
    "Suicide and Attempted Suicide among Students:
    Problem, Prediction, and Prevention"   **433**
    from *Understanding A Child's World: Readings in Infancy
    through Adolescence*

Ego Strengths of Adolescence
    Kenneth Keniston
    "Youth: A 'New' Stage of Life"   **444**
    from *The American Scholar*

PART SIX   DISTURBANCES IN A CHILD'S WORLD

Chapter 15   Personality Development   **463**

The Preschool Years
    Erik H. Erikson
    "The Theory of Infantile Sexuality"   **463**
    from *Childhood and Society*

The Middle Years
    Virginia Axline
    "Chapter One"   **470**
    from *Dibs in Search of Self*

Adolescence and Youth
    Hannah Green
    "Chapter 5" and "Chapter 6"   **480**
    from *I Never Promised You a Rose Garden*

Help for the Severely Disturbed Child
    B. G. Tate and George S. Baroff
    "Aversive Control of Self-injurious Behavior in a Psychotic Boy"   **493**
    from *Behavior Therapy and Research*

Preface

The purpose of this reader is to present psychology as the study of human nature, a field which is attempting to explore such basic questions as what factors shape our emotions and our personalities. I have concentrated on what appear to be important areas of psychology while avoiding topics and jargon which are geared to the academician.

What I hope I have brought to this reader is what I hope to bring to my students. I want to open their eyes to the joys and problems of others, to help them to learn how to help a child reach his or her full potential, to learn that it is much better to give pleasure than to inflict pain, and that it is easier to hug a child than to hit one. This book should help future parents, teachers, nurses, and anyone who is interested in children to see psychology as exciting and real.

This book is different. There is, to my knowledge, no other book which offers a similar collection of current selections combined with classic materials. While it is important to be timely, it is equally important to retain the valuable material which was formulated in the past. Just as we would not remove the study of Freud from a course in psychopathology because he did not formulate his theories within recent years, so we should not remove the study of Harlow's work or the

theories of A. S. Neill or Robert Coles simply because they did not publish their theories within the past year.

The level of the selections, while generally not advanced, is purposely designed to have a wide appeal to students with varying backgrounds, fields of interest, and levels of preparation. No one group of students, regardless of the level of the course, is truly homogeneous. Levels of preparation and degrees of psychological sophistication and interest vary. A book comprised entirely of popular magazine articles or technical journal articles will miss a large number of students in any group. This book attempts to bridge the interest gap by providing something for everyone.

The approaches covered in the selections are also varied so as to provide exposure to the relevant theories—psychoanalytic, maturational, cognitive, and learning theory—as well as to major theorists such as Erikson, Gesell and Ilg, and Piaget.

The selections have been chosen from best-loved novels such as *I Never Promised You a Rose Garden*, *Lord of the Flies*, and *Dibs in Search of Self*; from popular magazines such as *Redbook*, *Esquire*, and *Playboy*; from contempory books such as *Birth without Violence*, *The First Three Years of Life*, and *Children of the Kibbutz*; from classic books such as *Summerhill, Childhood and Society,* and *Children of Crisis*; as well as from professional journals such as *American Scientist, Child Development,* and *The American Journal of Psychoanalysis.*

My purpose is to show that psychology is not reserved for the laboratory but is all around us. The materials I have presented are easy to relate to, enjoyable to read, and possible to apply. They are materials which students say they would read even if the selections were not assigned. The readings are not dry or technical, as they were chosen to appeal to the interests of students with a practical involvement in child development. The articles do not require an extensive knowledge of psychology—only an interest in human nature.

My book is geared toward the students I have been teaching for the past six years; students in child development, education, nursing, social work, adolescent psychology, clinical psychology, and counselor education who are not interested in running rats or in mastering highly technical journals. They want to know what makes children loving or aggressive, how to help them to handle frustration and anger, what role the father plays in development, what is the impact of divorce on the life of a child or of poverty on the life of the adolescent. They want to explore the nature of the human personality, of early affective development, of alternative educations or of psychopathology. The book covers the areas of child and adolescent development which are most relevant to today's students: natural childbirth, breast-feeding, day care, sex-role stereotypes, maternal employment, child abuse, television violence, discipline and death, among others.

The introduction to each article begins with

a quotation from the body of the selection in order to promote interest in the article. Then a discussion of the selection and of the topic under consideration follows. The introductions are personal and, I hope, engaging.

This reader has been carefully designed to mesh exactly, chapter by chapter, with *A Child's World: Infancy through Adolescence,* by Diane Papalia and Sally Wendkos Olds, a major text in the field of child development. The Papalia and Olds book covers the areas of child and adolescent development which are most relevant to today's students, and it does so in an extremely interesting manner. This reader could, therefore, be used in conjunction with Papalia and Olds, be utilized by itself, or be used in conjunction with any of the major texts in child and adolescent development.

This book was begun while I was pregnant with my daughter, Lauren, and is being completed after her second birthday. I had wanted to finish it long ago, but both the book and I have profited from the delay. While it has been nearly impossible to be a mother, wife, full-time teacher at a university and also serve a private clinical practice, appear on television and radio, and give speeches, it has been fruitful. The information which I am now able to bring to the book—information which no amount of theoretical training can provide and which comes from the experience of giving birth, nursing, waking up in the middle of the night for weeks on end, watching a child learn language and deal with happiness and frustration—has brought a great deal to my understanding of child psychology. I now understand that I will never understand. Each child is unique.

Pamela Cantor

Part One

The Prenatal Period

Chapter 1

Conception and Birth

THE PRENATAL ENVIRONMENT

The Prenatal Development of Behavior

John Paul Scott

Estimates indicate that each human being carries, on the average, two recessive lethal genes. . . . As a rule, however, the vast majority of babies are born with a reasonably good combination of genes and no crippling defects. Heredity thus operates very much like a lottery, but one in which the results are biased in favor of the gambler rather than against him.

Editor's Introduction

People have always been fascinated with the question of how life begins. A look at "recent" history will give some indication of the various theories which have dominated scientific knowledge at different times. In the Middle Ages, it was thought that the child was held in the womb, complete with all human qualities, as a miniature human being. In the 1500s, Leonardo Da Vinci proposed the theory, which was quite advanced for his times, that the infant in the womb was, in fact, attached to the mother and reliant upon her systems for survival. In the 1600s and 1700s, biologists held two prevalent views. The "homunculists" said that the individual existed in the head of the sperm and that the female served only as the incubator for the already formed being. The "ovists" believed that the preformed individual was contained entirely in the mother's ovaries and that the male sperm served only as the mechanism which incited the baby to expand. In 1759, Kaspar Wolff refuted these two theories and proposed the theory that both parents were equally responsible for the development of life. Fifty years later, Karl von Baer discovered the human egg cell under his microscope. In the 1800s, George Coghill studied embryonic behavior and expanded our knowledge of human prenatal development.

The following article, written in the 1970s, presents our current knowledge of prenatal development; it discusses the egg as environment and the effects of the prenatal environment on human development. We must remind ourselves, however, of the distinct possibility that just as we now examine and replace the "truths" of the earlier centuries, biologists will, a hundred years from today, replace the "absolutes" of the 1970s.

Pamela Cantor

When does behavior begin? The early biologists thought that human beings were preformed in the egg and that the embryo was a miniature baby which only had to swell up to the usual size in order to be born. However, the invention of the microscope soon showed them that human life, like all other life, begins as a single cell, the fertilized egg. Although chemical activity and movement occur inside it the egg shows no behavior, if behavior is defined in the strict sense of activity of the whole organism. Behavior therefore has to be developed, and developed under the influence of all sorts of internal and external factors.

Nevertheless, the egg develops in a very predictable fashion. Obviously, the human egg, if it develops at all, always develops into a human being rather than into a chicken or a rabbit or a fox. This predictable element in development is often attributed to heredity alone, but as we shall see, heredity is only one of many organized systems which control the development of behavior, and variations in any one of these will modify it in various ways. The end result is that, while all human eggs normally develop into recognizable human beings, no two of these things are ever exactly alike—not even identical twins.

HEREDITY AND BEHAVIOR

The first organized system to affect development is that of heredity. By this we mean the collection of fifty thousand or more gene pairs which are carried on the chromosomes of each individual. Each of these gene pairs can vary through the process of mutation, and the total genetic system of the human species consists of all of the genes carried by the billions of individuals now living. This is often called the "gene pool," because each individual withdraws a particular set of genes at birth and returns some of them to the common pool in the keeping of his own offspring.

The Chemical Nature of the Genes

It is now known that genes are composed of highly complex proteins known as nucleic acids and that they produce their effects through chemical action, either directly or by producing enzymes which affect other chemical reactions. This means that heredity can directly affect only chemical reactions, and therefore that all genetic effects on behavior must be indirect. Some genes affect growth and may produce the difference between a tall, long-legged individual who thus has some aptitude for jumping and a short-legged person who has less of this aptitude. Other genes affect the chemistry of pigment formation and so may determine the difference between a blond and a brunette, and thus influence his or her attractiveness to certain members of the opposite sex. But gene action can take place in other ways than through growth or structure. It may also affect any chemical reactions going on in the body at any time during life, including those processes directly concerned with nerve action. Therefore, these genetic differences can appear very early in development or at any time in later life. A well-known example of early effects is the disease of phenylpyruvic oligophrenia, marked by the accumulation of an unmetabolized chemical, phenylalanine, beginning at birth. This substance in turn inhibits intellectual development unless the condition is controlled. At the other end of life, the symptoms of Huntington's chorea, a degenerative disease of the nervous system produced by the presence of a dominant gene, may not appear until sometime in the forties, the individual having led a normal life up to that point.

The Principle of Variation

The heredity of any species of animals is an organized system which has the general function of producing similar individuals. At the same time, the system of transmission which involves the chromosomes carrying the genes is also one which has an opposing function, that of producing dissimilar individuals. Each parent transmits to a particular child only half of his chromosomes, and these are chosen purely at random. Since the genes carried on the chromosomes vary through the process of mutation, the chromosomes of each child are never exactly alike. Through the process of "crossing over," or exchange of genes between chromosome pairs, identical chromosomes are never available for successive offspring. Each time a sperm or an egg cell is formed, the chromosomes pair together, break in various places, and reconnect with the opposite member of the pair. The location of a break is a matter of chance. Consequently it is almost impossible for two genetically identical individuals to be produced except in the rare case of identical twins which come from the same egg. Even in this case, the two twin embryos grow up in different parts of the uterus and therefore live in different environments from the very first moments of life.

Yet this genetic variation can exist only within certain limits. If a mutation or an unusual combination of genes produces too great a disturbance in the total genetic system, the individual may not be able to develop properly and may die at some stage of development.

Genic Disturbances of Development

When a gene is chemically altered, the result is called a mutation. The nature of such changes has been extensively studied in fruit flies and also in bacteria. Mutation rates vary considerably, as some genes are much more stable than others; but on the average a particular gene will mutate in one out of every million individuals in each generation under normal conditions. This rate can be greatly speeded up by X rays. In fact, radiation either from X rays used as clinical tools or from radioactive materials forms a major modern hazard to the genes.

Newer discoveries of the chemical nature of the genes have made it possible to produce mutational changes in bacteria deliberately. Unlike mutations produced by X rays, these are specific in nature, and geneticists now anticipate the future possibility of producing controlled mutations in the higher animals and in man.

However, a gene is one part of an extremely complex system composed of 50,000 or more similar parts, all adjusted to and interacting with each other. A change in any one gene is much more likely to disturb the normal functioning of the system than to improve it. To use a mechanical analogy, reaching into an automobile engine and turning a screw at random is much more likely to disturb the running of the engine than to improve it. Similarly, the effect of the vast majority of chance mutations is deleterious. Many of them result in the early death of the embryo, and others produce various anatomical and physical malfunctions which may have an effect upon behavior.

Chromosomal Disturbances of Development

Changes in the normal form and numbers of chromosomes may occur as the result of faulty cell division. Ordinarily the pairs of chromosomes divide and separate equally, and each daughter cell gets the normal number. Occasionally, however, a chromosome pair may stick together, with the result that one cells lacks a chromosome and the other has one too many. The condition of Mongolian idiocy is produced by such a chromosomal accident; here the individual has three of one particular chromosome instead of the usual pair. Very frequently such chromosomal abnormalities result in early death of the embryo, but in this case the individual is viable enough to be born and live for at least a few years, although he is highly susceptible to certain kinds of disease.

Similar abnormalities in the distribution of other chromosomes also have anatomical and behavioral consequences, and those concerning the sex chromosomes have particularly interesting effects on behavior. Ordinarily, the female human being has two X chromosomes,

and the male has an XY. When two chromosomes do not separate, the result may be more than the usual number of either X or Y chromosomes. In the human species, the result can be to suppress or distort the development of the various sex organs and thus affect both bodily appearance and fertility.

The assortment and transmission of either chromosomal or genic abnormalities are almost completely matters of chance, and their occurrence can consequently be predicted only in terms of probabilities. Estimates indicate that each human being carries, on the average, two recessive lethal genes. Whether or not these affect the next generation depends upon whether or not the individual selects a mate who carries the same lethal genes. The frequencies of genes which are not lethal but have deleterious effects on behavior are known in some cases. For example, albinism, which totally removes pigment from the skin, hair, and eyes, occurs in about one out of 20,000 individuals and affects behavior in that the eyesight of an albino individual is very weak and in that he cannot expose himself to sunlight without suffering burns.

As in the case of albinism, most genes that produce unfavorable effects tend to be rare. Perhaps the commonest gene of this sort is that producing color blindness, which affects one out of twelve males and one out of 100 females. As a rule, however, the vast majority of babies are born with a reasonably good combination of genes and no crippling defects. Heredity thus operates very much like a lottery, but one in which the results are biased in favor of the gambler rather than against him. There is always an element of risk, but an individual has a good chance to draw a favorable combination of genes from the gene pool.

THE EGG AS AN ENVIRONMENT

The genes themselves operate within the environment of a cell, and the first contact of the newly organized genetic system formed by fertilization is with the cytoplasm of the egg. This itself is a system of organic chemicals organized under the influence of the mother's genes and developed in the environment provided by her ovary. Experiments with the eggs of lower animals show that even if the nucleus is removed, a properly stimulated egg will go through the first few cell divisions without the presence of the genes. The cytoplasmic system comes under genic control only gradually, and its condition modifies the action of heredity.

After the egg is formed in the ovary, half of the chromosomes and the genes carried with them are discarded, with the result that when the set of chromosomes from the father is brought into the egg with the sperm, the new individual has the same number as the parents. This means that in every case the genes of the new individual begin operations in an environment (the egg) which was produced under the influence of a different set of genes. Ordinarily this produces no difficulty, but if the genes are sufficiently different, development may be disturbed. This effect is shown by experiments in which the nuclei from salamander eggs are removed and those from a different species are substituted. In some cases development proceeds fairly well, but in others it soon comes to a halt, indicating that there must be a different chemical organization of eggs developed under different heredities. This principle would also apply, but with less drastic effects, to eggs normally produced and fertilized in the same species.

In addition to these gene-induced differences in the composition of the cytoplasm, the eggs can be modified by environmental factors or simply by the passage of time. There have been few attempts to actually alter the chemical constitution of eggs, but it is well established that if an egg is not fertilized soon after being shed from the ovary, the chance of normal development decreases. Presumably the egg deteriorates with age; in other words, a stale egg has a lessened chance of normal development.

Ordinarily eggs are developed under highly protected conditions within the body and so provide a highly uniform environment for the action of the genes. Each mother should therefore produce eggs closely similar to each other, except for rare environmental accidents and, of course, the fact that each one carries a different set of genes.

PRENATAL ENVIRONMENT

Homeostasis

As the French physiologist Claude Bernard pointed out long ago, a great many physiological processes are concerned with maintaining a constant internal environment. The American physiologist Walter Cannon called the phenomenon *homeostasis* and established it as one of the broad general principles of physiology.

As a result of homeostatic activity, human body temperature is ordinarily regulated within a fraction of a degree and with a dependability not exceeded by the finest of mechanical thermostats (there are few thermostats that will continue to operate for 70 or 80 years). Consequently the human embryo develops at a uniform temperature within its mother's body. In the early stages its cells and tissues are extremely delicate, and it is protected from the effects of touch and contact by being bathed in fluids. As it grows older the embryo develops within the amnion, a fluid-filled sac. Thus it is actually living under water, receiving equal support in all directions, and is little affected by gravity. No light reaches the embryo, and sound can reach it only through vibrations in the surrounding fluid.

The chemical environment is likewise highly regulated. The mother's liver has the function of regulating the food substances in the blood so that there is no wave of new chemical substances after each meal. This organ also has the ability to denature many poisonous substances which may enter the blood stream. Oxygen and carbon dioxide are kept at relatively constant levels by alterations in rates of the mother's breathing and blood circulation.

Under ordinary conditions, a cyclical fluctuation occurs in the female hormones connected with the menstrual cycle. During pregnancy, a more stable condition is maintained with the result that the embryo is given a uniform environment in this aspect throughout prenatal development.

In spite of all these mechanisms for maintaining stability, homeostasis may sometimes be upset, as it is in the case of disease which produces a fever. In a time of famine, a mother who is actually starving may be unable to maintain a sufficient supply of food substances within her blood stream to maintain the growing embryo. Under other conditions, the liver may be unable to manage certain drugs and poisons, especially if the mother takes these in large quantities. At very high altitudes, the mother may be unable to supply the embryo with enough oxygen. Finally, hor-

monal balance may be upset by violent emotional experiences which affect the hormones produced by the adrenal glands.

The possible effects of upsetting homeostasis and thus altering the prenatal environment can only be ascertained by experiment, and studies are now being made with various lower animals. While the results cannot be transferred directly to human development, certain general principles have been established regarding the times at which variations in the prenatal environment produce important effects.

The Principle of Critical Periods

Table 1-1 shows the major periods of early human development and their approximate timing. In general, the most drastic effects upon development are produced before the fetal period, which begins at approximately three months. Furthermore, in the periods preceding this, the earlier a disturbance is produced, the more general and the more drastic are its effects. For example, a disturbance during the period of cleavage may result in the separation of the egg and the production

Table 1-1   Major Periods of Prenatal Human Development

Period	Approximate age after conception	Major processes
Cleavage	0	Cell division; growth begins
Implantation	9–10 days	Improved nutrition, acceleration of growth
Germ-layer formation	2 weeks	Organization of growth processes
Embryonic organ formation	3 weeks	Nerve tube, somites, limb buds, etc., formed by differential growth
Adult organ formation	5 weeks	Embryonic organs transformed by tissue formation into functional organs
Fetal	8 weeks–9 months	First motor behavior; organization through nervous stimulation begins

of identical twins or, less fortunately, in the production of Siamese twins or even a double monster. Disturbances in the period of germ-layer formation may result in part of the brain failing to develop.

The time of implantation is a critical period, for if the egg does not become attached to the uterus it is discharged and lost. Likewise, the period of forming the attachment of the placenta is critical, because without this form of nutrition normal development cannot proceed.

Most injuries during these early periods either result in the death of the embryo or in such a drastic alteration of form that the individual cannot survive beyond birth. However, during the period of embryonic organ formation damage may be much more specific and not as lethal. A dramatic example of a non-lethal effect resulted from the administration of thalidomide to pregnant women. This drug has a specific effect on the development of the limb buds, with the result that otherwise normal infants were born without arms or legs.

Minor disturbances affecting the embryonic organs result in less drastic effects. The embryonic eye is one of the most susceptible of these organs, because even a minor change in the shape of the lens or eyeball will drastically upset its future function. A large number of eye defects are probably caused by accidental embryonic damage.

The general principle of critical periods is based on the fact that any organ or part of the body which is undergoing rapid organization—and hence rapid growth—is unusually susceptible to damage. In the early periods of development when whole areas of the body are being organized, the effects of such damage are widespread and general. Later on, when specific organs or parts are being organized, the results are less drastic. We can therefore say that for each sort of effect there is a critical period at some time in development.

This same principle of critical periods limits the effects both of the chemical action of the genes and of chemical disturbances produced by various environmental accidents. There is no way of determining by inspection whether a particular kind of variation in development is produced by heredity or environmental factors. The only way to be sure is to experimentally demonstrate that the altered development is preceded by a specific change, or to show that the same condition is also present in the individual's relatives in a pattern consistent with Mendelian inheritance.

The Effects of Experience during the Fetal Period

The fetal period is usually defined as starting when movement of the body begins, and extending up to birth. It is therefore the time during which behavior actually begins. The fetus is far less susceptible than the early embryo to environmental changes, and the period is characterized primarily by growth in size rather than by rapid changes in organization.

One would expect, therefore, that environmental factors in this period would have their chief effect on growth. For example, experiments with other animals show that the size of the mother has considerable effect upon the size of the baby, irrespective of genetics.

Horses belonging to the very large breed of draft animals known as Shires have been crossed experimentally with Shetland ponies. The colt receives the same heredity no matter which way the cross is made, but the newborn colt born to a Shetland pony mother is smaller than one born to a Shire mother. The difference is apparently caused by the fact that a larger placenta develops in the Shire. Consequently, more food is received by the growing embryo. The same principle has been established even more clearly by taking fertilized eggs from a small breed of sheep and transplanting them into a mother from a large breed. The newborn lambs are much larger than they would have been had they developed within the body of a small mother (Hammond, 1961).

The only human evidence we have of such uterine environmental effects is that afforded by twins, which are smaller on the average than babies from a single birth and hence have a somewhat smaller chance of survival. Here again, there is probably only a limited amount of room within the uterus for the development of a placenta or placentas.

Because the fetus grows so remarkably within the space of six months—from an embryo an inch or two in length to a newborn baby weighing six pounds or more and measuring approximately ten times as long—we should not suppose that the development of the various organs is complete. Of particular importance is the development of the endocrine system, which exercises chemical control over physiology and behavior.

The fetal period is also the time during which many of the basic biological characteristics of sex are determined. It has long been known that if the male hormone is accidentally given to a female fetus, it will produce masculinization. Such masculinization frequently appears in the case of twins in cattle. If a male and female are born together and there has been some intermixture of blood in the two placentas, the female turns out to be sterile and is called a freemartin.

Why does a human mother not show the effects of the male hormone when she is carrying a baby boy? Male hormones are sometimes given to women for medical reasons, and one of the undesirable side effects is the growth of facial hair in a masculine pattern. However, pregnant women are completely resistant to the virilization effects of the hormone. During pregnancy a mother produces as excessive amount of the female hormone, estrogen, and this apparently protects her against the action of the male hormones of her unborn boy.

As we have seen above, unborn female infants (at least in some species) are not protected against the effects of male hormones. Young and his co-workers (1964) have shown that injecting male hormones into a pregnant monkey bearing a genetically female fetus will produce a masculinized infant that not only shows sex organs which appear to be those of a male but also exhibit more masculine behavior than normal females. The hormone therefore modifies the development of the nervous system during the fetal stage, as well as modifying the external appearance of the individual.

Ordinarily, the developing fetus is protected against the kind of drastic interference with development which can be produced experimentally, but various accidents happen often enough so that pseudo-hermaphrodites do occasionally occur among newborn human babies. Is such a baby doomed to abnormal behavior? As we shall see in a later chapter, human behavior is highly adaptable, and up to a certain age the human infant can readily adapt himself to either sex role, even though lacking the complete biological basis for it.

Another part of the endocrine system that develops rapidly during the fetal period is that which regulates physical reactions to the stress of pain, injury, and emotional excitement. This regulation is accomplished chiefly through the hormone cortisone, produced by the cortex of the adrenal gland. Thompson and his colleagues (1962) have trained female rats to become fearful and nervous by giving them electric shocks in a particular box. After they have become pregnant, they are placed again in the box and repeatedly given the same treatment but without the electric shock. The effect is to make them afraid without actually hurting them while they are carrying their unborn young. The offspring of these rats are more nervous and fearful than those from control mothers, even if they are raised by foster mothers which have never had the frightening experience. These results correlate with the observation made on wild rats brought into the laboratory that there is a considerable reduction in "wildness" after two or three generations even when no genetic selection is made for tamer animals.

Whether or not this effect could be duplicated with experiments on human mothers is still unknown, and in fact, verification would be almost impossible because of the tremendous individual variation among human beings, even if mothers would consent to being frightened. The most that can be said at present is that such a possibility does exist, and it is known that the unborn babies of mothers undergoing emotional disturbances are more active than those of calmer mothers. Many circumstances, however, determine whether being an anxious and nervous individual is an asset or a liability. In times of real danger, a nervous individual might be more likely to survive than a stolid one.

Moreover, this maternal effect on emotionality is not the same phenomenon as that described in the old wives' tales of "prenatal impressions," which were based on notions of sympathetic magic. According to these tales, a mother frightened by a horse might have a baby with a birthmark which looked like a horse, and so forth. No known mechanism exists by which such an effect could be produced.

Prenatal experience may affect later behavior in more severely damaging ways than the above. Determining the time when a prenatal disturbance of the maternal environment took place is not always easy, but in any woman whose medical history is known, it is at least possible to know that complications of pregnancy such as toxemia have actually occurred. Pasamanick and Knobloch (1961) studied the relationship between prenatal experience and certain behavioral disorders and found that cerebral palsy, epilepsy, mental deficiency, and behavior disorders were correlated both with complications of pregnancy and with prematurity. They believe that these effects were probably the result of oxygen deficiency produced by such conditions as toxemia and maternal bleeding.

They further found that these damaging prenatal experiences and their associated behavioral deficiencies were more commonly found in mothers coming from lower socio-economic levels than in mothers from more prosperous homes. Since a disproportionate number of Negroes were found in lower economic levels, the figures for defective children were proportionately higher among Negroes. In addition, the experimenters found that an unusual number of neonatal deaths resulted from pregnancies initiated in the spring, that is, in pregnancies whose first three months occurred during hot weather. Again, the effects were much more severe for mothers in the lowest economic levels. While no 1:1 correlation exists between poverty and prenatal damage, it is difficult to avoid the conclusion that the condition of poverty in our society produces a circular effect. Children born of poor parents are more likely to have certain defects, and because of these will be less likely to be able to provide their own children with a favorable prenatal environment.

Providing the unborn infant with an adequate supply of oxygen appears to be particularly important in the last stages of pregnancy when the fetus is becoming quite large. Babies born at high altitudes—especially those of over 10,000 feet—show a much higher rate of prematurity and hence run a much greater risk of neonatal death (Grahn and Kratchman, 1963). This condition applies to a few areas in the Rocky Mountain states and is, of course, much more severe in some of the South

American equatorial highlands, where many people live and work at altitudes of 14,000 feet or more. Historical records show that in the early days of the Spanish conquest there were no living children born to Spanish families at the high-altitude city of Potosi (13,120 feet) in a period of over fifty years (Monge, 1948). When one child finally did survive, the event was officially listed as a miracle. Presumably by a process of selection, the native Indian children were and still are better able to survive at these high altitudes, but even they as adults show the physical effects of stress produced by lack of oxygen and exposure to ultra-violet rays.

In addition to the disturbances of the prenatal environment produced by unfavorable external conditions, the mother in any environment herself changes with age and so affects prenatal development. Figures on neonatal mortality show high death rates both in babies carried by young girls and by older women, indicating that the most favorable period for child bearing is the early twenties, with a moderately favorable period on either side extending from 15 to 35 (see Table 1-2).

Similar results are obtained with other mammals. Very young mothers are less efficient, both physiologically and behaviorally, than those who are fully mature, while very old mothers have weaker offspring and are less able to suckle them. This does not mean that an individual is inevitably doomed because he is born to a very young or a relatively old mother; in human populations many normally hardy and healthy children are born under these circumstances. The probabilities of good health, however, are somewhat poorer for them than for children born to mothers in the mid-range. Parents who have a choice are wise to have their children during the most favorable age period.

In addition to these studies of the indirect effects of fetal experience upon later behav-

Table 1-2   Fetal Death Ratios by Age of Mother in 34 States in the U. S.

(Gestation 20 Weeks or Longer)*

Age of mother (years)	Ratio: 1000 live births
Under 15	26.6
15–19	14.7
20–24	11.7
25–29	13.7
30–34	19.0
35–39	26.9
40 and over	38.7
Total, all ages	15.5

*Most states do not require registration of deaths taking place before 20 weeks, so that the great majority of miscarriages are not included in these figures. Note that the most favorable age of the mother for fetal survival is 20–24 years.
Source: Vital Statistics of the United States, 1964, U.S. Public Health Service.

ior, many studies have been made of fetal behavior itself. As any mother knows, her unborn baby becomes active enough to be felt at about four months of age and becomes increasingly so as it grows older. Early fetuses obtained as a result of operations or miscarriages show reactions to tactile stimulation as long as they survive. Such results indicate that much of the reflex behavior of a neonate appears long before birth.

Perhaps the most interesting studies are those of behavior of babies being carried by normal mothers who cooperated with the Fels Institute for the Study of Human Development (Sontag, 1944). Observers could readily detect and measure kicking, squirming, and hiccoughs through the abdominal wall of the mother, and found that babies are active about 15 per cent of the time at four months of pregnancy, increasing to 35 per cent by eight months. If a sudden vibration is applied to the mother's abdomen, the result is the startle or Moro reflex, accompanied by an increase in heart rate. The fetus will also respond to loud sounds received by the mother's abdomen through the air. The fetus is of course surrounded by water, which is an excellent transmitter of sound. Moreover, the mother is continually stimulating it by producing changes in internal pressures through breathing and other bodily movements.

Attempts have been made to condition the prenatal startle reflex, but the difficulty with all these experiments is that it is almost impossible to stimulate the fetus with anything that is not perceived by the mother. Since the fetal infants seem to condition more readily than neonates, it is quite probable that the mother is the one who is being conditioned rather than her offspring. In any case, the amount of information that a fetal infant could learn and organize within the highly protected and stable environment of a normal mother's body would be extremely limited, even if it possessed good learning capacities. Attempts to put adult individuals into similar situations in tanks of warm water and without sensory stimulation tend to produce disassociation and disorganization of behavior.

It is therefore possible to conclude that the effects of changes in the prenatal environment are largely physiological rather than psychological in nature. From the biological viewpoint, fetal behavior has chiefly a physiological adaptive function. Movements promote circulation, prevent the formation of adhesions to the surrounding membranes, and help develop and strengthen bones and muscles.

GENERAL EFFECTS OF PRENATAL EXPERIENCE

Prenatal development proceeds under the general control of three organized systems: the heredity of the individual, the egg and the composition of its contents, and the prenatal environment produced by the mother. Disturbances in any one of these systems can pro-duce variations whenever they occur in the course of development, and hereditary and environmental factors can operate to produce such disturbances at any time in prenatal existence. The effect of a disturbance depends largely upon the stage of development. The most drastic effects are produced when particular processes are proceeding most rapidly. Thus numerous critical periods occur in development, that for one process being different from that in another, or perhaps overlapping with it. The same process may take place at different times in different organs, so that the timing of critical periods may be different for different organs. In general, the earlier the disturbance is produced, the more drastic the effects.

In this chapter we have given many examples of the deleterious effects of prenatal experience, chiefly because these are the ones which are easiest to produce and measure experimentally. However, there must be many minor effects which are less harmful and even beneficial.

The preponderance of harmful effects may also be related to the fact that it is easier to upset a highly organized system than to change it to produce a superior kind of organization. Moreover, we cannot deny the importance of such upsets. At least 20 per cent of all human pregnancies never come to term, and the figures for animal experiments, where the data are more accurate, run as high as 40 per cent. In human cases many terminated pregnancies undoubtedly occur without being reported, and if the egg dies early enough, the mother may never even notice it.

Such prenatal deaths should not be considered as tragedies, as the vast majority of them concern highly defective individuals produced by variations in either heredity or environment. In most cases it is a much greater tragedy if such a highly defective individual survives beyond birth.

Obviously, most variations in the prenatal environment are completely outside conscious control. The most that a mother can do is to make sure that she is leading a healthful existence and to give herself good physiological care and relatively placid surroundings. Most environmental accidents to which she herself is subjected will be taken care of by the normal homeostatic processes of her body. She should, however, guard against prolonged exposures to strong chemicals or drugs, which may enter her body either through food or through the air she breathes. She can also consult a clinic on medical genetics if she suspects that heredity diseases which she might transmit to her child are present in her family.

STUDIES IN SPECIAL TOPICS

De Fries, J. C. Prenatal maternal stress in mice: Differential effects on behavior. *Journal of Heredity*, 1964, 55, 289–295. The effect of prenatal stress depends upon the heredity of both mother and offspring.

Grahn, D., and Kratchman, J. Variation in neonatal death rate and birth rate in the United States, and possible relations to environmental radiation, geology, and altitude. *American Journal of Human Genetics*, 1963, 15, 329–352. High altitudes tend to cause premature births and greater neonatal mortality.

Hammond, J. Growth in size and body proportions in farm animals. In M. X. Zarrow (Ed.), *Growth in living systems*. New York: Basic Books, 1961. Pp. 321–334. Effects of maternal body size on prenatal growth.

Monge, C. *Acclimatization in the Andes*. Baltimore: Johns Hopkins Press, 1948. Fascinating historical account of the effects of high altitude on reproduction and mortality.

Pasamanick, B., and Knobloch, M. Epidemiologic studies on the complications of pregnancy and the birth process. In G. Caplan (Ed.), *Prevention of mental disorders in children*. New York: Basic Books, 1961. Pp. 74–94. Studies of the effect of the environment on maternal health and resulting behavioral defects of children.

Sontag, L. W. Differences in modifiability of fetal behavior and physiology. *Psychosomatic Medicine*, 1944, 6, 151–154. Studies on human behavior before birth.

Thompson, W. R., Watson, J., and Charlesworth, W. R. The effects of prenatal stress on offspring behavior in rats. *Psychological Monographs No. 557*, 1962, 1–26. The effects of maternal emotional states on the behavior of young rats.

REFERENCES

Anderson, V. E. Genetics in mental retardation. In H. A. Stevens and R. Heber (Eds.), *Mental retardation*. Chicago: University of Chicago Press, 1964. Pp. 348–394. Review of genetic factors affecting human intelligence.

McKusick, V. A. *Human genetics*. Englewood Cliffs, N. J.: Prentice-Hall, 1964. Defects produced by hereditary factors.

Reed, S. C. *Counseling in medical genetics*. Philadelphia: W. B. Saunders, 1963. Practical human problems resulting from genetically produced defects.

Young, W. C., Goy, R. W., and Phoenix, C. H. Hormones and sexual behavior. *Science*, 1964, *143*, 212–218. Prenatal effects of the sex hormones.

Chapter 2

Heredity and Environment

**INTERACTION BETWEEN "NATURE"
AND "NURTURE"**

Heredity or Environment

Peter Wolfe

From the moment of conception to the moment of birth, heredity and environment contribute to development as inseparable factors. Although the distinction between heredity and environment may still be useful for some technical discussions, it is an artificial abstraction that has no direct reference to actual developmental processes.

Editor's Introduction

Are personalities made or are they born? What part does environment play in shaping behavior? Notions about the relative importance of heredity and environment are part of our popular folklore. There are those who believe that heredity is the sole determinant of behavior, while others believe that the environment can cause limitless modifications in behavior. The environmentalists are presently enjoying greater favor in academic circles due to the current political, social, and historical trend to conceive of all persons as identical genetically except for the genes which determine appearance. It is out of vogue to suggest that other differences exist. Further support for the environmentalists has come from research which indicates that the appearance of a particular trait at birth is not proof of its genetic origin but instead may be due to prenatal influences. For instance, an infant's emotions at the time of birth may be due to tranquilizers or other drugs given to the mother during her pregnancy or during the birth process rather than to the infant's genetic heritage.

Despite the current dominance of the environmental theories, heredity is of great importance. Differences in susceptibility to stress, preference for alcohol, and also motivation and temperament are thought to be determined largely by heredity. In fact, it has been found that in the first months of life infants display a predominant temperament or behavioral pattern which persists relatively unchanged into adulthood. Aspects of behavior such as activity level, rhythmicity, adaptability, the tendency to approach or withdraw from novel situations, mood, threshold of pain, and attention span may be biologically determined. If these traits are due to heredity it is then possible that compatibility or incompatability will come to exist between a child's innate temperament and his environment. Compatability of innate traits with a child's environment will generally mean a healthy development while incompatability may lead to disturbance in behavior. In other words, a very active child may be born to parents who also have a very high activity level and all will be well. But if the same child were born to parents with far more lethargic temperaments, an incompatability might result which could lead to problems for the child.

So in actuality, heredity and environment interact with each other in determining an individual's behavior, although heredity and environment make proportionately different contributions to different traits.

Pamela Cantor

At some point in her pregnancy every woman wonders what her child will be like. Will it be a boy or girl? Will he resemble either of his parents? How will he behave? Did the pregnancy leave any harmful effects? Will his behavior in early infancy be any indication of what he is to become?

Most of these questions go back to an age-old controversy about the influence of heredity and environment on the developing child. Primitive peoples who pondered the same questions tried to answer them in their mythologies. Universal concerns about the effects of the environment are also reflected in the superstitions and folkways by which parents try to protect the unborn child against harmful influences. As late as the last century many persons still believed that a woman who had seen a rabbit (hare) in pregnancy might produce a child with a cleft (hare) lip. Even today one sees pregnant women in rural America and Western Europe who wear amulets to ward off the evil eye or other malign influences.

In the sixteenth century some philosophers advanced elaborate arguments to establish at what precise moment the soul enters the human fetus. One school of physiology pictured the fetus as a tiny but completely formed human being (the *homunculus*) who entered the mother's womb in the male sperm and there simply marked time until he reached sufficient size to be born. This naïve explanation of fetal growth and development did not stand up against the systematic study of anatomy and physiology any better than the environmentalist view, but in its essence the philosophy of predeterminism survived well into the nineteenth century as a psychological doctrine that assumed that the child is ready-made and complete in all his faculties before he is born.

Advocates of either the extreme environmentalist or preformist positions have lost ground, yet the controversy goes on. Is environment or is heredity the major influence on the traits of the offspring? One might expect that by now the vast apparatus of modern science would have found the answers. Yet when we get down to the all-important details, the same debate still engages students of behavior. How completely determined at birth is the future course of development? To what extent are intelligence, temperament, appearance, and personality already fixed at birth? How much influence does the environment exert to bring about radical changes in young babies? It turns out that no collection of facts can resolve this issue because environment and heredity are only arbitrary distinctions about a single unitary developmental process.

To attempt here an explanation of all that is known or surmised about the genetic (inherited) influences on development would take us far afield, but we can sketch certain crude facts (necessarily oversimplified) to give some perspective. We know that forty-six microscopically visible, rod-shaped structures called *chromosomes* are to be found in each one of the millions of cells in the human body. These chromosomes carry the *genes*, which are the basic material for the transmission of inherited traits. In the past ten years, we have learned a great deal about the complex protein chemistry of these genes, but the ultimate meaning of these discoveries tends to fade when we try to apply our current knowledge to those aspects of human behavior with which parents are primarily concerned. Can we say that the genes have *caused* this or that specific trait in the fully formed infant? Usually not. On rare occasions we can say that a specific deviation from the expected norm in structure or behavior—that is, a variation from the pattern we see in the great majority of infants—is genetic in origin. However, it makes no sense to discuss genetic factors as if they alone were responsible for the enormously complicated patterns of structure and behavior that in sum compose an individual personality.

Some persons have blue eyes, others brown. In the last hundred years, . . . scientists have found a simple and quite consistent mathematical relation between the color of the eyes of married couples and the color of the eyes of their descendants. When a blue-eyed man and a brown-eyed woman have children, it is possible to predict on a statistical basis how many of their grandchildren (but not which ones) will have blue eyes and how many will have brown. The further along the line of descent we go the more involved the mathematics becomes, but the principle holds, or so we believe. Our observations on the transmission of eye color in families have been so consistent that we feel justified in regarding this physical characteristic as an inherited trait that follows a precise genetic law.

Our certainty about the genetic basis of eye color comes from a combination of facts. Eye color is a well-defined, clearly visible, and limited difference between individuals. We have no trouble separating the blue-eyed from the brown-eyed members of a family, and we can count how many are in each set. We have *numbers* to deal with when we talk about eye color, and numbers are the language of science. With somewhat less assurance we can assert a genetic basis for some other physical differences among individuals, the color of skin or hair, say, but the less specific the trait is the more complex the genetic relationship becomes, and the more difficult the task of deciphering the mechanisms of inheritance. It is also possible to speak of inheriting particular diseases such as phenylketonuria (PKU) or hemophilia. In certain instances it is even possible to demonstrate that a single gene is responsible for the transmission of a disease from parent to offspring. But how do we account for the fact that all normal babies are born with two arms, two legs, and one head? Is the "genetic determination" of those "traits" the same sort of process as the "genetic determination" of PKU or blue eyes? The formation of arms on the human embryo depends on much more than a single or a single set of genes, and it is impossible to identify a particular gene or set of genes as being responsible, since a host of interrelated factors, perhaps an uncountable number of them, must be involved. Some of these will have to do with specific genetic properties of particular chromosomes but these do not "cause" the formation of arms or legs. They interact with many other factors as parts of a more inclusive plan, one that establishes the properties of all living systems and fixes the direction and the boundaries of growth as well as limiting the uses to be made of experience.

For most of the attributes that make the human baby what he is we cannot point to any single gene and say, "This is responsible." The gene does not operate in splendid isolation. Generally, a gene produces its effect in relation to other genes on the same chromosome and genes on other chromosomes. Even in the cell, the fundamental building block of a human being, it is impossible to make a clear separation between heredity and environment. The cytoplasm (intracellular tissue) surrounding the nucleus is not associated primarily with genetic functions, but it does contain substances that influence the direction of development by mechanisms similar to the functions of the nuclear genes. Each cell in turn is surrounded by other cells that are part of that cell's environment and influence its functions. Groups of cells compose an organ, and the organ itself is influenced by other organs. The embryo made up of many interrelated organs is embedded in the wall of the mother's uterus and derives all its nutrient from the mother's bloodstream. Throughout the pregnancy, therefore, the survival of the fetus depends on the adequacy of the physiological environment. From the moment of conception to the moment of birth, heredity and environment contribute to development as inseparable factors. Although the distinction between heredity and environment may still be useful for some technical discussions, it is an artificial abstraction that has no direct reference to actual developmental processes.

Identical twins are often considered to be nature's experiment for demonstrating the pure effects of heredity, because both organisms by definition have the same chromosomal or genetic constitution. Yet even identical twins may be very different in appearance and behavior at birth.

Identical twins may, in fact, differ considerably in their birth weights; and such differences appear to be associated, at least in a statistical sense, with differences in the course of their respective psychological developments. Although we have no clear idea at present why birth weight should make any difference in the course of psychological development, we can be reasonably certain it is not due to differences in genetic makeup. When the single egg from which the twins comes divides to make two separate organisms, the two embryos will be embedded in different regions of the uterus and their cords attached to different parts of the placenta. Hence, the twins will have different access to nutriment in the womb; in other words, they will be inhabiting different environments. At the moment of birth, one or the other of the twins must be born first, and he will prepare the way for his twin. Although he may experience difficulty during the birth process while widening the birth canal, his twin may be suffering some lack of oxygen while awaiting his turn. So despite their same genetic endowment, identical twins do undergo distinct experiences before, during, and after birth; and even in the earliest stages of development these different experiences help to make them into distinct individuals.

So it makes no sense to speak of *the* environment as if it were some well-defined feature that is sharply distinguishable from inheritance and remains constant throughout the individual's developmental life. But it is useful to make a first rough distinction between the *pre*natal and *post*natal environments of the infant. Let us think of the influence of the parental environment as limited to the provision of chemicals, nutriment, and oxygen to the cells and mechanical protection to the fetus—in other words, to maintenance of the minimal conditions necessary for the physiological growth and development of an embryo into a recognizable member of the human species. In the nine months of pregnancy the organism is not required to make delicate adjustments to the constant changes of our everyday physical world, but only to exist and grow in conformity to a built-in blueprint.

Immediately after birth the baby is bombarded with an infinite variety of novelties. This stimulating, specific new environment gives rise to the sensory impressions from which he will develop his knowledge of the world. To be sure, even in the mother's womb the fetus is not altogether isolated from the environment as we usually think of it. If the mother has been exposed to German measles in the first three months of pregnancy, if she has taken certain drugs or not been nourished adequately, the baby's development will be influenced, usually in a harmful direction. But the effects are almost always nonspecific and make themselves known only by their interference with normal development. As long as the prenatal environment remains relatively generous and neutral, the fetus will develop in a direction that is uniform for the species. Any individual differences noted at birth usually will be the expression of differences in genetic makeup collaborating with differences in the intrauterine environment.

Isolated experiments have suggested that babies can be "conditioned" before birth, more or less according to the methods outlined by the Russian physiologist Ivan Pavlov, who trained dogs to salivate in response to the ringing of a bell. For example, recent experimenters have reported using similar techniques to teach unborn infants to kick whenever they hear a particular sound through the walls of the mothers' abdomens. If these experiments could be corroborated more generally, we might have to modify our ideas about whether or not the prenatal environment can have a specific influence upon the unborn baby. In the same vein, there has been inconclusive speculation about the effects that the mother's emotional state can have on the unborn child. We know, for instance, that emotion can influence the hormone output of the mother's endocrine glands. We know also that major changes in the hormonal environment of the embryo can have a profound influence on the infant's behavior in later life. Since the mother's hormones can pass through the placenta to become part of the fetal environment, it is not unreasonable to speculate that they might have an indirect but specific effect on the behavior of the fetus. But in comparison to the radical changes that occur the instant a baby leaves the womb, these influences on the unborn are, as far as we know, of relatively minor importance—except, of course, in pathological situations.

From the state of comparative weightlessness provided by the amniotic fluid, the baby at birth passes almost instantaneously to a state where he must maintain his position against gravity. Now he must start breathing on his own and suck in order to feed. He is no longer protected against cold, or against noise and the painful knocks of the outside world. He must accommodate to constant change, which can at times be overwhelming. It is true that from the moment of conception the baby is subject to the effects of environment, but the process of birth represents an abrupt shift from a comparatively neutral environment to one making continual, and continually increasing, demands on him. How well equipped is he at birth to cope with this relentless external world?

Methodical observation of babies on a scientific scale to find out how they actually behave is a relatively recent undertaking. The first American to insist upon this approach to psychology was Dr. John B. Watson, founder of the Behaviorist school, who began his work at Johns Hopkins University around the time of World War I. He took the extreme position of picturing all human behavior as not much more than a mechanical response to external stimuli. Not many modern psychologists would accept this simple view, but Watson's influence has nevertheless been long lasting.

Until twenty years ago the prevailing picture of the baby (greatly influenced by Watson's original work) was an amorphous, vegetative creature able to suck, cry, sleep, urinate, and defecate and exhibiting a few isolated reflexes, but otherwise unstructured and for the most part indifferent to everything except those events that relieved his immediate bodily tensions. This view implied that the baby was not much more than an empty receptacle, whose development would depend almost entirely on the stimulus he received from his environment. In this scheme of things every act of a parent involving the baby was of vital importance because it was thought that parental actions and influences were filling the empty receptacle and thereby establishing the character and personality of the child.

Nowadays, our picture of the infant is quite different. The theoretical inferences that Sigmund Freud drew from his studies of adult psychiatric patients gave us a new conception of the psychology of the young organism. Anna Freud's clinical observations and the work of others along the same lines altered our view of the emotional development of young children. And from the meticulous studies of the Swiss biologist and psychologist Jean Piaget we have received a new interpretation of children's intellectual development. Empirical studies of the last two decades have taught us that the infant is remarkably well organized at birth, and not merely with respect to the reflexes required for maintaining posture, eating, eliminating, sleeping, and withdrawing from a painful stimulation.

We now recognize that the baby is not a passive being, haphazardly registering whatever sense impressions the environment may offer. He is an active organism that selectively takes in and processes those environmental events that have meaning for him. In other words, the baby participates in his own development, and to some extent guides its course.

A mother feeding her baby for the first time will discover that he "roots"; that is, he turns his head to the side where his cheek or lip is touched, and moves with considerable accuracy toward the touching nipple or finger. She may also notice that her baby grasps a finger when his palm is pressed. From the first day infants can fix on a light and follow it with their head and eyes when it is moved in their field of vision. They will turn to a source of a sound when it is presented at the right or the left side but not when it is presented above or below the head. Whether a newborn infant responds in different ways to different word-sounds remains a matter of debate, but babies do seem to react with greater interest to such complex noises as the human voice than they do to pure tones. Likewise, infants stare longer at some visual patterns than others; if the duration of gaze is a criterion of interest, then infants seem to "prefer" relatively complex visual patterns to simple figures.

The perceptual capacities of the newborn are probably far greater than we have dared to believe. We can infer much from our studies of animals. For instance, although the eyes of a newborn kitten are closed, the animal is born with a very detailed network of neural connections that link particular cells in the retina (the receptor region of the eye) with the various brain centers, including the visual cortex. When the kitten opens its eyes for the first time, this complex visual apparatus is capable of analyzing geometric shapes into particular brain patterns. We can only conclude that kittens are born with the capacity for pattern recognition. By inference, it is reasonable to assume that the human infant is similarly capable of pattern recognition long before he can show us that he has learned to discriminate forms.

It is far from settled how many of the older child's capacities are learned, or how many of those capacities have been there all the time as latent abilities, awaiting only the appropriate environmental conditions to show themselves. The recognition of "size constancy" is an example of such latent abilities. This is the ability to perceive that two identical objects are of the same size even when they are presented at different distances from the eye. Though the closer object projects a larger image on the retina, we still know that the objects are of the same size. If our knowledge of the real world depended purely on sense impressions, we would always see the nearer of two identical objects as being larger than the more distant one. Because of our capacity for "size constancy" we are able to make the appropriate adjustments that take distance into account when judging size. Whether size constancy can be taught at any age is questionable. Certainly, it is difficult to imagine how a child learns it in the first several weeks—yet we know from experiment that normal infants have acquired size constancy by the end of the first month.

Linguists have pointed out that the capacity to learn a language cannot be taught, yet with very little in the way of specific instruction the child manages to learn at least the rudiments of the particular language of his environment. In consequence, linguists assume that the infant is born with latent capacities to decode and abstract some general features of the language from samples of speech he hears, and that from this very limited information he can put together new sentences of his own, which are grammatically correct. Whether the rules of language can be taught at an early age or not, at least the child exhibits a feeling for grammar long before anyone has ever taught him grammar.

On the strength of current observations, it is likely that the patterns of crying in the infant—the pitch, the intensity, the duration of the sound—vary with the provoking cause. We have no proof that the infant *intends* to vary his cries and no way at present of finding out what the baby does intend. Yet he can send out different kinds of vocal signals depending on his different discomforts. Among lower animals such systems of vocal communications are far better developed, and although their sounds are not a true language in the human sense, they nevertheless constitute a complex system of vocal communication. The human infant's signals are not so differentiated or specific.

Whether the human newborn does or does not smile is a question that resolves itself into an argument over definitions. Certainly, the grimace we call a smile appears in the newborn; indeed, it can be seen in premature infants born ten weeks before term. Moreover, the newborn's smile is not just a sign of "gas," as many persons (including some pediatricians) contend, since we can get the infant to smile more or less on order by making certain sounds. We cannot say whether the infant is "happy" when he smiles, for we have some reason to assume that the smile is at first not a signal of social recognition at all but the reflex response to certain stimulations. But to accept this limitation is not to deny that the mechanism for smiling is present at birth.

As we saw earlier in this chapter, babies can be "conditioned" even before birth. Further experiments have shown that newborn infants can "learn," that is, that they can be trained to respond consistently to signals when the signals are accompanied by "reinforcement." By certain modification of Pavlov's classic conditioning methods, young infants can be trained to turn their heads to the right side when they hear a pure tone or to the left side when they see a flashing light. They can also be trained to make refined visual discriminations. Such experiments make it clear that the newborn infant can indeed "learn" in a limited sense.

At the same time, we must remember that the range of response to which the infant can be conditioned is probably quite limited. Almost certainly, the psychologist's methods of conditioning are qualitatively different from the intellectual processes required for acquisition of language, formation of symbols, and mathematical abstractions. While the baby does "learn" through conditioning, it would be meaningless and mischievous to assert that with these techniques one can train the baby to do almost anything as long as the teaching materials are properly programmed, or to argue that the acquisition of intellectual skills is determined by the same "laws" of learning that have been found so successful in teaching rats to run mazes or seals to jump through hoops. The human baby is neither a black box nor a rat but a well-structured organism with his own ground plan, his own timetable of development, and his own style of acquiring knowledge about the real world.

A comprehensive list of things that babies can do on their own at birth, or can be made to do by environmental controls, would be much longer than the foregoing discussion suggests. The picture that emerges from even these few examples is a far cry from the concept of the helpless, amorphous organism that vegetates in blissful indifference to the world around it. Despite his apparent helplessness, the infant is actively engaged with his surroundings. He takes in sights, sounds, smells, and other sensations and organizes them into experiences with meanings; moreover, he sends out social signals that exert some control over the people who are biologically "programmed" or psychologically willing to respond.

Nevertheless, there are obviously many things that the young baby cannot do for himself. In many ways he is truly helpless, so that a generous and compliant environment must always be available if he is to survive. He is particularly helpless when it comes to changing the physical environment by his own motor action, and he of course must be nurtured for months and years before he can fend for himself. To be fed and kept clean and warm are his most immediate needs requiring outside attention. Since he is acutely sensitive to the novelties of the environment, he must also be protected against excessive stimulation. Yet he appears to thrive better when he is regularly exposed to a moderate amount of patterned stimulation. Keeping him too long in total isolation from the normal environment (as may sometimes happen in the sterile surroundings of a nursery or orphanage) may retard his development. The evidence on this point is fragmentary, and should not precipitate us into a hysterical program of overstimulating young babies. Our current impressions in this matter have been influenced by observations of premature infants who for good medical reasons were isolated from human contact for long periods of time. Premature infants were found to become more active and to gain weight faster when they were picked up and handled as often as possible and as early as good medical practice would permit.

Another source of evidence leading to the view that children need stimulation, particularly human stimulation, comes from clinical observations on institutionalized children and more recently from reports about children growing up in the hopeless circumstances of unrelieved poverty and social disorganization. Orphans, for instance, may receive the best physical care, but if it is given under sterile conditions where human contact is kept to a minimum, the children are much more susceptible to illness and infection. They gain weight more slowly and may even die from the effects of social isolation. In contrast, infants in the same institution who are picked up regularly by caretakers and exposed to the usual amount of human contact will develop normally. Certainly thriving or not thriving does not depend on a mysterious love substance that flows between mother and infant, and the critical factors can probably be rationalized in scientific terms. The fact remains that infants (and probably newborn infants) fare better when they are in close proximity to a caretaking person, who in most cases will be the mother. Up to six months or even beyond, it does not seem to matter very much whether this person is always the same individual. One caretaker can replace another without doing the infant great harm.

The experiences of the children brought up in the communal setting of the kibbutzim in Israel suggest that the constant presence of a single mothering figure (the ideal of our conception of the nuclear family) is not as essential to healthy development of the child as we have been led to believe. Within the well-defined social organization of the group nursery designed especially for the life of the kibbutz, children do prosper, even though they spend most of the day apart from their parents. Nevertheless, we should not draw unwarranted conclusions from these special conditions. Success in the case of the kibbutzim probably rests on the fact that the social context of the nursery is an integral part of the kibbutz society as a whole, not an idiosyncratic pattern of child rearing adopted by some individual families. The experience with children of the kibbutz cannot simply be lifted out of its context and applied in other, alien circumstances. In our society here in the United States, for instance, prolonged separation from her infant may be psychologically harmful for a mother because it may interfere with the development of her maternal intimacy with the child. As the person designated by our society to be the child's primary caretaker, she needs this sense of intimacy in its fullest development. Physical contact in the early months is just as important for the mother as for the child, because it helps to seal the bond that establishes the two as a mother-infant couple.

Many mothers wonder whether the newborn infant's individual characteristics will set the course for later development. Will the easygoing baby boy become an easygoing man? Must the very sensitive infant inevitably grow into an irritable adult? And will the infant who peers intently at everything crossing his visual field remain alert and inquisitive?

This question of the relationship between the traits of infancy and the traits of adulthood has goaded child psychologists to pursue the study of individual differences among babies. Their great hope, of course, is that one day they will be able to predict the future development of a child from his behavior in the early weeks of life. But if we exclude from consideration babies with major congenital malformations or birth injuries and infants who are unique in some other significant way, all the questions about the persistence of individual differences become extremely complex. No two infants have precisely the same experiences in the early years, and even if they did, the experiences would not have the same meaning for both children. Unless the children are siblings, they are not likely to be exposed to similar parents. We all know that siblings and even twins provoke consistently different reactions from their parents and hence will experience a different social feedback from the same parents. At every turn some new complication prevents us from predicting what course the adult personality will take. Usually we cannot hold one factor in the child's development constant while we study the effects of another factor in shaping the course of development. The outcome is always a mixture of the infant's initial condition (including his genetic endowment), and the experience he undergoes in relation to a particular set of parents, in a particular social environment, at a particular time in history.

At present, we know too little about the processes of human change to be able to trace this or that trait of the adult back through a direct chain of cause and effect to the infant. Where we do find some simple correlations or parallel differences at birth and at five or twenty years, these similarities are usually quite superficial and, even then, may not represent direct developmental lines.

It is important to remember that the baby is not just a miniature edition of the adult. To say, "The child is father to the man," is really quite misleading, because development is more than a simple increase in weight, height, size, physical skills, and intellectual sophistication. A baby is just as much an organism in his own right as the adult, and in psychological terms the young infant is not *quantitatively inferior*, but qualitatively different from the adult. Some functions may be superficially similar in infancy and maturity, but they will surely be different in terms of the significance they have for the child and in terms of the way they fit together as parts of the total organism.

For an exaggerated example of the changes that biological organisms may undergo in their life cycles, consider the butterfly. In its early stages this organism is a caterpillar, which must crawl because it has no wings. Nothing about its shape or color or behavior suggests that the lowly caterpillar will one day become the fluttering butterfly. Yet caterpillar and butterfly are the same creature even though there probably is very little of the physical substance of the caterpillar that remains in the butterfly, and even less of its behavior. Still, we correctly insist upon regarding them biologically as only different forms of the same organism. In what sense, then, is "the child the father of the man"? No outward change as drastic as the metamorphosis of the caterpillar separates the baby from the child or the child from the adult, but less obvious changes of equal or greater magnitude occur in psychological development. Just as we cannot regard the baby as merely an adult in miniature, so conversely we cannot infer from the superficial similarities of infantile and adult behavior that the "immature" adult is merely a child. Child and man are distinct and qualitatively different organizations.

This is by no means to deny the possibility of consistent individual differences in the behavior of infant and adult. It is just that we have not yet found the proper level at which to specify such similarities. Experienced parents and professionals who observe babies in clinical practice often agree that very soon after birth babies seem to take on personalities that persist throughout life. There are studies also that seem to point to the persistence of certain differences among children into adolescence. At the lowest denominator it seems certain that female babies are feminine and boys are masculine long before they are aware of themselves or of the differences between the sexes. Some children seem to be born with what in an adult would be called a sense of humor; they are sly or coy, or they laugh a lot and seem to retain a happy disposition throughout childhood. Some from the start are outgoing and aggressive; others give the impression of being serious, even reflective. At present our methods are inadequate to prove or disprove the constancy of traits of personality, but we have no reason to doubt that temperamental differences may persist over time. It is important, however, to keep in mind that constancies or inconstancies in development do not depend on the child alone. The child's personality does not develop in a vacuum. The original source of a child's restlessness and hypersensitivity may be traced to genetic differences, stresses of birth, poor diet, or too much excitement, but the restless baby does not grow into an irritable child just because he was born that way. His peculiarities have influenced his parents' response to him, and this response may well have aggravated his peculiarities. Under more soothing parents, the same baby might have become a quieter child, more tolerant of his environment.

Some traits that distinguish babies are probably so fixed in life that they are irreversible and relatively beyond reach of experience. Others are merely transitory phenomena that will drop away, no matter what happens to the child. Still other characteristics go through complex transformations and may even swing around into their opposites before they take on definitive forms. From the little we know about psychological development, it is impossible to say which traits will remain unchanged, which are transitory, which go through radical transformation, and which are most susceptible to change by parental intervention. Clearly the child does not travel a fixed path—he grows up in the context of his family, which will influence him as much as he influences them. His personality at birth determines how his parents react to him; their reaction to him in turn influences him either to continue on the original path or to take a new direction. In order to predict successfully the outcome of any individual's development, we would have to separate and examine one by one all the complicated factors contributing to his personality, and then study how these factors interact; the gene in relation to the cell, the cell in relation to the organs, the organs in relation to the other organ systems, and finally the young infant in relation to his parents, his siblings, his society, and his time.

Part Two

Birth to Age Three

Chapter 3

Birth

THE BIRTH PROCESS

The Cultural Warping of Childbirth

Doris Haire, International Childbirth Education Association

Many professionals contend that a "good experience" for the mother is of paramount importance in childbearing. They tend to forget that, for the vast majority of mothers, a healthy undamaged baby is the far more important objective of childbirth. . . . To expose a mother to the possibility of a lifetime of heartache or anguish in order to insure her a few hours of comfort is misguided kindness, . . . the price of a narcotized mother may be a narcotized or damaged newborn infant whose ultimate potential for learning is forever diminished.

Editor's Introduction

The infant mortality rate for the United States is higher than that of thirteen other developed countries in the world. Sweden and Norway compete for the distinction of having the lowest incidence of infant deaths per thousand live births. Our position is outrageous.

The United States is reputed to lead all other developed countries in the rate of infant deaths due to birth injury or respiratory distress such as postnasal asphyxia and atelectasis.

An infant born in the United States is four times more likely to die on the first day of life than an infant born in Japan. But survival of the birth process is not the only goal. There are likely to be many American infants who survive, but with neurological impairment.

According to the National Association of Retarded Children there are at least 6 million retarded children and adults in the United States. Research on birth defects makes it appear that the use of obstetrical medication may play a large role in the incidence of retardation and neurological impairment.

The management of labor may be of even greater importance than the management of birth in determining the future health of an infant. In order to avoid pain during labor, mothers are offered medications. Almost all obstetrical medications—sedatives, muscle relaxants, diuretics, tranquilizers, local anesthesia, or general anesthesia—tend to cross the placental barrier and enter the circulatory system of the yet unborn infant within minutes after administration to the mother. The placenta is actually not a barrier but, according to Virginia Apgar, a "bloody sieve."

It is evident that the use of obstetrical medication tends to alter the fetal environment. The respiratory center of the unborn infant is highly sensitive to anesthetic drugs administered to the mother, and such medication may jeopardize the onset of respiration in the infant at birth. Sedatives containing barbiturates, given to laboring mothers, have been shown to adversely affect the sucking responses of the newborn for five days after birth. Regional anesthesias, although an improvement over general anesthesia, tend to alter the fetal environment and compromise the mother's ability to effectively push the baby down the birth canal. This, in turn, increases the need for forceps and uterine stimulants, which are not always in the best interest of the baby. And there is some research which indicates that even the widely used regional anesthesias—such as the pudendal block or paracervical block—can influence a decrease in the fetal heartbeat, and a decrease in the heartbeat usually indicates a decrease in the oxygen supply to the fetus. How much oxygen depletion can be sustained without neurological damage is not yet fully understood. But certainly no one would purposely, without very good cause, inject medication into a newborn infant which might decrease the oxygen supply.

The lack of concern for the problem in the past may have been due to a lack of knowledge. It is now evident, however, that drugs administered to the mother in labor do alter the fetal environment and cause risk to the unborn infant.

Certainly there are indications for the use of obstetrical medication, but the practice of applying these procedures routinely to all mothers is not in the best interests of either the mother, her infant, or society. If mothers can be taught to recognize the importance of accepting some discomfort in order to avoid having drugged or damaged babies, perhaps these cultural patterns can be changed.

The elective induction of labor appears to increase the risk of fetal death. Shaving the birth area appears to do little toward the reduction of infection and a great deal toward the increase of discomfort to the mother. There is no evidence that the routine episiotomy reduces the incidence of vaginal "ripping" or structural damage to the vaginal orifice or that the procedure reduces stress to the baby. Requiring the mother to assume the lithotomy position, flat on her back with her knees spread wide apart and her feet held in stirrups, tends to alter the normal process of childbirth. This makes spontaneous birth more difficult and is like asking a woman to have a baby against the forces of gravity. It is similar to trying to have a bowel movement while lying flat on your back, a position no one would voluntarily assume.

Why, then, do these practices exist? While the answer is complex, the author of the following selection quotes one European professor of obstetrics and gynecology as having made the following comment: "Since all the physician can really do to affect the course of childbirth for the 95% of mothers who are capable of giving birth without complication is to offer the mother pharmacological relief from the discomfort of pain and to perform an episiotomy, there is probably an unconscious tendency for many professionals to see these practices as indispensable."

Perhaps educating mothers for the childbirth experience and improving the nature of the emotional support given to mothers during labor and delivery will reduce the need for obstetrical medication and reduce the frequency with which these other presently accepted practices occur.

Pamela Cantor

Permitting the Mother to Face Childbirth Uninformed of Ways in Which She Can Help Herself to Cope with the Discomfort of Labor and Birth

All mothers should be offered the opportunity to be physically and emotionally prepared to cope with the discomfort of childbirth because circumstances frequently preclude the use of obstetrical medication, even if the mother requests it. Dr. Charles Flowers, former Chairman of the Committee on Obstetric Analgesia and Anesthesia of the American College of Obstetricians and Gynecologists, states "Gymnastics are not necessary in the preparation of the patient for childbirth but the ability of a person to know what to do and how to relax and how to breathe during labor is of fundamental importance."[*]

A well-controlled research program by Enkin[2] of Canada demonstrated that mothers

[*]Superior numbers refer to references at the end of this reading.

who were prepared for the possibility of effectively participating in the birth process tended to experience significantly shorter labors, to require less medication and less obstetrical intervention and to remember the experience of birth more favorably than did those mothers who were motivated to ask to be prepared to cope with childbirth but could not be accommodated in classes.

According to Dr. Pierre Vellay, a pioneer in childbirth education, the ability to relax is the key to pain relief during labor and birth and the breathing patterns act as a distraction from painful stimuli. Experience in several countries indicates that the type of controlled breathing patterns, either chest or abdominal, taught in class or in the labor room is relatively unimportant since it is the mother's intense concentration on the controlled breathing patterns, and not the breathing patterns in themselves, which makes her less aware of the discomfort or pain of her contractions.

The psychoprophylactic method of childbirth training, developed and still used successfully in Russia, involves no controlled breathing patterns. While controlled breathing patterns may be unnecessary in the future, such patterns serve a useful purpose at this point in our culture. The recent deemphasis on breathing patterns will help to avoid hyperventilation (according to McCance hyperventilation rarely occurs in animals[3]) and will help to bring childbirth educators into greater agreement.

Requiring All Normal Women to Give Birth in the Hospital

While ICEA does not encourage home births, there is ample evidence in the Netherlands and in Chicago (Chicago Maternity Center) to demonstrate that normal women who have received adequate prenatal care can safely give birth at home if a proper system is developed for home deliveries. Over half of the mothers in the Netherlands give birth at home with the assistance of a professional midwife and a maternity aide. The comparatively low incidence of infant deaths and birth trauma in the Netherlands, a country of diverse ethnic composition and intermarriage, is evidence of the comparative safety of a properly developed home delivery service.

Dutch obstetricians point out that when the labor of a normal woman is unhurried and allowed to progress normally, unexpected emergencies rarely occur. They also point out that the small risk involved in a Dutch home delivery is more than offset by the increased hazards resulting from the use of obstetrical medication and obstetrical tampering which are more likely to occur in a hospital environment, especially in countries where professionals have had little or no exposure to normal labor and birth in a home environment during their training. We cannot justify deprecating a system of care which rarely produces a newborn infant with an Apgar score less than 9 when we in the U.S. have a predicted yearly increase of more than 100,000 retarded infants. If the increasing American trend to-ward home deliveries is to be contained, it is imperative that an effort be made to make birth in the hospital as normal, as homelike and as inexpensive as possible.

Elective Induction of Labor

The elective induction of labor (where there is no clear medical indication) appears to be an American idiosyncrasy which is frowned upon in other countries. In discussing elective induction of labor in *Williams Obstetrics, 14th Ed.*, Hellman and Pritchard caution that the conveniences of elective induction are not without the attendant hazards of prematurity, prolonged latent period with intrapartum infection, and prolapse of the umbilical cord. They report that studies involving almost 10,000 elective inductions indicate that perinatal deaths due to premature elective inductions occur despite efforts to comply with specific criteria.[3]

In reviewing the results of 3,324 elective inductions of labor at the University of Pennsylvania Hospital, Fields stresses the importance of caution in the selection of candidates for elective induction. He states,

Amniotomy carries with it the risk of injury to the mother or fetus and displacement of the presenting part, resulting in malposition, prolapsed cord, prolonged latent period and infection. The hazards of the use of oxytocin in labor are related directly to the dose for a given individual. Overdosage results in uterine spasm with possible separation of the placenta, tumultuous labor, amniotic fluid embolus, afibrinogenemia, lacerations of the cervix and birth canal, postpartum hemorrhage and uterine rupture. There may be water intoxication due to the antidiuretic effect of oxytocin. There may be fetal distress due to anoxia and intracranial hemorrhage, and trauma may result from tumultuous uterine contractions. Fetal and/or maternal mortality are, of course, ever-present dangers.[4,5]

The elective induction of labor has been found to almost double the incidence of fetomaternal transfusion and its attendant hazards.[6] But perhaps the least appreciated problem of elective induction is the fact that the abrupt onset of artificially induced labor tends to make it extremely difficult for even the well prepared mother to tolerate the discomfort of the intensified contractions without the aid of obstetrical medication. When the onset of labor occurs spontaneously the normal, gradual increase in contraction length and intensity appears to provoke in the mother an accompanying tolerance for discomfort or pain.

Since the British Perinatal Hazards Study[7] found no increase in perinatal mortality or impairment of learning ability at age 7 among full term infants, unless gestation had extended beyond 41 weeks, there would appear to be no medical justification for subjecting a mother or her baby to the possible hazards of elective induction in order to terminate the pregnancy prior to 41 weeks gestation. The elective induction of labor, when there is no specific medical indication, could be considered obstetrical interference in the normal physiology of childbirth and may leave the participating accoucheur legally vulnerable unless the mother is offered accurate information as to the possible hazards of elective induction of labor.

Separating the Mother from Familial Support during Labor and Birth

Research indicates that fear adversely affects uterine motility and blood flow[8] and yet many American mothers are routinely separated from a family member or close friend at this time of emotional crisis. Mice whose labors were environmentally disturbed experienced significantly longer labors, as much as 72% longer under some conditions, and gave birth to 54% more dead pups than did the mice in the control group. Newton cautions that the human mammal, which has a more highly developed nervous system than the mouse, may be equally sensitive to environmental disturbances in labor.[9]

In most developed countries, other than the United States and the Eastern European countries, mothers are encouraged to walk about or to sit and chat with a family member or supportive person in what is called an "Early Labor Lounge." This lounge is usually located near but outside the labor-delivery area in order to provide a more relaxed atmosphere during much of labor. The mother is taken to the labor-delivery area to be checked periodically, then allowed to return to the labor lounge for as long as she likes or until her membranes have ruptured.

The rapid acceptance by professionals of permitting the mother to be emotionally supported by a family member during birth is perhaps the most dramatic change in obstetrical care throughout the developed countries. However, in some countries where multiple bed delivery rooms are prevalent, such as in the eastern European countries and Asia, husbands are usually excluded.

Confining the Normal Laboring Woman to Bed

In virtually all countries except the United States, a woman in labor is routinely encouraged to walk about during labor for as long as she wishes or until her membranes have ruptured. Such activity is considered to facilitate labor by distracting the mother's attention from the discomfort or pain of her contractions and to encourage a more rapid engagement of the fetal head. In America, where drugs are frequently administered either orally or parenterally to laboring mothers, such ambulation is discouraged—not only for the patient's safety but also to avoid possible legal complications in the event of an accident.

The disadvantages to the fetus resulting from the mother's lying in a recumbent position during labor have been recognized for several years.[10,11] It is not unlikely that research will eventually find that the peasant women who labored in the fields up until the moment of birth may have been well served by this physical activity.

Shaving the Birth Area

Research involving 7,600 mothers has demonstrated that the practice of shaving the perineum and pubis does not reduce the incidence of infection. In fact, the incidence of infection was slightly higher among those mothers who were shaved.[12,13] Yet this procedure, which tends to create apprehension in laboring women, is still carried out routinely in most American hospitals. Clipping the perineal or pudendal hair closely with surgical scissors is far less disturbing to the mother and is less likely to result in infection caused by razor abrasions.

Withholding Food and Drink from the Normal Unmedicated Woman in Labor

The effect on the fetus of depriving a mother of food and drink for many hours, as is the custom in the United States, has not been sufficiently investigated. Intravenous feeding, as a substitute for light eating, only adds to the pathologic environment of an American hospital birth. In most developed countries one of the incentives for an expectant mother to take advantage of prenatal care is the fact that she will be allowed to eat and drink lightly during labor only if her prenatal examinations show her to be normal. Since anesthesia is not routinely administered during childbirth, light eating and drinking has not been found to increase the incidence of maternal morbidity or mortality in these countries.

The inhalation of gastric fluids by itself can be hazardous to the anesthetized mother. Therefore, to avoid this hazard obstetricians in most countries require that the mother's stomach be emptied or special precautions be taken if for any reason she must be anesthetized for delivery.

Professional Dependence on Technology and Pharmacological Methods of Pain Relief

Most of the world's mothers receive little or no drugs during pregnancy, labor or birth. The constant emotional support provided the laboring woman in other countries by the nurse-midwife, and often by her husband, appears to greatly improve the mother's tolerance for discomfort. In contrast, the American labor room nurse is frequently assigned to look after several women in labor, all or most of whom have had no preparation to cope with the discomfort or pain of childbearing. Under the circumstances drugs, rather than skillful emotional support, are employed to relieve the mother's apprehension and discomfort (and perhaps to assuage the harried labor attendant's feeling of inadequacy).

The fallacy of depending on the stethoscope to accurately monitor the effects of obstetrical medication on the well-being of the fetus has been demonstrated by Hon.[14,15] While electronic fetal monitoring is more accurate, the fact that some monitoring devices require that a mother's membranes be ruptured and that the electrode penetrate the skin of the fetal scalp creates possible hazards of its own. Therefore, obstetrical management which reduces the need for such monitoring is advisable.

Many professionals contend that a "good experience" for the mother is of paramount importance in childbearing. They tend to forget that, for the vast majority of mothers, a healthy, undamaged baby is the far more important objective of childbirth. The two objectives are not always compatible. Human maternal response has not been demonstrated to be adversely altered by a stressful, unmedicated labor if the mother has been prepared for the experience of birth. To expose a mother to the possibility of a lifetime of heartache or anguish in order to insure her a few hours of comfort is misguided kindness, for while analgesia and anesthesia for the laboring woman may be the easier route for the nurse, midwife or physician, the price of a narcotized mother may be a narcotized or damaged newborn infant whose ultimate potential for learning is forever diminished.[16,17,18]

Chemical Stimulation of Labor

Oxytocic agents are frequently administered to American mothers in order to intensify artificially the frequency and/or the strength of the mother's contractions, as a means of shortening the mother's labor. While chemical stimulation is sometimes medically indicated, often it is undertaken to satisfy the American propensity for efficiency and speed. Hon suggests that the overenthusiastic use of oxytocic stimulants sometimes results in alterations in the normal fetal heart rate.[14] Fields points out that the possible hazards inherent in elective induction are also possible in artificially stimulated labor unless the mother and fetus are carefully monitored.[4,5]

The British Perinatal Study appears to consider 24 hours as an outside limit for the first stage of labor, with a second stage of 2 or 3 hours or more. The average labor is about 13 hours for a primipara and about 7 1/2 hours for a multipara.[19] Shortening the phases of normal labor when there is no sign of fetal distress has not been shown to improve infant outcome. Little is known of the long term effects of artificially stimulating labor contractions. During a contraction the unborn child normally receives less oxygen. The gradual buildup of intensity, which occurs when the onset of labor is allowed to occur spontaneously and to proceed without chemical stimulation, appears likely to be a protective mechanism that is best left unaltered unless there is a clear medical indication for the artificial stimulation of labor.

Moving the Normal Mother to a Delivery Room for Birth

Most of the world's mothers, in both developed and developing countries, give birth in the same bed in the same hospital room in which they have labored. Since most European labor-delivery beds do not have adjustable backrests, mothers are supported into a semi-sitting position for birth by their husbands or a midwife. The midwife assists the mother, and if necessary, performs an episiotomy from the side of the bed, rather from the end of the bed. The suturing of an episiotomy is done from the side of the bed, or the bed may be "broken."

American nurse-midwives, especially those who have been trained abroad, are now beginning to permit American mothers the same privilege. This may seem innovative to many Americans until we realize that there is no research or evidence which indicates that a normal, essentially unmedicated mother should be required to give birth in a delivery room, rather than in a labor room which is equipped with portable or permanent sources of oxygen, suction and high intensity lighting. The pathological environment of the modern American delivery room is not conducive to a relaxed, normal childbirth experience.

The low temperature of the average delivery room has in the past been more suitable for the staff than for the infant. The American Academy of Pediatrics, acting as the infant's advocate, now recommends that the temperature of the delivery room should be maintained between 71.6 and 75.2° F.[20]

Delaying Birth until the Physician Arrives

Because of the increased likelihood of resultant brain damage to the infant, the practice of delaying birth by anesthesia or physical restraint until the physican arrives to deliver the infant is frowned upon in most countries. Yet the practice still occurs occasionally in the United States and in countries where hospital-assigned midwives do not routinely manage the labor and delivery of normal mothers. One of the benefits of husband-attended deliveries noted by many chiefs of American obstetrical departments is the tendency for obstetrical coverage by attending physicians to immediately improve.

Requiring the Mother to Assume the Lithotomy Position for Birth

Some contend that the low incidence of spontaneous births among American mothers is due to the disparity in the size between the parents, resulting from the differences in their ethnic background. However, there is gathering scientific evidence that the unphysiological lithotomy position (back flat, with knees drawn up and spread wide apart by "stirrups") which is preferred by most American physicians because it is more convenient for the accoucheur, tends to alter the normal fetal environment and obstruct the normal process of childbearing, making spontaneous birth more difficult or impossible.

The lithotomy and dorsal positions tend to:

1 Adversely affect the mother's blood pressure, cardiac return and pulmonary ventilation.[1,10,21]
2 Decrease the normal intensity of the contractions.[21,22,23]
3 Inhibit the mother's voluntary efforts to push her baby out spontaneously.[21,22,24]
4 Increase the need for forceps and increase the traction necessary for a forceps extraction.[22]
5 Inhibit the spontaneous expulsion of the placenta[24] which, in turn, increases the need for cord traction, forced expression or manual removal of the placenta[25]—procedures which significantly increase the incidence of fetomaternal hemorrhage.[6]
6 Increase the need for episiotomy because of the increased tension on the pelvic floor and the stretching of the perineal tissue.[21] The normal separation of the feet for natural expulsion is about 15 to 16 inches, or 38 to 41 centimeters, which is far less separation than is allowed by the average American delivery table stirrups.

Australian, Russian and American research bears out the clinical experience of European physicians and midwives—that when mothers are supported to a semi-sitting position for birth, with their feet supported by the lower section of the labor-delivery bed, mothers tend to push more effectively, appear to need less pain relief, are more likely to want to be conscious for birth and are less likely to need an episiotomy.[21,24]

The fact that the extended delivery table or bed spares the mother the common but often unspoken fear of involuntarily expelling her baby onto the floor before the doctor or midwife is ready to receive the infant, or the fear that the accoucher might accidentally drop her baby may inhibit the mother's ability to relax her perineum during the second stage of labor.

The increased efficiency of the semi-sitting position, combined with a minimum use of medication for birth, is evidenced by the fact that the combined use of both forceps and the vacuum extractor rarely exceeds 4% to 5% of all births in the Netherlands, as compared to an incidence of 65% in many American hospitals. (Cesarean section occurs in approximately 1.5% of all Dutch births.) These differences are even more striking when one considers that in modern Holland, which has a population almost as heterogeneous as our own, the average pelvic measurements of the Dutch mother and the average circumference of her baby's head are the same as those of their American counterparts.

Manual removal of the placenta occurs in approximately .6% of all Dutch births despite the fact that oxytocin is not administered to mothers routinely.

Although the author knows of no specific research which verifies the incidence, clinical experience in the United States suggests that mothers who give birth in the semi-sitting position, with their legs resting on the bed, are less likely to sustain postpartum backache and fracture of the coccyx. A scientific investigation is long overdue.

The Routine Use of Regional or General Anesthesia for Delivery

In light of the current shortage of qualified anesthetists and anesthesiologists and the frequent scientific papers now being published on the possible hazards resulting from the use of regional and general anesthesia, it would seem prudent to make every effort to prepare the mother physically and mentally to cope with the sensations and discomfort of birth in order to avoid the use of such medicaments. Regional and general anesthesia not only tend to adversely affect fetal environment pharmacologically, which has been discussed previously herein, but their use also increases the need for obstetrical intervention in the normal process of birth, since both types of anesthesia tend to prolong labor.[19] Johnson points out that peridural and spinal anesthesia significantly increase the incidence of midforceps delivery and its attendant hazards.[26] Pudendal block anesthesia not only tends to interfere with the mother's ability to effectively push her baby down the birth canal due to the blocking of the afferent path of the pushing reflex but also appears to interfere with the mother's normal protective reflexes, "thus making an explosive" birth and perineal damage more likely to occur.

While there are exceptions, the use of regional and general anesthesia usually dictates that:

1 The mother must be restricted from eating or drinking from the onset of labor.
2 The mother's uterine contractions must frequently be pharmacologically stimulated.
3 The mother must be moved to a delivery room which is equipped for obstetrical emergencies (obstetrical medication tends to increase the need for resuscitative measures for the infant).
4 The mother must be placed in the lithotomy position for delivery since she will not be in control of her legs.
5 Fundal pressure and/or the use of forceps and an episiotomy will be needed to facilitate the delivery of the infant.
6 The infant's umbilical cord will be clamped early to facilitate immediate resuscitative measures for the infant and to shorten the infant's accumulation of obstetrical medication.
7 Fundal pressure or manipulation, cord traction, pharmacological stimulation of contractions or manual removal of the placenta will be employed in order to facilitate the prompt delivery of the placenta to prevent maternal hemorrhage. . . .

The Routine Use of Forceps for Delivery

There is no scientific justification for the routine application of forceps for delivery. The incidence of delivery by forceps and vacuum extractor, combined, rarely rises above 5% in countries where mothers actively participate in the births of their babies. In contrast, as mentioned previously, the incidence of forceps extraction frequently rises to as high as 65% in some American hospitals. Research in Europe, where there are more natural births to serve as controls, has demonstrated that when forceps are used for delivery in order to relieve maternal distress, those infants so delivered are more likely to sustain intracranial hemorrhage and damage to the facial nerve or the brachial plexus.[27] There are obviously times when indications of fetal distress dictate the use of forceps to facilitate the safe delivery of an infant, but there is no scientific support for the routine application of forceps during birth.[7]

Routine Episiotomy

There is no research or evidence to indicate that routine episiotomy (a surgical incision to enlarge the vaginal orifice) reduces the incidence of pelvic relaxation (structural damage to the pelvic floor musculature) in the mother.

Nor is there any research or evidence that routine episiotomy reduces neurological impairment in the child who has shown no signs of fetal distress or that the procedure helps to maintain subsequent male or female sexual response.

Pelvic Relaxation The incidence of pelvic floor relaxation appears to be on the decline throughout the world, even in those countries where episiotomy is still comparatively rare. The contention that the modern washing machine has been more effective in reducing pelvic relaxation among American mothers than has routine episiotomy is given some credence by the fact that in areas of the United States where life is still hard for the woman, pelvic relaxation appears in white women who have never borne children. Interviews with gynecologists in many countries suggest that the incidence of pelvic relaxation is strongly influenced by genetics. The condition, although comparatively rare in both Fiji and Kenya, occurs more frequently among Indian women in those countries than among black women, although the living habits and fertility rate of both groups of women are much the same. Whether a resistance to pelvic relaxation is due to diet, physical activity, practices or position used during birth or any other factor is not clear. The fact remains, however, that susceptibility to pelvic relaxation appears to be a genetic weakness which has not been shown to be eliminated or reduced by routine episiotomy.

Neurological Impairment Shortening the second stage of labor by performing an episiotomy when there is no sign of fetal distress has not been shown to be beneficial to the infant. The scientific evaluation of 17,000 children, born in one week's time and followed for 7 years in Great Britian, indicates that a second stage of labor lasting as long as two and one-half hours does not increase the incidence of neurological impairment of the full-term, average-for-gestational age infant who shows no signs of fetal distress.[7]

Sexual Response In developed countries where episiotomy is comparatively rare, the physiotherapist is considered an important member of the obstetrical team—before, as well as after the birth. The physiotherapist is responsible for seeing that each mother begins exercises the day following birth which will help to restore the normal elasticity and tone of the mother's perineal and abdominal muscles. In countries where every effort is made to avoid the need for an episiotomy, interviews with both parents and professionals indicate that an intact perineum which is strengthened by postpartum exercise is more apt to result in both male and female sexual satisfaction than is a perineum that has been incised and reconstructed.

Why then, is there such an emotional attachment among professionals to routine episiotomy? A prominent European professor of obstetrics and gynecology recently made the following comment on the American penchant for routine episiotomy:

> Since all the physician can really do to affect the course of childbirth for the 95% of mothers who are capable of giving birth without complication is to offer the mother pharmacological relief from discomfort or pain and to perform an episiotomy, there is probably an unconscious tendency for many professionals to see these practices as indispensable.

Interviews with obstetrician-gynecologists in many countries indicate that they tend to agree that a superficial, first degree tear is less traumatic to the perineal tissue than an incision which requires several sutures for reconstruction. There is no research which would indicate otherwise. It would appear callous indeed for a physician or nurse-midwife to perform an episiotomy without first making an effort to avoid the need for an episiotomy by removing the mother's legs from the stirrups and bringing her up into a semi-sitting position in order to relieve tension on her perineum and enable her to push more effectively.

Early Clamping or "Milking" of the Umbilical Cord

Several years ago De Marsh stated that the placental blood normally belongs to the infant and his failure to get this blood is equivalent to submitting him to a rather severe hemorrhage. Despite the fact that placental transfusion normally occurs in every corner of the world without adverse consequences, there is still a great effort in the United States and Canada to deprecate the practice. One must read the literature carefully to find that placental transfusion has not been demonstrated to increase the incidence of morbidity or mortality in the placentally transfused infant.[28]

Routine early clamping or milking of the umbilical cord may appear to save the professional a few minutes time in the delivery room, but neither practice has been demonstrated to be in the best interest of either the essentially unmedicated mother or her infant.[29] Placental transfusion resulting from late clamping, whereby the infant receives approximately an additional 25% of his total blood supply, is part of the physiological sequence of childbirth for most of the world's newborn infants in both developed and developing countries where the dorsal, squatting or semi-sitting position is preferred for birth. The lithotomy position for birth, preferred by the American obstetrician because it is more convenient for him, makes placental transfusion inconvenient since there is no end of the bed on which the obstetrician can place the wriggling infant. The practice of "milking" the cord in order to save 3 minutes time does not appear to be in the best interests of the newborn infant.[30]

Early clamping has been demonstrated by research to lengthen the third stage of labor and increase the likelihood of maternal hemorrhage, retained placenta or the retention of placental fragments.[25]

... Whether early clamping increases the incidence of anemia in the rapidly growing child has not been sufficiently investigated, but research has demonstrated that the red cell volume of late clamped full term infants increases by 47%.[28]

Routine Suctioning with a Nasogastric Tube

Although the use of a nasogastric tube attached to a deLee trap is now a widely used method for removing mucous from the newborn infant's nasopharynx, Cordero and Hon suggest that blind suctioning with a nasogastric tube is a hazardous procedure. They point out that the procedure can cause severe cardiac arrhythmias and apnea—conditions which do not tend to develop when the suctioning is accomplished by the use of a bulb syringe.[31]

Apgar Scoring by the Accoucheur

No one can be completely impartial in judging his own skills, no matter how objective he or she may try to be. As one pediatrician put it, "Asking the person who delivers the infant to determine that infant's score on the Apgar scale is like asking a student to fill out his own report card." In countries where obstetrical medication is the exception rather than the rule, the Apgar score of the majority of newborn infants seldom falls below 9. Therefore, it would appear that an infant's Apgar score is possibly more influenced by the management of labor and delivery than the physical condition of the mother.

Although there is a "maximum dosage" level and time interval recommended by the manufacturers of most obstetrical medications there are no recommendations, guidelines or restrictions on the use of several medications administered to the mother at the same time. Nor is there any recommendation or guideline for determining safe time intervals between administration of multiple medication. A review by the hospital joint obstetric-pediatric committee of any Apgar score of 7 or below would very likely tend to improve infant outcome.

Treatment of a slow learner or retarded child may be facilitated by knowing the Apgar score of the child under observation. Since the Apgar score of an individual is not always accessible several years after birth (many hospitals discard birth records after 7 to 10 years) parents should be given a copy of their baby's Apgar score for retention, even if the score is coded.

Obstetrical Intervention in Placental Expulsion

The most common mismanagement of the third stage of labor involves an attempt to hasten it.[19] Cord traction, the use of uterine stimulants, such as oxytocin, ergonovene, etc., manipulation of the fundus and manual removal as means of accelerating the expulsion of a reluctant placenta, are pathological procedures which tend to increase the incidence of fetomaternal transfusion, maternal blood loss and the incidence of retained afterbirth or placental fragments.[6,25,32,33,34] Such obstetrical intervention is rarely found necessary when (a) the mother has received little or no medication, (b) she has been supported to a semi-sitting position for birth and (c) where placental transfusion has reduced the volume of the placenta.[32,25]

Separating the Mother from her Newborn Infant

There is no evidence that the full term infant of a relatively unmedicated mother will suffer an abnormal drop in temperature if he is dried off quickly, wrapped in a prewarmed blanket and placed in his mother's arms during the

recovery period.[35] Experience at Yale-New Haven Hospital in Connecticut indicates that when the above procedure is followed and the mother is allowed to hold her baby for two hours or so, the infant's body temperature remains stable. In light of the present concern over the possible hazard of infant warming devices in the delivery room, perhaps we should recommend one of the most logical of warming devices—the mother's arms.

A Mother-Baby Recovery Room staffed with skilled nursing personnel makes it possible for even the high-risk or postoperative mother to be with her baby during the first hours of life.

Recent research by Klaus[36] and Salk[37] has demonstrated that the conventional hospital postpartum routine tends to inhibit rather than engender maternal response and nurturing. The first 24 hours following birth appear to be a critical period for the establishment of the normal mother-infant bonds. Separating the mother from her infant during this time tends to interfere with the mother's normal responses to her baby. Salk suggests that the mother's increased sensitivity to her newborn infant during the first 24 hours following birth may be a biochemical mechanism which is not yet understood. Both Salk and Klaus have demonstrated that maternal response and nurturing are adversely affected a full one month after birth when the mother and her baby have been restricted to the usual hospital postpartum schedule (a glimpse of the baby shortly after birth, brief contact and identification at 6 to 12 hours, and then 20 to 30 minutes every four hours for feeding). How long this initial restrictive pattern of contact adversely affects maternal behavior is yet to be assessed. . . .

Delaying the First Breast-Feeding

The common American practice of routinely delaying the time of the first breast feeding has not been shown to be in the best interest of either the conscious mother or her newborn infant. Clinical experience with the early feeding of newborn infants has shown this practice to be safe.[38] If the mother feels well enough and the infant is capable of suckling while they are still in the delivery room, then it would seem more cautious, in the event of tracheoesophogeal abnormality, to permit the infant to suckle for the first time under the watchful eye of the physician or nurse-midwife rather than delay the feeding for several hours when the expertise of the professional may not be immediately available.

In light of the many protective antibodies contained in colostrum, it would seem likely that the earlier the infant's intake of species specific colostrum the sooner the antibodies can be accrued by the infant.

Research on several species of animals suggest that the earlier the newborn's intake of colostrum and maternal milk the earlier gut closure will occur. Gut closure, whereby the colostrum acts as a sealant to the intestinal lining, appears to prevent or lessen the passage of harmful bacteria or foreign protein through the intestinal lining.[39] Although similar research has not been carried out on the human infant, it is not unlikely that such a similar protective mechanism exists.

Offering Water and Formula to the Breast Fed Newborn Infant

The common American practice of giving water or formula to a newborn infant prior to the first breast-feeding or as a supplement during the first days of life has not been shown to be in the best interests of the infant. There are now indications that these practices may, in fact, be harmful. Glucose water, once the standby in every American hospital, has now been designated a potential hazard if aspirated by the newborn infant, yet it is still used in many American hospitals.

It is a comment on the American penchant for the artificial that there has never been any research carried out in the U.S. which attempts to evaluate the safety of colostrum as the infant's first intake of fluid, yet nature obviously intended the initial fluid intake of the newborn infant to be of the same consistency as the relatively thick, viscous colostrum.

Whether the human infant experiences such a gut closure, as is seen in animals, and whether the administering of water or formula initially to the infant who is to be breast-fed will interfere with normal gut closure has not been scientifically investigated. Experts in the raising of cows make great effort to see that species specific bovine colostrum, not milk or water, is the first fluid received by the newborn calf. It is ironic that we do not give the same consideration to human newborns.

Unless the physician or the nurse can be absolutely sure that an infant has no familial history of allergy it would be cautious to obtain the mother's permission before offering her infant formula in the nursery. Offering the infant formula in the nursery interferes with the normal progress of lactation in so many ways that the subject cannot be adequately discussed herein.[40] For those who wish more information on the subject I suggest you read references 41 and 42.

Restricting Newborn Infants to a Four Hour Feeding Schedule and Withholding Night Time Feedings

Although widely spaced infant feedings may be more convenient for hospital personnel, the practice of feeding a newborn infant only every four hours and not permitting the infant to breast-feed at all during the night cannot be justified on any scientific grounds. Such a regimen restricts the suckling stimulation necessary to bring about the normally rapid onset and adequate production of the mother's milk. In countries where custom permits the infant to suckle immediately after birth and on demand from that time, first time mothers frequently begin to produce breast milk for their babies within 24 hours after birth. In contrast, in countries where hospital routines prevent normal, demand feeding from birth, mothers frequently do not produce breast milk for their babies until the third day following birth. . . .

Preventing Early Father-Child Contact

Permitting fathers to hold their newborn infants immediately following birth and during the postpartum hospital stay has not been shown by research or clinical experience to increase the incidence of infection among newborns, even when those infants are returned to a regular or central nursery. Yet, only in the eastern European countries is the father permitted less involvement in the immediate postpartum period than in the United States (eastern European fathers are usually not permitted to enter beyond the foyer of the maternity hospital and are not allowed to see their wives or babies for the entire 7 to 9 day stay). Research has consistently confirmed the fact that the greatest source of infection to the newborn infant are the nursery and nursery personnel.[43,44] One has only to observe a mother holding her newborn infant against her bathrobe, which has probably been exposed to abundant hospital borne bacteria, to realize the fallacy of preventing a father from holding his baby during the hospital stay. . . .

REFERENCES

1 Flowers, C.: *Obstetric Analgesia and Anesthesia*, Hoeber, Harper & Row, N.Y., 1967.

2 Enkin, M. et al: *"An Adequately Controlled Study of the Effectiveness of P.P.M. Training,"* III Int'l Congress of Psycho. Med. in Obstet. & Gynec., London, April, 1971.

3 McCance, R.: *"The Maintenance of Stability in the Newborn,"* Arch. Dis. Childh., 34:361–370, 1959.

4 Fields, H.: *"Complications of Elective Induction,"* Obstet. & Gyneco., 15:476–480, 1960.

5 Fields, H.: *"Induction of Labor: Methods, Hazards, Complications and Contraindications,"* Hospital Topics, 63–68, Dec. 1968.

6 Beer, A.: *"Fetal Erythrocytes in Maternal Circulation of 155 Rh-Negative Women,"* Obstet. & Gynec., 34:143–150, 1969.

7 Butler, N.: *"A National Long Term Study of Perinatal Hazards,"* Sixth World Congress, Fed. Int'l. Gynec. & Obstet., 1970.

8 Kelly, J.: *"Effect of Fear Upon Uterine Motility, "* Am. J. Obstet. Gynec., 83:576–581, 1962.

9 Newton, N.: *"The Effects of Disturbance on Labor,"* Amer. J. Obstet. and Gynec. 101: 1096–1102, 1968.

10 James, L.S.: *"The Effects of Pain Relief for Labor and Delivery on the Fetus and Newborn,"* Anesthesiology, 21:405–430, 1960.

11 Veland, K. & Hansen, J.: *"Maternal Cardiovascular Dynamics*, Posture & Uterine Contractions,"* AM. J. Obstet. & Gynec., 103:1, Jan. 1969.

12 Burchell, R.: *"Predelivery Removal of Pubic Hair,"* Obstet. & Gynec., 24:272–273, 1964.

13 Kantor, H., et al: *"Value of Shaving the Pudendal-Perineal Area in Delivery Preparation,"* Obstet. & Gynec., 25:509–512, 1965.

14 Hon, E.: *"Direct Monitoring of the Fetal Heart, "* Hosp. Prac. 91–97, Sept. 1970.

15 Hon, E. and Quilligan, E.: *"Electronic Evaluation of Fetal Heart Rate,"* Clin. Obst. & Gynec. 145–167, March, 1968.

16 Bowes, W. et al: *"The Effects of Obstetrical Medication on Fetus and Infant,"* Monographs of the Society for Research in Child Development, No. 137, Vol. 35, June 1970.

17 Windle, W.: *"Brain Damage by Asphyxia at Birth,"* Scient. Amer. 77–83, Oct. 1969.

18 Lewis, M. et al: *"Individual Differences in Attention,"* Amer. J. Dis. Child., 113:461–465, 1967.

19 Hellman, L. & Pritchard, J.: *Williams Obstetrics*, 14th Ed. Appleton, Century-Crofts, New York, 1971.

20 American Academy of Pediatrics, *Standards and Recommendations for Hospital Care of Newborn Infants*, Fifth Edition, 1971.

21 Blankfield, A.: *"The Optimum Position for Childbirth,"* Med. J. Australia, 2:666–668, 1965.

22 Howard, F.H.: *"Delivery in the Physiologic Position,"* Obstet. & Gynec., 11:318–322, 1958.

23 Gritsiuk, I.: *"Position in Labor,"* Ob-Gyn Observer, Sept. 1968.

24 Newton, N. and Newton, M. *"The Propped Position for the Second Stage of Labor,"* Obstet. & Gynec., 15:28–34, 1960.

25 Botha, M.: *"The Management of the Umbilical Cord in Labour,"* S. Afr. J. Obstet. 6(2):30–33, 1968.

26 Johnson, W.: *"Regionals Can Prolong Labor,"* Medical World News, Oct. 15, 1971.

27 Hubinont, P. et al: *"Effects of Vacuum Extractor and Obstetrical Forceps on the Fetus and Newborn—A Comparison,"* V World Congress Gynaec. & Obstet., Sydney, Australia, 1967.

28 Saigal, S. et al: *"Placental Transfusion and Hyperbilirubinemia in the Premature."* Pediatrics, 49:406–419, 1972.

29 Avery, M.: *"Decreased Blood Volume,"* The Lung and Its Disorders in the Newborn Infant, 1:130–131, W.B. Saunders Co., Philadelphia.

30 Duckman, S., et al: *"The Importance of Gravity in Delayed Ligation of the Umbilical Cord,"* Am. J. Obstet. & Gynec., 66:1214–1223, 1953.

31 Cordero, L. and Hon, E.: *"Neonatal Bradycardia Following Nasopharyngeal Stimulation,"* J. Pediat., 78:441–447, 1971.

32 Walsh, S.: *"Maternal Effects of Early and Late Clamping of the Umbilical Cord,"* Lancet, 1:996–997, 1968.

33 Doolittle, J. & Moritz, C.: *"Prevention of Erythroblastosis by an Obstetric Technic,"* Obstet. & Gynec., 27: 529–531, 1966.

34 Weinstein, L., Farabow, W. and Gusdon, J.: *"Third Stage of Labor and Transplacental Hemorrhage,"* Obstet. & Gynec., 37:90–93, 1971.

35 Dahm, L. and James, L.: *"Newborn Temperature: Heat Loss in Delivery Room,"*: Pediatrics 49:504–513, 1972.

36 Klaus, M. et al: *"Maternal Attachment–Importance of the First Post-Partum Days,"* N.E.J. of Med. 286:460–463. March 2, 1972.

37 Salk, L.: *"The Critical Nature of the Post-Partum Period in the Human for the Establishment of the Mother-Infant Bond: A Controlled Study,"* Dis. Ner. Sys., 31:Suppl:110–116, Nov. 1970.

38 Eppink, H.: *"Time of Initial Breast Feeding Surveyed in Michigan Hospitals,"* Hospital Topics, 116–117, June 1968.

39 Lecce, J. et al.: *"Effects of Feeding Colostral and Milk Components on the Cessation of Intestinal Absorption of Large Molecules Closure in Neonatal Pigs,"* J. Nutrition, 78:263–268, 1962.

40 Newton, M. and Newton, N.: *"Normal Course and Management of Lactation,"* Clin. Obst. and Gynec., 5:44–63, 1962.

41 Haire, D. & Haire, J.: *"The Nurse's Contribution to Successful Breast-Feeding,"* Int'l Childbirth Ed. Ass'n, Milwaukee, Wisconsin, 1971.

42 Newton, M.: *"Human Lactation,"* in Milk: The Mammary Gland and its Secretion, Vol. 1, edited by S. Kon and A. Cowie, N.Y. Academic Press, 1961.

43 Gezon, H., et al: *"Some Controversial Aspects in the Epidemiology of Hospital Nursery Staphylococcal Infections,"* Amer. J. of Public Health, 50:473–484, 1960.

44 Ravenholt, R. and LaVeck, G.: *"Staphylococcal Disease—An Obstetric, Pediatric & Community Problem,"* Amer. J. of Public Health, 46:1287–1296, 1956.

Birth without Violence

Frederick Leboyer

Is there anything we can do?
Happily, there is some hope.
"You will give birth in pain," says the Bible.
But today a woman can give birth joyfully.
A miracle.
But how can she be joyful when her child is still being crucified?
It cannot be.
Should the woman then renounce her joy?
No, certainly not.
We must simply do for the child what we have already done for the mother. Or at least we
must try.

Editor's Introduction

Each time I read Leboyer's book and look at the photographs of the newborn infant serenely smiling, I cry and ache with sadness—a profound sadness for the treacherous birth experience which my daughter Lauren endured, for her shrill cries of pain.

I do remember her birth vividly and have previously thought of it only with a good deal of joy. I was fully awake and able to watch her being born and to hold her moments after her birth. Her father was there with us; although, as a surgeon, he had delivered many infants himself, he wept with relief and elation as she emerged.

But I now think of her birth with great anguish, not for myself, but for Lauren, for the fact that there were alternatives to the brutality which she experienced. I wish I had been aware of Leboyer's method and had had the opportunity to save her from her pain.

Leboyer feels that the suffering that the newborn experiences stems from the huge contrast between the peaceful environment of the womb and the shock of what is experienced at birth: the glare of operating room lights, the loud noises, the sudden straightening of the previously curved spine and the abrupt separation from the mother. Most infants are not treated as human beings but rather regarded as objects. Yet if the fetus in the mother's womb can see, feel, and hear, it must be able to continue to do so outside the womb. On leaving the womb, the infant experiences a weight and density with which he or she is totally unfamiliar; the result is pain, confusion, and fear.

Leboyer has sought to make the transition from internal to external life a more gradual development by prolonging the sensations which the fetus felt while in the uterus. In the womb, sounds are softened by the amniotic fluid. When the baby leaves the womb, sounds are perceived all over the skin surface, and they become explosive. Inside the womb, the fetus is in total darkness. Outside, the infant is met by intense light. Leboyer delivers babies in total silence and complete darkness. He waits at least five minutes before cutting the umbilical cord so that the baby may still receive oxygen through the blood pulsating through the cord. He handles the spine with great care. The newborn is held delicately and allowed to uncurl at a natural speed; it is not jerked upside down and straightened with one sudden, callous motion. Leboyer believes—like Freud, Rank, and Reich—that the treatment given to the infant at birth is bound to leave its mark throughout life. He does not wish to hasten the infant's physical or emotional separation from the mother. The baby has just been taken from the womb, and there is no need to take it instantly from its mother. He states that the baby's senses of sight, sound, and touch are raw at birth. To wrap an infant's fragile skin in a coarse hospital gown is a cruelty akin to wrapping a burned child in barbed wire. He places the naked newborn on the mother's bare abdomen. The infant lies on its tummy so that it will uncurl from the fetal position at its own rhythm, in its mother's arms, being stroked by her loving hands. A bath is made ready and the newborn is slowly immersed in water up to the neck. The baby, again weightless as in the uterus, relaxes, stretches, plays, and smiles—smiles within a few minutes after birth. When a child is born in silence and in darkness, is held and caressed by the mother, is gently hugged to ease the pain of separation, is immersed in a sea of warm water, is wrapped in a loose warm cotton cloth and is again held safely by the mother, the experience becomes one of pleasure instead of pain.

Leboyer has himself delivered more than 10,000 babies. The last 1,000 have been brought into this world by the method he describes in the following pages. The babies delivered in this fashion do not scream in agony. They babble and smile.

Why, then, have we delivered babies with violence? Not because we are cruel but because we have never thought of the infant. We have simply assumed that birth had to be ugly. Leboyer's words and his photographs of newborns with expressions of peace cannot fail to convince us that there is an alternative to yet the most brutal aspect of the warping of childbirth.

Pamela Cantor

"Do you believe that birth is an enjoyable experience—for the baby?"

"Birth? . . . Enjoyable?"

"You heard me. . . . Do you believe that babies feel happy coming into this world?"

"You're joking."

"Why should I be joking?"

"Because babies are just babies."

"What is that supposed to mean?"

"That babies aren't capable of intense feeling."

"What makes you so certain?"

"Babies don't have fully developed feelings."

"How do you *know*?"

"Well, don't you agree?"

"If I did, I wouldn't be asking."

"But everybody knows they don't."

"Since when has that ever been a good reason to believe anything?"

"True. But newborn babies can't see or even hear, so how can they feel unhappy?"

"Even if they can't see or hear, that doesn't stop them from crying their hearts out."

"A baby has to test its lungs. That's common knowledge."

"Nonsense."

"Well, that's what people say."

"People say all kinds of stupid things. But do you really believe that babies feel nothing at all while they're being born?"

"Obviously they don't."

"I'm not so sure. After all, young children suffer overwhelming agonies about things that seem quite trivial to us—they feel a thousand times more intensely than we do."

"Yes, I know, but newborn babies are so tiny."

"What does size have to do with it?"

"Well . . ."

"And why do they scream so loud if they're not in some kind of pain or misery?"

"I don't know—a reflex I suppose. But I'm sure they're not feeling anything."

"But *why* aren't they?"

"Because they have no conscious awareness."

"Ah. So you think that means they have no soul."

"I don't know about the soul."

"But this consciousness . . . why is it so important?"

"Consciousness is the beginning of being a person."

"Are you trying to tell me that babies aren't fully human because they're not fully conscious? Tell me more. . . ."

How many times have I heard that kind of discussion. It leads nowhere.

Things are simple. It's we who complicate them.

When children come into the world, the first thing they do is cry. And everyone rejoices.

"My baby's crying!" the mother exclaims happily, astonished that something so small can make so much noise.

And how does everyone else react?

The reflexes are normal. The machine works.

But are we machines?

Aren't cries always an expression of pain?

Isn't it conceivable that the baby is in anguish?

What makes us assume that birth is less painful for the child than it is for the mother?

And if it is, does anyone care?

No one, I'm afraid, judging by how little attention we pay to a baby when it arrives.

What a tragedy that we're all so determined to believe that this "thing" can't hear, can't see, can't *feel* . . .

So how could "it" feel pain?

"It" cries, "it" howls. So?

In short, "it" is an object.

But what if "it" is already a *person*?

Already a person! That is a contradiction of everything we believe.

Common sense suggests we begin by looking at the facts.

Which tell us absolutely nothing.

Because babies can't actually "tell" us anything. They don't speak in words.

Nor do porpoises. Or birds. But that doesn't prevent *them* from communicating.

Are there languages without words? Of course. We know there are, only our vanity keeps us from acknowledging them.

Just watch someone accidentally swallow something boiling hot, and you see how eloquently he speaks—without words!

He leaps up, hops from foot to foot, frantically waves his hands. His face is contorted, his eyes are watering. Whether he is from Moscow, Mombasa, or Miami, he's managed to say, "I've burned myself"—and say it without using a single word.

And compared to being born, burning your throat is nothing at all. If there's one thing a newborn baby doesn't lack, it's the ability to express itself.

Newborn babies don't talk?

Let's wait a moment before making up our minds.

What more proof do we need?

That tragic expression, those tight-shut eyes, those twitching eye-brows . . .

That howling mouth, that squirming head trying desperately to find refuge . . .

Those hands stretching out to us, imploring, begging, then retreating to shield the face—that gesture of dread.

Those furiously kicking feet, those arms that suddenly pull downward to protect the stomach.

The flesh that is one great shudder.

This baby is not speaking?

Every inch of the body is crying out: "Don't touch me!"

And at the same time pleading: "Don't leave me! Help me!"

Has there ever been a more heartrending appeal?

And yet this appeal—as old as birth itself—has been misunderstood, has been ignored, has simply gone unheard.

How can this have been? How can this still be?

A newborn baby doesn't speak?

No. It is we who do not listen.

And so we begin to wonder.

This little creature already a person?

Suffering? Howling with grief?

But it's so young, so small . . .

Again! Something in us resists, doesn't wish to hear, refuses to believe. We close our eyes, we guard our precious peace of mind.

Clearly we find it intolerable to look . . . to see . . .

Pictures of newborn infants are just not bearable. They could equally well be pictures of criminals who have undergone torture and are about to die.

People turn away and say: "No! I can't stand it."

Or: "Suffering? Do you really believe they are suffering?"

What you won't see can't hurt you.

Others try to argue: "But it isn't possible. Birth isn't like that, or we'd know about it. You're showing us an infant being tortured, a baby in the hands of sadists."

No. It's nothing like that.

It's only birth.

No monsters, no sadists. Just people like you and me. People whose minds are elsewhere.

"They have eyes but do not see."

Blind men and women whose eyes are wide open. Do you want to watch them at it?

Watch.

A small creature has just been born. The father and mother gaze at it with delight. The young practitioner shares their joy.

One dazzling smile lights up all their faces. They radiate happiness.

All of them, that is, except the child.

The child?

Oh, dear God, it can't be true!

This mask of agony, of horror. These hands—above all, these hands—clasping the head . . .

This is the gesture of someone struck by lightning. The gesture you see in the mortally wounded, the moment before they die.

Can birth hold so much suffering, so much pain? While the parents look on in ecstasy, oblivious.

No, we can't accept it.

And yet . . . it's true.

Why is the young doctor smiling, why does he look so pleased? Out of happiness for the child? Not really.

He's completed "his" delivery. He's succeeded at something that's not always so easy. The infant is there, crying loudly, as it's "supposed" to be. The mother is safe. Everything has turned out for the best.

The doctor smiles with relief. He is justifiably pleased . . . with *himself*!

What about the mother?

Radiant expression, ecstatic smile. But what is she smiling about? The beauty of her child? Not really.

She's smiling because it's over.

She has completed "her" delivery without all the suffering she was dreading. She's amazed. And relieved. And—justifiably— proud of herself.

She's smiling with delight.

She's pleased . . . with *herself*.

And who can blame her?

Finally, what about the father?

A happy man. There will be a new generation . . . a baby who will grow up to reproduce, trait for trait, its father's perfections.

And finally, this man who may never before have truly created anything has created a child.

And so he is proud. And pleased. But pleased with *himself*.

Yes, everyone is pleased. With themselves. As for the child . . .

Is there anything we can do?

Happily, there is some hope.

"You will give birth in pain," says the Bible.

But today a woman can give birth joyfully.

A miracle.

But how can she be joyful while her child is still being crucified? It cannot be.

Should the woman then renounce her joy?

No, certainly not.

We must simply now do for the child what we have already done for the mother. Or at least we must try.

Nature, they say, doesn't move forward in sudden leaps.

Yet birth is just such a leap forward. An exchange of worlds, of levels.

How can we resolve this contradiction? How does Nature make smooth a transition whose very essence is so violent?

Very simply.

Nature is a strict mother, but a loving one. We misunderstand her intentions; then we blame her for what follows.

Everything about birth is arranged so that both leap and landing are made as easy as possible.

The danger the child faces during birth has quite properly been stressed. This danger is anoxia: a deficiency of the precious oxygen to which the nervous system is so acutely sensitive.

If it happens that the child fails to receive oxygen, the result is irreparable damage to the brain: a person maimed for life.

So at all costs, the child must not lack oxygen at birth, not even for an instant.

As the experts tell us.

As Nature has always known.

She has arranged it so that during the dangerous passage of birth, the child is receiving oxygen from two sources rather than one: from the lungs *and* from the umbilicus.

Two systems functioning simultaneously, one relieving the other: the old one, the umbilicus, continues to supply oxygen to the baby until the new one, the lungs, has fully taken its place.

However, once the infant has been born and delivered from the mother, it remains bound to her by this umbilicus, which continues to beat for several long minutes: four . . . five . . . sometimes more.

Oxygenated by the umbilicus, sheltered from anoxia, the baby can settle into breathing without danger and without shock. At leisure. Without rush.

In addition, the blood has plenty of time to abandon its old route (which leads to the placenta) and progressively to fill the pulmonary circulatory system.

During this time, in parallel fashion, an orifice closes in the heart, which seals off the old route forever.

In short, for an average of four or five minutes, the newborn infant straddles two worlds. Drawing oxygen from two sources, it switches gradually from the one to the other, without a brutal transition. One scarcely hears a cry.

What is required for this miracle to take place? Only a little patience. Only a refusal to rush things. Only knowing enough to wait, giving the child time to adjust.

We can see that education is required; otherwise, how can we bear to wait five long minutes doing absolutely nothing? When *everything* inclines us to act: our mental laziness, our automatic assumptions, our habits. And our everlasting impatience.

For the baby, it makes an enormous difference.

Whether we cut the umbilical cord immediately or not changes everything about the way respiration comes to the baby, even conditions the baby's taste for life.

If the cord is severed as soon as the baby is born, this brutally deprives the brain of oxygen.

The alarm system thus alerted, the baby's entire organism reacts. Respiration is thrown into high gear as a response to aggression.

Everything in the body-language of the infant—in the frenzied agitation of its limbs, in the very tone of its cries—shows the immensity of its panic and its efforts to escape.

Entering life, what the baby meets is death. And to escape this death it hurls itself into respiration. The act of breathing, for a newborn baby, is a desperate last resort. Already the first conditioned reflex has been implanted, a reflex in which breathing and anguish will be associated forever. What a welcome into this world!

How do things unfold when we refrain from interfering, when we protect the umbilicus?

Doubly supplied with oxygen, the baby's brain is never threatened, even for a minute. Nothing occurs to set off the alarm system. Consequently, no attack, no anoxia, no panic or anguish.

Rather, a slow and gradual progression from one state to another . . . the blood changes course without sudden disruption.

The lungs are not convulsed into action.

When the infant emerges, it utters a cry. This is because the thorax—which until now has been constricted by external pressure—is suddenly relaxed and opens wide.

A void is created. The air rushes in. It is the first breath. A passive acceptance.

It is also a burning.

Wounded, the child responds by breathing out, furiously expelling the air—this is the cry.

And then, quite often, everything stops.

As if stunned by such pain, the baby pauses. Sometimes it cries two or three times before pausing.

And the pause terrifies us. So . . . we slap the infant, smack the infant, spank the infant.

But now, better trained to control the impulses, trusting in nature and in the steady, continuing pulse of the umbilical cord, we refrain from interfering. And the baby's breathing begins again . . . by itself. Hesitantly, cautiously at first—still pausing now and again. The baby, still receiving oxygen from the umbilicus, is able to take its time discovering just how much of the burning it can tolerate.

A pause, then another breath. The baby is getting used to this sensation and gradually begins to breathe deeply. Soon it is taking pleasure in what a few moments ago was pain.

In a little while, this breathing is full and abundant, easy and joyous.

The child will have uttered no more than one cry. Or two. Or three. And we will have heard no more than some strenuous gasps— powerful, startled, punctuated by tiny cries— exclamations of surprise and an outburst of energy.

Besides the breathing, we hear other noises: noises the baby makes with its lips, nose, throat.

Lots of noises. A whole language. But no howls of terror, no cries of despair, of agony, of hysteria.

When a child comes into the world, must there be a cry?

Yes, there is no question about it.

But there is no need for weeping.

Enjoying this new experience, the baby easily loses all memory of the world it just left.

Our baby's birth is an awakening from a happy sleep.

Why should a baby cling to the past when it is so content in this new present?

So. When the umbilicus has finally stopped beating we cut it.

Actually, we cut nothing. It is a dead link that is ready to fall away of itself.

The infant has not been torn from its mother; the two have merely separated.

Later—when this infant takes its first step, ventures into the world standing up—the mother will offer her own friendly support.

The child, still shaky in the legs, will clutch its mother's hand . . . release her, then reach for her, only to let her go again. Until one day, finally steady on its own legs, it will have no further need of her support, will forget the hand that has been held out for so long.

The hand can then be withdrawn; the child has no more use for it. But what if the mother withdrew her hand while the child was still taking that first step? You might think that in this way she was hastening the child's progress, encouraging its instinct for independence. The odds are that she would be accomplishing the opposite: discouraging, not encouraging her baby.

All of this is equally true in relation to the umbilicus. By not immediately cutting the cord, we let the mother accompany her infant's first steps into the world of breathing. She goes on breathing for them both until her child is safely established in its new domain.

Cutting the umbilicus at the first cry, withdrawing the hand at the first step—they are one and the same thing.

We must behave with the most enormous respect toward this instant of birth, this fragile moment.

The baby is between two worlds. On a threshold. Hesitating.

Do not hurry. Do not press. Allow this child to enter.

What an extraordinary thing: this little creature, no longer a fetus, not yet a newborn baby.

This little creature is no longer inside his mother, yet she's still breathing for them both.

An elusive, ephemeral moment.

Leave this child. Alone.

Because this child is free—and frightened.

Don't intrude: stay back. Let time pass.

Grant this moment its slowness, and its gravity.

The rest is detail.

Once the respiratory system is functioning, everything has succeeded. (Or if it is not, then the failure is irreparable.)

But even now the details are of vital importance.

How should one place this child on the

mother's belly? On its side? Flat on its own belly? On its back?

Never on its back. This, in a single spasm, would straighten the spinal column, which has been curved for so long.

The energy that is stored there would be released with such great force, such great violence, that the shock would be unendurable.

Once again, we must remember that it is necessary to let the infant uncoil its spine and stretch its back at its own pace.

Besides, each child is born with its own character, its own temperament.

Some, when they are barely out of their mothers' wombs, straighten out proudly, flex their muscles, stretch their arms.

Their spinal columns straighten out with the force of a tightly strung bow releasing its arrow.

It can also happen that, shaken by their own temerity, they retract and huddle up again.

Others, curled in a ball at first, open themselves more gradually: venture out with great caution.

Since we cannot anticipate what is to come, it is best to place the child on its belly, arms and legs folded under.

This is the age-old, familiar posture, the one that best allows the abdomen to breathe freely and permits the infant to work its way (at its own speed) toward the final unbending.

The stretching, the triumphant extension of self. Moreover, by placing a child on its stomach, we can see its back, watch it in action, observe how it breathes.

In fact, this unbending of the spinal column, this stretching of the back, this start of free respiration are all one.

Watching this breathing, we can see how it pervades the infant's whole body. Not only the thorax but the stomach and—especially—the sides.

Soon the infant appears to be *all* breathing; one sees the powerful waves course through

its back from bottom to top, from top to bottom, from the tip of the head to the coccyx.

And then—cautiously emerging from beneath the stomach—an arm, usually the right arm.

The arm stretches out. A hand lightly touches, caresses the mother's stomach—then withdraws.

The other hand ventures out . . . slowly, as if astonished to encounter no resistance, surprised that the space around it is so vast . . .

And now the legs begin to move. First one and then the other stretches itself nervously. Then both begin to kick, and thrash—alarmed because there is no longer any barrier to impede them.

To calm their panic, we can offer them support; the touch of a hand, offering gentle resistance even while letting itself be pushed away.

This overcomes the child's horrible sense of having lost its foothold.

And then, suddenly everything is moving together, harmoniously. There is no part of the little body that is not caught up in this movement.

The baby stretches more and more boldly, thrusting, probing.

At this point the child may be placed on its side—its limbs are more relaxed in this position. Its spine adopts the posture that is most comfortable for it.

We move the baby slowly, always lending support, placing one hand under the infant's buttocks, and the other high against its back.

It is best not to touch the head at all; the head is extremely sensitive. This was the part of the child that bore the full weight of the birth drama, of the descent into hell; it was this head that cleared the path. Even the slightest touch can now arouse memories that are still too raw.

Finally, when we are sure that everything is functioning well, we place the infant on its back.

Not permanently—the baby is still not comfortable in this new straightening of the spine—but simply as a stage of adjustment.

The child is now prepared.

The umbilicus has since been cut when it ceased to beat.

And we are ready for the next step—to raise this baby upright.

Is this not the posture Man has striven for? But even now certain precautions are necessary. We must ease the child *slowly* into a sitting position, always supporting the wavering head. The child's own muscles are not yet strong enough to hold it erect without our help.

A word about the hands holding the child.

It is through our hands that we speak to the child, that we communicate.

Touching is the primary language.

"Understanding" comes long after "feeling."

Among blind people, this touching has never lost its subtlety and importance.

Immediately, we sense how important such contact is, just how important is the way we hold a child.

It is a language of skin-to-skin—the skin from which emerge all our sensory organs. And these organs in turn are like window-openings in the wall of skin that both contains and holds us separate from the world.

The newborn baby's skin has an intelligence, a sensitivity that we can only begin to imagine.

It is through this skin that the unborn child once knew its entire world: that is, its mother. It was through the entire surface of its back that it knew her uterus: our backs are, literally, our past.

Now the baby is born. And suddenly this contact is gone. Forever.

Hands touch him. Hands so unlike the uterus in temperature, in weight, in the way they move, in their power, and in their rhythm.

This is the baby's first contact with the unknown, with the new world, with that which is "other."

And our hands that touch and hold the baby, these unknowing, unfeeling hands, have no understanding at all of everything the baby has experienced until this moment.

Our hands are instruments of our intelligence, our will.

They are obedient to the muscles. Voluntary, agile muscles. Their movements are quick, brief, almost brusque.

And terrifying to the infant who has experienced only the slow internal rhythms of the womb.

How could the child *not* panic at this new kind of touch? And how, then, ought we to touch—to handle—a newborn baby?

Very simply: by remembering what this infant has just left behind. By never forgetting that everything new and unknown might terrify and that everything recognizable and familiar is reassurance.

To calm the infant in this strange, incomprehensible world into which it just emerged, it is necessary—and enough—that the hands holding him should speak in the language of the womb.

What does this mean?

That the hands must "remember" the slowness, the continuous movement of the uterine contraction, the "peristaltic wave" the child grew to know so well during the final months before its birth.

This is another reason why it is necessary to first place the child flat on its stomach—so that, in massaging it, we "speak" to its back.

And what should our hands say? Exactly what the mother and her womb have been saying.

Not the womb as it was during final labor, not the violent womb that expels and banishes. But the womb of the early, happy days.

The womb that pressed slowly, tenderly. The womb that embraced. The womb that was pure love.

It was an infinitely sensual, amorous relationship that existed between the child and its mother, between the uterus and its prisoner.

What is needed is neither a brisk rubbing motion nor a caress, but a deep and slow massage.

Our hands travel over the infant's back, one after the other, following each other like waves. One hand still in contact as the other begins. Each maintaining its steady rhythm until its entire journey is concluded. Without rediscovering this visceral slowness that lovers rediscover instinctively, it is impossible to communicate with the child.

But, people will say, you're making love to the child!

Yes, almost.

To make love is to return to paradise, it is to plunge again into the world before birth, before the great separation. It is to find again the primordial slowness, the blind and all-powerful rhythm of the internal world, of the great ocean. Making love is the great regression.

What we are doing here is softening the pain of an almost total upheaval by carrying the past forward into the present. We are giving the child company on its journey. We are soothing by sending the echo of the familiar and loving uterine waves along its back.

Yes, making love is the sovereign remedy for anguish: to make love is to rediscover peace and harmony. In the cataclysm of birth is it not fit that we should call upon this sovereign comfort?

But our hands may also remain immobile.

The hands that touch the child reveal everything to it: nervousness or calm, clumsiness or confidence, tenderness or violence.

The child knows if the hands are loving. Or if they are careless. Or worse, if they are rejecting.

In attentive and loving hands, a child abandons itself, opens itself up.

In rigid and hostile hands, a child retreats into itself, blocks out the world.

So that before we even think of recreating the prenatal rhythms which once flowed around this little body, we must let our hands lie on it motionless.

Not hands that are inert, perfunctory, distracted.

But hands that are attentive, alive, alert, responsive to its slightest quiver.

Hands that are light. That neither command nor demand. That are simply there.

Light . . . and heavy in the weight of tenderness. And of silence.

Whose hands should hold the child? The mother's, naturally, provided that these hands know . . . everything we have been saying.

But that cannot be taught. Although it can be forgotten.

How many mothers briskly pat their babies! Or shake them, while believing that they're rocking and caressing them . . .

How many have hands that are stiff, lifeless, lacking understanding!

How many preoccupied by their own emotions actually threaten to smother their children!

Happily, in most cases the woman who has delivered her baby naturally knows her own body. She is ready to hold and touch her baby. She has had to rediscover her own body, to control its negative impulses.

Such a woman, despite the joy which fills her, will not overwhelm her child.

When the newborn child is placed on her stomach, when she lays her hands on it, she will remember, "My trial is over. But not my baby's."

Yes, the delivery is over but the baby's awakening has just begun. The baby is on the first step of a glorious adventure—and yet is transfixed with fear.

Do not move. Do not add to the baby's panic.

Just be there. Without moving. Without getting impatient. Without asking anything.

At this point, out of consideration for her child, out of real—not egocentric—love, a woman will simply place her hands on its body. And leave them there, immobile.

Hands that are not animated, agitated, trembling with emotion, but are calm and light. Hands of peace.

Through such hands flow the waves of love which will assuage her baby's anguish.

REFLEX BEHAVIORS

The Newborn's Equipment

T. Berry Brazelton

Much of the complex behavior we use later in our human development is anticipated in early infancy in the form of reflexes. The infant builds upon these reflexes. After they appear, they may go underground and, with a lapse of time, return as controlled, voluntary behavior. Walking is an example of this.

Editor's Introduction

As the work on this book was beginning, my pregnancy was nearing completion. The birth of my daughter has allowed me to witness and share my impressions of the capabilities of the newborn, which is the topic of Brazelton's article.

The newborn is endowed with particular patterns of behavior which are called reflexes, since they operate from the lower centers of the brain and are evidence of noncortical functioning. The higher brain centers, which are responsible for rational thought, do not manifest themselves for a period of several weeks.

As a psychologist and as a student of human development, I am well aware of the fact that the reflex capacities are part of the equipment of every newborn. As a mother, however, I marveled at the wonders of my own child.

Like all newborn infants, she was provided with particular responses which, upon appropriate stimulation, were automatically elicited and allowed her to adapt to her extrauterine environment. While still on the delivery table, she looked at me as I held her and she sucked. She soon found her mouth with her hand and she stuffed all five fingers inside. This *hand-to-mouth-reflex* is probably the forerunner of thumbsucking and may be a way in which nature has equipped the newborn to handle tension. If her cheek was stroked, she would turn her mouth toward the stroking object, be it a finger or—as nature intended—the mother's breast. This is the *rooting reflex*. It is completely automatic and helps the baby to find the source of milk before she actually knows where the food is to be found. While the sucking and rooting reflexes are helpful in directing the baby to the source of nourishment, my daughter, Lauren, would "root" on anything available, be it an arm, a shoulder, or a nose.

Lauren startled when she was abruptly moved. Her arms and legs flailed, moving outward and upward, while her hands opened wide and then clenched tightly as though she were trying to grasp at something to prevent her fall. This response is known as the *startle* or *Moro reflex*, Dr. Moro having been the physician who first described it. This reflex is thought to be evidence of our ancestral linkage with the primates, for whom this grasping mechanism had survival value. (That is, the ape could thus grasp a tree limb in order to gain support.)

If pressure was applied to Lauren's hands or feet, her fingers or toes would grasp the pressing object. This *grasp reflex* is taken as additional evidence of our phylogenetic history. It is thought that it aided the newborn primate in holding onto the mother's furry body while allowing the mother's arms to be free for climbing trees.

If I supported Lauren by holding her under her arms and moved her across a surface, her legs would make movements which were very much like those of walking. This is a reflexive response to movement and pressure of the feet. When placed in a prone position, she would make swimming or crawling movements, lift her head off the surface, and lift herself up on her arms. A sudden drop in the temperature of the room would cause Lauren to pull her legs up in order to conserve heat before she began to shiver. If one of her legs was gently stroked, she would automatically move the other leg over to push the stroking object away. She reflexively withdrew from any painful stimulus. She closed her eyes in bright light. She also showed the capacity to habituate; for example, she responded with a startle to a sudden loud noise and then ignored it completely. Immediate repetition of the noise elicited no response.

While Lauren had many adaptive reflexes at birth, there were many responses yet to develop, such as the first time she intentionally looked into my eyes and the first time she showed a social smile that was more than an expression of general well-being. It was also a while before she was able to reach for an object with visually guided attention. Her natural endowment was remarkable but, like the first part of this book, it was only the beginning.

Pamela Cantor

Each newly born infant is equipped with a potential for physical, mental, and emotional development. Because the human animal has the longest period of childhood dependency in which he may unfold, he learns not only how to survive but also how to utilize all of this potential in a complex fashion for learning and thinking. How he does this is intimately dependent on the experiences that he has with the world around him.

The newborn's capacity for behavior resides in the central part of the brain (or midbrain) during the first three months of life. He reacts largely with reflexes and uses a rather primitive setup by which he receives stimuli and reacts to them. His brain's higher center (or cortex) is playing only a monitoring and storage role at best, according to neurologists, not the fully determining one it will play later.

At birth there are pathways throughout the entire nervous system, like electric circuits, that are ready to be set off by the appropriate signals. A mother automatically uses these signals as part of her mothering. An example could be the first feeding. She stimulates his lips and mouth as she inserts the nipple and as she holds him in a way that allows his rooting, sucking, and swallowing mechanisms to start into chainlike action. The infant's cortex is ready to learn with each reaction and to store up the effects of this experience.

THE IMPORTANCE OF STIMULATION

The infant is constantly receiving and reacting to stimuli. Each stimulus adds to the new baby's experience. The stimulus sets off a pathway of reactions. The "receptor" nerves that receive the signal transmit it to the baby's nervous system. A long, complex train of reactions are set off along this pathway that end in a reflex or automatic reaction. Since the newborn's nervous system is largely at the mercy of such stimulus-response systems, many repetitions of this go into the "learning" or "conditioning" that will eventually result in his ability to react with the discrimination characteristic of the human animal. With each stimulus reaction an infant's brain has the opportunity to store up experience for future learning.

How can an infant "learn" in the face of a bombardment of many kinds of new stimuli? He must already have the ability to select which one he will receive and react to. He must have predetermined pathways that will select an "appropriate" versus an "inappropriate" signal. He must have the ability to "prefer" one reaction at a particular moment over the other. These assumptions about a brand-new baby may well evoke wonder or criticism from those who have never really looked at or played with a baby.

The infant in the delivery room seems to have strong preferences and strong dislikes. He will react to a loud noise once, but will shut it out the second and third times. Soon after birth, he will alert with a start, control his startle reaction, and turn to a soft rattle or a crooning voice.

More impressive mechanisms are available to him in this selecting process. Even while he is asleep he is receiving stimuli but is able to suppress disturbing reactions to them. He deals with them effectively in sleep so that he need not react in the usual manner to them. In fact, a newborn can be "put to sleep" by a series of strong or changing stimuli that disturb him at first, then begin to quiet him. Finally he goes to sleep in the face of a barrage of disturbing events.

I saw a striking example of this suppressive mechanism in a newborn who was being tested in the hospital. He was brought into the room for a cardiogram and an electroencephalogram or brain-wave test. The rubber bands were tightly placed around his scalp like a headband, and around his wrists. Both were constricting enough to cause swelling of his flesh on either side of the bands and must have been painful. The infant screamed for a few seconds, then quieted abruptly. He kept his arms and legs pulled up into a fetal position and remained motionless throughout the rest of the testing period. He seemed asleep except that his extremities were tightly flexed. A series of bright lights and sharp noises seemed barely to disturb him. All those in the room said, "See, he's asleep!" His brainwave showed the pattern of sleep. When the stimulation ceased, however, and the tightly constricting bands were removed, he immediately roused and cried lustily for fifteen minutes. Why hadn't he cried during the ordeal? This apparent sleep seemed to be a more successful way of shutting out disturbing stimuli. The infant's amazing capacity for handling such an upsetting situation makes one realize how well he is equipped at birth to withstand disturbances and insults from the outside world.

Lack of stimulation is a much more devastating kind of experience to the growing neonate. Too much handling and anxious stimulation may create such reactions as excessive crying and even "colic." But as the infant matures, he becomes able to handle and assimilate these stimuli, even though they may not have been the most appropriate. Too little stimulation is worse, for it can lead to subtler forms of interference with development and growth. Just as an infant's physiological growth depends on proper nutrients fed at natural intervals, his emotional growth needs encouragement and a kind of nurturing stimulation. Without them, he will pass through critical periods of development with no progress from one stage to the next. Institutionalized children who are maintained physically, but not fed necessary emotional nutrients, demonstrate the effect of such privation. They may start out as normally demanding babies. They make their needs known by crying and react to attention with smiles. As those around them respond with infrequent, sterile encouragement, the babies' responses become less frequent, and their demands less forceful. Their cries become weaker, their smiles fade, and they turn inward. They begin to roll their heads, play weakly with their hands or hair or clothes, or stare at the walls with an empty look. Their social responses to an outside person consist of an apathetic curiosity or faint anxiety followed almost immediately by turning away.

Inner forces that propel an infant from one stage of development to the next are: (1) a drive to survive independently in a complex world; (2) a drive toward mastery made evident in the observable excitement that accompanies each development step; and (3) the drive to fit into, to identify with, to please, and to become part of his environment. The first force comes from within the child and is constantly being fed by the second, his own delight in mastery. The third falls to the mother and father to nurture. It constantly surprises me how early an infant picks up cues from his environment that lead him to "want" to become a part of it. That he can sense the climate around him is by now well known. But the fact that he is able to tune in and out when stimulation is appropriate or inappropriate to his particular state of the moment or to his stage of development can be a reassuring, exciting discovery for his parents. He can choose what he needs from his environment,

as long as someone gives him something to choose from.

SENSORY REACTIONS AND REFLEX BEHAVIOR

The newborn shows a capacity to react differentially to stimulation. He will respond in a positive way to a stimulus that is appropriate to him. He will shut his eyes tightly and will keep them shut after being exposed to a bright white light, but he will alert and look intently at a red or soft yellow object dangled before him. As he looks, his face brightens, his body quiets, and his eyes glisten. He will follow it with his eyes, even turning his head when the object is moved slowly from one side to the other. He can even follow it up and down. This complicated visual responsiveness can be seen in a baby in the delivery room, at a time when we know he has had no previous experience with vision. Mothers comment that they can see their new infants looking at them as they hold them, but they have been taught to believe that a newborn can't see. A newborn can and does respond to visual objects that are within a particular range of sensory values which, in turn, are *appropriate* to his particular stage of development.

This same differentiation of responses can be seen in his hearing. As was stated before, a loud noise or series of noises causes him to startle or shudder. Thereafter, he can suppress his reaction to more loud sounds so that he seems almost not to hear them. In the newborn nursery, I have been able to produce and reproduce fleeting smiles by the use of soft noises. Research has shown that neonates (before learning can have been a determining factor) exhibit more consistent quieting and alerting to a soft, high-pitched voice than to a low one. Perhaps this is nature's preparation for a mother's voice in preference to a father's. At least it justifies the high-pitched baby talk that many of us use in dealing with babies.

The importance of a newborn of tactile experiences has been outlined by the late Lawrence Frank. He equates touch to a language or communication system for infants, and feels that one of the major reasons for defective development in institutional babies is the infrequent handling that they receive. All of us have experienced the thrill of having a baby quiet from active crying when he is picked up or held. Many fussing babies will quiet when a hand is simply placed on their abdomens, or when an extremity, such as an arm or leg, is restrained firmly. Swaddling has this effect, and it is an old remedy for a fussing, "colicky" baby. I think this involves a number of things for the infant. The quiet, soothing aspect of touch plus the effects of firm, steady pressure join to quiet the baby. By restraining any part of his body, one interferes with a reflex reaction that is called the Moro reflex.

The Moro is a reflex that is a remnant of our ape ancestry. When the baby experiences a sudden change in position that causes him to drop his head backward, he startles, throws out his arms and legs, extends his neck, cries briefly, then rapidly brings his arms together and flexes his body as if to clasp the branch of a tree or his mother as he falls. This reflex is a disturbing one to him, one that he sets off for himself repeatedly when he is crying. Thus, as he cries, he startles, cries because of the startle, and sets up a vicious circle. Any steady pressure on a part of his body seems to break into this circle, and results in calming the baby.

Stroking the infant in special parts of his body will set up special reactions. He will "root" or turn toward the stroking object if his cheek or the area around his mouth is touched. This rooting reflex is important in helping the infant find the breast. The sucking reflex will follow and is intimately tied up with initial rooting. The rooting and sucking reflexes are best stimulated by touching the mucous membranes of the mouth. The inside of the mouth is more sensitive than the area around it. Even a sleepy infant will suck when his soft palate is stimulated.

When the palm of the infant's hand or sole of his foot is stroked, he will close on the object in a grasp that is strong and determined. The more premature he is, the more determined and unremitting his grasp may be. Seven-month premature babies can be picked up by their hand grasps and held in the air, clinging to the examiner's fingers, as if they were holding on to a tree branch for dear life. A more mature infant has a grasp that comes and goes with rhythmic relaxation, but he, too, can support his own weight with his hands, and one can lift his leg off the bed by using his toe grasp.

Stroking the soles of the infant's foot can set up two opposing reflexes in the toes. One is the grasp, described above, that is set off by pressing the end of the foot at the base of the toes. The other, called a Babinski, is set off by stroking the outside of the sole. The toes spread out and the largest toe extends up in the air.

There is a hand-to-mouth reflex that is set off by stroking either the cheek or the palm of the hand. The simple stroking of one end or the other of this hand-mouth chain causes the infant's mouth to root, his arm to flex, and bring his hand up to his mouth. His mouth opens in anticipation, and he brings his fist up to it. Infants will complete this hand-to-mouth cycle in the first few days, and they need very little stimulation to set it off. In fact, it is likely that hand-to-mouth activity and finger-sucking are common activities for infants in the uterus. It is often reinforced after delivery by their initial fight to clear their respiratory tracts. I have seen a seven-month premature baby suck on her thumb when she was attempting to choke down mucus and clear her airway in order to survive. She was able to bring her fingers to her mouth, to suck on them, and, because of the sucking, to swallow the mucus. The tactile gratification around the mouth and hand is coupled with the infant's ability to reproduce *for himself* the sucking experience which is satisfied every time he feeds. I have come to feel that an intentional bringing of his hand to his mounth during periods of stimulation is evidence of good ability on the part of a newborn.

There are protective reflexes that are available to the infant and demonstrate his amazing capacity to survive under adverse conditions. When an object that could conceivably stop his breathing is placed over the baby's nose and mouth, he begins to mouth it vigorously as if to displace it, and then twists his head violently from side to side. Finally, if these maneuvers of his head are unsuccessful, he begins to flail; each arm is brought across his face as he attempts to knock the object away.

Stroking one leg causes the other leg to flex, cross over, and push the stroking object away with the other foot. When an upper part of the body is stroked or tickled, his hand comes over to grasp the object. When one applies a painful stimulus to any part of the baby's body, he will withdraw from it if he can. Then his hands will try to push the painful stimulus away. He will bat at it over and over again. For instance, when I have to draw blood from an infant's heel, he pulls his foot away. When this doesn't work, the other foot comes over to push me away. The other foot may be quite difficult to keep out of the way.

Placed on his belly, head down, the infant has a set of reflexes that make it almost impossible for him to smother in that position. He picks his head up off the bed, then turns it to one side or the other. He begins to crawl with his legs, and can even lift himself up on his arms. Occasionally newborns flip themselves completely over to one side or the other—all as part of reflex responses with which they are equipped at birth.

Temperature changes from warm to cold may be most upsetting to an infant's body equilibrium. When a part of his body is exposed to a real temperature change (and we can see this by blowing cold air from a tube onto a small part of his belly, his whole body changes color and temperature in an effort to equalize the local temperature change. He becomes upset and will pull his legs and arms in to cut down on the amount of exposed body surface. Finally, he begins to cry and shiver in an effort to improve his body's circulation, and to protest the disturbing temperature change. When he is covered and warmed, he quiets down again.

The difference in performance that is apparent in a premature as opposed to a full-term infant demonstrates the importance of time and learning on his movements. The jerky, flinging, flailing of arms and legs that appear in a preemie are precursors to the smoother, cycling, self-monitored movements of a full-term baby. Many full-term babies demonstrate less mature movements. The more immature an infant is, the more such flailing is seen. They are rapid, cogwheel-like thrusts outward of arms and legs, with sudden flexion and return to his body. Twitches and convulsion-like movements are normal and common. The infant's preferred position may vary from a floppy frogleg and arms half extended on the bed to one of complete flexion with all extremities pulled into his body, as he must have been in the uterus.

There is a reflex present at birth that is a response to having the head turned to one side or the other. This is called the "tonic neck reflex" or T.N.R. When a baby's head is turned to one side, and even when he turns it himself, his whole body may arch away from the side to which his head is turned. The arm on the face side extends, the other arm flexes in a fencing position, and the leg on the face side may draw up in flexion. This reflex may be used in conjunction with several of the others we have mentioned, such as the Moro and the extension of the head in prone, to assist the baby in delivering himself from the uterus. The T.N.R. influences behavior for several months after delivery and helps him to learn to use one side of his body separately from the other.

When a baby, lying on his back, is pulled up by the arms to a sitting position, he tries to maintain his head upright. One feels his whole shoulder girdle tense as he helps to pull up his head. When his head flops forward, he will try to bring it up again. It will overshoot and flop backward. He tries to right it again and it falls forward. These attempts to keep his head in the upright position are part of his "righting reflexes." When he is pulled to sit, his eyes open in a "doll's eye reflex"—just like the old baby dolls that had weights attached to their china eyeballs.

When a baby is held in the examiner's hands and rotated toward one side, the infant's head turns toward the side to which he is being rotated, and his eyes also go ahead of the rotation. Rocking a baby from side to side in a moderately upright position may be the most successful way of getting him to open his eyes as a newborn. Most mothers seem to worry about their babies' eyes after delivery. This is a maneuver that may help them to open the infant's eyes.

If a newborn is suspended in the air by his legs, he may assume a fetal position, flexing his legs and arms, curling into an upside-down ball. Then he extends his legs and drops his arms, extending into a straight line, arching his head backward. Babies rarely cry in this position, and even quiet when suspended this way. It does not injure them if it is done gently; it must be reminiscent of their position in the uterus.

Another series of reflexes combines to propel an infant across a bed, or even through the water. An infant has available, like any amphibian, a rhythmical extension and flexion of his legs and arms, which can be accompanied by a swinging of his trunk from side to side. This activity looks like that of an amphibian, and relates us to them in the hierarchy of evolution. Added to this is an infant's capacity to inhibit breathing when his head is placed under water for a short period. Mothers who accidentally let their infant's head dip under water report that the babies seem to be less affected by it than they are themselves. Rarely do they choke and aspirate water. Their gag reflexes are still too strong.

The stepping reflex can be seen when a baby is held in a standing position. The sole of one foot, and then the other, is pressed gently on the bed. Each leg is drawn up in succession as he seems to walk. This walking reflex is similar to the voluntary attempts that come much later. A brand-new infant can be helped to walk across a bed. This early sign of the more complex act of walking is exciting to all of us who are interested in the evolution of behavior.

Much of the complex behavior we use later in our human development is anticipated in early infancy in the form of reflexes. The infant builds upon these reflexes. After they appear, they may go underground and, with a lapse of time, return as controlled, voluntary behavior. Walking is an example of this. Long after the newborn's walk reflex has disappeared, it reappears in the voluntarily controlled, complex act of walking.

Since every new parent is presented with an infant whose repertoire is made up of reflexes and poorly understood response systems, I hope that this sketchy documentation of some of them will increase his pleasure in watching and caring for the infant. As I stated in the paragraph on the importance of stimulation, any is better than none. However, stimulation geared to an understanding of the infant's own style is bound to be even more productive. Mothering is too complex and instinctive to teach, but understanding of what is going on in her infant can reinforce a mother's best judgment and instincts, and, above all, add to her pleasure. When parents enjoy interacting with their new baby, he, in turn, becomes more rewarding. This circular process can only add luster to each of the participants.

SENSORY CAPACITIES OF THE INFANT IN THE FIRST FEW WEEKS OF LIFE

The Determinants of Attention in the Infant

Jerome Kagan

A . . . source of support for the discrepancy hypothesis comes from experiments in which an originally meaningless stimulus is presented repeatedly (usually 5 to 10 times), and afterwards a variation of the original stimulus is shown to the infant. Fixation time typically decreases with repetitions of the first stimulus; but when the variation is presented fixation times increase markedly (McCall and Melson, 1966).

Editor's Introduction

Jerome Kagan suggests that there are three major factors which control an infant's attention to visual events. During the first two months of life, movement and black-white contour have the greatest ability to hold the attention of the infant. By 4 months of age, an event which is discrepant from the infant's usual environment will have the greatest power to hold his or her attention. The discrepancy hypothesis states that events which present a novel stimulus to the infant will elicit increased attention as long as the event is not so discrepant as to be frightening. In other words, for the infant, a small increment of change will be pleasant while extreme change will be disturbing. The third determinant of attention becomes apparent only after the infant reaches approximately 8 months of age. At this point the infant will begin to utilize hypotheses to represent discrepant events.

Kagan concludes that the central problem involved in the education of children is the maintenance of attention. Thus, the question of the determinants of attention is not limited to infancy alone. The major theoretical issue in the understanding of mental growth then becomes the identification of the factors which will predict how the infant, and later the child; will distribute his or her attention.

Pamela Cantor

A six-month-old infant displays a remarkable ability to focus his attention on interesting events, and he will maintain prolonged orientations to the face of a stranger, the movement

Reprinted by permission, *American Scientist*, Journal of Sigma Xi, The Scientific Research Society of North America, Inc.

of a leaf, or a lively conversation. He seems to be quietly absorbing information and storing it for future use. Since acquiring knowledge about the environment depends so intimately upon how the infant distributes his attention, and for how long, it is important to ask what governs these processes. This question has stimulated fruitful research from which an outline of preliminary principles is emerging.

EARLY DETERMINANTS OF FIXATION TIME: CONTRAST AND MOVEMENT

The most obvious index of attentiveness to visual events is the length of orientation to an object—called fixation time. Like any response it has multiple determinants; the relative power of each seems to change as the infant grows. Ontogenetically, the earliest determinant of length of orientation to a visual event derives from the basic nature of the central nervous system. The infant is predisposed to attend to events that possess a high rate of change in their physical characteristics. Stimuli that move or possess light-dark contrast are most likely to attract and hold a newborn's attention. A two-day-old infant is more attentive to a moving or intermittent light than to a continuous light source; to a design with a high degree of black-white contrast than to one of homogeneous hue (Haith 1966; Salapatek and Kessen 1966; Fantz 1966; Fantz and Nevis 1967). These facts come from experiments in which stimuli varying, for example, in degree of black-white contrast (e.g., a black triangle on a white background versus a totally gray stimulus) are presented to infants singly or in pairs while observers or cameras record the length of orientation to each of the stimuli. In general, the newborn's visual search behavior seems to be guided by the following rules: (1) If he is alert and the light is not too bright, his eyes open. (2) Seeing no light, he searches. (3) Seeing light but no edges, he keeps searching. (4) Finding contour edges, his eyes focus on and cross them (Haith 1968).

The attraction to loci of maximal contrast and movement is in accord with knowledge about ganglion potentials in the retinas of vertebrates. Some ganglion cells respond to a light going on; others to its going off; still others to both. Since an object moving across a visual field stimulates a set of cells for a short period, it creates onset and offset patterns similar to those of an intermittent light. Figures that contain dark lines on light backgrounds serve better as onset stimuli than do solid patterns because the change in stimulation created by the border of dark on light elicits more frequent firing of nerve cells, and this phenomenon may facilitate sustained attention (Kuffler 1952, 1953).

The preference for attending to objects with high contrast is dependent, however, on the size of the figure; there seems to be an optimal area that maintains fixation at a maximum. Four-month-old infants shown designs of varying areas (Figure 3-1) were most attentive to the moderately large designs (Figure 3-2) (McCall and Kagan 1967). Similarly there is a nonlinear relation between the total amount of black-white edge in a figure and attention. Consider a series of black-and-white checker-

Figure 3-1   One of a set of random designs shown to 4-month-old infants.

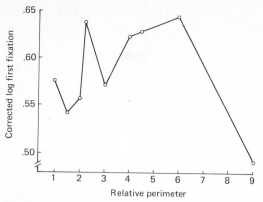

Figure 3-2 Relation between fixation time and approximate area of random design in 4-month-old infants.

boards of constant area but varying numbers of squares. The total number of inches at which black borders white increases as the number of squares increases. Karmel (1966) has suggested, on the basis of studies with young infants, that the longest fixations are devoted to figures with a moderate amount of edge.

Although indices of attention to auditory events are more ambiguous than those to visual ones, intermittent tones, which have a high rate of change, elicit more sustained interest, as evidenced by motor quieting, than continuous tones (Eisenberg 1964; Brackbill 1966). Nature has apparently awarded the newborn an initial bias in his processing of experience. He does not have to learn what he should examine, as the nineteenth-century empiricists argued. The preferential orientation to change is clearly adaptive, for the source of change is likely to contain the most information about the presence of his mother or danger.

THE ROLE OF DISCREPANCY FROM SCHEMA

The initial disposition to attend to events with a high rate of change soon competes with a new determinant based on experience. The child's encounters with events result, inevitably, in some mental representation of the experience, called a schema. A schema is defined as an abstraction of a sensory event that preserves the spatial or temporal pattern of the distinctive elements of the event. A schema is to be regarded as a functional property of mind that permits an organism to recognize and retrieve information. The schema does not necessarily involve a motor response. It is neither a detailed copy of the event nor synonymous with the language label for the event. An example from a recent experiment may be useful here.

A four-year-old looked through a set of 50 magazine pictures illustrating objects, people, or scenes, many of which he had never seen before and could not name when asked. He spent only a few seconds on each picture and flipped through the 50 in less than three minutes. He was then shown 50 pairs of pictures; one of each pair was the picture he saw earlier, the other was new. He was asked to point to the picture he saw before. Although he could recall spontaneously only three or four, the average four-year-old recognized over 45 of the 50 pictures. Some children recognized them all. Since some of the pictures showed objects the child had never seen (say, a lathe or a slide rule), it is unlikely that his performance can be totally explained by assuming that each picture elicited a language label or a fragmentary motor response. What hypothetical entity shall we invoke to explain the child's ability to recognize over 90 percent of the scenes? If we use the concept schema to refer to the processes that permitted recognition, we can say that each picture contained a unique configuration of salient elements, and the schema preserved that configuration, without necessarily preserving an exact spatial analogue of the event. Some psychologists might use the older term memory engram to convey the meaning we attribute to schema. The schema for a visual event is not a photographic copy, for minor changes in the scenes viewed initially do not produce changes in the child's performance. Nor is the schema synonymous with a visual image, for the child is also able to recognize a series of different melodies or sound patterns after brief exposure to each. Early twentieth-century biologists used the concept of the gene to explain demonstrated properties of cells and nuclear material, though no one knew the gene's structure. We use the concept of schema to account for properties of mind, even though we cannot specify its structure.

The notion of schema helps to explain the older infant's distribution of attention. Toward the end of the second month, fixation time is influenced by the degree to which the child's memory for a particular class of events resembles the specific external event encountered originally. Thus the length of orientation to a picture of a strange face is dependent on the child's schema for the faces he has seen in the past. Events which are moderately discrepant from his schema elicit longer fixations than very familiar events or ones that are completely novel and bear no relation to the schema. The relation of fixation time to magnitude of discrepancy between schema and event is assumed to be curvilinear; this assumption is called the discrepancy hypothesis.

The neurophysiologist describes this attentional phenomenon in slightly different language.

The prepotent role of novelty in evoking the orienting reflex suggests that this response is not initiated directly by a stimulus, in the customary sense of the term, but rather by a change in its intensity, pattern or other parameters. A comparison of present with previous stimulation seems of prime significance, with an orienting reflex being evoked by each point of disagreement. The concept of a cortical neuronal model . . . accounts for this induction of the orienting reflex by stimuli whose characteristic feature is their novelty. This model preserves information about earlier stimuli, with which aspects of novel stimulation may be compared. The orienting reflex is evoked whenever the parameters of the novel stimulus do not coincide with those of the model [Magoun 1969, p. 180].

Although an orienting reflex can often be produced by any change in quality or intensity of stimulation, duration of sustained attention seems to be influenced by the degree of discrepancy between event and related schema. Consider some empirical support for the discrepancy hypothesis. One- or two-week-old infants look equally long at a black-and-white outline of a regular face and a meaningless design, for contrast is still the major determinant of attention at this early age. Even the eight-week-old attends equally long to a three-dimensional model of a head and an abstract three-dimensional form (Carpenter 1969). But four-month-old infants show markedly longer fixations to the two regular faces . . . than to the design . . . (McCall and Kagan 1967). The four-month-old has acquired a schema for a human face, and the achromatic illustrations are moderately discrepant from that schema. However, if the face is highly discrepant from the schema, as occurs when the components are rearranged, . . . fixation time is reduced (Wilcox 1969; Haaf and Bell 1967). The moderately discrepant face elicits more sustained attention than the extremely discrepant form at 16 weeks, but not during the first eight weeks of life (Fantz and Nevis 1967; Wilcox 1969; Lewis 1969). The differences in length of fixation to a normal face and to an equally complex but distorted face is greatest between three and six months of age, when infants normally display long fixations to faces. After six months fixation times to photographs of faces drop by over 50 percent and are equally long for both regular and irregular faces (Lewis 1969).

This developmental pattern confirms the discrepancy hypothesis. Prior to two months, before the infant has a schema for a human face, photographs of either regular or irregular faces are treated as nonsense designs and elicit equal periods of attention. Between two and four months the schema for a human face is established, and a photograph of a strange face is optimally discrepant from that schema. During the latter half of the first year, the schema for a face becomes so firmly established that photographs of regular or irregular faces, though discriminable, elicit short and equal fixations.

A second source of support for the discrepancy hypothesis comes from experiments in which an originally meaningless stimulus is presented repeatedly (usually 5 to 10 times), and afterward a variation of the original stimulus is shown to the infant. Fixation time typically decreases with repetitions of the first stimulus; but when the variation is presented, fixation times increase markedly (McCall and Melson 1969). In one experiment four-month-old infants were shown a stimulus containing three objects (a doll, a bow, and a flower) for five 30-second presentations. On the sixth trial the infants saw a stimulus in which one, two, or all three objects were replaced with new ones. Most infants showed significantly longer fixations to the changed stimulus than to the last presentation of the original (McCall and Kagan 1970).

The most persuasive support for the curvilinear hypothesis comes from an experiment in which a new schema was established experimentally (Super, Kagan, Morrison, Haith, and Weiffenbach, unpublished). Each of 84 first-born Caucasian infants, four months old, was shown the same three-dimensional stimulus composed of three geometric forms of different shape and hue for 12 half-minute periods . . . . Each infant was then randomly assigned

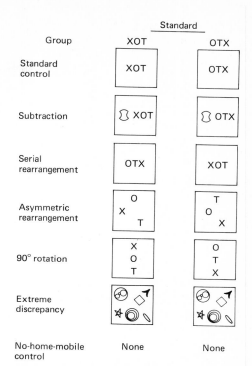

Figure 3-3 Schematic illustration of the mobiles infants saw at home for twenty-one days.

to one of seven groups. Six of these groups were exposed at home to a stimulus that was of varying discrepancy from the standard viewed in the laboratory. The mother showed the stimulus, in the form of a mobile, to the child 30 minutes a day for 21 days. The seven experimental groups were as follows (Figure 3-3).

Group 1: Control standard. These infants were exposed to the same stimulus they saw in the laboratory at four months.

Group 2: Subtraction. These infants were shown a four-element stimulus constructed by adding a fourth element to the three-element standard seen in the laboratory. ("Subtraction" referred to the later laboratory session [see below], which used only three elements.)

Group 3: Serial rearrangement. Infants exposed to a stimulus in which the three elements of the original standard were rearranged in the horizontal plane.

Group 4: Asymmetric rearrangement. Infants shown the three-element stimulus rearranged in an asymmetric form.

Group 5: Ninety-degree rotation. Infants shown a stimulus in which the three horizontal elements in the standard were rearranged in a vertical plane.

Group 6: Extreme discrepancy. Infants shown a mobile consisting of many more elements of different shapes and colors than those of the standard.

Group 7: No-mobile control. Infants exposed to no stimulus during the 21-day experiment period.

Three weeks later each subject was brought back to the laboratory and shown the same stimulus viewed initially at four months. The major dependent variable was the change in fixation time between the first and second test sessions. Figure 3-4 illustrates these changed scores for total fixation time across the first six trials of each sessions.

The infants who saw no stimulus at home are the referent group to which all the other

groups are to be compared. These infants showed no change in fixation time across the three weeks, indicating that the laboratory stimulus was as attractive on the second visit as on the first. The infants who developed a schema for the asymmetric and vertical rotation mobiles (moderate discrepancy) showed the smallest drop in interest across the three weeks. By contrast, the infants who experienced a minimal (groups 2 and 3) or major discrepancy (group 6) showed the greatest drop in interest. (Analysis of variance for total fixation time across the first six trials yielded an F ratio of 5.29 and a probability value of less than .05.) There was a curvilinear relation between attention and stimulus-schema discrepancy. Although the existing data are still not conclusive, they clearly support the discrepancy hypothesis.

The onset of a special reaction to discrepancy between two and three months is paralleled by other physiological and behavioral changes in the infant. . . . The Moro reflex—the spreading and coming together of the arms when the head is suddenly dropped a few inches—begins to disappear, crying decreases, babbling increases, decreased attention to repeated presentations of a visual event becomes a reliable phenomenon (Dreyfus-Brisac 1958; Ellingson 1967), and three-dimensional representations of objects elicits longer fixations than two-dimensional ones (Fantz 1966). Perhaps the infant's capacity to react to discrepancy at this age reflects the fact that the brain has matured enough to permit the establishment of long-term memories and their activation by external events.

THE EFFECT OF THE INFANT'S HYPOTHESES

As the child approaches the end of the first year, he acquires a new kind of cognitive structure which we call hypotheses. A hypothesis is an interpretation of some experience

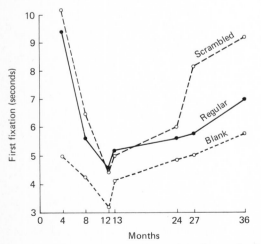

Figure 3-4 Change in fixation time for each of the experimental groups.

accomplished by mentally transforming an unusual event to the form the child is familiar with. The "form he is familiar with" is the schema. The cognitive structure used in the transformation is the hypothesis. Suppose a five-year-old notes a small bandage on his mother's face; he will attempt to find the reason for the bandage and may activate the hypothesis, "She cut her face." A five-month-old will recognize his mother in spite of the bandage but will not try to explain its presence.

To recognize that a particular sequence of sounds is human speech, rather than a telephone, requires a schema for the quality of a human voice. Interpretation of the meaning of the speech, on the other hand, requires the activation of hypotheses, in this case linguistic rules. The critical difference between a schema and a hypothesis resembles the difference between recognition and interpretation. Recognition is the assimilation of an event as belonging to one class rather than another. The performance of the four-year-old in the experiment with 50 pictures illustrates the recognition process. The child requires only a schema for the original event in order to answer correctly. Interpretation involves the additional process of activating hypotheses that change the perception of an event so that it can be understood. It is assumed that the activation of hypotheses to explain discrepant events is accompanied by sustained attention. The more extensive the repertoire of hypotheses—the more knowledge the child has—the longer he can work at interpretation and the more prolonged his attention. The child's distribution of attention at an art museum provides a final analogy. He may be expected to study somewhat unusual pictures longer than extremely realistic ones or surrealistic ones because he is likely to have a richer set of hypotheses for the moderately discrepant scenes. The richer the repertoire of hypotheses, holding discrepancy of event con-

stant, the longer the child will persist at interpretation. There is as yet no body of empirical proof for these ideas, but data that we shall consider agree with these views.

In sum, three factors influence length of fixation time in the infant. High rate of change in physical aspects of the stimulus is primary during the opening weeks, discrepancy becomes a major factor at two months, and activation of hypotheses becomes influential at around 12 months. These three factors supplement each other; and a high-contrast discrepant event that activates many hypotheses should elicit longer fixation times from an 18-month-old than a stimulus with only one or two of these attributes.

Two parallel investigations attest to the potential usefulness of the complementary principles of discrepancy and activation of hypotheses. In the first, one-, two-, and three-year-old children of middle class families in Cambridge, Massachusetts, and of peasant Indian families from a village in the Yucatan peninsula were shown color prints of male faces—Caucasian for the American children and Indian for the Mexican children (Finley 1967). Fixation time to the faces increased with age. The largest increase between two and three years of age occurred to the discrepant, scrambled face rather than to the nondiscrepant, regular face; the former required the activation of more hypotheses in order to be assimilated.

In the second study 180 white, firstborn boys and girls from the Cambridge area viewed . . . clay faces . . . repeatedly at 4, 8, 13, and 27 months of age. There was a U-shaped relation between age and fixation time. Fixation decreased from 4 to 13 months but increased between 13 and 27 months. The longer fixations at 4 months reflect the fact that these stimuli were discrepant from the infant's acquired schema for his parents' faces. Fixations decreased at 8 and 13 months because these masks were less discrepant but did not yet activate a long train of hypotheses in the service of assimilation. Between one and two years fixations rose because the child was activating hypotheses to resolve the discrepancy.

As with the first study, the largest increase in fixation time, between 13 and 27 months, occurred to the scrambled face. The children's spontaneous comments indicated that they were trying to understand how a face could be so transformed. "What happened to his nose? Who hit him in the nose?" asked a two-year-old. And, "Who that, Mommy? A monster, Mommy?" said another. The function resulting from combining the data of the two studies is illustrated in Figure 3-5. The U-shaped relation between fixation time and age is concordant with the theoretical argument given earlier.

SOCIAL CLASS AND FIXATION TIME

The number of hypotheses surrounding a class of events should covary, in part, with language competence. Hence any experiences that pro-

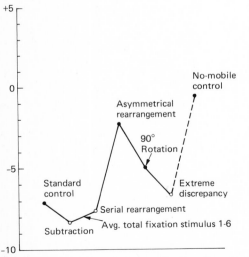

Figure 3-5 Relation between fixation time to faces and age of child.

mote acquisition of language should be associated with longer fixation times toward the end of the first year. The positive correlation between parental educational level and the child's linguistic competence is well known and well documented (see, for example, Cazden 1966). Thus a positive relation between parental education and fixation time should appear toward the end of the first year and grow with time. The data on 180 firstborns indicated that parental education was not highly related to fixation time to faces at 4 and 8 months but was moderately related (correlation coefficient [r]= about 0.4) at 13 and 27 months, and this relation was slightly stronger for girls than for boys. Since the majority of infants either increased in fixation time or showed no essential change between 13 and 27 months, we computed the change in first fixation between 13 and 27 months for each child and correlated that change with parental educational level as well as independent indexes of verbal ability at 27 months. There was a positive relation between increase in fixation time and parents' education level for the girls (r = .31) but not for boys (r = −.04); 27-month-old girls with the highest vocabulary scores showed the largest increases in fixation time.

It is not clear why the relation between parental education and sustained attention should be stronger for girls than for boys. Other investigators have also reported closer covariation in girls than boys between social class and various indexes of cognitive development including IQ scores and school grades. Moss and Robson (1968) studied the relation between amount of face-to-face interaction mother and infant had in the home and the three-month-old infant's fixation time to photographs of faces in the laboratory. The association was positive for girls (r = .61, p < .01) and close to zero for boys. Hess, Shipman, Brophy, and Bear (1968, 1969) and Werner (1969) have reported more substantial correlations for girls than boys between maternal education or verbal ability, on the one hand, and the child's IQ or level of reading achievement on the other. There seems to be a general tendency for indexes of maternal intellectual ability and, by inference, maternal concern with the child's mental development, to be better predictors of cognitive development in daughters than sons.

One interpretation of this puzzling phenomenon rests on the fact that girls are biologically less variable than boys (Acheson 1966). This implies that fewer infant girls would display extreme degrees of irritability, activity, or attentiveness. Let us assume the following principle: the more often the mother attempts to interest her child in an event the stronger the child's tendency to develop a general sensitivity to change and a capacity for sustained attention to discrepancy. This principle is likely to be less valid for infants who temperamentally have a tendency toward apathy or hypervigilance. There are many functional relations in nature that lose their validity when one of the variables assumes an extreme value, and this may be another instance of that phenomenon.

An alternative explanation of the stronger covariation for girls than boys between maternal intelligence and the child's mental development assumes greater differences between well and poorly educated mothers in their treatment of daughters than of sons, especially in maternal actions that promote attention and language acquisition. A mother seems more likely to project her motives, expectations, and self-image on her daughter than on her son, and is more likely to assume that her daughter will come to resemble her. Many poorly educated mothers feel less competent than the college graduate and have greater doubts about their daughters' potential for intellectual accomplishment. Such a mother may set or supply lower standards and less enthusiastic as well as less consistent encouragement to her infant girl to learn new skills. The well educated mother sets higher aspirations and acts as though she held the power to catalyze her child's development.

The situation with sons is somewhat different. Most mothers, regardless of class background, believe their sons will have to learn how to support a family and achieve some degree of independence. Hence mothers of all classes may be more alike in energizing the cognitive development of sons. The restricted range of acceleration of sons, compared with daughters, would result in closer covariation for girls between social class and indexes of cognitive development.

This argument finds support in observations of the mother-child interaction in the home. Well educated mothers are more likely to talk to their four-month-old daughters than mothers with less than a high school education. But this class difference in maternal "talkativeness" does not occur for sons. Observations of an independent sample of 60 mother-daughter pairs at 10 months of age (Tulkin, unpublished) also indicate that middle, in contrast to lower, class mothers spend significantly more time in face-to-face contact with their daughters, vocalize more often to them, and more frequently reward their attempts to crawl and stand. A final source of data is the home observations on some of the 180 children at 27 months. The observer noted each instance in which the mother reproved the child for disobeying a rule. Mothers of all social classes were more likely to reprove sons than daughters. However, reproval for incompetence at a task was most frequently meted out by the well educated mothers of daughters; there was no comparable class difference for mothers of sons.

Thus, independent and complementary evidence supports the idea that differential pressures toward intellectual competence are more likely to covary with social class for mother-daughter than for mother-son pairs. It has usually been assumed that the girl is more concerned with acceptance by parents and teachers than the boy, and that this particular motive for intellectual accomplishment covaries with social class; but intellectual achievement among boys is spurred by more varied motives, including hostility, power, and identification with competent male figures— motives less closely linked to social class. However valid these propositions, they are not operative during the first year of life.

IMPLICATIONS

The influence of contrast, discrepancy, and activation of hypotheses on distribution of attention is probably not limited to the first two years of life. Schools implicitly acknowledge the validity of these principles for older children by using books with contrasting colors and unusual formats and by emphasizing procedures whose aim is to ensure that the child has a relevant hypothesis available when he encounters a new problem. A child who possesses no hypothesis for solution of a problem is likely to withdraw from the task. Many children regard mathematics as more painful than English or social studies because they have fewer strategies to use with a difficult problem in arithmetic than for one in history or composition. The school might well give children more help in learning to generate hypotheses with which to solve problems, and put less pressure on them to accumulate facts.

The principles discussed in this paper are also related to the issue of incentives for acquiring new knowledge. The behaviorist, trying to preserve the theoretical necessity of the concept of reinforcement, has been vexed by the fact that the child acquires new knowledge in the absence of any demonstrable external reward. However, the process of assimilating a discrepant event to a schema has many of the characteristics of a pleasant

experience and therefore is in accord with the common understanding of a reward. The central problem in educating children is to attract and maintain focused attention. The central theoretical problem in understanding mental growth is to discern the factors that are continually producing change in schema and hypothesis. Solution of these two problems is not to be found through analyses of the environment alone. We must decipher the relation between the perceiver and the space in which he moves, for that theme, like Ariadne's thread, gives direction to cognitive growth.

REFERENCES

Acheson, R. N. 1966. Maturation of the skeleton. In F. Falkner, ed. *Human development.* Philadelphia: W. B. Saunders, pp. 465–502.

Brackbill, Y., G. Adams, D. H. Crowell, and M. C. Gray. 1966. Arousal level in newborns and preschool children under continuous auditory stimulation. *J. Exp. Child Psychol.* 3:176–88.

Carpenter, G.C. Feb. 1969. Differential visual behavior to human and humanoid faces in early infancy. Presented at Merrill-Palmer Infancy Conference, Detroit, Mich.

Cazden, C. B. 1966. Subcultural differences in child language. *Merrill-Palmer Quart.* 12:185–219.

Dreyfus-Brisac, C., D. Samson, C. Blanc, and N. Monod. 1958. L'électroencéphlograme de l'enfant normal de moins de trois ans. *Etudes néonatales* 7:143–75.

Eisenberg, R. B., E. J. Griffin, D. B. Coursin, and M. A. Hunter, 1964. Auditory behavior in the neonate. *J. Speech and Hearing Res.* 7:245–69.

Ellingson, R. J. 1967. Study of brain electrical activity in infants. In L. P. Lipsitt and C. C. Spiker, eds. *Advances in child development and behavior.* New York: Academic Press, pp. 53–98.

Fantz, R. L. 1966. Pattern discrimination and selective attention as determinants of perceptual development from birth. In A. H. Kidd and J. J. Rivoire, eds. *Perceptual development in children.* New York: International Universities Press.

Fantz, R. L., and S. Nevis. 1967. Pattern preferences in perceptual cognitive development in early infancy. *Merrill-Palmer Quart.* 13:77–108.

Finley, G. E. 1967. Visual attention, play, and satiation in young children: a cross cultural study. Unpublished doctoral dissertation. Harvard Univ.

Haaf, R. A., and R. Q. Bell. 1967. A facial dimension in visual discrimination by human infants. *Child Devel.* 38:893–99.

Haith, M. M. 1966. Response of the human newborn to visual movement. *J. Exp. Child Psychol.* 3:235–43.

Haith, M. M. March 1968. Visual scanning in infants. Paper presented at regional meeting of Society for Research in Child Development. Clark Univ., Worcester, Mass.

Hess, R. D., V. C. Shipman, J. E. Brophy, and R. M. Bear. 1968 and (follow-up phase) 1969. The cognitive environments of urban preschool children. Report to the Graduate School of Education, Univ. of Chicago.

Karmel, B. Z. 1966. The effect of complexity, amount of contour, element size and element arrangement on visual preference behavior in the hooded rat, domestic chick, and human infant. Unpublished doctoral dissertation, George Washington Univ., Washington, D.C.

Kuffler, S. W. 1952. Neurons in the retina: Organization, inhibition, and excitation problems. *Cold Spring Harbor Symposium in Quantitative Biology* 17:281–92.

Kuffler, S. W. 1953. Discharge patterns and functional organization of mammalian retina. *J. Physiol.* 16:37–68.

Lewis, M. 1969. Infants' responses to facial stimuli during the first year of life. *Devel. Psychol.* no. 2, pp. 75–86.

McCall, R. B., and J. Kagan. 1967. Attention in the infant: effects of complexity, contour, perimeter, and familiarity. *Child Devel.* 38:939–52.

McCall, R. B., and J. Kagan. 1970. Individual differences in the infant's distribution of attention to stimulus discrepancy. *Developmental Psychology* 2:90–98.

McCall, R. B., and W. H. Melson. March 1969. Attention in infants as a function of the magnitude of discrepancy and habituation rate. Paper presented at meeting of the Society for Research in Child Development. Santa Monica, Calif.

Magoun, H. W. 1969. Advances in brain research with implications for learning. In K. H. Pribram, ed., *On the biology of learning.* New York: Harcourt, Brace & World, pp. 171–90.

Moss, H. A. 1967. Sex, age and state as determinants of mother-infant interaction. *Merrill-Palmer Quart.* 13:19–36.

Moss, H. A., and K. S. Robson. 1968. Maternal influences on early social-visual behavior. *Child Devel.* 39:401–8.

Salapatek, P., and W. Kessen. 1966. Visual scanning of triangles by the human newborn. *J. Exp. Child Psychol.* 3:113–22.

Super, C., J. Kagan, F. Morrison, and M. Haith. An experimental test of the discrepancy hypothesis. Unpublished.

Tulkin, S. Social class differences in mother-child interaction. Unpublished.

Werner, E. E. 1969. Sex differences in correlations between children's IQs and measure of parental ability and environment ratings. *Devel. Psychol.* 1:280–85.

Wilcox, B. M. 1969. Visual preferences of human infants for representations of the human face. *J. Exp. Child Psychol.* 7:10–20.

IMPORTANT ISSUES CONCERNING THE NEONATE

Should You or Shouldn't You

Marvin S. Eiger and Sally Wendkos Olds

The "nursing couple"—mother and baby—forge an especially close and interdependent relationship. The baby depends upon his mother for sustenance and comfort, and the mother looks forward to feeding times to gain a pleasurable sense of closeness with her infant. If a feeding is too long delayed, both members become distressed: the baby because he is hungry and the mother because her breasts fill with milk. Each member needs the other, yearns for the other, is intimate with the other in a very special way.

Editor's Introduction

It is a commonly held assumption in our society that the bottle-fed baby who is held in the mother's arms is receiving an equivalent experience, both physiologically and psychologically, to the breast-fed baby. The authors of the following selection, however, feel that breast-feeding is uniquely different from artificial feeding in terms of a number of psychophysical and psychological variables.

In the past ten years the breast-feeding rate in the United States has dropped by half. As far back as history is recorded there has been a search for a reliable substitute for mother's milk. To avoid breast-feeding, mothers have hired wet nurses. Other milk substitutes have been tried over the centuries, ranging from the milk of goats and cows to combinations of foods prechewed by mothers and grandmothers. While the wet nurse has all but disappeared, the combination of a fairly adequate milk substitute and the freedom for the mother that the bottle provides has allowed the baby to be fed without the mother's physical presence. Formula-feeding has an appeal in today's technological society, since it appears to be so scientific and efficient.

Then we might ask, when bottle-feeding has proved satisfactory, why do so many mothers continue to breast-feed? The breast-fed baby has warm milk available in seconds. A mother has the urge to suckle as soon as her baby's hunger noises have triggered her milk letdown. The breast can be used not only to assuage hunger but also to calm all types of traumas and fears. This may foster a strong mother-infant attachment which can be duplicated in no other way. In other words, when the baby is breast-fed, nourishment and comfort will not be experienced away from the mother. Furthermore, human milk is not only easier than formula for babies to digest but also unlikely to provoke allergic reactions. Although babies can be allergic to artificial food none has been known to be allergic to mother's milk. In addition, breast-feeding prolongs the period of the infant's natural immunity to certain viral diseases.

While the physiological evidence strongly favors breast-feeding, the psychological effects of different feeding methods are less clearly understood. The relationship between breast-feeding and later personality development has been studied over four decades. One study demonstrated a correlation between a high measure on a test of security and having been breast-fed for more than one year (Maslow & Szilagyi-Kessler, 1946). Those with the lowest security scores were weaned between six and nine months. Those falling in the middle were breast fed for less than three months or not at all. Another study (Childers & Hamil, 1932) showed a relationship between neurotic behaviors and weaning between the first and sixth months of infancy. The group having the fewest problems had been nursed at least eleven months.

Thus, the data regarding the psychological impact of breast-feeding seem to point to the benefits of unrestricted breast-feeding for at least a year rather than the more common experience in our society of token breast-feeding, which is characterized by severe restrictions on the amount of time an infant is allowed to nurse, the number of nursings each day, and the length of time breast-feeding is continued before bottle-feeding replaces it.

It is highly probable, however, that a distressed breast-feeding mother may convey her feelings to her child more completely than the mother who feeds her child artificially because feeding and feelings are so closely interrelated physiologically. It is therefore best for a mother to respect her own feelings in making the decision, as nursing will not benefit the infant if it makes the mother unhappy. Difficulties face the new mother who is recently exhausted from the experience of childbirth, feeling unsure of her role, oversensitive and tired from a succession of sleepless days and nights, laden with diapers to wash, a house to tend, and thank-you notes to write and who is, on top of all this, socially isolated from other women who might offer advice or help. If she is also uncertain about breast-feeding, the struggles increase. Thus, the method of feeding may be far less important than the quality of the relationship between mother and infant.

I chose to breast-feed because of what seemed to me to be the overwhelming advantages of breast-feeding for the health of the infant as well as the emotional closeness that nursing would provide. I nursed Lauren for six months. She nursed almost constantly—except when she slept, which was not too often. I had little support from my husband, family, or friends. Their discouragement was direct: "Are you sure she is getting enough?" or "Why is she crying if you've just fed her?" or "Why don't you get dressed?" When I weaned Lauren, I had mixed feelings. I loved the closeness and intimacy breast-feeding afforded, while I resented the restrictions it placed on my sleep (as no one could take a feeding for me) and on my freedom. I have since learned that this conflict exists in every phase of motherhood. I am sorry that I gave up breast-feeding so early, just as I am now certain that I will regret the fact that Lauren's childhood is fleeing so rapidly, although I will again have more time for myself.

REFERENCES

Childers, A. T., & Hamil, B. M. Emotional problems in children as related to the duration of breast-feeding in infancy. *American Journal of Orthopsychiatry*, 1932, **2**, 134.

Maslow, A. H., & Szilagyi-Kessler, I. Security and breast-feeding. *Journal of Abnormal Social Psychology*, 1946, **41**, 83.

Pamela Cantor

Only in relatively recent times has there been any question at all as to whether a mother would breastfeed her baby. With the advent of dependable refrigeration and pasteurization, however, there is now a choice. You can decide whether you want to feed your baby the way mothers have done from time immemorial—or whether you want to take advantage of modern technology and provide your baby's nourishment in a bottle.

Many factors will enter into your decision—the customs of your community, the attitudes of your obstetrician, your pediatrician, your husband, your style of life, your personality, and your feelings about mothering. In some countries, it is taken for granted that a woman will breastfeed her children. Some governments, such as that in Switzerland, where the picture of a nursing mother appears on the fifty-franc note, actively encourage breastfeeding by paying nursing mothers.

In the United States, the nursing mother is the nonconformist, a member of a minority group. It seems, however, that the long-term trend away from breastfeeding is now being reversed, at least among better-educated, middle- and upper-class women. Since these women led the movement away from breastfeeding in generations past, perhaps their renewed interest will spur a similar resurgence in the country at large.

Before you decide how you will feed your baby, you will want to consider the advantages of breastfeeding for both baby and mother, and its ramifications in your personal situation.

BENEFITS FOR THE BABY

Health

From the physiological point of view, the breast is best. Recent studies do not show significant differences in rates of illness between breastfed and bottle-fed infants of middle- or upper-class parents in well-developed countries. However, among parents who are less medically sophisticated and in hot climates with less than optimal sanitary conditions, the picture changes radically. In tropical countries, the breastfed baby may have six times the chance for life as his bottle-fed cousin.

Breast milk can never be contaminated by the harmful bacteria that may multiply in standing animal milk; it is always served to the baby in a clean container. It cannot be over-diluted to save money. Mistakes cannot be made in its preparation.

There may be other reasons, too, why breast milk is healthier. Some medical researchers feel that specific antibodies against disease germs reach the infant through his mother's milk, while others attribute its immunological benefits to the action of "unspecific factors of unknown origin." There is also some speculation that breast milk contains no antibodies of its own, but is able to stimulate antibody production in the baby's system. There are definite indications that babies are protected from influenza, from polio, and from diarrhea by substances in their mothers' milk.

In highly developed countries such as ours, where sanitary conditions are generally good, the gap in health between the breastfed and the bottle-fed baby is narrowed considerably. In addition, modern antibiotic medicines can now vanquish many of the illnesses that used to be fatal to infants. Preventing an infection, however, is still better than curing it. And there *is* some basis for belief that breast milk does, indeed, have certain preventive, protective powers.

Digestibility

A baby can digest human milk more easily than he can digest the milk of other animals. Breast milk forms softer curds in the infant's stomach than cow's milk, and is more quickly assimilated into his system. While it contains less protein than does cow's milk, virtually all the protein in breast milk is used by the baby, whereas about half the protein in cow's milk is wasted, passing through his body and making extra work for his excretory system.

The breastfed baby is less apt to get diarrhea than the bottle-fed baby—and he can never become constipated, since breast milk cannot solidify in his intestinal tract to form hard stools. While he may soil every diaper in his early days or go several days without a bowel movement later on, neither of these situations will indicate intestinal upset.

Some premature infants and other babies with sensitive digestive systems are known to thrive only on breast milk. If their own mothers do not provide it, they must obtain it from other mothers.

Allergy

While most babies do well on either breast or formula, an occasional infant seems to be allergic to the formula he first receives. When such a baby suffers indigestion or diarrhea, the hunt is on to find a formula that will not upset the baby. The mother faced with this problem may feel like a chemist in the lab as, on the advice of her pediatrician, she tries different proportions and different kinds of milks and sugars, even going occasionally to such exotica as goat's milk or soybean milk.

The breastfeeding mother never has this concern, since no baby is allergic to breast milk. An occasional infant may, however, develop an allergic reaction such as vomiting, diarrhea, skin rash, hives, or sniffles, to some substance in his mother's diet that is transmitted through the milk. With a little trial and error, it is usually possible for the mother to identify the allergenic food and stop eating it as long as she continues to nurse.

Another rare condition, not precisely an allergy but a reaction by the infant to a substance in the mother's milk, is breast-milk

jaundice. Occasionally, a baby who develops this generally harmless condition has to be taken off the breast temporarily but can resume normal breastfeeding after only a few days.

Neither of these situations is a true allergic reaction to the breast milk itself. In fact, there are indications that breast milk may even prevent allergies. In one classic study of more than 20,000 infants, those who were fed artificially were seven times as likely to get eczema (a skin disorder associated with allergy) as those who were completely breastfed. If you or your husband is particularly allergy-prone, you have a special reason for nursing your baby.

Human Milk for Human Babies

Chemical analysis has shown that the milk of every species is different in its composition from every other milk. We can logically assume from this that each animal produces in its milk those elements most important for the survival of its young. While artificial formula can closely imitate mother's milk, it can never duplicate it exactly. No manufacturer has ever claimed that his formula product is just as good as or better than breast milk, and it is highly doubtful that such an audacious claim will ever be made. About fifteen years ago, leading infant formulas were found to be deficient in a substance called pyroxidine; only a couple of years ago, the amount of folic acid in baby formula was deemed insufficient. Who knows what other ingredients will be isolated and identified in mother's milk for the formula-makers to attempt to imitate?

The breastfed baby differs in so many respects from his bottle-fed counterpart that one pediatrician, Dr. Harry Bakwin, has said that he is practically a different animal. The ratio of vitamins in his system is different, as is the composition of various substances in his blood. In addition, the bacteria in his intestinal tract are strikingly different. While all human beings harbor a large and varied population of intestinal bacteria, a single innocuous species, *Lactobacillus bifidus*, makes up more than 90% and sometimes more than 99% of the total bacteria found in the feces of a nursing infant. *L. bifidus* is also present in the stool of the bottle-fed baby, but only as one of a crowd of many other species. It is possible that this harmless organism is the only intestinal microbe that can survive the highly acid environment of the nursling's intestinal tract.

The breastfed baby even grows differently from the bottle baby, who develops bigger and heavier bones during his first year of life—probably due to the larger amounts of calcium in cow's milk. Some people feel that breastfed babies are deficient in calcium, but it seems more likely that the formula-fed baby is exhibiting an artificial growth pattern—much like the force-fed Strasbourg geese.

Even though we don't know the precise reasons for, or the significance of, all the differences between the baby nourished at the breast and the baby fed by bottle, it seems logical to assume that the best first food for your baby is the one served up by Mother Nature.

The Natural Way

At a time when so much of our life has an unsettlingly unnatural aspect—with chemicals in the air we breathe, the clothes we wear, and the foods we eat—more and more of us are striving to recapture some of the natural joys of life on earth. When you breastfeed your baby, you know that you are giving him the natural food intended just for him. Its purity is tainted by no synthetic compounds, no preservatives, no artificial ingredients. Breast milk is the ultimate health food.

If you are concerned about the environment your baby will grow up in, we think you will agree that the breast is also best from the ecological point of view. Feeding the bottle-fed baby entails the use and disposal of dozens of cans of formula, the cardboard cartons in which they are packaged, and the baby's bottles and nipples which are also discarded either after one use, as in the case of disposable bottles, or after a few months use. To wash the baby's feeding utensils, soap or detergents, water, and the energy used to heat the water must all be expended.

Tooth and Jaw Development

Apart from the nutritional benefits of breast milk, suckling at the breast is good for your baby's tooth and jaw development. The infant at the breast has to use as much as sixty times more energy to get his food than does the baby drinking from a bottle. The nursling has to mouth the entire areola (the brown area surrounding the nipple), move his jaws back and forth, and squeeze hard with his gums to extract the milk. To accomplish this arduous task, your baby has been endowed with jaw muscles relatively three times stronger than those of his mother or father. As these muscles are strenuously exercised in suckling, their constant pulling encourages well-formed jaws and straight, healthy teeth.

One factor accounting for many dental malformations that eventually send youngsters to the orthodontist or the speech therapist is an abnormal swallowing pattern, known as "tongue thrust." This is very common among bottle-fed babies, but almost nonexistent among the breastfed. To understand why, we have to examine the mechanisms of feeding. The baby at the breast moves his lower jaw back and forth quite vigorously to stimulate the flow of milk. He pushes his tongue upward against the flattened nipple to keep it in his mouth. As the milk begins to come, he sucks it in and swallows. He then repeats the whole process, so that a feeding session involves a constant succession of chewing and suckling motions.

The bottle-fed baby does not have to exercise his jaws so energetically, since light suckling alone produces a rapid flow of milk. In fact, since the milk flows so freely from the bottle, the infant actually has to learn how to protect himself from an over-supply so that he will not choke. He pushes his tongue forward against the nipple holes to stem the flow to a level that he can easily handle. The tongue that should be pressing upward has instead come forward, and a swallowing pattern that will most likely persist throughout the child's life has begun. Many dentists feel that such forward tongue thrust can result in mouth breathing, lip biting, gum disease, and an unattractive appearance.

Of course, not all bottle-fed babies develop dental problems, and some breastfed babies do. In addition, a new type of "orthodontic" nipple, the Nuk Sauger, has been designed to avoid the development of "tongue thrust" and its effects. Despite its much closer approximation to the human nipple, however, there is no doubt that the "real thing" will continue to remain superior to all its imitators.

Besides the development of good swallowing habits, there is another factor that contributes to the breastfed child's healthy tooth and jaw development. Since he gets more of the sucking that most babies seem to need, he is less likely to suck his thumb. The bottle-fed baby must stop sucking the nipple as soon as his bottle is empty, to avoid ingesting air; the baby at the breast can continue in this blissful pastime until either you or he decides he's been at the well long enough.

Availability

Another advantage enjoyed by the nursling is the constant availability of milk. His dinner is always ready, always at the right temperature, always the same consistency. He never has to struggle to get milk from a nipple with scanty holes, nor does he have to gulp furiously to keep up with a gush from extra-large holes. No snowstorm, no flood, no car breakdown, no milk-drivers' strike can keep his food from him. As long as mother is near, so is dinner.

Emotional Gratification

A great deal has been written and said about the psychological benefits the baby derives from breastfeeding. Dr. Niles Newton, a psychologist who has devoted much of her professional career to studies of lactation in humans and in laboratory animals, has found many psychological differences between breast and artificial feeding, most of which seem to tip the scales in favor of breastfeeding. For example, lactating mice demonstrate a greater drive than non-nursing mice in overcoming obstacles to reach their infants, indicating some mechanism in lactation itself that triggers maternal behavior. Also, such factors as the more intimate interaction between the breastfeeding mother and child and the more immediate satisfaction of the nursing baby's hunger seem, from the psychological point of view, to augur healthier mental development.

However, as important as early feeding experiences may be to a child's later development, there are so many variables in a family relationship that it is impossible to say that breastfeeding per se produces a well-adjusted individual. The mother who breastfeeds only because she thinks it is her duty to do so communicates her resentment to her child. The mother who weans suddenly and traumatically can undo much of the good that has been built up in the nursing relationship. The frustration encountered by a hungry baby whose mother does not have enough milk can over-balance the benefits of breastfeeding. Partly for these reasons, it is virtually impossible to say that breastfeeding is always psychologically superior to bottle feeding.

And, while investigators have been conducting studies for the past forty years to try

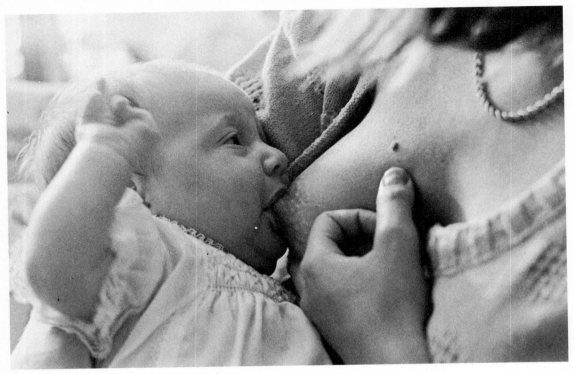

By permission of Sissy Krook, photographer.

to correlate method of infant feeding with later personality development, none of these studies have proved that either breast- or bottle-feeding—by itself—will guarantee that a baby will become a secure, well-adjusted person.

Psychiatrists and other students of human and animal nature do state categorically, however, that a baby does gain a sense of security from the warmth and closeness of the mother's body. When you breastfeed your baby, you cannot be tempted—even on your busiest days—to lay your baby down in his crib with a propped bottle. You *have* to draw him close to you for every single feeding. While the bottle-feeding mother can also show her love for her baby by holding him and cuddling him at feeding times, in actual practice she tends to do less of this. And, of course, she cannot

duplicate the unique skin-to-skin contact between the nursing mother and her infant. Many adults today are going out of their way to join encounter groups, sensitivity groups, T-groups, and other forms of group therapy in settings that encourage a large measure of hugging, hand-holding, and other forms of touching. It is possible that many of those who respond so well in these groups are trying to make up for that close bodily contact they missed as infants.

Babies also gain a sense of well-being from secure handling, and the mother who nurses her baby often seems more confident in her management of him. Whether the woman who is sure of her maternal abilities is more likely to breastfeed—or whether the experience of being a good provider infuses her with self-confidence—is difficult to answer. It does seem that the mother who nurses is more likely to know how to soothe her baby when he is upset—perhaps because the very act of putting him to the breast is such a comfort to him that she does not have to search for other ways of reassuring him. The breast is more than a pipeline for getting food into the baby. It is warmth, it is reassurance, it is comfort.

BENEFITS FOR THE MOTHER

Your primary reason for wanting to breast-feed is probably your awareness that it will be better for your baby. You may not have realized that nursing offers a world of benefits for you, too.

Good for the Figure

Nursing your baby will help you to regain your figure more quickly, since the process of lactation causes the uterus (which has increased during pregnancy to about twenty times its normal size) to shrink more quickly to its pre-pregnancy size. During the early days of nursing, you can actually feel the uterus contracting while your baby suckles. As he nurses, he stimulates certain nerves in the nipples which bring about the uterine contractions. These contractions hasten uterine involution (return to former size) and the expulsion of excess tissue and blood from the uterus.

Convenience

Breastfeeding is much easier than preparing formula. When asked why they decided to breastfeed, many women answer, "Because I'm lazy." We live in a world of conveniences, in which each manufacturer tries to outdo the other in providing "less work for the home-maker." In the area of infant feeding, no efficiency expert alive has been able to outdo nature. It's so easy just to wake up in the morning, pick up the baby and put him to the breast. You don't have to mix formula. You don't have to scrub and sterilize bottles and

nipples. You don't have to stagger to the kitchen in the middle of the night to heat a bottle. Your baby's daily batch of food prepares itself in its own attractive, permanent containers. You have the pleasure of feeding your baby, with none of the bother. You'll enjoy that extra hour or so you save by not having to sterilize bottles and make formula. And since your breastfed baby won't need solid foods for some two to three months later than the bottle baby, you'll be spared the spoon-feeding routine for a while, too.

When you breastfeed, you never have to make up an extra bottle at the last minute, nor throw out formula that your baby doesn't want. Working on the time-honored principle of supply and demand, your mammary glands produce the amount of milk your baby wants.

You'll find it easier to go visiting or traveling with your baby, since you won't have to take along bottles, nipples and formula, nor will you have to worry about refrigeration and dishwashing facilities.

Economy

Breastfeeding is cheaper. If you have already been maintaining a healthy, well-balanced diet, you need to eat nothing special to provide for the manufacture of milk. The small amounts of extra food that you'll be eating to make up for the calories you lose in the milk will cost you less than you would have to pay for bottles, nipples, sterilizing equipment, and formula. It is ironic that in our country, the women in the lowest income groups, where sanitary conditions are least favorable and finances least plentiful, are also the least likely to take advantage of the practical benefits of breastfeeding. . . .

Your Health

Every mother of an infant needs adequate rest. The many physiological changes of pregnancy, the hard work of labor and delivery, and the demanding care of a new baby all deplete your energy. When you breastfeed, you are forced to relax during your baby's feeding times, since you cannot prop a bottle or turn the baby over to someone else in the family while you run around straightening up the house.

Thromboembolism, a potentially dangerous disorder in which a blood clot breaks loose from its site of formation to block a blood vessel, is a rare complication of childbirth. Women who are over twenty-five, who have had several children, or who have had surgical deliveries have a slightly higher risk of thromboembolism. Two recent British studies found that these higher-risk patients were at even higher risk if lactation were suppressed. This may have been the result of the hormones administered to suppress lactation, or it may have been the result of the suppression itself. In any case, the evidence from these two studies suggests that the hormonal suppression of lactation may tip the scales against those women already predisposed to such clotting disorders.

It is also worth noting that some cancer researchers state that the risk of developing breast cancer is lowest for women who have borne and nursed children. . . .

Birth Control

Breastfeeding acts as a natural, albeit unreliable, means of spacing children. While your baby is receiving nothing but breast milk—no solid foods nor any formula at all—you are less likely to become pregnant than the non-nursing or partially nursing mother. This is because the fully lactating woman rarely ovulates. (She rarely menstruates, also, which might be considered another plus.) *Nursing a baby is not a guarantee against pregnancy, however.* While you are less likely to conceive while you are maintaining your baby solely on your milk, it is possible that you might become pregnant. If you want to plan the size and spacing of your family, you should use some form of contraception. . . .

Enjoyment

Very little attention is usually given to the fact that breastfeeding can be an intensely pleasurable, sensuous act. Suckling a baby gives rise to some of the same physical responses that occur during sexual intercourse, such as the discharge of the hormone *oxytocin*, contractions of the uterus, erection of the nipples, and an elevation of body temperature. Masters and Johnson, the researchers who have contributed so much to our knowledge of physiological sexual response, report in their book, *Human Sexual Response*, that women who nursed their babies were more interested in resuming sexual activity with their husbands than were non-nursing mothers. This may be because the nursing experience itself contains a measure of sexual stimulation—or perhaps because the woman who is more comfortable with her body is more likely to nurse her babies.

Feminine Fulfillment

All these benefits are real. Any one of them might be a valid reason for deciding to breastfeed. Yet the woman who has a choice between breast and bottle and decides to nurse her baby often makes her final decision on a completely different basis—the emotional satisfaction and enormous sense of fulfillment gained from breastfeeding an infant. As one young mother has said, "There is something very right about a system that makes one human being so happy about being responsible for another. I could never have the same good feeling of accomplishment by relying on the neighborhood store or the dairy for my baby's milk. Knowing that I was giving him something no one else could give him created a tie between us that became one of my deepest joys."

Women who have bottle-fed one baby and nursed another usually say that they felt closer to their nursing infants—even though as the babies grew, this difference did not continue to exist. A common reaction is reflected in this statement: "I never knew what I was missing by not nursing my first baby. I loved him and I enjoyed him, yes, but I never got so many of the little 'extras' that I get from this one—that little hand that touches my skin as she's nursing, the way she'll pull away from the breast, smile at me and go right back again, the happiness that I feel at being able to give her what she wants."

The "nursing couple"—mother and baby—forge an especially close and interdependent relationship. The baby depends upon his mother for his sustenance and comfort, and the mother looks forward to feeding times to gain a pleasurable sense of closeness with her infant. If a feeding time is too long delayed, both members become distressed: the baby because he is hungry and the mother because her breasts fill with milk. Each member needs the other, yearns for the other, is intimate with the other in a very special way. Because of this unique relationship, many women consider the nursing months among the most fulfilling times of their lives.

WHY SOME WOMEN DECIDE AGAINST BREASTFEEDING

The reasons why women decide not to breastfeed are almost as varied as the arguments in its favor. There are a very, very few instances when a woman cannot nurse her baby—when the mother has a serious infectious illness such as tuberculosis or whooping cough, for example, or when the infant has some condition making it impossible for him to nurse, such as cleft palate. Such cases are rare. Virtually every healthy woman can breastfeed her baby, and as late as 1900, almost every mother did.

Yet, breastfeeding in America has had such a drastic fall from favor that now only one mother in four breastfeeds her baby for the first few days, and less than one out of ten is still nursing him by the time he has attained the ripe age of four months. Surely in our scientifically advanced country, the reasons for this cannot be medical ones. Why, then, do so many mothers decide to substitute the milk of another species for the first-rate infant food already supplied to them?

Like most questions about a major cultural change, this one has no single simple answer. Women say they don't breastfeed because they're too embarrassed, or because the idea doesn't appeal to them, or because they don't want to be tied down, or because there's no reason to, now that ready-made formula is available, or because they're too nervous, or because the whole business just seems too complicated. The real reasons for the swing away from universal breastfeeding to almost universal bottle-feeding in the United States go far deeper than these statements and involve a wide variety of factors. These include the technological advances that spurred reliable refrigeration and a chemical approximations of mother's milk; changes in child-rearing styles; alterations in women's views of their own role; and the emergence of the female breast as a sexual object, with no apparent function other than the delectation of the male.

At the beginning of the twentieth century, psychologists and pediatricians, both members of new and rapidly growing professions, were convinced that babies developed best if they were raised according to certain hard-and-fast rules. Mothers were ordered by their doctors not to feed—or even pick up—their babies oftener than every four hours, no matter how piercing or pathetic the infants' wails. Bottle-feeding was far better adapted to these practices. For breastfeeding requires flexibility, not rigidity; understanding of a baby's needs, not the ability to tell time; and an intuitive maternal reaction, not an adherence to a cultural fad. Also, because the child-care experts insisted that only they knew what was best for the child, mothers believed them—and lost any confidence they might have had in their own maternal capabilities. Lack of confidence itself may be enough to sabotage successful breastfeeding.

At the same time these mothers were being intimidated in the nursery, they were asserting themselves on the street. Demonstrating to achieve the right to vote, smoking cigarettes in public, bobbing their hair, and daring to carve out their own careers, women were eager to free themselves from their traditional roles in the house. And the baby bottle became an instant symbol of emancipation. (Conversely, today's liberationist is just as likely to nurse her baby before going out to picket.)

Later on in the century, the breast was suddenly "discovered" as the most sexual element of a woman's body. After having been hidden under the tight binders of the flapper era, women's breasts were now molded into fashionable shapes by that new invention, the brassiere. By the time the 1940s came along, pin-up photos were gracing barracks walls, exhibiting the new ideal of feminine beauty—a pretty young woman with enormous breasts. EVEN the ideal shape of the pectoral area had changed: it now consisted of two pointed cones attached at right angles to the female chest. These unnatural-looking appendages became purely decorative in nature, valued for their sexiness and forgotten for their original function. Husbands began to look upon their wives' breasts as their own property— and some who were married to that rapidly dwindling species of mothers who nursed their babies, became unreasoningly jealous as they saw their little sons or daughters nursing.

Furthermore, as formulas became more satisfactory during the 1930s, the act of giving a bottle achieved a certain status of its own. Mothers who wanted to be modern wanted to bottle-feed. This urge to keep up, to be "modern," is still wooing rural and urban poverty groups away from the breast and to the bottle—with disastrous effects in some underdeveloped countries. When money is scarce, mothers dilute the milk and starve their babies, and when refrigeration and sanitation are inadequate, the milk becomes contaminated. The World Health Organization has mounted a major campaign to encourage women in underdeveloped countries to go back to safe, healthy breastfeeding.

A recent study in Sweden showed that mothers living in modern apartments breastfeed longer than do those living in old-fashioned houses. Nursing, among the best-educated Swedish women, is the "latest thing." In this country, too, change is in the wind. The very women who initially took up the bottle with such enthusiasm—the well-educated, progressive daughters of the middle and upper classes—are now showing greater interest in living their lives the natural way. Today's forward-thinking young woman is less likely to be wearing heavy makeup, an elaborate hairdo, or a padded bra. She is what she is—and is not embarrassed to be herself. She wants to look natural and she wants to act natural. And she is more likely to want to feed her baby according to nature's plan. Yet the modern woman may still have many questions about nursing. . . .

You may have all your questions answered, be assured that you can breastfeed your children, yet still be loath to do so. It may still seem like a foreign notion or a repulsive one. It may make you "feel like a cow." If you really do not want to nurse your baby, if the very idea repels you, don't do it. You should not embark upon the nursing adventure because you feel you ought to, to be a good mother. You should not do something you find abhorrent to please your husband, your doctor, your mother, or your best friend. If you do, you are doomed to failure.

How you feel about your baby is vastly more important than how you feed him. A baby raised in a loving home can grow up to be a healthy, psychologically secure individual no matter how he receives his nourishment. While successful nursing is a beautiful, happy experience for both mother and child, the woman who nurses grudgingly because she feels she *should* will probably do more harm to her baby by communicating her feelings of resentment and unhappiness, than she would if she were a relaxed, loving, bottle-feeding mother.

WHAT WILL YOU DO?

What will you do, then? We urge you to give nursing a try. You might look on it as a thirty-day guarantee or your money back. Suppose you begin to nurse your baby and you decide that it's not for you. You haven't lost anything, you haven't invested in anything; you can always stop. The stores will always have those bottles, nipples, sterilizers, and cans of formula. You haven't made a lifelong commitment. You can change your mind.

On the other hand, if you decide to bottle-feed right away, it's much harder to change your mind later. It has been done, by mothers who found that their babies needed breast milk to survive and by women who discoverd that bottle-feeding has its own set of problems, but deciding to nurse even after a week has gone by is far from easy. It requires a great deal of determination, persistence, and patience.

Suppose you never gave breastfeeding a chance—don't you think you might look back on this time in later years and wonder whether you and your baby missed one of life's greatest gifts—the bond shared by the nursing couple? The regrets we have in life are less often for the things we have done than for those missed opportunities that will never come again. This priceless chance to nurse your baby comes only once in each baby's lifetime. Make the most of it. You may count these nursing days among the most beautiful and fulfilling of your entire life.

Father's Child-Rearing Approach
David B. Lynn

They found that these fathers spent very little time talking with their infants. The average number of vocal interactions per day was 2.7 and the average number of seconds per day that the father vocalized to the baby was 37.7. Even the father who interacted the most averaged only 10½ minutes vocalizing to his infant each day. . . .

I suspect that fathers spend so little time with their infants partly because they simply do not understand the importance of early father-infant interaction on the later development of children. It is hard to believe that interaction with a tiny baby is so critical to its later development, but the child development literature defies common sense and long ago demonstrated its significance. . . .

Editor's Introduction

Until recently, psychological literature has concentrated almost entirely on the mother-child relationship and has excluded the father-child relationship from any systematic investigation. This focus was primarily due to the psychoanalytic emphasis on infancy as the critical period in human development and the fact that the role of the mother during infancy has been well established for centuries. The father has been accorded little importance in studies of child-rearing practices as his role has been ill defined.

The role of the father is in a state of flux due to the rapidity of change in today's society: the increasing number of women who pursue work outside the home, the changes in the heretofore rigid views of appropriate masculine and feminine behaviors, and the increasing awareness that child care can be a challenge for both parents. These controversial social changes potentially include an additional positive aspect if they allow men the freedom to assume a larger role in child care beginning at birth.

In reviewing the current research, Lynn discusses the issue of the father's role in child-rearing today. He states that fathers see their role as vital to the well-being of their children and perceive themselves as fathers in more than the biological sense. Yet the studies he cites indicate that most American fathers spend less than one hour a day with their infant children. Thus, a father may spend more time conceiving his children than fathering them.

To state that fathers themselves see their role as an important one and then to read that most fathers share minimal interaction with their children is a contradiction which saddens me. I am distressed because I share the opinion that the father's involvement is vital. But involvement, for either mother or father, should not be directly equated with the time the parent spends with the child, as there is little, if any, evidence to support the theory that the amount of time a parent spends with a child has a direct relationship to the degree of influence that parent has on the child or the degree of affection felt by the child toward the parent or by the parent toward the child. Perhaps there may even be an inverse relationship. Since the father is typically less available, it may be that his presence has a greater impact than that of the consistently more available mother. His time may be more influential precisely because of its limitations.

Thus, it is with little scientific data and strong emotion that I am campaigning for a future of fathers who father in more than name only. I know the importance of my own father to my sense of myself as a competent human being and to my view of myself as a woman, and I know of the deprivations young women in my clinical practice have expressed due to psychologically or physically absent fathers. As a result, it appears to me that two parents who share an intense commitment to child rearing will certainly be of benefit to a child. Only if both parents are able to work out their lives so that they can share equally in child care and share equally in all aspects of their own development as well can we expect that their children will grow up having experienced the maximum advantages that both men and women can offer.

In the following selection, Lynn discusses the major aspects of a father's child-rearing approach and how it influences the child. He assesses the father's participation in child rearing and his methods of child rearing. He also discusses the influence of the father as seen through the eyes of his children.

Pamela Cantor

Last night my child was born—
   a very strong boy with large black eyes. . . .
   If you ever become a father,
   I think the strangest and strongest sensation
of your life will be hearing for the first time
the thin cry of your own child.
Lafcadio Hearn

Papa's appearance has been described many times, but very incorrectly. . . . All his features are perfect, except that he hasn't extraordinary teeth. His complexion is very fair, and he doesn't ware a beard. . . .

Papa has a peculiar gait we like, it seems just to sute him, but most people do not; he always walks up and down the room while thinking and between each coarse at meals. *Susy Clemens, Mark Twain's daughter, age 13*

THE FATHER ROLE

Judson Landis' study (1962), in which he surveyed college students to determine the values their families held and the relationship the students had to each of their parents, illustrates the fact that Father is critical to the well-being of the family. A close father-child relationship was, more often than the mother-child relationship, associated with a cohesive family that held positive values.

Although an overly strong attachment between mother and son can be very damaging to the son's development, John Nash (1954) has reviewed evidence suggesting that a strong attachment between father and child does not often carry the same risks. Nash also concluded that a strong attachment between father and daughter is less inimical to the girl's normal development than is a strong mother-son attachment to the boy's. Assuming the validity of these studies, Father is therefore vital to a healthy family, and a strong father-child relationship carries few risks.

Father's role has been characterized by Parsons (Parsons & Bales, 1955) as "instrumental." Now let's examine the evidence to determine how Father's place in the family is described in research on this role's essential features. Father, even more than Mother, may stress explicit child-rearing values and goals. More often than she, he may consider agents outside the family beneficial to the child. For example, in interviews, fathers talked more than mothers did about providing emotional

security for their children and helping them to learn (Stolz, 1966). Whereas mothers emphasized helping the child to remain free from anxiety, fathers stressed education, moral values (especially responsibility), personal values, and safety. Fathers, more often than mothers, said that socializing agents other than parents (neighborhood, school, television) were beneficial to the child. Mothers were loath to accept the usefulness of agents other than the home. Note that many of these findings are consistent with Parsons' theory of Father as the parent concerned with relating the child to the larger society.

In contrast to mothers, fathers more often approved of punishment and favored stricter controls, although they also talked more about the negative effects of physical punishment. Both parents recognized that their own personal needs sometimes influenced their interactions with their offspring, but mothers discussed these needs—their interests, anxieties, fatigue, or illness—more often than fathers did.

Although fathers, more often than mothers, perceived the value to their children of agencies other than the home, they were much less responsive to outside advice on their own child-rearing practices. Mothers, not father, listened to and were influenced by child-rearing information from friends and relatives, the mass media, educational institutions, physicians, teachers, or clinics. Mothers were often influenced in their child-rearing practices by their own mothers, especially in regard to practices they did not wish to emulate. Fathers, more often than mothers, were influenced by their own fathers, but especially in regard to practices they wished to emulate in rearing their own offspring. Other researchers (Bronson, Katten, & Livson, 1959) elaborated on the influence of parents on their children's child-rearing practices. Their analysis of cumulative case histories indicates that parents' ideas gained from retrospective assessments of their own parents' treatment of them are seldom applied directly to their own child-rearing practices. There was, however, a tendency among mothers to emulate their own mothers if they viewed them as authoritarian, whereas fathers tended to resemble their own fathers if the fathers had shown them affection.

Do fathers view the paternal role as superfluous? Most fathers, when interviewed, said that they did not see their role in the family even as secondary, much less superfluous (Tasch, 1952). They thought of themselves not just as breadwinners, but as active participants in the child's daily care. They considered child rearing an integral part of their father role. These fathers valued companionship with their children highly, and, when the companionship was good, they considered it a major source of satisfaction in their lives. The few fathers who found their role unsatisfying often cited lack of companionship with their children as one reason for their discontent. Many of the fathers enjoyed spending time with their children and regretted that their need to earn a living limited the time they could spend with them. An earlier study (Gardner, 1943) with another group of fathers, however, revealed that they had ample time to spend with their children but did not use the opportunities available to them to do so.

Fathers reported in Tasch's interviews that they participated more in the daily care of their girls than in that of their boys and were more concerned about the girls' safety. They seemed to view girls as fragile and delicate. Fathers participated more in developing the motor abilities, skills, and interests of their boys. They made clear distinctions between boys' tasks and girls' tasks: girls iron, mind siblings, and wash clothes; boys take out garbage and help Father. After their children reached the age of 6, fathers engaged in much more rough-and-tumble play with their sons than with their daughters. Fathers also were more likely to spank boys.

Fathers may be less indulgent, affectionate, and patient than mothers. Radke (1946) found that fathers explained the reason for their discipline less frequently than mothers did. Fathers less often allowed children to have their own way. They lacked the easy rapport with their children that mothers enjoyed, taking less time to answer their questions and showing them less affection. Their children, in turn, did not so often share confidences with fathers. Fathers, however, did not deprive their children of privileges and pleasures so frequently as mothers did. Mothers more often played the role of chief supervisor of the child as well as that of the more affectionate and yielding parent.

Fathers may be on the whole less nurturant and more restrictive with their children, but they may differentiate between the sexes in asserting their power. Questionnaires administered to parents of children 6 to 10 years of age suggested that their fathers were less nurturant and more restrictive than their mothers. The fathers used power more freely with sons than with daughters, but the mothers exercised power more freely over daughters (Emmerich, 1962).

Although disobedience in children of both sexes runs high in fathers' concerns, fathers may be less extreme than mothers in their discipline. When Jackson (1956) asked mothers what they would do when facing certain contrived parent-child situations, they gave a wider variety of suggestions than did fathers, and they tended to suggest both milder and more severe punishments.

High-status fathers are usually more concerned with career goals for their sons than for their daughters, and they are distressed by behavior in their boys that is inconsistent with their high aspirations for them. Upper-middle-class fathers expected their sons to go to college and then to take up business or a profession, but they anticipated that their daughters would marry rather than take up a

By permission of Sissy Krook, photographer.

career (Aberle & Naegele, 1952). The behaviors that bothered fathers most in their boys were lack of responsibility and initiative, poor schoolwork, insufficient aggressiveness, athletic inadequacy, overconformity, excitability, excessive tearfulness, homosexual play, and childish behavior. These behaviors were mentioned in regard to girls, too, but much less frequently. Girls were to be pretty, sweet, affectionate, and nice. The authors felt that fathers had more definite ideas of what boys need for a successful adult role.

FATHER THROUGH THE CHILD'S EYES

We have just examined the typical roles fathers play through the eyes of the researcher. Now, let's look at the father through the eyes of the child.

The Instrumental Parent

Parsons' characterization of the father as the instrumental leader in the family has provided a useful way of organizing much of our material. Of course, young children do not use the jargon of the social scientist, but we can examine their perceptions of the father and say, with some assurance, whether they do or do not fit into Parsons' framework.

In one study (Eisenberg, Henderson, Kuhlmann, & Hill, 1967), for example, 6- and 10-year-old boys and girls filled out a questionnaire about men and women in general and about their parents in particular. The researchers classified their responses as representing instrumental nurturance, affectional nurturance, or punitiveness. One of the questions asked whom the child would ask for help in opening a heavy door. The act of helping the child open a heavy door was classified as instrumental nurturance. The experimenters also asked the child which parent kisses him the most. Kissing is an example of affectional nurturance. Another question asked the child which parent yells at him the most when both parents are at home; the response to this question was categorized under punitiveness.

In keeping with Parsons' theory, both boys and girls perceived the father (along with males in general) as more instrumentally nurturant and the mother as more affectionally nurturant. Fathers were also viewed as punitive more often than mothers. In several other investigations, boys and girls from preschool to high school viewed the father as less affectionally nurturant than the mother (Bronfenbrenner, 1961b; Droppleman & Schaefer, 1963; Emmerich, 1959b; Gardner, 1947; Kagan, 1956; Kagan, Hosken, & Watson, 1961; Kagen & Lemkin, 1960; Meissner, 1965; Ucko & Moore, 1963).

But whether Father is viewed as less affectionally nurturant than Mother may vary with the sex and age of the child. In a doll-play study (Ucko & Moore, 1963), 4-year-old boys and girls showed the mother doll as positive and helpful, but the 6-year-old boys showed the father doll in that role, whereas 6-year-old girls still displayed the mother as positive and helpful. In a study (Fitzgerald, 1966) of 14- and 15-year-olds, the boys viewed the mother as offering more affection and support, but half of the girls viewed the father as more affectionate and supportive. With few exceptions, however, the mother was viewed more often than the father in a way that fits Parsons' expressive role.

In several studies (Bronson,Katten, & Livson, 1959; Emmerich, 1959b; Emmerich, 1961; Gardner, 1947; Grace & Lohmann, 1952; Kagen, 1956; Kagen, Hosken, & Watson, 1961; Kagan & Lemkin ,1960; Meissner, 1965), children from preschool to high school were interviewed directly about their views of their parents (for example, "Whom are you more afraid of, your father or your mother?"). Boys and girls characterized the father, more often than the mother, as strong, powerful, potent, dominant, authoritative, competent, bossy, irritable, punitive, a nag, a frustrating agent, interfering, cold, indifferent, fearsome, dark, dirty, angular, threatening, and dangerous. If chased by a dog, 6- to 8-year-old children would run to Father, not to Mother. They presented the image of a nurturing mother and a somewhat frightening, strong, competent father. It is not easy for a woman, whose voice is not as strong and deep as a man's, who is not as large, and who cannot physically subdue a large boy, to present the same image of power that the father presents.

The research, however, does not consistently show that children view their father as described above. In the doll-play study mentioned (Ucko & Moore, 1963), 4-year-old girls attributed authority mainly to the mother and boys attributed it primarily to the father. The 6-year-old children of both sexes, however, showed the father doll as the more authoritarian parent. Moreover, the father doll, more often than the mother doll, was shown using nonpunitive methods of coping with the child doll's behavior.

The sex and age of the child may influence whether Father is viewed as the more controlling or punitive parent. Fourth-through eighth-grade children saw Father as *less* controlling than Mother (Armentrout & Burger, 1972). A questionnaire administered to children 7 to 15 indicated that boys tended to see Father as boss, whereas girls tended to see their parents as equal (Hess & Torney, 1962). Seventh-grade girls reported that their mothers used more overt, direct methods of punishment; their male counterparts reported that their fathers used these methods. They did not report, however, that their parents differed in strictness (Droppleman & Schaefer, 1963).

In one investigation of adolescent girls (Fitzgerald, 1966), half of them perceived Mother as more punishing and fearful than Father. The interview responses of 14- and 15-year-olds revealed that boys generally associated the punishing role with Father and feared him more than they feared Mother, half of the girls also saw Father as punishing and fearful, but the other half saw Mother in that role.

Two investigators (Grinder & Spector, 1965) administered a questionnaire to adolescents asking which parent had more control over a variety of activities and situations, such as their going to movies or parties, career choice, and privacy. More adolescent boys attributed this kind of control to the father and more girls attributed it to the mother.

One study (Bronfenbrenner, 1961b) found that adolescent girls considered Father less active than Mother in all the parent-child functions investigated. According to the same study, 15- and 16-year-old boys and girls reported that Mother performed 17 out of the 21 cited parent-child functions. Both sons and daughters reported that the mother, rather than the father, was their main source not only of nurturance and affection but also of protectiveness, general discipline, and material rewards, and that she was the chief decision maker. The adolescent girls generally reported that Mother exceeded Father in all aspects of the parental behavior studied. Sons, on the other hand, reported that Father, rather than Mother, punished them physically and participated with them in activities and projects. Finally, college students reported that, in general, Mother had punished them the most when they were children and that they preferred to be punished by her (Jackson, 1956).

If it is true that Mother loves you even if you have proved yourself a complete failure, but that you must earn your love from Father, children might be expected to consider Father less accepting than Mother. Children from the fourth through the eighth grade considered Father more accepting of them than Mother (Armentrout & Burger, 1972; Stehbens & Carr, 1970). From the sixth grade on, girls more often than boys reported that Mother was the more accepting parent (Armentrout & Burger, 1972).

If Father, as the less expressive parent, is less concerned than Mother with subtle interactions within the family, his children might be expected to consider him less devious in his methods of controlling their behavior. In support of this hypothesis, seventh-grade children reported that their father used more direct methods of control than their mother (Droppleman & Schaefer, 1963). In that study, girls saw Father and boys saw Mother as granting more independence. Girls reported receiving more love, affection, and nurturance from both parents. Boys reported more hostile and negative treatment and more overt and covert control from both Father and Mother.

Father may be seen to intrude less on the child's privacy but also to be less helpful than Mother. Fourteen- and 15-year-olds reported in an interview (Fitzgerald, 1966) that Father checked up on them less than Mother did, but that he did not help them so much in solving problems. The girls reported almost unanimously that Mother helped them more than Father. Their near unanimity in naming Mother as the one helping them with troubles may be explained by the nature of the problems faced by girls during puberty.

The parent assuming the instrumental role must be able to tolerate the inevitable hostility of family members. If father is the instrumental parent, we would expect him to engender less pleasant feelings in his children than the mother does and to receive more criticism from them. The evidence offers only partial support for this prediction. Fifth graders reported that they felt less pleasant feelings for their father than for their mother (Hawkes, Burchinal, & Gardner, 1957b). But in other investigations, fifth- and sixth-grade children criticized their father more than their mother (Gardner, 1947), but 10- and 11-year-olds criticized their mother and their father to the same degree (Stott, 1940). When very bright 12-year-olds responded to a sentence-completion test, the girls gave more positive reactions than the boys to both Father and Mother (Smith, 1963). In a free-association interview of children in grades 5 through 8, girls showed more hostility to Mother than to Father, and boys showed more hostility to Father (Meltzer, 1943).

If Father, as the instrumental parent, invests much of his energy in the larger society, his children might consider him less child-centered than Mother. Ninth-grade children, in response to a parental-behavior inventory, viewed the father as less important, less involved in their lives, less child-centered, and less accepting of their individuality. The boys described him as not so overprotective and controlling as the mother and as less likely to force himself into their peer relationships. The girls described their relationship with Father as less friendly than their relationship with Mother (Stehbens & Carr, 1970).

Father, the instrumental parent, may be considered less understanding than Mother, the expressive parent. As high school boys grow older, they become more rebellious and alienated from their parents. In a study by Meissner (1965), they described their father as more old-fashioned and less understanding than their mother. They reported that the mother was more reasonable but also more nervous. The expressive parent would be expected to show feelings more freely than the instrumental parent. Among college students, fathers were perceived as being more stoical than mothers in the face of illness (Mechanic, 1965).

If Father is the instrumental parent, we assume that he would be associated in the minds of his sons and daughters with powerful personages, such as the President or even God. This assumption proved valid in third-grade children's ratings of their father and the President; they described them in quite similar terms (Hess & Torney, 1967). The assumption did not prove true, however, in a study of the associations between father and God in the thinking of adolescents and adults. A researcher (Nelson, 1971) asked the latter to complete phrases such as, "When I think of father . . . ," "When I think of mother . . . ," and "When I think of God . . . ," and discovered that there was a higher association between God and whichever parent the subject preferred, regardless of the sex of the subject.

Children's perception of the father as the instrumental parent should be reflected in the roles they report that he performs in the society and in the home. In a study by Finch (1955), children 3 to 7 years old from professional families overwhelmingly described Father as the breadwinner and Mother as the one assigned to household chores and child care.

Ruth Hartley (1960) asked 5-, 8-, and 11-year-old children to engage in play and to respond to pictures, tests, and an interview in order to discover their view of sex roles in home and society. In general, men earn the living, women are homemakers; when an adult carries out a function that the child characterizes as appropriate to the opposite sex, that adult is seen as "crossing over" into foreign terrain in order to help the other parent with his duties.

One of Hartley's methods was to ask children how they would tell a visitor from Mars what men and women in this world need to know and what they are able to do. About two-thirds of the women's activities men-

tioned were traditional domestic tasks related to household management, child care, and relations with the husband. Only six percent of the items that were mentioned for women dealt with outside employment. Men, in striking contrast, were generally described as engaging in traditionally masculine activities requiring physical strength and stamina, and these activities were described as often done outside the home. Only six percent of the activities mentioned for men lay within the realm of traditional "women's work." Sons of working mothers, more often than sons of nonworking mothers, assigned work roles to women and domestic tasks to men. Sons of working men, more often than sons of upper-middle-class fathers, assigned such task to men, in keeping with findings that working men do in fact engage in more domestic chores. Boys and girls thought that both Mother and Father felt sad when they had to leave home and go to work. In general, these descriptions of parental roles closely fit Parsons' differentiation of instrumental and expressive functions.

The Preferred Parent

Which is the preferred parent in the eyes of the child? There is no clear answer to this question. In doll play, boys (but not girls) as young as 2 and 3 years old chose the father doll in some situations that seemed very much mother-oriented such as the one in which a parent fed the child (Ammons & Ammons, 1949; Lynn, 1969a). Given a choice of parent with whom to play an actual game, more boys (as young as 2) also chose their father, but more girls switched from their father at age 2 to their mother at age 4 (Lynn & Cross, in press).

Gardner (1947) found that fifth- and sixth-grade children preferred Mother over Father. But in still another investigation (Pishkin, 1960) of children ages 3 to 19, boys preferred Father and girls preferred Mother.

Cooper and Lewis (1962) asked high school students some direct questions on their preference for each parent. They were asked which parent they would prefer in a number of different situations. To which would they show a report card? To which would they go for advice? Which would they rather be with on a vacation? Whom would they prefer to work with for money, to resemble, or to be with during serious trouble? As one might expect, the parent the student wished to resemble was not always the one he preferred for the various situations described. The high school girls were split almost 50/50 in their parent preferences. Among the boys, 38 percent preferred their mother and 62 percent preferred their father.

When both adolescents and adults (ages 15 to 44) were questioned, however, they generally preferred their mother over their father (Nelson, 1971). Unlike Cooper and Lewis, Nelson found that the males chose their mother more consistently than did the females. The females more often expressed no preference. In a survey of studies reported from 1894 to 1936 (Stogdill, 1937), the mother was more often preferred over the father.

The Good Father and the Bad Father

What is a "good father" and a "bad father" in the eyes of his children? In a study reported in a French journal (Tap, 1972), subjects aged 13 to 20 were asked, "What are the qualities you would like in a father?" The qualities most frequently listed were that he be understanding, good natured, and assertive.

A research team (Schvanveldt, Freyer, & Ostler, 1970) interviewed preschool children and discovered that a good father does not spank, does not lock doors, and feeds you when your mother is not home. He washes the dishes, helps Mother, and picks up the garbage; he is to be sat upon and fought with. He reads stories, sings, and does things for you; he kisses and hugs and helps you get dressed. He works with Mother, sleeps with Mother, and likes her. He does not steal; he is nice to people and helps them get in and out of cars.

The bad father sends his child to bed or lets his child be naughty and does not spank him, slaps him on the face, and does not feed him when Mommy is not home. He does not come home to eat. He won't read stories to his child and isn't nice to him. He leaves Mommy and child. "The one we used to have, boy, was he mean." He does not read the newspaper, throws chairs at people, and smokes. He is big, dirty, and dumb. He does not like nice people. One father did "naughty things" to a child's sister. He is mean to everybody.

EXPECTANT FATHERS AND NEW FATHERS

Why do men want to be fathers in the first place? Perhaps if people could accurately foresee all the implications of parenthood they would never dare undertake the responsibility. For a man, having a child may be like going to war: if he were capable of accurately visualizing the full implications of what he was getting into, he would not go. Do young couples rush into parenthood because they are too blinded by the inexperience of youth to visualize precisely the implications of their acts? Perhaps cultures, in the service of their continuity, intuitively conceal from the young the drudgery and restrictions imposed by parenthood so that the young will rush headlong into producing children before they know what they have gotten into.

Now, of course, under the threat of overpopulation, the curtain is beginning to lift a little and adults are daring to admit that parenthood brings pain along with joy. Today, having children no longer assures the parent of old-age care in one of his children's homes; a retirement community will probably be his abode in his old age.

Perhaps one of the motivations men feel to become fathers (along with the obvious delights of experiencing the companionship of children and sharing with one's mate in planning, producing, and rearing them) is the immortality they offer. Unless a man is convinced of life after death or is so creative that he adds something to the culture that will exist after he ceases to, having children is the only way he can ensure that a part of him will continue living after his death.

The adjustments in a man's life demanded by the advent of his first child may be greater than those demanded by his marriage. Two studies (LeMasters, 1957; Feldman, no date) reported that most of the couples studied reported extensive or severe crises in adjusting to the birth of their first child. One investigator (Wainright, 1966) even found an association in men between fatherhood and mental illness. Parents with infants were more resentful of each other and had more arguments than those in any other stage of marriage. Other research (Dyer, 1963; Hobbs, 1965) found the incidence of crisis to be lower than originally thought; even so, in Hobbs' study, 75 percent of the fathers said that they were bothered by the interruption of their routine habits, such as sleeping and going places, and 60 percent said that they were bothered by increased money worries.

Father's troubles may begin long before the birth of the baby. The expectant father may experience a crisis (Arnstien, 1972). Most of the men interviewed in a study of expectant fathers (Liebenberg, 1967) expressed pleasure that the pregnancy was confirmed but worried about whether they could handle the emotional and financial responsibilities it implied; for example, one admitted that, although he had always wanted a child, he was pretending to be happy for his wife's benefit but was in fact sad and worried about money. Another expectant father admitted that he was frightened by the thought of the care another human being would require. During their wife's pregnancy, many of the men appeared to need their own mothers—they wrote more frequent letters to their parents and telephoned them more than usual, and a number of them wished to be at their parents' homes on Mother's Day.

Some of the expectant fathers seemed to envy their wife's pregnancy; sometimes they (in effect) denied the reality of her pregnancy by, for example, dragging their fatigued wife on long motor trips or camping expeditions, insisting that she lead a "normal life." Others seemed to identify with her, asking her to breast-feed the baby because it would "feel so good." Some supervised their wife's wardrobe and diet, shopped for maternity dresses, or described the details of their wife's pregnancy as though they were an anatomical part of her. On the other hand, others seemed uneasy and a few were repelled by the pregnancy.

Toward the end of their wife's pregnancy, some men reported difficulty in sleeping, restlessness, or anxiety, and a few became ill; one had pain whenever he took a deep breath and was bedridden, although medical examination revealed nothing wrong with him. Some men stopped drinking coffee and began to drink milk, as babies do. One expectant father complained of a little muscle sticking out from his stomach; in the eighth month of his wife's pregnancy, he fell across the bed, gasping for breath, with sharp pain in his abdomen. He was sent to the hospital, where medical examination revealed no physical basis for his symptoms, and the doctor could not feel the abdominal lump.

Several husbands began to drink heavily and became involved with other women. (The sexual exploits of expectant fathers will be elaborated later in connection with findings from another study.) Many husbands began to work frantically during the middle and late stages of the pregnancy. Over half of the husbands in the study were largely unavailable to their wives because of heavy work or class schedules. Liebenberg suggested, as possible explanations, that the husbands envied their wife's creativity or that they were using work as an excuse to get away from home in order to exclude themselves from the whole process.

Almost half of the sample also reported a sharp decrease in sexual activity during the pregnancy. The wives expressed disinterest during the first third because of a fatigue; the men lost interest after the beginning of fetal movement. Some men said they were afraid of hurting the baby, of crushing the baby's head—a physiological impossibility. Some said that the kicking of the baby disturbed their slumber so that they could not sleep in the same bed with their wife.

Some men had fears about the pregnancy, such as whether their wife was big enough, whether a baby could emerge from such a small place, or whether she would need surgery; one even wondered whether she was actually pregnant or had a tumor. Some also worried that the baby might be deformed or retarded. Almost all the expectant fathers expressed anxiety about getting their wife to the hospital on time, and one of them equipped his car with flares and emergency equipment in case the baby should be born in the car.

Several fathers described feelings that they had been abandoned or deserted during their wife's labor. They also expressed anger toward the obstetrician for failing to keep them sufficiently informed during labor. After the birth, several fathers were shocked at the newborn's appearance, describing it as "ugly," "like a newborn rat," "ghastly," and so on. These were the exceptions, however, and the usual response was positive.

Expectant fathers openly revealed their overwhelming preference for a male child—typical of men expecting firstborns. One husband talked in his sleep about "his son" even before the child was born. Liebenberg re-

ferred to Margaret Mead's (1949) explanation for men's strong desire for a son. Mead's reasoning is that a son, more than a daughter, embodies the father's desire for immortality.

Sometimes the birth of a child, particularly a male, brought up old dependencies in the husband and he became jealous of the baby. Some fathers became irritated with the child, and one even struck it when it cried, blaming the baby for maliciously disturbing him. One man complained that he and his wife had worked hard and saved money for a home, and, now that they were finally well off enough to enjoy life, they were tied down with the baby. More often, the father was unaware of his underlying rivalry with the child, but he expressed rivalry through his fears that something bad would happen to it—that it would die or become abnormal. Some expressed rivalry by insisting that their wives go back to work, saying it was wrong to let a baby run one's life. Forty-one percent of the husbands expressed rivalry in a different way: they competed with their wives over who could be a better parent to the child.

The researcher concluded by stating that the wife's pregnancy and the birth of the first child may intensify the husband's feelings of separation, reactivate his infantile conflicts with his own parents, and heighten his dependency.

In another psychiatric study of expectant fathers, Curtis (1955) concluded that men who were not referred to psychiatric consultation had adapted in a superior way to fatherhood by virtue of a stable and unconscious view of themselves as capable and loving fathers. Those referred for consultation with minor problems had achieved a less satisfactory identification with the father role but were nevertheless able to cope with a comfortable unconscious image of themselves in the role of a good mother or of an older child in the family. Men presenting serious problems were unable to form a stable identification as father, mother, or sibling.

The interview study of expectant fathers discussed previously (Liebenberg, 1967) mentioned that several husbands began to drink heavily and became involved with other women. Hartman and Nicolay (1966) asked whether the kind of offenses committed by expectant fathers who ran into trouble with the law might be disproportionately sexual in nature. They compared the police records of men whose wives were pregnant with those of men whose wives were not pregnant. They discovered that the number of sex offenses in the wife-pregnant group was far greater. The frequency of sexual offenses by the expectant fathers, ranked in descending order, were (1) exhibitionism, (2) sexual offenses against children, (3) rape or attempted rape, (4) lewd phone calls and letters, and (5) homosexual behavior, transvestism, possession of pornography, and voyeurism. Bear in mind that these facts do not imply that a large percentage of expectant fathers commit sexual offenses. It indicates, however, that among those few who do break the law, the frequency of sexual offenses is disproportionately high.

From her interviews with expectant fathers, Liebenberg reported that over half of the husbands were absent a great deal from their wives because of heavy work or class schedules. How available are fathers to their children during their infancy? Pedersen and Robson (1969) studied fathers' activities with their infants, until recently a neglected area of investigation. Unfortunately, they interviewed mothers instead of fathers to gather the information. They discovered that 6 out of 45 fathers of 8- and 9-month-old infants engaged in two or more caretaking tasks on a daily basis and that these fathers spent an average of 8 hours per week playing with the child, ranging from 45 minutes to 26 hours. Nine of the 45 fathers were extremely patient and

tolerant with fussy or irritable babies, but ten habitually became angry or irritated with their infants. Of those ten irritated fathers, eight were fathers of girls. Fathers also tended to be more apprehensive about the well-being of female infants. Seven fathers were very authoritarian in their conduct with the child, restrictive, and ready to slap or spank in order to enforce their will. On the other hand, eleven were very permissive and tolerant of the baby's getting into things. The fathers tended to roughhouse with their boys, but some criticized their wives for being too rough with the baby. Fathers were in the home while the baby was awake for an average of 26 hours per week.

The baby's attachment to the father was ascertained by his smiling, vocalizing, increased activity, and excitement upon seeing the father after separation. Approximately three-fourths of the babies showed intense attachment to their father. At around 8 months of age, two babies began to show distress or protest when the father held them. For boy babies, the father's caretaking, emotional involvement, and play with the infant were significantly associated with their attachment to him. The father's irritability with the baby was negatively associated with the baby's attachment.

There was a sex difference in the relationship between Father's child-rearing approach and the baby's attachment: compared with many relationships between the father and boy babies, the only significant relationship between the father and female infants was a negative association between the father's irritability and her attachment to him.

For boy babies, the father's authoritarian control was related to the baby's protest upon being separated from the *mother*. There also was a relationship between the father's playing with the boy baby and the baby's responding better to male than to female strangers.

For girl babies, there was an association only between the father's authoritarian control and the frequency of their sleep disturbances.

When more precise measuring instruments were used (Rebelsky & Hanks, 1971), a gloomier picture of father-infant interaction emerged. Beginning in the second week of a baby's life, 24-hour tape recordings of everything that happened to him were made approximately every two weeks for a 3-month period. A microphone about the size of a half-dollar with a 27-foot cord was attached to the infant's shirt. The researchers told the parents that they were studying how infants live, what they do, and so on. They explained that they did not wish to interfere in any way with the normal household schedule.

They found that these fathers spent very little time talking with their infants. The average number of vocal interactions per day was 2.7 and the average number of seconds per day that the father vocalized to the baby was 37.7. Even the father who interacted the most averaged only $10^1/_2$ minutes vocalizing to his infant each day. Unlike the mothers, who vocalized to the baby an increasing amount during the first three months of its life (Moss, 1967; Rebelsky, 1967), most of the fathers spent less time vocalizing during the last half of the study than during the first half. This decrease in vocalization over time was especially true of fathers of girl babies.

In fairness to fathers, the procedures in the Rebelsky and Hanks study (a microphone and a 27-foot cord attached to the infant's shirt) may have dampened the father's impulse to interact vocally with his baby. Neither did this study measure the father-infant interaction that took place without the father's vocalizing. I suspect that fathers spend so little time with their infants partly because they simply do not understand the importance of early father-infant interaction on the later development of children. It is hard to believe that interaction with a tiny baby is so critical to its later development, but the child development literature defies common sense and long ago demonstrated its significance (Goldfarb, 1945). . . .

SUMMARY

A close father-child relationship is more often associated with a cohesive family that holds positive values than a close father-mother relationship. Fathers are usually more punitive and stricter than mothers, although mothers may use a wider variety of punishments. Fathers frequently perceive their role as vital to the child's development, but some seem, nevertheless, to take insufficient advantage of the time available to them to spend with their child.

Fathers tended to participate more in the daily care of girls than in that of boys; they are more likely to use power with their sons and more likely to spank them. Father has a clearer definition of what a boy needs for a successful adult role than he has for a girl. Father tends to play a unique role in the family. He lacks the close, easy, affectionate rapport with his children enjoyed by the mother, but this detachment may be to his advantage in situations that require firmness.

The mother is viewed by children in a way that fits Parsons' expressive role. Children generally describe fathers as instrumentally nurturant, punitive, strong, powerful, and fearsome. Children usually see their fathers, compared with their mothers, as less accepting, using more direct methods of control, and less likely to "check up" on children; they are seen as less helpful, as evoking less pleasant feelings, as less important in their children's lives, and as more stoical in the face of illness.

Young children tend to associate their fathers with the President. College students associate God with their preferred parent, not necessarily with the father. Children generally see Father as the breadwinner and Mother as homemaker and child-rearer. Their descriptions of parental roles closely parallel Parsons' differentiation of instrumental and expressive functions.

The wife's first pregnancy and the birth of the baby are times of crisis for many men. These events may intensify the husband's feelings of separation, reactivate his infantile conflicts with his parents, and heighten his dependency. Expectant fathers who run into trouble with the law tend to commit a disproportionate number of sexual offenses.

The father's positive interaction with his baby boy is frequently associated with the baby's attachment to him and with the baby's responding better to male than to female strangers. For girl babies, there is a relationship between the father's authoritarian control and frequency of their sleep disturbances. Fathers also tend to become more irritated with girl babies and tend to play in a more rough-and-tumble way with boy babies. Fathers average very little time in vocal interaction with their babies, and their vocalization with their infant daughters decreases over time. . . .

REFERENCES

Aberle, D. F. & Naegele, K. D. Middle-class fathers' occupational role and attitude toward children. *American Journal of Orthopsychiatry*, 1952, **22**, 366–378.

Ammons, R. B. & Ammons, H. S. Parent preferences in young children's doll-play interviews. *Journal of Abnormal and Social Psychology*, 1949, 490–505.

Armentrout, J. A. & Burger, G. K. Children's reports of parental childrearing behavior at five grade levels. *Developmental Psychology*, 1972, **7**, 44–48.

Arnstien, H. The crisis of becoming a father. *Sexual Behavior*, 1972, **2**, 42–48.

Bronfenbrenner, U. Some familial antecedents of responsibility and leadership in adolescents. In L. Petrullo & B. M. Bass (Eds.), *Leadership and interpersonal behavior*. New York: Holt, Rinehart, & Winston, 1961. Pp. 239–271. (b)

Bronson, W. C., Katten, E. S., & Livson, N. Patterns of authority and affection in two generations. *Journal of Abnormal and Social Psychology*, 1959, **58**, 143–152.

Cooper, J. B. & Lewis, J. H. Parent evaluation as related to social ideology and academic achievement. *Journal of Genetic Psychology*, 1962, **101**, 135–143.

Curtis, J. A psychiatric study of 55 expectant fathers. *U. S. Armed Forces Medical Journal*, 1955, **6**, 937–950

Droppleman, L. F. & Schaefer, E. S. Boys' and girls' reports of maternal and paternal behavior. *Journal of Abnormal and Social Psychology*, 1963, **67**, 648–654.

Dyer, E. D. Parenthood as a crisis: A re-study. *Marriage and Family Living*, 1963, **25**, 196–201.

Eisenberg, J., Henderson, R., Kuhlman, W., & Hill, J. P. Six- and ten-year-olds' attribution of punitiveness and nurturance to parents and other adults. *Journal of Genetic Psychology*, 1967, **111**, 233–240.

Emmerich, W. Young children's discriminations of parent and child roles. *Child Development*, 1959, *40*, 403–419. (b)

Emmerich, W. Family role concepts of children ages six to ten. *Child Development*, 1961, **32**, 609–624.

Emmerich, W. Variations in the parent role as a function of the parent's sex and the child's sex and age. *Merrill-Palmer Quarterly*, 1962, **8**, 3–11.

Feldman, H. Development of the husband-wife relationship. Mimeographed grant application, E-228, undated.

Finch. H. M. Young children's concepts of parent roles. *Journal of Home Economics*, 1955, **47**, 99–103.

Fiztgerald, M. P. Six differences in the perception of the parental role for middle and working class adolescents. *Journal of Clinical Psychology*, 1966, **22**, 15–16.

Gardner, L. P. A survey of the attitudes and activities of fathers. *Journal of Genetic Psychology*, 1943, **63**, 15–53.

Gardner, L. P. An analysis of children's attitudes toward father. *Journal of Genetic Psychology*, 1947, **70**, 3–28.

Goldfarb, W. Effect of psychological deprivation in infancy and subsequent adjustment. *American Journal of Orthopsychiatry*, 1945, **15**, 247–255.

Grace, H. A. & Lohmann, J. J. Children's reaction to stories depicting parent-child conflict situations. *Child Development*, 1952, **23**, 61–67.

Grinder, R. E. & Spector, J. C. Sex differences in adolescents' perceptions of parental resource control. *Journal of Genetic Psychology*, 1965, **106**, 337–344.

Hartley, R. E. Children's concepts of male and female roles. *Merrill-Palmer Quarterly*, 1960, **6**, 83–91.

Hartman, A. A. & Nicolay, R. C. Sexually deviant behavior in expectant fathers. *Journal of Abnormal Psychology*, 1966, **71**, 232–234.

Hawkes, G. R., Burchinal, L. G., & Gardner, J. Pre-adolescents' views of some of their relaions with their parents. *Child Development*, 1957, **28**, 393–399. (b)

Hess, R. D. & Torney, J. V. Religion, age, and sex in children's perceptions of family authority. *Child Development*, 1962, **33**, 781–789.

Hess, R. D. & Torney, J. *The development of political attitudes in children*. Chicago: Aldine, 1967.

Hobbs, D. F. Parenthood as crisis: A third study. *Journal of Marriage and the Family*, 1965, **27**, 367–372.

Jackson, P. W. Verbal solutions to parent-child problems. *Child Development*, 1956, **27**, 339–351.

Kagan, J. The child's perception of the parent. *Journal of Abnormal and Social Psychology*, 1956, **53**, 257–258.

Kagan, J., Hosken, B., & Watson, S. Child's symbolic conceptualization of parents. *Child Development*, 1961, **32**, 625–636.

Kagan, J. & Lemkin, J. The child's differential perception of parental attributes. *Journal of Abnormal and Social Psychology*, 1960, **61**, 440–447.

Landis, J. T. A re-examination of the role of the father as an index of family integration. *Marriage and Family Living*, 1962, **24**, 122–128.

LeMasters, E. E. Parenthood as crisis. *Marriage and Family Living*, 1957, **19**, 352–355.

Liebenberg, B. Expectant fathers. *American Journal of Orthopsychiatry*, 1967, **37**, 358–359.

Lynn, D. B. Indiscriminate father preference as an index of masculine-role striving. 1969 supplement to D. B. Lynn, *The Structured Doll Play Test*. Burlingame, California: Test Developments, 1959. (a)

Mead, M. *Male and female*. New York: Morrow, 1949.

Mechanic, D. Perception of parental responses to illness: A research note. *Journal of Health and Human Behavior*, 1965, **6**, 253–257.

Meissner, W. W. Parental interaction of the adolescent boy. *Journal of Genetic Psychology*, 1965, **107**, 225–233.

Meltzer, H. Sex differences in children's attitudes to parents. *Journal of Genetic Psychology*, 1943, **62**, 311–326.

Moss, H. A. Sex, age and state as determinants of mother-infant interaction. *Merrill-Palmer Quarterly*, 1967, **13**, 19–36.

Nash, J. The psychology of deprivation. Unpublished doctoral dissertation, University of Edinburgh, 1954.

Nelson, M. O. The concept of God and feelings toward parents. *Journal of Individual Psychology*, 1971, **27**, 46–49.

Parsons, T. & Bales, R. F. *Family, socialization and interaction process*. Glencoe, Illinois: Free Press, 1955.

Pedersen, F. A. & Robson, K. S. Father participation in infancy. *American Journal of Orthopsychiatry*, 1969, **39**, 466–472.

Pishkin, V. Psychosexual development in terms of object and role preference. *Journal of Clinical Psychology*, 1960, **16**, 238–240.

Radke, M. J. *The relation of parental authority to children's behavior and attitudes*. Minneapolis: University of Minnesota Press, 1946.

Rebelsky, F. G. Infancy in two cultures. *Nederlands Tijdschrift voor de Psychologie*, 1967, **22**, 379–385.

Rebelsky, F. & Hanks, C. Fathers' verbal interaction with infants in the first three months of life. *Child Development*, 1971, **42**, 63–68.

Schvaneveldt, J. D., Freyer, M., & Ostler, R. Concepts of "badness" and "goodness" of parents as perceived by nursery school children. *Family Coordinator*, 1970, **19**, 98–103.

Smith, R. M. Sentence completion differences between intellectually superior boys and girls. *Journal of Projective Techniques*, 1963, **27**, 472–480.

Stehbens, J. A. & Carr, D. L. Perceptions of parental attitudes by students varying in intellectual ability and educational efficiency. *Psychology in the Schools*, 1970, **7**, 67–73.

Stogdill, R. Survey of experiments on children's attitudes toward their parents 1894-1936. *Journal of Genetic Psychology*, 1937, **51**, 293–303.

Stolz, L. M. Old and new directions in child development. *Merrill-Palmer Quarterly*, 1966, **12**, 221–232.

Stott, L. H. Adolescents' dislikes regarding parental behavior and their significance. *Journal of Genetic Psychology*, 1940, **57**, 393–414.

Tap, P. Etudes différentielles de la représentation des qualités paternelles à l'adolescence. *Enfance*, April 1971, No. 3, 249–289. Abstract No. 8483, *Psychological Abstracts*, 1972, **49**, 959.

Tasch, R. J. The role of the father in the family. *Journal of Experimental Education*, 1952, **20**, 319–361.

Ucko, L. E. & Moore, T. Parental roles as seen by young children in doll play. *Vita Humana*, 1963, **6**, 213–242.

Wainright, W. H. Fatherhood as a precipitant of mental illness. *American Journal of Psychiatry*, 1966, **123**, 40–44.

Chapter 4

Physical Development

**MOTOR DEVELOPMENT OR WHAT THE
BABY DOES**

Mrs. James Potty-Trains Mickey

Nathan H. Azrin and Richard M. Foxx

Then she asked him, "Mickey, do you have dry pants?" Mickey looked down at his pants. "Feel them—see if they're dry." Mickey put his hands on his pants. "Mickey, are they dry?" Mickey said, "Yes," they were. "Mickey, you're a big boy too! What do big boys get?" she asked. "Candy!" he shouted.

Editor's Introduction

Azrin and Foxx describe the traditional method of toilet training as requiring the mother to seat her child on the potty. The child remains seated until urination occurs. If the child has urinated, the mother may reciprocate with praise or a reward. If the child takes a long time, she may provide encouragement. If the child urinates after rising from the potty chair, she may scold.

This procedure requires a considerable amount of time on the part of the mother as she must undress the child, seat him or her on the potty, remain in attendance for extended periods of time, and empty the potty after urination has occurred. The mother must be constantly available at a moment's notice in order to get the child to the potty whenever the urge to urinate arises. Faced with numerous accidents, the mother may begin to nag. Then, having failed to live up to expectations, the child may become frustrated, throw temper tantrums, or become secretive, concealing wet pants in order to avoid punishment.

Azrin and Foxx claim they have developed a method by which the average child requires less than four hours to be trained. After that time, the child determines when he or she has to urinate, goes to the potty alone, lowers his or her pants without assistance, urinates or defecates, wipes up if necessary, arises, pulls up his or her pants, empties the potty into the larger toilet, flushes the toilet, and returns the potty to the potty seat. No supervision or effort from the mother is required.

The authors have followed many theoretical orientations in the development of their approach to toilet education. They have incorporated (1) the psychoanalytic emphasis on the possible effects of punitive toilet training procedures on subsequent personality development and (2) the learning-theory principles of the association of sphincter relaxation with the stimulus of the potty and the generous use of reinforcement following the desired responses. Finally, (3) a doll that wets is used, as part of social learning procedure to encourage imitation. This is done by teaching the child to train and reward the doll for the proper behavior.

The authors advise the parent not to begin toilet training until the child is ready for it, as indicated by sufficient bladder control and the ability to follow instructions. Their objective is to make toilet training a pleasant experience for the child and one through which the child can achieve a feeling of competence. Spanking and anger are excluded. During the training, the child is praised and hugged and made the center of attention. It is the authors' hope that the child will enjoy the process and respond enthusiastically.

The premise is sound. I read the book and followed the instructions. Lauren had Oscar the Grouch, her doll, urinate in the potty, and we both rewarded Oscar with graham crackers at the appropriate times. Lauren drank large quantities of ginger ale and ate candy and crackers for three days. She loved it. She learned this method so well that she urinated in the potty at least thirteen times every day, expecting a reward not only each time she urinated but also all the times in between, when she remained dry. She was terrific. As the tangible food rewards were diminished, according to the instructions, Lauren's patience with this procedure also diminished. After the fourth day she refused to urinate on the potty; on eight different occasions she chose the floor instead. I then realized that I was asking Lauren's cooperation to accomplish my goal. I was overeager and Lauren was frustrating me by not cooperating, which was her way of saying "enough." We decided to relax the whole intensive procedure. She now urinates in the potty whenever she is without her diaper and urinates in her diaper whenever she is wearing it (contrary to the Azrin and Foxx instructions, which are never to return to a diaper once the training has begun). She shows great pride in her accomplishments, and I am sure that in short order or in good time, as Lauren prefers, she will train herself.

Whatever method or combination of methods is chosen, I fully agree with Azrin and Foxx that it is best to avoid contests of will between parent and child, pressure to reach the potty before having an accident, and shame about failure. If we view this process as a cooperative venture which continues for months, the child's interest and participation will probably be enlisted. One day the child may forget or may prefer to urinate or defecate in the old manner. Meanwhile, it is best to encourage the successes and not be troubled by the failures. After several months, success should become fairly frequent. It is also my opinion that to overreact to each success as if it were a work of art may cause difficulty. Some children, feeling that their urine or feces are so highly prized, may become reluctant to part with them and be distressed with the idea of flushing away such valuable products. The most important motive should be the child's own pleasure in his or her achievements.

Many parents do not understand how difficult it is for a young toddler to postpone the urge to urinate or defecate; they do not know that normally the process of toilet training can take many months, with many relapses in between. Surely a toddler can learn to urinate in the potty in a day, or in ten minutes for that matter; but to expect a child to completely master the tasks of toileting within a day is to create undue pressures for both the child and the parents. It is my belief that if a small child is to achieve total control in such a short time, a great deal of pressure will necessarily be involved. This, in turn, may compromise the permanence of the training or perhaps lead to problems in other areas of control.

Pamela Cantor

. . . Mrs. James decided to conduct the training in her kitchen. The kitchen was large enough so that neither she nor Mickey would feel confined. The drinks could be kept cold in the refrigerator, and the floor was linoleum, so that any spillings or wettings could be wiped up easily. She brought the potty chair and doll into the kitchen. She lifted the pot out of the potty chair to make sure that it could be removed easily and checked to make sure the urine-signaling device was working. Then she took a piece of paper and made a reminder sheet to use during the training. On this reminder sheet she would record the time of each dry-pants inspection, prompted toileting, and accident, as a reminder to herself to conduct these various procedures. When she had finished making up the Training Reminder sheet, she went over a reminder list of questions, checking to make sure she could answer each question satisfactorily. When she encountered a question she felt unsure of, she reread the section of the procedure that answered the question. Now that she had "passed" the reminder test, she felt ready to begin Mickey's training.

Mickey was still wearing the diaper that she had put on him before breakfast. She rolled up Mickey's undershirt and pinned it so that it was about two inches above his training pants, where it would not hinder his attempts to lower or raise his pants. Mrs. James removed the diaper, told Mickey to sit on the floor, and guided his feet through the legs of a pair of old training pants. When Mickey's feet were through the pants legs, she told him to stand up. When he was standing, she told him, "Mickey, pull up your pants," guided him to bend forward slightly, and then guided his hands to the waistband of the pants. She guided his hands in grasping the waistband and then guided them in raising the pants. As he began pulling up the pants, she reduced the guidance by lifting her hands off his hands. She kept her hands close by, however, almost touching, so that she could resume the guidance should he stop. She praised him each time he attempted to raise the pants himself: "That's good, Mickey: you're pulling up your pants, like a big boy." She gave him a big hug and kiss when he had pulled the pants all the way up.

She had found it difficult to refrain from pulling up his pants for him. Although she knew that he had to learn to dress himself in order to potty independently, her natural inclination had been to do it for him, just as she had always done for Ronnie and Renée. After all, it was always faster to dress your child than to stop and wait for him to painstakingly dress himself. Fortunately, the new potty-training procedure had given her some tips on how to accomplish dressing training rapidly. And since her objective was to teach Mickey to potty by himself, she was willing to be patient and teach him to dress.

Mrs. James offered Mickey a glass of orange soda. She wanted him to drink as much as possible so that he would have the urge to urinate shortly. She had begun giving him a lot to drink at breakfast. Mickey took a sip and handed the glass back to her. She said, "Mickey, that's a good drink, isn't it? Would you like some more?" and handed the glass back to him. This time he took two sips before handing the glass back to her. She continued to praise him for drinking and continued to hand him the glass until he had drunk almost the entire glassful. She set the glass aside and said, "Mickey, let's give the doll a drink. Do you want to help the doll drink?" Mickey said yes, that he would.

Mrs. James handed him the doll and a plastic baby bottle filled with water. "Mickey, give the baby a drink. That's right. Lay her down so she can drink." When she saw that the bottle was empty, Mrs. James said, "Mickey, the dolly has to pee-pee. Let's help her sit on the potty." She picked up the doll by one of its arms and offered the doll's other arm to Mickey. After she and Mickey carried the doll

to the potty, she said, "Mickey, let's help her pull down her pants." She guided him in pulling the doll's pants down. She was careful to keep the doll in a partly prone position, since the water came out when the doll was in an upright position. "Mickey, set the doll on the potty. That's right. You're a big helper."

When Mickey had placed the doll on the chair, Mrs. James told him to "Watch the dolly. The dolly is about to pee-pee." She knew the doll would begin to leak water now that it was set up straight. As the water dripped from between the doll's legs, she pointed to it and said, "Mickey, see Dolly pee-peeing in the potty." She paused a moment to make sure that Mickey was looking at the droplets of water. Then she clapped her hands and said, "Mickey, Dolly's a big girl. She's pee-peeing in the potty. Is Dolly a big girl?" Mickey nodded his head up and down and said, "Yes." Mrs. James handed Mickey a piece of candy from her apron and said, "Mickey, give the dolly a piece of candy for being such a big girl."

As Mickey held the candy to the doll's mouth, Mrs. James told him that he could eat it if he would be a big boy and go pee-pee in the potty as the dolly had. Mickey nodded his head affirmatively and ate the candy. She then said, "Mickey, Dolly is finished pee-peeing; help lift her off the potty." When they had lifted the doll from the chair, she said, "Mickey, help the dolly pull up her pants." She waited a moment before guiding his hands, to see if he would begin pulling up the doll's pants himself. He began immediately, but was having trouble pulling the pants over the doll's bottom. Mrs. James placed her hands on Mickey's to help guide him in pulling up the pants. When the pants were pulled up, Mrs. James praised him, just as she had throughout his attempts to raise the doll's pants, and then set the doll aside on the nearby kitchen table.

Then she told him, "Mickey, help the dolly by carrying her pot to the big toilet." She guided him in lifting the plastic pot from the chair. "Hold on to it tight so it won't spill." When she was sure that he had a good grip on the pot, she said, "Carry it to the big toilet in the bathroom." He started for the bathroom.

On the way to the toilet, she walked beside Mickey, always staying within arm's reach so that she could steady the pot should he start to drop it or spill its contents. When they reached the toilet, she told him, "Mickey, dump the pee-pee into the toilet." Then she guided him in turning the potty sideways so that its contents emptied into the toilet. "That's right— make sure the pee-pee is all out." She lifted her hands from his when she saw that he was following her instructions. "Now, flush the toilet." He tried to set the pot down before flushing the toilet, but she told him to hold it with his left hand and use his right hand to flush, since he was right-handed. "That's right. Put your hand on the handle. Just like Mommy does when she is finished pee-peeing."

Mickey had reached for the handle automatically. He had seen all of the family flush the toilet many times before. He had no trouble pushing the handle downward. She noticed that he seemed to enjoy flushing the toilet, probably because of the flushing noise. "Now, take the pot back to the potty." Again she remained close to him on the return trip, so as to be ready to intervene should he wish to set the pot down. When he reached the potty chair, she said, "Mickey, put the pot in the chair." He bent down and placed the pot in the chair. "Turn it around so that it fits straight. That's right," she said, as she guided his hands ever so slightly in turning the pot to its correct position.

Now she would have him inspect the doll's pants to see if they were dry. "Mickey, does Dolly have dry pants? Let's see." She guided Mickey over to the table and told him to put his hands on the doll's pants. "Why, they're dry. The dolly has dry pants. Does she have dry pants?" "Yes," he answered. "She's a big

girl. Are you proud of the dolly?" she asked. Mickey nodded yes. Mrs. James continued, "Dolly has dry pants; let's give her some candy. She's a big girl. Big girls get candy for dry pants. Mickey, can you tell her she's a big girl?" "Big girl," he said. "Here, you give the dolly candy for having dry pants." She handed Mickey a piece of candy, which he pushed toward the doll's mouth.

Then she asked him, "Mickey, do you have dry pants?" Mickey looked down at his pants. "Feel them—see if they're dry." Mickey put his hand on his pants. "Mickey, are they dry?" Mickey said, "Yes," they were. "Mickey, you're a big boy too! What do big boys get?" she asked. "Candy!" he shouted. "That's right." Making sure that his hand was still touching his pants, she told him to eat the piece of candy he was holding in his other hand. "Mickey, you're a big boy. You have dry pants. You get candy," she said. Turning from the doll she asked, "Mickey, do you want a drink?" He said, "Yes." "You do? Are your pants dry?" He felt his pants again and said very excitedly, "Dry." She handed him a glass of orange soda while saying, "Mickey, you're a big boy. You have dry pants. Big boys can have drinks." After a few swallows, he handed the glass back to her. In the next five minutes, she had Mickey check the doll's pants and then his own pants two more times, each time giving him a snack treat and then a drink of soda.

Now Mickey would learn why he should not have accidents. While he was drinking, Mrs. James spilled water on the doll's pants. Then she directed Mickey's attention to the doll. "Mickey, let's see if the dolly has dry pants. Does the doll have dry pants?" "Yes," he said. "Mickey, feel her pants," she said, guiding his hand to the doll's wet pants. He pulled his hand back when he felt the wetness. "Wet," he said. "That's right. The doll wet her pants. She's a baby," Mrs. James said sternly. "Mickey, is the dolly a baby?" Mickey nodded affirmatively. "We love Dolly but we don't want her to wet her pants. Do we love Dolly?" Mickey said, "Yes." "Do we like her to wet her pants?" "No," he answered. She was pleased by his answers. They showed that he understood that wetting was bad but that the person who wet was still loved.

"When Dolly wets her pants, she has to practice going potty," she said. "She must learn not to pee-pee in her pants. Will you help her practice?" Mickey said that yes, he would. She told him to carry the doll to the potty rapidly, to help lower her pants rapidly, to set her on the potty for a moment, to help raise her pants, and to carry her rapidly back to where she had "had the accident." Whenever necessary, Mrs. James provided instruction and manual guidance throughout the practice trials. Mickey helped the doll practice three times. For each action Mrs. James said, "Mickey, Dolly must practice fast. Help her practice fast."

After the last practice trial, she said, "Mickey what happens when Dolly wets her pants?" He just looked at her. "She must practice," Mrs. James said. "Practice," Mickey said, looking at the doll. "What happens if you wet your pants?" she asked. "Practice," he said. "That's right. You don't want to practice, do you?" "No," he said resolutely. "Now, feel her pants. Are they wet?" she asked. "Yes," he said. "Dolly has wet pants. Do we love Dolly?" "Yes," he said. "What don't we like?" she asked. "Wet pants," he said loudly. "That's right," she said approvingly. "Mickey, are you going to wet your pants?" "No," he said. "Are you a big boy with dry pants?" He felt his pants. "Big boy," he said loudly. "That's right—big boys have dry pants." she said. "You can have the candy. Your pants are dry." "Dry," he said, putting the candy in his mouth.

Approximately ten minutes had elapsed since the training had begun. She began asking him a series of questions, all of which were designed to inform him of how happy all his family, friends, and heroes would be when he was a big boy who could potty by himself. She also wanted to point out to him that all of these people used the toilet by themselves and thereby kept their pants dry. She wanted him to identify with and emulate these people. She began by asking, "Mickey, does Daddy wet his pants?" She had waited until he was looking at her before she asked the question; that way she could be sure that he was listening to her. Mickey shook his head and said, "No." She repeated his answer: "No, Daddy doesn't wet his pants. Daddy is a big boy. He keeps his pants dry. He pees in the potty. Does Daddy wear diapers?" "No," Mickey said. "Are you a big boy?" "Yes," Mickey answered. "Will you keep your pants dry?" "Yes." he said. "Does Ronnie wet his pants?" "No." "Does Renée wet her pants?" "No." "Does Mommy wet her pants?" "No." "Only babies wet their pants. Are you a baby?" "No." "That's right. You don't wet your pants. You're not a baby. You're a big boy!"

She would now describe to him all of the acts necessary for him to toilet himself. She would repeat this description many times that morning as a reminder of what he would be doing. She would ask him a question after each statement to ensure that he was paying attention to what she was saying. "Mickey, when you have to pee-pee, you'll go to the potty. Right?" "Yes." "Where will you go?" "Potty." "You'll pull your pants down and sit on the potty. Right?" "Yes." "Then you'll pee-pee. Is that right?" "Yes," he said. "Will you pee-pee in your pants?" "No!" "And then you'll pull your pants up. Right?" "Right," he said loudly and happily. "Then you'll pick up the pot and carry it to the toilet. Right?" "Right." "Where will you carry the pot?" He pointed toward the bathroom. "Right. And dump the pee-pee in the toilet?" "Yes." "And flush the toilet?" "Yes." "Flush it just like Daddy does?" "Yes." "And then carry the pot back to the potty?" "Yes." "Where do you carry the pot?" "Potty." He pointed to the chair. "That's right, you carry it there. And put it back in the potty?" "Yes."

Now that she had had him verbally rehearse and visualize all of the toileting acts, she would suggest that he go to the potty. He had drunk over a glass of soda, so she knew he would be ready to urinate any time now. She wanted his first urination of the day to be in the potty. That would start the day's training with a success! "Mickey, sit on the potty now." She walked with Mickey over to the potty. "Mickey, pull your pants down." He looked at her, then started to sit down. "Wait, you've forgotten something." She pointed to his pants. Mickey looked down, started to reach for his pants, then stopped. She knelt down beside him and said, "Pull your pants down." He paused as if he weren't sure what to do. "Put your hands on your pants," she said again as she grasped his hands with her thumb and forefinger and guided them to the waistband of his pants. "Now, grab your pants." She placed his hands on the waistband so that his thumbs were inside next to his skin and his fingers outside, grasping the training pants. "Pull down, down," she said as she slowly guided his hands in lowering the pants about an inch. She released his hands as he began lowering his pants himself. "That's right—down past your knees. Just like a big boy!" She continued praising until he had his pants all the way down and then kissed him.

When his pants were down a few inches below his knees, she pointed to the potty chair, and he sat down. "Mickey, try and go pee-pee in the potty. Big boys pee-pee in the potty. Does Daddy pee-pee in the potty?" "Yes," he said. "Yes, he does. Well, you be a big boy too. Tell me when you pee-pee. What will you say when you pee-pee?" she asked. "Pee-pee," he answered. "That's right. You'll say pee-pee," she said. Then she stopped talking to him, because she didn't want to

distract him any further. She knew that he had to relax before he could urinate; if she talked to him, he might not relax long enough to do so. After a minute or so, he started to stand up. "Wait, not yet. Sit down on the potty until you pee-pee," she said as she placed her hand on his shoulder and gently guided him back to a seated position.

I'm certainly acting differently during this training from the way I did when I trained Ronnie and Renée, she thought. Especially when I trained Ronnie; it seemed as if I were always yelling at him. Whenever he couldn't follow my instructions, which was often, I would give him the instructions again in an angry tone of voice. When he still would not follow the instructions, I would become even angrier and often spank him. I wish I had known about this physical-guidance procedure back then. I would not have gotten angry, because I could have always made sure that he followed my instruction. Even if Mickey becomes a little difficult later, I won't let myself become angry. Rather, I'll just guide him through the task until he begins doing it himself. I think the training and especially the guidance permits a mother to be more patient. Also, my instructions this time are simpler, which should make it easier for Mickey to understand what I want him to do.

While he sat on the potty, she looked closely between his legs into the potty. Four minutes after he had been sitting, she saw him urinate. He had done it! Immediately she clapped her hands and said, "Mickey, you're a big boy! You pee-peed in the potty! I'm so proud of you!" She waited until the urine stopped, then hugged and kissed him. "You're my big boy. You pee-peed in the potty." She reached in her apron and took out a large piece of candy and handed it to him. "Here's candy for pee-peeing in the potty. Big boys get candy." He took the candy and ate it. She waited a few moments to make sure that he had finished urinating, since she didn't want him to stand up until he had finished. "Okay. You can stand up. You are finished when you pee-pee in the potty."

Mickey stood up and turned around to lift the pot out of the chair. "Wait a minute. You've forgotten something." He turned and looked at her. "Your pants," she said, pointing toward his pants. He reached down and pulled up his pants so that they were just below his buttocks. He kept pulling at the pants, but he couldn't get them up over his bottom. She reached down and took his right hand in hers. She guided his right hand from the side of his pants to the back of his pants so that he was grasping the pants with his palm facing outward. "Mickey, pull your pants up." With his palm facing outward, the pants were pulled out from and over his bottom easily. "That's the right way to pull up your pants. Now pick up the potty." He reached down with one hand. "Use both hands so that it won't spill." He looked up at her momentarily, then placed both hands on the pot. The pot fitted tightly, but he managed to lift it from the seat. "Mickey, take it to the toilet," she said. She walked beside him, as she had done earlier when he was emptying the potty for the doll. She remained close enough to help him steady the pot, if necessary. He walked from the kitchen through the living room to the bathroom with no trouble.

The last time they were in the bathroom, she had left the toilet lid up so that it wouldn't be in the way. She was extremely pleased when he poured the contents of the pot into the toilet without being told. "Tip it over just a little bit more. That's right. Now all the pee-pee will be in the toilet." He started to set the pot on the floor. She didn't want him to do this, because he would forget to pick it up after he had flushed the toilet. She wanted him to be ready to carry the pot back to the potty chair. "Hold the potty in one hand. That's right. Now flush the toilet with your other hand. Good. That's a big boy."

As she had noticed earlier, Mickey seemed to enjoy flushing the toilet, for he smiled when he heard the flushing sound, and he had begun flushing almost before she told him to do so. He carried the pot back to the kitchen without any trouble and smiling broadly. When he reached the potty chair, he set the pot in the chair, but in a crooked position, so that it did not fit into the chair correctly. He had started to rise up and move away when Mrs. James told him, "Mickey, fix the pot so that it is straight." She bent over him and, taking his hands in hers, guided him in turning the pot around. She stopped guiding his hands as soon as he began turning the pot in the correct direction.

Once the pot was in place, she said, "Mickey, are your pants dry?" He reached down and felt the crotch of his pants with his right hand. "Dry," he said. "That's good. Your pants are dry. You're a big boy, just like Ronnie. Big boys can have a treat." She took one each of several different candies and chips from her apron and offered him his choice. "Which would you like?" He picked a corn chip. I'm glad he likes salted treats, she thought: they'll make him thirsty and he'll want more to drink. When he had eaten the corn chip, she asked him if his pants were dry and then offered him a drink. Again, as she had done with the food, she offered him his choice of milk, orange soda, cola, and fruit punch. He chose the orange soda. He took a few sips and then handed the glass back to her. After a brief moment, she handed the glass back to him and asked him if he wanted to drink some more, which he did. After he had drunk a few swallows, he said he didn't want any more. She wanted him to drink as much as possible, so she lifted the glass to her lips and said, "May I have some of your soda?" He said, "Yes." After she had pretended to drink, she handed him the glass. Much to her delight, he drank seven or eight more swallows. She recorded the time of the dry-pants inspection on her Training Reminder List so that she would be reminded in five minutes to make another inspection. She had been recording the time of each dry-pants inspection since the beginning of the training.

Since Mickey had just urinated, he wouldn't be ready to urinate again for at least fifteen minutes. In the interim before she sent him to the potty again, Mrs. James used several procedures. She used the "Friends-Who-Care" procedure to let him know how much everyone wanted to see him potty by himself. She pointed out to Mickey that all of those people toileted themselves. She wanted his identification with friends and relatives and heroes to motivate him to toilet himself. At other times, she described to him all of the various toileting acts, asking him if he would and could do them. She also continued to have him check his pants every five minutes or so and rewarded him if they were dry, with praise and a snack. Every few minutes, she offered him a choice of drinks. Each time the drinks were offered, she also checked his pants.

Almost a half-hour had passed since she had begun the training. She would now have Mickey train the doll again before sending him to the potty. That way, she might not have to use very much instruction to get him to go to the potty. After this time, the doll would be used only once more. That would be fifteen minutes later. Mrs. James felt that after Mickey had trained the doll three times, he would have a good grasp of why and how he should be toileting himself. Thus, once Mickey was sufficiently familiar with the overall training objective, she would discard the doll. After Mickey had helped the doll toilet herself, emptied her pot, given her a dry-pants check, and reacted to another accident by the doll, Mrs. James set the doll aside.

She would now send Mickey to the potty. She would send him using some sort of general suggestion that he go rather than the direct instruction she had used the last time. If he urinated, she would reward him. If not, she would leave him on the potty for only five minutes. For each toileting act, she would use less physical guidance and direct instruction than she had the last time. Thus, Mickey would be performing each of these acts more independently each time.

She gave him the general suggestion: "Mickey, remember, big boys pee-pee in the potty. Where do big boys pee-pee?" "Potty." "You should go to the potty when you have to pee-pee." He did not move. "Is the dolly a big girl when she pee-pees in the potty?" "Yes," he said. "That's right. Can you pee-pee in the potty?" "Yes," he said, and he started pulling his pants down. He lowered them just to below the crotch and began to sit down. "Mickey, wait, pull them down a little farther." He looked at her, then down at his pants. He grasped the pants and attempted to push them down still farther. "That's right," she said. "You're pulling your pants down."

He was having difficulty, however. The pants had bunched up when he had first lowered them, making it difficult for him to lower them farther. She placed her hands on his hands, which were still grasping the waistband. She gently guided his hands in pulling the pants out from his thighs and then sliding them down. They were lowered easily to a point just above his knees. Next time he would know how to do it without her help. "That's right. You're a big boy. Big boys can pull their pants down." She had helped him lower his pants because she knew that if they were not lowered to his knees, they might bunch up when he sat down and he thus might accidentally wet them while sitting on the potty. With his pants down, he sat down by himself without being told. She was delighted; he had walked to the potty, pulled his pants down, and sat down, all without being told directly. While he sat there, she recorded the time of this prompted toileting on her Training

Reminder List and then went to the refrigerator for fresh ice for his glass.

The only thing she had said to him after he sat down was that he should try and go pee-pee. Other than that, she said nothing, since she didn't want to distract him. She knew that he had to relax in order to urinate; if she talked to him, he would be too interested in what she was saying to relax. She appreciated this brief respite, since it gave her time to review what had occurred so far. She spread his knees slightly apart so she could look into the pot.

Shortly after Mickey had sat down, she saw him urinate. As before, she praised, hugged, and gave him a snack. He had finished urinating, but was making no attempt to stand up. "Mickey, if you are finished pee-peeing, you can stand up," she said. He still didn't move, so she reached down and touched him lightly on the shoulder. He stood up and immediately bent over and raised his pants. Mrs. James could hardly believe her eyes. She was ecstatic. He had raised his pants without being told, and he had raised them perfectly, with no trouble and little effort. She hugged him and told him what a big boy he was. She had waited to praise him until he had finished pulling up his pants, since he was raising his pants without any help.

He turned and looked at the potty chair, then bent down and began to lift the pot from the chair. Again, he was beginning one of the toileting acts without being told. He was having a little trouble placing his fingers under the rim of the pot. She bent down and, taking his right hand, guided his fingers under one edge of the pot. With an edge to grip, he lifted the pot easily and carried it to the toilet, emptied it, flushed the toilet, brought it back to the potty chair, and reinserted it. He had needed assistance when reinserting the pot only in turning it around so that it fitted in the chair correctly. Mrs. James's heart was pounding; he had done so much by himself. He had learned the entire sequence for emptying the pot. It could be only a matter of time now before he pottied himself. Now she would have to remember to praise him only at the completion of the pottying sequence, since she did not want to distract him while he was doing so well.

During the next fifteen minutes she gave him three pants checks—one every five minutes—and continued to talk to him about the benefits of toileting himself and how happy everyone would be with his newfound skill. He had begun to drink less, so she began offering the drinks more often and varying the types of drinks. He had gone to the potty again when she had asked him to show her his potty. He had walked over to it and touched it and then begun lowering his pants. He had lowered his pants by himself and had sat down on the potty chair. We're getting close, she thought; now he can raise and lower his pants by himself. He also knows how to empty the pot by himself. He urinated within a minute after sitting down. Mrs. James was extremely pleased that he had urinated so soon after sitting down. This meant that he had learned what he was to do in the potty. Now all he had to do was go to the potty without her telling him to and he would be trained. . . .

Chapter 5

Mental Development

LEARNING THE LANGUAGE

Suggestions from Studies of Early Language Acquisition

Courtney B. Cazden

C: *Nobody don't like me.*
M: *No, say "Nobody likes me."*
C: *Nobody don't like me.*
    (eight repetitions of this dialogue)
M: *No. Now listen carefully; say "Nobody likes me."*
C: *Oh! Nobody don't likes me!*

(McNeill, 1966)

Editor's Introduction

There are two basic theories which attempt to account for the acquisition of language. The learning theory approach, states that language learning may be described as learning elements of language piece by piece and building up a repertoire of verbal behaviors. Children learn language by interacting with their environment. They hear, imitate, and are reinforced by other people. Children learn to speak because speaking has specific effects on the environment which are reinforcing to the child. There is no reference to any innate language abilities to explain the development of speech. The transformational-grammar theory states that a child is born knowing the principles of language. Children use their innate capacities to build the abstract rule system of their language. Thus, the child's capacity to learn is not based upon the ability to imitate or upon corrections or reinforcements of speech patterns. While experience does affect language development, language is primarily a function of a fixed schematic structure and of language universals. Human beings are predisposed to produce sounds, to reproduce them, and to order them into structures which generate meaning. When children learn language, they learn the rules for the relationship between the underlying and surface structure of a sentence and then extend these rules to new sentences with similar structures. The learning of language is the learning of rules which enable the child to generate sentences once the rules have been learned.

Many linguists believe that there is truth in both positions, that there is both a biological and a social basis for language. According to Cazden, reinforcement or imitation do not account for language acquisition. She argues that a theory that relies totally on imitation fails to explain how children produce or understand novel sentences which they have never heard before. While imitation and reinforcement may be a part of language development, Cazden states that it appears to be primarily the inference of rules combined with maturational readiness which account for language learning. Further, there are stages of language development, each of which is characterized by a different set of rules. For instance, if at the first stage a child has learned that in order to talk about things which have already happened, the sound "ed" must be added to a word, he or she might say, "I walked, I batted, I goed." No matter how many times another might correct this and say, "Say went 'instead of goed,' the child will stick to the rule.

Courtney Cazden discusses what she believes to be the myth of imitation and the myth of being corrected, indicating that these are not the processes by which children learn language.

Pamela Cantor

When we say that a child has learned his native language by the time he enters first grade, what do we mean he has learned? A set of sentences from which he chooses the right one when he wants to say something? The *meaning* of a set of sentences from which he chooses the right interpretation for the sentences he hears? Even if the sets of sentences and interpretations were enormous, the result would still be inadequate. Outside of a small and unimportant list of greetings like *Good morning* and clichés like *My, it's hot today*, few sentences are spoken or heard more than once. Any speaker, child or adult, is continu-

ously saying and comprehending sentences he has never heard before and will never hear or comprehend again in the same way. Creativity in expressing and understanding particular meanings in particular settings to and from particular listeners is the heart of human language ability.

The only adequate explanation for what we call "knowing a language" is that the child learns a limited set of rules. On the basis of these rules he can produce and comprehend an infinite set of sentences. Such a set of rules is called a grammar, and the study of how a child learns the structure of his native language is called the study of the child's acquisition of grammar.

When we say that a child knows a set of rules, of course we don't mean that he knows them in any conscious way. The rules are known nonconsciously, out of awareness, as a kind of tacit knowledge. This way of knowing is true for adults too. Few of us can state the rules for adding /s/ or /z/ or /iz/ sounds to form plural nouns. Yet if asked to supply the plurals for nonsense syllables such as *bik* or *wug* or *gutch* (Berko, 1958), all who are native speakers of English could do so with ease. Most six-year-old children can too. We infer knowledge of the rules from what adults or children can say and understand.

Children learn the grammar of their native language gradually. Might one assume, therefore, that the stages they pass through on their way to mature knowledge could be characterized as partial versions of adult knowledge? Not so! One of the most dramatic findings of studies of child language acquisition is that these stages show striking similarities across children but equally striking deviations from the adult grammar.

For example, while children are learning to form noun and verb endings, at a certain period in their development they will say *foots* instead of *feet*, *goed* instead of *went*, *mines* instead of *mine* (Cazden, 1968). Children do not hear *foots* or *goed* or *mines*. These words are overgeneralizations of rules that each child is somehow extracting from the language he does hear. He hears *his*, *hers*, *ours*, *yours* and *theirs*; and he hypothesizes that the first person singular should be *mines*. Human beings are pattern- or rule-discovering animals, and these overgeneralizations of tacitly discovered rules are actively constructed in each child's mind as economical representations of the structure of the language he hears.

Rules for formation of sentences show the same kinds of deviations. In learning how to ask a question, children will say, *Why I can't go?*, neglecting temporarily to reverse the

auxiliary and pronoun (Bellugi-Klima, in press). And their answer to the often-asked question, *What are you doing?*, will temporarily be, *I am doing dancing* (Cazden, 1968). If the answer to *What are you eating?* takes the form, *I am eating X*, the child hypothesizes that the answer to *What are you doing?* is, *I am doing X-ing*. Only later does he learn that answers with *doing* require the exceptional form *I am X-ing*.

The common-sense view of how children learn to speak is that they imitate the language they hear around them. In a general way, this must be true. A child in an English-speaking home grows up to speak English, not French or Hindi or some language of his own. But in the fine details of the language learning process, imitation cannot be the whole answer, as the above examples show.

Sometimes we get even more dramatic evidence of how impervious to external alteration the child's rule system can be. Jean Berko Gleason's conversation with a four-year-old is an example:

> She said, *My teacher holded the baby rabbits and we patted them.*
> I asked, *Did you say your teacher held the baby rabbits?*
> She answered, *Yes.*
> I then asked, *What did you say she did?*
> She answered, again, *She holded the baby rabbits and we patted them.*
> *Did you say she held them tightly?* I asked.
> *No*, she answered, *she holded them loosely.* (Gleason, 1967, p. 1)

Impressed by the confidence with which the child continued to use her own constructions despite hearing and comprehending the adult form, Gleason conducted a variation of her older test (Berko, 1958) with first-, second- and third-grade children. She asked the children to give irregular plural nouns or past tense verbs after she had supplied the correct form as she asked the question. "In the case of the verbs, they were shown a bell that could ring and told that yesterday it rang; then they were asked what the bell did yesterday" (Gleason, 1967, p. 3). Even under these conditions, only 50 percent of the first-graders (seven out of 14) said *rang*; six said *ringed* and one said *rung*. Gleason concludes:

> In listening to us, the children attended to the sense of what we said, and not the form. And the plurals and past tenses they offered were products of their own linguistic systems, and not imitations of us. (1967, p. 8)

When sophisticated parents try deliberately to teach a child a form that does not fit his present rule system, the same filtering process occurs. The following conversation took place when a psychologist tried to correct an immaturity in her daughter's speech:

> C: *Nobody don't like me.*
> M: *No, say "Nobody likes me."*
> C: *Nobody don't like me.*
>   (eight repetitions of this dialogue)
> M: *No. Now listen carefully; say "Nobody likes me."*
> C: *Oh! Nobody don't likes me!* (McNeill, 1966, p. 69)

It happens that irregular verbs such as *went* and *came* are among the most common verbs in English. Children usually learn the irregular forms first, evidently as isolated vocabulary words, and later start constructing their own overgeneralizations *goed* and *comed* when they reach the stage of tacitly discovering that particular rule. Finally, they achieve the mature pattern of rule plus exceptions. Stages on the way to the child's acquisition of mature behavior may look for the moment like regressions, like new errors in terms of adult standards, and yet be significant evidence of intellectual work and linguistic progress.

With a very few pathological exceptions, all children learn to speak the language of their parents and home community. They do so with such speed and ease, at an age when other seemingly simpler learnings such as

identification of colors are absent, that one wonders how they do it, and how the environment helps. Here we can contrast research knowledge with common folk beliefs.

MYTH: CHILDREN LEARN LANGUAGE BY IMITATION

The common-sense view of how children learn to speak is that they imitate the language they hear around them. In a general way, this must be true. A child in an English-speaking home grows up to speak English, not French or some language of his own. But in fine details of the language learning process, imitation cannot be the whole answer. As *foots* and *goed* and *holded* show, children use the language they hear as examples of language to learn from, not samples of language to learn.

While imitation is not as important as commonly believed, identification with particular models is very important. How any person speaks depends not only on who he is, but on how he sees himself in relation to others, on who he wants to be. From the beginning of the language learning process, children pick their models. This is not done consciously, but we have already noted how powerful nonconscious knowledge can be. If children didn't pick their models, there would be no way to explain why Black children, for example, speak like their parents or peers despite considerable exposure to standard English on television. The power of attitudes to influence language learning is of critical importance for education. They influence teachers' responses to children as well as children's responses to teachers. We will return to this point in a later section.

MYTH: CHILDREN LEARN LANGUAGE BY BEING CORRECTED

Just as the common-sense view holds that the child's language learning process is basically imitation, so it holds that the adult's contribution is to shape the child's speech by correcting him when he is "wrong" and reinforcing him when he is "correct." Here too the folk belief is wrong. All analyses of conversations between parents and children whose language is developing well show that neither correction of immature forms nor reinforcement of mature forms occurs with sufficient frequency to be a potent force. Studies have shown that this is true for white children in Cambridge, Massachusetts (Brown, Cazden & Bellugi, 1969), and Madison, Wisconsin (Friedlander, in press); for Black lower socioeconomic class children in Rochester, New York (Horner, 1968), and Oakland, California (C. M. Kernan as reported in Slobin, 1968).

During conversations with their children, parents do correct misstatements of fact (like when a particular television program comes on); they clarify word meanings (like the difference between *beside* and *under*); and they correct socially inappropriate language. Ursula Bellugi-Klima's picture of one family's conversations applies to all:

The mother and child are concerned with daily activities, not grammatical instruction. Adam breaks something, looks for a nail to repair it with, finally throws pencils and nails around the room. He pulls his favorite animals in a toy wagon, fiddles with the television set, and tries to put together a puzzle. His mother is concerned primarily with modifying his behavior. She gives him information about the world around him and corrects facts. Neither of the two seems overtly concerned with the problems that we shall pursue so avidly: the acquisition of syntax (1968).

In modifying behavior, supplying information about the world and correcting facts, mothers of young children do seem to use simpler language than they address to other adults. At least, this is indicated in the only study in which the mother's utterances to her child and to another adult have been compared. The utterances to her child were both shorter and simpler (Slobin, 1968). Presumably, as the child's utterances become longer and more complex, so do the mother's. Other than this simplification, there is no sequencing of what the child has to learn. He is offered a cafeteria, not a carefully prescribed diet. And, seemingly impelled from within, he participates in the give-and-take of conversation as best he can from the very beginning, in the process takes what he needs to build his own language system and practices new forms to himself, often at bedtime (Weir, 1962). As far as we can tell now, all that the child needs is exposure to well-formed sentences in the context of conversation that is meaningful and sufficiently personally important to command attention. Whether the child could learn as well from an exclusive diet of monologues or dialogues in which he did not participate—as he could get from television—we don't know and, for ethical reasons, may never be able to find out.

The foregoing picture of how children learn their native language *before* school is fairly certain, though still incomplete. Implications for how to help children continue their learning *in* school are far less certain—indeed, are controversial in the extreme—and evidence on which the controversy might be resolved is insufficient. The most obvious implication is that teachers should act the way parents have acted: talk with children about topics of mutual interest in the context of the child's ongoing work and play. This recommendation is made by many people in early childhood education in this country and in infant schools in England. And see Hawkins' (1969) sensitive account of "the language of action and its logic" in six four-year-old children who are deaf. Controversy arises because, so far, experimental comparison of various preschool programs that focus on language development have failed to demonstrate the effectiveness of those programs based on the above philosophy (see Blank & Solomon, 1969, for one such comparison).

Two different explanations of this apparent anomaly can be very tentatively suggested. First, our diagnosis of children's communication problems may be inadequate. Children who need help with language may need very specific kinds of help: help in specific language knowledge such as work meanings, in specific communication skills such as communicating information accurately through words alone, in specific school language games such as answering questions posed by an adult who obviously knows the answers; or help in very general cognitive strategies like focusing attention in school and on tests. In short, maybe the kind of linguistic knowledge that has developed so well in the conversational setting of the home is not a problem in school at all, even for children from "disadvantaged" environments, and the problems that do exist respond better to more structured educational programs. Second, the test results in the more structured programs may look deceptively good. What the child has learned well enough to express on a test may not have been assimilated into his total linguistic and cognitive system (see Glick, 1968, and Kohlberg, 1968, for words of caution).

Hopefully, this controversy will be resolved in the near future. It is an issue of both practical and theoretical importance.

REFERENCES

Bellugi-Klima, U. *The Acquisition of the System of Negation in Children's Speech.* Cambridge, Mass.: Massachusetts Institute of Technology Press, in press.

Berko, J. The child's learning of English morphology. *Word*, 1958, 14, 150–177. Also in S. Saporta (Ed.), *Psycholinguistics.* New York: Holt, Rinehart & Winston, 1961, Pp. 359–375.

Blank, M. & Solomon, F. How shall the disadvantaged be taught. *Child Development*, 1969, 40, 47–61.

Brown, R., Cazden, C. B. & Bellugi, U. The child's grammar from I to III. In J. P. Hill (Ed.), *1967 Minnesota Symposium on Child Psychology.* Minneapolis: University of Minnesota Press, 1969. P. 28–73.

Cazden. C. B. The acquisition of noun and verb inflections. *Child Development*, 1968, 39, 433–448.

Cazden, C. B. *Child Language and Education.* New York: Holt, Rinehart & Winston, 1972.

Friedlander, B. Z. Listening, language and auditory environment. In J. Hellmuth (Ed.), *Exceptional Infant. Vol 2: Studies in Abnormality.* New York: Brunner/Mazel, in press.

Gleason, J. B. Do children imitate? *Proceedings of the International Conference on Oral Education of the Deaf, June 17–24, 1967.* 1967, Vol. II, 1441–1448.

Glick, J. Some problems in the evaluatin of preschool intervention programs. In R. D. Hess & R. M. Bear (Eds.), *Early Education.* Chicago: Aldine, 1968. Pp. 215–221.

Hawkins, F. P. *The Logic of Action: From a Teacher's Notebook.* Boulder: University of Colorado Elementary Science Advisory Center, 1969.

Horner, V. M. The verbal world of the lower-class three-year-old: A pilot study in linguistic ecology. Unpublished doctoral dissertation, University of Rochester, 1968. Shorter version appears as V. M. Horner & J. D. Gussow. John and Mary: A pilot study in linguistic ecology. In C. B. Cazden, V. P. John & D. Hymes (Eds.), *Functions of Language in the Classroom.* New York: Teachers College Press, 1972. Pp. 155–194.

Kohlberg, L. Early education: A cognitive-developmental view. *Child Development*, 1968, 39, 1013–1062.

McNeill, D. Developmental psycholinguistics. In F. Smith & G. A. Miller (Eds.), *The Genesis of Language: A Psycholinguistic Approach.* Cambridge, Mass.: Massachusetts Institute of Technology Press, 1966. Pp. 15–84.

Slobin, D. I. Questions of language development in cross-cultural perspective. Paper prepared for symposium on "Language learning in cross-cultural perspective," Michigan State University, September, 1968.

Weir, R. H. *Language in the Crib.* The Hague: Mouton, 1962.

MEASURING INFANT INTELLIGENCE

From Eight to Fourteen Months of Age

Burton White

In addition to the notion that somewhere between the first and third birthdays children are beginning to reveal where they are headed in later years, we have come to the conclusion that to begin to look at a child's educational development when he is two years of age is already much too late, particularly in the area of social skills and attitudes.

Editor's Introduction

White states that in the brief span extending from ages 8 to 18 months, a mother's actions will do more to determine her child's competence than at any time before or after. According to White, "the mother is right there on the hook, just where Freud put her." She can turn her child into a highly competent human being or she can produce a young social and intellectual failure who will stand little chance for change. Yet, according to White, nowhere can a mother find the information necessary to make intelligent decisions about a child's life, as this early period of life had not yet been studied. Until recently even professional psychologists were unaware of the importance of this period in the determination of competence.

So White and his staff at the Harvard Preschool Project began studying children. They first studied two groups of children aged 3 to 6: one group which they rated as exceptionally competent in all areas of development and another which they rated as incompetent. They studied these two groups to find out how they differed. In motor skills, the groups appeared to be quite similar. The differences became apparent in social and intellectual skills. But even more startling was the discovery that the competent 3-year-olds already possessed the same skills which were indicative of competency in the 6-year-olds. In other words, the researchers had arrived too late. Whatever had caused the divergence in competencies had occurred before the child had reached its third birthday.

The more closely the researchers looked, the earlier the differences became apparent. Even at age one-and-a-half, the child's path seemed predictable. Yet at ten months the differences were not clearly observable. Thus, White and his staff concluded that somewhere between 10 and 18 months, things happened which determined the child's future development. It is conceivable that the differences which seem to appear between the 10- to 18-month period may have their origins in an even earlier period. In fact, while Freud felt that personality was fairly well established at age five, White states that intellectual and social competence are determined at age one-and-a-half, and some psychologists believe that the most critical period of human development occurs during the first few weeks of life. In any discussion of determinism, however, it is largely the mother who is held responsible for her child's development.

All mothers want to produce competent children. "Professor White," I ask,

"What's a mother to do?" According to White, most effective mothers do not devote most of their time to child rearing. They have their own interests or part-time jobs. They are extremely effective, however, as designers of their child's environment and as consultants for their children's lives. They design a home which is open to exploration and in no way stifles the child's curiosity. The use of restrictive devices such as playpens or high chairs for long periods of time every day is felt to severely restrict a child's intellectual development. The effective mother also sets up guidelines for her child's behavior. She is, however, generally permissive and indulgent, encouraging the great majority of her child's explorations in spite of the mess involved. White states that there may be an inverse relationship between competence and a mother's desire to preserve the contents and neatness of her home. As a consultant, the mother is available to her child for brief 10- to 20-second intervals in which she may answer a question, share some language, encourage the child's curiosity, and generally reinforce the important skill of using an adult as a resource when the child discovers something particularly exciting or confronts a situation which he or she is unable to control. These interactions are oriented toward the child's interests rather than toward those of the mother.

According to White, a good mother needs some practical guidelines, knowledge of cognitive development, and a vast amount of energy. The guidelines that follow are a few of the highlights of those which are being developed for use in training mothers to be aware of what they should do—in White's estimation—to foster optimal emotional, social, and intellectual development.

1 Provide access to as much of the house as possible. Allow a child to explore. The child's natural tendencies are toward nonmalicious destructiveness.

2 White suggests a wide range of exploratory materials which do not necessarily require any expense. Simple household items are, in fact, preferable.

3 The mother should be available to her children at least half their waking hours. Thus, mothers should not consider working full-time when their children are young but should rather work part time or develop other interests in addition to child-centered activities. White cautions about constant hovering but advises accessibility for frequent consultations, assistance, or support.

In short, the researchers have learned that love is not enough. The major resources necessary for excellent child rearing are energy and patience. A young child who is slow relative to adult standards, who has modest abilities, and who insists on repetitive behavior (Lauren asked me to sing "It's Raining, It's Pouring, the Old Man Is Snoring" 36 times yesterday afternoon), can be very trying to an adult. A mother needs time with her child, but not as much as the researchers first thought. Even effective mothers who were home all the time spent less than 10 percent of their time interacting with their infants, and many of the excellent mothers worked half time.

White and his colleagues are convinced that they have unraveled one of the mysteries of child development and have discovered the crucial time period and the crucial processes for the effective shaping of a competent child. Essentially competent mothers produce competent children . . . and all before age 2.

Pamela Cantor

THE SPECIAL IMPORTANCE OF THIS PERIOD OF LIFE

With the onset of Phase V, the parent assumes a new, challenging, and considerably more significant role. Whereas most families in this country today get their children through the first six to eight months of life reasonably well educated and developed, I have come to the conclusion that *relatively few families, perhaps no more than ten percent, manage to get their children through the eight- to thirty-six-month age period as well educated and developed as they can and should be*. This statement underlies my dedication to the subject of education in the first years of life.

Not all professionals agree with me. There are people in child psychiatry, for example, who think that the first weeks of life are the most important and that prospective parents must be educated in the best way to establish a healthy mother-child relationship. My response is that I am as much an advocate of love and a close emotional relationship as anybody, but I do not believe that there really are very many parents who do *not* establish a good solid relationship with their children in the first months of life.

There are, of course, exceptions. Tragically, every day of the year some small fraction of our families is doing an apparently abominable job with young children. There are children who are abused physically, children in family situations so burdened with problems that neglect takes a heavy toll, and of course there is the special case of children afflicted with disease or physical anomalies. But my remarks are not addressed to these extreme cases. They are addressed to the ninety percent or more of our families who do not have to cope with such extraordinary difficulties.

There is a good deal of information that suggests that sometime during the middle of the *second* year of life, children begin to reveal which way they are headed developmentally. Most children of this age begin to produce performances on achievement measures that increasingly represent the kinds of levels of achievement they will be reaching and attaining in the years to follow, including the school years. Put another way, in the earlier phases—I through IV—and at the beginning of Phase V as well, what a child scores on tests of intelligence, motor ability, language, and social skills does not seem to bear any meaningful relationship to what he will score on similar tests when he is two or three years of age. The only exception to this concerns the children in the five percent group who look seriously weak from birth and who, in tests during the first year of life, consistently score very much below most of the population.

The fact that test scores in the first year of life generally have no predictive power is an old, very well-established finding. It is a finding that people who emphasize development in the first months of life have great difficulty explaining away. To be sure, there is always the possibility that problems created in the first months of life may not reveal themselves until considerably later in the child's life. Nevertheless, there is also the real possibility that what people are claiming as problems in the first months are not indeed so very important. My own feeling is that *the reason we do not see dramatic evidence of poor development in the first year of the lives of most children who will do poorly later is simply that they have not yet actually developed the deficits.*

Groups of children who go on to underachieve in the elementary grades almost never look particularly weak in terms of achievement at one year of age, but only begin to lag behind as a group sometime toward the end of the second year of life. Such children, on standardized language and intelligence tests, for example, will pretty clearly reveal where they are headed educationally by the time they are three years of age. In report after report—whether from low-income urban

American children or from children from low-income homes in Africa, India, or other places in the world—the pattern of findings is pretty much the same. These disadvantaged children make a fairly good showing during the first year of life on standard baby tests like the Gesell, even if they have not had the best of nutrition, and even if their parents have had little or no education. It is not until they reach the middle of the second year of life, at the earliest, that scores begin to slide. Subsequently, it is all downhill. That is, it is all downhill for such *groups* of children, not necessarily for every *individual* child within those groups.

It is very important to point out that many low-income children are *not* underachievers. Vast numbers of these children, both in this and other countries around the world, develop just about as well as any children during the first two years of their life. Many do average or above-average work from the elementary grades right on through graduate school. To be born into a low-income family is very far from being a guarantee of academic underachievement. . . .

THE EFFECT OF REARING CONDITIONS ON DEVELOPMENT

Let us move on to a subsidiary point which I want to keep separate in an attempt to avoid confusion. During the ten years I spent studying the role of experience in the development of children in the first six months of life, I learned many interesting things concerning the rate of development as a function of different kinds of experiences in those early months. Through experimentation with physically normal children, I became convinced that the rate at which children acquire abilities in the first six months of life, at least in regard to visual motor skills and foundations of intelligence, can be modified rather dramatically by the manipulation of rearing conditions.

It has long been known that you can easily

prevent a child from reaching any significant level of development in the first six months of life. What we also learned in our ten years of research was that if you provide certain circumstances for the young child in those first months of life, he can achieve some kinds of skills considerably earlier than what is typical for the average child—indeed, in some cases even earlier than the precocious child.

Take the skill of visually directed reaching which, as we have seen, is normally acquired at about five to five and one-half months of age by children in this society, as well as in most others that have been tested. Our studies, in which we provided objects for children to look at, bat, feel, and play with, starting from when they were three or four weeks of age, resulted in the acquisition of mature reaching at about three months of age. Not only is this a considerable acceleration of the acquisitional process, but, perhaps more important, the children involved had a marvelous time engaging in these activities. During the fourth month they were full of enthusiasm, giggled excitedly, played with the objects around them, looked happily into a mirror that we had placed overhead, and did a good deal of vocalizing. You can see how this kind of pleasurable and occasionally exciting play fits into the aforementioned goals of supporting the development of specific skills while nurturing the zest for life and curiosity of a child. The children who went through those studies seemed to be spirited and terribly interested children at six and seven months of age, much more so than children who were like them at the outset but who had not gone through those particular experiences. . . .

What all of this adds up to is that we now have information at hand which will enable us to provide future children, at least in principle, with circumstances that are more suited to their earliest needs and interests than the circumstances to which they are normally exposed. It also means, very probably, that what we now call a normal rate of development will be considered—thirty or forty years from now—to be a slow pace. . . .

But let us get back to today. In the research of the last several years we arrived at another telling conclusion. In addition to the notion that somewhere between the first and third birthdays children are beginning to reveal where they are headed in later years, we have come to the conclusion that *to begin to look at a child's educational development when he is two years of age is already much too late, particularly in the area of social skills and attitudes.* We find the two-year-old is a rather complicated, firmly established social being. We find it not uncommon that a two-year-old is already badly spoiled and very difficult to live with, or in more tragic situations, alienated from people, including his own family. We have seen these phenomena over and over again. On the other hand, we rarely see an eight-, nine-, or ten-month-old child who in any way seems to be spoiled or particularly well differentiated socially. Up through Phase IV a child is, comparatively speaking, a very simple social creature.

You can trace your child's evolutions as he goes from eight to twenty-four months of age by keeping a step-by-step journal and taking movies of him, preferably sound movies, if possible. This will confirm the fact that the twenty-four-month-old child is as different from the eight-month-old as the eight-month-old is from the newborn. Human growth is a remarkable process.

From the above discussion you can see that the period that starts at eight months and ends at three years is a period of primary importance in the development of a human being. And the period eight to fourteen months of age is the first major phase of that exciting time span.

Educational Goals

Over the years three useful ways of describing educational goals of the period from eight months through three years have emerged. One deals with the child's major interest patterns. We have found that all healthy eight-month-old children seem motivated by three major interests aside from the fundamental physiological needs such as hunger, thirst, freedom from pain, etc. These three major interests are: the primary caretaker, exploration of the world as a whole, and mastering newly emerging motor abilities. These interests have obvious specific survival value. They start out vigorous and in balance in all healthy eight-month-old babies. When development goes well, they each grow steadily and the balance is maintained. Very often, however, they develop unevenly between eight and twenty-four months of age, and the results are mildly or severely debilitating. . . .

A second way of discussing educational goals is to talk of emerging competencies of special importance. These competencies are by no means guaranteed to develop well. I'm referring to the pattern of intellectual, linguistic, perceptual, and social competencies our research has found typical of beautifully developed three- to six-year-old children. These processes sometimes overlap with the processes to be discussed under the other ways of dealing with educational goals. . . . At this point, I would like to single out three social competencies that emerge in Phase V for special mention. Toward the end of the first year, children begin to realize older people can be helpful. They begin to deliberately seek assistance from them. This behavior we call using an adult as a resource. Shortly after the first birthday, two other very important social potencies emerge. Seeking approval for a simple motor achievement or for a "cute" behavior seems to indicate the first feelings of pride in achievement. Finally, at about the same time, children begin to manifest simple make-believe or fantasy behavior. Common examples are "talking" on a toy telephone or pretending to be driving a toy truck, car, or airplane. Each of these emergents

emergents seems to play a special role in educational development. More on this topic will follow.

The third way is to emphasize four key goals which are commonly accepted by most people knowledgeable in early human development. These goals are language development, the development of curiosity, social development, and nurturing the roots of intelligence.

Language Development

We have seen that while children may respond to words in some simple fashion during the first six or seven months of life, there is no indication whatsoever that they understand the meaning of those words. Their response is really an affair that involves the sound qualities of the words—the association of the particular patterns of a mother's voice, for example, with the pleasure in her presence. But they do not respond differently to their own name or to some other name. They do not know, for example, that the word "Mommy" means only one person. But at about seven or eight months of age, they begin to learn language.

By three years of age, experts estimate that most children understand most of the language that they will use for the rest of their lives in ordinary conversation. Notice I said most children *understand* most of the language they will use in ordinary conversation. There is an important difference between the growth of *understanding* language and the growth of *producing* language. Children begin to learn to understand language earlier and at a more rapid rate than they learn to use it orally. The first five or six words should be fairly well understood by the time a child is nine or ten months of age. But he may not *say* five or six words until he is two years of age or even older. Nevertheless, in both cases he may be a very normal child.

Language, like so many of the issues we will talk about, is interrelated during the first years of life with other major developments. There is no way that a young child can do well on an intelligence test at three or four years of age, for example, unless his language development is good. You can usually predict a child's IQ once he gets to be three or four years of age with reasonable accuracy from any reliable assessment of his language skills.

Over and above language's fundamental role in the development of intelligence, it plays an extremely important part in the development of social skills. So much of what transpires between any two people involves either listening to or expressing language. And so, in a very significant way, good language development underlies good social development.

The Development of Curiosity

Just about everyone knows that kittens go through a stage during which they are incredibly curious. We also know that monkeys and puppies are similar in this regard. Indeed, it appears that almost all young mammals go through an early period when they are consumed by the need to explore. This is even true, I learned recently, of young horses. We have never really pinpointed such a stage with man before, and I think this is simply because the people charged with the responsibility of doing research on early human development have left much of that research undone to this point in time. We believe, however, that we have filled this informational gap through extensive home observations of a wide variety of children.

We have never come across an eight-month-old child who was not incredibly curious. We have never come across an eight-month-old child who needed to be reinforced for exploration of the home once he could crawl. Bear in mind that to have a very strong exploratory drive is vitally important for humans in that unlike most other animals humans go through a very long developmental period, and come equipped with fewer in-

By permission of Sissy Krook, photographer.

stincts than other animals with which to cope with the world.

Nothing is more fundamental to solid educational development than pure uncontaminated curiosity.

Social Development

The two-year-old child is an extremely complicated and sophisticated social creature. His social world, for the most part, revolves around his primary caretaker (who is usually his mother); and ordinarily he has worked out with her an extraordinary contract full of ifs, ands, and buts which describes a great deal about the various possibilities for him within the home. He has learned specifically what he can and cannot play with in each room in the home. He has learned how much he can get away with with his mother or, more sadly, he may have developed into an overindulged child who constantly badgers his mother, particularly if there is a younger child in the

home. He may become, in other words, extraordinarily difficult to live with and regularly unpleasant. Even sadder is the case of the child who at two has been consistently turned off by people, who has learned to be an isolate, one who has never had the pleasure of a free and easy rewarding relationship with another human being.

These are the three major patterns we have seen. There are all sorts of variations on these themes, but it seems to us that the process which leads to one or another of these states, or something similar to them, begins in earnest somewhere around seven or eight months of age.

Nurturing the Roots of Intelligence

As we have seen, in Piaget's system the child of eight months of age has turned a corner wherein he leaves behind his early introduction to the world and to his own basic motor skills and starts to focus on the world of objects. The year or so that follows is a period of active exploration of simple cause-and-effect mechanisms; of the movement patterns of objects; of their texture qualities, shapes, and forms. This is an incredibly rich time during which the child's mind is undergoing basic development with respect to the prerequisites of higher forms of thinking. Surely, as far as education is concerned, few things are more central than the substructure of sensorimotor explorations upon which higher levels of intelligence are built.

In my opinion, *every one of the four educational goals and processes is at risk during the period from eight months to two years.* What do I mean by *at risk*? I mean that unlike the achievements of the first six or seven months of age, which I propose are more or less assured by virtue of their simple requirements and the characteristics of the average expectable environment, the educational goals of the eight-month to twenty-four-month period are by no means assured. It is not at all inevitable that a child will learn language as well as he might. It is not at all inevitable that he will have his curiosity deepened and broadened anywhere near as well as he might. It is not at all inevitable that his social development will take place in a solid and fruitful manner. And it is not at all inevitable that the substructure for intelligence will be built well. Indeed, I must repeat that on the basis of all I have learned in close to two decades, no more than one child in ten achieves the levels of ability in each of these four fundamental areas that he could achieve.

OBSTACLES TO OPTIMAL ACHIEVEMENTS IN THE FOUR FUNDAMENTAL EDUCATIONAL PROCESSES

As I see it, there are three kinds of obstacles to successful educational development in the eight- to twenty-four-month age range. They are ignorance, stress, and lack of assistance.

Ignorance

Typical young parents are quite unprepared for the responsibility of educating their first baby. As noted earlier, we do nothing in this country, in a systematic way, to educate couples for the responsibility of parenting young children. Even if we did, there would be yet another fundamental problem, the fact that we simply did not have enough useful information.

We know, of course, when the typical baby starts to walk, to sit unaided, to wave bye-bye, and so forth. But sophisticated, extensive, and detailed information about the growth of the young human, and especially about the causes of good or poor growth, has been in remarkable short supply in spite of all the opinions and all the words that have been written on the topic. The problem is simply that the people who are supposed to produce the information—that is, psychological and educational research people—while acknowledging the importance of the processes developing in the first three years of life, have not, for one

reason or another, developed the necessary knowledge. After all, if you wanted to do research on a very young child, up until very recently the only way you could do it would be to go out to his home or to make an appointment for him to come into your office or your laboratory. Going out to the home is a relatively inconvenient affair. It is also an extremely inefficient way to do research. It is much easier to have a group of college sophomores beating a path to your laboratory, where then can be researched upon for thirty minutes at a time. Studying a child in his own environment not only necessitates transportation to and from his home but, more important, does not provide conditions good for this kind of research. The college sophomore coming into a psychology laboratory to be a subject does not bring his parents along. He is not overly apprehensive about what might happen to him, and he has been conditioned for many years to do what he is told, particularly when he is told to do something by someone with high prestige or someone who is going to give him a grade in a course. Furthermore, there are so many different kinds of children. It is not scientifically proper to make general statements about children on the basis of one middle-class Protestant child. Samples must be drawn from all the major types of children, depending on the particular topic under study. And, of course, on one day a child of two years of age may do one thing in a test situation or in his spontaneous behavior; the next day, or even an hour later, he may do something else. You cannot assume that if you have gone to a home one, two, three, four, or five times that you have gotten a fair sample of a child's behavior.

All in all, it is not surprising that the actual basic building of a science of human development has made so little progress in spite of hundreds of millions of dollars poured into the enterprise by the federal government and private foundations. In spite of the fact that during the last ten years or so this situation has been improving, as I look about my office at the several hundred books on young children that line my shelves, I know that parents cannot find in them the basic information they ought to have.

Such a situation, by the way, is an ideal one to stimulate all sorts of misinformation to be offered to the public, and indeed, you can find many programs in existence which purport to help the parent in this regard. Scratch the surface of the programs, however, and look for the basis on which the recommendations about child-rearing are made and you will generally find that the basis is very shallow. There are a few exceptions. By and large, up until very recently, if you wanted legitimate information about raising a very young child, I frankly think you would have been better off asking an intelligent well-put-together mother of four or five children than if you had tried almost any other approach to the problem.

The Problem of Stress

Not only are families unaware of what they should know about early human development, but in addition they are put under a fair degree of stress in trying to do their job. When I say *they*, I am referring for the most part to the young mother, because by and large she is the one most likely to have the almost-total responsibility for a baby's upbringing. Major stress occurs routinely when the baby starts to crawl about the home, because he is then actually in physical danger. He is in danger because houses are not ordinarily designed for eight-month-old crawling babies; because babies are incredibly curious about everything they see and can reach; because they use their mouths as exploring organs; because they do not know very much about the characteristics of objects and about physical dangers; and because they are inadequate masters of their bodies.

What it all adds up to is a worried parent, and rightly so. The period from ten to thirty months of age, for example, is the time when

something in the order of eighty percent of all reported accidental poisonings involving children take place. Remember that the child, when crawling about the kitchen, the living room, the bedroom, or the bathroom for the first few times, finds everything new. He has seen some of these things from a distance but he has never been able to come up close to such intriguing objects as the shut-off valve behind the john; bits of beautiful shiny glass from a broken jar that happened to fall in an out-of-the-way place; and interestingly frayed sections of lamp cords.

Babies do not know which physical objects are sturdy enough to support their weight and which will fall if leaned upon. And babies have poor memories at this point. There is nothing of more universal appeal to a ten-month-old than a set of stairs. Put him at the bottom and you can bet money (with confidence) that he will attempt to climb. Some ten-month-olds are pretty good at climbing three, four, or five stairs. Very commonly they will then pause, and in the moments that follow they may be distracted, perhaps by a mark on the bannister that captivates them or by a small toy left there by another child. This may cause them to forget where they are and simply turn around and fall down the stairs. No wonder anyone who is reasonable and loving worries about the safety and well-being of the child who is crawling about the home for the first time.

In addition to the stress from the worry about physical danger, there is also the stress from the extra work that a child of this age produces. If you give him a chance to roam about the home, you will find yourself spending more time during the course of the day straightening up the house, particularly if you or your husband happen to be compulsive about household neatness. Babies create clutter. It is as natural as breathing. A cluttered house with a ten-month-old baby is, all other things being equal, a good sign. In fact, an immaculately picked-up house and a ten-month-old baby who is developing well are, in my opinion, usually incompatible. If more husbands were aware of this contradiction, it would save a lot of grief.

Another source of stress at this time has to do with the actual damage a young child can do to a home. Babies of this age are not exactly graceful, nor are they aware of the value of objects. From time to time costly breakages may occur.

A fourth major source of stress which is extremely important has to do with ill feelings from older siblings directed toward the baby, particularly when the older sibling is a first child and less than three years older than the baby. It is extremely common to find deeply rooted feelings of anger and outright dislike on the part of the older sibling for the baby. This may express itself in nasty behavior to and even physical battering of the younger sibling, which at times can produce serious physical harm, and in many other ways which are difficult for most mothers to tolerate. We have found over and over again that when we begin to talk with mothers of five- to eight-month-old babies about that child's educational development, they pour their hearts out to us about the difficulties they are having with the two- or three-year-old. They simply cannot attend to the problems of the younger child until we give them some sort of assistance in coping with the havoc that is created by the older child. . . .

The final form of stress to the system has to do with the negativism that emerges with most children in the second half of the second year. Although the eight- to fourteen-month-old baby creates a good deal of stress because of the aforementioned reasons, there does not seem to be anything personal in his behavior. He is simply acting in accordance with his nature, rather than deliberately trying to aggravate or stress his parents. Not so the child of fifteen or sixteen months of age. It is perfectly normal for such children to begin to vie for supremacy in the home with the primary caretaker. Resistance to simple requests becomes very common at this time, and some parents find this behavior extremely difficult to take. This is an age when you see the spectacle of a young mother in a dawn-to-dusk struggle with the one and one-half-year-old child, trying somehow or other to regain control over the situation. If there is more than one young child around this can be a very trying time for a young family. . . .

Lack of Assistance

The final obstacle to facilitating optimal educational development has to do with the fact that by and large young parents have to go through these processes alone. Very often the mother does not even have the benefit of a sympathetic husband, and has to cope with his dissatisfaction during this period on top of everything else. Pediatricians vary in the degree to which they provide support; the ones that do provide intelligent support are revered, at least in my acquaintance. Very often, however, the pediatrician does not have any extensive background in these topics and is ill equipped to cope effectively with this part of his practice. The public educational system is gradually beginning to consider whether it should try to lend a helping hand, but by and large there are very few programs where educators assist parents in this situation. Occasionally public-health nurses, visiting nurses, home-study people, and child-study-association people provide some support. Indeed, there are even occasions where a young mother is on good terms with her mother or mother-in-law, in which case she can profit from the wisdom that experience and good sense often present in the minds of practiced mothers. By and large, however, the typical young family—and particularly the mother—has to go it alone. . . .

Chapter 6

Personality Development

WHAT EMOTIONS DO BABIES HAVE?

How a Baby Learns to Love

Selma Fraiberg

. . . by the end of the first year the baby has gone through a sequence of phases in his human attachments—from simple recognition of the mother to recognition of her as a special person to the discovery that she is the source of joy, the satisfier of body hungers, the comforter, the protector, the indispensable person in his world. In short he has learned to love.

Editor's Introduction

Love! What is love? Our songs proclaim it, we all know that we want it, and our bumper stickers read "Make love, not war." But what is it and how does it develop? Does love appear in full bloom with the birth of the infant, or is it a quality that develops in mother, father, and infant over a period of time? Are there critical periods in the development of love? How much love does an infant need? Are there differences between infants who receive love and those who do not? And what is it we are defining? Is it physical stimulation, a feeling of affection, the inability to live without the other, the willingness to give your life for another, unconditional acceptance, or some combination of all these factors?

Selma Fraiberg's sensitive article confronts the question "How does a child learn to love?" Since a nonverbal infant is unable to say to its mother, "I love you," Fraiberg has had to look at the other signs of attachment and love during the first eighteen months of life. She states that during the first six months a baby has the rudiments of love: the smile and the cooing sounds. A little later something new begins to emerge and the baby begins to show another way in which he or she places a special value on the mother. Having previously been very sociable for all assorted visitors, the baby now becomes frankly antisocial, screaming at the sight of each new face. While parents are quick to apologize, the change is actually a sign of sound mental health. It is called *stranger anxiety*, and it simply means that the mother has become the center of the baby's world. This attachment and exclusive possession of the mother by the child will continue for some time to come. Lauren, who is now almost two and exceedingly verbal, will announce in her clearest voice when Jeanne, her favorite baby sitter, arrives, that "Jeanne should go home." She wants only to be with her Mommy. She will say to Mommy, when a special visitor arrives, even with gift in hand, "Tell her to leave now, I do not want her to visit today." Again, she wants Mommy's exclusive attention. This behavior embarrasses me, because even as a psychologist I sometimes forget that all love begins with a feeling of exclusiveness.

In institutions, babies usually do not have mothers or mother substitutes. The infants are bathed and fed by a rotating staff and are often left alone in their cribs and fed by means of propped-up bottles in order to save time. In follow-up studies of adult behavior, these infants, who had been reared in institutions and given inconsistent and inadequate emotional care, were found to be unable to form stable human bonds—they were unable to love. They were rootless and incapable of staying with one partner because no one partner was valued. Since they had never known physical closeness as infants, they took little pleasure in intimacy as adults. Their sexual behavior was impoverished or bizarre. A major conclusion that Fraiberg draws is that the love we experience as infants will set the stage for our capacity to love as adults, and that without a unique loving relationship to one person in infancy we will be less able, or perhaps unable, to develop a unique loving relationship in later life.

What is it that occurs between babies and their parents which guarantees the capacity to love in later life? In the biological program of mother and baby, there are built-in guarantees for the initial formation of human bonds; the mother will cradle her baby, caress and nuzzle it, and thus provide the necessary physical closeness. When the mother is the primary caretaker, the baby will recognize her earlier and begin to respond to her as a special person. In my experience, love—both maternal love and infant love—do not appear automatically at birth but are feelings which develop through the physical closeness, the joys, and the pains of shared experiences. The agonies are great, but the rewards are immeasurable. There is the maternal pain of extreme fatigue, the necessity of being constantly present, and the drain of caring for a helpless baby who needs you as much as you need it. But there is also the joy of the baby's first smile, hug, and kiss; the pleasure of seeing the child walk for the first time, say its first words and then sentences, create imaginary playmates, learn the alphabet, and sing a first song with a diva's enthusiasm.

This morning I was helping Lauren make her cream of wheat. She was sitting on the kitchen counter and I was standing in front of her to make sure that she did not topple off. As she was pouring her cereal into her bowl she looked up, threw open her arms, and said "Hold me, Mom. I love you. You're a wonderful Mom." No matter how the theorists define it, for me that is love, and it makes it all worthwhile.

Pamela Cantor

During the past two decades a number of child-development specialists have started a new trend in the scientific study of babies. They began to sneak off one by one from their consulting rooms and their laboratories and camped out in homes where new babies had just arrived. I was one of them. We took along pencils and paper, cameras and tape recorders, and said to baffled mothers, "Don't mind us. Just do everything you ordinarily do in the course of the day. We want the baby to teach *us* a few things."

The mothers quite frankly thought we had lost our minds. But if the doctors wanted to learn how to diaper an infant or how to get a spoonful of mashed peas into a baby with a mind of his own, the mothers felt, Well, just go ahead. Actually there were no benefits to the parents; but sometimes if a mother needed an hour of emergency baby sitting, it was a comfort to know that a Harvard professor was available who could entertain the baby with the Audubon bird whistle he kept in his kit.

Among the many things we scientists wanted to learn in this camp-out was one very elusive question: How does the baby learn to love? Since no infant has ever been known to say to his mother, "I love you," the scientific work had to attack the problem by inference. What are the *signs* of love and attachment during the first eighteen months of life?

Over a period of years many of the scientists found agreement about certain signs. If we follow the growth of the infant's human attachments from the first day of his life to the end of his first year, we find that he responds to his mother and his father in ways that show increasing preference. And finally we see that he values his parents above all other persons in his small world. And because the mother is the primary figure during the *first* year of life, the selective responses to the mother became a sound guide for all the scientists engaged in this work.

What are the signs?

During the first six months the baby has the rudiments of a love language; there is the language of the smile, the language of vocal sound-making, the language of the embrace. It's the essential vocabulary of love before we can yet speak of love. (In 18 years, when the baby is grown and "falls in love" for the first time, he will woo his partner through the language of the smile, through the utterance of endearments and the joy of the embrace.)

How does the smile become part of the vocabulary of love? The smile is innate, the universal greeting sign of our species. Already in the early weeks of life it appears in deep sleep; then gradually it is elicited more and more frequently by external stimuli. At three months of age the one stimulus that will automatically produce a smile is the human face. At this age *any* human face will elicit a smile, which seems a poor reward for maternal devotion, but between three months and six months the smile becomes a smile of preference—for the mother.

The baby smiles more frequently for his mother than for others and his smiles for her

By permission of Sissy Krook, photographer.

are bigger and more joyful. During the same period he "talks" more, jabbers more fluently, with his mother than with a stranger. And if he is frightened or has taken a bad bump, he cannot be comforted by "just anyone" any longer; he seeks the comfort of his mother's arms. His mother's arms and her lap, the closeness of her body, have a magical quality in soothing him and creating the feeling that all is well.

At this stage, then, the baby has discriminated his mother from others, shows preference for her and associates her with the satisfaction of his hunger and body needs. But, we ask ourselves doubtfully, is this "love"? Not yet, perhaps. But these are signs of selection, of intimate exchange and partnership, that will lead him to love.

Between six and 12 months something new begins to emerge. The baby now begins to

show us another way in which he places special value upon his mother. While he has always been sociable and smiled for the uncle who wiggled his ears or for the lady in the red dress, he now begins to become downright unsociable. In place of a smile they may get a look of cold scrutiny, or a frown, or—regrettably—a howl of indignation.

The infant's parents are quick to offer apologies. "I don't know what's got into him! He used to be so friendly." What's-got-into-him is something the baby specialists call *stranger reaction*, perfectly normal behavior between six and 15 months. It means, very simply, that his mother for the time being is the center of his world and the "stranger" is somehow an intruder, someone who unsettles the intimacy and safety of the private world. Typically, after the baby produces a negative reaction to the stranger his eyes will begin to search the room for his mother, and when he finds her face he bestows a big smile upon her and then may make overtures to be picked up.

Odd as it may sound, this behavior toward strangers is one of the signs of the baby's increasing affection for his mother. All love, even in later life, begins with a feeling of exclusiveness. "You are the one who matters—only you." It's the magic circle of love that in infancy includes the father and a few other choice people but not yet the stranger. In a few months, by the way, the baby will receive strangers quite hospitably again, but that's because he is secure enough to feel that the magic circle is no longer threatened by outsiders.

At around the same time, about eight months of age, the baby shows his growing love for his mother in still another way. He complains when he is separated from her. He may not object if she leaves him to go to the kitchen, but his face is very likely now to pucker up when he sees her in her hat and coat. And his baby sitters may report that he complains loudly for a time after she leaves.

"Do you think he's spoiled?" some mothers and fathers will ask. But he's not spoiled. At this time his mother is still the most important person in his world. And he behaves the way all of us behave when a loved person is absent for a while: "I can't bear to be without you. I am lost. . . . I am not myself when you're gone. . . . You are my world, and without you the world is empty."

If all this seems too extravagant to put into the minds of babies, we need only watch an infant of this age whose mother has been called away on an emergency for several days or a baby who has been isolated from his mother in a hospital. The face of grief is no different at eight months from that at 30 years of age. Loss of appetite, sleeplessness, refusal of comfort from someone else—for both ages the symptoms are the same.

From this short sketch we can see that by the end of the first year the baby has gone through a sequence of phases in his human attachments—from simple recognition of the mother to recognition of her as a special person to the discovery that she is the source of joy, the satisfier of body hungers, the comforter, the protector, the indispensable person of his world. In short, he has learned to love.

This is what we learned from scientific camping out in the homes of babies.

Another group of scientists chose to study babies who had been reared from birth in institutions as well as babies reared in their own families. And they emerged with a different story.

In the institutions—even the best ones—no baby has a mother or a mother substitute. There may be 12 to 30 babies in a ward with two to four nurses or aides for each of three shifts. No one person, no matter how much she loves babies, can serve as mother substitute under these circumstances. The infant is fed, bathed and changed by a rotating staff. In many institutions it saves staff time to feed the baby by means of a propped-up bottle. A good

part of his time is spent in a crib during the first year of life.

At three months of age, when our home-grown babies smiled in response to the human face, the babies in institutions smiled too. The smiles were not as frequent, some of the scientists noted, but they were there. The babbling sounds that babies make at three months were made by the institutional babies, also—but their vocalizations were less frequent than those of family-reared babies and seemed to have a more limited range of sounds.

Then between three months and 12 months of age something that should happen to the smile and something that should happen to vocalizations did not appear in the institutional babies. At a time when the home-reared baby showed preference with huge smiles for mother and father, the institutional baby smiled indifferently at everyone he saw. And around six to 12 months, the time when the family baby reserved his smile for the members of the magic circle and showed negative reactions toward strangers, the institutional baby behaved no differently toward the daily nurses and attendants and casual visitors to the nursery whom he had never seen before.

Everyone had equal value in his eyes because no one had special value. Anyone who created a diversion in the monotony of the nursery day could get a smile.

During a period when the family-reared infant began to carry on "conversations" in gibberish with his mother and father and when he began to imitate sounds (around eight months of age), the institutional baby had a restricted range of sounds. He was not imitating sounds; and the melodies of speech, which emerge at this time like an absurd parody of English, were not present at all.

How odd! we think. These institutional babies were exposed to all the ordinary conversational exchanges of nurses and aides; they were not being reared in isolation. But findings such as these are very common among institutional babies. From this we learn that while the brain is "programmed" so that a full range of articulations are available to every normal infant, the organization of these sounds into patterns and the use of these sounds for communication is entirely dependent upon the existence of human partners.

We can confirm this very simply as adults. It is possible to live in a foreign country for months, exposed to the native language day after day, and not acquire even the rudiments of discourse in that language if there is no relationship with a native who speaks the language, someone who provides the conditions for dialogue.

The institutional babies had heard the sounds of English all around them, but because there were no partners to provide the intimate exchange that is vital to the acquisition of language, they were slow to acquire the sounds and the cadences of that language. And if they remained in the institution for the early years of life, speech became one of the areas of severe retardation in their development.

How did the institutional infants react to separation from the nurses and aides who were the only representatives of a human world? We know that babies reared in their own homes show distress at a mother's absence, and if absence is prolonged, there is terrible grief. We understand that pain at separation is another measure of the child's love for his mother. But the institutional baby showed no signs that the absence of one or another of the people who cared for him had any meaning to him. If the red-haired nurse took a two-week vacation, there were five other nurses who performed identical duties and were interchangeable parts in the human machine that fed, bathed and changed him.

In many of the institutions, babies were placed in foster homes in the second and third years, and the possibilities of human bonds were opened up to them. But some of the babies spent their early years in the institution without human partners, without intimacy. And these children offered science the most chilling testimony for the power of love.

At the age of three and four they were already different from other children. They continued to show by their behavior that one adult was interchangeable with any other adult, and they were measurably retarded in speech and abstract thinking.

In follow-up studies in later childhood and in adult life the scientists found many of them in social agencies, in clinics and in courts. Their life problems were in all cases different, of course, but they all suffered from the most extreme effects of a love-starved infancy. They had one thing in common—they were unable to form stable human bonds, unable to love. They were rootless and unbound, without partners—or, often, with casual and shifting partners, since no one partner was valued.

Of the children who had spent their early years in institutions, some managed to become relatively well-adjusted adults, able to make meaningful, if limited, human associations. But many of the children who had never known physical closeness or the certainty of satisfaction of body hungers became men and women who seemed to have no pleasure in body intimacy and whose sexual appetites were impoverished or bizarre. Aggression, which is normally modified in the early years through the agency of love, appeared in these loveless men and women in erratic forms, sometimes fused with eccentric sexual practices. The human capacity for empathy, for feeling oneself into another personality, was simply absent. And because there can be no conscience without the capacity to feel for another, there was a vacant space in personality where conscience should have been.

Once again the scientific question led back to the first years of life. What was it, we asked ourselves, that transpired between an ordinary baby and his parents that usually guaranteed the capacity for love in later life? Surely since the dawn of mankind and in every society the human family has produced and nurtured babies who grew into men and women capable of experiencing enduring love and physical joy. In contemporary "primitive" societies, simple and illiterate parents achieve this miracle by simply doing what their ancestors have been doing for thousands of years.

It appears that the "program" for infant-mother attachment was laid down in our biological ancestry. It has much in common with the infant-rearing practices of all mammals and has close resemblance to infant rearing among the higher primates.

In the biological program we inherit, an infant leaves intrauterine life and comes into a radically changed environment. He is cushioned against the shock of the journey—from the water world to the land world, from enclosed space to unclosed space—but he brings little instinctive baggage into the world to ensure his adaptation or his survival. As a specimen of our genus, he is unfinished by comparison with the newborn of other species.

At the end of his journey there are provisions in the program that the woman who sheltered and nourished him in intrauterine life should be the woman to shelter and nourish him outside the womb. Body intimacy, the shelter of enclosing arms and nourishment are all marvelously contrived in the program to center around the mother's breast.

In breast feeding, the infant is cradled in the mother's arms. Pleasure in sucking, the satisfaction of hunger, intimacy with the mother's body, are united with his recognition of her face. The baby learns to associate *this* face, his mother's face, with an enjoyable and comforting experience. As we watch the nursing baby we see how gradually the skin surface of the body is suffused with pinkness—a sensual glow of pleasure and well-being.

When the baby is held at his mother's breast the entire ventral surface of his body is in contact with her body. And this sensual pleasure heightens his awareness of his own body. Nursing mothers also experience sensual pleasure through the baby's sucking. This should lead to no embarrassment. It is simply one of the rewards, one of the ways in which *mutual* sensual pleasure binds the mother to her baby and the baby to her.

Breast feeding virtually guarantees that the baby and his mother are bound to each other for the duration of the nursing period. And while it is possible (as we see in many breast-feeding societies) for another lactating woman to take over a feeding in the mother's absence, the regulation of the milk supply depends upon emptying of the breast, and the baby's own mother must have continuity and regularity in her nursing or she will cease to lactate.

The nursing period itself is extremely variable, even in primitive societies, but where so-called modern theories of baby rearing have not influenced practices of infant care, babies are nursed for one to two years, on the average. In scientific terms this means that for the critical period of the formation of human bonds the breast-fed baby has had one mother, even if he has had several assistant mothers, and this person is united in his experience with pleasure, with the satisfaction of hunger and needs and the alleviation of discomfort and fears.

Need and the satisfaction of need are the indispensable components of all primary human bonds. Love is a special form of need and need satisfaction, in which the giver of satisfaction and pleasure becomes valued over all other persons. As psychiatrist René Spitz reminds us, we cannot speak of love if all partners are exchangeable.

In the biological program of mother and baby there are built-in guarantees for the satisfaction of the baby's needs that ensure the formation of human bonds in the first 18 months of life. The mother is the primary "need satisfier," and that need satisfaction should lead the infant through a series of stages in the first year in which the mother is loved more than any other person in his small world.

Of course, it is entirely possible that even with a breast-feeding regimen the biological program can be derailed or may *not* result in a strong attachment between baby and mother. But in the main, when a baby and his mother are united through an extended nursing period it will most often lead to a strong attachment.

The bottle-fed baby, we have learned, also can follow a normal route toward the development of strong bonds with his mother. This is particularly so when the mother follows the ancient traditions of nursing and when she approximates breast-feeding conditions.

Most mothers who bottle-feed their babies will cradle the baby in their arms during feedings, and the caresses and nuzzling and crooning that normally go with this intimacy give the baby the body closeness and sensual pleasure that are the first requirements of love. Many mothers who feed by means of the bottle choose to take over all or most of the feedings themselves. There is probably no reason why Father or Grandma cannot take over an occasional feeding. But when Mother is the main person who feeds him, the baby will *recognize* her earlier and begin to respond to her as a very special person, another requirement of love.

Thus most mothers have maintained the traditions while substituting the bottle for the breast. But today in many thousands of families, as well as in institutions for the care of infants, the old traditions have been lost. In many busy households or nurseries the baby is fed by means of a propped-up bottle and is deprived of one of the vital nutriments for love. Alone with his bottle in his crib, he will not learn to associate feeding with body inti-

macy and the face of his mother. And in cases when a baby is fed during his bottle feeding by someone other than his mother he may not associate feeding with pleasure and intimacy in relation to a central person—which disturbs the conditions for the love bonds.

The bottle gives a mother far more mobility than the breast, which is one of the reasons for its growing popularity during the past two decades. And a baby today experiences many more separations from his mother than the baby in the traditional breast-feeding societies. How does this affect the stability of the bonds to his mother?

At this point none of us can know for certain how changes in baby rearing have affected the development of children in our society during the past 20 years. I have cited the evidence from extreme cases, the babies in institutions who received no mothering. What we have learned from these tragic life stories is sobering, but the lesson also should be read as a testimony for love. It means that something goes on between an ordinary baby and ordinary mothers and fathers that creates and ensures the capacity for love in infancy and in later life. It tells us that love and pleasure in the body begin in infancy and progress through childhood and adolescence to a culminating experience, "falling in love," the finding of the permanent partner, the achievement of sexual fulfillment.

In every act of love in mature life there is a prologue that originated in the first year of life. There are two people who arouse in each other sensual joy, feelings of longing and the conviction that they are absolutely indispensable to each other—that life without the other is meaningless. Separation from each other is intolerable. In the wooing phase and in the prelude to the act of love the mouth is rediscovered as an organ of pleasure and the entire skin surface is suffused with sensual joy. Longing sees its oldest posture, the embrace.

In the first falling in love, every pair of

lovers has the conviction that "nothing like this has ever happened to me before. I never knew what love could be." And this is true, but only in a certain sense. The discovery of the partner, the one person in the world who is the source of joy and bliss, has its origin in the discovery of the first human partner in infancy. What is new is the *new* partner and the experience of genital arousal with longing for sexual union. Yet the pathway to full arousal in mature life was laid down in infancy, long before the genitals could play a dominant role in experience. It was the infant's joy in his own body, the fullness of infant sensuality, that opened the pathways to fulfillment in maturity.

Freud said all this 65 years ago and there were few who believed him.

THE INFANT IN THE FAMILY

Play Behavior in the Year-Old Infant: Early Sex Differences

Susan Goldberg and Michael Lewis

Boys and girls showed striking differences in their behavior toward their mothers. First, upon being removed from their mothers' laps, girls were reluctant to leave their mothers. When the S's [subjects] were placed on the floor by their mothers, significantly more girls than boys returned immediately—in less than 5 seconds.

Editor's Introduction

Are the differences between men and women due to genetic or biological factors or are they the result of conditioning by society? This expression of the nature-nurture controversy may be oversimplified. Predisposition may be genetic while complex behavior patterns may be largely influenced by environment.

On the basis of anthropological, ontogenetic, and physiological evidence, genetic predispositions are thought to exist. With regard to anthropological data, in most societies the females assume the primary responsibility for child care and males assume responsibility for protection of the females and young. Ontogenetic studies reveal behavioral differences, which appear very early in infancy, between males and females; the earlier a particular difference appears—so it is thought—the more likely it is to be determined largely by biological factors. Physiological differences are evident even while the fetus is in the mother's womb, and the heart of the female fetus often beats faster. (My obstetrician was certain that Lauren was a boy because her heartbeat was not as rapid as he would have expected for a female. His later surprise when she proved to be a girl shows that this method of

Reprinted from *Developmental Psychology*, 1974, *10*, pp. 204–228. Copyright 1974 by the American Psychological Association. Reprinted by permission.

predicting the sex of a child is not entirely reliable.) Newborn females react more quickly to touch and pain and—as early as 3 months of age—females display a preference for looking at pictures of human faces as opposed to geometric figures. Male infants, on the other hand, show no initial preference, although they later prefer figures of cars, shapes, and other objects over faces. Female infants are quicker in learning to talk and count, although male infants are generally more adept at mathematical and spatial reasoning. These differences in ability may be due to sex-linked differences in the brain, to social contingencies, or to some combination of both. Thus, the female's verbal superiority may be due to the presence of female hormones in the brain or to the fact that mothers tend to talk to female infants more than they do to male infants. Or perhaps, as Michael Lewis and Susan Goldberg suggest, mothers talk more to their girls because, for biological reasons, the female infant offers more frequent responses to mother's verbalizations, thus stimulating her to keep talking. There is further evidence to suggest the interaction of biology and environment, as it has been reported that boys and girls who possess unusually fine verbal abilities have mothers who tend to be overprotective and who offer frequent suggestions and praise, while girls who have unusual mathematical abilities have mothers who encourage them to work alone, with less mother-child verbal interaction.

Jerome Kagan (1964, pp. 137–167) reports experiments which show that 1-year-old girls will respond to fear by moving toward their mothers, boys cope with the fear situation by trying to find something interesting to occupy their time and attention, and girls are twice as likely to cry when frightened as boys are. Kagan states that these differences, which can also be seen in some primates, support the theory that biological predispositions strongly influence psychological and behavioral development.

Lewis and Goldberg have tried to discover the extent to which sex differences can be attributed to biological differences by examining variations in the behavior of infants toward mother, play, and frustration. In examining thirty-two boys and thirty-two girls at 13 months of age, they found significant differences in behavior directed toward the infant by the mother and in the infants' play. Girls were less willing to leave their mothers in order to explore or play and most likely to return to them without provocation. In a situation of frustration, the girls stood crying and helpless while the boys made active attempts to defeat the barrier which was causing them the frustration. There were significant sex differences in the ways in which toys were used and in activity levels; girls were more docile and dependent while boys were more active and vigorously independent in their play. The data demonstrate that these patterns of what are considered to be sex-appropriate behaviors are already present in the first year of life. Whether these behaviors can therefore be considered to be of biological origin is still an unresolved question. While it is true that the earlier in development a particular trait appears the more likely it is to be of a biological nature, it is still possible that the parents reinforce, even in the first year, those behaviors they consider appropriate to their infant's sex (such as male autonomy or female dependence) and that the child then learns these behaviors. While there is little doubt that maternal encouragement or discouragement of particular behaviors plays a major role in the shaping of personality, there is also little doubt as to the biological basis of particular traits such as physical strength, activity level, rhythmicity, adaptability to stress, and sensitivity to pain (Thomas, Chess, Birch, Hertzig, & Korn, 1963).

REFERENCES

Kagan, J. Acquisition and significance of sex-typing and sex-role identity. In M. L. Hoffman and L. W. Hoffman (Eds.), *Review of child development research.* (vol 1) New York: Russell Sage Foundation, 1964.

Thomas, A., Chess, S., Birch, H., Hertzig, M., & Korn, S. *Behavior individuality in early childhood*, New York: New York University Press, 1946.

Pamela Cantor

Until recently, the largest proportion of studies in child development gave attention to nursery and early grade school children. The literature on sex differences is no exception. A recent book on development of sex differences which includes an annotated bibliography (Maccoby, 1966) lists fewer than 10 studies using infants, in spite of the fact that theoretical discussions (e.g., Freud, 1938 [originally published in 1905]; Piaget, 1951) emphasize the importance of early experience. Theoretical work predicts and experimental work confirms the existence of sex differences in behavior by age 3. There has been little evidence to demonstrate earlier differentiation of sex-appropriate behavior, although it would not be unreasonable to assume this occurs.

Recently, there has been increased interest in infancy, including some work which has shown early sex differences in attentive behavior (Kagan & Lewis, 1965; Lewis, in press). The bulk of this work has been primarily experimental studying specific responses to specific stimuli or experimental conditions. Moreover, it has dealt with perceptual-cognitive differences rather than personality variables. There has been little observation of freely emitted behavior. Such observations are of importance in supplying researchers with the classes of naturally occurring behaviors, the conditions under which responses normally occur, and the natural preference ordering of behaviors. Knowledge of this repertoire of behaviors provides a background against which behavior under experimental conditions can be evaluated.

The present study utilized a free play situation to observe sex differences in children's behavior toward mother, toys, and a frustration situation at 13 months of age. Because the Ss were participants in a longitudinal study, information on the mother-child relationship at 6 months was also available. This made it possible to assess possible relations between behavior patterns at 6 months and at 13 months.

METHOD

Subjects

Two samples of 16 girls and 16 boys each, or a total of 64 infants, were seen at 6 and 13 months of age (±6 days). All Ss were born to families residing in southwestern Ohio at the time of the study. All were Caucasian. The mothers had an average of 13.5 years of schooling (range of 10–18 years) and the fathers had an average of 14.5 years of schooling (range of 8–20 years). The occupations of the fathers ranged from laborer to scientist. Of the 64 infants, 9 girls and 10 boys were first-born and the remaining infants had from 1 to 6 siblings.

The 6-Month Visit

The procedure of the 6-month visit, presented in detail in Kagan and Lewis (1965), included two visual episodes and an auditory episode where a variety of behavioral responses were recorded. The infant's mother was present during these procedures. At the end of the experimental procedure, the mother was interviewed by one of the experimenters, who had been able to observe both mother and infant for the duration of the session. The interviewer also rated both mother and infant on a rating scale. The items rated for the infant included: amount of activity, irritability, response to mother's behavior, and amount of affect. For the mother, the observer rated such factors as nature of handling, amount of playing with the baby, type of comforting behavior, and amount of vocalization to the baby. Each item was rated on a 7-point scale, with 1 indicating the most activity and 7 the least. For the purpose of this study, it was necessary to obtain a measure of the amount of physical contact the mother initiated with the child. Since scores on the individual scales did not result in sufficient variance in the population, a composite score was obtained by taking the mean score for each mother over all three of the touching-the-infant scales. These included: amount of touching, amount of comforting, and amount of play. The composite touch scores (now called the amount of physical contact) resulted in a sufficiently variable distribution to be used for comparison with the 13-month touch data.

The 13-Month Visit

Kagan and Lewis (1965), who employed the same 64 infants for their study, described the procedures used at 6 months, which were similar to those of the present (13-month) study. The only addition was a free play procedure, which will be discussed in detail below.

The playroom, 9 by 12 feet, contained nine simple toys: a set of blocks, a pail, a "lawnmower," a stuffed dog, an inflated plastic cat, a set of quoits (graduated plastic doughnuts stacked on a wooden rod), a wooden mallet, a pegboard, and a wooden bug (a pull toy). Also included as toys were any permanent objects in the room, such as the doorknob, latch on the wall, tape on the electrical outlets, and so forth. The mother's chair was located in one corner of the room.

Procedure

Each S, accompanied by his mother, was placed in the observation room. The mother was instructed to watch his play and respond in any way she desired. Most mothers simply watched and responded only when asked for something. The mother was also told that we would be observing from the next room. She held the child on her lap, the door to the playroom was closed, and observation began. At the beginning of the 15 minutes of play, the mother was instructed to place the child on the floor.

Measurement

Two observers recorded the S's behavior. One dictated a continuous behavioral account into a tape recorder. The second operated an event recorder, which recorded the location of the child in the room and the duration of each contact with the mother.

Dictated Recording During the initial dictation, a buzzer sounded at regular time intervals, automatically placing a marker on the dictated tape. The dictated behavioral account was typed and each minute divided into 15-second units, each including about three typewritten lines. The typed material was further divided into three 5-second units, each unit being one typed line. Independent experimenters analyzed this typed material. For each minute, the number of toys played with and amount of time spent with each toy was recorded.

Event Recorder To facilitate recording the activity and location of the child, the floor of the room was divided into 12 squares. For each square, the observer depressed a key on the event recorder for the duration of time the child occupied that square. From this record it was possible to obtain such measures as the amount of time spent in each square and the number of squares traversed. A thirteenth key was depressed each time the child touched the mother. From this record, measures of (*a*) initial latency in leaving the mother, (*b*) total amount of time touching the mother, (*c*) number of times touching the mother, and (*d*) longest period touching the mother were obtained.

The data analysis presented in this report provides information only on sex differences (*a*) in response to the mother and (*b*) in choice and style of play with toys. Other data from this situation are presented elsewhere (Lewis, 1967).

RESULTS

Response to Mother (13 Months)

Open Field　Boys and girls showed striking differences in their behavior toward their mothers (see Table 6-1). First, upon being removed from their mothers' laps, girls were reluctant to leave their mothers. When *S*s were placed on the floor by their mothers, significantly more girls than boys returned immediately—in less than 5 seconds ($p < .05$ for both samples by Fisher Exact Probability Test). This reluctance to leave their mothers is further indicated by the time it took the children to first return to their mothers. Girls, in both samples, showed significantly shorter latencies than boys. Out of a possible 900 seconds (15 minutes), girls returned after an average of 273.5 seconds, while boys' average latency was nearly twice as long, 519.5 seconds. This difference was highly significant ($p < .002$, Mann-Whitney *U* test). All significance tests are two-tailed unless otherwise specified.

Once the children left their mothers, girls made significantly more returns, both physical and visual. Girls touched their mothers for an average of 84.6 seconds, while boys touched their mothers for only 58.8 seconds ($p < .03$, Mann-Whitney *U* test). Girls returned to touch their mothers on an average of 8.4 times, and boys 3.9 times ($p < .001$, Mann-Whitney *U* test). For the visual returns, the number of times the child looked at the mother and the total amount of time spent looking at the mother were obtained from the dictated material. The mean number of times girls looked at the mother was 10.8 (as compared with 9.2 for boys), a difference which was not significant.

Table 6-1　Summary of Infant Behavior to Mother in Free Play Session

Behavior	Girls	Boys	*p*
Touching mother:			
x latency in seconds to return to mother	273.5	519.5	<.002
x number of returns	8.4	3.9	<.001
x number of seconds touching mother	84.6	58.8	<.03
Vocalization to mother:			
x number of seconds vocalizing to mother	169.8	106.9	<.04
Looking at mother:			
x number of seconds looking at mother	57.3	47.0	<.09
x number of times looking at mother	10.8	9.2	NS
Proximity to mother:			
x time in squares closest to mother	464.1	351.4	<.05
x time in squares farthest from mother	43.8	44.3	NS

Table 6-2 Summary of Infant Behavior during Barrier Frustration

Behavior	Girls	Boys	p
x number of seconds crying	123.5	76.7	$<.05$
x number of seconds at ends of barrier	106.1	171.0	$<.001$
x number of seconds at center	157.7	95.1	$<.01$

The total amount of time looking at the mother was 57.3 seconds for girls and 47.0 seconds for boys ($p <.09$, Mann-Whitney U test).

Finally, vocalization data were also available from the dictated material. The mean time vocalizing to the mother was 169.8 seconds for girls and 106.9 seconds for boys ($p <.04$, Mann-Whitney U test).

Another measure of the child's response to his mother was the amount of physical distance the child allowed between himself and his mother. Because the observers recorded which squares the child played in, it was possible to obtain the amount of time Ss spent in the four squares closest to the mother. The mean time in these squares for girls was 464.1 seconds; for boys, it was 351.4 seconds ($p < .05$, Mann-Whitney U test). Moreover, boys spent more time in the square farthest from the mother, although the differences were not significant.

Barrier Frustration At the end of the 15 minutes of free play, a barrier of mesh on a wood frame was placed in such a way as to divide the room in half. The mother placed the child on one side and remained on the opposite side along with the toys. Thus, the child's response to stress was observed.

Sex differences were again prominent, with girls crying and motioning for help consistently more than boys (see Table 6-2). For both samples, amount of time crying was available from the dictated record. Girls' mean time crying was 123.5 seconds, compared with 76.7 seconds for boys ($p < .05$, Mann-Whitney U test). Boys, on the other hand, appeared to make a more active attempt to get around the barrier. That is, they spent significantly more time at the ends of the barrier than girls, while girls spent significantly more time in the center of the barrier—near the position where they were placed ($p < .01$, Mann-Whitney U test).

Toy Preference (13 Months)

A second area of experimental interest was toy preference. When the nine toys were ranked in order of the total amount of time they were played with, girls and boys showed similar patterns of preference.

Table 6-3 presents each toy and the amount of time it ws played with. Play with the dog and cat were combined into one category. The toys which were used most were the lawn-mower, blocks, and quoits, and those that were used least were the stuffed dog and cat. On a *post hoc* basis, it seems as if the toys which received the most attention were those that offered the most varied possibilities for manipulation.

Although there were no sex differences in overall toy preference, there were significant sex differences in the amount of time spent with individual toys and in the ways toys were used. Girls played with blocks, pegboard, and with the dog and cat (the only toys with faces) more than boys did ($p < .03$, $p < .03$, $p < .01$, respectively, Mann-Whitney U Test).

In terms of style of play, there were also sex differences. Observation of girls' play indicates that girls chose toys which involved more fine than gross muscle coordination, while for boys, the reverse was true—building blocks and playing with dog and cat versus playing with mallet and rolling the lawnmower over other toys. Moreover, boys spent more time playing with the nontoys (doorknob, covered outlets, lights, etc.; $p < .005$, Mann-Whitney U test).

In terms of overall activity level, boys were more active than girls. Girls tended to sit and play with combinations of toys ($p < .05$, Mann-Whitney U test), while boys tended to be more active and bang the toys significantly more than girls ($p < .05$, Mann-Whitney U test). In addition, the children were rated by two observers on the vigor of their play behavior; a rating of 1 was given for high vigor, 2 was given for medium vigor, and 3 for low vigor. These ratings were made from the dictated material for each minute, so that the final score for each S represented a mean of 15 vigor ratings. The interobserver reliability was $p = .78$. The boys played significantly more vigorously than girls (mean for boys was 2.45, varying from 1.2 to 3.0; for girls, the mean was 2.65, varying from 1.9 to 3.0 [$p < .05$, Mann-Whitney U test]). This vigor difference was also seen in the style of boys' play; for example, boys banged with the mallet and mowed over other toys. Thus, there were not only significant differences in the choice of toys, but also in the way the toys were manipulated. The data indicate that there are important and significant sex differences in very young chil-

dren's response to their mothers, to frustration, and in play behavior.

Mother-Infant Touch (6 Months) One possible determinant of the child's behavior toward the mother in the playroom is the mother's behavior toward the child at an earlier age. The 6-month data indicated that mothers of girls touched their infants more than mothers of boys. On the composite score, where I indicated most touching and 7 least, there were twice as many girls as boys whose mothers were rated 1–3 and twice as many boys as girls whose mothers were rated 5–7 ($p < .04$, x^2 test). Moreover, mothers vocalized to girls significantly more than to boys ($p < .001$, Mann-Whitney U test), and significantly more girls than boys were breast-fed rather than bottle-fed ($p < .02$, Mann-Whitney U test). Thus, when the children were 6 months old, mothers touched, talked to, and handled their daughters more than their sons, and when they were 13 months old, girls touched and talked to their mothers more than boys did. To explore this relationship further, mothers were divided into high, medium, and low mother-touch-infant groups (at 6 months), with the extreme groups consisting of the upper and lower 25 per cent of the sample. For

Table 6-3   Mean Time Playing with Toys, by Sex

	Girls	Boys	p
Total time with:			
Mallet	51.7	60.8	—
Bug	50.2	45.3	—
Pail	34.6	22.9	—
Blocks	126.5	77.5	<.03
Lawnmower	220.3	235.6	—
Cat plus dog (combined)	31.0	9.1	<.01
Quoits	122.7	130.3	—
Pegboard	37.2	28.7	<.05
Nontoys	6.9	31.0	<.005
Putting toys in pail	28.2	43.0	—
Banging toys	19.7	34.8	<.05
Lawnmowing on other toys	2.8	9.8	—
Other manipulation of two toys	28.2	10.3	<.05

the boys at 13 months, the mean number of seconds of physical contact with the mother indicated a linear relation to amount of mother touching (14, 37, and 47 seconds for the low, medium, and high mother-touch groups, respectively; Kruskal-Wallis, $p < .10$). Thus, the more physical contact the mother made with a boy at 6 months, the more he touched the mother at 13 months. For the girls, the relation appeared to be curvilinear. The mean number of seconds of touching the mother for the low, medium, and high mother-touch groups was 101, 55, and 88 seconds, respectively (Kruskal-Wallis, $p < .10$). The comparable distribution for number of seconds close to the mother was 589, 397, and 475 seconds (Kruskal-Wallis, $p < .03$). A girl whose mother initiated very much or very little contact with her at 6 months was more likely to seek a great deal of physical contact with the mother in the playroom than one whose mother was in the medium-touch infant group.

Observation of the mothers' behavior when their infants were 6 months old revealed that five of the seven mothers of girls who showed little physical contact were considered by the staff to be severely rejecting mothers. The data suggest that the child of a rejecting mother continues to seek contact despite the mother's behavior. This result is consistent with Harlow's work with rejected monkeys (Seay, Alexander, & Harlow, 1964) and Provence's work with institutionalized children (Provence, 1965; Provence & Lipton, 1962) and suggests that the child's need for contact with his mother is a powerful motive.

DISCUSSION

Observation of the children's behavior indicated that girls were more dependent, showed less exploratory behavior, and their play behavior reflected a more quiet style. Boys were independent, showed more exploratory behavior, played with toys requiring gross motor activity, were more vigorous, and tended to run and bang in their play. Obviously, these behavior differences approximate those usually found between the sexes at later ages. The data demonstrate that these behavior patterns are already present in the first year of life and that some of them suggest a relation to the mother's response to the infant in the first 6 months. It is possible that at 6 months, differential behavior on the part of the mother is already a response to differential behavior on the part of the infant. Moss (1967) has found behavioral sex differences as early as 3 weeks. In interpreting mother-infant interaction data, Moss suggests that maternal behavior is initially a response to the infant's behavior. As the infant becomes older, if the mother responds contingently to his signals, her behavior acquires reinforcement value which enables her to influence and regulate the infant's behavior. Thus, parents can be active promulgators of sex-role behavior through reinforcement of sex-role-appropriate responses within the first year of life.

The following is offered as a hypothesis concerning sex-role learning. In the first year or two, the parents reinforce those behaviors they consider sex-role appropriate and the child learns these sex-role behaviors independent of any internal motive, that is, in the same way he learns any appropriate response rewarded by his parents. The young child has little idea as to the rules governing this reinforcement. It is suggested, however, that as the child becomes older (above age 3), the rules for this class of reinforced behavior become clearer and he develops internal guides to follow these earlier reinforced rules. In the past, these internalized rules, motivating without apparent reinforcement, have been called modeling behavior. Thus, modeling behavior might be considered an extension or internalization of the earlier reinforced sex-role behavior. However, it is clear that the young child, before seeking to model his behavior, is already knowledgeable in some appropriate sex-role behavior. In that the hypothesis utilizes both early reinforcement as well as subsequent cognitive elaboration, it would seem to bridge the reinforcement notion of Gewirtz (1967) and Kohlberg's cognitive theory (1966) of identification.

The fact that parents are concerned with early display of sex-role-appropriate behavior is reflected in an interesting clinical observation. On some occasions, staff members have incorrectly identified the sex of an infant. Mothers are often clearly irritated by this error. Since the sex of a fully clothed infant is difficult to determine, the mistake seems understandable and the mother's displeasure uncalled for. If, however, she views the infant and behaves toward him in a sex-appropriate way, our mistake is more serious. That is, the magnitude of her displeasure reveals to us the magnitude of her cognitive commitment to this infant as a child of given sex.

Regardless of the interpretation of the observed sex differences, the free play procedure provides a standardized situation in which young children can be observed without interference from experimental manipulation. While behavior under these conditions may be somewhat different from the young child's typical daily behavior, our data indicate that behavior in the play situation is related to other variables, that behavior can be predicted from earlier events, and that it is indicative of later sex-role behavior. The results of the present investigation as well as the work of Bell and Costello (1964), Kagan and Lewis (1965), and Lewis (in press) indicate sex differences within the first year over a wide variety of infant behaviors. The fact that sex differences do appear in the first year has important methodological implications for infant research. These findings emphasize the importance of checking sex differences before pooling data and, most important, of considering sex as a variable in any infant study.

REFERENCES

Bell, R. Q. & Costello, N. S. Three tests for sex differences in tactile sensitivity in the newborn. *Biologia Neonatorum*, 1964, **1**, 335–347.

Freud, S. Three contributions to the theory of sex. Reprinted in *The basic writings of Sigmund Freud*. New York: Random House, 1938.

Gewirtz, J. The learning of generalized imitation and its implications for identification. Paper presented at the Society for Research in Child Development Meeting, New York, March, 1967.

Kagan, J. & Lewis, M. Studies of attention in the human infant. *Merrill-Palmer Quarterly*, 1965, **11**, 95–127.

Kohlberg, L. A cognitive-developmental analysis of children's sex role concepts and attitudes. In E. Maccoby (Ed.), *The development of sex differences*. Stanford, Calif.: Stanford University Press, 1966.

Lewis, M. Infant attention: response decrement as a measure of cognitive processes, or what's new, Baby Jane? Paper presented at the Society for Research in Child Development Meeting, symposium on "The Role of Attention in Cognitive Development," New York, March, 1967.

Lewis, M. Infants' responses to facial stimuli during the first year of life. *Developmental Psychology*, in press.

Maccoby, E. (Ed.) *The development of sex differences*. Stanford, Calif.: Stanford University Press, 1966.

Moss, H. Sex, age and state as determinants of mother-infant interaction. *Merrill-Palmer Quarterly*, 1967, **13**, (1), 19–36.

Piaget, J. *Play, dreams and imitation in childhood*. New York: Norton, 1951.

Provence, S. Disturbed personality development in infancy: a comparison of two inadequately nurtured infants. *Merrill-Palmer Quarterly*, 1965, **2**, 149–170.

Provence, S. & Lipton, R. C. *Infants in institutions*. New York: International Universities Press, 1962.

Seay, B., Alexander, B. K., & Harlow, H. F. Maternal behavior of socially deprived rhesus monkeys. *Journal of Abnormal and Social Psychology*. 1964, **69**(4), 345–354.

The Nature of Love

Harry F. Harlow

We were not surprised to discover that contact comfort was an important basic affectional or love variable, but we did not expect it to overshadow so completely the variable of nursing; indeed the disparity is so great as to suggest that the primary function of nursing as an affectional variable is that of insuring frequent and intimate body contact of the infant with the mother. Certainly man cannot live by milk alone.

Editor's Introduction

Harry Harlow, once called "The Monkey Man of Madison" by *Life* magazine, has been director of the Primate Laboratory of the University of Wisconsin. He has been researching the behavior patterns of the rhesus monkey for over forty years in the hope of applying his discoveries to human infants.

Harlow has identified five love systems or affectional patterns in the development of the monkey; the maternal, infant to mother, paternal, peer, and heterosexual. The focus of this selection is that of the mother's role in child development. Harlow did not accept the commonly accepted theory that food or the satisfaction of the basic hunger drive was the primary bond which held the infant to the mother. In order to test his theory, he designed two surrogate monkey mothers, both made of wire mesh but one left bare and the other covered with soft terry cloth. Even when the bare wire mother was fitted with a nursing bottle and the cloth-covered mother left without a source of food supply, the infants invariably preferred the cloth-covered mother. Harlow concluded that contact comfort was the single most important variable in the determination of infant-maternal attachment. The conclusion to be drawn is that the manner in which a child is fed is more important than the food the child is given. Breast-feeding provides the greatest amount of surface body contact and thus might be the most satisfactory method of feeding; but it is the holding and cuddling that is the critical ingredient, not the container in which the milk is held. Thus father with a nursing bottle might be just as adequate as mother. Harlow allows, however, that it is entirely possible that because of its structure, a man's body is not as comforting on contact as a woman's; but a man would certainly be a better mother than three propped-up pillows.

Harlow contends that contact comfort is the most important variable in the formation of the infant-maternal love bond and that learning to love cannot be postponed without disastrous effects. When a monkey is brought up without contact comfort, indiscriminate violent behavior and bizarre sexual behavior invariably follows.

Harlow's work has confirmed the possibly lethal and certainly devastating effects of severe maternal deprivation, especially the deprivation of physical contact. His work has left little doubt that infants who suffer from insufficient body contact and inadequate response from their caretakers suffer serious psychological and physical damage.

Of course, Harlow is working with monkeys. Is there any evidence that his theories are applicable to human infants? René Spitz (1946, pp. 313–342) observed

Excerpts reprinted from *The American Psychologist*, December 1958, XIII, pp. 673–685. Copyright 1958 by the American Psychological Association. Reprinted by permission.

children who differed in the amount of affection which was offered to them. In the "nursery" group mothers took care of the infants. In the "foundling home" group, overworked nurses cared for the children. The development of the "foundling home" group was severely retarded, and the incidence of death among this group was close to 40 percent; while none of the "nursery" children died. Subsequently Spitz coined the phrase *anaclitic depression* to characterize a syndrome which consists of a progressive reaction to separation from the mother. It begins with increased demandingness and weepiness and rapidly moves to weight loss, an arrest in developmental progress, refusal to make contact with other human beings, lying in a prone or fetal position with an averted face, insomnia, further weight loss, recurrent physical ailments, and rigidity of emotions and facial expressions. It culminates in retardation, lethargy, and—not infrequently—death. If, within a critical period of three to five months, the mother is returned to the child or an adequate substitute is found, the condition is corrected with surprising rapidity. John Bowlby (1953) has described a similar condition which he has called *marasmus*, a wasting away of infants as a result of an inadequate amount of loving attention.

The results are convincing. It is sad that in our advanced society we make it so difficult for a child to receive a great deal of physical contact comfort. We make it difficult by making one person alone responsible for supplying these needs and placing her in an isolated household where additional contact with caring others and with peers is hard to find. And we encourage infants and mothers to give up nursing or bottles in favor of the cup as early as possible so as to encourage independence.

Although Harlow feels that physical contact from the mothering person is important, he also stresses the need for affection between young playmates. He calls this peer love and contends that without it the human infant is destined to encounter sexual and social difficulties upon reaching adulthood. Here again Harlow is reiterating what Spitz observed with human infants. Spitz found that peer comfort was just as effective in countering the negative effects of maternal separation as was restitution of the mother.

Harlow's research stems from established human data. He has tried to apply the human concepts to primates and then back to humans again. After all, we are all animals. And when I observe what our advanced technological society has done to the functions of motherhood, I often feel that it is the monkeys who are advanced, certainly with regard to emotional health.

REFERENCES

Bowlby, J. *Child care and the growth of love*, Middlesex, England: Penguin Books, Ltd., 1953.

Spitz, R. Anaclitic depression: An inquiry into the genesis of psychiatric conditions in early childhood. *Psychoanalytic study of the child* (Vol. 2). New York: International University Press, 1946.

Pamela Cantor

The position commonly held by psychologists and sociologists is quite clear: The basic motives are, for the most part, the primary drives—particularly hunger, thirst, elimination, pain, and sex—and all other motives, including love or affection, are derived or secondary drives. The mother is associated with the reduction of the primary drives—particularly hunger, thirst, and pain—and through learning, affection or love is derived.

It is entirely reasonable to believe that the mother through association with food may become a secondary-reinforcing agent, but this is an inadequate mechanism to account for the persistence of the infant-maternal ties. There is a spate of researches on the formation of secondary reinforcers to hunger and thirst reduction. There can be no question that almost any external stimulus can become a secondary reinforcer if properly associated with tissue-need reduction, but the fact remains that this redundant literature demonstrates unequivocally that such derived drives suffer relatively rapid experimental extinction. Contrariwise, human affection does not extinguish when the mother ceases to have intimate association with the drives in question. Instead, the affectional ties to the mother show a lifelong, unrelenting persistence and, even more surprisingly, widely expanding generality.

Oddly enough, one of the few psychologists who took a position counter to modern psychological dogma was John B. Watson, who believed that love was an innate emotion elicited by cutaneous stimulation of the erogenous zones. . . .

The psychoanalysts have concerned themselves with the problem of the nature of the development of love in the neonate and infant, using ill and aging human beings as subjects. They have discovered the overwhelming importance of the breast and related this to the oral erotic tendencies developed at an age preceding their subjects' memories. Their theories range from a belief that the infant has an innate need to achieve and suckle at the breast to beliefs not unlike commonly accepted psychological theories. There are exceptions, as seen in the recent writings of John Bowlby, who attributes importance not only to food

and thirst satisfaction, but also to "primary object-clinging," a need for intimate physical contact, which is initially associated with the mother.

As far as I know, there exists no direct experimental analysis of the relative importance of the stimulus variables determining the affectional or love responses in the neonatal and infant primate. Unfortunately, the human neonate is a limited experimental subject for such researches because of his inadequate motor capabilities. By the time the human infant's motor responses can be precisely measured, the antecedent determining conditions cannot be defined, having been lost in a jumble and jungle of confounded variables.

Many of these difficulties can be resolved by the use of the neonatal and infant macaque monkey as the subject for the analysis of basic affectional variables. It is possible to make precise measurements in this primate beginning at two to ten days of age, depending upon the maturational status of the individual animal at birth. The macaque infant differs from the human infant in that the monkey is more mature at birth and grows more rapidly; but the basic responses relating to affection, including nursing, contact, clinging, and even visual and auditory exploration, exhibit no fundamental differences in the two species. Even the development of perception, fear, frustration, and learning capability follows very similar sequences in rhesus monkeys and human children.

Three years' experimentation before we started our studies on affection gave us experience with the neonatal monkey. We had separated more than 60 of these animals from their mothers 6 to 12 hours after birth and suckled them on tiny bottles. The infant mortality was only a small fraction of what would have obtained had we let the monkey mothers raise their infants. Our bottle-fed babies were healthier and heavier than monkey-mother-reared infants. We know that we are better monkey mothers than are real monkey mothers thanks to synthetic diets, vitamins, iron extracts, penicillin, chloromycetin, 5% glucose, and constant, tender, loving care.

During the course of these studies we noticed that the laboratory-raised babies showed strong attachment to the cloth pads (folded gauze diapers) which were used to cover the hardware-cloth floors of their cages. The infants clung to these pads and engaged in violent temper tantrums when the pads were removed and replaced for sanitary reasons. Such contact-need or responsiveness had been reported previously by Gertrude van Wagenen for the monkey and by Thomas McCulloch and George Haslerud for the chimpanzee and is reminiscent of the devotion often exhibited by human infants to their pillows, blankets, and soft, cuddly stuffed toys. . . . The baby, human or monkey, if it is to survive, must clutch at more than a straw.

We had also observed during some allied observational studies that a baby monkey raised on a bare wire-mesh cage floor survives with difficulty, if at all, during the first five days of life. If a wire-mesh cone is introduced, the baby does better; and, if the cone is covered with terry cloth, husky, healthy, happy babies evolve. It takes more than a baby and a box to make a normal monkey. We were impressed by the possibility that, above and beyond the bubbling fountain of breast or bottle, contact comfort might be a very important variable in the development of the infant's affection for the mother.

At this point we decided to study the development of affectional responses of neonatal and infant monkeys to an artificial, inanimate mother, and so we built a surrogate mother which we hoped and believed would be a good surrogate mother. In devising this surrogate mother we were dependent neither upon the capriciousness of evolutionary processes nor upon mutations produced by chance radioac-

tive fallout. Instead, we designed the mother surrogate in terms of modern human-engineering principles. . . . We produced a perfectly proportioned, streamlined body stripped of unnecessary bulges and appendices. Redundancy in the surrogate mother's system was avoided by reducing the number of breasts from two to one and placing this uni-breast in an upper-thoracic, sagittal position, thus maximizing the natural and known perceptual-motor capabilities of the infant operator. The surrogate was made from a block of wood, covered with sponge rubber, and sheathed in tan cotton terry cloth. A light bulb behind her radiated heat. The result was a mother, soft, warm, and tender, a mother with infinite patience, a mother available twenty-four hours a day, a mother that never scolded her infant and never struck or bit her baby in anger. Furthermore, we designed a mother-machine with maximal maintenance efficiency since failure of any system or function could be resolved by the simple substitution of black boxes and new component parts. It is our opinion that we engineered a very superior monkey mother, although this position is not held universally by the monkey fathers.

Before beginning our initial experiment we also designed and constructed a second mother surrogate, a surrogate in which we deliberately built less than the maximal capability for contact comfort. . . . She is made of wire-mesh, a substance entirely adequate to provide postural support and nursing capability, and she is warmed by radiant heat. Her body differs in no essential way from that of the cloth mother surrogate other than in the quality of the contact comfort which she can supply.

In our initial experiment, the dual mother-surrogate condition, a cloth mother and a wire mother were placed in different cubicles attached to the infant's living cage. . . . For four newborn monkeys the cloth mother lactated and the wire mother did not; and, for the other

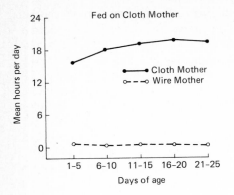

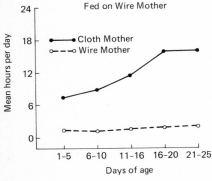

Figure 6-1   Time spent on cloth-and-wire mother surrogates.

four, this condition was reversed. In either condition the infant received all its milk through the mother surrogate as soon as it was able to maintain itself in this way, a capability achieved within two or three days except in the case of very immature infants. Supplementary feedings were given until the milk intake from the mother surrogate was adequate. Thus, the experiment was designed as a test of the relative importance of the variables of contact comfort and nursing comfort. During the first 14 days of life the monkey's cage floor was covered with a heating pad wrapped in a folded gauze diaper, and thereafter the cage floor was bare. The infants were always free to leave the heating pad or cage floor to contact either mother, and the time spent on

the surrogate mothers was automatically recorded. Figure 6-1 shows the total time spent on the cloth and wire mothers under the two conditions of feeding. These data make it obvious that contact comfort is a variable of overwhelming importance in the development of affectional responses, whereas lactation is a variable of negligible importance. With age and opportunity to learn, subjects with the lactating wire mother showed decreasing responsiveness to her and increasing responsiveness to the nonlactating cloth mother, a finding completely contrary to any interpretation of derived drive in which the mother-form becomes conditioned to hunger-thirst reduction. The persistence of these differential responses throughout 165 consecutive days of testing is evident in Figure 6-2.

One control group of neonatal monkeys was raised on a single wire mother, and a second control group was raised on a single cloth mother. There were no differences between these two groups in amount of milk ingested

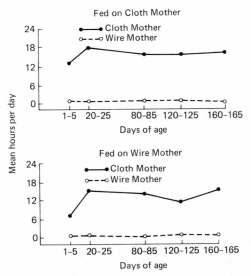

Figure 6-2   Long-term contact time on cloth-and-wire mother surrogates.

or in weight gain. The only difference between the groups lay in the composition of the feces, the softer stools of the wire-mother infants suggesting psychosomatic involvement. The wire mother is biologically adequate but psychologically inept.

We were not surprised to discover that contact comfort was an important basic affectional or love variable, but we did not expect it to overshadow so completely the variable of nursing; indeed, the disparity is so great as to suggest that the primary function of nursing as an affectional variable is that of insuring frequent and intimate body contact of the infant with the mother. Certainly, man cannot live by milk alone. Love is an emotion that does not need to be bottle- or spoon-fed, and we may be sure that there is nothing to be gained by giving lip service to love.

A charming lady once heard me describe these experiments; and, when I subsequently talked to her, her face brightened with sudden insight: "Now I know what's wrong with me," she said, "I'm just a wire mother." Perhaps she was lucky. She might have been a wire wife.

We believe that contact comfort has long served the animal kingdom as a motivating agent for affectional responses. Since at the present time we have no experimental data to substantiate this position, we supply information which must be accepted, if at all, on the basis of face validity.

One function of the real mother, human or sub-human, and presumably of a mother surrogate, is to provide a haven of safety for the infant in times of fear and danger. The frightened or ailing child clings to its mother, not its father; and this selective responsiveness in times of distress, disturbance, or danger may be used as a measure of the strength of affectional bonds. We have tested this kind of differential responsiveness by presenting to the infants in their cages, in the presence of

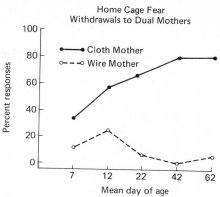

Figure 6-3 Differential responsiveness in fear tests.

the two mothers, various fear-producing stimuli. The data on differential responsiveness are presented in Figure 6-3. It is apparent that the cloth mother is highly preferred over the wire one, and this differential selectivity is enhanced by age and experience. In this situation, the variable of nursing appears to be of absolutely no importance: the infant consistently seeks the soft mother surrogate regardless of nursing condition.

Similarly, the mother or mother surrogate provides its young with a source of security, and this role or function is seen with special clarity when mother and child are in a strange situation. At the present time we have completed tests for this relationship on four of our eight baby monkeys assigned to the dual mother-surrogate condition by introducing them for three minutes into the strange environment of a room measuring six feet by six feet by six feet (also called the "open-field test") and containing multiple stimuli known to elicit curiosity-manipulatory responses in baby monkeys. The subjects were placed in this situation twice a week for eight weeks with no mother surrogate present during alternate sessions and the cloth mother present during the others. A cloth diaper was always available as one of the stimuli throughout all sessions. After one or two adaptation sessions, the infants always rushed to the mother surrogate when she was present and clutched her, rubbed their bodies against her, and frequently manipulated her body and face. After a few additional sessions, the infants began to use the mother surrogate as a source of security, a base of operations. . . . They would explore and manipulate a stimulus and then return to the mother before adventuring again into the strange new world. The behavior of these infants was quite different when the mother was absent from the room. Frequently they would freeze in a crouched position. . . . Emotionality indices such as vocalization, crouching, rocking, and sucking increased sharply. . . . Total emotionality score was cut in half when the mother was present. In the absence of the mother some of the experimental monkeys would rush to the center of the room where the mother was customarily placed and then run rapidly from object to object, screaming and crying all the while. Continuous, frantic clutching of their bodies was very common, even when not in the crouching position. These monkeys frequently contacted and clutched the cloth diaper, but this action never pacified them. The same behavior occurred in the presence of the wire mother. No difference between the cloth-mother-fed and wire-mother-fed infants was demonstrated under either condition. Four control infants never raised with a mother surrogate showed the same emotionality scores when the mother was absent as the experimental infants showed in the absence of the mother, but the controls' scores were slightly larger in the presence of the mother surrogate than in her absence. . . .

Affectional retention was . . . tested in the open field during the first 9 days after separation and then at 30-day intervals, and each test condition was run twice at each retention interval. The infant's behavior differed from that observed during the period preceding separation. When the cloth mother was present in the post-separation period, the babies rushed to her, climbed up, clung tightly to her, and rubbed their heads and faces against her body. After this initial embrace and reunion, they played on the mother, including biting and tearing at her cloth cover; but they rarely made any attempt to leave her during the test period, nor did they manipulate or play with the objects in the room, in contrast with their behavior before maternal separation. The only exception was the occasional monkey that left the mother surrogate momentarily, grasped the folded piece of paper (one of the standard stimuli in the field), and brought it quickly back to the mother. It appeared that deprivation had enhanced the tie to the mother and rendered the contact-comfort need so prepotent that need for the mother overwhelmed the exploratory motives during the brief, three-minute test sessions. No change in these behaviors was observed throughout the 185-day period. When the mother was absent from the open field, the behavior of the infants was similar in the initial retention test to that during the preseparation tests; but they tended to show gradual adaptation to the open-field situation with repeated testing and, consequently, a reduction in their emotionality scores.

In the last five retention test periods, an additional test was introduced in which the surrogate mother was placed in the center of the room and covered with a clear Plexiglas box. The monkeys were initially disturbed and frustrated with their explorations and manipulations of the box failed to provide contact with the mother. However, all animals adapted to the situation rather rapidly. Soon they used the box as a place of orientation for exploratory and play behavior, made frequent contacts with the objects in the field, and very often brought these objects to the Plexiglas box. The emotionality index was slightly higher than in the condition of the available cloth mothers, but it in no way approached the emotionality level displayed when the cloth mother was absent. Obviously, the infant monkeys gained emotional security by the presence of the mother even though contact was denied.

Affectional retention has also been measured by tests in which the monkey must unfasten a three-device mechanical puzzle to obtain entrance into a compartment containing the mother surrogate. All the trials are initiated by allowing the infant to go through an unlocked door, and in half the trials it finds the mother present and in half, an empty compartment. The door is then locked and a ten-minute test conducted. In tests given prior to separation from the surrogate mothers, some of the infants had solved this puzzle and others had failed. . . . On the last test before separation there were no differences in total manipulation under mother-present and mother-absent conditions, but striking differences exist between the two conditions throughout the post-separation test periods. Again, there is no interaction with conditions of feedings.

The over-all picture obtained from surveying the retention data is unequivocal. There is little, if any, waning of responsiveness to the mother throughout this five-month period as indicated by any measure. It becomes perfectly obvious that this affectional bond is highly resistant to forgetting and that it can be retained for very long periods of time by relatively infrequent contact reinforcement. During the next year, retention tests will be conducted at 90-day intervals, and further plans are dependent upon the results obtained. It would appear that affectional responses may show as much resistance to extinction as has been previously demonstrated for learned fears and learned pain, and such data would be in keeping with those of common human observation. . . .

We have already described the group of four control infants that had never lived in the presence of any mother surrogate and had demonstrated no sign of affection or security in the presence of the cloth mothers introduced in test sessions. When these infants reached the age of 250 days, cubicles containing both a cloth mother and a wire mother were attached to their cages. There was no lactation in these mothers, for the monkeys were on a solid-food diet. The initial reaction of the monkeys to the alterations was one of extreme disturbance. All the infants screamed violently and made repeated attempts to escape the cage whenever the door was opened. They kept a maximum distance from the mother surrogates and exhibited a considerable amount of rocking and crouching behavior, indicative of emotionality. Our first thought was that the critical period for the development of maternally directed affection had passed and that these macaque children were doomed to live as affectional orphans. Fortunately, these behaviors continued for only 12 to 48 hours and then gradually ebbed, changing from indifference to active contact on, and exploration of, the surrogates. The home-cage behavior of these control monkeys slowly became similar to that of the animals raised with the mother surrogates from birth. Their manipulation and play on the cloth mother became progressively more vigorous to the point of actual mutilation, particularly during the morning after the cloth mother had been given her daily change of terry covering. The control subjects were now actively running to the cloth mother when frightened and had to be coaxed from her to be taken from the cage for formal testing. . . .

Consistent with the results on the subjects reared from birth with dual mothers, these late-adopted infants spent less than one and one-half hours per day in contact with the wire mothers, and this activity level was relatively constant throughout the test sessions. Although the maximum time that the control monkeys spent on the cloth mother was only about half that spent by the original dual mother-surrogate group, we cannot be sure that this discrepancy is a function of differential early experience. The control monkeys were about three months older when the mothers were attached to their cages than the experimental animals had been when their mothers were removed and the retention tests begun. Thus, we do not know what the amount of contact would be for a 250-day-old animal raised from birth with surrogate mothers. Nevertheless, the magnitude of the differences and the fact that the contact-time curves for the mothered-from-birth infants had remained constant for almost 150 days suggest that early experience with the mother is a variable of measurable importance. . . .

Before the introduction of the mother surrogate into the home-cage situation, only one of the four control monkeys had ever contacted the cloth mother in the open-field tests. In general, the surrogate mother not only gave the infants no security, but instead appeared to serve as a fear stimulus. The emotionality scores of these control subjects were slightly higher during the mother-present test sessions than during the mother-absent test sessions. These behaviors were changed radically by the fourth post-introduction test approximately 60 days later. In the absence of the cloth mothers the emotionality index in this fourth test remains near the earlier level, but the score is reduced by half when the mother is present, a result strikingly similar to that found for infants raised with the dual mother-surrogates from birth. The control infants now show increasing object exploration and play behavior, and they begin to use the mother as a base of operations, as did the infants raised from birth with the mother surrogates. However, there are still definite differences in the behavior of the two groups. The control in-

fants do not rush directly to the mother and clutch her violently; but instead they go toward, and orient around her, usually after an initial period during which they frequently show disturbed behavior, exploratory behavior, or both.

That the control monkeys develop affection or love for the cloth mother when she is introduced into the cage at 250 days of age cannot be questioned. There is every reason to believe, however, that this interval of delay depresses the intensity of the affectional response below that of the infant monkeys that were surrogate-mothered from birth onward. In interpreting these data it is well to remember that the control monkeys had had continuous opportunity to observe and hear other monkeys housed in adjacent cages and that they had had limited opportunity to view and contact surrogate mothers in the test situations, even though they did not exploit the opportunities.

During the last two years we have observed the behavior of two infants raised by their own mothers. Love for the real mother and love for the surrogate mother appear to be very similar. The baby macaque spends many hours a day clinging to its real mother. If away from the mother when frightened, it rushes to her and in her presence shows comfort and composure. As far as we can observe, the infant monkey's affection for the real mother is strong, but no stronger than that of the experimental monkey for the surrogate cloth mother, and the security that the infant gains from the presence of the real mother is no greater than the security it gains from a cloth surrogate. Next year we hope to put this problem to final, definitive, experimental test. But, whether the mother is real or a cloth surrogate, there does develop a deep and abiding bond between mother and child. In one case it may be the call of the wild and in the other the McCall of civilization, but in both cases there is "togetherness."

In spite of the importance of contact comfort, there is reason to believe that other variables of measurable importance will be discovered. Postural support may be such a variable, and it has been suggested that, when we build arms into the mother surrogate, 10 is the minimal number required to provide adequate child care. Rocking motion may be such a variable, and we are comparing rocking and stationary mother surrogates and incliñed planes. The differential responsiveness to cloth mother and cloth-covered inclined plane suggests that clinging as well as contact is an affectional variable of importance. Sounds, particularly natural, maternal sounds, may operate as either unlearned or learned affectional variables. Visual responsiveness may be such a variable, and it is possible that some semblance of visual imprinting may develop in the neonatal monkey. There are indications that this becomes a variable of importance during the course of infancy through some maturational process.

John Bowlby has suggested that there is an affectional variable which he calls "primary object following," characterized by visual and oral search of the mother's face. Our surrogate-mother-raised baby monkeys are at first inattentive to her face, as are human neonates to human mother faces. But by 30 days of age ever-increasing responsiveness to the mother's face appears—whether through learning, maturation, or both—and we have reason to believe that the face becomes an object of special attention.

Our first surrogate-mother-raised baby had a mother whose head was just a ball of wood since the baby was a month early and we had not had time to design a more esthetic head and face. This baby had contact with the blank-faced mother for 180 days and was then placed with two cloth mothers, one motionless and one rocking, both being endowed with painted, ornamented faces. To our surprise the animal would compulsively rotate both faces 180 degrees so that it viewed only a round, smooth face and never the painted, ornamented face. Furthermore, it would do this as long as the patience of the experimenter in reorienting the faces persisted. The monkey showed no sign of fear or anxiety, but it showed unlimited persistence. Subsequently it improved its technique, compulsively removing the heads and rolling them into its cage as fast as they were returned. We are intrigued by this observation, and we plan to examine systematically the role of the mother face in the development of infant-monkey affections. Indeed, these observations suggest the need for a series of ethological-type researches on the two-faced female.

Although we have made no attempts thus far to study the generalization of infant-macaque affection or love, the techniques which we have developed offer promise in this uncharted field. Beyond this, there are few if any technical difficulties in studying the affection of the actual, living mother for the child, and the techniques developed can be utilized and expanded for the analysis and developmental study of father-infant and infant-infant affection.

Since we can measure neonatal and infant affectional responses to mother surrogates, and since we know they are strong and persisting, we are in a position to assess the effects of feeding and contactual schedules; consistency and inconsistency in the mother surrogates; and early, intermediate, and late maternal deprivation. Again, we have here a family of problems of fundamental interest and theoretical importance.

Infancy

Melford E. Spiro

There is much evidence to indicate that after the babies become adjusted to the group, they feel secure within it and object to being separated from it. The babies seldom cry in the evening when the adults leave the Nursery, for example, and it is not an unlikely hypothesis that the presence of their group is at least partially responsible for this behavior.

Editor's Introduction

The Israeli kibbutzim constitute what is probably the most significant social experiment in our times. *Kibbutz* is the Hebrew word for *group*. In the kibbutz children are raised outside the home in group care from shortly after birth until late adolescence. When the children are a few days old, they are brought to the nursery, where they live with approximately fifteen peers and are cared for by the *metapelet*, or woman in charge of the nursery. The infants remain in this nursery until they reach approximately 1 year of age. They are visited at least once a day by their fathers and more frequently by their mothers, especially during the nursing period. This frequent visitation lasts until the infant is 6 months old. At six months, the infants begin to visit with their parents in the parental home for approximately two hours a day. When the children reach the age of 1 year, they are moved to the toddler house, where they acquire a new caretaker and a new physical environment. It is here that the children learn to feed, dress, and toilet themselves. The infants sharing the nursery tend to remain together as a group throughout childhood as they move to the toddler house, new *metapelets*, and new teachers. Thus the peer group becomes a primary agent of socialization.

When the kibbutz movement first began, there was great concern about how effectively children could be reared outside the traditional nuclear-family structure. The main question was: Could children be reared away from their mothers without long-lasting negative consequences and without a severe weakening of the mother-child bonds that were felt to be essential for sound mental health? Advocates of this social system claim that the fears have been unfounded. Research has shown that strong family loyalties have developed and that the kibbutz children's perceptions of parental sex roles do not differ greatly from those of children raised elsewhere. In brief, the picture of emotionally flat, repressed children with limited capacities for intimate relationships projected by early fears stands in sharp contrast to the warm, responsive, outgoing children who are the actual products of a kibbutz upbringing. Adherents claim that the vast majority of children who are raised as kibbutzniks later remain and raise their own children in this manner. They also state that the benefits to society, with regard to particular personality traits, are important. Delinquency, for example, is nearly nonexistent in the kibbutz. This may be related to the fact that the community provides for all economic needs. It may also be related to the fact that the young person in the kibbutz has an extended family system—the group—as well as a nuclear family to which to belong. Thus, there appear to be fewer grounds for feelings of alienation and lack of belonging than there are in our American culture.

In 1948, in coming to the land of their fathers, the Jews were leaving fear, war, torment, and ghettos behind them; their desire to build a new way of life gave rise to the kibbutz. A major focus of the new way of life was the family, but the kibbutz radically changed the family as these post-World War II Israelis had known it. There no longer was the authoritarian father and the selfless, devoted mother. The women took an equal place with the men in the establishment and maintenance of the kibbutz, and they feared that this might exclude child rearing. The solution— group care—radically changed the social and familial structure of Israel in spite of the fact that only 9 percent of Israel's population actually live in the kibbutzim.

Spiro is one observer among many of the Israeli social structure. I have chosen this selection because it focuses on the early years of child rearing and education in Israel (which differ so strongly from the practices of American middle-class families) and because these years markedly affect the lives of the young Israeli children. This selection addresses the most important issue in looking at the kibbutz system: What is the importance of the absence or presence of parents and the traditional family structure in the emotional development of children?

Pamela Cantor

INTERACTION

There are various categories of persons with whom the infants interact and from whom, presumably, they learn. Their most frequent contact is with the nurses.

Nurses

Aside from their mothers, the infants are in the care of two full-time, trained nurses, one trained nurse who works only a half-day, and one untrained nurse. The latter serves as a replacement for any regular nurse who may be absent. The nurses' schedules are staggered (so that not all are present all the time) to ensure the presence of at least one nurse from the time the babies awaken in the morning until their parents visit them in the evening. There are three nurses on duty in the early morning, one in the late morning and early afternoon, and two in the late afternoon. The nurses' workday ends shortly after the parents arrive to visit their babies. There is no nurse on duty in any children's house at night. There is, however, a night watch (*shomeret lailah*) who goes from house to house to check on all the children. Each round requires approxi-

mately one hour. Babies (with the exception of nursing infants) awaken infrequently at night, but when they do, the watch attempts to pacify them. She also covers those whose blankets have slipped off, and in general sees that their needs are met. Should a nursing infant cry from hunger long before his mother is scheduled to feed him, she will call the mother.

The primary duties of the nurse are, necessarily, of a caretaking nature. Almost her entire day is devoted to caring for the physical needs of seventeen babies and to cleaning the house. The affection she is able to bestow on her charges must therefore always come in the course of these caretaking duties. Most nurses perform their duties with a maximum of warmth and affection, but occasionally a nurse cares for a baby in a perfunctory manner, with a minimum of stimulation for the baby. . . .

In general, then, nurses are warm and affectionate with the babies; and it may be assumed that the attitudes of love and permissiveness that pervade the Nursery ensure a high level of gratification for the babies, despite the fact that their opportunities to interact with the nurses are usually limited to those which arise in the process of caretaking. If a baby experiences frustration, therefore, it is primarily because his individual needs cannot always be satisfied in a system based on routine. Differences in need are often great, not only because each infant has his own rhythms, but because there is an age difference of one year separating the youngest from the oldest; and yet they are all expected to conform to the same schedule.

The most frequent occasion for frustration as a result of institutional routine is prolonged crying without attention. Ideally, say the nurses, a baby is not allowed to cry, and when he does a nurse always goes to see what is wrong. This statement is only partially true, however, and often depends upon the particular nurse and the particular baby. An experienced nurse, such as the head nurse, can identify every baby by, and knows the meaning of, his cry. Hence she can distinguish between serious and other kinds of crying and can regulate her responses accordingly. Others not so experienced may allow serious cries to go unheeded for some time. The nurses' statement is true, moreover, if a nurse happens to be in the room where the baby is crying. If, however, she is busy elsewhere and the cry does not sound too serious to her, she may wait five or ten minutes—or even longer—before she goes to see what is wrong. . . .

It should be noted . . . that the nurse not only waits for some time before she attends to the baby's needs, but that her attention consists in a mechanical manipulation of the baby rather than of the giving of warmth and affection. Although this is entirely understandable in terms of the nurse's busy routine, the baby's emotional needs may still remain unsatisfied.

On the other hand, nurses attempt to recognize individual differences and to deal with them to the extent that their schedule permits them to do so. If a baby cries from hunger much before his scheduled feeding, the nurse may bring him his food early. So, too, if an infant finds it difficult to sleep when other babies are present, an attempt is made to give him some privacy.

The Parents

We have noted that the mother of a young infant has considerably more contact with him at this age than she will when he is older, for she comes to the Nursery several times a day to nurse. She may, furthermore, visit her baby at other times of the day as well, if she happens to be free. But although the mother's primary contacts with her infant occur during the feeding period, the interaction between mother and child is not confined solely to nursing. For at these times, she also changes her baby's diaper, plays with him, bathes him if necessary, and puts him back to sleep. The average mother spends from forty-five minutes to one hour with her baby when she comes to nurse him. Thus the infant has frequent and intimate contact with his mother, and it is not surprising therefore that she is the first individual for whom he shows recognition.

In the past, this characterization of the mother-infant relationship would not have applied. Until about fifteen years ago, the Nursery was viewed as a hospital, in which order and cleanliness reigned supreme. The mother was allowed to visit her baby only at the scheduled feeding periods, and when she arrived the nurse had prepared everything for her—the baby was already bathed and his diaper had been changed. The present head nurse, upon assuming her position, insisted that the Nursery be a "house" and not a "hospital," and that the mothers be allowed to care for their infants in other ways as well. At first, some nurses resisted these changes, for the order that had formerly prevailed was destroyed. Even a few mothers objected, for they had been accustomed to the nurses' doing everything for them. It is apparent, however, that today almost every mother enjoys the opportunity to care for her baby when she visits him. While she does not attempt to prolong the feeding time unduly, neither does she attempt to shorten it by encouraging the baby to "hurry up" or by failing to "play" with him, change his diaper, and stay with him a few minutes after returning him to his crib.

Today, too, fathers are encouraged to visit their infants whenever they please, although permission to enter the room during nursing depends upon the attitudes of the mothers who are nursing at that time.[1] Aside from those infrequent occasions when a father, arriving early in the evening, may undertake to feed his baby, his sole role from the very beginning is that of playmate to his child. In general, it may be said that most fathers display an interest in their infants immediately, holding them, bouncing them, discussing with their wives and the other mothers their baby's particular characteristics, and proudly heralding the appearance of each new accomplishment. This interest in and interaction with the baby increases as the infant develops new skills.

Peers

A source of constant stimulation for the baby is his peer-group. The babies are together the entire day. They sleep in the same rooms, eat at the same time, and play on the floor together. They stimulate each other. Babies were observed to recognize and to be aware of individual babies by the age of five months. By this age they look at other babies and show definite signs of awareness such as laughing, babbling, waving of arms and legs, and touching. This awareness, of course, increases with age. . . .[2]

There is much evidence to indicate that after the babies become adjusted to the group, they feel secure within it and object to being separated from it. The babies seldom cry in the evening when the adults leave the Nursery, for example, and it is not an unlikely hypothesis that the presence of their group is at least partially responsible for this behavior.

That the babies feel most secure when in the presence of their peers may be inferred from other evidence as well. The babies object to being separated from the group, for example, whether the separation takes the form of isolation in a separate room within the Nursery or in their parental rooms. One baby became so upset when her bed was moved to another room that she refused to nurse. Another baby, when compelled to stay in his parents' room for a short time because the other babies in his group were ill, cried most of the time and would not permit his parents to leave the room. This behavior disappeared as soon as he returned to the Nursery. Babies show signs of disturbance, moreover, even when their cribs are rearranged so that they are no longer near the babies with whom they had previously interacted.

This attachment to the group is most perceptible in the case of the older babies, those ten months and older, who have already begun to form their own selective in-group. They play most frequently with each other, and generally play within an area which makes them visibly a social group.[3] Indeed, a baby no more than a month younger than they has difficulty in becoming part of the group. They interact with him much less frequently than with each other, and it may take several days before he is completely accepted.

[1]The group of nursing mothers observed during this study did not object to the presence of a father of a nursing infant. They did object, however, to the suggestion that I—not a member of "the family"—be present.

[2]The recognition of adults is earlier. According to the head nurse, an infant can recognize his mother during the second month and the head nurse by the end of that month.

[3]Their contacts with each other are more frequent than their contacts with the younger babies, for these older babies sleep in a separate room, their cribs are placed together on the porch, and they are more often placed on the terrace to play.

SOME BEHAVIOR SYSTEMS AND THEIR SOCIALIZATION

Motor Behavior

At the time of observation, there were seventeen babies in the Nursery—twelve males and five females, who ranged in age from four days to twelve months. All were considered to be normal and healthy babies, both in terms of nurses' reports and of the researchers' observations based on American norms.

There appears to be little difference between the motor development of American infants and the oldest kibbutz infants. According to the norms established by Gesell,[4] American infants sit alone and creep by forty weeks. By twelve months, the American infant stands and cruises. At the time of our observations in the Nursery, three children, ages ten months, ten and one-half months, and eleven and one-half months, respectively, were already standing and cruising. They also sat alone and crawled. A fourth infant stood at nine months and began to creep at that age. He could also sit alone. A fifth baby was able to crawl at eight months, and at nine months was making definite attempts to stand. He was already able to sit without support. One nine-month-old baby began to raise his head and chest at that age, and at ten months began to scoot. This case of retardation was not viewed by the nurses as cause for alarm, as it was felt that his retardation was due to his unusually large head—merely too large for him to support as yet.[5] Of the three other babies in the last quarter of their first year, one was trying to sit alone at eight months, and it was obvious that she would soon be successful in her attempts; the other two, aged nine months, did not yet sit alone, crawl, or stand. They could, however, roll over, raise their heads and chests, and showed definite signs of alertness and interest in their surroundings.

Some kibbutz mothers claim that living in a group accelerates the maturation processes of the babies, for they stimulate each other to talk, stand, and walk, so that kibbutz babies are precocious by comparison with city children in the development of these behaviors. Our observations did not substantiate these claims. For if the infants who were in the Nursery at the time of our study may be said to have constituted a representative sample of kibbutz infants, then the above summary of motor development would seem to disconfirm the hypothesis that communal living accelerates the process of motor development.[6] Nor is there any evidence for the converse hypothesis—that lack of adult encouragement retards such development. Although babies are permitted to develop motor skills at their own pace without special urging or stimulation from the nurses, the observations indicate that their rate of development conforms to American norms. (It is our impression, however, that although the nurses do not encourage the development of motor skills, the parents do.)

As for language development, no words were actually used by any infant, although many parents claimed that their babies could say 'a-ba' ("Daddy"), and so the older ones could—but there is no evidence that they actually used it in reference to their fathers.

---

[4]A. Gesell and C. S. Amatruda, *Developmental Diagnosis* (New York: Hoeber, 1941). A. Gesell et al. *The First Five Years of Life* (New York: Harper, 1940).

[5]Although the infant's mother expressed some concern, she was reminded by the nurse that her older child had also had this difficulty as an infant, but had later been able to catch up with his age group.

[6]There does seem to be some indication in the older groups of acceleration in both motor and social development as a result of group living. However, the influence is from the older children in the group to the younger; the younger attempt to emulate the older children. This matching behavior is particularly pronounced when two groups of slightly different ages are combined into one; the nurses report that there is almost always a rapid spurt in the development of the younger children as a result.

Babbling and jabbering appeared to be normal, however.[7]

Feeding

All kibbutz mothers, according to a nurse, are eager to nurse their children (although there was one exception to this rule in the recent past) and they do "anything they can" in order to have milk. Mothers, furthermore, wish to defer complete weaning as long as possible. The mothers have a "myth," says one nurse, that mother's milk is the best food for babies, so that even after the babies are eating solids, some mothers insist on nursing their babies before giving them the solids. For some mothers, moreover, nursing is a source of personal gratification, and they are reluctant to give it up even though their babies may receive little nourishment from the milk.

Today, the entire process of nursing, weaning, and self-feeding is relaxed and permissive. But this was not true in the past. Until approximately ten years prior to this study,

babies were forced to eat even if they were not hungry, and many feeding problems resulted from this policy. The policy of forcing an infant to nurse was based on the physician's insistence that every baby should weigh at least eleven kilos at the age of one year.[8]

In the past, moreover, the kibbutz ideal of equality was applied as strictly to infants as it was to adults. Since it was believed, for example, that all babies should weigh the same number of kilos, it was agreed that they should all receive the same quantities of food. Individual differences among infants were not recognized.[9] This rigidity applied to weaning as well. Eating from a cup or spoon, for example, was introduced abruptly, and babies who wished to continue nursing from either the breast or bottle were not permitted to do so.

Within the past ten years, however, this rigidity has been almost entirely replaced by an emphasis on individualization. The ideal of equality is no longer felt to apply to infant development. Hence, infants are not com-

---

[7] . . . a few observations about the role of the nurse [in motor and verbal development] may be made here. Again, as in the Nursery, little attempt is made by the nurses to hasten their development. Each child is permitted to develop such skills at his own pace, and, indeed, one occasionally has the impression that the nurse's behavior tends to discourage, rather than to encourage, achievement. The nurse does not always have the time to wait for a new toddler to slowly walk from one room to another, and in her haste to get on with her work she will often carry such a child, thus preventing him from learning to walk as quickly as he might. On the other hand, should a child be unusually slow in learning to walk, the nurse, insofar as her time permits, will often encourage him to walk—helping him to do so by holding his hands and walking with him, or holding out her arms and asking him to walk to her. Such a child may also receive special exercises from the physical therapist to hasten his development.

While the nurses make no specific attempts to hasten the children's acquisition of language skills, they are concerned with it and quick to praise such development. "Oh," says one nurse, "Chanele is speaking Hebrew so nicely now—you have no idea!" "Iris," says another, "that's not right. Don't say, *chultza-ah*, say, *chultz-a*." "Amir, it's *pee-pee*, not *pee-pee-ee-ee*." "Oy," groans the nurse. "All the children talk like that, it's terrible."

[8] Interestingly enough, many of the babies who were compelled to eat did not attain the prescribed weight—a situation that induced anxieties in both nurses and mothers.

[9] This emphasis on equality was applied not only to the gaining of weight and the intake of grams, but to all other matters as well. Parents, for example, were enjoined not to show more affection to their own babies than to others in the Nursery, and all babies were quite literally to be regarded as one's own. The anxieties engendered by the effort to scatter one's love and affection without discrimination soon brought the state of affairs to "absurdity," and a more relaxed and natural approach came to be accepted. Today it is apparent that parents, while primarily absorbed in their own children, have a definite affection for the older babies in the Nursery and especially for those other babies who share their infant's room. It is also apparent, however, that a mother's primary love and attention goes to her own baby. When, for example, a mother works as a nurse in the Nursery, she goes immediately to her own baby if he cries or needs attention. If it is another baby in need of attention, however, she takes her time about helping him. This preference seems to be unconscious, and is denied when another nurse points it out.

pelled to eat if they do not wish to; no arbitrary optimal weights are established, and the entire weaning process is a gradual one. When cereal, for example, is added to the evening meal, it may be fed to the baby in a bottle, and those who do not eat well from a cup also receive their vegetables in a bottle. As one nurse remarked, they no longer believe in "arguing with the baby," so that the bottle is not eliminated until the baby no longer wants it.

The mother nurses the infant for the first time twelve hours after birth, so that his sucking may stimulate her flow of milk. For the same reason the baby is not given any food except tea which he receives in a bottle according to a fixed schedule of five or six times a day, for it is believed that by keeping the baby hungry he will want to suck. Being hungry, the babies not only cry frequently during the first few days but lose weight as well.

Upon returning to Kiryat Yedidim the new mother nurses her baby six times a day for six weeks. This is the period, it will be remembered, in which she enjoys a complete vacation from her work, so that the midnight feeding which this schedule imposes upon her is not unduly burdensome. This latter feeding is gradually omitted during this six week period by progressively deferring the time of the feeding from 12:00 to 1:00, to 2:00, to 3:00, etc., until the baby sleeps the entire night without waking for a feeding. Should the baby cry at night much before the mother is scheduled to nurse him, the night watch will call her. In the past, however, the mother was not called and the watch tried to appease the baby. The present system of calling the mother was instituted about fifteen years ago by the new head nurse over the objections of the mothers, who complained that it was an unwelcome burden, particularly in the winter months. Many women still object to the night feeding and, according to one informant, "they wait for the day when the nurses tell them they need not come any more."

Before describing the nursing situation, mention should be made of those few mothers who have no milk. Today a baby is put on a formula as soon as it is discovered that his mother is unable to nurse. In the past, however (until about fifteen years ago), the baby was nursed by other nursing mothers, a procedure consistent with the original notions of collectivism and equality that were rigidly enforced in Kiryat Yedidim. One of the nurses characterized this practice as "a mess," as it created tensions for everyone concerned. The baby, however hungry, was forced to wait for his feeding until his wet nurse had nursed her own baby. The wet nurse, moreover, did not always have sufficient milk for two babies, so that the infant was often nursed by more than one woman. But this practice was hard on the other babies as well. Since it was thought that the principle of equality demanded that all infants weigh the same, it was agreed that all babies be given the same amount of milk at each feeding. Thus even if a woman's own baby wanted one hundred and fifty grams, the feeding stopped at one hundred grams—the prescribed amount—so that she would have enough milk for the other baby. For the mother herself the use of a wet nurse had unhappy consequences. Although the other mothers did not derogate her for her "deficiency," she nevertheless felt inferior to them.[10] Moreover, since she was unable to nurse her infant, it was ruled that she should return to her work immediately—for she was not needed in the Nursery. Hence, such a mother was able to see her baby only after she had completed her day's work.

Eventually the protests of the mothers resulted in the abolition of wet or communal nursing, and infants whose mothers had no milk were instead given a formula by the

[10]According to the nurses, the attitude of nursing mothers toward mothers with no milk is "neutral." But, given the prevailing belief that mother's milk is the "best" for the baby, it is not surprising that some mothers who are unable to nurse develop strong feelings of inadequacy.

nurses. This still meant that such mothers had little contact with their babies. This final inequity was officially recognized by The Federation a few years ago when it ruled that mothers who were unable to nurse should be permitted to give the formula until their babies were four months old.

Although collective nursing of a baby whose mother has no milk has long been abolished, all nursing takes place within a communal framework. All the nursing babies sleep in the same room, and it is there that they are nursed by their mothers. And since all the mothers adhere to the same feeding schedule, they nurse their babies at the same time as well as in the same place. Hence, from infancy, eating for the sabras is a shared experience, and even the intimacy of mother-love is not private. For the mother, nursing becomes a social occasion in which gossip and conversation can be shared with other mothers while she shares her milk with her baby.

The weaning process begins about the age of three months, at which time a cup of fruit puree, consisting generally of mashed banana and/or apple and orange juice, is given to the baby at his 1:30 P.M. feeding. The mother first offers the baby the "solids," either with a spoon or directly from the cup.[11] In most instances the cup presents no problem because of the gradualness with which it is introduced. If the baby rejects the cup when it is first presented, the mother is instructed by the nurse to remove it immediately. They try again on succeeding days until the baby accepts it, a process which rarely takes more than a week. If the baby continues to reject the cup or spoon, the food is offered to him in a bottle.[12] After the baby either accepts or rejects the solid, the mother nurses him. She continues this process, gradually increasing the amount of fruit, until the nursing is completely eliminated. By the sixth month the babies generally double their weight, which may be taken as a clue to the adequacy of the feeding routine.[13]

Weaning is generally completed by the end of the eighth month for it is rare that the

[11]The cups used are large china cups which are sterilized prior to each feeding by being filled with boiling water.

[12]At the time of observation, however, only two babies—one nine months old, the other eight months—were taking bottles, and this occurred only at the 5:30 P.M. feeding.

[13]The following represents a detailed summary of the weaning process. In the fourth month, the 9:30 A.M. nursing is supplemented with a vegetable puree, consisting generally of tomatoes, carrots, potatoes, and later, ground liver. If the mother has sufficient milk to continue nursing, this diet will continue until the sixth month. If, however, she begins to lose her milk, other feedings will be supplemented as well. At the 5:30 P.M. feeding, for example, the baby is introduced to *daisa*, a combination of very rich milk, cereal (corn starch), and much sugar. Once the weaning is completed, this is the form in which the baby receives all his milk.

At the age of six months, the infant's 10:00 P.M. feeding is eliminated, so that the baby is then fed four times a day. If the mother has sufficient milk, all feedings will include nursing. There is, however, considerable individualization in this routine. If the baby is feeding well and appears to want to continue the night feeding, the mother may continue to nurse him at night beyond his sixth month. If he is not eating well, however, this night nursing may be eliminated even before the sixth month. The procedure adopted depends upon the individual baby's needs. Since most mothers are eager to give up the night nursing, the mother's attitude, as well as the infant's needs, plays its part in this flexibility.

At six months, also, the 10:00 A.M. nursing is eliminated, and egg yolk and butterfat are added to the vegetable puree. By the age of approximately seven months, the 1:30 P.M. nursing is eliminated. By this time, the mother is usually beginning to lose her milk, and she is almost fully reintegrated into her work routine, so that it is difficult for her to come to the Nursery. At this time, a raw egg may be added to the infant's fruit.

At the eighth month, the 5:30 nursing is eliminated, for by this time most mothers have little milk left. If a mother has sufficient milk, however, and wishes to do so, she may continue this nursing until the ninth month. Since the mother does not have to leave her work for this nursing, but comes after she has finished for the day, economic factors do not play a part in determining the conclusion of this nursing period. For most babies, however, this nursing is eliminated by the eighth month, and they receive only *daisa*.

The early morning nursing, at 6:00 A.M., is the last to be eliminated. The reason for this is that the mothers are rested from their night's sleep, and it is assumed that their milk will be both nourishing and sufficient.

mother has enough milk to nurse beyond the beginning of the ninth month. Many babies, moreover, do not wish to nurse beyond that time and become angry if they are offered the breast. Others want either the mother's milk or the solids, but not both. Hence the general policy is to eliminate the mother's breast entirely by no later than the beginning of the ninth month, and the morning meal then consists of daisa.

Although weaning is not completed until the end of the eighth month, the nurses begin to feed the babies before that time. In general this occurs at the sixth month, when the mother gives up the 10:00 A.M. feeding. If a mother wishes to feed her baby herself, however, and if she can leave work at that time, she may do so. Most mothers do wish to feed their babies, so that the shift from mother to nurse as the giver of food is generally a gradual one. If the baby is not taking solids well, however, the nurse will not permit the mother to feed her baby, as he will want to nurse—and the point is to eliminate the nursing at this time.

Once the babies are old enough to be fed by the nurses, they are fed in the following manner. The food is wheeled on a little table into one of the bedrooms (or onto the porch) where the babies are usually fed. The nurses sit in chairs beside the table and feed the babies, who sit on their laps.

The behavior of the nurse while feeding the babies varies. Sometimes she sings to the baby as she feeds him; sometimes she talks to him or coos at him. At other times, when the baby is first learning to eat at the table or when he appears apathetic, the nurse may pretend to drink from the cup (although she does not put her mouth on the cup) and smack her lips, hoping to stimulate the baby to drink. Frequently, however, the nurses converse with each other while they feed the babies. In any event, feeding is a rapid process, seldom lasting more than twelve or fifteen minutes. The babies are usually hungry and eat rapidly and well, and the nurses do not encourage leisurely eating or playing after the meal.

This rapid feeding by the nurse may be contrasted with the more leisurely feeding by the mother, who spends at least forty-five minutes nursing and/or feeding her infant. Even in the last days of weaning, when she gives her baby only solids, she prolongs the feeding. This sudden shift to a rapid feeding constitutes a discontinuity in the feeding experience of the baby.[14]

The babies are first trained to feed themselves at about the age of nine months, which is also the age at which weaning comes to an end. As is true of many aspects of collective education, there is a wide range within which this training occurs. Since the nurses do not have the time to devote to the training of one child, they wait until a group of children has attained the maturity necessary for the training. Hence, although no baby is trained to feed himself before the age of nine months, some do not receive such training until they are twelve months old, at which time a number of babies are trained at the same time. In general, the principle concerning such matters is a simple one: in those training areas which demand a certain stage of maturation, the younger child is not accelerated beyond his maturation state in order to accommodate to the group; rather, the older child is retarded until the younger ones reach the required stage.

When this training begins, the four or five babies who are ready for training are seated at a miniature table—exactly like the ones they will use for the next few years. The nurse places a bowl of food before each child, and permits him to hold a spoon. She feeds each

[14]One may speculate on the relationship between this rapid feeding in infancy and the hurried eating that characterizes the sabra at his meal. The adolescent and adult sabras eat rapidly, and the former leave the table only a few minutes after they sit down.

child in turn. If a baby attempts to feed himself, she encourages him by guiding his hand from the bowl to his mouth; if, however, the baby does not take the initiative in feeding himself, the nurse makes no attempt to encourage him. At the time of observation, none of the five babies who had begun to sit at the table made any attempts to feed themselves. The goal in the Nursery, however, is not actually to train the child in self-feeding, but merely to accustom him to sitting at a table with his own bowl of food and his own spoon, so that when he moves to the Toddlers' House, this arrangement will not be new to him and genuine training can begin.[15]

Because of the generally permissive nature of the nursing and feeding situation, there are seldom any feeding problems in the Nursery. Minor feeding problems do occur, however, when some babies begin to teethe, and they must then be fed with great care. When feeding problems do arise in the Nursery, they are, according to the nurses, almost always the result of a mother's forcing her child to eat. If the mother persists in this behavior, the nurse will intervene and insist that the mother adopt a more permissive attitude. In those rare instances when a mother fails to conform to the nurse's dictum, and the child continues to refuse to eat, the nurse may even refuse to permit the mother to feed her baby.

Two elements of the feeding process in the Nursery—its routinization and its communal nature—result in certain negative consequences for the child. Because the babies are all fed on the same schedule, a baby may cry from hunger for a long time before he is fed. If a nursing baby cries for food when his mother

is at work, nothing can be done about it.[16] Some babies were observed to awaken as much as thirty minutes before the scheduled arrival of their nursing mothers and cry the entire time or else cry themselves to sleep again. In the case of at least one infant, the mother invariably arrived late—as much as half an hour—for her feeding (much to the nurses' indignation), and the baby cried with hunger the entire time. A nurse tried, unsuccessfully, to pacify him. Babies who are already weaned may also cry from hunger and often they too are allowed to cry until their scheduled mealtime. In some instances, however, when a baby cries long before mealtime, and cannot be pacified, the nurse may go to the kitchen to bring him his food early.

Again, since all babies are fed on schedule, it is sometimes necessary to awaken them for a feeding. When this occurs, the baby often cries and becomes irritable. . . .

A second potentially disturbing element in nursing inheres in its communal nature. We have already observed that both nurses and mothers spend much of their feeding periods in conversation with each other. At times these discussions become heated and may cause the infant to stop nursing or to be ignored by the adult who is feeding him. . . .

Toilet and Sexual Behavior

Training in eating and self-feeding is the only formal training that babies receive in the Nursery. In the past, however, when babies remained in the Nursery until the age of eighteen months, it was there that they received their first toilet training. Now that they leave the Nursery at the age of one year, such training does not begin until after they enter the Toddlers' House. "Training" in this con-

---

[15]Soon after the weaning is completed, other foods in addition to those already mentioned are added to the babies' diet. At the 10:00 A.M. feeding, a meatball and mashed potatoes are added to the meal and, at twelve months, biscuit or bread is added. At the 5:30 P.M. feeding, cottage cheese, in a semi-liquid form, and a cookie or piece of bread are added to the meal.

[16]Pacifiers are not used in the Nursery. The nurses know that pacifiers are now commonly used in the United States, but they point out that the problem of accounting for and keeping clean seventeen pacifiers makes their use in the Nursery impractical.

text refers to formal training, for even in the Nursery nurses and parents communicate their attitudes about excretion to the babies; and in some cases, this communication is so effective that the babies modify their behavior as a result. One nurse, for example, explained that she does not like the babies to defecate on her and that, moreover, they don't. At first she was puzzled by this, for she observed that these babies did defecate on their parents and other nurses. Then she remembered that whenever she holds a baby and he seems about to urinate or defecate, she holds him away from her. Thus the babies learn not to excrete on her, for, "They know I don't like it."

In these ways, negative attitudes toward excretion are communicated to the babies long before formal training is instituted. In general, however, the attitude is permissive. In the past, for example, when babies frequently played in the nude, they had many opportunities to play with their feces—which they were allowed to do with impunity. Since they are rarely nude today, they have much less opportunity for such play, but if they do, the response of the nurse is permissive.

This permissive attitude prevails also in the changing of diapers. The nurse's routine obviously prevents her from changing a baby's diaper immediately after he has wet or soiled. The youngest babies seem to find a wet diaper uncomfortable, for they cry until their diapers are changed. As they grow older, however, they apparently become adjusted to what had formerly been an uncomfortable sensation, for they no longer cry.

The same permissive attitude applies to sexual manifestations. Masturbation at this age was rarely observed in the course of this study. The nurses say that it now happens infrequently, but that in the past, when the babies were kept nude for long periods, masturbation was not infrequent. In her fifteen years in the Nursery, the head nurse recalls only one case of a persistent masturbator.

PHYSICAL AND EMOTIONAL HEALTH

In general, it may be said that infants lead relatively secure lives in the Nursery, and that attempts are made by those who care for them to provide them with a high degree of physical and emotional gratification. So far as physical health is concerned the kibbutz provides optimum facilities, prophylactic and therapeutic alike.

In addition to the medical care provided by the kibbutz physician and nurse, the babies' health is supervised by a pediatrician, who comes once a month to examine all of them. Infant mortality is low and, while no statistics were obtained, we were told of only two infant deaths in the recent past, both of which occurred while the infants were still in the hospital. Epidemics are relatively unknown, and the incidence of disease does not appear to be greater in the kibbutz than among infants elsewhere. Immediate quarantine (in separate rooms, separate buildings, or in the hospital) is one factor in the absence of epidemics. Shots and vaccinations for smallpox, typhoid, diphtheria, and tetanus are administered during this first year by the kibbutz nurse.[17]

The babies seem to be emotionally healthy, as well, and one's general impression from observing them is of a group of happy, contented babies. At times, however, they display forms of behavior which are generally regarded as symptoms of disturbance. Thumbsucking, for example, is manifest, and occurs both when the babies are in bed and at play on the floor. Jouncing occurs frequently, particularly at bedtime. Babies jounce when asleep as well as when awake. Some few babies bump their

---

[17]During the period of observation in the Nursery, four infants were ill. One who developed "swollen glands" was hospitalized for a short time; the others who displayed symptoms of fever, excessive crying, and occasional vomiting, were immediately quarantined, and the illnesses lasted only a few days. The nurses reported instances of occasional high temperature, but with one exception there were no serious illnesses.

heads against their beds or against the wall, and the nurses claim they do this when they are frustrated. Although every instance of these symptoms was not recorded, they are noted many times in the record, and babies are characterized as being thumbsuckers, jouncers, and so on. Of the eleven babies who were six months or older at the time of observations, ten were noted as being thumbsuckers. The one exception, a male, was the baby who was nursed for a longer period (through the ninth month) than any other baby in the Nursery at that time. Of the ten babies who sucked their thumbs, four also manifested jouncing behavior, and three were observed to bump their heads against cribs or walls. In sum, three of eleven babies manifested all three symptoms of disturbance, one manifested two symptoms (thumbsucking and jouncing), and six displayed only thumbsucking behavior. One baby manifested no such symptoms. Of the six babies in the Nursery who were less than six months of age, two were characterized by the observer as thumbsuckers.

TRANSITION TO TODDLERS' HOUSE

Since such frustrations as are experienced by infants result primarily from the routinization that must inhere in any collective framework, rather than from lack of interest, understanding, or warmth, it would appear that the first important trauma in the lives of these infants probably does not occur until after they leave the Nursery and enter the Toddlers' House at the age of approximately one year. As a rule, babies do not make this move individually; rather, four or five of the oldest infants who have attained the age of one year are moved as a group, and later, whenever other infants in the Nursery have matured sufficiently, they are added to the group to form the new kevutza of eight toddlers. When they move,

they acquire a new nurse; they move into an entirely new physical environment (a new house); and, for some of them, there is a change in their peer-group as well, for they may be placed in a group with several children whom they either do not know or do not remember.

The education authorities are not unaware of the emotional disturbance that such a configuration of abrupt changes may create for the children, and an attempt is made to mitigate some of the more disturbing consequences by ensuring some continuity in nurses. This the kibbutz hopes to achieve by assigning the new nurse to work in the Nursery for several weeks prior to the babies' departure—thus providing an opportunity for them to form an attachment to her in a familiar and secure setting. There are, nevertheless, occasions when this palliative is not applied, and when the babies have no contact with their new nurse prior to moving to their new dwelling. During the course of this study, for example, the nurse assigned to the new kevutza arrived at the Nursery one morning and abruptly moved the five oldest babies—with no previous preparation for them—to the Toddlers' House.

This abrupt transition from familiar faces, house, and schedule—it can be assumed—is highly disturbing for these babies (it will be recalled that the mere shifting of cribs in the same room is sufficient to upset them). Unfortunately, however, we were unable to observe these five babies at the time of their transition. Some months later, however, one baby was moved from the Nursery to the new kevutza, and he was observed at this time.

Ron (thirteen months) is in the crib in the front yard; the others are in the back. He was moved without any previous preparation and without any previous acquaintance with the nurse. He has just awakened, and looks groggy and crabby. But his face also indicates past crying, and I

(A.G.S.)[18] have the feeling that this was a period of suffering for him. He recognizes me, and I pick him up. The nurse comes out, and I remark that he does not seem happy. She replies that, of course he isn't—everything is still so new for him, and he is not yet adjusted. I take him into the backyard and set him in the pen with the other babies. He looks "at home" immediately, busies himself with the toys there, crawls around, stands, smiles at me, and seems to accept the other babies casually—as they seem to accept him.

Five days after this observation, the first interaction between Ron and any other child in the group was noted. Three days later, he was observed to laugh for the first time. During this initial period, he ate little, slept frequently, and—when the observer was present—rarely left her side. For Ron, she was the only point of continuity, for he had known her in the Nursery.

Some months following this addition to the group, two more babies were added to complete the kevutza of eight, but their move was made with a nurse who had been working with them for several weeks in the Nursery and who then became the assistant nurse in the new kevutza. These two babies had previously been observed in the Nursery, so that their behavior in the Toddlers' House could be compared with their previous behavior. In the Nursery, both babies had been characterized as "active, alert, and outgoing" (although not in equal degree). Immediately after their move, both appeared quiet, passive, and withdrawn (in equal degree). Their initial reactions were in sharp contrast to their previous behavior. . . .

Regrettably, this study came to an end shortly after these two babies were moved, so that we were unable to follow their behavior and to discover how much time elapsed before they became adjusted to their new situation. From the recorded observations, however, it is clear that the passivity and withdrawal with which these babies responded to their move continued for at least two weeks, although toward the end of that period they began to display some interest in the other children and in their surroundings.

---

[18]Since the children's response to the observer may be a function of his sex and general personality characteristics, and since I observed some of the groups and my wife observed others, it is desirable that the reader be aware of the identity of the observer. The initials, A.G.S., refer to my wife; the initials, M.E.S., are mine.

Part Three

The Preschool Years

Chapter 7

Physical Development

ABUSED AND NEGLECTED CHILDREN

Violence against Children

David G. Gil

Strong support for considering child abuse as endemic in American society was provided by the public opinion survey, which revealed that nearly 60 percent of adult Americans thought that "almost anybody could at some time injure a child in his care." That survey also indicated that several millions of children may be subjected every year to a wide range of physical abuse, though only several thousands suffer serious physical injury and a few hundred die as a consequence of abusive attacks.

Editor's Introduction

Jeannie is 6 years old and very pretty. She is also blind. Until 16 months ago she had beautiful blue eyes that sparkled with childish excitement when she talked. Then it happened—her mother, in a fit of anger, threw an empty glass at Jeannie, and it smashed in her face. Jeannie put her hands to her face and inadvertently rubbed glass slivers into her eyes. Her sight was destroyed. She was taken to the hospital by police, called by her mother. Doctors worked over Jeannie in the emergency room. They injected a sedative into her arm to relax her nerves and put her to sleep. Then they were able to examine the tiny round face. They lifted tiny slivers of glass from her chin and cheeks using tweezers. Larger slivers were pulled from her forehead and eyes. Her mother was nearly hysterical in a waiting room near the emergency room. She told her story to a nurse who wrote on a white block of paper. The mother said Jeannie had a sore throat and wouldn't stop whining. Finally, in a rage, the mother said she flung the glass at the girl. (Carr, 1976, p. 1. Reprinted courtesy of the Boston Globe.)

Jeannie is an abused child. She is only one of the abused and neglected children in our country. There are estimated to be about 3 million such children. Child abuse has become a national tragedy.

What is the difference between abuse and neglect? According to Gil, abuse is "the intentional, nonaccidental use of physical force, or intentional, nonaccidental acts of omission on the part of a parent or other caretaker interacting with a child in his care, aimed at hurting, injuring or destroying that child" (1970, p. 6). A neglected child is one whose physical or emotional condition is seriously impaired as the result of the failure to provide food, shelter, clothing, and protection or medical care which are necessary to sustain life.

Most abusive parents love or care about their children and are ashamed and concerned about what they did. According to authorities in the area of child abuse, almost any parent is a potential child abuser under certain stress conditions. It is just that the vast majority are able to cope with stress and redirect their angry feelings elsewhere, away from the child, to the benefit of both the child and society.

Gil states that one of the most important insights gained from the nationwide study reported in *Violence against Children* was that abusive treatment toward children is not a rare occurrence. He feels that it may be endemic in our society because of a child-rearing philosophy which encourages the use of physical force in disciplining children.

Furthermore, it became clear that abuse of children committed or tolerated by society as a whole, by permitting millions of children to grow up under conditions of severe deprivation, was a much more serious social problem than abusive acts toward children committed by individual caretakers. Not surprisingly it was also learned that while child abuse is known to occur among all groups in the population, children living in deprived circumstances were, for a variety of reasons, more likely than other children to be subjected to abusive acts by their caretakers.

Thus he feels that the dynamics of child abuse are rooted in the faults of our society, and that the notion that this problem is the result of individual psychopathology is too narrow an interpretation of the causes of child abuse.

Other researchers—notably Kempe and Helfer (1971), pioneers in the investigation of child abuse—disagree. They state that in the histories of abusing parents we find histories of abuse to the parent, either in the form of physical abuse or intense demands or criticisms from their own parents. This pattern repeats itself when the children grow up and have children of their own. Most of these abusive parents were deprived of love in their own infancy; they expect their infants to satisfy their emotional needs, and children who do not satisfy these requirements are punished.

Gil believes that the conventional treatment which is derived from the view of abuse as a function of individual pathology might aid some children and their families, but it would not prevent or even reduce significantly the overall incidence of child abuse. He feels that we must change the prevailing child-rearing philosophy which sanctions physical force in disciplining children, and we must eliminate poverty, which allows so many children to be at risk for abuse and neglect. Although his position is arguable, it seems that some combination of these approaches might provide the most fruitful solution. Regardless of whether the abusive parents are seen as victims of their culture or of their childhood background, changes in both areas would help to decrease the number of beaten and terrified children who produce some of our most heartbreaking statistics.

REFERENCES

Carr, R. B. Child abuse—a growing U.S. tragedy. *Boston Globe*, March 30, 1976.

Gil, D. G. *Violence against children: Physical child abuse in the United States.* Cambridge, Mass.: Harvard University Press, 1970.

Kempe, H., & Helfer, R. E. *Helping the battered child and his family.* Philadelphia: Lippincott, 1971.

Pamela Cantor

American society has often been described as child-centered. This idealized image seems, however, contradicted by various destructive aspects of child life in the United States such as widespread poverty, hunger, malnutrition, neglect and exploitation; stultifying education and inadequate health care; and an ample measure of physical violence inflicted upon children in their homes, in schools, in child care facilities, and in various children's institutions. There can be little doubt that all these phenomena tend to block opportunities for growth and development of many millions of children, and that they prevent the realization of their innate human potentialities.

Physical violence against children has attracted considerable interest during recent decades in this country and overseas among pediatricians, psychiatrists, social workers, lawyers, public authorities, communications media, and the general public. Yet in spite of this widespread interest and concern, which is reflected in numerous studies and demonstra-

tion projects, conferences, seminars, articles and books, the underlying dynamics of physical child abuse are still insufficiently understood, and its real incidence and prevalence rates throughout the population and among various population segments are unknown (U.S. Children's Bureau, 1969).

The somewhat sensational concern with individual cases of child abuse seems, at times, to have a quality of "scapegoating," for it enables the public to express self-righteous feelings of anger, disgust, resentment, and condemnation toward an individual abusing parent while the entire society is constantly guilty of massive acts of "societal abuse" of millions of children, about which relatively little is said, and even less has been done in recent decades.

One consequence of the extensive interest in child abuse seems to have been the now widely help assumption that its incidence was on the increase. This claim, however, can neither be substantiated nor refuted since no systematic data are available in the form of time series on incidence. One other consequence of the professional and public concern with child abuse was the swift passage throughout the United States of legislation requiring or urging physicians, hospitals and others to report child abuse incidents to appropriate local public authorities. This legislation had been initiated and promoted vigorously by the United States Children's Bureau in order to protect children who had been abused, and to prevent further abuse of these same children and of others in their families. However, since the dynamics of child abuse were not adequately understood at the time reporting legislation was enacted, no proven strategies and policies for prevention and treatment were incorporated into these laws, and their impact on incidence rates is consequently not expected to be significant (U.S. Children's Bureau, 1962; 1966).

The failure of clinical investigators and of various professional groups to unravel the complex underlying dynamics of violence against children in American society seems due mainly to a significant, built-in bias of the social and behavioral sciences, and of the general system of beliefs of our society. This bias is the deeply rooted, yet untested, assumption that behavioral manifestations which are viewed by the majority of society as "deviant" are the result of personal characteristics, failings, problems, maladjustment, or dysfunction. Whatever label is used, the source of all deviance is conceived to be in the individual or his primary group, his family, rather than in characteristics of the society. This general conception of the dynamics of deviance seems to derive from a politically "conservative" premise, according to which American social structure is basically sound except, perhaps, for a few minor, necessary adjustments. Since the design and the findings of social and behavioral research tend to depend on the questions and hypotheses investigated, and since these questions and hy-

potheses in turn tend to be generated within the framework of the general assumptions of a scientific discipline and its societal context, it is not surprising that most investigations of child abuse in the United States were clinically oriented, and found this phenomenon to be the result of psychological disorders of the perpetrators or, at times, of the abused children themselves, and/or certain pathological aspects of family relationships. This interpretation of the causal context of child abuse is matched logically by intervention strategies aimed mainly at changing the disorders of individuals and the pathology of families, rather than aspects of the social context in which these "disordered" individuals and "pathological" families live.

The series of nationwide studies of physical child abuse discussed here tried to avoid the limitations inherent in the foregoing assumptions concerning the "individual as source" of behavioral deviance. The causal model guiding these investigations was that behavioral phenomena perceived to be deviant tend to result from interaction effects of societal and individual forces rather than from one or the other of these sets of forces acting independently of each other. The corresponding intervention model or social policy perspective of these studies is that intervention at the societal level is likely to be more effective in terms of prevention than intervention at the individual level since intervention aimed at modifying the societal force field can be expected to have a more far-reaching impact on the causal context of deviance posited here. This intervention model does, of course, not preclude direct protection and treatment of individuals and family groups involved in incidents of child abuse or in other deviant phenomena.

STUDY DESIGN AND DEFINITION OF SUBJECT

The general causal model of deviance sketched here led to a comprehensive psychosocial-cultural conception of child abuse. To study this phenomenon from such a perspective required an epidemiologically oriented survey design involving systematic review of large numbers of child abuse incidents from all over the country rather than a clinically oriented design involving intensive analysis of small samples in specified settings and localities. Accordingly, the nationwide surveys gathered standardized information on every incident of child abuse reported through legal channels throughout the United States during 1967 and 1968, nearly 13,000 incidents. This broadly based survey was supplemented by more comprehensive case studies of nearly 1400 incidents reported during 1967 in a representative sample of 39 cities and counties. Further data sources, especially concerning the cultural roots of child abuse, were interviews in October of 1965 with 1520 adults from across the country selected at random so as to be representative of the entire U.S. adult population, and a six months survey during 1965 of daily and periodical newspapers and magazines published throughout the United States.

Studies of child abuse were hampered in the past not only by a certain preconception of the causal context but also by the lack of an unambiguous definition of the phenomenon itself. Definitions were usually derived from observable consequences of violent acts against children rather than from the acts themselves and the underlying behavioral dynamics. However, consequences of abusive acts seem to be an inappropriate basis for developing a conceptually valid definition since such consequences are likely to be affected by chance factors as much as by the intentional behavior of perpetrators, and since their evaluation depends on subjective standards or judgments.

In an effort to minimize ambiguity in defining physical abuse of children, the following conceptual definition was developed. This definition is based only on the behavior of perpetrators, rather than on the variable consequences of such behavior.

> Physical abuse of children is intentional, nonaccidental use of physical force, or intentional, non-accidental acts of omission, on the part of a parent or other caretaker in interaction with a child in his care, aimed at hurting, injuring, or destroying that child.

The foregoing definition seems sound conceptually, but is not completely satisfactory as an operational definition since it may not always be possible to differentiate between intentional and accidental behavior. Also, the presence of intentional elements in the behavior of perpetrators does not imply complete absence of chance elements. An added difficulty is the fact that behavior which appears to be accidental may be determined in part by "unconsciously intentional" elements. Thus, while the boundary between "pure" accidents and physical abuse can be drawn clearly on a conceptual level, it may, at times, be difficult to differentiate between them without examination of the motivations which underlie manifest behavior in given incidents.

Apart from the difficulty of ascertaining the presence of elements of intentionality, which, by definition, constitute a *sine qua non* of child abuse, the definition reduces ambiguity by including *all* use of physical force and *all* acts of omission aimed at hurting, injuring, or destroying a child, irrespective of the degree of seriousness of the act, the omission, and/or the outcome. Thus, the relativity of personal and community standards and judgments is avoided.

SELECTED FINDINGS FROM THE NATIONWIDE SURVEYS

The Scope of Child Abuse

During 1967 child abuse registries throughout the United States received 9,563 reports. The number of reports rose to 10,931 in 1968.

Screening the reports against the conceptual definition of physical child abuse resulted in the elimination of over 37 percent of the 1967 cohort and of over 39 percent of the 1968 cohort, leaving 5,993 children for 1967 and 6,617 for 1968. The post-screening nationwide reporting rate per 100,000 children under age 18 was thus 8.4 in 1967 and 9.3 in 1968. . . .

Characteristics of Legally Reported Abused Children

Slightly more than half the children reported as abused during 1967 and 1968 were boys. Boys outnumbered girls in every age group under age 12, but were outnumbered by girls among teen-aged victims of child abuse. Shifts in the sex distribution during different ages seem to reflect culturally determined attitudes. Girls are viewed as more conforming than boys during childhood and physical force tends to be used less frequently in rearing them. However, during adolescence parental anxieties concerning dating behavior of girls lead to increasing restrictions, conflicts, and use of physical force in asserting parental control. With boys physical force tends to be used more readily prior to adolescence. However, during adolescence, as the physical strength of boys begins to match their parents' strength, the use of physical force in disciplining boys tends to diminish.

The age distribution of the reported children indicates that physical abuse is not limited to early childhood. Over 75 percent of the reported victims were over two years of age, and nearly half of them were over six years. Nearly one-fifth were teen-agers. Age distribution was similar for all ethnic groups.

Non-white children were over-represented in the study cohorts. Nationwide reporting rates per 100,000 white children were 6.7, and per 100,000 non-white children 21.0. This over-representation of non-white children seems due partly to reporting bias but mainly to the higher incidence of poverty and poverty related social and psychological deviance, and to the higher rate of fatherless homes and large families among non-white population segments, all of which were found to be strongly associated with child abuse. Finally, the possibility of real differences in child rearing practices among different ethnic groups cannot be ruled out as a contributing factor to observed differences in reporting rates. Such differences in the use of physical force in child rearing may reflect the violence inflicted upon many generations of non-white minorities in American society.

About 29 percent of the children revealed deviations in social interaction and general functioning during the year preceding the abusive incident, nearly 14 percent suffered from deviations in physical functioning during the same time span, and nearly eight percent revealed deviations in intellectual functioning. Among the school-age children over 13 percent attended special classes for retarded children or were in grades below their age level. Nearly three percent of the school-aged children had never attended school. Nearly 10 percent of children in the sample cohort had lived with foster families sometime during their lives prior to the incident, and over three percent had lived in child care or correctional institutions. Over five percent had appeared before Juvenile Courts on other than traffic offenses. Taken together, these items suggest a level of deviance in excess of the level of deviance of any group of children selected at random from the population at large.

Over 60 percent of the children had a history of prior abuse. It thus seems that physical abuse of children is more often than not an indication of a prevailing pattern of caretaker-child interaction in a given home rather than of an isolated incident. This impression is supported also by data on involvement in previous abuse by parents, siblings, and other perpetrators.

The Families of Abused Children

Nearly 30 percent of the abused children lived in female-headed households. The child's own father lived in the home in 46 percent of the cases, and a stepfather in nearly 20 percent. Over two percent of the children lived in foster homes, and 0.3 percent lived with adoptive parents. The child's own mother was not living in his home in over 12 percent. Ten percent of the mothers were single, nearly 20 percent were separated, divorced, deserted, or widowed, and over two-thirds were living with a spouse. The homes of non-white children were less frequently intact than those of white children. The data on family structure suggest an association between physical abuse of children and deviance from normative family structure, which seems especially strong for non-white children.

The age distribution of parents of abused children does not support observations according to which parents tend to be extremely young.

The proportion of families with four or more children was nearly twice as high among the families of the reported abused children than among all families with children under 18 in the U.S. population, and the proportion of small families was much larger in the U.S. population. The proportion of larger families among non-white families in the study was significantly higher than among white families.

Educational and occupational levels of parents were markedly lower than of the general population. Non-white parents ranked lower on these items than white ones. Nearly half the fathers of the abused children were not employed throughout the year, and about 12 percent were actually unemployed at the time of the abusive act. Unemployment rates were higher for non-white fathers. Table 1 shows the distribution of income for all sample families, for white, black and Puerto Rican families in the sample, and for all families in the United States.

Compared to all families in the United States, the income of families of abused children was very low and that of families of non-white abused children even lower. At the time of the abusive incident over 37 percent of the families were receiving public assistance. Altogether nearly 60 percent of the families had received public assistance at some time preceding the abusive incident.

Data concerning the personal history of the parents of the reported abused children suggested a level of deviance in areas of psychosocial functioning which exceeds deviance levels in the general population.

Table 1   Family Income 1967

Income in dollars	Percent of Sample Cohort				Percent of all U.S. Families*
	All families	White	Negro	Puerto Rican	
under 3,000	22.3	17.7	24.8	34.5	12.5
3,000 to 4,999	26.1	21.9	28.6	41.9	12.8
5,000 to 6,999	16.2	18.5	14.1	9.7	16.1
7,000 to 9,999	12.7	15.9	11.7	5.4	24.3
10,000 to 14,999	2.6	3.1	1.9	1.1	22.4
15,000 and over	0.4	0.9	0.2	0.0	12.0
unknown	19.8	22.2	18.6	7.5	0.0
	N=1380	N=536	N=630	N=93	N=49,834,000

*Consumer Income, Bureau of the Census, Current Population Reports, Series P-60, No. 59, April 1969.

The Incidents and the Circumstances Surrounding Them

In nearly 50 percent of the incidents a mother or stepmother was the perpetrator and in about 40 percent a father. However, since about 30 percent of the homes were female-headed, the involvement rate of fathers was actually higher than that of mothers. Two-thirds of incidents in homes with fathers or stepfathers present were committed by fathers or stepfathers, while mothers or step-mothers were the perpetrators in less than half the incidents occurring in homes with mothers or stepmothers present. Over 70 percent of the children were abused by a biological parent, nearly 14 percent by a stepparent, less than one percent by an adoptive parent, two percent by a foster parent, about one percent by a sibling, four percent by other relatives, and nearly seven percent by an unrelated caretaker. Fifty-one percent of the children were abused by a female perpetrator.

Perpetrators tended to have little education and a low socioeconomic status. About 61 percent of them were members of minority groups, 56.8 percent had shown deviations in social and behavioral functioning during the year preceding the abuse incident and about 12.3 percent had been physically ill during that year. Nearly 11 percent showed deviations in intellectual functioning, 7.1 percent had been in mental hospitals some time prior to the incident, 8.4 percent before Juvenile Courts, and 7.9 percent in foster care. Under 14 percent had a criminal record. About 11 percent had been victims of abuse during their childhood, and 52.5 percent had been perpetrators of abuse prior to the current incident.

The . . . tabulation of injuries is based on medical verification in 80.2 percent of the cases and the reliability of the diagnoses is therefore quite satisfactory. The injuries were considered to be "not serious" in 53.3 percent. They were rated "serious, no permanent damage expected" in 36.5 percent, "serious with permanent damage" in 4.6 percent, and fatal in 3.4 percent. It is noteworthy that 90 percent of the reported incidents were not expected to leave any lasting physical effects on the children, and that over half the incidents were not considered to be serious at all. Even if allowance is made for under-reporting, especially of fatal cases, one must question the view of many concerned professional and lay persons, according to which physical abuse of children constitutes a major cause of death and maiming of children throughout the nation.

Analysis of the relationship between severity of injury and age reveals that injuries of children under age 3 were serious or fatal in 65 percent of the cases while injuries of children over age 3 were serious in 35 percent of the cases only.

Severity of injuries was also found to be related to ethnicity. The injuries of white children were judged not serious in 61.6 percent and serious or fatal in 35.2 percent. The injuries of Negro and Puerto Rican children were judged not serious in 47.3 percent and serious in 52.0 percent.

While severity of injury was thus associated with the age and the ethnic background of the victim, it was found not to be associated with the victim's sex. Severity of injury was about equal for boys and girls.

Several less pronounced associational trends were revealed concerning the severity of injuries sustained by abused children. Severe injuries were more likely to be inflicted by parents and other perpetrators under age 25 than by older ones, by women than by men and especially by single women. Parents who had appeared before Juvenile Courts and who experienced some form of foster care were more likely than other parents to inflict serious injury. Finally, injuries were more likely to be serious or fatal in families whose annual income was under $3,500.

The extent of medical treatment is another crude indicator of the degree of severity of physical abuse sustained by children. The injuries of nearly 60 percent of the children did not seem to require hospitalization, and in nearly 25 percent no medical treatment seemed indicated at all. Of those requiring hospitalization, over 41.7 percent were discharged in less than one week. Hospitalization beyond one week was required by 21.3 percent of the children, and this group seems to represent the segment of severe injury of the child abuse spectrum.

Official Actions Following Abuse

. . . Over 36 percent of the abused children were placed away from their families after the abuse incidents. In 15.4 percent of the cases, not only the victims but also siblings living in the same homes were placed away from their families. Placement away from the child's home was more likely to be used when injuries were serious and when children had been abused before. Homemaker service was made available to 2.2 percent of the families, and counseling services were made available to 71.9 percent.

The suspected perpetrators were indicted in 17.3 percent of the incidents. They were convicted in 13.1 percent and jailed in 7.2 percent. Court action was more likely to be taken when children were seriously or fatally injured.

A TYPOLOGY OF CHILD ABUSE

Based on observations throughout the study, the conclusion was reached that physical abuse of children is not a uniform phenomenon with one set of causal factors, but a multidimensional phenomenon. In order to explore the many possible contributing causal contexts which may precipitate incidents of physical abuse of children, lists were prepared of circumstances which may or may not have been present in any given case. The items on the checklist were not designed to be mutually exclusive. Associations between two or more types were therefore expected in many incidents. Responses concerning the circumstances of abuse of 1,380 cases of a sample cohort suggest the following observations concerning types of physical child abuse:

One major type involves incidents developing out of disciplinary action taken by caretakers who respond in uncontrolled anger to real or perceived misconduct of a child. Nearly 63 percent of the cases were checked as "immediate or delayed response to specific act of child," and nearly 73 percent were checked as "inadequately controlled anger of perpetrator."

A second important type seems to involve incidents which derive from a general attitude of resentment and rejection on the part of the perpetrator towards a child. In these cases, not a specific act but the "whole person," or a specific quality of the person such as sex, looks, capacities, circumstances of birth, etc., are the object of rejection. In these cases, too, specific acts of the child may precipitate the acting out of the underlying attitude of rejection. The item "Resentment, rejection of child . . ." was checked in 34.1 percent of the cases. This type was associated with "Repeated abuse of same child by perpetrator," and also "Battered child syndrome" (Kempe, 1962).

A third type is defined by the item "Persistent behavioral atypicality of child, e.g., hyperactivity, high annoyance potential, etc." Cases checked positively on this item may be considered as child-initiated or child-provoked abuse. This item was checked in 24.5 percent of the cases. This type was found to be associated with "Misconduct of child."

A fourth type is physical abuse of a child developing out of a quarrel between his caretakers. The child may come to the aid of one parent, or he may just happen to be in the midst of a fight between the parents. Sometimes the child may even be the object of the fight. The item reflecting this type was checked in 11.3 percent of the cases. It was associated with "Alcoholic intoxication of perpetrator."

A fifth type is physical abuse coinciding with a perpetrator's sexual attack on a child. This item was checked in 0.6 percent of the cases. It was found to be associated with the sixth type, "Sadistic gratification of the perpetrator."

The seventh type may be referred to as sadism sublimated to the level of child rearing ideology. The item was worded on the checklist: "Self-definition of perpetrator as stern, authoritative disciplinarian." It was checked in 31.0 percent of the cases, and was associated with the first type.

Type Number 8 was called "Marked mental and/or emotional deviation of perpetrator." It was checked in 46.1 percent of the cases and was associated with "Mounting stress on perpetrator."

Type Number 9 is the simultaneous occurrence of abuse and neglect. Contrary to observations of many investigators who consider abuse and neglect as mutually exclusive phenomena, this type was checked in 33.7 percent of the cases. It was associated with type Number 2, "Resentment, rejection. . . ."

"The battered child syndrome" (Kempe, 1962) constitutes type Number 10. This item was checked in 13.6 percent of the cases.

"Alcoholic intoxication of the perpetrator at the time of the abusive act" constitutes type Number 11. It was checked as present in 12.9 percent of the cases and was associated with "Caretaker quarrel," and "Mother temporarily absent—perpetrator male."

A very important type is Number 12, "Mounting stress on perpetrator due to life circumstances." It was checked as present in 59.0 percent of the cases and was associated with "Mental, emotional deviation of perpetrator."

Type Number 13 is an important "typical constellation" which frequently tends to precipitate physical abuse of a child: The mother or substitute are temporarily absent from the home, working or shopping, or for some other reason, and the child is left in the care of a boyfriend or some other male caretaker. This type was the context for the abuse in 17.2 percent of the cases and seems to deserve special attention in preventive efforts. It was found to be associated with "Physical and sexual abuse coincide," "Sadistic gratification of perpetrator," and "Alcoholic intoxication."

The last type, Number 14, is similar to type Number 13, but quantitatively much less important as a typical context for child abuse. It is the temporary absence of the mother or substitute during which the child is cared for and abused by a female baby-sitter. This item was checked in 2.7 percent of the cases.

The foregoing typology is quite crude. However, it may be of interest to note that this typology seems to have successfully covered most of the circumstances of abuse observed by social workers who completed the checklists. This is reflected in the fact that a residual item—"other circumstances"—was checked only in 2.7 percent of the cases.

Data underlying the foregoing empirically derived typology were subjected to a factor analysis. The final results of this analysis suggest that the typology can be reduced to the following underlying seven factors of legally reported physical child abuse:

1. Psychological Rejection
2. Angry and Uncontrolled Disciplinary Response
3. Male Babysitter Abuse
4. Personality Deviance and Reality Stress
5. Child Originated Abuse
6. Female Babysitter Abuse
7. Caretaker Quarrel

In a certain sense, the seven factors of the spectrum of legally reported physical abuse of children summarize the findings of the nationwide surveys by reducing them into a concentrated paradigm which reflects the underlying structure of the phenomenon. A more comprehensive conceptual summation of these findings, and a set of recommendations derived from them, are presented below.

A CONCEPTUAL MODEL OF PHYSICAL CHILD ABUSE

1 Culturally Sanctioned Use of Physical Force in Child Rearing One important conclusion of the nationwide surveys was that physical abuse of children as defined here is not a rare and unusual occurrence in our society, and that by itself it should therefore not be considered as sufficient evidence of "deviance" of the perpetrator, the child, or the family. Physical abuse appears to be endemic in American society since our cultural norms of child rearing do not preclude the use of a certain measure of physical force toward children by adults caring for them. Rather, such use tends to be encouraged in subtle, and at times not so subtle, ways by "professional experts" in child rearing, education, and medicine; by the press, radio and television; and by professional and popular publications. Furthermore, children are not infrequently subjected to physical abuse in the public domain in such settings as schools, child care facilities, foster homes, correctional and other children's institutions, and even in juvenile courts.

Strong support for considering child abuse as endemic in American society was provided by the public opinion survey, which revealed that nearly 60 percent of adult Americans thought that "almost anybody could at some time injure a child in his care." That survey also indicated that several millions of children may be subjected every year to a wide range of physical abuse, though only several thousands suffer serious physical injury and a few hundred die as a consequence of abusive attacks. Against the background of public

sanction of the use of violence against children, and the endemic scope of the prevalence of such cases, it should surprise no one that extreme incidents will occur from time to time in the course of "normal" child rearing practices. It should be noted that in most incidents of child abuse the caretakers involved are "normal" individuals exercising their prerogative of disciplining a child whose behavior they find in need of correction. While some of these adults may often go farther than they intended because of anger and temporary loss of self-control, and/or because of chance events, their behavior does, nevertheless, not exceed the normative range of disciplining children as defined by the existing culture. Moreover, their acts are usually not in conflict with any law since parents, as well as teachers and other child care personnel, are in many American jurisdictions permitted to use a "reasonable" amount of corporal punishment. For children are not protected by law against bodily attack in the same way as are adults and, consequently, do not enjoy "equal protection under the law" as guaranteed by the XIVth Amendment to the U.S. Constitution.

While, then, culturally sanctioned and patterned use of physical force in child rearing seems to constitute the basic causal dimension of all violence against children in American society, it does not explain many specific aspects of this phenomenon, especially its differential incidence rates among different population segments. Several additional causal dimensions need therefore be considered in interpreting the complex dynamics of physical child abuse.

2 Difference in Child Rearing Patterns Among Social Strata and Ethnic Groups Different social and economic strata of society, and different ethnic and nationality groups tend to differ for various environmental and cultural reasons in their child rearing philosophies and practices, and consequently in the extent to which they approve of corporal punishment of children. These variations in child rearing styles among social and economic strata and ethnic groups constitute a second set of causal dimensions of child abuse, and are reflected in significant variations in incidence rates among these strata and groups. Thus, for instance, incidence rates tend to be negatively correlated with education and income. Also, certain ethnic groups reveal characteristic incidence patterns. Some American Indian tribes will never use physical force in disciplining their children while the incidence rates of child abuse are relatively high among American blacks and Puerto Ricans.

Lest the higher incidence rates among black and Puerto Rican minority groups be misinterpreted, it should be remembered that as a result of centuries of discrimination, non-white ethnic minority status tends to be associated in American society wth low educational achievement and low income. The incidence rates of child abuse among these minority groups are likely to reflect this fact, as much as their specific cultural patterns. Furthermore, exposure of these minority groups to various forms of external societal violence to which they could not respond in kind is likely to have contributed over time to an increase in the level of frustration-generated violence directed against their own members. Relatively high rates of homicide among members of these minority groups seem to support this interpretation.

Higher reporting rates of physical child abuse, and especially of more serious incidents among the poor and among non-white minority groups may reflect biased reporting procedures. It may be true that the poor and non-whites are more likely to be reported than middle class and white population groups for anything they do or fail to do. At the same time there may also be considerable under-reporting or reportable transgressions not only among middle class and white population groups but also among the poor and the non-white minorities. The net effect of reporting

bias and of overall and specific under-reporting with respect to child abuse can at this time not be estimated.

It should not be overlooked, however, that life in poverty and in minority group ghettoes tends to generate many stressful experiences which are likely to become precipitating factors of child abuse by weakening a caretaker's psychological mechanisms of self-control and contributing, thus, to the uninhibited discharge of his aggressive and destructive impulses toward physically powerless children. The poor and members of ethnic minority groups seem to be subject to many of the conditions and forces which may lead to abusive behavior toward children in other groups of the population and, in addition to this, they seem to be subject to the special environmental stresses and strains associated with socioeconomic deprivation and discrimination. This would suggest that the significantly higher reporting rates for poor and non-white segments of the population reflect a real underlying higher incidence rate among these groups.

It should also be noted that the poor and non-whites tend to have more children per family unit and less living space. They also tend to have fewer alternatives than other population groups for avoiding or dealing with aggressive impulses toward their children. The poor tend to discharge aggressive impulses more directly as they seem less inhibited in expressing feelings through action. These tendencies are apparently learned through lower class and ghetto socialization, which tends to differ in this respect from middle class socialization and mores.

Middle class parents, apparently as a result of exposure to modern psychological theories of child rearing, tend to engage more than lower class parents in verbal interaction with their children, and to use psychological approaches in disciplining them. It may be noted, parenthetically, that verbal and psychological interaction with children may at times be as violent and abusive in its effects, or even more so, than the use of physical force in disciplining them. Life in middle class families tends to generate tensions and pressures characteristic of the dominant individualistic and competitive value orientations of American society, and these pressures may also precipitate violence against children. However, middle class families are spared the more devastating daily tensions and pressures of life in poverty. They also tend to have fewer children, more living space, and more options to relax, at times, without their children. All this would suggest a lower real incidence rate of physical child abuse among middle class families.

Deviance and Pathology in Bio-Psycho-Social Functioning of Individuals and Families

A further set of causal dimensions of violence against children involves a broad range of deviance in biological, psychological, and social functioning of caretakers, children in their care, and of entire family units. This is the causal context which had been identified and stressed by most clinical investigators of child abuse. It is important to note that this dimension of child abuse is by no means independent of the basic cultural dimension discussed above. The choice of symptoms through which intra-psychic conflicts are expressed by members of a society tends to be influenced by the culture of that society. Symptoms of personality deviance involve often exaggerated levels of culturally sanctioned trends. It would thus seem that violent acts against children would less likely be symptoms of personality disorders in a society which did not sanction the use of physical force in rearing its young.

The presence of this third dimension of child abuse was reflected in findings from our surveys, which revealed relatively high rates of deviance in bio-psycho-social circumstances and functioning of children and adults involved in many reported incidents. Often manifestations of such deviance had been observed during the year preceding an incident. Deviance in functioning of individuals was also matched by high rates of deviance in family structure reflected in a high proportion of female-headed households, and of households from which the biological fathers of the abused children were absent.

Environmental Chance Events

A final, but not insignificant causal dimension of child abuse is environmental chance events which may transform "acceptable" disciplinary measures into serious and "unacceptable" outcomes. It is thus obvious that physical abuse of children, like so many other social problems, is a multidimensional phenomenon rather than a uni-dimensional one with a single set of causal factors. This multidimensional conception of child abuse and its dynamics suggests a corresponding multidimensional approach to the prevention or reduction of the incidence rate of this destructive phenomenon.

IMPLICATIONS FOR SOCIAL POLICY

Violence against children constitutes a severe infringement of their rights as members of society. Since distribution of rights in a society is a key aspect of its social policies, modifications of these policies are necessary if the rights of children to physical safety are to be assured (Gil, 1970). For social policies to be effective they must be based on a causal theory concerning the etiology of the condition which is to be corrected or prevented. Accordingly, social policies aimed at protecting the rights of children to bodily safety should be designed around the causal dimensions of child abuse presented in the conceptual model of this phenomenon.

Since cultural sanctions of the use of physical force in child rearing constitute the common core of all physical abuse of children in American society, efforts aimed at gradually changing this aspect of the prevailing child rearing philosophy, and developing clear-cut cultural prohibitions and legal sanctions against such use of physical force, are likely to produce over time the strongest possible reduction of the incidence and prevalence of physical abuse of children.

Suggesting to forego the use of physical force in rearing children does not mean that inherently non-social traits of children need not be modified in the course of socialization. It merely means that non-violent, constructive, educational measures would have to replace physical force. It needs to be recognized that giving up the use of physical force against children may not be easy for adults who were subjected to physical force and violence in their own childhood and who have integrated the existing value system of American society. Moreover, children can sometimes be very irritating and provocative in their behavior and may strain the tolerance of adults to the limit. Yet, in spite of these realities, which must be acknowledged and faced openly, society needs to work toward the gradual reduction, and eventual complete elimination, of the use of physical force against children if it intends to protect their basic right of security from physical attack.

As a first, concrete step toward developing eventually comprehensive legal sanctions against the use of physical force in rearing children, the Congress and legislatures of the states could outlaw corporal punishment in schools, juvenile courts, correctional institutions and other child care facilities. Such legislation would assure children the same constitutional protection against physical attack outside their homes as the law provides for adult members of society. Moreover, such legislation is likely to affect child rearing attitudes and practices in American homes, for it would symbolize society's growing rejection of violence against children.

To avoid misinterpretations it should be noted here that rejecting corporal punishment does not imply favoring unlimited permissiveness in rearing children. To grow up successfully, children require a sense of security which is inherent in non-arbitrary structures and limits. Understanding adults can establish such structures and limits through love, patience, firmness, consistency, and rational authority. Corporal punishment seems devoid of constructive educational value since it cannot provide that sense of security and nonarbitrary authority. Rarely, if ever, is corporal punishment administered for the benefit of an attacked child, for usually it serves the immediate needs of the attacking adult who is seeking relief from his uncontrollable anger and stress.

The multiple links between poverty and racial discrimination and physical abuse of children suggest that one essential route toward reducing the incidence and prevalence of child abuse is the elimination of poverty and of structural social inequalities. This objective could be approached through the establishment of a guaranteed decent annual income for all, at least at the level of the Bureau of Labor Statistics' "low" standard of living. No doubt this is only a partial answer to the complex issue of preventing violence toward children, but perhaps a very important part of the total answer, and certainly that part without which other preventive efforts may be utterly futile. Eliminating poverty by equalizing opportunities and rights, and by opening up access for all to all levels of the social status system, also happens to be that part of the answer for which this nation possesses the necessary know-how and resources, provided we were willing to introduce changes in our priorities of resource development, and to redistribute national wealth more equitably.

Deviance and pathology in biological, psychological, and social functioning of individuals and of family units were identified as a third set of forces which contribute to the incidence and prevalence of physical abuse of children. These conditions tend to be strongly associated with poverty and racial discrimination, and, therefore, eliminating poverty and discrimination are likely to reduce, though by no means to eliminate, the incidence and prevalence of these various dysfunctional phenomena. The following measures, aimed at the secondary and tertiary prevention and amelioration of these conditions and their consequences, and at the strengthening of individual and family functioning, should be available in every community as components of a comprehensive program for reducing the incidence of physical abuse of children, and also for helping individuals and families once abuse has occurred:

1 Comprehensive family planning programs including the repeal of all legislation concerning medical abortions: The availability of family planning resources and medical abortions are likely to reduce the number of unwanted and rejected children, who are known to be frequently victims of severe physical abuse and even infanticide. . . .

2 Family life education and counseling programs for adolescents and adults in preparation for, and after marriage. . . .

3 A comprehensive, high quality, neighborhood based, national health service, financed through general tax revenue, and geared not only to the treatment of acute and chronic illness, but also the promotion and maintenance of maximum feasible physical and mental health for everyone.

4 A range of high quality, neighborhood based social services geared to the reduction of environmental stresses on family life and especially on mothers who carry major responsibility for the child rearing function. Any measure which would reduce these stresses would also indirectly reduce the incidence rate of child abuse. . . . It should be recognized, however, that unless a decent income is assured to all families, these social services are unlikely to achieve their objectives.

5 Every community needs also a system of social services and child care facilities geared to assisting families and children who cannot live together because of severe relationships and/or reality problems. Physically abused children belong frequently to this category.

The measures proposed herewith are aimed at different causal dimensions of violence against children. The first set would attack the culturally determined core of the phenomenon; the second set would attack and eliminate major conditions to which child abuse is linked in many ways; the third set approaches the causes of child abuse indirectly. It would be futile to argue the relative merits of these approaches as all three are important. The basic question seems to be, not which measure to select for combating child abuse, but whether American society is indeed committed to assuring equal rights to all its children, and to eradicate child abuse in any form, abuse perpetrated by individual caretakers, as well as abuse perpetrated collectively by society. Our affluent society certainly seems to possess the resources and the skills to eradicate the massive forms of abuse committed by society collectively as well as the physical violence perpetrated by individuals and societal institutions against children in their care.

REFERENCES

Gil, D. G. A systematic approach to social policy analysis. *The Social Service Review*, 44 (December), 1970.

Kempe, D. H. *et al.* The battered child syndrome. *Journal American Medical Association*, 181 (17), 1962.

U.S. Children's Bureau. *The abused child: Principles and suggested language on reporting the physically abused child.* Washington, D.C.: U.S. Government Printing Office, 1962.

U.S. Children's Bureau. *The child abuse reporting laws—A tabular view.* Washington, D.C.: U.S. Government Printing Office, 1966.

U.S. Children's Bureau. *Bibliography on the battered child.* Washington, D.C.: Clearinghouse for Research on Child Life, U.S. Government Printing Office, 1969.

Chapter 8

Mental Development

COGNITIVE CONCEPTS OF THE PRESCHOOL CHILD

Giant in the Nursery

David Elkind

The second stage (usually 2–7 years), which Piaget calls the preoperational stage, bears witness to the elaboration of the symbolic function, those abilities which have to do with representing things. . . .

At the beginning of this stage the child tends to identify words and symbols with the objects they are intended to represent. He is upset if someone tramps on a stone which he has designated as a turtle. And he believes that names are as much a part of objects as their color and form.

Editor's Introduction

Piaget is perhaps the most influential theorist of cognitive development in this century. Piaget's work has shown that while the content of the child's conceptual world may be highly variable from child to child and from background to background, the organization of the child's world will be characterized by defined developmental levels. These levels do not vary with each individual. Thus, Piaget's theories of cognition are oriented toward the form in which the child organizes his or her conceptual knowledge and away from the particular content of the child's thought. According to Piaget, the order of the stages through which a child progresses is invariable, but the age at which a child will reach a particular stage is a variable which partially depends upon the child's native endowment.

Piaget believes that cognitive development proceeds in an orderly sequence, and he traces the interaction of the child and the environment over distinct stages which lead to mature thought. The first stage, the sensorimotor, lasts from birth to two years of age. This stage exists prior to the child's acquisition of symbolic language. In the second stage, the preoperational stage, which extends roughly from two to seven years, the child begins to use language to organize mental life. It is during the stage of concrete operations, which lasts approximately from ages seven to eleven, that the child is able to organize his or her mental processes into concepts and rules. The stage of concrete operations is followed by the stage of formal operations, which is said to characterize adolescent and adult thought.

These stages may be viewed as a description of the different developmental tasks which the child solves at each level. As problems are solved at one level, new problems are formed; these create disequilibrium and prompt the child to reduce the conflict by solving the new problems and thus to move to the next higher level.

Piaget's theories evolve from his observations. He does not formulate a hypothesis, devise an experiment, and test his theories. Instead, he observes the child, explores the thoughts of the child, and formulates his theories as a result of his observations. Piaget's technique for assessing the thoughts of children is unique. First, he begins with a question which the child might ask, and he allows the child the opportunity to discover the answer. Piaget believes that lecturing or instructing prevents the child from making discoveries. Lectures by another person have no real educational value for a child. If a child is allowed to experiment and thus arrive at independent conclusions, he or she will comprehend rather than just repeat what the adult has said. The role of teacher or parent, according to Piaget, is not so much knowing what question to ask but rather knowing how to let a child ask questions and knowing what questions not to answer. Second, Piaget does not refute the child's answer or criticize it as incorrect. He accepts the child's response as valid for the child, since the errors made are often quite reasonable at the child's level. The child's response may be different from that which an adult might give, but it is not necessarily wrong—just different. Third, Piaget uses the child's response to help the child explore the reasoning behind his or her response. He may suggest alternatives not in order to force a change of mind but rather to determine whether the child has given a reasoned response or just repeated something that was overheard or made up for the moment.

Piaget's work has had a tremendous impact on American psychological and educational theories in the past twenty years. The following selections, although not written by Piaget, reflect his warmth and empathy. "Giant in the Nursery" offers a good discussion of Piaget's maturational theory of cognitive development. "What Does Piaget Say to the Teacher" discusses the implications of Piaget's work for education. The major goal of education, according to Piaget, is to promote each child's spontaneous development. Adults should act as guides not by providing answers but by creating situations in which the child can solve the problem and learn independently.

Pamela Cantor

In February, 1967, Jean Piaget, the Swiss psychologist, arrived at Clark University in Worcester, Mass., to deliver the Heinz Werner Memorial Lectures. The lectures were to be given in the evening, and before the first one a small dinner party was arranged in honor of Piaget and was attended by colleagues, former students and friends. I was invited because of my long advocacy of Piaget's work and because I had spent a year (1964-65) at his Institute for Educational Science in Geneva. Piaget had changed very little since I had last seen him, but he did appear tired and mildly apprehensive.

Although Piaget has lectured all over the world, this particular occasion had special significance. Almost 60 years before, in 1909, another famous European, Sigmund Freud, also lectured at Clark University. Piaget was certainly aware of the historical parallel. He was, moreover, going to speak to a huge American audience in French and, despite the offices of his remarkable translator, Eleanor Duckworth, he must have had some reservations about how it would go.

Piaget's apprehension was apparent during the dinner. For one who is usually a lively and charming dinner companion, he was surprisingly quiet and unresponsive. About half way through the meal there was a small disturbance. The room in which the dinner was held was at a garden level and two boys suddenly appeared at the windows and began tapping at them. The inclination of most of us, I think, was to shoo them away. Before we had a chance to do that, however, Piaget had turned to face the children. He smiled up at the lads, hunched his shoulders and gave them a slight wave with his hand. They hunched their shoulders and smiled in return, gave a slight wave and disappeared. After a moment, Piaget turned back to the table and began telling stories and entering into animated conversation.

Although I am sure his lecture would have been a success in any case and that the standing ovation he received would have occurred without the little incident, I nonetheless like to think that the encounter with the boys did much to restore his vigor and good humor.

It is Piaget's genius for empathy with children, together with true intellectual genius, that has made him the outstanding child psychologist in the world today and one destined to stand beside Freud with respect to his contributions to psychology, education and related disciplines. Just as Freud's discoveries of unconscious motivation, infantile sexuality and the stages of psychosexual growth changed our ways of thinking about human personality, so Piaget's discoveries of children's implicit philosophies, the construction of reality by the infant and the stages of mental development have altered our ways of thinking about human intelligence.

The man behind these discoveries is an arresting figure. He is tall and somewhat portly, and his stooped walk, bulky suits and crown of long white hair give him the appearance of a thrice-magnified Einstein. (When he was at the Institute for Advanced Study at Princeton in 1953, a friend of his wife rushed to a window one day and exclaimed, "Look, Einstein! Madame Piaget looked and replied, "No, just my Piaget.") Piaget's personal trademarks are his meerschaum pipes (now burned deep amber), his navy blue beret and his bicycle.

Meeting Piaget is a memorable experience. Although Piaget has an abundance of Old-World charm and graciousness, he seems to emanate an aura of intellectual presence not unlike the aura of personality presence conveyed by a great actor. While as a psychologist I am unable to explain how this sense of presence is communicated, I am nevertheless convinced that everyone who meets Piaget experiences it. While talking to me, for example, he was able to divine in my remarks and questions a significance and depth of which I was entirely unaware and certainly hadn't intended. Evidently one characteristic of genius is to search for relevance in the apparently commonplace and frivolous.

Piaget's is a superbly disciplined life. He arises early each morning, sometimes as early as 4 A.M., and writes four or more publishable pages on square sheets of white paper in an even, small hand. Later in the morning he may teach classes and attend meetings. His afternoons include long walks during which he thinks about the problems he is currently confronting. He says, "I always like to think on a problem before reading about it." In the evenings, he reads and retires early. Even on his international trips, Piaget keeps to this schedule.

Each summer, as soon as classes are over, Piaget gathers up the research findings that have been collected by his assistants during the year and departs for the Alps, where he takes up solitary residence in a room in an abandoned farmhouse. The whereabouts of this retreat is as closely guarded as the names of depositors in numbered Swiss bank accounts; only Piaget's family, his longtime colleague Bärbel Inhelder and a trusted secretary know where he is. During the summer Piaget takes walks, meditates, writes *and* writes. Then, when the leaves begin to turn, he descends from the mountains with the several books and articles he has written on his "vacation."

Although Piaget, now in his 72d year, has been carrying his works down from the mountains for almost 50 summers (he has published more than 30 books and hundreds of articles), it is only within the past decade that his writings have come to be fully appreciated in America. This was due, in part, to the fact that until fairly recently only a few of his books had been translated into English. In addition,

American psychology and education were simply not ready for Piaget until the fifties. Now the ideas that Piaget has been advocating for more than 30 years are regarded as exceedingly innovative and even as avant-garde.

His work falls into three more or less distinct periods within each of which he covered an enormous amount of psychological territory and developed a multitude of insights. (Like most creative men, Piaget is hard put to it to say when a particular idea came to him. If he ever came suddenly upon an idea which sent him shouting through the halls, he has never admitted to it.)

During the first period (roughly 1922-29), Piaget explored the extent and depth of children's spontaneous ideas about the physical world and about their own mental processes. He happened upon this line of inquiry while working in Alfred Binet's laboratory school in Paris where he arrived, still seeking a direction for his talents, a year after receiving his doctorate in biological science at the University of Lausanne. It was in the course of some routine intelligence testing that Piaget became interested in what lay behind children's correct and particularly their incorrect, answers. To clarify the origins of these answers he began to interview the children in the open-ended manner he had learned while serving a brief interneship at Bleuler's psychiatric clinic in Zurich. This semiclinical interview procedure, aimed at revealing the processes by which a child arrives at a particular reply to a test question, has become a trademark of Piagetian research investigation.

What Piaget found with this method of inquiry was that children not only reasoned differently from adults but also that they had quite different world-views, literally different philosophies. This led Piaget to attend to those childish remarks and questions which most adults find amusing or nonsensical. Just as Freud used seemingly accidental slips of the tongue and pen as evidence for unconscious motivations, so Piaget has employed the "cute" sayings of children to demonstrate the existence of ideas quite foreign to the adult mind.

Piaget had read in the recollections of a deaf mute (recorded by William James) that as a child he had regarded the sun and moon as gods and believed they followed him about. Piaget sought to verify this recollection by interviewing children on the subject, and he found that many youngsters do believe that the sun and moon follow them when they are out for a walk. Similar remarks Piaget either overheard or was told about led to a large number of investigations which revealed, among many similar findings, that young children believe that anything which moves is alive, that the names of objects reside in the objects themselves and that dreams come in through the window at night.

Such beliefs, Piaget pointed out in an early article entitled "Children's Philosophies," are not unrelated to but rather derive from an implicit animism and artificialism with many parallels to primitive and Greek philosophies. In the child's view, objects like stones and clouds are imbued with motives, intentions and feelings, while mental events such as dreams and thoughts are endowed with corporality and force. Children also believe that everything has a purpose and that everything in the world is made by and for man. (My 5-year-old son asked me why we have snow and answered his own question by saying, "It is for children to play in.")

The child's animism and artificialism help to explain his famous and often unanswerable "why" questions. It is because children believe that everything has a purpose that they ask, "Why is grass green?" and "Why do the stars shine?" The parent who attempts to answer such questions with a physical explanation has missed the point.

In addition to disclosing the existence of children's philosophies during this first period, Piaget also found the clue to the egocentrism of childhood. In observing young children at play at the *Maison des Petits*, the modified Montessori school associated with the Institute of Educational Science in Geneva, Piaget noted a peculiar lack of social orientation which was also present in their conversation and in their approaches to certain intellectual tasks. A child would make up a new word ("stocks" for socks and stockings) and just assume that everyone knew what he was talking about as if this were the conventional name for the objects he had in mind. Likewise, Piaget noted that when two nursery school children were at play they often spoke *at* rather than *to* one another and were frequently chattering on about two quite different and unrelated topics. Piaget observed, moreover, that when he stood a child of 5 years opposite him, the child who could tell his own right and left nevertheless insisted that Piaget's right and left hands were directly opposite his own.

In Piaget's view, all of these behaviors can be explained by the young child's inability to put himself in another person's point of view. Unlike the egocentric adult, who can take another person's point of view but does not, the egocentric child does not take another person's viewpoint because he cannot. This conception of childish egocentrism has produced a fundamental alteration in our evaluation of the preschool child's behavior. We now appreciate that it is intellectual immaturity and not moral perversity which makes, for example, a young child continue to pester his mother after she has told him she has a headache and wishes to be left alone. The preschool child is simply unable to put himself in his mothers position and see things from her point of view.

The second period of Piaget's investigations began when, in 1929, he sought to trace the origins of the child's spontaneous mental growth to the behavior of infants; in this case, his own three children, Jaqueline, Lucienne, and Laurent. Piaget kept very detailed records of their behavior and of their performance on a series of ingenious tasks which he invented and presented to them. The books resulting from these investigations, "The Origins of Intelligence in Children," "Play, Dreams and Imitation in Children," and "The Construction of Reality in the Child" are now generally regarded as classics in the field and have been one of the major forces behind the scurry of research activity in the area of infant behavior now current both in America and abroad. The publication of these books in the middle late nineteen-thirties marked the end of the second phase of Piaget's work.

Some of the most telling observations Piaget made during this period had to do with what he called the *conservation of the object* (using the word conservation to convey the idea of permanence). To the older child and to the adult, the existence of objects and persons who are not immediately present is taken as self-evident. The child at school knows that while he is working at his desk his mother is simultaneously at home and his father is at work. This is not the case for the young infant playing in his crib, for whom out of sight is literally out of mind. Piaget observed that when an infant 4 or 5 months old is playing with a toy which subsequently rolls out of sight (behind another toy) but is still within reach, the infant ceases to look for it. The infant behaves as if the toy had not only disappeared but as if it had gone entirely out of existence.

This helps to explain the pleasure infants take in the game of peek-a-boo. If the infant believed that the object existed when it was not seen, he would not be surprised and delighted at its re-emergence and there would be no point to the game. It is only during the second year of life, when children begin to represent objects mentally, that they seek after toys that have disappeared from view. Only then do they attribute an independent existence to objects which are not present to their senses.

The third and major phase of Piaget's endeavors began about 1940 and continued until the present day. During this period Piaget has studied the development in children and adolescents of those mental abilities which gradually enable the child to construct a world-view which is in conformance with reality as seen by adults. He has, at the same time, been concerned with how children acquire the adult versions of various concepts such as number, quantity and speed. Piaget and his colleagues have amassed, in the last 28 years, an astounding amount of information about the thinking of children and adolescents which is only now beginning to be used by psychologists and educators.

Two discoveries made during this last period are of particular importance both because they were so unexpected and because of their relevance for education. It is perhaps fair to say that education tends to focus upon the static aspects of reality rather than upon its dynamic transformations. The child is taught how and what things are but not the conditions under which they change or remain the same. And yet the child is constantly confronted with change and alteration. His view of the world alters as he grows in height and perceptual acuity. And the world changes. Seasons come and go, trees gain and lose their foliage, snow falls and melts. People change, too. They may change over brief time periods in mood and over long periods in weight and hair coloration or fullness. The child receives a static education while living amidst a world in transition.

Piaget's investigations since 1940 have focused upon how the child copes with change, how he comes to distinguish between the permanent and the transient and between appearance and reality. An incident that probably played a part in initiating this line of investigation occurred during Piaget's short-lived flirtation with the automobile. (When his children were young, Piaget learned to drive and bought a car, but he gave it up for his beloved bicycle after a couple of years.) He took his son for a drive and Laurent asked the name of the mountain they were passing. The mountain was the Salève, the crocodile-shaped mass that dominates the city of Geneva. Laurent was in fact familiar with the mountain and its name because he could see it from his garden, although from a different perspective. Laurent's question brought home to Piaget the fact that a child has difficulty in dealing with the results of transformations whether they are brought about by an alteration in the object itself or by the child's movement with respect to the object.

The methods Piaget used to study how the child comes to deal with transformations are ingenuously simple and can be used by any interested parent or teacher. These methods all have to do with testing the child's abilities to discover that a quantity remains the same across a change in its appearance. In other words, that the quantity is conserved.

To give just one illustration from among hundreds, a child is shown two identical drinking glasses filled equally full with orangeade and he is asked to say whether there is the "same to drink" in the two glasses. After the child says that this is the case, the orangeade from one glass is poured into another which is taller and thinner so that the orangeade now reaches a higher level. Then the child is asked to say whether there is the same amount to drink in the two differently shaped glasses. Before the age of 6 or 7, most children say that the tall, narrow glass has more orangeade. The young child cannot deal with the transformation and bases his judgment on the static features of the orangeade, namely the levels.

How does the older child arrive at the notion that the amounts of orangeade in the two differently shaped glasses are the same? The answer, according to Piaget, is that he discovers the equality with the aid of reason. If the child judges only on the basis of appearances he cannot solve the problem. When he compares the two glasses with respect to width he must conclude that the wide glass has more while if he compares them with respect to the level of the orangeade he must conclude that the tall glass has more. There is then no way, on the basis of appearance, that he can solve the problem. If, on the other hand, the child reasons that there was the same in the two glasses before and that nothing was added or taken away during the pouring, he concludes that both glasses still have the same drink although this does not appear to be true.

On the basis of this and many similar findings, Piaget argues that much of our knowledge about reality comes to us not from without like the wail of a siren but rather from within by the force of our own logic.

It is hard to overemphasize the importance of this fact, because it is so often forgotten, particularly in education. For those who are not philosophically inclined, it appears that our knowledge of things comes about rather directly as if our mind simply copied the forms, colors and textures of things. From this point of view the mind acts as a sort of mirror which is limited to reflecting the reality which is presented to it. As Piaget's research has demonstrated, however, the mind operates not as a passive mirror but rather as an active artist.

The portrait painter does not merely copy what he sees, he interprets his subject. Before even commencing the portrait, the artist learns a great deal about the individual subject and does not limit himself to studying the face alone. Into the portrait goes not only what the artist sees but also what he knows about his subject. A good portrait is larger than life because it carries much more information than could ever be conveyed by a mirror image.

In forming his spontaneous conception of the world, therefore, the child does more than reflect what is presented to his senses. His image of reality is in fact a portrait or reconstruction of the world and not a simple copy of it. It is only by reasoning about the information which the child receives from the external world that he is able to overcome the transient nature of sense experience and arrive at that awareness of permanence within apparent change that is the mark of adult thought. The importance of reason in the child's spontaneous construction of his world is thus one of the major discoveries of Piaget's third period.

The second major discovery of this time has to do with the nature of the elementary school child's reasoning ability. Long before there was anything like a discipline of child psychology, the age of 6 to 7 was recognized as *the age of reason*. It was also assumed, however, that once the child attained the age of reason, there were no longer any substantial differences between his reasoning abilities and those of adolescents and adults. What Piaget discovered is that this is in fact not the case. While the elementary school child is indeed able to reason, his reasoning ability is limited in a very important respect—he can reason about things but not about verbal propositions.

If a child of 8 or 9 is shown a series of three blocks, ABC, which differ in size, then he can tell by looking at them, and without comparing them directly, that if A is greater than B and B greater than C, then A is greater than C. When the same child is given this problem, "Helen is taller than Mary and Mary is taller than Jane, who is the tallest of the three?" the result is quite different. He cannot solve it despite the fact that it repeats in words the problem with the blocks. Adolescents and adults, however, encounter no difficulty with this problem because they can reason about verbal propositions as well as about things.

This discovery that children think different-

ly from adults even after attaining the age of reason has educational implications which are only now beginning to be applied. Robert Karplus, the physicist who heads the Science Curriculum Improvement Study at Berkeley has pointed out that most teachers use verbal propositions in teaching elementary school children. At least some of their instruction is thus destined to go over the heads of their pupils. Karplus and his co-workers are now attempting to train teachers to instruct children at a verbal level which is appropriate to their level of mental ability.

An example of the effects of the failure to take into account the difference between the reasoning abilities of children and adults comes from the New Math experiment. In building materials for the New Math, it was hoped that the construction of a new language would facilitate instruction of set concepts. This new language has been less than successful and the originators of the New Math are currently attempting to devise a physical model to convey the New Math concepts. It is likely that the new language created to teach the set concepts failed because it was geared to the logic of adults rather than to the reasoning of children. Attention to the research on children's thinking carried out during Piaget's third period might have helped to avoid some of the difficulties of the "New Math" program.

In the course of these many years of research into children's thinking, Piaget has elaborated a general theory of intellectual development which, in its scope and comprehensiveness, rivals Freud's theory of personality development. Piaget proposes that intelligence—adaptive thinking and action—develops in a sequence of stages that is related to age. Each stage sees the elaboration of new mental abilities which set the limits and determine the character of what can be learned during that period. (Piaget finds incomprehensible Harvard psychologist Jerome Bruner's famous hypothesis to the effect that "any subject can be taught effectively in some intellectually honest form to any child at any stage of development.") Although Piaget believes that the order in which the stages appear holds true for all children, he also believes that the ages at which the stages evolve will depend upon the native endowment of the child and upon the quality of the physical and social environment in which he is reared. In a very real sense, then, Piaget's is both a nature and a nurture theory.

The first stage in the development of intelligence (usually 0-2 years) Piaget calls the sensory-motor period and it is concerned with the evolution of those abilities necessary to construct and reconstruct objects. To illustrate, Piaget observed that when he held a cigarette case in front of his daughter Jaqueline (who was 8 months old at the time) and then dropped it, she did not follow the trajectory of the case but continued looking at his hand. Even at 8 months (Lucienne and Laurent succeeded in following the object at about 5 months but had been exposed to more experiments than Jaqueline) she was not able to reconstruct the path of the object which she had seen dropped in front of her.

Toward the end of this period, however, Jaqueline was even able to reconstruct the position of objects which had undergone hidden displacement. When she was 19 months old, Piaget placed a coin in his hand and then placed his hand under a coverlet where he dropped the coin before removing his hand. Jaqueline first looked in his hand and then immediately lifted the coverlet and found the coin. This reconstruction was accomplished with the aid of an elementary form of reasoning. The coin was in the hand, the hand was under the coverlet, the coin was not in the hand so the coin is under the coverlet. Such reasoning, it must be said, is accomplished without the aid of language and by means of mental images.

The second stage (usually 2-7 years), which Piaget calls the preoperational stage, bears witness to the elaboration of the symbolic function, those abilities which have to do with representing things. The presence of these new abilities is shown by the gradual acquisition of language, the first indications of dreams and night terrors, the advent of symbolic play (two sticks at right angles are an airplane) and the first attempts at drawing and graphic representation.

At the beginning of this stage the child tends to identify words and symbols with the objects they are intended to represent. He is upset if someone tramps on a stone which he has designated as a turtle. And he believes that names are as much a part of objects as their color and form. (The child at this point is like the old gentleman who, when asked why noodles are called noodles, replied that "they are white like noodles, soft like noodles and taste like noodles so we call them noodles.")

By the end of this period the child can clearly distinguish between words and symbols and what they represent. He now recognizes that names are arbitrary designations. The child's discovery of the arbitrariness of names is often manifested in the "name calling" so prevalent during the early school years.

At the next stage (usually 7-11 years) the child acquires what Piaget calls concrete operations, internalized actions that permit the child to do "in his head" what before he would have had to accomplish through real actions. Concrete operations enable the child to think about things. To illustrate, in one study Piaget presented 5-, 6- and 7-year-old children with six sticks in a row and asked them to take the same number of sticks from a pile on the table. The young children solved the problem by placing their sticks beneath the sample and matching the sticks one by one. The older children merely picked up the six sticks and held them in their hands. The older children had counted the sticks mentally and hence felt no need to actually match them with the sticks in the row. It should be said that even the youngest children were able to count to six, so that this was not a factor in their performance.

Concrete operations also enable children to deal with the relations among classes of things. In another study Piaget presented 5-, 6- and 7-year-old children with a box containing 20 white and seven brown wooden beads. Each child was first asked if there were more white or more brown beads and all were able to say that there were more white than brown beads. Then Piaget asked, "Are there more white or more wooden beads?" The young children could not fathom the question and replied that "there are more white than brown beads." For such children classes are not regarded as abstractions but are thought of as concrete places. (I once asked a pre-operational child if he could be a Protestant and an American at the same time, to which he replied, "No," and then as an afterthought, "only if you move.")

When a child thought of a bead in the white "place" he could not think of it as being in the wooden "place" since objects cannot be in two places at once. He could only compare the white with the brown "places." The older children, who had attained concrete operations, encountered no difficulty with the task and readily replied that "there are more wooden than white beads because all of the beads are wooden and only some are white." By the end of the concrete operational period, children are remarkably adept at doing thought problems and at combining and dividing class concepts.

During the last stage (usually 12-15 years) there gradually emerge what Piaget calls formal operations and which, in effect, permit adolescents to think about their thoughts, to construct ideals and to reason realistically about the future. Formal operations also en-able young people to reason about contrary-to-fact propositions. If, for example, a child is asked to assume that coal is white he is likely to reply, "But coal is black," whereas the adolescent can accept the contrary-to-fact assumption and reason from it.

Formal operational thought also makes possible the understanding of metaphor. It is for this reason that political and other satirical cartoons are not understood until adolescence. The child's inability to understand metaphor helps to explain why books such as "Alice in Wonderland" and "Gulliver's Travels" are enjoyed at different levels during childhood than in adolescence and adulthood, when their social significance can be understood.

No new mental systems emerge after the formal operations, which are the common coin of adult thought. After adolescence, mental growth takes the form—it is hoped—of a gradual increase in wisdom.

This capsule summary of Piaget's theory of intellectual development would not be complete without some words about Piaget's position with respect to language and thought. Piaget regards thought and language as different but closely related systems. Language, to a much greater extent than thought, is determined by particular forms of environmental stimulation. Inner-city Negro children, who tend to be retarded in language development, are much less retarded with respect to the ages at which they attain concrete operations. Indeed, not only inner-city children but children in bush Africa, Hong Kong and Appalachia all attain concrete operations at about the same age as middle-class children in Geneva and Boston.

Likewise, attempts to teach children concrete operations have been almost uniformly unsuccessful. This does not mean that these operations are independent of the environment but only that their development takes time and can be nourished by a much wider variety of environmental nutriments than is true for the growth of language, which is dependent upon much more specific forms of stimulation.

Language is, then, deceptive with respect to thought. Teachers of middle-class children are often misled, by the verbal facility of these youngsters, into believing that they understand more than they actually comprehend. (My 5-year-old asked me what my true identity was and as I tried to recover my composure he explained that Clark Kent was Superman's true identity.) At the other end, the teachers of inner-city children are often fooled by the language handicaps of these children into thinking that they have much lower mental ability than they actually possess. It is appropriate, therefore, that pre-school programs for the disadvantaged should focus upon training these children in language and perception rather than upon trying to teach them concrete operations.

The impact which the foregoing Piagetian discoveries and conceptions is having upon education and child psychology has come as something of a shock to a good many educators and psychological research in America, which relies heavily upon statistics, electronics and computers, Piaget's studies of children's thinking seem hardly a step beyond the pre-scientific baby biographies kept by such men as Charles Darwin and Bronson Alcott. Indeed, in many of Piaget's research papers he supports his conclusions simply with illustrative examples of how children at different age levels respond to his tasks.

Many of Piaget's critics have focused upon his apparently casual methodology and have argued that while Piaget has arrived at some original ideas about children's thinking, his research lacks scientific rigor. It is likely that few, if any, of Piaget's research reports would have been accepted for publication in American psychological journals.

Other critics have taken somewhat the opposite tack. Jerome Bruner, who has done so much to bring Piaget to the attention of American social scientists, acknowledges the fruitfulness of Piaget's methods, modifications of which he has employed in his own investigations. But he argues against Piaget's theoretical interpretations. Bruner believes that Piaget has "missed the heart" of the problem of change and permanence or conservation in children's thinking. In the case of the orangeade poured into a different-sized container, Bruner argues that it is not reason, or mental operations, but some "internalized verbal formula that shields him [the child] from the overpowering appearance of the visual displays." Bruner seems to believe that the syntactical rules of language rather than logic can account for the child's discovery that a quantity remains unchanged despite alterations in its appearance.

Piaget is willing to answer his critics but only when he feels that the criticism is responsible and informed. With respect to his methods, their casualness is only apparent. Before they set out collecting data, his students are given a year of training in the art of interviewing children. They learn to ask questions without suggesting the answers and to test, by counter-suggestion, the strength of the child's conviction. Many of Piaget's studies have now been repeated with more rigorous procedures by other investigators all over the world and the results have been remarkably consistent with Piaget's findings. Attempts are currently under way to build a new intelligence scale on the basis of the Piaget tests, many of which are already in wide-spread use as evaluative procedures in education.

When it comes to criticisms of his theoretical views, Piaget is remarkably open and does not claim to be infallible. He frequently invites scholars who are in genuine disagreement with him to come to Geneva for a year so that the differences can be discussed and studied in depth. He has no desire to form a cult and says, in fact, "To the extent that there are Piagetians, to that extent have I failed." Piaget's lack of dogmatism is illustrated in his response to Bruner:

> Bruner does say that I "missed the heart" of the conservation problem, a problem I have been working on for the last 30 years. He is right, of course, but that does not mean that he himself has understood it in a much shorter time. . . . Adults, just like children, need time to reach the right ideas. . . . This is the great mystery of development, which is irreducible to an accumulation of isolated learning acquisitions. Even psychology cannot be learned or constructed in a short time.

(Despite his disclaimer, Piaget has offered a comprehensive theory of how the child arrives at conservation and this theory has received much research support.)

Piaget would probably agree with those who are critical about premature applications of his work to education. He finds particularly disturbing the efforts by some American educators to accelerate children intellectually. When he was giving his other 1967 lectures, in New York, he remarked:

> If we accept the fact that there are stages of development, another question arises which I call "the American question," and I am asked it every time I come here. If there are stages that children reach at given norms of ages can we accelerate the stages? Do we have to go through each one of these stages, or can't we speed it up a bit? Well, surely, the answer is yes . . . but how far can we speed them up? . . . I have a hypothesis which I am so far incapable of proving; probably the organization of operations has an optimal time . . . For example, we know that it takes 9 to 12 months before babies develop the notion that an object is still there even when a screen is placed in front of it. Now kittens go through the same sub-stages but they do it in three months—so they're six months ahead of the babies. Is this an advantage or isn't it?

> We can certainly see our answer in one sense. The kitten is not going to go much further. The child has taken longer, but he is capable of going further so it seems to me that the nine months were not for nothing. . . . It is probably possible to accelerate, but maximal acceleration is not desirable. There seems to be an optimal time. What this optimal time is will surely depend upon each individual and on the subject matter. We still need a great deal of research to know what the optimal time would be.

Piaget's stance against using his findings as a justification for accelerating children intellectually recalls a remark made by Freud when he was asked whatever became of those bright, aggressive shoeshine boys one encounters in city streets. Freud's reply was, "They become cobblers." In Piaget's terms they get to a certain point earlier but they don't go as far. And the New York educator Eliot Shapiro has pointed out that one of the Negro child's problems is that he is forced to grow up and take responsibility too soon and doesn't have time to be a child.

Despite some premature and erroneous applications of his thinking to education, Piaget has had an over-all effect much more positive than negative. His findings about children's understanding of scientific and mathematical concepts are being used as guidelines for new curricula in these subjects. And his tests are being more and more widely used to evaluate educational outcomes. Perhaps the most significant and widespread positive effect that Piaget has had upon education is in the changed attitudes on the part of teachers who have been exposed to his thinking. After becoming acquainted with Piaget's work, teachers can never again see children in quite the same way as they had before. Once teachers begin to look at children from the Piagetian perspective they can also appreciate his views with regard to the aims of education.

"The principal goal of education," he once said,

is to create men who are capable of doing new things, not simply of repeating what other generations have done—men who are creative, inventive and discoverers. The second goal of education is to form minds which can be critical, can verify, and not accept everything they are offered. The great danger today is of slogans, collective opinions, ready-made trends of thought. We have to be able to resist individually, to criticize, to distinguish between what is proven and what is not. So we need pupils who are active, who learn early to find out by themselves, partly by their own spontaneous activity and partly through materials we set up for them; who learn early to tell what is verifiable and what is simply the first idea to come to them.

At the beginning of his eighth decade, Jean Piaget is as busy as ever. A new book of his on memory will be published soon and another on the mental functions in the preschool child is in preparation. The International Center for Genetic Epistemology, which Piaget founded in 1955 with a grant from the Rockefeller Foundation, continues to draw scholars from around the world who wish to explore with Piaget the origin of scientific concepts. As Professor of Experimental Psychology at the University of Geneva, Piaget also continues to teach courses and conduct seminars.

And his students still continue to collect the data which at the end of the school year Piaget will take with him up to the mountains. The methods employed by his students today are not markedly different from those which were used by their predecessors decades ago. While there are occasional statistics, there are still no electronics or computers. In an age of moon shots and automation, the remarkable discovereies of Jean Piaget are evidence that in the realm of scientific achievement, technological sophistication is still no substitute for creative genius.

What Does Piaget Say to the Teacher?
David Elkind

For more than fifty years, Jean Piaget has been studying the development of intelligence (adaptive thinking and action) in children. His research and theory have, during the past decade, become widely disseminated in American education. Piaget's work, has, however, had its greatest impact in the domain of the new curriculums that were the main educational thrust of the sixties. The "New Math," "Man, a Course of Study," and the "Science Curriculum Improvement Study" materials were, in part at least, influenced by Piaget's work. Less well known, but equally important, are the implications of Piaget's writings for the practice of teaching. It is this aspect of Piaget's work I want to talk about here.

While the curriculum work started from Piaget's findings regarding the child's conceptions of the world at different age levels, the implications of his work for teaching derive from Piaget's method of investigation. This method is the "semiclinical interview," a relatively nondirective open discussion with a child that deals with a particular issue or problem. The nature of this interview and the way in which it is conducted exemplify an orientation toward children and toward learn-

Reprinted from *Today's Education* (NEA Journal), November 1972, pp. 47-48. Reprinted by permission of the author and publisher.

ing and instruction which is probably present in all effective teaching.

In the first place, Piaget starts with questions that children themselves have posed. For example, Piaget overheard a child ask, "Why does the moon follow me at night?" This remark suggested a particular view of the world in which inanimate objects have their own volition and motor force. Piaget used this remark to model a number of questions about the physical world which revealed the young child's belief that all objects are alive and that all things are made by and for man.

By starting with questions posed by children themselves, Piaget was able to get at their genuine intellectual concerns. This method of starting where children are intellectually has a number of implications for teaching. For one thing, it suggests the value of *thematic* education: instruction in all subjects by relating them to a common theme. If children express an interest in, say, stars and planets, then language units, math units, social study units, and natural science units can all be tied to the common theme. This is one of the features of the open classroom that seems to have considerable psychological validity. (Thematic education also supports some facets of Dewey's project method.)

In addition to starting where children are in terms of interest, Piaget also starts where they are in terms of language and conceptual development. Language growth proceeds much more rapidly than conceptual growth so that the child's verbal facility is far in advance of his intellectual comprehension. By selective inquiry, Piaget tries to distinguish between what a child knows verbally and what he understands conceptually.

The implication for teaching is clear. Our teaching at the elementary school level is generally much too verbal and abstract because we have been misled by the children's verbal prowess. Throughout the elementary school years, children need to concretize their

language by relating words to things. The child's natural propensity in this regard is obvious from his penchant for collecting things and for making and doing. These propensities need not be extracurricular and could be incorporated into the regular school program as a way of helping children tie up their words with experience. There is so much in the world of nature and technology that children can learn to label, order, classify, and seriate that teachers do not need to rely solely on kits and prepared curriculum materials.

Starting where the child is has special importance because of the attitude or orientation which it conveys on the part of the teacher toward children. By starting where the child is, teachers reflect the attitude that adults do not know everything and that they have something to learn from children. And it means that teachers are willing to listen, really listen, to what children are saying and to take what they are saying seriously.

In short, the attitude implicit in the Piagetian interview is that it is a true interpersonal exchange in which there is mutual respect and in which each participant expects to learn as well as to impart information to the other person. The effective teacher of children is the one who is himself constantly learning and growing from his teaching experience.

A second feature of the Piagetian interview is that the adult accepts as valid for the child whatever responses the child produces. If the child is asked why the moon follows him when he takes a walk at night and he replies, "Because he likes me," the adult accepts the response as valid for the child, although it may not be correct from an adult's point of view. The same is true at older age levels. A nine-year-old may insist that Honda is a city in Japan. Rather than immediately telling a child he is wrong, that it is, in fact, a Japanese-made motorcycle, the Piagetian approach would accept the answer as valid for the child and by questioning seek to understand how he came to the idea. Such questioning may lead the child to discover for himself that he is mistaken.

The readiness to accept the child's ideas as valid for him again reflect more deep-seated and abiding attitudes toward children and teaching. One of these attitudes is that a child's ideas can be different from our own without, therefore, being wrong. When a child says that if he eats spaghetti he will be Italian, he expresses an idea that is foreign to adults. It suggests that one can change his nationality simply by changing the food he eats. If at this point the adult smiles and says that this is not correct, the major effect is to inhibit the child from freely expressing himself in the presence of adults. On the other hand, if one accepts such ideas as different rather than wrong, the child is encouraged to express himself further.

At this point, it is necessary to answer a question I get asked every time I do a live demonstration of the Piagetian interview technique. The question is "Why do you praise children when they are wrong?" I do indeed praise children—not for "wrong" answers but for "different" ones. If a little girl standing opposite me says my right hand is opposite hers, I may respond, "Very good." It is a praiseworthy achievement for a child of five to know her right and left hands even if she doesn't know mine. My "reinforcing" her "wrong" response will not impede her learning the correct concepts of right and left. Praising her for what she knows and ignoring what she does not know encourages the child to be free and open about her ideas.

Please understand, I am not saying that indications of "right" and "wrong" are always inappropriate in teaching. Obviously, there are many times when an answer is incorrect—particularly in the matter of factual material, such as names, dates, spelling, and solutions to arithmetic problems. What I am saying is that the right/wrong orientation need not per-

vade the educationl enterprise. Evaluations of "right" and "wrong" have less of a place in the realm of concepts about the social and biological worlds than they do in the realms of physics and mathematics. In the social domain, particularly, children have to recognize that because individuals or groups are different they are not necessarily "wrong" for that reason.

It is probably fair to say that when the right/wrong orientation dominates a child's thinking, it can have many negative results. The child concentrates on being "right" rather than understanding. And it makes him reluctant to entertain or consider ideas contrary to his own. Unfortunately, when the right/wrong orientation is carried over to the social domain, it results in prejudice, bigotry, and narrow-mindedness.

The last feature of Piaget's interview procedure of interest to the practice of teaching is what Piaget calls . . . the counter proof. When a child says that he thinks dreams come into the window at night, one can accept this as valid for him and yet still inquire further about it. Was it an idea that just popped into his head, did he overhear it, or is it a conclusion that he arrived at himself?

To test these possiblities, one suggests alternatives to the child. "Yes, but perhaps dreams come down the chimney. What do you think about that?" If the child really believes in what he said, he will stick to his guns. If not, he will respond to the examiner's suggestion and change his mind.

What this procedure implies with regard to teaching is the importance of helping children to consider how they come by their ideas. That is to say, one thing Piaget emphasizes as a goal of education is to get children to check their ideas and not to accept as valid the first thought that comes to mind. Presenting alternative ideas, as in the contr'épreuve, is a way of getting children to check their ideas without the onus of right or wrong, particularly when the alternative idea is presented tentatively.

In my opinion, this is "discovery" teaching and learning in the truest sense. Children really have no trouble discovering new ideas and hypotheses. Their difficulty lies in learning to check and evaluate the ideas they have, regardless of the domain. Here again, of course, I am talking about a change of emphasis and am not ruling out the practice of helping children to arrive at innovative ideas. All I am arguing is that the Piagetian view would give as much weight to helping children check their ideas as it would to helping children arrive at new ideas and hypotheses.

In summary, I have suggested three aspects of Piaget's interview procedure that, to me, have implications for teaching. Piaget's use of the child's own productions as a starting point for discussion suggests that the child's intellectual level and spontaneous interests be considered in setting up curriculum for him. Piaget's emphasis upon the child's ideas as different rather than wrong or right suggests that this approach might be given more emphasis in teaching than it has received up to now. Finally, helping children check their ideas by posing alternative ones should receive as much attention as getting children to discover new ideas.

Certainly Piaget's work has more implications for teaching, and most effective teachers already use these suggestions. I have simply tried to describe some of the rationale for teaching implicit in his methods and explicit in effective teaching.

LEARNING IN PRESCHOOLERS

Infant Day Care and Attachment

Bettye M. Caldwell, Charlene M. Wright, Alice S. Honig, and Jordan Tannenbaum

Day care and institutional care have only one major feature in common: children in groups. Characteristics of institutional children that day care children do not share — prolonged family separation, a sameness of experience, absence of identity, isolation from the outside world, often no significant interpersonal relationship — undoubtedly far outweigh the one characteristic that the groups have in common.

Editor's Introduction

About seven decades ago it was assumed that infants might be better off in institutions than in neglectful homes. Two decades ago the report *Maternal Care and Mental Health* (1951) by John Bowlby was published, and the influence of this report is still being felt. Much of the concern about children being raised in institutions can be traced to this report, as it has had a profound effect on social policy and attitudes. Bowlby frightened us all, professional and lay person alike. He

From *American Journal of Orthopsychiatry*, 40, 3 (April 1970), pp. 396–412. Copyright © 1970 by the American Orthopsychiatric Association, Inc. Reproduced by permission.

warned of the irreparable damage which results from the absence of adequate mothering, especially within the first two years of life. His work has been of great importance as it led to the making of provisions designed to avoid the ill effects of life in children's homes, where the care of the child was particularly inadequate. However, as a result of his warning, many individuals have assumed that a day-care center is an institution, or that children who attend day-care centers will develop the problems associated with institutional life.

Bettye Caldwell (1971) states that one of the reasons that mothers have resisted day care has been the fear that it would weaken the bonds between children and their families. This fear has been based on the irrational equation of day care with institutional care. "Day care — daily separation followed by nightly reunion in the context of social relationships that permit a sense of identity to be formed — appears to have none of the socially toxic effects of prolonged institutional care, or even of temporary separations (such as hospitalization) during which family contacts might be terminated for a given time" (p. 49). Although children in day care do experience separation from their mothers, it is not fair to assume that they therefore suffer maternal deprivation. Day-care children clearly know to whom they belong, spend time with their families, and do experience extensive mothering. Caldwell and her colleagues have tried to demonstrate that two-and-a-half-year-olds who had been in day care since one year of age were as attached to their mothers as were the group of comparable children who had never had such day-care experiences.

One may still maintain, however, that group care for children under two years of age presents serious concern for the physical and emotional health and safety of the infants. Historically speaking, day care received its definition as care and protection from such hazards as insufficient food, inadequate supervision, poor shelter, or physical abuse. Day care is no longer seen as a substitute for inadequate care but rather as a supplement to the care the child receives from his or her parents. According to Caldwell and other researchers, the data appear to show that a clean, airy facility with healthy children and a ratio of one warm, intelligent, concerned adult to every four or five children can be beneficial to the children. Unfortunately there are centers which have insufficient personnel or personnel without the proper training to understand the psychological complexities of a group of very young children. One of the major requisites for success in a day-care experience, according to Caldwell, is that the infant in the center should not be exposed to a large number of continually changing adults. The centers need to learn from and to duplicate the advantages of the family unit and provide the child with consistent adults who will respond to the child's needs as would a sensitive parent. In sum, the day-care center should be organized to maximize attachment and stimulation in order to facilitate the benefits which can be derived from good group care during the early years.

Today we have more working mothers than ever before, and the figures are expected to double in the next decade. Nearly one-third of all mothers with preschool children are working. Yet we have no network of subsidized child care where parents can be sure that their child will receive a full range of developmental services as well as the opportunity to relate to other children.

Instead, we have at least 8 million children who are cared for by a succession of sitters, looked after by older siblings who are forced to drop out of school to care for them, or left to take care of themselves.

There is nothing radical about making group care available to children. During World War II, the government provided child care to over a million mothers who were working in defense plants. Currently, however, the major aim of child care is to reduce the number of families on welfare. This attitude leads to the isolation of poor and minority-group children in day-care centers. Child-care facilities should be available to all families regardless of economic status.

Day care, properly and wisely designed, can provide numerous opportunities of which many children would be deprived in a home setting. This does not apply only to children of families on welfare. Day-care facilities can help children to learn cooperation rather than rivalry, free children from the anxiety created by hovering parents, provide a remedy for the loneliness fostered by uncaring parents, offer peers for children who live in areas where playmates are not easily accessible, and provide facilities that the average home cannot reproduce. Thus, Caldwell and her associates point out that day care need not result in deficiencies in maternal attachment or in any other area. Perhaps those children who are not exposed to the benefits of day care might prove to be the ones who are deprived.

REFERENCES

Bowlby, J. *Maternal care and mental health*. World Health Organization, Monograph No. 2. London: His Majesty's Stationery Office, 1951.

Caldwell, B.M. A timid giant grows bolder. *Saturday Review*, February 20, 1971, 47–49, 65–66.

Pamela Cantor

Day care for infants has had a slow crawl toward social respectability. Boosted on the one hand by zealots who see in it an antidote for many of today's social ills, it has been denounced on the other hand as destructive of a child's potential for normal social and emotional development. Such partisanship has made it somewhat difficult to operate innovative programs with sufficient objectivity to permit collection of the data needed to establish guidelines for current and future programs.

The authors and their colleagues have been engaged in operating a day care program for infants and preschoolers for four years. The broad aim of the program was to create an environment which would foster optimal cognitive, social, and emotional development in young children from disadvantaged families. As data from other studies suggested that by age 3 such children already showed cognitive deficits, the logic of the Syracuse program was to devise a delivery procedure which could get certain types of critical environmental experiences to the children prior to age 3 and thus hopefully circumvent the process of gradual decline. As there are few if any facilities through which large numbers of very young children in this society can be reached, it seemed necessary to devise a new kind of facility. The pressing clamor from working mothers for better child care facilities for their children presented the opportunity to set up a delivery process, and in 1964 the Children's Center, a day care center for infants and preschoolers, was established.

At that time the developers of the program (see Caldwell and Richmond[6]) were acutely aware that there might be certain inherent risks in group day care for infants. For one thing, little was known about the health consequences of bringing substantial numbers of infants into daily contact. For another, there was concern stemming from an awareness of the consistent findings that experiences which diluted the normal mother-infant relationship were likely to produce (be associated with) serious emotional, social, and cognitive impairment. When the plan to offer group day care for infants was announced, many persons expressed alarm that such an arrangement would surely produce deleterious social and emotional consequences, regardless of what benefits it might foster in the cognitive domain. Particularly it was feared that exposure of an infant to large numbers of adults might weaken his primary maternal attachment. If this were to happen, what price gains in any other area?

The question of whether such dilution actually occurs as a consequence of infant day care cannot be answered overnight. It is much easier to report gains or losses in the cognitive area because they can be measured more precisely (though not necessarily more meaningfully) and because they might register at least temporary effects more quickly. However, a certain passage of time is required before one can examine data for the relatively long-term effects upon the basic mother-child relationship of group day care for infants.

Informal checks have been made from the beginning, partly through the use of outside consultants who were experts in early development and objective and unbiased about possible effects of infant day care. Such impartial evaluations have on occasion identified areas of concern, yet offered reassurance that social and emotional development was not suffering. However, none of the outside consultants had the opportunity to observe the children interacting with their own mothers, seeing them instead with the day care staff. Accordingly, the Center staff members who were on duty at arrival and departure times were alerted to signs of healthy attachment. For example, resistance to separation upon being brought to the Center, calling for the mother during times of distress during the day, positive emotional responses shown upon sighting a returning parent, and scampering to gain proximity when the mother comes upon the scene have all been looked for and noted in the day care children. However, it still appeared necessary to conduct a formal evaluation to determine whether there were basic differences in the strength of attachment in a group of day care and a comparable group of home reared infants.

What is Attachment?

Attachment is a term which is somewhat elusive of a conceptual definition and one about which there is not unanimity of opinion as to appropriate definition. Ainsworth[3] has attempted to distinguish among the terms *object relations*, *dependency*, and *attachment*. She suggests that attachment refers to an affectional tie to a specific person which may wax and wane as a function of the situation but which has an enduring quality which can survive even adverse socio-emotional circumstances. Attachment is characterized essentially by maintenance of proximity, by mutual pleasure in a relationship, and by reciprocal need gratification.

The importance of maternal attachment for healthy development has been perhaps more inferred than demonstrated. That is, some infants reared in circumstances which did not permit the formation of an exclusive child-mother attachment have developed deviant patterns of affective relationships with other people (see Goldfarb,[11] Provence and Lipton,[14] and summaries by Bowlby,[5] Yarrow,[17] and Ainsworth[1]). From such findings the inference has been drawn that the absence of a one-to-one relationship is the causative factor which explains the deviance. This inference has been challenged by Casler[9] and others, who proposed the alternative interpretation that the deficits shown in nonattached children are more the product of inadequate environmental stimulation than of maternal deprivation per se. The findings of Freud and Dann[10] that mother-separated children who have had prolonged contact with one another show intense peer attachment have been interpreted as indicating that reciprocal peer attachments can possibly substitute for maternal attachment. Also on the basis of his studies of nonhuman primates, Harlow[12] has suggested that peer attachments are actually more critical for subsequent species-normal social and sexual behavior than is maternal attachment. Mead,[13] referring to the need of children in today's world to be able to go many places without fear and to interact with many people, questions the advocacy of a very close tie between mother and child, suggesting that perhaps wider experiences "in the arms of many individuals in different degrees of intimacy, if possible of different races," might represent the more adaptive experience for young children.

Empirical studies of attachment are scarce in the literature. Schaffer and Emerson[16] studied longitudinally 60 infants ranging in age from 21 to 78 weeks of age. They found indiscriminate attachment behavior during the second quarter and specific attachments during the third quarter of the first year of life. Mothers whose interaction with their children was more intense tended to have infants who were more intensely attached to them. Attachment was unrelated to whether the attachment object had had major responsibility for the child's physical care. Maternal availability to child did not differentiate significantly infants who formed exclusive attachments from those who attached to more than one object. Children who had extensive contacts with other people, independent of the nature of the mother-child relationship, tended to show broader attachment patterns than did children who had limited contacts with other people.

By far the greatest amount of empirical work on the topic of attachment has been carried out by Ainsworth[2,4] and her associates. In a group of 28 Uganda babies she categorized 15-month-old infants in terms of strength and security of attachment as: unattached, insecure-attached, and secure-attached. She then compared the infants in these groups on certain maternal variables. Warmth of the mother, care by people in addition to the mother, and use of scheduled versus demand feeding bore no relationship to strength of attachment. The only variables that showed a clear relationship were total amount of care given by the mother, mother's excellence as an informant, and positive attitudes toward breast feeding. Whether the mother had an ample milk supply was marginally related to attachment. In regard to the multiple caretaker variable, Ainsworth[2] concluded that "there is no evidence that care by several people necessarily interferes with the development of healthy attachment." In a sample of American babies and mothers studied throughout the first year of life, Ainsworth and Wittig[4] found that sensitivity of the mother in responding to the baby's signals and the amount and nature of the interaction between the mother and the infant were additional variables which bore a relationship to strength of attachment.

Attachment during the preschool years, at which time the primary child-mother attachment should weaken somewhat and new attachments form, has been studied to only a very limited extent.

Objectives of This Study

The main question asked by the present study was: are there differences in child-mother attachment and mother-child attachment between a sample of home-reared children and a sample of children who have participated in a group day care program since infancy? Stated in the null version, the formal hypothesis would be that there are no differences between the groups. Additional questions addressed to the data related to whether there are associations between attachment and sex, race, and developmental level of child, and between attachment and stimulation and support available for development within the home.

METHOD
Subjects

Subjects for the study were 41 children who had been followed since early infancy in a longitudinal study relating infant and child development to the social and physical environment. Data for this study were collected as close to each child's 30-month birthday as possible. Twenty-three of the children had received their primary care from their mothers from birth until the time of data collection, except for brief periods during which the mother might have had temporary work or might have been out of the home because of illness. Eighteen of the children had been enrolled in the Children's Center from the time they were about a year old, with all but two of the children having been enrolled prior to 15 months of age. At the time data were collected for this study, the mean duration of day care attendance was 18.8 months, with a range of 5 to 24 months.

Demographic characteristics of the sample can be seen in Table 8-1. Most of the subjects were from lower-class families, with 25% being from one-parent families. As enrollment in the day care program was limited to children whose parents requested the service, certain desirable touches of methodological

elegance—such as matching sex and ethnicity—could not be achieved. The Home group contained a disproportionate number of males and Caucasian children.

On a gestalt of home characteristics the two groups were, at the time of the present analysis, quite comparable. This is perhaps best supported by current scores on the Inventory of Home Stimulation.[7] The Home sample had a mean of 52.8 and the Day Care sample a mean of 54.7 (t = .98, p = NS). However, Stimulation Inventory scores of 53.4 and 49.5 for the Home and Day Care samples when the study children were 12 months of age indicated a marginal difference (t = 1.87, p = .10) in favor of the Home sample at that time. The closer contact between the parents of the Day Care sample and staff of the project, plus continued exposure to the philosophy of the day care program, presumably (and hopefully) accounted for the higher Home Stimulation scores that were earned by the Day Care families at the current assessment. Objectively the Day Care group would be described as having been somewhat more "disadvantaged" in the customary connotation of that term at the time their children entered the day care program; clinically and subjectively, there was no doubt but that they were.

The Day Care Program

The generalizability of results from any scientific study is limited by the fidelity with which the sample represents the characteristics of the population from which it was drawn and by the replicability of the experimental procedures. At the outset it should be stated that the experimental procedure of the present study—the infant day care program—is not duplicated in every facility that advertises itself as a day care center. It is a very special day care center. A technical description of the program may be found in Caldwell and Richmond,[8] but at least a few descriptive sentences must be offered here.

Table 8-1 Demographic Characteristics of the Sample

	Home	Day Care	Total
Sex			
Boys	14	4	18
Girls	9	14	23
Race			
White	19	9	28
Nonwhite	4	9	13
Parents in household			
1 parent	3	7	10
2 parents	20	11	31
No. of siblings			
None	6	6	12
One	11	6	17
Two	4	1	5
Three or more	2	5	7
Mother's education			
Some High School	9	12	21
High School Graduate	12	2	14
Some College	2	4	6
Father's education			
Some High School	10	7	17
High School Graduate	8	3	11
Some College	2	1	3
Not Applicable	3	7	10
Social class			
Lower Social Class	20	14	34
Middle Social Class	3	4	7
IQ (current mean)	107.2	108.8	
Stim score			
(current mean)	52.8	54.7	

The establishment of the Center effected a rather unique blend of social concern for the welfare of young children with the challenge of an intellectual idea—that disadvantaged children will benefit maximally if environmental supports are made available during the first three years of life. "Enrichment" in this carefully planned environment is not merely cognitive enrichment but is an atmosphere in which people and objects give proper levels and quantities of stimulation to young children in a context of emotional warmth, trust, and enjoyment. Teachers, research staff, and office personnel alike are selected partly on the basis of such personal characteristics as warmth and affection for children, empathy for (and often experience with) the problems of the poor, understanding of the complexities and difficulties of family life, and personal convictions about the importance of early experience. Visitors have repeatedly, over the years, commented on such things as the large number of rocking chairs (almost always containing an assortment of adults and children) in the Center, the fact that everybody seems to know everybody else's name, the apparent confidence in adults shown by the children, and the zest for their task displayed by all adults working in the program.

Vital statistics include an average daily attendance of 65 or 70 children ranging in age from 6 months to 5 years, with group assignment based roughly on developmental age. The largest group (the older children) contains 16 children, and the adult-child ratio is approximately one to four. The total group is racially balanced, but the goal of having approximately equal numbers of boys and girls is seldom achieved. Although some middle-class children are accepted into the program, preference for all openings is always given to socially and economically needy families.

The daily schedule is arranged to permit alternating cycles of action and rest, of adult-initiated and child-initiated activity, of group activities and pursuit of individualized interests, of playing for fun and working to learn. One cannot walk into a classroom without thinking, "This is a place where children will be happy." The authors are justified in offering this seemingly immodest and somewhat emotional description, as they are only peripherally involved in the daily programming and can take no credit for the creation of this special milieu for the children. It is hoped that the reader can forgive the immodesty, for knowledge about the program is essential to a correct interpretation of the material to follow.

Procedure

Primary data for the study were obtained from three sources: (1) an intensive, semistructured interview; (2) a home visit; and (3) developmental testing. All procedures were scheduled as close together in time as possible, with an interview and the developmental test usually administered on the same day. Also used in the data analysis was the developmental test administered to the subjects when they were one year of age.

Interviews and Ratings   Most of the assessment procedures employed in this project were designed to cover some specific and relatively circumscribed aspect of child and/or family functioning. The interview conducted for the present study was deliberately planned to achieve the opposite purpose—namely, to obtain a broad picture of the mother-child interaction and of child behavior in settings not ordinarily open to observation by the research staff. All interviews were conducted by a research-oriented social worker (CMW) in a room at the Children's Center comfortably furnished to encourage a relaxed atmosphere. The mothers were told simply, "We want to talk with you about your child's activities and about some of the things you and he (she) are doing now." The study child was present during the interview, and ratings were based on both maternal report and maternal and child behavior. The interview was observed through a one-way mirror by a second staff member, and immediately after the session the interviewer and the observer independently rated both mother and child.

Although the interview deliberately covered a broad array of topics, ratings made from the interviews mainly dealt with clusters of behavior representing attachment and achievement. For the present analysis only those concerned with attachment were used.

Each variable was defined as ranging along a 9-point continuum, with all odd-numbered points described and behaviorally anchored in terms of either maternal or child behavior. The mothers were rated on all variables in terms of their behavior toward the study child, not toward other persons. For example, a mother might be very close to her husband but very distant and remote from the study child; only the latter behavior entered into the ratings used for this data analysis. Each child was rated on the attachment variables twice, once in terms of his relationship with his mother and once in terms of his behavior toward other people. These latter ratings were, of course, based entirely upon maternal report.

Both the interviewer and the observer rated the children and the mothers on these scales immediately following the interview and then, within a few hours, held a discussion and arrived at a rating consensus. Identical ratings were recorded on the final data sheet and were not discussed. Differences of one point were resolved in the direction of the more extreme rating (away from the midpoint of the scale), and differences of two points were reconciled by recording the intermediate rating. When the ratings differed by more than two points, the two raters reassessed the interview and defended their ratings until a consensus emerged. Although this form of rating obviates the need for conventional inter-rater reliability figures, a check was made on the extent of agreement between the raters. On four protocols across all scales the two raters agreed within two points on the material ratings on an average of 87% of the ratings (range 80% to 93%). On the child ratings the average agreement was 91% (range 83% to 96%).

It should be noted here that both the interviewer and the rater knew whether a particular mother-child dyad belonged in the Home or the Day Care sample. In a project like the present one, such knowledge will be unavoidable until a fiscal millenium is reached which permits the luxury of completely blind assessment by impartial assessors. However, the analytic strategy was not discussed with the interviewer until all the interviews had been completed and the ratings filed. She was not told at the outset that the interviews would be used for a comparison between the responses of the Home and Day Care samples. She knew only that the children's age ($2^1/_2$ years) had been designated as a major assessment point at the time the longitudinal study of the Home babies began. The interviewer's assignment was identical to that communicated to the mothers: to get a broad picture of the mother-child relationships and the development of the

children, not to look for "strength of attachment." Furthermore, one of her major functions in the total project was to maintain rapport with the Home families. Therefore, she was actually closer to and friendlier to the Home than to the Day Care mothers, and any bias might have been in their favor. Thus it is the honest conviction of the authors that as much objectivity was maintained as is possible under such circumstances.

Inventory of Home Stimulations This is an experimental procedure developed within the research program of which the present study is a component.[7] It represents an attempt to assess those qualities of the home environment impinging directly upon the young child which have the potential to inhibit or support development. The Inventory contains 72 binary items, about one-half of which depend entirely upon observation of home conditions for their score. It is scored on the basis of a home visit which usually lasts about two hours. Inter-observer reliability in terms of percent of agreement has been found to average around 95% for persons trained in the administration of the Inventory.

Developmental Examinations The instrument used was the Stanford-Binet Intelligence Scale unless the child was somewhat slow and did not attain the basal age of two years. In such instances, and in all assessments of children younger than two, the Cattell Infant Intelligence Scale was used. Most of the examinations were given by the same person (ASH).

Operational Definition of Attachment

For this study attachment was defined operationally as involving the behavior characteristics sampled in the maternal interviews and rated on seven scales. The variables defined in terms of the behavior considered descriptive of the most intense manifestation for both mothers and children are as follows:

Affiliation. Mother: actively responsive to child; initiates nonroutine contacts; likes to be with child. Child: initiates contacts with mother with high frequency; protests being left alone; follows mother around; resists separation.

Nurturance. Mother: initiates support of child; tries to gratify needs; extremely helpful. Child: highly responsive to mother's activities; child's behavior reinforcement for mother's actions; is helpful.

Hostility. Mother: openly hostile; disapproves of much of child's behavior; imposes own schedule upon child; perceives child negatively. Child: expresses anger toward mother; demanding; negativistic, uncooperative; resists manipulation.

Permissiveness. Mother: lets child have own way much of time; invites manipulation and control by child. Child: extremely submissive to maternal control; yields to mother's wishes.

Dependency. Mother: hates to separate from child; extreme emotional involvement with this child to the exclusion of other persons; activities exclusively child-centered; enjoys company of child. Child: strong attachment to mother; is dependent upon mother; maintains proximity; resists separation when proximity is possible; likes to be with or near mother.

Happiness. Mother: expresses great happiness and pleasure in relation to child; child is the emotional high spot in mother's life. Child: extremely happy in interaction with mother; laughs, smiles, shows positive affect.

Emotionality. Mother: persistent extreme overt emotional expression displayed to child; frequently laughs or cries or becomes upset in interactive sessions. Child: persistent extreme overt emotional expression displayed to mother; interaction characterized by high affect rather than apathy and lack of involvement.

All scales except Hostility were expected to co-vary positively with attachment; low ratings on the Hostility scale were interpreted as indicative of strong attachment.

Data Analysis

For data analyses involving the behavior ratings, a distribution-free statistic was needed, and chi square and Fisher's exact test were used. When the developmental tests and the Inventory of Home Stimulation were examined internally, the *t* test for independent samples was used. For this type of study, it was felt that *t* Type II decision error (accepting the null hypothesis when it was actually false—i.e., inferring no difference when actually there were differences between the groups) carried greater interpretive risks. Therefore, it was decided to report and discuss *p*-values of .10.

RESULTS
Attachment and Early Child Care

Child-Mother Attachment The major hypothesis tested by the present study was that there would be no significant difference between child-mother attachment patterns shown by a sample of children who had been home-reared since birth and a sample who had been enrolled in a group day care program since roughly one year of age. The hypothesis was tested by dichotomizing the behavior ratings (above and below the median for the total sample of 41) and examining the obtained distributions for disproportionality related to membership in the Home or the Day Care samples by means of chi square. Results of this analysis are summarized in Table 8-2. From the first column it can be seen that there were no significant differences between the Home and Day Care samples on any of the ratings of the child's relationship with his mother. This failure to disconfirm the null hypothesis indicates that such group experience as that provided in our Center can occur without producing deviant child-mother relationship.

Child-Other Relationships In Column 2 of Table 8-2 are presented data on the way the children in the Home and Day Care samples relate to other people in their environment. These data were gathered and analyzed in order to determine whether children who see a larger number of people in an emotionally supportive context might not relate more positively to other people. Schaffer and Emerson's[16] finding that infants who had more contact with persons other than the mother formed broader attachment patterns would lead to this prediction, as would Rheingold's[15] finding that infants in an experimentally mothered group were more socially responsive than the controls to a neutral person in the environment as well as to the person who had supplied the extra mothering. In the present study there was only one scale on which a difference significant at the .10 level was found. This was on the Dependency scale, on which the Day Care children were found to have higher ratings than the Home children. As defined in the present scales, dependency connotes proximity-seeking more than help-seeking and perhaps indicates an enjoyment of interaction with others more than anything else. Although the difference is of marginal statistical significance, it offers some confirmation of previous findings related to the breadth of interest in other people shown by children who have extensive nonfamily contacts.[1]

Mother-Child Attachment Of perhaps equal relevance to the child's attachment to the

Table 8-2 Summary of Chi Square Analyses of Distribution of Ratings (Above and Below Median) for Home and Day Care Children*

	Child-Mother	Child-Other	Mother-Child
1. Affiliation	.24	.05	.00
2. Nurturance	.40	.20	.03
3. Hostility	.00	.96	.24
4. Permissiveness	.50	.17	5.49[b](H)
5. Dependency	1.45	3.39[a](DC)	.24
6. Happiness	1.04	.59	.96
7. Emotionality	.59	1.62	.09

[a]Significant at .10 level.
[b]Significant at .05 level.
*All chi squares have $df = 1$ and represent 4-cell tables enumerating numbers of persons in Home (H) and Day Care (DC) samples rated above or below the median or the total sample on the behavior ratings. Letters in parentheses (H, DC) after significant chi squares identify the group excessively represented in the above-median cell.

mother is the mother's attachment to the child. If early day care in any diminishes the intensity of the emotion which the mother brings to the relationship with her baby, then this might also have negative consequences for the child no matter how normally the child's own attachment pattern might develop. The data in Column 3 of Table 8-2 indicate that this does not appear to be a valid threat. On six out of the seven ratings, there were no significant differences between the mothers of the Home and the Day Care samples. On the remaining scale, Permissiveness, the Day Care mothers were rated lower than were the Home mothers. Whether this reflects a general concern with achievement, "looking good" as a parent, or a basic personality characteristic of early Day Care mothers cannot be determined. It may reflect the fact that the Day Care mothers are more attuned to parent education literature and perceive permissiveness as being currently out of favor.

Sex and Race Differences

If the samples for the two groups had been more perfectly matched in terms of all possi-

---

[1]In reacting to an earlier version of this paper, Dr. John Bowlby (personal communication) suggested that the slightly higher ratings of the day care children on the dependency scale in terms of their interactions with persons other than the mother might indicate that these children show an "overanxious" attachment. One manifestation of this would be apprehension about breaking contact with an adult and a tendency to maintain constant proximity with the adult at the expense of exploration. Experimental tests of this would have been desirable and will indeed be made in future studies.

bly influential variables, the finding of only one significant difference as a function of group membership (Home or Day Care) could be interpreted more unequivocally. It will be recalled from Table 8-1 that girls were overrepresented in the Day Care sample and that Negroes were underrepresented in the Home group. Differences in either of these variables might conceivably mask differences related to early child care experience. As so many recent research studies have reported sex differences in behavioral characteristics measured during early childhood, an analysis by sex was considered especially relevant.

In order to determine whether there were differences in ratings as a function of sex or race, the same kind of analysis described above and summarized in Table 8-2 for infant care pattern was carried out for sex and then for race. In the child-mother and child-other ratings, there was only one significant disproportion. That was on the Nurturance scale in the child's relationships with his mother (see definition under Method). On this scale girls were found (chi square = 3.81, p = .10) to be more responsive and helpful to their mothers—a difference which certainly fits the cultural stereotype for sex-typed behavior. There were no significant differences as a function of sex in the child-other ratings or in the mother-child ratings.

On the racial variable there were no significant differences between the groups on the child-mother or child-other variables. On the mother-child attachment variables, however, there were three that attained significance: Affiliation (whites high: chi square = 3.35, p = .10), Permissiveness (whites high: chi square = 3.69, p = .10), and Emotionality (whites high: chi square = 10.81, p = .001). This appearance of a fairly consistent pattern on three out of the seven maternal attachment scales suggests that in this particular sample the Negro infants received slightly less intense affective responses from their mothers. These relationships also suggest that the earlier re-

ported findings of relatively greater concern with control (low permissiveness) on the part of the Day Care mothers (see Table 8-2, Column 3) may be confounded by the fact that Negro infants are slightly overrepresented in the Day Care sample in relation to the Home sample.

In general these data strengthen the interpretation of no major differences in attachment patterns associated with Home or Day Care group membership. Unbalanced sex distribution made essentially no contribution, and racial differences in the mothers, if anything, should have increased the likelihood of significant differences as a function of group membership. Thus the unbalanced representation in the two infant care groups of sex and race cannot be cited as obscuring differences that might have existed as a function of child care group membership.

Developmental Level and Attachment

Although the major task of this project was to ascertain whether there were differences in attachment patterns of mothers and children as a function of child care history, the research program of which this project is but one part is concerned with broader aspects of child development. As stated previously, a major orientation of the program has been an attempt to develop a model of infant care that would support a child's development and provide certain critical experiences necessary to normalize development. It was conceivable that the child-mother and the mother-child attachment systems might in some way interact with the rate of development shown by the child.

Ratings on the attachment variables were examined for an association with child's developmental level at 30 months, with the results shown in Table 8-3. Only one of the maternal variables, Nurturance, achieved marginal significance, thus suggesting that in this sample child's developmental level bore little or no relation to strength of maternal attachment. In terms of child-mother attach-

Table 8-3   Summary of Chi Square Analyses of Attachment and Child's Developmental Level

	Child-Mother	Mother-Child
Affiliation	.59	.00
Nurturance	3.69[a](HH)*	2.81[a](HH)
Hostility	3.69[a](HL)	.02
Permissiveness	1.77	.15
Dependency	1.77	1.95
Happiness	7.00[b](HH)	.12
Emotionality	.02	.33

[a]Significant at .10 level.
[b]Significant at .01 level.
*H (High) and L (Low) in parentheses indicate patterns of significant disproportionalities on the two variables.

ment, however, there is a definite suggestion that the better developed infants tend to be more strongly attached to their mothers. This finding should be especially reassuring to those who are concerned that cognitive enrichment might be fostered at the expense of social and emotional development. These obtained associations suggest quite the contrary, namely, that rate of development and strength of attachment co-vary positively.

In view of the fact that cognitive enrichment was one of the goals of the research program, it appeared valid to examine the developmental quotients of the children in order to determine whether there were demonstrable differences between the Home and Day Care samples on this variable both in terms of current functioning and in terms of development prior to entering day care. The results of the analysis are shown in Figure 8-1 Data in Figure 8-1 show that the two groups were not comparable with respect to developmental level at 12 months of age (another situation that one must live with in research where random assignment of subjects is not possible). The difference between the DQ's obtained on the children at that time is significant at the .01 level of confidence. The Home children show the decline in DQ over time that has been consistently reported for disadvan-

taged children. The Day Care children, while not showing any astronomical rise in developmental level, have managed to avoid decline and have, in fact, shown a slight rise. The difference between the groups at 30 months is not statistically significant. This finding, coupled with the above results pointing to comparable attachment patterns in the two groups, demonstrates the feasibility of devising programs which circumvent developmental decline without damaging the child's capacity to relate to his mother or her capacity to relate to him.

Home Characteristics and Attachment
The remaining assessment procedure used for this study was the Inventory of Home Stimulation. The score obtained by a given mother on this Inventory should provide some information about whether the verbal report and behavior which formed the basis for the attachment ratings were at all representative of child and maternal behavior. Accordingly, scores on the Inventory were dichotomized and related to dichotomized ratings on the attachment variables for the total sample of 41 children. Data from this analysis are presented in Table 8-4.

From Column 2 of Table 8-4 it is obvious that the mother-child ratings were rather consistently related to independent data about mother and child gathered during a visit to the home. On five of the seven attachment variables, high ratings on the interview data were

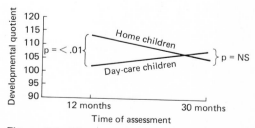

Figure 8-1   Time trends in developmental quotients for home and day-care children at 12 and 30 months.

Table 8-4 Summary of Chi Square Analyses of Home Stimulation and Attachment Behavior (Above and below Median on STIM, above and below Median on Attachment Scales)

	Child-mother*	Mother-child*
Affiliation	7.06[c]	3.38[a]
Nurturance	10.51[c]	5.11[b]
Hostility	1.71	.09
Permissiveness	.00	.85
Dependency	.00	7.06[c]
Happiness	.20	4.89[b]
Emotionality	1.96	6.93[c]

[a]Significant at .10 level.
[b]Significant at .05 level.
[c]Significant at .01 level.
*Significant disproportionalities were consistently of the High-High pattern.

associated with high scores on the Home Stimulation Inventory. Similarly, on two of the child-mother ratings, there was an association between amount of stimulation available in the home and the intensity of the child's attachment to his mother. These data give support to the reliability of the behaviors sampled in the rating scales and also provide clues as to factors in the home situation which can be expected to correlate with strength of attachment.

Home Characteristics and Development

So far in this paper we have shown that child-mother and mother-child attachment were not adversely affected by the kind of early day care experience provided in this setting. We have further shown that attachment patterns are to some extent associated with developmental level of the child and are rather strongly associated with amount and quality of stimulation available to the child within the home. The data collected for this study also lent themselves to an examination of the relationship between home stimulation, pattern of early child care, and development. Results of this analysis are presented in Table 8-5. Here the association between child's developmental level (above or below a quotient of 100 at 30 months) and family score on the Home Stimulation Inventory (above or below the median) is examined separately for the Home sample, the Day Care sample, and the total group of children and families. The results of this analysis are again quite reassuring from the standpoint of the contribution that early day care can make to the total welfare of the developing child. In the Home sample, there is a statistically significant association (Fisher's exact test) between score on the Home Stimulation Inventory and developmental level—that is, children from homes low in stimulation tend to score below the median on the intelligence test. A similar association exists for the total sample. However, for the Day Care sample the distribution of scores on the variables of home stimulation and developmental level is random. Thus it appears that infant day care intrudes into the relationship between home stimulation and developmental level; it can, in effect, offer at

Table 8-5 Distribution of Home Stimulation Scores and Developmental Quotients for Home, Day Care, and Total Samples

	Home		Day care		Total	
	Hi stim	Lo stim	Hi stim	Lo stim	Hi stim	Lo stim
Above 100	9	3	7	4	16	7
Below 100	3	8	4	3	7	11
	$p = .05$		NS		$p = .05$	

least some of the resources and some of the influences of a "second home." It is clearly not the absence of a home.

DISCUSSION AND CONCLUSION

At the time the project of which this study is a part was introduced to the scientific literature, the following statement of goals was made:

> This paper describes a recently initiated program which has as its aim the development of a day care program for children three years of age and under to foster their subsequent educability. In order to accomplish this aim, an attempt will be made to program an environment which will foster healthy social and emotional development as well as provide stimulation for cognitive growth during a developmental period that is critical for its priming. . . . The basic hypothesis to be tested is that an appropriate environment can be programmed which will offset any developmental detriment associated with maternal separation and possibly add a degree of environmental enrichment frequently not available in families of limited social, economic, and cultural resources.[6]

The data reported in this paper demonstrate that at least with respect to the social-emotional variables of child-mother and mother-child attachment, we can claim some success at this point. We *have* offered environmental enrichment, and we *have* shown that it is possible to do this without producing the classical picture of maternal deprivation. It is our hope that these findings will offer encouragement and reassurance to all persons interested in obtaining for children the benefits of high quality infant day care but cautious about jumping into premature programming lest the welfare of the children be forgotten. We ourselves are reassured.

These findings do not guarantee that a socioemotional deficit would never be associated with infant day care. In the strict statisti-

cal sense, we can generalize only to samples participating in similar programs. As such programs are so scarce in America, the generalizability of the findings is sharply restricted. What they do show is that one *can* have infants in quality day care without having jeopardized the child's primary emotional attachment to his mother. In the present program, great pains were taken to avoid this jeopardy. For example, no infants were taken into the program prior to the age of six months, by which time rudimentary forms of attachment have developed. In point of fact, most children who enter the program during infancy do so around one year of age. Also the program is one which offers a generous adult-child ratio and which features in abundance the kinds of behavior shown to be associated with strength of attachment (intensity of response, sensitivity to child's needs, and general competence as adults).

Results of this study provide some extremely valuable information about the range of acceptable variability in patterns of social care for young infants which can be tolerated without damaging the developing children. The implicit equation of infant day care with institutionalization should be put to rest. Infant day care *may* be like institutionalization, but it does not have to be. Day care and institutional care have only one major feature in common: children in groups. Characteristics of institutional children that day care children do not share—prolonged family separation, a sameness of experience, absence of identity, isolation from the outside world, often no significant interpersonal relationship—undoubtedly far outweigh the one characteristic that the groups have in common.

The group with which we are working offers sufficient variation on both child and maternal dimensions to permit further investigations of factors influencing attachment and other important types of social and emotional development. For example, second in importance only to the development of child-mother and mother-child attachments is the development of peer attachments and other types of child-adult and adult-child attachments. One of the findings of the Schaffer and Emerson[16] study referred to earlier was that exclusivity of maternal care was not related to strength of child-mother attachment, but its opposite, wide child care experiences, bore a slight relationship to the tendency of the infant to develop broader attachment patterns. In this study our concern has been primarily with the influence of infant day care upon the basic child-mother attachment; only incidentally did we address ourselves to the influence of such an infant care experience upon attachment to others. We are currently designing new research strategies to determine whether infant day care tends to be associated with strong attachments to more than one person without weakening the basic child-mother attachment.

When we talk about "group care for infants," it is easy to sound as though we are proposing something radically deviant for the children. In the Western world of today with its tract houses, Dick and Jane and mother and dad readers, and our carefully nurtured concern for territoriality and for "mine" and "yours," it is easy to forget that until very recent times isolation of the nuclear family from relatives and friends was rare. Many children living and developing in a small amount of space was the rule, not the exception. Furthermore, the prevalence of extended family living arrangements made for interpersonal environmental settings not unlike that which exists in our infant day care setting: that is, a small group of infants cared for by several friendly and supportive adults but with never a question about who belongs to whom. Our teachers and nurses no more wish to usurp the maternal and paternal role than did relatives and friends who still help perform the child care functions in nonliterate societies and did so in our own country until some 60-70 years ago. We would like to claim that our program is truly innovative, but we must at least consider the possibility that it represents a return toward a pattern that is normal and adaptive for the species. At the same time, we fervently hope that it represents progression toward the goal of more complete utilization of society's resources to foster optimal development for its children.

REFERENCES

1 Ainsworth, M. 1962. Reversible and irreversible effects of maternal deprivation on intellectual development. Child Welfare League of America: 42–62.

2 Ainsworth, M. 1967. Infancy in Uganda. Johns Hopkins Press, Baltimore.

3 Ainsworth, M. 1969. Object relations, dependency, and attachment: a theoretical review. Child Devel. 40:969–1026.

4 Ainsworth, M., and Wittig, B. 1968. Attachment and exploratory behavior of one-year-olds in a strange situation. *In* Determinants of Infant Behavior IV, B. M. Foss, ed. Methuen, London and John Wiley & Sons, New York.

5 Bowlby, J. 1952. Maternal Care and Mental Health. World Health Organization, Geneva, Switzerland.

6 Caldwell, B., and Richmond, J. 1964. Programmed day care for the very young child—a preliminary report. J. Mar. and Fam. 26:481–488.

7 Caldwell, B., Heider, J., and Kaplan, B. 1966. The Inventory of Home Stimulation. Paper presented at meeting of Amer. Psychol. Assn., Sept. 1966.

8 Caldwell, B., and Richmond, J. 1968. The Children's Center in Syracuse, New York. *In* Early Child Care: The New Perspectives, L. L. Dittmann, ed. Atherton Press, New York: 326–358.

9 Casler, L. 1961. Maternal deprivation: a critical review of the literature. Monographs of the Society for Research in Child Development, 26(2).

10 Freud, A. and Dann, S. 1951. An experiment in group unbringing. Psychoanal. Study of Child, 6:127–168.

11 Goldfarb, W. 1955. Emotional and intellectual consequences of psychological deprivation in infancy: a revaluation. *In* Psychopathology of Childhood, P. H. Hoch and J. Zubin, eds. Grune and Stratton, New York: 105–119.

12 Harlow, H., and Harlow, M. 1966. Social deprivation in monkeys. *In* Human Development, M. L. Haimowitz and N. R. Haimowitz, eds. Thomas Crowell, New York: 230–235.

13 Mead, M. 1957. Changing patterns of parent-child relations in an urban culture. Int. J. Psychoanal. 38(6):1–10.

14 Provence, S., and Lipton, R. 1962. Infants in Institutions. International University Press, New York.

15 Rheingold, H. 1956. The modification of social responsiveness in institutional babies. Monograph of the Society for Research in Child Development 21(2).

16 Schaffer, H., and Emerson, P. 1964. The development of social attachments in infancy. Monograph of the Society for Research in Child Development, 29(3).

17 Yarrow, L. 1964. Separation from parents during early childhood. *In* Review of Child Development Research, Vol. I, M. L. Hoffman and L. W. Hoffman, eds. Russell Sage Foundation, New York: 89–130.

PLAY IN THE LIFE OF THE PRESCHOOL CHILD

Children at Play

Brian Sutton-Smith

From the analysis of play in animals we know that play increases as we ascend the phylogenetic order. The more complex the animal, the more it plays. From cross-cultural studies we know also that as cultures become more complex, more types of games are added; and that different types of games are systematically related to other cultural variables. For example, games of strategy appear in cultures when diplomacy, class stratification, and warfare are institutionalized. Games of chance appear when survival conditions are uncertain.

Editor's Introduction

As the father of five children, Brian Sutton-Smith has had the opportunity to observe a great deal of play. In addition, he has been systematically studying children's play throughout the world for over twenty years. In the following selection, Sutton-Smith defines play and discusses the relationship between play and cognition.

Play, in our culture, has been considered trivial by most. Yet, according to Sutton-Smith, play is a subject worthy of study, since all forms of play are actually based upon one of the four basic ways in which we come to know the world. In attempting to define play, the author examines four ways of knowing—imitation, exploration, testing, and model building—as they apply to the child's world of play.

The earliest forms of play involve the baby imitating the parent and the parent imitating the baby. This circular, imitative play later extends to other important people in the child's environment. Exploratory play for the very young child resides in his or her actions. As the child develops, the play may involve both actions and verbal explorations. Exploratory play produces novel sensations and novel relationships for the child. Play as testing is a form of self-validation. Most testing games are contests which deal with some aspect of the child's emotional life and which change in form with each subsequent developmental level. Model building involves putting together the elements of experience in unique ways which utilize the child's imagination.

Thus, Sutton-Smith's article suggests that play and games are functional in our society even though many people may be in the habit of considering them inconsequential. Play is both a voluntary system which is indicative of an individual's fantasy life and a system which is imitative of the larger culture.

Pamela Cantor

Our civilization has not paid much rational attention to play. Rather, we have considered it to be irrational, trivial, ephemeral—not really critical. The seventeenth-century creation of an "innocent" childhood has led us, until recently, to consider play unimportant in adult existence. Although in the past fifty years some intuitive investigators have sought to rescue something from this pejorative definition by saying that play is a child's work, little has been accomplished in the systematic understanding of play.

The Genevan psychologist Jean Piaget demonstrated that much of what we had called play is really the activity of intelligence. From the very first days of life, the child is learning discriminations and forms of effective behavior. A generation of American psychologists showed that much of the time a child is intently "exploring" his world and that we should not call that play either.

What then is play? To answer this question we need to say something about the special feelings, the special volitions, and the special structure of play. Entering into play seems to involve a relaxation of feelings. A baby who has had his bottle and is "playfully" sucking and tonguing in his mouth has a quiescent, euphoric, ruminative quality. Paradoxically, once play gets under way, new forms of feeling and tension often arise. For example, a championship chess player was recently quoted as saying, "For the most part chess is everything. It's a tight world of 64 squares. It's an unreal fascination. You're always thinking. You're always in the present time. You know you're alive. You're always being challenged and threatened."

Perhaps play has a temporal sequence: first, a relaxation of customary feelings; then the induction of new, play-appropriate tensions, followed by relaxation at the end. The "pleasure" of play has a distinctive alternation between relaxed and heightened affect.

Play and game involvement are customarily voluntary. The player begins because he wants to, and once in the play he makes his own choices and behaves in the novel ways he wishes. The player has more freedom and can sustain his chosen activity without interference for considerable periods. Being active rather than passive before fate may account for the immediately euphoric quality of play, while the exigencies of the new game may account for the novel tensions that then arise.

These considerations lead us to define play briefly as a transformation of feelings, volitions, and thoughts for the sake of the excitements of the novel affective, cognitive, and behavioral variations that then occur. In play the ends are indeed subordinated; the means justify the ends. Within this context, play of children can be usefully divided into four categories: imitative, exploratory, testing, and model building.

IMITATIVE PLAY

In the first year of life, the earliest forms of imitative play usually involve the child imitating the parent imitating the child. The baby can only do well what he has already done. The mother who imitates the six-month-old baby's sucking sound may then induce the baby to reproduce that same sound. The difference between the original sucking and the new sucking noise causes them both to laugh during this game. By the end of the first year a number of mother-child games (for example, handclapping) have this circular imitative basis.

By the second year the infant can imitate other people by himself. This deferred imitation is illustrated when the 18-month-old child "pretends" to rub the face cloth all over his face as if washing, although he is nowhere near the washbasin. If he does this washing at the basin, we might say that it is intelligent imitation, a mode of knowing. If he does it nowhere near its proper setting, we can say it is imitative play. In this second year of life most of the imitative play will be partial acts borrowed from sleeping, eating, and washing.

In the third year, children show a greater awareness of their own pretence and tend to copy other people as a whole. They become mothers and fathers. The imitation of whole people can be difficult in some modern societies where the father's work is outside the child's sphere. For example, in a suburban nursery school, children did not like to be assigned the role of "father" in their dramatic play. Most of them refused. One boy, who reluctantly took the part, rapidly rode his bicycle (car) away from the "house," turned around at the end of the room, tore back, clasped "mother" in his arms and gave her a loud kiss, stretched, and said, "Well, I guess I'll take a nap."

In most of this early imitative play the child imitates the important and powerful people in his life. In homes or in cultures where the parents are highly authoritarian and inflexible, play throughout early childhood is usually rigidly imitative. Alternatively, in cultures where adults have much greater flexibility in their roles as adults and in their adult-child relationships, at about the fourth year the characters in children's play become increasingly imaginary and less faithful copies of rigid parental prototypes. Cross-cultural information suggests that the rigid imitation of parental power has been the rule throughout most of human history, and that the rather imaginative play we have come to observe in modern nursery schools is a late product in cultural development.

Similarly, toys may reflect the children's needs for exact replication of overpowerful superiors or for more flexible venture into novel worlds. The social play of the fourth year also reflects these differences. In the more rigid tradition the play involves a dominant child forcing the less powerful children into inferior roles. The dominant child arbitrarily fixes the parts the other children shall play and refuses to reverse the roles. This order of events is then maintained by threats and bribes. In modern nursery schools there is more readiness to take turns and to alternate the desirable roles.

Between four and six, imitative social play tends to be governed by one player acting as a central person and the others acting in satellite roles, or by players taking turns and alternating the roles, or by all the players doing much the same thing at the same time.

In earlier times in America this age group performed a number of circular group-singing and rhythmic pastimes that emphasized choral imitative behavior. These circle pastimes are still found in some nursery schools and in certain rural or immigrant environments. Many were simple group pantomimes such as "ring-around-a-rosy," "baloo, baloo, balight," "looby loo," "mulberry bush," but most were choral celebrations of marriage or funeral customs, such as "Poor Alice is a-weeping," "Sally Waters," "Knights of Spain," "Green Grow the Rushes, Oh," "Green Gravels," and others.

Today we see less of these traditional pastimes, and more informal, imitative group games known by such names as "houses," "cars," "trucks," and "schools." These latter games have seldom been studied systematically, perhaps because they are found in homes and neighborhoods more often than in the more accessible school playgrounds. Whatever the reason, the meaning behind these games probably could give us a better indication of how our civilization is going than anything else that children have to tell us.

EXPLORATORY PLAY

It is difficult to separate exploratory play from exploration. When a child discovers a novel object and examines it, he is not playing. But what if the novel object is a toy that the child is examining in his unsual play milieu? Is that play? Because the answer lies in the child's attitude at the time, it is difficult to provide an answer, particularly for the first two years of life when play consciousness is not clearly differentiated.

Still, even in the first six months the child occasionally seems relaxed and pleased when he plays with his tongue and lips or his hands and fingers. This might well be exploratory play. And in the second six months, play with the parents' face and hair is often accompanied by smiling and laughter. In the second year, exploratory activities that may well give rise to exploratory play include tasting, scribbling, emptying, filling, inserting, putting in and out, pulling, stacking, rolling, and climbing into and under small places.

By the third year this exploration grows increasingly complex. Various patterns of organization become manifest. The child ar-

ranges, heaps, combines, transfers, sorts, and spreads. The child is also aware that he is playing and that his objects are toys. He piles the blocks in new and amusing ways. Novel manipulations and effects excite him. Much so-called destructive block play has this character. Towers of blocks make marvelous effects as they crash to the ground or get higher and higher before falling. Blocks do odd things when a child pushes one against another, then another against the first one, and then another and another. Clay can be pushed and squeezed and torn into pieces that yield funny shapes and feel different to his fingers. Sand pours from buckets and over his legs in pleasant ways. There are again novel feelings, novel effects, and novel relationships in a familiar setting.

At the same age level, from three to four years, we should not neglect the extensive verbal exploratory play that children exhibit. They put words and sounds together in novel combinations, most frequently while sitting in bed early in the morning or before sleep at night.

In childhood today, exploratory play is facilitated by innumerable toy models—cars, ships, and skeletons. These models partly confine play, but children often build fantasies during their examination and construction of the toys. Verbal exploratory play is also conventionalized in childhood through prescribed humor and nonsense. Riddles expose the child to novel contingencies in semantic relationships: "Why did the dog get out of the sun? He didn't want to be a hot dog." Nonsense yields absurd possibilities: "I took a chair and sat down on the floor."

TESTING PLAY

In many types of play and playful contests, the child is testing himself. During his second year, he does a great deal of large motor testing. He crawls under and into things, pulls wagons, lifts objects, pushes, hammers, splashes, rides, balances, climbs, digs, opens, closes, runs, throws. Much of this is not play, but direct testing and adaptation in a given situation. At times, however, an exuberance to the pulling, the pushing, the creeping into cupboards makes it play. Testing play is a form of self-validation.

As the child becomes older, the tests he enjoys increase in variety and character. The baby climbing the stairs gives way to the child jumping down them three at a time or sliding down the bannister. The most obvious way in which testing takes place in play is in the social form of games. In these games the child obtains his self-validation by using others as his standard of competence. He seeks out competitors with talents matching his own. Against them he can measure his progress.

Most testing games are contests that deal with some of the major forms of emotional life. There are games of approach and avoidance, incorporating the behaviors of withdrawal and escape (hide-and-seek), in which the emotion of fear and the adaptive function of protection are tested out. There are games of attack, in which anger and the adaptive function of destruction are tested (dodge ball). There are games of choice, in which joy or sadness, mating or deprivation are tested (flashlight kissing); games of observation in which expectancy, sensory functions, and exploration are exercised (memory); games of impulse-control, in which surprise, stopping, and orientation are critical (priest of the parish).

Each of these types of contests can be arranged in a developmental sequence that children go through between the ages of five to twelve years. This development can be illustrated through four levels of approach and avoidance games. At each level in the game there are particular spatial and temporal relationships, different approach and avoidance actions, and special relationships between the players.

Level I (Hide-and-Seek, Tag) First played extensively between five and six years, these games continue for many years, particularly in the play of girls. There is one central person (the *It*) who has most of the power (he can select whom to chase, when to run) and a number of other fugitive persons who try to hide or escape by holding on to a safe base or saying some safe term. The players' actions are reversible. The space is differentiated into "hiding places," or "safe" spaces, and dangerous territory. These two qualities of space (security versus danger) may be analogous to the division of religious and mythic spaces into the sacred and the profane. The temporal arrangement is episodic. Each incident is of equal weight, and one follows the other interminably. When the *It* tags another player, he is replaced by that player and the game continues.

Level II (Release and Ring-a-lievo) In these games, which become popular at seven to eight years, a central *It* figure again attempts to capture the other players. But now these other players can harass him and rescue each other. While the *It* is accumulating the captured at his base, all the captured players can be freed if one of the free players rushes through that base and cries "release." As well as "hideaways," there is now a "captive base." Space has been differentiated into these two special types of territory. Time has also changed. It is now cumulative. Each episode adds to the previous one until the *It* catches all players and is then relieved of his role.

Level III (Red Rover) In this game, which is popular among nine- and ten-year-olds, the *It* player calls the others across from one base to the next. As they race from base to base he attempts to catch them. If he succeeds, the captured player joins him in the middle and helps him catch the other players. The play takes place now within defined boundaries, with two safe bases at each end. At some

Reprinted by permission of Marcia Keegan, photographer, from *Natural History Magazine*, December 1971.

middle point, the play resembles a team game with half the players on each side. The play reaches an exciting climax when everyone except the last player has been caught. He is the fastest, the most cunning of all, and all the other players join to capture him. The game has a crescendo effect, and the exciting capture of that last player is a climax time.

Level IV (Prisoners' Base) In a complex game usually played first at 11 or 12 years of age, two relatively undifferentiated teams pursue each other over a large, but defined, territory. The pursued players attempt to return to base before they can be hunted down. There are home bases and prisoners' bases and one team attempts to eliminate the other. When this is done, the game is over.

In these four levels of play, the child first tests his powers against "magical" *It* figures, and finally, at an older age, against other players of relatively the same skill. The actions in this sequence evolve from chasing and escaping to capturing and rescuing, with the final game of prisoners' base containing both sets of elements. Each level has a new form of spatial and temporal arrangement, which corresponds to parallel forms of cognitive organization in children of these age levels. But the spatial and temporal qualities take on a vividness in games that they may not have in other situations. Notions like episodic, cumulative, and climax time are also illustrated in the picaresque stories, folktales, and dramas for children. Some cross-cultural data show that games of chase, escape, capture, and rescue exist in cultures where children are made anxious about independence. The children's running back and forth between bases may represent attempts to come to terms with their apprehensions about becoming independent as against remaining dependent. In these games they test their ability to hide, to escape, to capture, to rescue without becoming overwhelmed by fear.

Similar levels can be illustrated for the other types of games. The relationships between the levels in games seem to be additive. Rather than disappearing, the younger elements are added to the next level of games. A sport of adults, such as football, may include many elements of child play.

When game progress is viewed in this developmental fashion, it seems clear that as children proceed through the series, they gain an understanding of social relations, social actions, space, and time.

MODEL-BUILDING PLAY

Although difficult to observe in the very young, model-building play becomes explicit by about four years when the organization of houses, tea-parties, blocks, cities, trucks reaches a peak. It becomes a different type of play when the child puts elements of his experience together in unique ways, especially when these involve flights of his imagination. During childhood, play with model worlds of trains, dolls, and cars may be facilitated by commercial toys. This is the play that the psychoanalyst Erik Erikson has suggested is the analog of the adults "planning" activity. There is a widespread, but unsubstantiated, belief among many adults that because children today have so many toys and models they spend less of their time in these solitary constructive pursuits. Actually the problem may lie less with the toys than with the parents' inability to provide examples of creative adult activities.

In today's society (as indicated by movies and television), fantasies about novel human interrelationships are a key form of model building. The industrious, product-oriented play that we of an older generation encourage in our children is more related to nineteenth-century industrialism than to tomorrow's customers. I have been impressed at the speed with which today's children construct gregarious fantasies with humor and versatility in their informal play. Here is another fitting area for research into the future of our own society.

A great deal of systematic observational work, probably with video tapes, will be necessary before we can decide what we mean when we say a child is at play. I am certain, however, that most readers will be unsatisfied with this state of affairs. They will want to know what play does. Why is it so important to define it? Unfortunately, answers to this sort of question must be even more imprecise than the missing observations.

From the analysis of play in animals we know that play increases as we ascend the phylogenetic order. The more complex the animal, the more it plays. From cross-cultural studies we know also that as culture becomes more complex, more types of games are added; and that different types of games are systematically related to other cultural variables. For example, games of strategy appear in cultures when diplomacy, class stratification, and warfare are institutionalized. Games of chance appear when survival conditions are uncertain. Studies of devoted game players in our own culture show that they have distinctive attributes that go along with their game playing. The players seem to be molded by their games, they don't just "play" them.

Such general discoveries indicate that play and games are functional in culture. Just what this functionality is, however, is another question. I suspect that the primary function of play is the enjoyment of a commitment to one's own experience. In play, the player makes the choices. In modern society, where individuals are increasingly aware of their alienation, such a commitment may have considerable survival value.

Once the player begins the game, the uniqueness, nonsense, triviality, distortion, or serendipity that follows may well bring secondary gains. The experience of play heightens the player's flexibility and imaginative capacity in addition to improving his physical and strategic competence. But these secondary gains are clearly indirect.

Games are in part imitative of the larger culture and therefore embody its processes and attitudes. But because play is voluntary, it admits madness as well as sanity. So that what ensues may be only partly a rehearsal for any specific cultural outcome. The primary purpose of play has a deeper importance for every individual. Playing children are motivated primarily to enjoy living. This is the major rehearsal value of play and games, for without the ability to enjoy life, the long years of adulthood can be dull and wearisome.

Chapter 9

Personality Development

SEX TYPING

Liberating Young Children from Sex Roles: Experience in Day Care Centers, Play Groups and Free Schools

Phyllis Taube Greenleaf

"Mommy I dreamed last night that I was a pilot. But I know that's silly because girls can't be pilots, we can only be stewardesses."

Editor's Introduction

"When a girl learns that it is not 'feminine' to be strong and when a boy learns that it is not 'masculine' to be emotional and when both the girl and boy begin to adjust their behavior to the normal expectations for their sex, the crippling process has begun." It is this crippling process, the manner in which adults—both consciously and unconsciously—teach sex-role stereotypes, which is the topic of the following selection.

Reprinted from Liberating Young Children from Sex Roles: Experience in Day Care Centers, Play Groups and Free Schools. Sommerville, Mass.: New England Free Press. Copyright © 1972, 1973 by Phyllis Taube Greenleaf.

How do we teach prejudices and preconceived notions of appropriate sex-role behavior? It begins early and almost unconsciously. Blue clothes for male infants, pink clothes for females. Gently soothe and sing to your little girl, play rough games with your son. Dolls, carriages, and brooms for girls; baseballs, footballs, and erector sets for boys. Skiing lessons, camping, and diving for John; ballet classes, art lessons, and cooky-baking for Jane. Children are smart; they get the message. Boys are expected to take risks, be strong, compete. Girls are expected to be cautious, fragile, and demure.

Although individual parents may be aware of the damage which is done by programming children into categories, denying them the right to develop their full potential, denying them access to experiences which are appropriate for human beings—not just for boys or for girls—their efforts can be thwarted by children's literature, the educational system, and the media. Cultural brainwashing is pervasive and insidious.

Lauren's favorite fairy tale is Rumplestiltskin. In this story, the miller's daughter is faced with a difficult problem: she must turn straw into gold. How does she handle this? She cries, of course. But wait; a little man will help her out of her dilemma and she will be rewarded—the King will marry her (the ultimate dream for every young girl). Then there is Peter Peter Pumpkin Eater who had a wife and couldn't keep her; so he stuffed her in a pumpkin shell, and that was all right with everyone. And we all know about Mistress Mary quite contrary, poor frightened Miss Muffet, and the Old Woman Who Lived in a Shoe with so many children and no welfare check. Then there is Cinderella, whose life was made worthwhile by a handsome prince because she was delicate enough to stuff her dainty foot into a petite glass slipper, and the princess who won her prince because she was sensitive enough to feel a pea under 40-odd mattresses. She too won her man and her castle. At least as a princess she probably did not have to wash all that bed linen herself. And, no doubt, it was a female maid who helped her keep her castle in shape.

Schoolbooks are not much better. Jane bakes pies and Dick builds bridges. Sally adds 4+4+4=12 while Jim multiplies 4×3=12. How clever of him. And the media are even worse. Quiz shows are always hosted by a confident, virile man who awards washing machines and dishwashers to giggling, hysterical women who foolishly scream with joy. Sometimes the host is aided by a beautiful lady whose sole taxing task is to hand him an envelope while she smiles, much like the receptionist in a big office. And how about George Burns and dumb Gracie, or scatterbrained Lucy, or poor Edith under Archie's domination? In all these situation "comedies" (I do not find the situations comical), Mom washes dishes and Dad brings home the bread and butter, Mom is stupid and Dad is smart—or at least Mom is smart enough to let Dad think he is smart in order to protect his male ego and to save her marriage. The Flintstones, another one of Lauren's favorites, shows smart wives and dumb husbands, but the wives have to plot to conceal their intelligence in order to make their husbands feel important even while the latter cavort at a Water Buffalo Lodge meeting. And Sesame Street, while it has made laudable innovations, still portrays traditional families with Mom in the kitchen and Dad at work, gruff boy monsters and silly girl monsters. Television commercials are so bad as to need little comment. Women drink diet soda in order to remain slim and thus keep their husbands' attention; men drive expensive cars in order to impress the pretty young women.

Even the teaching practices of the schools reinforce the sexual stereotypes. Boys and girls line up separately, are provided with separate sports equipment, are asked to take on different tasks and to play with sexually segregated toys.

How can I help Lauren to grow up emancipated from sex-role stereotypes? It is not possible unless the institutions which affect her life are altered. She may receive exposure to shared roles at home, but how will it be possible to deal with the fact that the only teachers she will see will be female, the only administrators she will see will be male, the guidance counselor will try to program her into a feminine occupation or no occupation at all, and the people she meets will expect her to become a secretary and not an executive or a nurse and not a doctor! The cultural traps are ever-present.

Sexual stereotyping is almost as constraining for boys as it is for girls. While girls are expected to be emotional, weak, and helpful, boys are expected to be unemotional, strong, and tough enough to fight wars to defend the country and other sorts of battles to support the family. Children need the freedom to express themselves, not the constraint of expressing only programmed role identities. The following selection describes some of the ways in which teachers have begun to challenge the ideology of sexism as it is reflected in the attitudes of young children. The children Phyllis Greenleaf is talking about are young, but in some ways they are already too old. They have already gotten the message.[1]

[1]Yesterday, as Lauren and I were leaving the house to go to the playground, she asked me, "Where is Daddy?" I replied, "Daddy is at work." She asked, "Seeing patients?" I said, "Yes, Daddy is seeing patients." Lauren said, "Daddy is a doctor." I said, "Yes, he is. Did you know that Mommy is a doctor too?" She replied, "You're not a doctor. You're a *woman*!" Lauren is only 2 and I fear I have already failed.

Pamela Cantor

Boys have trucks
Girls have dolls

Boys are strong.
Girls are graceful.

Boys are doctors.
Girls are nurses.

Boys are policemen.
Girls are metermaids.

Boys are football-players.
Girls are cheerleaders.

Boys are pilots.
Girls are stewardesses.

Boys fix things.
Girls need things fixed.

Boys invent things.
Girls use what boys invent.

Boys build houses.
Girls keep houses.

I'm glad you're a boy.
I'm glad you're a girl.

We need each other.

These statements quoted from the children's book *I'm Glad I'm A Boy, I'm Glad I'm A Girl*, published by Simon and Schuster in 1970, blatantly teach attitudes and beliefs about sex role differences that parents, teachers, and the mass media teach in more subtle ways. Learning to conform to these sex roles has been considered a normal and healthy part of human development.

When we were growing up the physically agile and aggressive girl was labeled "tomboy" and considered to be going through a temporary stage of development. The boy who cried or was too sensitive was labeled sissy and girlish. Tomboy girls soon learned to inhibit their spirit of adventure; sissy boys stopped crying. Female and male children learned their proper sex roles and so were considered well-adjusted and "normal."

The Women's Liberation Movement has forced us to question whether our ideas about normal development are consistent with our goals for healthy development—for both sexes. The Movement has made many women and men realize that our beliefs about normalcy are a basic part of the ideology of sexism, a system of ideas, values and expectations that prescribes and therefore cripples the full development of both sexes. When a young girl learns it is not "feminine" to be strong and when a young boy learns it is not "masculine" to be emotional and when both the girl and boy begin to adjust their behavior to the normal expectations for their sex, the crippling process has begun. As they grow up they will also learn that a normal relationship between a man and a woman is one in which the man is dominant and superior, while the woman is dependent and inferior. They will learn that a woman's role is to care for her children and husband, while the role of men is to support their families and achieve. From early childhood onward, we learn to accept this ideology of sexism. As adults we play our roles quite unconsciously and naturally.

When *I'm Glad I'm A Boy, I'm Glad I'm A Girl* was discussed recently by a group of preschool teachers, it was felt that the book's clarity and simplicity regarding sex role differences would be helpful to children's development. Most of the teachers believed that boys and girls should be socialized in different ways. Boys should be prepared to assume roles of leadership and action; while girls should be prepared to be more "feminine," which meant dependent and passive. Their attitudes toward the book probably would have been different had it read:

Whites are doctors.
Blacks are nurses.

The rich are strong.
The poor are graceful.

The rich build houses.
The poor keep houses.

Americans invent things.
Asians and Africans use what Americans invent.

At least intellectually, most teachers and parents do not believe in doctrines of class, race and national superiority. Therefore few adults would intentionally select books for children that openly taught them that "black people are stupid, while white people are smart." Nor do most adults consciously want to teach children national racism—that being North American makes one better than being Asian or African.

One could argue that in some respects all of those statements contrasting whites and blacks, boys and girls, rich and poor, do indeed describe reality: the existing dominant-dependent relationships between those people with power and privilege and those without. Most doctors in this country are white and men. Most architects are rich. And, indeed, most housework—paid and unpaid—is done by women. But while children are learning about such realities, we also want them to learn that reality can be questioned and changed and that not everyone fits the pattern. We want children to have enough confidence in themselves to know that they can make new choices in their own lives.

The purpose of this paper is to first discuss how adults consciously and unconsciously teach sex role sterotypes, and then to describe ways that some teachers have begun to challenge the ideology of sexism as it is expressed in the play of young children.

By permission of Sissy Krook, photographer.

TEACHING SEX ROLE STEREOTYPES

All adults have values which influence the way they work with and care for young children. Often certain values are unintentionally communicated. At other times teachers are fully conscious of their goals and very intentionally try to communicate them to children. In 1965 I intentionally dealt with the issue of race with the children and adults in the preschool where I taught. Having learned through study and experience that before the age of five, children already begin to accept our society's racist attitudes, I realized the importance of openly discussing this issue with the children. My goal was to help develop in children positive self-concepts that included an acceptance and respect for their own racial identity.

Yet while consciously trying to counter the learning of racial stereotypes and the ideology of racism, I unconsciously was teaching sex role stereotypes and the ideology of sexism.

When I used to say, "I need some big strong boys to help me carry this table," I was communicating to all of the children that I did not expect the girls to be physically strong, and that I assumed that all the boys were stronger than the girls. I expected the girls to set and clear the table for snack times. The lesson was well learned: "Boys are strong, girls are graceful." No girl ever offered her assistance in moving tables or other heavy objects. My expectations were fulfilled.*

I encouraged the boys much more often

*See *Pygmalion in the Classroon: Teacher Expectation and Pupils' Intellectual Development* by Robert Rosenthal and Lenore Jacobson (Holt, Rinehart and Winston, 1968) for an excellent study of how expectations become self-fulfilling prophecies.

than the girls to "channel their aggression" into hammering, sawing, or block building. If a group of boys excluded the girls in their dramatic play—chainting, "No girls here, no girls here . . . " I would smile, confident that this excluding behavior was normal to four year olds and therefore not harmful. Likewise, if some girls excluded the boys from cooking in the housekeeping corner, I felt no need to intervene in their "free" play. The children and I silently accepted the traditional pattern of male-female division of labor.

On the other hand, I would have intervened if a group of white kids excluded blacks by saying, "No blacks can play here," or a group of rich kids excluded poor kids from their play. But since I believed that boy-girl exclusive play was a normal part of developing a "healthy sex-role identity," it never occurred to me that children's exclusion of each other on the basis of sex could be harmful. Nor did I think that a girl's self-exclusion from "masculine" activities or a boy's self-exclusion from "female" activities was anything to be concerned about.

Yet believing in "free" choice, I never discouraged a child from "testing out" any role. In fact, a traditional goal of early childhood education has been to let kids test out different roles—occupation and sex—in preparation for later "normal" adjustment. We say they should have the opportunity to explore all areas of interest in order to develop physical and intellectual self-confidence. Yet while believing that it is normal to try out different roles in early childhood, we have failed to recognize that boys and girls might continue to enjoy and be challenged by those activities traditionally assigned to the opposite sex if it were not for the attitudes and expectations that adults express to them.

Seven years ago I did not recognize that helping children adjust to traditional sex roles was contradictory to helping them develop their potential. Yet for children to make such

an adjustment, they must severely limit their development—literally shut off parts of their personalities and cut themselves off from many physical and intellectual challenges.

Like most adults, I was unintentionally tracking children according to their sex, programming their development, rather than expanding it. Becoming conscious of this contradiction resulted in my wanting to change the way I was teaching.

For the past two years a group of Boston area teachers in child care centers and nursery schools have been trying to figure out ways to confront the sex role stereotyping that young children express in their play. In the remaining three sections of this paper, I will describe several incidents that took place in our centers—what the children did and how we responded.* The first situations involve incidents in which children of each sex openly excluded the opposite from her or his "female" or "male" realm. The second group of situations will describe how teachers have helped some children break out of a stereotype they had already begun to accept in themselves. The last part of the paper discusses how adults can act as living examples to counter the learning of sex roles.

CONFRONTING CHILDREN'S ACTS OF EXCLUSION

"Boys don't cook! You can't play here, Larry."

Early in the fall, three year olds Linda and Joanna were playing house in the outdoor

---

*Most of the experiences described in this paper demonstrate that adults' actions with children regarding the issue of sex roles can bring about positive and visible change. However, it must be recognized that, given the social pressures of the media, family, etc., efforts to help children grow up in a new way can meet with frustration, and change is often slow and not as visible as in the experiences discussed here. In fact, working with children between the ages of 2 and 4 years gives one a rare opportunity to promote new attitudes and self-concepts which is not the case when working with older kids.

kitchen. Larry, a somewhat shy boy, hesitantly walked into the playhouse to join them. He was instantly stopped by Joanna, who asserted confidently, "No, Larry, you can't play here. Boys don't cook." Linda nodded in agreement. Larry, looking somewhat rejected, began to retreat.

At this point the teacher said, in a matter of fact way, "Joanna, I know lots of men who like to cook, and I know many women who don't enjoy cooking."

The kids looked up at the teacher with puzzled and interested expressions.

"Yes, my daddy cooks," Linda proudly asserted to the other kids.

"You know, I'm a woman and I don't like to cook—at least not all the time. So my husband and I both cook," the teacher added.

Joanna especially looked baffled. Nevertheless, Larry joined the girls in cooking. For the moment Joanna accepted this. . . .

The next situation took place in an experimental elementary school; the children involved were in a "family group" that ranged in age from five to ten.

Seven year olds Eddy and John were engrossed in playing with hot wheels on an elaborate home-made ramp structure. After watching them race a while, Linda, a sturdy five year old, walked up, picked up a car and silently joined the boys in their racing.

"You can't play here, Linda," asserted one boy.

Without responding she continued playing with her car. Both boys repeated their demand for her to leave, getting progressively louder and more annoyed. Over and over they repeated, "Girls don't play with cars!" While she didn't appear to be intimidated, she finally stood up, stared at them, holding on to one car. For a few moments she simply stood there and looked at them, unsure of what to do next.

At this point the teacher intervened, saying, "Girls can play with cars as well as boys can."

The boys looked bothered by the teacher's statement.

"We'll talk more about this later, but right now I think you will have to let her play." Play resumed; although the boys played separately from Linda, excluding her from the racing and measuring.

At their regular group discussion time that day the teacher brought up the incident and asked the kids why it was that boys and girls did not play together.

"Sometimes we want to play alone," one boy said.

"Why do girls ever need to play with cars? They don't drive cars," another boy commented.

A nine year old girl responded, "Look, that's silly to say because ladies drive cars. Like Marian (the teacher), so we can play with cars, too."

Another girl pointed out that one of the bus drivers was a woman. The teacher asked them about their own parents. It came out that mothers drove as often as fathers. The result of that discussion was to show that the boys' line of argument was simply not true: both men and women drive.

The teacher continued the discussion by asking, "Why do you think that boys usually play with cars and trucks and girls with dolls? I want you to go home and think about this for the next few days. Look at your toys and at your sisters' and brothers' and try to think why boys and girls play in different ways."

At the suggestion of a child the teacher reintroduced the issue a few days later. She began the discussion by asking if the children had noticed if their fathers ever helped out with the babies or with housework. Most of their fathers helped only on Mother's Day or when their mothers were sick. This happened whether both parents worked or not.

"How do fathers get that way? How come that happens?" the teacher asked.

"That's why young boys should take care of

babies, 'cause they are going to be fathers and fathers should help too," one older girl replied.

"Yeah, that's why boys should play house with girls; they need to learn how to do that kind of thing," added another girl.

It was quite clear that the kids understood that role playing in childhood taught people their adult roles.

"Look, remember our problem was the business of boys and girls playing with cars together?"

"But that's how it should be," insisted one boy.

"How did you learn that?"

"Tonka."

"Where do you see Tonka?"

"On TV, only the boys play with the trucks."

Then proceeded a very involved 45-minute discussion about other things that kids see on TV regarding roles: mothers cooking with their girls, using Pillsbury; fathers fishing or hiking with their sons, smoking Kent, etc.

"Do you girls like to play with trucks?"

"I do." "Sure." "Yeah." "Not me." "Sometimes."

And do you boys like to play with dolls?"

"Yeah." "Sure." "Sometimes." "Me too."

"Where do you do it?"

"I play with my sisters' dolls," a few boys commented. The same was true of girls using their brothers' trucks. When the teacher suggested that the boys ask their parents for dolls, and the girls ask for trucks for their next birthdays, the response was a united "No" from all the kids. The teacher's final comment was to point out how early in their lives they had learned from their parents and TV what they could and could not do.

Throughout the year this topic cropped up in various ways. The kids, even though they didn't dramatically change their own behavior, certainly became aware of how they got that way. . . .

HELPING INDIVIDUAL CHILDREN BREAK OUT

The focus of this section will be on individual children whose behavior expresses an unspoken acceptance of sex role stereotypes. In these cases the adults deal with problems of self-exclusion and even self-rejection that appear to be related to a child's attitude toward her or his sexual identity. . . .

"I Don't Want To Be A Girl."

At the age of three a little girl named Jessica appeared insulted when her teacher commented to her when she was wearing a firehat, "Here comes Jessica, the firewoman."

"I'm not a firewoman, I'm a fireman," she said sternly.

At first the teacher did not know how to respond. Then she said. "Jessica, it is true that right now not many people who put out fires are women. Most of them are men. But this is changing. You are a young girl now, but when you are older and become a woman, you could probably be a firewoman, if you wanted to."

"But I'm not a girl! I don't want to be a girl," Jessica answered with anger in her voice.

At this point the teacher felt at a loss. Fortunately for the frustrated teacher, Jessica ran off to continue playing fireman with her boy companions.

The teacher told Jessica's mother what had happened. The incident did not surprise the mother, as Jessica had already made the declaration to her parents that she was a boy and did not want to be a girl or to play with them. Both at school and at home Jessica avoided activities that most girls participated in—doll play, art, cooking, etc. She clearly preferred vigorous activities and the company of active boys.

The mother and teacher were not bothered by her preference for energetic play, but they were concerned about Jessica's rejection of her sexual identity. She seemed to believe that one had to be a boy to take part in "boy" activities. Girls did not belong in those activities, so therefore she decided—or wished herself—not to be a girl.

A later realization that Jessica had never gone to the bathroom* at the center raised the question that her shyness about possibly being seen on the toilet could be related to her not wanting other children to know that she was a girl.

The teachers helped Jessica's parents to become more aware of the importance of assuring their daughter that she could be a person of action and still be a girl. Yet they knew what awaited Jessica in the public schools—sexually segregated sports, with the emphasis and prestige on boys' sports. Yet their daughter was a natural athlete, not a cheerleader or spectator type. They realized that unless they worked with other parents and teachers, who felt the same way, to change the schools, Jessica would have a lonely battle ahead.

The teachers wondered at the end of the year if they had really done their job in helping Jessica to enjoy and participate in the activities she had avoided. The emphasis had been on integrating girls into the "boys" activities, and to a lesser extent on involving boys in "girls" activities. They may have communicated a preference for outdoor play over playing house. In other words, the teachers' own prejudice that "woman's work" is less

important might have been expressed to Jessica, giving support to her rejection of girlhood.**

One year later Jessica's mother told her former teacher:

> She is beginning to resolve that although she is a girl she can still do the things that interest her. She is really involved in carpentry and works very independently. This year she is playing with dolls, but when she plays house with her girlfriend, she always is the father. I once came into the room when Jessica, as father, was lying down on the bed directing the other girl, the wife, to 'bring me some food.' And what upsets both my husband and me is how Jessica gets mad when her father does any housework. Once she asked, "Why does Daddy have to do the dishes?" . . . We were also really disturbed when she came in and told us that she had to be a nurse, when all last summer she was talking about being a doctor.

Jessica's conclusion about her medical aspirations parallels a statement made this year by a four year old girl from another center: "Mommy, I dreamed last night that I was a pilot. But I know that's silly because girls can't be pilots, we can only be stewardesses."

It seems that to both these girls an acceptance of their girlhood has meant giving up their "male" goals. Even having teachers and parents who have tried to counter the stereotypes, it is hard to stand up against the larger social pressures.

Boys and Dolls: "Dolls Are for Girls, Sissy."

While girls are usually not encouraged to develop themselves physically, boys are not

---

*At this particular center, when children observed each other in the bathroom, the teachers occasionally and informally would comment about the differences between female and male sex organs in order to help children deal with their shame, confusion or curiosity. For instance, one teacher once commented to a group of giggling, gaping children in the bathroom, "Boys pee out of their penises and girls pee from their vaginas." (Actually, this comment is incorrect; the word **vulva** describes the whole outer area of the female genital region. While the **urethra** is the actual vehicle for urination, males have an urethra too. It is a real issue to decide what is the best label to use to describe the difference between the ways boys and girls pee. But the mere fact that adults matter-of-factly comment on sex differences makes children realize that there is nothing "nasty" about their "private" parts.)

**What Jessica's rejection calls to mind is what a four year old black boy replied when asked, "Is this boy (a brown doll) like you?"

"No, 'cause I don't want him to be. But he looks like me."

This child and Jessica made "wishful identifications." The quote is from *Race Awareness in Young Children* by Mary Ellen Goodman.

encouraged to develop themselves emotional-ly. In fact, the capacity to be compassionate and the ability to take care of others—and babies in particular—have been considered instinctive qualities of women. Yet it is quite clear from watching young children from in-fancy on that boys can be as gentle and sensitive as girls.

Being deprived of the experience of playing with dolls, little boys have much less oppor-tunity than girls to express and develop nur-turant feelings. Furthermore, rarely in our society are older brothers or teenage boys expected to be responsible for the care of younger children—at home or as neighbor-hood babysitters. By not encouraging boys to play with dolls or take care of babies and young children, adults are, in effect, promot-ing the development of emotional hardness and inhibition—qualities all too common in adult men, who, as fathers cannot relate easily to their babies. The next incident illustrates the importance of dolls in the life of a three year old boy named Mark.

Mark was a bright, intense, physically ag-gressive boy. Usually he played alone, and when he made contact with another child, it was usually to take away a toy that he or she was using.

One day Mark seemed at loose ends. While normally able to get involved in one activity, on this day he went from activity to activity—restless, silent and somber. All at once he ran to the cradle in the housekeeping area, picked up a baby doll, found a baby bottle and sat down in a rocking chair. For the next fifteen minutes he rocked, talked and sang to the baby doll, smiling frequently.

The adults who saw this happen made sure that Mark was not disturbed by the other kids, and they also left him alone. They had never in the six months at the center seen Mark as peaceful and affectionate as he was with that doll. For the remaining part of the day Mark played with the other kids in an unusually relaxed and flexible way.

In the following week one of the teachers described the incident to Mark's mother, and asked her if Mark ever played with dolls at home.

"Oh, yes, he often plays with his sister's dolls."

"Does Mark have any dolls of his own?"

"No, I've never thought of giving him one. And I know my husband would not permit it, or at least he would not approve."

In spite of her husband's attitude, she agreed with the teacher that it was important that her son be encouraged to play with dolls and that meant giving him his own dolls. Both the mother and the teacher felt that playing with dolls would help free Mark emotionally. They were both aware that through doll play children could express feelings, both affec-tionate and hostile, that otherwise might not get expressed.

For the rest of the school year Mark contin-ued to play with dolls; not as often as most of the girls, but more often than the other boys. The teachers noticed that Mark would choose to play with dolls at times when he was in a bad mood and feeling tense. His mother in-formed the teachers that Mark never played with dolls in front of his father; she felt that Mark did this to avoid his father's ridi-cule.

By the end of the year Mark, the solitary, intense achiever, was becoming a warmer, more relaxed social being, able to work inde-pendently as well as enjoy the company of his peers.

"But Its Not Nice to Hit."

While Mark needed to develop the capacity to be sensitive to other people, Judy, in the following situation, needed to become more able to stand up for herself.

Judy and Jerry, two four year olds, were the oldest kids in a parent cooperative playgroup. Judy liked to please others. Her consideration for other children, her cooperative attitude with adults, and her capacity to get absorbed in art activities and doll play all made her an easy child to work with.

Jerry was the rough, tough leader of the group. His physical aggression and speed helped to give him that role. In the fall he continually picked on Judy—knocking her down, grabbing things from her, or shoving her out of the way. Her response to his aggression was a pitiful, defenseless wailing, calling to the adults for comfort. The adults' usual reaction was to get mad at Jerry, try to find out why he hit her, tell him it wasn't nice to hit people—he should use words instead—and then to comfort poor, frail Judy. In other words, Jerry could create a big event when he hit Judy.

Two of the mothers decided that instead of trying to stop Jerry from bullying Judy, it might be better for both kids if Judy would hit him back. They felt that Judy should be encouraged to defend herself. A few days later, one of these mothers saw Jerry shove Judy out of the way. Instead of bawling out Jerry, she quickly came up to Judy, who was on the verge of tears and said, "Say, Judy, you can hit him back when he does that to you."

"But it's not nice to hit."

"Maybe if Jerry knew you could hit back, he wouldn't bother you so much."

Judy looked at this mother with disbelief and confusion, and then commented with a somewhat put-on coyness, "Well, I don't really want to hit him anyway," and walked away.

A week after that conversation, as he was running through a museum, Jerry rammed into Judy full force, knocking her to the floor. At first she appeared stunned. Then all of a sudden, she got up, ran up to him and with a determined look on her face, she socked him hard on the back.

He turned around and stared at her. For the next few seconds they both stood still staring at each other in silence. It seemed as though neither child could believe what had just happened. Then Jerry ran off.

The mother who had just watched the whole event, the same person who had encouraged Judy to fight back, came up to Judy, saying approvingly, "Judy, you can hit back when you need to! Now Jerry knows that you can defend yourself." Judy nodded and smiled, obviously pleased with herself.

After that event (as well as a few repeat performances), the parents noticed that Jerry and Judy played together more often, and that she participated more frequently in active play. Jerry's play became more constructive, especially when he was with Judy. He rarely hit her, and when he did, her typical response was to yell at him angrily. Angry words and the occasional use of force replaced her defenseless crying.

Their relationship became more give and take. He seemed to realize that a girl could be his equal. Judy only occasionally played the frail female role: she no longer seemed intimidated by his physical power. This probably grew out of a new recognition of her own strength. The other children in the group also benefited from Judy's example. Though younger than Jerry, they began to get mad at him, at least occasionally, instead of being intimidated when he hit them.

In Defense of Self-Defense and Self-Expression

What these mothers did in openly encouraging Judy to hit back goes against the "we-don't-hit-at-this-school" policy, the traditional line toward physical aggression among professionals in early education. Teachers in nursery schools and day care centers have been trained to get the aggressor to "verbalize" feelings or to "channel" the aggressive energy into other activities. Attention is usually focused on stopping the child who uses physical force, rather than encouraging the kids who are intimidated to fight back.

Yet it is quite common for adults to quietly encourage "weakling" boys to fight back when attacked by other boys. Most parents will encourage their sons to stand up for themselves. But it is uncommon—especially among middle income families—for parents to encourage girls to physically defend themselves against boys. Boys learn early in life that it is not proper to fight girls, frail creatures that they are. When a boy does hit a girl, the adult intervenes to stop him and protect her. His sin is not simply hitting, but hitting a girl.

By protecting girls instead of encouraging them to fight back, we are training them to accept the role of the retreating and impotent female. And while girls are trained to be defenseless, boys are pressured into being the brave defenders; they are not permitted to feel frightened or cry when in pain. "Big boys don't cry," we tell our boys, training them to control the expression of their emotions. As adults these big boys have little capacity to feel deeply and express those feelings freely—physically or verbally. Beginning in early childhood, boys learn to hold back feelings of hurt behind clenched teeth and determined eyes—instead of allowing their emotions to be expressed in words—asking for help; in tears—feeling the pain; or with their bodies—in warm embraces.

But regardless of our sex we need to develop strength—physical and emotional. But having strength does not mean that people will not experience moments and periods of weakness. What is most healthy is when a person can express and share her or his strengths and weaknesses with others, able to be independent yet also dependent. In fact, unless women can be independent and strong as men, men and other women will not be able to depend on them.

CHILDREN'S FEARS

The Kingdom Where Nobody Dies
Robert Kastenbaum

At the beginning the child does not know that he is supposed to be afraid of death, that he is supposed to develop a fabric of evasions to protect himself, and that his parents are not to be relied upon for support when it really counts.

Editor's Introduction

Robert Kastenbaum has spent many years investigating the ideas of children, adolescents, and adults concerning the meaning of death. "The Kingdom Where Nobody Dies" summarizes some of his observations regarding how children learn about death. He states that "curiosity about death and 'where things go' is part of a child's early motivation for discovering his environment."

A few days ago, as Lauren and I were outside walking though the garage, Lauren noticed some dead spiders and announced that "they are sick and resting, and then they will get better and get up." This interpretation stemmed from the reason she is often given for having to rest when she is not feeling well. I then explained that when people or animals get sick and rest, they usually get better and get up.

But sometimes people or animals get sick and they do not get better or get up. They die. These spiders had died. They were no longer living. Lauren has always liked to visit our neighborhood bugs, spiders, moths, and ants to examine them and to explore their environment. Now she tries hard to distinguish between those things which are living and those which are dead and to call my attention to the "no-longer-living spider," the "no-longer-living moth," and the surviving ones. She still, however, would like to make the "no-longer-living" bugs live again if she could. This morning, because she wanted it to be alive, she told me that a spider was living when she knew it was not.

Actually, her first confrontation with death occurred a few months ago with the death of Gerbie, her friend's gerbil. Her friend had taken the gerbil out of the cage to play with it. Being a strong and energetic three-year-old, she handled it a bit too briskly and squeezed it to death inadvertently (we hope). Susan was told that the gerbil had gotten very still and that he was buried and would go to heaven with the bunnies. Lauren was told that the gerbil had been handled too roughly and had died.

Subsequently she observed her goldfish getting sick, although she did not actually see them die. Her father felt that an explanation of death might be inappropriate and told her that the fish were sick and had to be taken back to the pet store to get well. While I did not want to contradict this story, I was concerned, as I want Lauren to know that she can trust us to tell her the truth.

I feel, as Bob Kastenbaum does, that it is important to be direct and honest with children. They can understand much more much earlier than we tend to believe. Allowing children to deal with death openly as the natural resolution of life allows them to grow intellectually and to trust that you and other adults upon whom they rely will tell them the truth. I am convinced that the realities of death will frighten children far less than evasive answers or lies.

The topic of death is shrouded in the prevailing cultural taboos. This makes it extremely difficult for an adult to help a child cope with an experience of death. Psychologists who have worked with children engaged in coping with loss suggest that there should be no unspoken barriers. Children are capable of talking about death and seem to profit by doing so. Silence only teaches them that the subject is forbidden. It is my belief that the best explanation for a young child is one that is simple and direct and that draws as much as possible from the child's own experiences. After an honest explanation has been given, the adult should ask the child to explain again what he or she has been told. This would offer the opportunity to correct any misinterpretations the child may have.

It is better to explore the child's own ideas than to allow unspoken fears to grip his or her imagination. A child might, for instance, believe that death need not be permanent if someone would only look after the dead person properly. This view could cause anxiety when the child learns that the body has been buried rather than nurtured back to life. Or children capable of magical thinking may believe that their thoughts may cause the death of another. Children who have felt anger toward a parent may feel responsible for that parent's death. If children believe that their thoughts can kill, they may hold themselves responsible or see a parent's death as a punishment for evil thoughts. While grieving is an awesome experience for the adult, it is even more difficult for the child, who is so vulnerable to separation and loss. Until children can cope with the finality of death, they may deny it. A child can be so deeply affected by the loss that he or she may pretend it has not happened, and this denial may serve as a defense against anxiety. Adults who use euphemisms in explaining death—such as "your grandfather has gone on a long trip" or "your grandmother has taken a long nap"—will only reinforce the child's process of denial and may find that this will further increase the fear of death. The child may then fear that a long trip or a nap may lead to his or her own death. It is important to be honest in explaining death and in exploring a child's feelings.

Children probably should be allowed to grieve with the rest of the family. Leading children away to a friend's house to spare them pain and sorrow may only make death seem more frightening and mysterious. The children may be angry, resentful, and deeply saddened by their loss. Denying them the opportunity to share these feelings with the rest of the family will most likely decrease their ability to deal with them and compound the grief that they are not allowed to share.

In an attempt to investigate children's ideas about death, Kastenbaum discusses a study done by Marie Nagy (1948, pp. 3–27). Nagy, in studying the ideas of children aged 3 to 10, has looked at the development of the concept of death from the ontogenetic standpoint. She has examined children's thoughts regarding death without concern for the content of each individual child's responses but rather in terms of the developmental stages which these responses represent.

While the content of the child's responses is not Nagy's main concern, and while the individual responses are not recorded in Kastenbaums's article, it is striking to note that few of the children she interviewed actually expressed fear of death. It is further observed that such fears generally do not appear until the later childhood years.

Nagy has shown that a child's ideas about death are quite different at various ages. Only as children approach adolescence are they able to understand that death is the final dissolution of bodily life. This difference in understanding may add to the difficulty of explaining to a child what has happened when death has occurred and to share feelings of loss in a way that will help the child to adapt and to grow appropriately.

REFERENCES

Nagy, M. The child's view of death. *Journal of Genetic Psychology*, 1948, *73*.

                                                                    Pamela Cantor

Children are playing and shouting in the early morning sunshine near the end of Alban Berg's opera *Wozzeck*. They are chanting one variant of a very familiar rhyme: "Ring-a-ring-a-roses, all fall down! Ring-a-ring-a-roses, all. . . . " The game is interrupted by the excited entry of other children, one of whom shouts to Marie's child, "Hey, your mother is dead!" But Marie's child responds only by continuing to ride his hobbyhorse, "Hop, hop! Hop, hop! Hop, hop!" The other children exchange a few words about what is "out there, on the path by the pool," and race off to see for themselves. The newly orphaned child hesitates for an instant and then rides off in the direction of his playmates. End of opera.

What begins for Marie's child? Without knowing the details of his fate, we can sense the confusion, vulnerability, and terror that mark this child's entry into the realm of grief and calamity. Adult protection has failed. The reality of death has shattered the make-believe of childhood.

Children are exposed to death on occasions much less dramatic than the sudden demise of a parent. A funeral procession passes by. A pet dies. An innocent question is raised at the dinner table: "Was this meat once a real live cow?" In a society such as ours that has labored so diligently to put mortality out of sight and out of mind, most of the questions children ask about death make parents uncomfortable. It is often thought that there is no appropriate answer that would not be alarming or threatening to children. Therefore, the subject of death is mostly evaded entirely or fantasized.

The intrusion of death places typical parents in an awkward position. They are not able to relax and observe—much less *appreciate*—how the child orients himself toward death. Yet much can be learned by indulging this curiosity. By dropping the adult guard that directs us to protect children from morbid thoughts and threatening events and by concentrating instead upon how children themselves react to death, surprising insights begin to emerge. We find from psychological research, clinical experience, folkways, and incidents shared with children in and around home that, despite the lack of explicit references, death is an integral part of growing up.

A child's fascination with death occurs almost any time, almost any place. Mortality is a theme that wends its way into many of the child's activities, whether solitary or social. Consider games for example. Ring-around-the-rosy is a popular childhood play theme in both this country and Europe. Our own parents and grandparents delighted in "all fall down," as did their ancestors all the way back to the fifteenth century. The origin of this game, however, was anything but delightful.

Medieval society was almost totally helpless against bubonic plague—Black Death. If adults could not ward off death, what could children do? They could join hands, forming a circle of life. They could chant ritualistically and move along in a reassuring rhythm of unity. Simultaneously acknowledging and mocking the peril that endangered each of them individually, the children predicted and participated in their own sudden demise: "all fall down!" This was a playing-at-death, but it utilized highly realistic materials. Ring-around-the-rosy had one distinct advantage over its model—one could arise to play again. While the game provided the vehicle to conquer or survive death, it was also a way of saying, "I know that I, too, am vulnerable, but I will enjoy the security of other young, living bodies around me." An exercise in make-believe? Perhaps. Nevertheless, this familiar game also deserves respect as an artful response to harsh and overwhelming reality.

Death has been ritualized in many other children's games as well. In the playful romping of tag, what is the hidden agenda or mystery that makes the chaser "It"? Could "It" be the disguise for death? We may be reluctant even to speculate that the touch of death is at the symbolic root of the tag games that have flourished for so many centuries throughout so much of the world. Yet Death (or the Dead Man) certainly is central to at least some of the chase games beloved to children. In the English game "Dead Man Arise" the central player lies prostrate on the ground while other children either mourn over him or seek to bring him back to life. When least expected, up jumps John Brown, the Dead Man, the Water Sprite, Death himself, or whatever name local custom prefers. The children flee or freeze in surprise as the chaser whirls toward them for a tag that will bestow Dead Man status upon the victim.

Although children today continue to participate in rituals that can be traced centuries back, other death-attuned merriments such as "bang, bang, you're dead!" are of more recent origin, and the repertoire is constantly freshened. When everyday group games do not provide a sufficient outlet for death-oriented play, children are likely to express their own special thoughts and feelings individually through inventive play. Suffocating and burying a doll is an instance of fulfilling a death fantasy. Similarly, a game of repeatedly crashing toy cars into each other or a model plane into the ground effectively permits a youngster to test out feelings that are evoked in certain real situations. Should an adult happen to interrupt this brutal type of play, the youngster may offer some reassuring comment, such as "Nobody gets killed bad" or "All the people come home for supper."

How death becomes a vital element in what we call child's play was illustrated by my eight-year-old son at home just a few weeks ago. David, for no ostensible reason, went to the piano and improvised. A short while later he moved to the floor near the piano and began stacking his wooden blocks. These two spontaneous actions did not have any apparent relationship to each other, nor did they bear the mark of death awareness. Yet the only way to appreciate David's behavior is in terms of response to death and loss. The piano playing and block building occurred within a half-hour of the time David and I had discovered our family cat lying dead in the road. Together we acknowledged the death, discussed the probable cause, shared our surprise and dismay, and removed the body for burial in the woods. David then went his own way for a while, which included the actions already mentioned.

When I asked what he was playing on the piano, David answered, "Lovey's life story." He explained how the various types of music he had invented represented memorable incidents in the life of his lost cat (e.g., "This is music for when she scratched my arm"). The wooden blocks turned out to be a monument for Lovey. A close look revealed that the entire building was constructed in an *L* shape, with several other *L*s at salient points.

If there had been no sharing of the initial death experience, I probably would not have guessed that David's play had been inspired by an encounter with mortality. Adults often fail to fathom the implications of children's play because they have not had the opportunity to perceive the stimulus. It is very easy to misinterpret what children are doing, because the nature of their play does not necessarily convey the meaning behind the activity (children go to the piano or their blocks for many other reasons than memorializing). The fact that a particular behavior does not seem to be death-related by no means rules out the possibility that it must be understood at least partially in those terms.

More systematically now, let us explore the child's relationship to death from encounters with both tragedy and games, starting in infancy. Although the young child does not comprehend death as a concept in the strictest sense of the term, death themes certainly engage his mind very early in life, and they are intimately related to the central development of his personality.

There are two different, although related, realizations that children must eventually develop. The first is that other people die, and the second is that they themselves will die. One of the earliest inquiries into the psychology of death touched upon the question of the child's exposure to the death of others. Around the turn of the century G. Stanley Hall, one of the most distinguished of this nation's first generation of psychologists, and one of his students conducted a study on adult recollections of childhood. Several of the questions they asked concerned early encounters with death. Interestingly, many of the earliest memories involved death in one form or another.

When asked specifically about their earliest

experiences with death, many of Hall's respondents answered with considerable detail. He later wrote that

... the first impression of death often comes from a sensation of coldness in touching the corpse of a relative and the reaction is a nervous start at the contrast with the warmth that the contact of cuddling and hugging was wont to bring. The child's exquisite temperature sense feels a chill where it formerly felt heat. Then comes the immobility of face and body where it used to find prompt movements of response. There is no answering kiss, pat, or smile . . . often the half-opened eyes are noticed with awe. The silence and tearfulness of friends are also impressive to the infant, who often weeps reflexly or sympathetically.

Taking careful note of mental reactions to the elaborate funeral proceedings of the era, Hall observed that

little children often focus on some minute detail (thanatic fetishism) and ever after remember, for example, the bright pretty handles or the silver nails of the coffin, the plate, the cloth binding, their own or others' articles of apparel, the shroud, flowers, and wreaths on or near the coffin or thrown into the grave, countless stray phrases of the preacher, the fear lest the bottom of the coffin should drop out or the straps with which it is lowered into the ground should slip or break, a stone in the first handful or shovelful of earth thrown upon the coffin, etc. The hearse is almost always prominent in such memories and children often want to ride in one.

Some adult memories of death went back to age two or three. A child that young could not interpret or symbolize death in anything approaching the adult mode. Yet the exposure to death seemed to make a special impression. Possibly what happens is that the memory is preserved in details of the perception. The scene, or some of its elements that are easily overlooked by an adult, remains charged with emotion and vividly etched in the child's mind. When the adult turns the pages back to early childhood, he cannot show us the text, only the pictures. We do not yet know very much about the place of these early death portraits in the process of individual development, nor can we say with certainty what happens when such seldom-reviewed memories are brought to light in the adult years. However, it is likely that many of us have death perceptions engraved at some level of our memory that predate our ability to preserve our experiences in the form of verbal concepts.

Another way to study the impact of death upon a young child is to learn how he responds to the actual loss of somebody close to him. Albert Cain and his colleagues at the University of Michigan have found that a pattern of disturbed behavior often follows a death in the family. The symptoms occasionally become part of the child's personality from that time forward. One of Cain's studies focused upon responses to the death of a brother or sister. Guilt, as might be expected, was one of the more frequent reactions. "In approximately half our cases," reports Cain, "guilt was rawly, directly present. So, too, was trembling, crying and sadness upon mention of the sibling's death, with the guilt still consciously active five years or more after the sibling's death. Such children felt responsible for the death, sporadically insisted that it was all their fault, felt they should have died, too, or should have died instead of the dead sibling. They insisted they should enjoy nothing, and deserved only the worst. Some had suicidal thoughts and impulses, said they deserved to die, wanted to die—this also being motivated by a wish to join the dead sibling. They mulled over and over the nasty things they had thought, felt, or said to the dead sibling, and became all the guiltier. They also tried to recall the good things they had done, the ways they had protected the dead sibling, and so on."

Many other types of problems were noted in the same study. Some young children developed distorted ideas of what is involved in both illness and death, leading them to fear death for themselves at almost any time or to fantasize that the adults had killed their siblings—fantasies often fed by misinterpretations of emergency respiration and other rescue procedures. The surviving children sometimes became very fearful of physicians and hospitals or resented God as the murderer of their siblings. A few children developed major problems in mental functioning; they suddenly appeared "stupid," did not even know their own age, and seemed to lose their sense of time and causation.

The loss of an expected family member who was not yet born also proved unsettling to many of the children observed by Cain. Although miscarriage, as an event, was difficult for the young child to understand, it was clear enough that something important had gone wrong. Evasive answers by anxious parents increased the problem for some children. In the absence of accurate knowledge they created fantasies that the fetus had been abandoned or murdered. One child insisted that his mother had thrown the baby into a garbage can in a fit of anger; another associated the miscarriage with guppies that eat their babies. At times the insistent questioning by the child had the effect of further unsettling his parents, who had not yet worked through their own feelings about the miscarriage.

Not all children become permanently affected by death in their family. Some weather the emotional crisis with the strong and sensitive help of others. The point is simply that death registers in the minds of young children whether or not adults are fully cognizant of the phenomenon. It need not be either a sibling death or a miscarriage. The death of a playmate, the man across the street, a distant relative, a pet, a sports hero, or a national political figure all make an impression some-

where in the child's mind. Real death is not a rare event in the child's world.

There is no precise way of knowing which death will make the greatest impact upon which child. The death of a pet, especially if it is the first death exposure or occurs in a striking manner, sometimes affects a youngster more than the subsequent death of a person. There is nothing automatic about the different responses to death, even in childhood. Nor can the seemingly inconsequential or remote death be disregarded if we wish to understand the child's thoughts and feelings on mortality.

Whatever the impact of other deaths, however, the loss of a parent has the most signal and longest-lasting influence on children. Bereavement in early childhood has been implicated as the underlying cause of depression and suicide attempts in later life. In one British study, for example, it was found that boys age four or younger who had lost their fathers were especially vulnerable to severe depression in adulthood. Many of the fathers died in combat. Perhaps some of the psychiatric and physical casualties of our involvement in Vietnam eventually will include the suicide committed in 1990 by the son whose father did not return. The death of a young father, however, does not automatically determine his son's fate. There is no way to predict the surviving child's response. In fact, the responses themselves cannot be explained entirely on the basis of parental death alone. What registered in the child's mind when his parent died? By what process did this first response develop into a way of life or into a sort of psychological time bomb set for later detonation? How might the child have been protected or guided? These questions have been raised only sporadically, and the answers are still elusive.

The significance of experiencing another's death during childhood has prompted many psychotherapists to look for such encounters in their adult patients. Psychiatrist David M. Moriarty, for example, has described a depressed woman who had attempted suicide on three occasions and had received electroshock therapy twice without notable improvement in her behavior. When she was three years old, her mother died of appendicitis. In the course of treatment she would call her psychiatrist in a panic, feeling that the world was coming in on her. The thought behind this fear was traced to the graveyard scene, when a shovelful of dirt had been thrown on the lowered coffin. Dr. Moriarty concluded that "Mrs. Q. lived most of her life afraid that she would lose other people whom she loved. The most impressive fact was that she talked and thought about the death of her mother as if it had just happened. This tragic event of forty years ago was still uppermost in her mind."

Of all the methods used to piece together the meaning of death during childhood, none can replace the sharing of a direct death experience with a young child. It is only in such moments of fortunate sharing that we have a clear glimpse into the child's face-to-face encounger with death. There is something indescribably poignant about the way in which the young child attempts to attune himself to threat, limitations, and mortality at a time when he would appear to be innocent of dark concerns. In a journal that I have kept for each of my children, I recorded my son's first encounter with death.

David, at eighteen months, was toddling around the back yard. He pointed at something on the ground. I looked and saw a dead bird, which he immediately labeled "buh . . . buh." But he appeared uncertain and puzzled. Furthermore, he made no effort to touch the bird. This was unusual caution for a child who characteristically tried to touch or pick up everything he could reach. David then crouched over and moved slightly closer to the bird. His face changed expression. From its initial expression of excited discovery and later of puzzlement, now it took on a different aspect: to my astonishment, his face was set in a frozen, ritualized expression resembling nothing so much as the stylized Greek dramatic mask of tragedy. I said only, "Yes, bird . . . dead bird." In typically adult conflict, I thought of adding, "Don't touch," but then decided against this injunction. In any event, David made no effort to touch.

Every morning for the next few days he would begin his morning explorations by toddling over to the dead-bird place. He no longer assumed the ritual-mask expression but still restrained himself from touching. The bird was allowed to remain there until greatly reduced by decomposition. I reasoned that he might as well have the opportunity of seeing the natural processes at work. This was, to the best of my knowledge, David's first exposure to death. No general change in his behavior was noted, nor had any been expected. The small first chapter had concluded.

But a few weeks later a second dead bird was discovered. David had quite a different reaction this time. He picked up the bird and gestured with it. He was "speaking" with insistence. When he realized that I did not comprehend his wishes, he reached up toward a tree, holding the bird above his head. He repeated the gesture several times. I tried to explain that being placed back on the tree would not help the bird. David continued to insist, accompanying his command now with gestures that could be interpreted as a bird flying. All too predictably, the bird did not fly when I returned it to the tree. He insisted that the effort be repeated several times; then he lost interest altogether.

There was a sequel a few weeks later—by now autumn. David and I were walking in the woods, sharing many small discoveries. After a while, however, his attention became thoroughly engaged by a single fallen leaf. He tried to place it back on the tree himself. Failure. He gave the leaf to me with "instructions" that the leaf be restored to its rightful place. Failure again. When I started to try once more, he shook his head no, looking both sober and convinced. Although leaves were repeatedly seen to fall and dead animals were found every now and then, he made no further efforts to reverse their fortunes.

David's look of puzzlement and his repeated efforts to reverse death suggest that even the very young child recognizes a problem when he sees one. Indeed, the problem of death very well might be the prime challenge that sets into motion the child's curiosity and mental questing. Instead of constituting only an odd corner of the young child's mental life, death and its related problems may, in fact, provide much of the motivation for his intellectual development. Children obviously do not possess the conceptual structures of the adult; nevertheless, they do try to understand. Curiosity about death and "where things go" is part of a child's early motivation for exploring his environment. While many developmentalists have observed how the young child comes to an appreciation of object constancy, few have noted that this mental achievement is not possible unless there is also an appreciation of inconstancy. In other words, the young child must be aware of changes, losses, and disappearances if he is eventually to comprehend what "stays," what "goes," and what "comes and goes." Even very young children encounter losses, ends, and limits. Without an ability to fathom these experiences, they could not form protoconcepts of constancies, beginnings, and possibilities.

The death of animals, relatives, or friends undoubtedly has some relationship to the child's discovery of his own mortality, but there are other observations that are more germane. Adah Maurer, a school psychologist in California, suggests than an infant as young as three months old has the glimmerings of death awareness. For a while the baby alternates between sleeping and waking states, with biological imperatives having the upper hand. Soon, Maurer says,

the healthy baby is ready to experiment with these contrasting states. In the game of peek-a-boo, he replays in safe circumstances the alternate terror and delight, confirming his sense of self by risking and regaining complete consciousness. A light cloth spread over his face and body will elicit an immediate and forceful reaction. Short, sharp intakes of breath, vigorous thrashing of arms and legs removes the erstwhile shroud to reveal widely staring eyes that scan the scene with frantic alertness until they lock glances with the smiling mother, whereupon he will wriggle and laugh with joy. . . . To the empathetic observer, it is obvious that he enjoyed the temporary dimming of the light, the blotting out of the reassuring face and the suggestion of a lack of air, which his own efforts enabled him to restore, his aliveness additionally confirmed by the glad greeting implicit in the eye-to-eye oneness with another human.

Babies a few months older begin to delight in disappearance-and-return games. Overboard goes a toy, somebody fetches it, then overboard again. The questions When is something gone? and When is it gone "forever"? seem very important to the young explorer. He devises many experiments for determining under what conditions something is "all gone." Maurer suggests that we "offer a two-year-old a lighted match and watch his face light up with demonic glee as he blows it out. Notice the willingness with which he helps his mother if the errand is to step on the pedal and bury his banana peel in the covered garbage can. The toilet makes a still better sarcophagus until he must watch in awed dismay while the plumber fishes out the Tinker-toy from the overflowing bowl."

It makes sense to take these activities seriously. They provide early clues as to how children begin to grasp what "all gone" means. Once children are old enough to begin talking in sentences, part of their verbal repertoire usually includes death words. One conversation between a four-year-old girl and her eighty-four-year-old great-grandmother illustrates the preschool-age child's concept of death: "You are old. That means you will die. I am young, so I won't die, you know." This excerpt suggests that the little girl knows what it means to die, even if she has not entirely grasped the relationship between age and death. However, a moment later she adds: "But it's all right, Gran'mother. Just make sure you wear your white dress. Then, after you die, you can marry Nomo [great-grandfather] again, and have babies."

The words "dead" and "die" are fairly common in children's conversation and often are used with some sense of appropriateness. Yet an extra comment such as "you can marry Nomo again" or a little adult questioning frequently reveals that a child's understanding of death is quite different from an adult's. Psychologist Maria Nagy, studying Hungarian children in the late 1940s, discovered three phases in the child's awareness of personal mortality. Her interpretation of death ideas expressed by three- to ten-year-olds in drawings and words are classic.

Stage one: present until about age five. The preschool child usually does not recognize that death is final. Being dead is like being less alive. The youngest children regard death as sleep or departure. Still, there is much curiosity about what happens to a person after he dies. The children "want to know where and how he continues to live. Most of the children connected the facts of absence and funerals. In the cemetery one lives on. Movement . . . is limited by the coffin, but for all that, the dead are still capable of growth. They take nourishment, they breathe. They know what is happening on earth. They feel it if someone thinks of them and they even feel sorry for themselves." Death disturbs the young child because it separates people from each other and because life in the grave seems dull and unpleasant.

Stage two: between the ages of five and nine. The distinguishing characteristic of this stage is that the child now tends to personify death. Death is sometimes seen as a separate person—for example, an angel or a frightening clown. For other children death is represented by a dead person. Death usually makes his rounds in the night. The big shift in the child's thinking from stage one is that death now seems to be understood as final: it is not just a reduced form of life. But there is still an important protective feature here: personal death can be avoided. Run faster than the Death Man, lock the door, trick him, and you will not die, unless you have bad luck. As Nagy puts it, "Death is still outside us and is also not general."

Stage three: ages nine to ten and thereafter. The oldest children in Nagy's study recognized that death was not only final but also inevitable. It will happen to them, too, no matter how fast they run or how cleverly they hide. "It is like the withering of flowers," a ten-year-old girl explained to the psychologist.

Nagy's stages offer a useful guide to the development of the child's conception of death, but not all observations fit neatly into these three categories. There are instances in which children as young as five realize their own inevitable mortality. A six-year-old boy worked out by himself the certainty of death. In a shocked voice he revealed, "But I had been planning to live forever, you know." A five-year-old reasoned aloud: "One day you [father] will be died. And one day Mommy will be died . . . . And one day even Cynthia [little sister], she will be died. I mean dead, too . . . . [pause] And one day *I* will be dead . . . . [long pause] *Everybody* there is will be dead . . . . [long, long pause] That's sad, isn't it?" This insight is several years ahead of schedule and is even farther ahead of what one would expect from most theories of mental growth.

Apparently, it is possible to grasp the central facts of death at a surprisingly early age. Children probably tend to retreat from this realization when it comes so early and for several years fluctuate between two states of belief: that death is final and inevitable, and that death is partial, reversible, and perhaps avoidable.

My research indicates that the orientation many adolescents have toward death also fluctuates between a sense of invulnerability and a sense of impending, castastrophic wipe-out. Some adults reveal a similar tendency to function at two levels of thought: they "know" that death is final and inevitable, of course, but most of their daily attitudes and actions are more consistent with the belief that personal mortality is an unfounded rumor.

Sooner or later most children come to understand that death is final, universal, and inevitable. Parents might prefer that children remain innocent of what is happening in their lives and sheltered from emotional stress, shock, and anguish. But it is our own make-believe, not theirs, if we persist in behaving as though children are not attuned to the prospect of mortality. It is important to remember that in this century millions of children around the world have grown up literally in the midst of death and the threat of death. They have fewer illusions on the subject than do many adults.

"The kingdom where nobody dies," as Edna St. Vincent Millay once described childhood, is the fantasy of grownups. We want our children to be immortal—at least temporarily. We can be more useful to children if we can share with them realities as well as fantasies about death. This means some uncomfortable moments. Part of each child's adventure into life is his discovery of loss, separation, nonbeing, death. No one can have this adventure for him, nor can death be locked in another room until a child comes of age. At the beginning the child does not know that he is supposed to be scared of death, that he is supposed to develop a fabric of evasions to protect himself, and that his parents are not to be relied upon for support when it really counts. He is ready to share his discoveries with us. Are we?

HOW CHILD-REARING TECHNIQUES AFFECT
PERSONALITY DEVELOPMENT

Congressional Inquiries into TV Violence

Robert M. Liebert, John M. Neale, and Emily S. Davidson

Many of the researchers associated with the project felt that their work had been represented inaccurately, at least to the extent of minimizing what seemed a clear relationship between viewing of TV violence and youngsters' aggressive behavior.

Editor's Introduction

American children are addicted to television. Three-year-olds view an average of 45 minutes of television each day, and five-year-olds spend approximately two hours a day watching television. After age 5, children spend one-sixth of each day watching television (Schramm, Lyle, & Parker, 1961). The average American household spends six hours per day watching television (Nielsen, 1965). The aggregate of children under 12 spend 70 million hours per day watching TV. Thus, television is the most extensive experience all American children share (Rogers, 1969, pp. 314–316).

While television has been called "chewing gum for the eyes" (Maccoby, 1963), and I think it is an appropriate description, it does, however, have positive aspects. It is an educational medium and it offers diversion from life's harassments. It is a powerful influence which can prepare children to enter school and promote reading and other academically related skills.

It can influence children in slightly less desirable areas as well. Lauren sings all the commercials, especially the "Mr. Potato Head I love you" commercial, and asks for Fruity Pebbles and Honey Comb cereals for breakfast by jingle instead of by name. Children may become passive, with a "come entertain me" attitude, and television can be an obstacle to doing homework or observing bedtime.

Clearly it has serious negative effects as well. Television viewing has been said to influence epidemics of delinquency and violence and to promote the imitation of characters who are devious or fraudulent. Television has been cited as a major cause of death and injury among children (Somers, 1976).

Television has been reported to increase fears and nightmares (Podolsky, 1952; Witty, 1955). In a study done almost twenty years ago, children indicated that their greatest fear was fear of their fathers. Today murder has assumed the number-one rank, with robbery and rape following close behind, and fear of Daddy has dropped to sixth place. A causal relationship between homicide and television is difficult to prove, but the relationship between television and fear appears difficult to dispute.

Studies suggest that aggression in children may be heightened by frequent exposure to televised violence, crime, horror, and war programs (Eron, Laulicht, Walder, Farber, & Spiegel, 1961; Bandura, 1965). In fact, television may be as potent for children as viewing the real act, because for many children—particularly young ones—television is real. I did a television program last week, and while I was at the studio filming the broadcast Lauren was at home watching. The babysitter reports that when Lauren first saw me she smiled with the joy of recognition and then suddenly and abruptly began to cry hysterically saying "I want my Mommy home, I don't want her in the TV, I want her home. She belongs to me." I can only assume, with adult logic imposed on her statement, that she believed that if I went into the television set I would not return. Perhaps she believes that people who are on television actually live in the set or cannot be real—an appropriate line of logic for the Ernie or Bert muppets on Sesame Street but not for Dinah Shore or Mommy.

Children see many hours of fighting and crime in a week of viewing. There is evidence to support the theory that children who observe aggressive models either in real life or on TV tend to display precisely imitative responses, that aggressive programs tend to arouse aggressive impulses, and that watching destructive cartoons leads to destructive play (Lovaas, 1955; Bandura, Ross, & Ross, 1961; Bandura, 1965). It has been found that the viewing of fighting does not serve as a means of discharging anger; rather, it increases aggression (Liebert & Baron, 1972) and the effects may be long range. One study has shown that boys who viewed a moderate amount of violence at age 8 were significantly more aggressive at age 18 than boys who viewed little televised aggression at age 8. Another study has stated that aggressive behavior at age 19 can be better predicted by the amount of violence a child watched while in third grade than by any other variable. These studies support a possible causative relationship between the violent content of television programs and subsequent aggressive behavior.

While the conclusions of the various researchers may be tentative, their results should be strongly considered. Most American children spend more time watching television than in any other activity except sleeping. And even if television actually contributes only a fraction of the estimated amount to violence among children, it should be of social concern.

And we must not be concerned only with the content of children's programs. First graders spend 40 percent of their viewing time watching adult shows; this rises to 80 percent by sixth grade (Maccoby, 1963). To consider the effects of television on children, we must consider the whole range of shows they watch, children's and adults' programs alike.

REFERENCES

Bandura, A. Behavioral modifications through modeling procedures. In L. Krasner & L. P. Ullmann (Eds.), *Research in behavior modification.* New York: Holt, 1965.

Bandura, A., Ross, D., & Ross, S. A. Transmission of aggression through imitation of aggressive models. *Journal of Abnormal and Social Psychology*, 1961, *63*, 575–782.

Eron, L. D., Laulicht, J. H., Walder, L. O., Farber, I. E., & Spiegel, J. P. Application of role and learning theories to the study of the development of aggression in children. *Psychological Reports*, 1961. *9* (Sup. No. 2-V9), 291–334.

Liebert, R. M., & Baron, R. A. Some immediate effects of televised violence on children's behavior. *Developmental Psychology*, 1972, **6**(2), 469–475.

Lovaas, O. I. Effect of exposure to symbolic aggression on aggressive behavior. *Child Development*, 1961, **32**, 37–44.

Maccoby, E. The effects of television on children. In William Schramm (Ed.), *The science of human communication.* New York: Basic Books, 1963.

Neilsen, A. C. *Television '65: A Nielsen Report*. A. C. Neilsen Co., 1965.
Podolsky, E. Horrors. *California P.T.A. Journal*, Dec. 23, 1952.
Rogers, D. Television, In Dorothy Rogers (Ed.), *Issues in child psychology*. Belmont, Calif.: Wadsworth, 1969.
Schramm, W. A., Lyle, J., & Parker, E. B. *Television in the lives of our children*. Stanford, Calif.: Stanford, Calif.: Stanford University Press, 1961.
Somers, A. R., Violence, television and the help of American youth. *New England Journal of Medicine*, April 8, 1976, 811–817.
Witty, P. A. Comics, television and our children. *Today's Health*, February 1955.

Pamela Cantor

As early as 1954, Senator Estes Kefauver, then Chairman of the Senate Subcommittee on Juvenile Delinquency, questioned the need for violent content on television entertainment. Network representatives claimed at that time that research on the effects of violence viewing upon children was inconclusive, although they admitted that some risk existed. In addition, Harold E. Fellows, President and Chairman of the Board of the National Association of Broadcasters, promised that the NAB would undertake research on the impact of television programming on children.

THE DODD HEARINGS

In 1961, Senator Thomas Dodd, then chairman of the same subcommittee, inquired about violence on children's television. Testimony during hearings revealed that the television industry's use of violence had remained both rampant and opportunistic.[2]

> An independent producer was asked to "inject an 'adequate' diet of violence into scripts." . . . Another network wrote "I like the idea of sadism." . . . "Give me sex and action," demanded one executive. (p. 40)

Also it was clear that the previously promised research had not been carried out. Leroy Collins, the new president of the NAB explained:[2]

> Soon [after Mr. Fellows' testimony] the television code review board undertook a pilot study of "viewer attitudes" to determine the feasibility of a broader study, but about that time the Columbia Broadcasting System announced that it was engaged in sponsoring a survey which, while broader, would cover essentially the same ground. In view of this overlapping inquiry, NAB deferred to CBS in order that the larger survey could go ahead in preference to the narrower inquiry which the NAB had initiated. It is anticipated that the CBS project will be completed by the end of this summer [1961] *and that the final report will be published before the end of this year*. (pp. 593–594)

The report in question was published in 1963 by Gary Steiner.[3] The title, *The People Look at Television*, indicates clearly the subject matter of the volume: the attitudes and beliefs of parents and other viewers about the effects of television on children, not the actual effects as determined by scientific investigation.

But the earlier hearings did have an impact, which one observer described this way:[4]

> [The subcommittee staff for the 1961 Dodd hearings] noted that many network series mentioned

in early testimony as especially violent were being syndicated, and shown on independent stations throughout the country. One committee aide observed: "It's as if they used our 1961 hearings as a shopping list!" Many of the programs were scheduled at earlier hours than before, and were reaching younger audiences. (p. 203)

In 1961, industry spokesmen again promised more research.[1]

> . . . we are moving significantly in this area [of research on effects of television on children] now. At a meeting of our joint radio and television board of directors last week approval was given to proceed with the initial planning of an NAB research and training center in association with one of the leading universities in the nation. (p. 594)

James T. Aubrey and Frank Stanton, executives of CBS, as well as executives of NBC and ABC agreed to participate in industry-wide research.

In 1962, the industry co-sponsored the Joint Committee for Research on Television and Children, along with the United States Department of Health, Education and Welfare. This committee, which consisted almost entirely of network personnel, solicited research proposals from various members of the scientific community. Unfortunately, it became clear in 1964 that few of these proposals were being carried out. In fact, only three papers were even begun as a result of the work of the joint committee. The first, by Dr. Ruth Hartley, constituted a criticism and analysis of the inadequacies of research which was detrimental to the industry, not an investigation of the actual effects.[5] A second was conducted by Dr. Seymour Feshbach, a leading proponent of the catharsis hypothesis.[16] The third study was not even completed.

In 1964, as Senator Dodd's hearings contin-

ued, network executives again promised to do more research. By this time the excuses had become rather pathetic. When asked by Dodd what had been done, NBC Executive Vice President Walter D. Scott replied this way:[1]

> I have aked the same question, Senator, because I have wondered why there has not been more in the way of results up to this point. I have been reminded by our people who are working very actively and closely with the Committee that it is appropriate to bear in mind that the work of scholars frequently sets its own pace and that time may be the price we must pay for meaningful results. As I understand it, they have had work done by a very large number of competent scholars in the field of social sciences, I understand that there have been something like one hundred separate projects that have been studied, that these have been narrowed down, that they are now at the stage of being ready to go ahead with, I believe, either five or six specific projects, out of which they hope to get some meaningful answers. (p. 595)

No new research was ever published or reported by the Committee. Scott went on to become NBC's board chairman.

THE VIOLENCE COMMISSION

In 1968, the National Commission on the Causes and Prevention of Violence held hearings on the role of the mass media. Once again, network executives were questioned about the promised research; once again, it was not forthcoming. By this time, the networks were arguing that *they* should not be doing research anyway. One ABC executive stated:[2]

> Research should be done from an objective standpoint and one that the public would be satisfied with as being done objectively, rather than that which is directly financed by our particular company. (p. 598)

The networks evidently felt no responsibility to determine the effects of television for their own use in determining program content.

Network executives also suggested that research was impossible due to the lack of adequate research design. Dr. Frank Stanton, then president of CBS and himself a Ph.D. psychologist, remarked:[2]

> It isn't unwillingness on the part of the industry to underwrite the research. It is that no one in the thirty-odd years I have been in the business has come up with a technique or methodology that would let you get a fix on this impact. . . . These people from the outside [of the industry] have been given every encouragement, every funding they have asked for to come up with methodology, and this is the field that is very illusive [sic] and it doesn't do any good to spend a lot of money and come up with facts somebody can punch his fingers through. (p. 598)

Less than 2 years later "people from the outside" funded by the Federal government had come up with a number of research plans which did permit "a fix on this impact." It was possible all along.

THE SURGEON GENERAL'S NIMH INQUIRY

In 1969, Senator John O. Pastore, Chairman of the Senate Sub-Committee of the Senate Commerce Committee sent a letter to Health, Education, and Welfare Secretary Robert Finch, which said in part:[7]

> I am exceedingly troubled by the lack of any definitive information which would help resolve the question of whether there is a causal connection between televised crime and violence and antisocial behavior of individuals, especially children. . . . I am respectfully requesting that you direct the Surgeon General to appoint a committee comprised of distinguished men and women from whatever professions and disciplines deemed appropriate to devise techniques

> and to conduct a study under his supervision using those techniques which will establish scientifically insofar as possible what harmful effects, if any, these programs have on children.

Secretary Finch directed Surgeon General William H. Stewart to select a committee to authorize and examine evidence relevant to questions about the effects of television on children. The Surgeon General, announcing that he would appoint an advisory panel of scientists respected by the scientific community, the broadcasting industry, and the general public, requested nominations from various academic and professional associations (including the American Sociological Association, the American Anthropological Association, the American Psychiatric Association, and the American Psychological Association), distinguished social scientists, the NAB and the three major networks. From the many names suggested, the office of the Surgeon General drew up a list of 40, and sent it to the presidents of the National Association of Broadcasters and the three national commercial broadcast networks. The broadcasters were asked to indicate "which individuals, if any, you would believe would *not* be appropriate for an impartial scientific investigation of this nature." They responded with a list of seven names:

Leo Bogart, executive vice president and general manager of the Bureau of Advertising of the American Newspaper Publishers Association. Dr. Bogart had previously published a book on television.

Albert Bandura, professor of psychology at Stanford, and an internationally acknowledged expert on children's imitative learning. Bandura, now president-elect of the American Psychological Association, had published numerous research articles which demonstrated that children can learn to be more aggressive from watching TV.

Leonard Berkowitz, Vilas professor of psychology at the University of Wisconsin, principal investigator of an extensive series of studies showing that watching aggression can stimulate aggressive behavior. Author of two books on aggression, Berkowitz served as a consultant to the 1969 Task Force on Mass Media and Violence.

Leon Eisenberg, professor and chairman of the Department of Psychiatry at Harvard University.

Ralph Garry, then professor of educational psychology at Boston University, author of a book on children's television, and a principal consultant to the U.S. Senate Subcommittee on Juvenile Delinquency. He is now at the Ontario Institute for Studies in Education.

Otto Larsen, professor of sociology at the University of Washington and editor of *Violence and the mass media*.

Percy H. Tannenbaum, then professor of psychology and communication at the University of Pennsylvania, and prominent for his theoretical analyses of the arousing effects of media entertainment depicting violence and sex. He has recently been appointed professor in the Graduate School of Public Policy, University of California at Berkeley.

While these distinguished men were blackballed, the industry secured 5 of the 12 positions for its own executives and consultants. They were:

Thomas Coffin, vice president of NBC
Ira H. Cisin, CBS consultant
Joseph T. Kapper, director of CBS social research
Harold Mendelsohn, CBS consultant
Gerhart D. Wiebe, former CBS executive

This odd selection procedure, of systematic inclusion and exclusion, was not intended to be a matter of the public record. Even the non-network members of the committee, all of whom are well respected by the scientific community, were not told anything about it.

When the procedure was uncovered by Stanford professor Edwin Parker and Senator Lee Metcalf, HEW Secretary Robert Finch tried to explain away the travesty as handily as he could, saying that the selection was designed to assure impartiality. James J. Jenkins, then chairman of the American Psychological Association's board of professional affairs, took a different view. He described the procedure as deplorable and analogized:[8]

> It looks like an exemplar of the old story of the "regulatees" running the "regulators" or the fox passing on the adequacy of the eyesight of the man assigned to guard the chicken coop (pp. 951-952)

It is important, though, that the Committee was not directly involved in the commissioning of new research. Instead, 1 million dollars was made available for support of independent projects through the National Institute of Mental Health. About 40 formal proposals were submitted. They were then reviewed by *ad hoc* panels of prominent scientists who were not themselves members of the Committee (by then known as the Surgeon General's Scientific Advisory Committee on Television and Social Behavior). Twenty-three projects were selected and funded in this way: the investigators were free to proceed with their contracted research without interference, and to prepare technical research reports of their findings and of any conclusions they deemed appropriate.

The Advisory Committee Report

Prior to the publication of the individual investigators' reports the committee reviewed them, as well as previous research, and submitted a report to the Surgeon General. The post had changed hands since the project began, having passed to Jesse Steinfeld who released both a brief summary, as well as the Committee's full report in January 1972.

Although indicating that a causal relationship between violence viewing and aggression by the young had been found, the Committee report was unfortunately worded so as to lead to misunderstanding, and the summary was flatly misleading. One journalist, Jack Gould of the *New York Times*, wrote a "scoop" story of the report with the headline, "TV Violence Held Unharmful to Youth."[9]

The Committee's hedging may or may not have been predictable, given its diverse composition and the political pressure to produce a unanimously signed document. At any rate, the private goings on were surely not dull. According to John P. Murray, research coordinator for the project and one of the few non-Committee members who was present during the deliberations:[10]

There was a big move by Government officials to get a consensus report. There was a lot of anger, the meetings were extremely tense with the warring factions sitting at either end of the table, glaring at each other, particularly toward the end. (p. 28)

The result was undoubtedly a compromise, with the "network five" scoring its share in the battle. According to *Newsweek*, in a story "correcting" its earlier interpretation:[11]

At one point during the committee meetings . . . former CBS consultant Wiebe raised his eyes from a particularly damning piece of evidence and grumbled: "This looks like it was written by someone who hates television." But the most ardent defender of the industry was CBS research director Joseph Klapper, who lobbied for the inclusion, among other things, of a plethora of "howevers" in the final report. (p. 55)*

Many of the researchers associated with the project felt that their work had been repre-

*Copyright Newsweek, Inc., 1972. Reprinted by permission.

sented inaccurately, at least to the extent of minimizing what seemed a clear relationship between viewing of TV violence and youngsters' aggressive behavior. Dr. Monroe Lefkowitz, Principal Research Scientist at the New York State Department of Mental Hygiene wrote in a letter to Senator Pastore:

The Surgeon General's Scientific Advisory Committee on Television and Social Behavior in my opinion ignores, dilutes, and distorts the research findings in their report, "Television and Growing Up: the Impact of Televised Violence." As a contributor of one of the technical reports whose study dealt with television violence and aggressive behavior . . . I feel that the Committee's conclusions about the causal nature of television violence in producing aggressive behavior are hedged by erroneous statements, are overqualified, and are potentially damaging to children and society. . . .

Lefkowitz' response is strong, but it is by no means unique. Matilda Paisley, in a report of Stanford University's Institute for Communication Research *(Social policy research and the realities of the system: violence done to TV research),* indicates that fully half of the researchers who replied to her questionnaire stated that the results of their own research had not been adequately reported by the Committee.[10] Some typical replies, with letters substituted for respondents' names, appear below:

Respondent B commented that, "In fact, they went too deep on some of our extraneous findings, in order to obscure the main conclusion." Respondents G, L, and P spoke of "strange emphases," "misleading focus," and "selective emphases," respectively. Respondents E and F spoke of errors in reporting their research. Respondent T stated that "the conclusions are diluted and overqualified."

One item on the Paisley questionnaire read:

"Whatever the findings of your own research suggest,* which of the following relationships of violence viewing to aggressiveness do you feel now is the most plausible?"

    (a) viewing television violence increases aggressiveness;
    (b) viewing television violence decreases aggressiveness;
    (c) viewing television violence has no effect on aggressiveness;
    (d) the relationship between the violence viewing and aggressiveness depends on a third variable or set of variables:
    (e) other, please specify?

None of the 20 investigators who responded to this question selected answer (b); none selected (c). Clearly, then these researchers felt that there was a relationship between TV violence and aggressiveness, and that the long touted catharsis hypothesis was untenable. Seventy percent of the respondents simply selected response (a): viewing television violence increases aggressiveness. All of the remainder qualified their replies with some version of alternatives (d) or (e).

The Pastore Hearings

In March 1972, shortly after the publication of the technical reports, Senator Pastore held further hearings to clarify the situation.[12] When questioned by Senator Pastore and members of his subcommittee, Ithiel de Sola Pool, a member of the Surgeon General's Advisory Committee, commented:

> Twelve scientists of widely different views unanimously agreed that the scientific evidence indicated that the viewing of television violence by young people causes them to behave more aggressively. (p. 47)

---

*Almost half of the investigators were involved in projects which did not bear directly on this question.

By permission of Sissy Krook, photographer.

Alberta Siegel, another Committee member, remarked:

> Commercial television makes its own contribution to the set of factors that underlie aggressiveness in our society. It does so in entertainment through ceaseless repetition of the message that conflict may be resolved by aggression, that violence is a way of solving problems. (p. 63)

Pool and Siegel were among the academic members of the Committee; they had pressed for a strong report on the basis of the data all along. But even Ira Cisin, Thomas Coffin, and the other "network" Committee members agreed that the situation was sufficiently serious to warrant some action.

The networks' chief executives also testified. Julian Goodman, President of NBC, stated:

> We agree with you that the time for action has come. And, of course, we are willing to cooperate in any way together with the rest of the industry. (p. 182)

Elton H. Rule of the American Broadcasting Company promised:

> Now that we are reasonably certain that televised violence can increase aggressive tendencies in

some children, we will have to manage our program planning accordingly. (p. 217)

Surgeon General Steinfeld made the unequivocal statement that:

Certainly my interpretation is that there is a causative relationship between televised violence and subsequent antisocial behavior, and that the evidence is strong enough that it requires sane action on the part of responsible authorities, the TV industry, the Government, the citizens. (p. 28)

Although few social scientists would put the seal "Absolutely Proven" on this, or any other body of research, the weight of the evidence and the outcry of the news media did become sufficient to produce a belated recognition of the implications of the research. Testimony and documentation at the Hearings of the Subcommittee on Communications, U.S. Senate, were overwhelming. Senator Pastore now had his answer. It is captured entirely in the following interchange, late in the hearings, between Pastore and Dr. Eli Rubinstein. (Rubenstein was Vice-Chairman of the Surgeon General's Committee and, in Dr. Steinfeld's absence, monitored the research and refereed the Committee.)

Senator Pastore: And you are convinced, like the Surgeon General, that we have enough data now [about the effects of television on children] to take action?

Dr. Rubinstein: I am, sir.

Senator Pastore: Without a re-review. It will only substantiate the facts we already know. Irrespective of how one or another individual feels, the fact still remains that you are convinced, as the Surgeon General is convinced, that there is a causal relationship between violence on television and social behavior on the part of children?

Dr. Rubinstein: I am, sir.

Senator Pastore: I think we ought to take it from there. . . . (p. 152)

REFERENCES

1. Baker, R. K. The views, standards, and practices of the television industry. In R. K. Baker and S. J. Ball (Eds.), *Violence and the media.* Washington, D.C.: U.S. Government Printing Office, 1969. Pp. 593-614.

2. Johnson, N. *How to talk back to your television set.* Boston: Atlantic-Little, Brown and Company, 1967.

3. Steiner, G. A. *The people look at television.* New York: Alfred A. Knopf, 1963.

4. Barnouw, E. *A History of broadcasting in the United States. Vol. III—from 1953: The image empire.* New York: Oxford University Press, 1972. P. 203. (Copyright©1972 by Erik Barnouw.)

5. Hartley, R. L. *The impact of viewing "aggression": Studies and problems of extrapolation.* New York: Columbia Broadcasting System Office of Social Research, 1964.

6. Feshbach, S., & Singer, R. *Television and aggression.* San Francisco: Jossey-Bass, 1971.

7. Cisin, I. H., Coffin, T. E., Janis, I. L., Klapper, J. T., Mendelsohn, H., Omwake, E., Pinderhughes, C. A., Pool, I. de sola, Siegel, A. E., Wallace, A. F. C., Watson, A. S., & Wiebe, G. D. *Television and growing up: The impact of televised violence.* Washington, D.C.: U.S. Government Printing Office, 1972.

8. Boffey, P. M., & Walsh, J. Study of TV violence. Seven top researchers blackballed from panel. *Science*, May 22, 1970, Vol 168 pp. 949-952. (Copyright © 1970 by The American Association for the Advancement of Science.)

9. Gould, J. TV violence held unharmful to youth. *The New York Times*, January 11, 1972.

10. Paisley, M. B. *Social policy research and the realities of the system: violence done to TV research.* Institute of Communication Research: Stanford University, 1972.

11. Violence revisited. *Newsweek*, March 6, 1972, pp. 55-56. (Copyright Newsweek, Inc. 1972. Reprinted by permission.)

12. U.S. Congress, Senate. Hearings before the subcommittee on Communications of the Committee on Commerce, March 1972.

Parental Control and Parental Love

Diana Baumrind

. . . It appears from the data that parental control and nurturance interact collaborative-ly, and that a pattern of parental behavior high in control and high in nurturance is more likely to produce self-assertive, self-confident, and self-controlled behavior in young children than is any other pattern of parental behavior.

Editor's Introduction

Discipline is defined by the rules and regulations which regulate a child's conduct. In an effort to determine the most effective and constructive methods of child discipline, Baumrind has conceptualized three types of parent discipline approaches. Authoritarian parents expect their children to conform to a set of standards and punish swiftly when children do not obey. This restricts the children's autonomy. Permissive parents avoid imposing their standards and allow their children to regulate their own behavior. This allows too much autonomy. Authoritative parents maintain control while providing affection and warmth. This does not stifle autonomy or initiative. These parents depend to a great degree on verbal reasoning.

Baumrind found that authoritarian parents produce children who are discontented, withdrawn, submissive, distrustful, and most likely to express displaced aggression. Permissive parents produce children who are immature, lacking in self-reliance and self-control. Authoritative parents produce children who are self-assertive, self-confident, and self-controlled. She concludes that there appears to be a correlation between particular personality traits and patterns of parental discipline. Thus, parents do create their children psychologically as well as physically.

Baumrind's conclusions are in accord with the present climate of opinion regarding child rearing. During the early part of the 1900s, theorists believed that children should not be coddled. The result was the advent of detention halls and the use of extreme control in the schools. Later, permissiveness arrived, largely due to the admonitions of psychologists that the thwarting of innate tendencies would produce neurosis. "Spare the rod and spoil the child" was changed to "Wield the rod and warp the child." Currently psychologists are advocating a middle-of-the-road concept of flexibility combined with firmness and warmth. The formula which is advocated is to try to structure the environment so as to encourage good behavior and reward it as frequently as possible. If it becomes necessary to punish in order to achieve discipline, try to be consistent and to make the punishment fit the crime.

Punishment is a word which is often used synonomously with *discipline*. The two words are not equivalents. While the effects of punishment are not Baumrind's main concern, the pervasive misuse of punishment—both the word and the deed—deserves some discussion. Punishment means creating an unpleasant

From "Parental Control and Parental Love," Children (now Children Today), U.S. Department of Health, Education and Welfare: Children's Bureau, *12*, 6 (November – December 1965), pp. 230-234. Reprinted by permission of the author and publisher.

situation for the child after he or she has done something that is not approved of. Most often, punishment is associated with the infliction of physical pain. The effectiveness of physical punishment, however, depends more upon the interruption of parental love than on the severity of pain. Thus, physical punishment from a parent who is usually warm and affectionate is far more effective than it would be coming from a parent who is normally cold or distant, since in the latter situation, the child has little to lose.

Over the long term, however, punishment has been found to be ineffective in eliminating the behavior it was meant to get rid of. Physical punishment is not only largely ineffective but also potentially destructive due to the lesson it demonstrates. It teaches children that the way to deal with anger and frustration is to hit, that "might makes right," and that someone bigger than the child has the right to hit. It is also potentially damaging, as a spanking may relieve the guilt which the child feels for the transgression and leave the child free to repeat the misdeed, since the price has already been paid.

Punishment, if it is to be used at all, should, in my opinion, not be of a physical nature. It should fit the crime both qualitatively and quantitatively. Thus, I would not tell a child who refuses to take a bath on Tuesday that he or she cannot go to the football game with Daddy next Sunday. This is inappropriate both in degree of severity and in temporal relationship to the crime. My feeling is that if it becomes necessary to punish I would ask the child to determine the punishment with me. The child would probably set a more severe restriction than I would have designed. I am then free to reduce the severity. I would warn the child in advance of the punishment so that the child could be given the choice of behaving or accepting the punishment. If I did threaten punishment, I would try to carry it out. At the same time, I would like to be able to alter a restriction which I imposed in haste. Punishment disassociated from the regulations regarding the event, punishment used injudiciously when there has been no misbehavior, punishment far in excess of the crime, or punishment that does not take place at the time of the transgression is potentially harmful. Punishment and reward do alter a child's behavior, but they are not equally effective.

Baumrind discusses the effects of parental discipline on the personality of the child. She concludes that permissive environments produce so little guidance that the children become anxious about doing the right thing. Authoritarian environments produce such strict control that children are not given reasoned discipline and therefore do not learn to reason for themselves. They are coerced into behavior by fear of the consequences without understanding the standards or rules. Authoritative homes, where reasonable expectations and reasoned standards have been used, produce children who can judge their own behavior and determine appropriate standards for themselves.

Pamela Cantor

Since the turn of the century, behavioral scientists have shown increasing interest in child-rearing practices. However, theoretical formulations from one period to the next have been in sharp contradiction. The proscriptions of early behavioral theory intended to prevent spoiling became the prescriptions of psychoanalytic and non-directive theory, in order to avert frustration and submission. The procedures advised by the behaviorist Watson in the early part of this century were specific and pertinent, but, according to later theorists, had injurious side effects on the young child. Watson's proscriptions on coddling and tending to the baby's comfort violated normal maternal desires to nurture their young. However, the theory of psychosexual development from which the later child-rearing ideology arose often frightened and bemused the conscientious parent who was cautioned to "behave naturally" but not to overstimulate, restrict, or express hostility toward her child.

Child-rearing theory of today has synthesized many of the central tenets of the conflicting theories of the past. In the past, Watson emphasized the control functions of child rearing while Freud and Rogers emphasized the nurturing functions. However, today's theories suggest that the lack of parental discipline may make a child insecure about parental love, and conversely that an unloving parent is not likely to successfully control her child's behavior.

This hypothesis and its reverse—that a combination of parental warmth and discipline produces a self-reliant, buoyant, self-controlled child—has received some support through an investigation undertaken in 1963 at the Institute of Human Development, University of California, Berkeley. The purpose of the study was to determine whether preschool children who are self-reliant, self-controlled, buoyant, and affiliative (Pattern I in the investigation) are reared by their parents in a different fashion from children who are discontented, withdrawn, and distrustful (Pattern II), or children who have little self-control or self-reliance and tend to retreat from novel experiences (Pattern III).

Thirty-two children who manifested these three prototypic social attributes to a high degree were selected for three study groups (composed of 13, 11, and 8 children) from among 110 normal pre-school children, who attended the H. E. Jones Child Study Center at Berkeley, after 5 months of observation in nursery school and laboratory settings. Parent-child interaction data were obtained by means of interviews, home visits, and structured observations. All parents whose children were chosen for the investigation cooperated in the study.

The interviews and observations were designed to obtain characteristic expressions of four interaction dimensions—parental control, parental maturity demands, parent-child communication, and parental nurturance.

Parent control refers to the socializing functions of the parent, that is, to those parental acts which are intended to shape the child's goal-oriented activity, modify his expression of dependent, aggressive, and playful behavior, and promote internalization of parental standards.

Parental maturity demands refers to the observed and reported expectations which the parent has of the child in intellectual, social, and emotional spheres, relative to the child's age, abilities, and past performance.

Parent-child communication refers to the extent to which the parent shares with the child her objectives for the child, solicits his opinions and feelings, exhibits attentive and patient interest in the child's efforts to communicate, and comprehends the child's perspective in adult-child interactions.

Parental nurturance refers to the predilection of the parent to perform the caretaking functions. Nurturance is composed of *warmth* and *involvement*. By *warmth* is meant the parent's personal love and compassion for the child expressed by sensory stimulation of the child, verbal approval, and tenderness of expression. By *involvement* is meant identification by the parent with the behavior and feelings of the child, her pride and pleasure in the child's accomplishments, and her conscientious protection of the child's welfare.

CONCEPTUAL APPROACH

Before going into the details of the study, it seems pertinent to describe the conceptual approach to parent-child relations from which it proceeds. This assumes that the physical, cognitive, and moral development of pre-school children is largely a consequence of parental attitudes and child-rearing practices.

A child's energy level, vigor, and alertness are set not only by genetic structure but also by the diet and health regimen provided by his parents. The child's inherent cognitive potential is stimulated by a rich, complex environment—or inhibited by impoverished surroundings. He is taught language, how to interpret and use his experience, and how to reason logically. Parents also teach their children how to relate to others, whom to like and emulate, whom to avoid and derogate, how to express love and animosity, and when to withhold response. The child learns to aspire toward the noble and the ideal—or to be satisfied with the ordinary and the tangible. The child, by seeing himself through his parent's eyes, learns to know his own characteristics and what value to place upon his attributes.

Later, the child's self-image is enhanced, or otherwise altered, by the attitudes toward him of other adults and children. He is evaluated by these others without the leniency expected from loving parents. He is loved if he is lovable, enjoyed if he is personable, avoided if he is irritating, and humiliated if he is incompetent. He is evaluated and reacted to in ways determined by attributes which his parents have to a large extent already shaped, by their own actions or the actions of others whose influence upon the child they have invited.

Although it has been fashionable for some time to pretend that children are not, or at least should not be, their parents' creations, both research findings and common sense demonstrate that, with varying degrees of consciousness and conscientiousness, parents do in many ways create their children psychologically as well as physically. Children commonly model themselves after their parents. The parents' use of reinforcement, whether punishment or reward, will be effective to the

extent that the underlying parent-child relationship becomes one of mutual love, respect, and trust.

Normally, as the child matures, the parent's current influence upon him diminishes and the influence of peers increases. However, the more the child has internalized the parent's value the more likely he is to seek parental guidance and to come to decisions which his parents can affirm. At the same time, the parent learns to trust his child sufficiently to learn, through him, the values and wisdom known best to the new generation.

The assumptions about the meaning of love implicit in the child-rearing models prevalent in the forties and fifties may have deterred parents from fulfilling certain important parental functions. Love was seen as coterminous with kindness, understanding, and self-sacrifice. Such "kind love" is passive with respect to its object, not requiring that its object become good, or knowledgeable, or disciplined—only that it be happy. It appreciates the child as he is and does not try to shape or alter his autonomous development. It is content with providing nourishment and understanding. It gives generously and demands little from the loved one.

The effect on the child of kind, understanding, self-sacrificing mother love may not be entirely salubrious. Once the child enters the larger community, the parents are forced to restrict or deprive. Accustomed as the child is to immediate need gratification and tension reduction, he suffers greater deprivation at such times than the child who is consistently disciplined by his parents. Acting as she is against her love ethic, the mother feels ambivalent about restriction and punishment.

Instances in which praise is used contiguously with punishment tend to nullify or reverse the deterrent effect of punishment. The use of praise in this way also tends to hamper the child in his ability to distinguish between good and bad acts. The parent's ambivalence and resultant guilt and self-depreciation may add to the child's burden of anger and frustration at being restricted or punished.

The mother who expressed love only by kindness, understanding, and self-sacrifice expects of the child, in relation to herself, a reciprocal, not an imitative, response. She permits the child to be selfish and demanding while she herself is not. If the child identifies with the mother's image of herself but is not punished when he behaves in disaccordance with it, he is likely to feel shame at what he is and conflict about what he should become.

Parental love need not be viewed as coterminous with kindness, understanding, and self-sacrifice, although these are among its ingredients. The parental love ethic may include authority, demanding of the parent active, vigorous interaction with the child. The authoritative mother rises actively to meet the developing adult within the child even as she enjoys his predominantly childlike qualities. Such a mother recognizes herself as a senior member of the family—one therefore required to be nobler, stronger, wiser, and more reasonable than the child. She recognizes that, as his creator, she has, in the eyes of her preschool child, divine attributes. Instead of denying this role, she tries to behave toward her child in a way that will justify the child's trust in her authority and maintain his respect even after he surrenders belief in her omnipotence.

The authoritative mother may use the experience of parenthood to become more admirable, to base her authority increasingly on reason and virtue and not on the child's relative impotence. Here authority has, as its aim, shaping the child in accordance with her image of the noble, the beautiful, and the best, and imparting this image to the young child as an initial model upon which he can create his own ideal.

Unlike the *authoritarian* parent, the *authoritative* parent maintains control without impeding the child's autonomous thrust, and encourages rather than suppresses free expression of divergent opinions. The authoritative mother does not mute the conflict which her demands upon the child, and his upon her, engender. But through it all, she asks for his best; she applauds the real, and stands for the ideal, until the child is ready to construct personal ideals which are consistent with the tasks of his own generation. The kind of parent-child conflict which is produced by authoritative parental love tends to free the child to know, and then surpass, his parents; to respect, yet finally overcome, their power and the precedents set by their generation.

THE STUDY

On the basis of these conceptions our study hypotheses were as follows:

Effects of Parental Control

High parental control should be associated in the preschool child with high self-control, self-reliance, and buoyant mood, if parental nurturance is at least average for the population studied. Low parental control combined with higher nurturance should be associated with low self-reliance, avoidant behavior, and low self-control, in the nonclinic preschool child.

Effects of Parental Maturity Demands

The effects of high maturity demands upon the child's self-reliance should vary, depending on the degree of parental nurturance and parent-child communication. When the parents are highly nurturant and communicative, high maturity demands should increase the child's self-reliance. When the parents are nonnurturant or noncommunicative, high maturity demands should be associated with medium or variable self-reliance in the child. Low parental demands for maturity should be associated with low self-reliance and low impulse control in the child.

Effects of Parent-Child Communication

High parent-child communication should augment the effects of high control and high maturity demands on the child. It should contribute to the child's sense of well-being and his interpersonal competence, as do other manifestations of nonindulgent nurturance.

Effects of Parental Nurturance

Low parental nurturance will be associated in the child with discontent and withdrawn, distrustful behavior. High parental nurturance should accentuate both the positive effects of high parental control, and the negative effects of low parental control.

Specifically, it was predicted that:

1. When contrasted with other parents, parents of Pattern I (mature) children will be rated high in control, maturity demands, parent-child communication, and nurturance.
2. Parents of Pattern II (disaffiliated and discontented) children will demonstrate less nurturance than parents of Pattern I and Pattern III children, and less parent-child communication than parents of Pattern I children.
3. Parents of Pattern III (immature) children will demonstrate less control than parents of Pattern II and Pattern I children, and make fewer maturity demands than parents of Pattern I children.

SETTING AND PROCEDURES

The interaction dimensions were defined operationally for the structured and natural settings. During the structured observation at the child study center, mother and child were offered teaching and play material designed to elicit theoretically meaningful behavior in standardized form but without interfering with the spontaneous interplay of mother and child. The home visit, on the other hand, permitted observation of all family members in a natural setting providing spontaneous instances of the phenomena later coded in prearranged categories. In both situations, natural and structured, an attempt was made to preserve the phenomena observed by the method of reporting and the system of categorization.

The Home Visit

The home is the most convenient natural setting in which to observe family interaction, the one which permits observation of all family members engaged in their customary pursuits and using familiar paraphernalia. Even with an observer present, members tend to demonstrate habitual response tendencies to the normal but urgent demands of home life at crucial periods during the day.

The family was observed in the home during two periods selected to elicit a wide range of critical interactions under different conditions of stress. The first period, lasting from just before dinner to the child's bedtime, was chosen so that the family would be seen during a period of maximum interaction and stress. The second period, by contrast, was chosen by the mother as a time which she thought of as least stressful for the child and for herself. Each visit lasted 3 hours.

During the home visits, the observers described in detail those parent-child interactions in which one member attempted overtly to influence the behavior of another. All interactions were coded after the home visits were concluded. Control sequences and noncontrol sequences were identified. A control sequence consists, by definition, of two or more causally related acts containing a single message and involving the same two family members as participants in an interchange initiated by one of them to alter the behavior of the other and ending with the other's compliance or noncompliance. A noncontrol sequence has no initiator or outcome, but otherwise has the same definition. If more than two family members were involved in an interchange, sequences were scored for all pairs of participants separately.

Coded elements of the sequence included the participants; substantive message; degree of power and kind of incentive used by the parent to motivate the child; the manner in which the child complied or failed to comply; and, where appropriate, child satisfaction.

Three kinds of sequences were identified:

1. *Parent-initiated control sequences*, intended to control or alter the child's behavior or future capacity to act. In this type, the parent directs the child's behavior, impelling the child by power, incentive, or both. The child responds by complying or not complying. He makes a decision immediately, or following a number of interpersonal maneuvers with the parent who initiated the sequence. These maneuvers and the results, in terms of compliance and noncompliance, are called the control-outcome rating. The nature of the demand made upon the child determines the message code. The following is a Type I sequence in which the parent uses minimal power and the child complies after the parent persists:

Mark gets up from the table.
Father: "What do you say, Mark?"
Mark: "I wanna go."
Father: "What do you say, Mark?"
Mark: "Excuse me, please."

2. *Child-initiated control sequences*, in which the child makes a demand of the parent with which the parent complies or fails to comply immediately, or after further interaction with the child. The following is a Type II sequence with which the parent fails to comply, although the child uses increasingly greater power:

John: "Can I go out?"
Mother: "Yes. Oh no, I guess you can't. I didn't realize how late is was."
John: "But why didn't you tell me the time?"
Mother: "You have to take a bath now."

John: "Please, Mother. (Crying, beseeching, being terribly cute.) I never get to go down the street."
Mother: "Not tonight, dear."

3. *Parent-initiated noncontrol sequences*, in which both parent and child participated without intending to alter behavior and usually for mutual pleasure. The following is a Type III sequence:

Mother: "Shall we have dessert now?"
Everyone rushes to the table and the family chats amiably while eating.

The Structured Observation

The structured situations consisted of a teaching situation in which the mother was asked to teach the child elementary numerical concepts, using appropriate equipment and an attractive play situation in which the mother could interact or not with the child, as she chose. The play equipment included a miniature city, toy kitchen center, and water play materials.

The teaching situation was arranged in the playroom with the child facing the play materials. This had the effect of producing a divergence of interests between mother and child, thus eliciting instances of parental control which could be observed. During the structured observation, items of behavior describing the mother-child interaction were checked. Following the observation, the experimenter and an observing psychologist filled out summary ratings independently.

CONCLUSIONS

Selection procedures do not permit drawing obligatory causal conclusions from our data since the number of children and parents observed was restricted by the pattern requirements. Nonetheless, it appears from the data that parental control and nurturance interact collaboratively, and that a pattern of parental behavior high in control and high in nurturance is more likely to produce self-assertive, self-confident, and self-controlled behavior in young children than is any other pattern of parental behavior.

In other studies,[1,2,3] where contrary findings have shown parental control to be positively associated with discontent or dependence, the operational definition of control has generally emphasized severity of penalties, restrictiveness, parental disapproval, or lack of communication between parent and child. It is reasonable to conclude that one or more of these variables was the crucial antecedent resulting in discontent or dependency, as was the case with Pattern II parent-child pairs.

Parents of Pattern II children, when compared with parents of Pattern I children, fitted the usual definition of the authoritarian parent in that they reasoned less, inflicted severer penalties, used more disapproval, and were more coercive in their use of power. Since parents of Pattern I children were rated even higher in control than parents of Pattern II children, but were not rated as authoritarian or non-nurturant, it seems reasonable to conclude that the disaffiliation and discontent shown by these children resulted not from high control but from low nurturance, or authoritarian parental behavior, or both.

To the extent that our results are generalizable, self-sufficiency and impulse control in the child are not as affected by parental nurturance as by parental control, since Pattern III children, whose parents were markedly low in control but higher in nurturance, were low in impulse control and low in self-sufficiency, although they were not discontented and socially withdrawn.

The thesis can be supported, from these results, that the processes we call control and nurturance are synergic and that the approach designated as authoritative love integrates the two central parental functions of control and nurturance, so that these functions are perceived by parent and child as unified manifestations of parental love.

[1]Schaefer, Earl S.; Bayley, Nancy: Maternal behavior, child behavior and their intercorrelations from infancy through adolescence. *Monographs of the Society for Research in Child Development,* vol 28, no. 3 (Series no. 87), 1963.

[2]Becker, Wesley C.; Peterson, Donald R.; Luria, Zella; Shoemaker, Donald J.; Hellmer, Leo A.: Relations of factors derived from parent-interview ratings to behavior problems of 5-year-olds. *Child Development,* September 1962.

[3]Kagan, Jerome; Moss, Howard A.: Birth to maturity: a study in psychological development. John Wiley & Sons, New York. 1962.

Part Four

The Middle Years

Chapter 10

Physical Development

HEALTH PROBLEMS OF CHILDREN

Hidden Children

Robert Coles

I only remember thinking to myself that here was yet another person in the ghetto who as a child had gone through repeated bouts of severe illness, and as a grown-up was still troubled by illness, seemingly more complicated illness—a person who nevertheless had never gone to a clinic, a hospital, a doctor's office, had never been visited at home by a school nurse or physican, had never in her life ever seen a physician.

Editor's Introduction

In his books, *Migrants, Sharecroppers and Mountaineers*, and *The South Goes North*, Robert Coles writes about poverty in rural America and in urban slums. In actuality, he is writing about the 25 million impoverished and deprived Americans who are misunderstood and patronized. His message is clear: the stereotyped view of these children as morally deficient or psychologically ill is wrong. He believes that they possess incredible strengths and remarkably courageous spirits.

The statement that the poor must be fed and the sick must be cared for certainly does not originate with Coles. But Coles goes further. He believes that America cannot help its children unless it understands them and it cannot understand them without discarding the pervasive stereotypes and attempts to change individuals without regard for their present needs or their past lives. As one woman living in a Northern ghetto said to Coles, "They tell you they want to help you, but if you ask me they want to make you into them and leave you without a cent of yourself to hang on to." A major tenet of Cole's work is that understanding will change the efforts to remedy poverty from welfare handouts, which make the poor passive recipients, to inclusion in society, which will allow individuals to take an active role in determining their own destinies.

The changes must come soon; for many of the children it is already too late. Although the young migrant children are without homes and live rootless lives, they are "quick, animated and tenacious of life." But this does not last long, as disease, poverty, and feelings of entrapment soon show their effects. Migrant children often become apathetic and self-destructive or openly violent, largely because they see no way out of their despair. Coles describes the migrants as captives who are paid nothing on the excuse that they owe their bosses wages for the little food and shelter which is provided or for their transportation to their jobs. The children come close to living in physical bondage to their bosses, and they are in psychological bondage to the stereotypes surrounding their lives. They are not uninterested in education, but they are often told by their teachers that they are hopeless in academic subjects, ". . . so maybe we should just wear the crayons down every day." There appears to be so little to gain by going to school. They are not apathetic about change, they are simply so beaten so often that Coles feels that they are simply being realistic about the chances of altering their lives.

The black child of the Northern ghetto is subject to stereotypes in much the same way as the child of rural America. The ghetto child is seen as the victim of a disorganized family life and a socialization process that is ineffective and unconcerned with improvement. The case is hopeless by the time the child reaches first grade. And like the children from Appalachia, these ghetto children begin life full of strength and love, only to become, all too soon, tired and full of hate.

In the two selections which follow, Coles discusses the most serious health problem among American children today: poverty. When people do not have enough money, they do not eat well, they do not live in adequate housing, and they do not go to doctors or to dentists. These problems often begin before birth. Poor mothers do not eat well during pregnancy and do not get prenatal attention. Newborn infants do not receive pediatric examinations and abnormalities are not noticed, nor are attempts made at treatment. Later, " . . . accidents and injuries and illnesses are part of life, and either 'take' the child or 'spare' him or her. Fractures heal or they don't. . . . Burns and lacerations and cuts and sores and rashes either 'clear up' or 'stop themselves' or 'leave the child' or they don't, with obvious results: worse and worse pain, more and more incapacity and disability . . . "

The health problems of the poor are not limited to rat bites and lead poisoning but are problems which have pervasive effects on intellectual and emotional development. While not ignoring the imperative need for health services, Coles stresses the role that American society must take to alter the social conditions which breed poverty and disease. Coles hopes to break the cycle of poverty and despair by breaking the stereotypes which prohibit change. He does so by asking us to listen, listen as he speaks without scientific jargon, speaks unabashedly from his heart.

Pamela Cantor

My kids, they're good; each of them is. They're good kids, and they don't make for trouble, and you couldn't ask for them any better. If he had asked me, the man out of the East, Washington or someplace, I would have told him that, too. We all would have. But he didn't want to ask us anything. All he wanted was to tell us he had this idea and this money, and we should go ahead and get our little kids together and they would go to the church during the summer and get their first learning, and they would be needing it, because they're bad off, that's what he must have said a hundred times, how bad off our kids are, and how the President of the United States wants for them to get their teeth fixed and to see a doctor and to learn as much as they can. You know what my wife whispered to me? She said, he doesn't know what our kids have learned, and still he's telling us they haven't learned a thing and they won't. And who does he think he is anyway? I told her it's best to sit him out and we could laugh out loud later when we left the church.

Later, when they left the church, they went home to their children, who were rather curious about the reason their parents had seen fit to go out to a meeting after supper in the middle of the week. There are five of those children and they range from four months to nine years. All the children were born in Swain County, North Carolina, as were their parents and grandparents and greatgrandparents going back a century and more. Nor does Mrs. Allen want her children to be born anyplace else, or for that matter, under any other circumstances:

This is good country, as anybody will likely admit once he's seen it, and there's no reason to leave that I can see. You ask about the children I've borne; well, they're all good children, I believe they are. I've lost two, one from pneumonia we

thought, and one had trouble from the moment he was alive. He was the only child that ever saw a doctor. We brought him down to Bryson City and there was a doctor there, waiting to see him. The Reverend Mason had called over, and he went with us.

The doctor looked over the child real good, and I kept on fearing the news was going to be bad, the longer he looked and the more tests he did. Then he said he'd need extra tests, even beyond what he did, and we would have to come back. Of course I told him we'd try, but it's real hard on us to get a ride, and there's the other children I have, and my mother's gone, so they have to be left with one another the whole day, and there's a baby that needs me for feeding. The doctor said he could understand, but he needed those tests, and he was going to have to call some other doctor way over in Asheville or someplace and ask him some things. Mr. Mason said he'd drive us again, and we'd better do what the doctor said. Mr. Mason asked the doctor if there was much hope, even if we did everything and kept on coming back, so long as we had to, and the doctor shook his head, but he didn't say anything, one way or the other. But then my husband, Mr. Allen, he decided we'd better ask right there and then what was happening, and he did. He told the doctor that we're not much used to going to see doctors, and we'd like to know where we stand—it's just as plain and simple as that. The doctor asked if he could talk to Mr. Mason alone, and we said yes, that would be fine by us, but please couldn't they decide between themselves and then come and tell us something before we go back. And they did. They didn't talk too long before they came out, and said they would be honest with us, like we wanted, and the problem was with little Edward's muscles, and they weren't good from the start, and chances are they'd never be much good, and if we come back for the tests we might find out the exact disease, but he was pretty sure, even right then the doctor was, that Edward had a lot of bad trouble, and there wasn't much that could be done for him, and we might as well know it, that he'd not live to be grown up, and maybe not more than a year was the best we could hope for.

I was real upset, but I was relieved to be told; I was thankful as can be for that. I guess Jim and I just nodded our heads and since we didn't say a word, and it was getting along, the time, the doctor came over and he asked if we had any questions to ask of him. I looked at Jim and he looked at me, and we didn't think of anything, and then Mr. Mason said it was all right, because if we did think of something later, we could always tell him and he could tell the doctor. The doctor said yes, and he said we were good people, and he liked us for being quiet and he wished he could do more. Jim said thank you, and we were glad he tried to help, and to be truthful we knew that there was something real bad wrong, and to us, if there isn't anything we can do, then chances are there isn't anything that anyone can do, even including a doctor, if he didn't mind us saying so. Mr. Mason said he wasn't sure we were in the right, and I said we could be wrong, and maybe they could have saved little Anne from her fever that burned her up—it was the pneumonia, we were sure. The doctor said there wasn't much use going back to what was over and done with, and I agreed. When we left, Mr. Mason said we could take the child back to the doctor anytime and he would drive us, and the doctor told the reverend he wouldn't charge us, not a penny. But Edward died a few weeks later. He couldn't breathe very good, like the doctor explained to us, because of his muscles, and the strain got to be more than he could take, so he stopped breathing, the little fellow did, right there in my arms. He could have lived longer, they said, if we'd have let them take him and put him in a hospital, you know, and they have motors and machines, to work on you. But I don't believe the Lord meant for Edward to go like that, in a hospital. I don't.

Her words read sadder than they sounded. She is tall, thin, but a forceful and composed woman, not given to self-pity. She has delicate bones, narrow wrists, thin ankles, decidedly pale blue eyes, and a bit surprisingly, a very strong, almost aquiline nose. She was thirty and, I thought, both young and old. Her brown hair was heavily streaked with gray, and her skin was more wrinkled than is the case with many women who are forty or even fifty, let alone thirty. Most noticeable were her teeth; the ones left were in extremely bad repair, and many had long since fallen out—something that she is quite willing to talk about, once her guest has lost *his* embarrassment and asked her a question, like whether she had ever seen a dentist about her teeth. No, she had never done anything like that. What could a dentist do, but take out one's teeth; and eventually they fall out if they are really no good. Well, of course, there *are* things a dentist can do—and she quickly says she knows there must be, though she still isn't quite sure what they are, "those things." For a second her tact dominates the room, which is one of two the cabin possesses. Then she demonstrates her sense of humor, her openness, her surprising and almost awesome mixture of modesty and pride:

If you want to keep your teeth, you shouldn't have children. I know that from my life. I started losing my teeth when I started bringing children into the world. They take your strength, your babies do, while you're carrying them, and that's as it should be, except if I had more strength left for myself after the baby comes, I might be more patient with them. If you're tired you get sharp all the time with your children.

The worst tooth to lose is your first one, after that you get used to having them go, one by one. We don't have a mirror here, except a very small one and it's cracked. My mother gave it to me. When I pick it up to catch a look at myself I always fix it so that I don't see my teeth. I have them in front of the crack instead of the glass. I'd like to have the teeth back, because I know I'd look better, but you can't keep yourself looking good after you start a family, not if you've got to be on the move from the first second you get up until right before you go to sleep. When I lie down on the bed, it's to fall asleep. I never remember thinking about anything. I'm too tired. So is Jim; he's always out there working on something; and so are the kids, they're real full of spirits. No wonder I lost so many teeth. When you have kids that are as rowdy and noisy as mine, they must need everything a mother's got even before they're born. Of course, even now Jim and I will sacrifice on their account, though they'll never know it.

I always serve myself last, you know. I serve Jim first, and he's entitled to take everything we have, if he wants to, because he's the father, and it's his work that has brought us what we have, all of it. But Jim will stop himself, and say he's not so hungry, and nod toward the kids, and that means to give them the seconds before him. We don't always have seconds, of course, but we do the best we can. I make corn bread every day, and that's filling. There's nothing I hate more than a child crying at you and crying at you for food, and you standing there and knowing you can't give them much of anything, for all their tears. It's unnatural. That's what I say; it's just unnatural for a mother to be standing in her own house, and her children near her, and they're hungry and there isn't the food to feed them. It's just not right. It happens, though—and I'll tell you, now that you asked, my girl Sara, she's a few times told me that if we all somehow could eat more, then she wouldn't be having trouble like me with her teeth, later on. That's what the teacher told them, over there in the school.

Well, I told Sara the only thing I could tell her. I told her that we do the best we can, and that's all anyone put here on this earth can ever do. I told her that her father has worked his entire life, since he was a boy, and so have I, and we're hoping for our kids that they may have it a lot better than us. But this isn't the place to be, not in Swain County here, up in this hollow, if you want to sit back and say I'd like this and I'd like that, and you'd better have this and something else, because the teacher says you should. I told Sara there's that one teacher, and maybe a couple more, and they get their salaries every week, and do you know who the teacher's uncle is—he's the sheriff over there in Needmore. Now, if Sara's daddy made half that teacher's salary in cash every week, he'd be a rich man, and I'd be able to do plenty about more food. But Sara's daddy doesn't get a salary from no one, no one, you hear! That's what I said to her, word for word it was. And she sat up and took notice of me, I'll tell you. I made sure she did. I looked her right in the eyes, and I never stopped looking until I was through with what I had to say. Then she said, 'Yes, ma'am,' and I said that I didn't want any grudges between us, and let's go right back to being friends, like before, but I wanted her to know what the truth was, to the best of my knowledge, and nothing more. She said she knew, and that was all that was said between us.

Vitality and Violence, Life and Death
Robert Coles

A DOCTOR CAN KEEP A POOR HEART BEATING

One day Leona took sick. She'd been having headaches, you know, like everyone has. She'd been having bad digestion, like I do. Then all of a sudden, right in front of the missus, she got a bad headache and her stomach started hurting something terrible, and then she threw up all she'd had over there to eat, and she fell to the floor and passed out. I guess she'd told the missus her head was hurting bad and her stomach, and the next thing she was down, right beside the refrigerator, we heard. The missus acted as though someone of her own was sick. She called her husband, and he called the hospital, and they made a special case of it and took Leona right over and put her in a room, all to herself. There were no colored there, and the room Leona had, it was reserved for the rich ones of the whites.

Well, it was an awful thing. They wouldn't let us come visit her, only the missus. My daddy lost his good sense and started being funny with my mother. He said Leona had suddenly turned white and that was what had happened—she'd collasped on her face and turned white and so naturally they won't let us see her, because she's all locked up there in the hospital with the white people, while they try to figure out what to do. He never should have talked like that, because Leona died—it was hardly a day or two after she fell sick and went there, went to the hospital. We never learned what it was that happened to her. The missus told us she wasn't sure, either. She said the doctors told her that Leona had about a dozen things wrong with her, that's right, and maybe even more than that.

She was called by God; that's what I believe. She must have been upset there, in the hospital. She never was inside a place like that, I'm sure. It was a brick building, large and with glass doors. We went and looked at it. We asked them if they please wouldn't just let Leona look out of the window, so that we could see her and wave to her, and she could see us and wave to us. The nurse told us to go, and the faster the better. So we did. Leona went too—do you see? Leona knew the doctors wanted to help her. The missus said Leona told her she knew that. I'm sure she did. But Leona never before had asked anyone in this world to help her but God. I do believed that she must have prayed extra-special hard to Him when she woke up and found herself in that place, all by herself, in a room she was, with the white people doing things to her—to help her, I know, to help get her better. Now she's *really* better, thank God.

The longer she talks the more apparent it becomes that she is not to be immediately judged as afraid, pure and simple—afraid of hospitals and doctors through "ignorance" and all the other things one could so easily ascribe to her. Of course her aunt's quick death in a hospital that barred her and other visitors cannot be forgotten. Of course she has no real awareness of how doctors and hospitals work, especially in a city like Boston. . . .

A doctor, what can a doctor do to change our lives, even if he would come here, right over here to our building, and give us all the medicines he had? Could they make him fix those stairs and get rid of the garbage? Could they help us with our children, so they can find jobs and earn the money they need? I don't blame anyone and not the doctors, not them. We never heard of them in Alabama, and we've only been up here a year, and maybe it's real different up her, but it's not all *that* different. The welfare lady, she tried to make that landlord come here and kill all those rats, those rats that bite my children all the time, but she can't get him to lift a single finger of his big fat hand. Could a doctor get him to be a better Christian man? I don't believe it. Landlords, a lot of them, have the devil in them, like the bossmen down South. I sure have the devil in me. The landlord won't do what he should, and I want to go kill him, like he should be killing the rats. The Bible says we should forgive; we should be forgiving. I can't be; I can't feel that way. I guess that's one reason God makes me suffer, and my children, too.

I was hardly born before I almost died, so maybe God was keeping his eye on me way back then and trying to warn me about being bad and losing my temper. I threw a brick at the man who collects the rent. I missed. He said he'd have the police here, but he didn't call them. He told the next-door people that he didn't blame us for the way we felt, but all he does is collect the rent, not own the place.

Like I said, I don't remember anything, but they tell me I nearly went several times, I nearly did, as a baby. I can remember later on, when I

was my Mary's age, when I was six or so, I
guess—then I can remember my mother looking
over me, and the minister and his wife, and they
prayed and prayed and prayed, and my mother
just kept on holding my hand in her hand, and I
do believe she got me better that way. When a
child of mine falls ill, I hold him, I hold her. I hold
them and hold them. I pray for them, and God
will listen—sometimes. I remember being hot,
and the sweat was coming out all over me, and it
was summer out, down there in Alabama, but I
was so hot my mother said I was hotter than the
sun was, even then, in the middle of the hottest
day you could want. She had my daddy bring the
water in, a pail at a time from the well, and she'd
wet the cloth and then cover up my forehead with
it, the cool, cool cloth. After a while I stopped
being so hot. Then I got better, I guess.

I can remember other times. I hate to think of
them. I'm going through the same troubles with
my own children. They get the chills. They get
the fevers. They get the rat bites. They tell me
they're not getting all the food they want to eat,
just like I used to tell my mother the same thing.
Up here you can get welfare if there's no work,
but only if your husband leaves you. My husband
won't leave. I don't want him to go. The welfare
people give us emergency money, they call it, and
they're always trying to get work for my husband. But even when they do get him work for a
while, then they don't need him any more, the
people he works for. So, we don't have the
money to keep up with the food prices and to buy
clothes for my children and pay all that rent, and
it's as bad as it was down there in Sweet Water,
Alabama, yes sir.

Oh, I hope everything will get better someday,
I do. I'd like to be able to get up in the morning
and not be tired and not be worried and not have
my body hurting, hurting, all the time giving me
hurt to feel. I know there are the doctors, and I
know they are smart, as smart as can be. Now
that we're up here in the North we have a
television, and we can see the doctors, how they
come and do their work on the people and be of
use to them. There aren't the doctors near here,
though. I've not yet tried the other part of the
city. I've not yet figured out where to go. They

say you can get the welfare people to help you;
they'll call a taxi and take you, if the worker is
good. Some of them are; some of them aren't, the
welfare workers. But we have tried to stay clear
of welfare. We have tried to be on our own. We
tried that in Alabama, too. We were tenants
there. We paid the bossman for using his land. By
the time we finished paying him there wasn't
much left. There was nothing left, I'll tell you.
Here, there's nothing left, too. My husband will
get a job doing sweeping, or it'll be washing cars,
and when he brings home the money, it isn't
hardly enough for us, just enough to let us eat
something and keep them away from us, the
court people that try to throw you out if you
don't give over your rent money.

No sooner is there a job that seems all right,
than they tell my husband they're closing shop,
or they have to cut down on things, so we're
without money again, just like we always were
down South, except that here there's no vegetables to grow, and there's that collection man
knocking on your door all the time for rent. I
never thought I'd wish for the sight of the old
bossman from Sweet Water, Alabama, but I do,
every time that rent-collection man comes, I do.

My children have troubles. In school they tell
them they need to have their eyes looked at, and
their teeth. They say I'm not feeding them the
right food. That's what the teacher told my Mary.
She said we're new to the North, and we should
pick up the way people live here—we should take
better care of ourselves, that's what she said to
Mary. I'm trying, I am. I'm going to do it; I'm
going to get the children looked at someplace, in
a hospital, and buy them the clothes that they
need. All I lack is the money, then I can go and do
those things they tell you to go do; take the taxis,
and visit the teachers, and go to the hospital, and
demand your rights at the welfare office, and all
that. The way I see it, though, is that there's not
much you can demand when you're someone like
me. The civil rights people come and tell you
there's a lot you can demand, and maybe they're
right and I'm wrong. But I can see with my eyes;
we have people in this building who have been
here years and years, not a little time, like us, and
they're no better off than us. They even go to the

hospital and get pills to take, and they're still no better off. They hurt, and they tell me they do. I said to one of them, I asked her why she kept going to the doctor and fighting with her welfare worker. She said because the doctor might help, and the welfare worker, too. Then I said she looked to be in trouble with her breathing, like me; and her heart and her stomach, the doctor told her they're both ailing her; and her boy got bit, like mine, by the rats. So, there you have it; there's the proof that she shouldn't expect much from the hospital and from the city hall, where she goes. She told me the doctor agreed with me. She told me he told her that a lot of us, we've got a lot of things wrong with us, and we haven't seen them, the doctors, all our life, and when we do get to see them, when we get up here, it's too late, and there's a limit to what they can do, a limit.

Perhaps that mother, Mrs. Rosa Lee Welch, that relative newcomer to a northern ghetto, is a little more sad, a little less hopeful, than other ghetto mothers are—or at least should be, say we doctors or lawyers or teachers or activists, who believe that things are getting better, slowly perhaps, but definitely. Perhaps that mother will find out how significantly different Roxbury, Massachusetts, is from Sweet Water, Alabama, and especially different with respect to the kind of medical services offered. Yet much of Mrs. Welch's despair is shared by her neighbors, even those who have lived in Roxbury years longer than she has. I could easily call upon psychological words like fear and depression and suspiciousness and skepticism to explain such attitudes, such lack of hope and confidence, and I could, of course, add the familiar sociological or anthropological facts that give external justification to those "internal" matters, those states of mind which in this woman's case, and in the case of hundreds of thousands like her, reflect what is real in their particular world. I would much rather, however, use her own words and her own medical history and her

husband's and children's—as nearly as they all can be reconstructed by a listener.

In Sweet Water, Alabama, a family such as the one Aunt Leona and her nieces and nephews come from learns to deal with birth, illness or death on its own. Aunt Leona's sudden ending, for all the examinations done on her, the tests taken, the equipment brought into her room, was clearly an exceptional, surprising and fearful experience, and one not easily forgotten by those who came and looked at that hospital building—as outsiders not only at that particular moment, but also as permanent outsiders, who would have felt no less overwhelmed had they, after all, been admitted to the dying woman's room. Aunt Leona's niece, whom I have quoted at such length, was in fact delivered by Aunt Leona and another aunt, Josephine, who herself later died giving birth to a baby. To slip into medical language, a child's destiny in Sweet Water, if he is black and poor *or* white and poor, is to be born to a mother who has received no prenatal care, to be born outside a hospital, in a rural cabin, attended either by a midwife (with various degrees of experience and training) or simply by a relative. Then the newborn infants gets no pediatric examination, no injections or "shots" to prevent this or that disease, no vitamin supplements, no evaluation, no treatment of any kind. The heart is not heard, nor the lungs. Abnormalities are not noticed, nor are attempts made at correction. Advice is not given, nor reassurance. Worst of all, accidents and injuries and illnesses are part of life, and either "take" the child or "spare" him or her. Fractures heal or they don't, often without the benefit of splints or casts. Infections go away or they don't. Burns and lacerations and cuts and sores and rashes either "clear up" or "stop themselves" or "leave the child" or they don't, with obvious results: worse and worse pain, more and more incapacity and disability—and always those complications, which themselves get no more care and attention and treatment than whatever kind of "pathology" caused the "sequelae" in the first place.

I find it hard at a moment like this to list some of the untreated diseases I have seen—both in places like Marengo County, Alabama, and in places like Roxbury. Indeed, among infants and children and their parents in rural areas of the South or Appalachia, a visiting doctor need only recall the various "systems" of the body he learned in anatomy and physiology, and the various classifications of diseases he learned in those medical and surgical clerkships—and then one by one take note of what he sees: cuts and bruises and infections of the skin; unrepaired injuries to bones due to accidents, or the bowing and bending of bones that rickets causes; weakness of muscles; evidence of hemorrhages or anemia; abnormal neurological responses, like the sensation of tingling or numbness or burning. Symptomatically one hears everything, and clinically one sees everything: fatigue, pains and spasms and cramps and itches; indigestion and vomiting, with the food often enough blood-streaked; headaches and backaches and a throbbing or pounding in the chest, or a sharp, piercing kind of hurt there; loss of appetite, loss of energy, loss of alertness, loss of ability to sleep and "just plain loss of everything," a nondescript and unscientific summary that usually can be heard spoken quietly rather than angrily, and tied to all sorts of concrete diseases, ones easy to document, were there doctors in Marengo County, Alabama, or Wolfe County, Kentucky, of a mind to do so, and were all those law-abiding, out-of-the-way, utterly penniless individuals to become patients.

The fact is that information about such individuals is nowhere recorded in our nation's rich accumulation of statistics. Aunt Leona's birth was never registered, nor was her death. Her illness, her income, her very existence as an American citizen were a matter between her and a bossman or two and her and her family, her kin, her neighbors—but not her and Washington, D.C., or Montgomery, Alabama, or Linden, where Marengo County's courthouse stands. If our federal government's statistics show the infant mortality rates for such counties to be double and triple what they are for other American children, I fear we have to conclude that matters are even worse than all those numbers and percentages can possibly tell us. There are people in this country who never see officials from the Census Bureau, who never see registrars of this or that or county officials whose job it is to keep track of things. They are people who are migrant farmers, hence live everywhere and nowhere, or sharecroppers and tenant farmers, hence a particular bossman's virtual property and out of everyone's sight but his, or mountaineers, hence up a hollow and beyond anyone's range of concern or even awareness. And in the cities they are those very same people, some newcomers to streets and alleys, some who move about from place to place, apartment to apartment, neighborhood to neighborhood, and some who hide themselves with a degree of success hard for the rest of us to imagine, so proud are we of where we live, what we are, whom we know and depend upon and visit and welcome as visitors.

Here, for example, is one landlord, a slum landlord I suppose he could be called:

I wouldn't even try to tell you how many people, how many families, live in my buildings. I couldn't find out even if I wanted to. I couldn't find out if I was working for the United States Government, for the census people, and if I had some soldiers with me when I knocked on those doors. They come here from far away usually, because there's a relative or a friend here, a contact they have, and they move in, and their idea of a crowd isn't yours or mine. All I do is collect my rents. I wouldn't dare try to poke inside those doors. Of course, one day an apartment will be full, packed full, and the next they're all gone, *all* of them. I'd like to see the FBI track them down, that's right, the FBI. What could they go on, any of those detectives? These people aren't recorded anyplace. No one has ever taken their fingerprints for a job or anything else. They don't have birth certificates. They've never had a "residence" up here. It's hard to explain all that to people. You drive by and all you see is the fronts of the buildings. I'm supposed to know what goes on inside them, but I don't. I try to keep the heat going in winter, and the water going, and the hallways lighted; I even try to install screens every summer and take them out in the fall, but as for that, the screens, it's a ridiculous business, because they ruin them—in a week or two they've been torn and punched and pushed out. It's terrible, what they must have gone through before they came here, but it's our cities that have to pay the price. I guess it's the price of everything that used to be wrong, everything that happened *before*—long before they ever came here. I read someplace that the ghetto is one big disease. I've owned property here for twenty years, and until five years ago this was no ghetto, this neighborhood. I should have sold my property then, before that. If it's one big disease here, landlords like me didn't cause the disease. No one in this city caused it; the disease was brought in from other places, and it was a real bad disease.

To be sure, he was speaking metaphorically, but many diseases have literally been carried into his buildings by the latest newcomers. Aunt Leona never made it North, but her niece and her niece's children and their many, many cousins did. They brought with them parasites and anemias and chronic sinusitis and rheumatic heart disease and teeth in poor repair and congenital diseases and vitamin-deficiency diseases like rickets and beriberi and pellagra. They brought with them scars and lumps; they brought high blood pressure and kidney infections, swollen ankles and

joints that don't quite work the way they were meant to work. We each of us get sick, of course, but the illnesses I have just mentioned are not even considered sicknesses—not by those in our ghettos who have always had them, and expect to have them until the end, until that Healer they mention so often with one sweep of His hand does away with all of a person's troubles, all that has gone wrong in body and mind.

I do not deny that in rural areas ("primitive areas" they are called by some who shun the notion that "plundered areas" might be more to the point) efforts are made to do away with all those complaints. Remedies are indeed sought and taken—herbs, roots, mixtures of things. Old ladies possessed of healing powers are visited, and they all the time reach out for those victims, "lay the hand on them," on sufferers and their enemies—sore spots and ailing limbs and bodies that seem seized by "a thousand million devils," as I once heard it put in Marengo County. For solace and reassurance and, just possibly, relief of some sort, there are even the mysteries of voodoo, of curses, of snakes held and danced with by desperate people willing to remind themselves of the Bible, each and every part of it, willing to do anything, say anything, call upon anything, lean upon anybody, all in the hope that a little, a very little might be done to change things, to make the body feel better, to make the breathing easier, to make the heart feel steadier and less fitful and less ominously pounding, to make the pus stop, the worms go away, the stomach settle down, the "soreness" leave. That is the word I hear in Marengo County and Wolfe County, the word used by white and black people, poor people driven from the land; they say it all in the "soreness" they claim to feel, or the "sorriness" they talk about, which is what we would rather more awkwardly, more pretentiously, call the "psychiatric component" of their various sicknesses. Those words "soreness" and "sorriness" are also the two words I have heard in Roxbury, Massachusetts, and in Cleveland's Hough section, and in the west and the south and the north sides of Chicago, heard used by former sharecroppers or tenant farmers, by mountaineers, by the descendants of slaves, by the descendants of yeomen, Scotch-Irish yeomen who are now "up in the city for a spell" and quite openly willing to say they "have come to naught," but also at the slightest sign of pity ready with a flash of sullen and unyielding and thoroughly combative pride.

Now they are all in the cities, and there to stay, however much they dream of the return, however often they make those brief pilgrimages back. Now they live not far from us doctors, more or less within our sight; they live near us and near us they struggle to live—not only to make a living but, literally, to catch their breaths, to get through another day. And often enough they fear and shun us doctors—to our frustration and sadness, because many of us, many more I believe than an overly critical public would acknowledge, really would like in some way to reach out, be of help, offer our skills to them. That is the problem, though; I refer to "them." They feel to us like a "them," even as we, well intentioned or not, feel the same—also a "them." History has made for the distance between "us" and "them," through generations and generations of experiences, some of which I can only try here to suggest or cite. We cannot wipe out that history with a wave of the hand, even the most dedicated hand, cradling a stethoscope or pointing to the finest, best-equipped, most concerned and responsive of hospitals, of clinics, of newly thought-out urban medical settings. But to quote a phrase often called upon both by John F. Kennedy and Robert F. Kennedy, two Americans who

meant so very much to all those people, black and white, "we can begin." We can begin by looking at what has happened to the people whose aches and pains do eventually lead them to the hospitals of our cities; and what has happened to make for suspicion and withdrawal and apparent unconcern and even hate; what has happened, medically, to destroy good vision and good sense.

Fortunately, Aunt Leona's niece did at long last take herself and her children to one of Boston's hospitals, not at my prodding but at her own initiative. She did so reluctantly, fearfully, with little expectation that any real cures would be the result; but she did it. She and her children caused their doctors to be seriously confused, appalled at what they found, troubled and annoyed with the "attitudes" of such patients; but she and her children have kept going to those various doctors. Months later, she could say this:

It's not a new life I have, but I sure feel like the old life is easier to live. A doctor can do that; a doctor can keep a poor heart beating. He can keep the heart alive, so you're alive. I can breathe better. I'm not so jittery. I'm up to facing the day, and my children, too, they're in better spirits. It's the same old troubles we have, you know, but they're not on top of us, just all around. If you can stand up and not be hurting all over, then troubles aren't on top of you any more.

She went on to thank the doctors profusely for what they have done, and I would imagine that they have good cause to thank her for what she allowed them to learn—about her and her kind, and about things and conditions and situations we all somehow never heard of, never realized existed, never counted as immediately present and pressing, matters of life and death for doctors, and for a great nation, too.

Chapter 11

Mental Development

**MORAL DEVELOPMENT IN THE
SCHOOL-AGE CHILD**

The Child as a Moral Philosopher

Lawrence Kohlberg

Adults seldom listen to children moralizing. If a child throws back a few adult clichés and behaves himself, most parents—and many anthropologists and psychologists as well— think that the child has adopted or internalized the appropriate parental standards.

Editor's Introduction

Through a longitudinal study of American boys followed from ages 10 to 15 and 25 to 30, and through cross-cultural studies (Taiwan, Yucatan, Turkey, Great Britain, Canada, and Israel), Kohlberg has concluded that there is an invariant sequence of stages in the development of moral thinking. Accordingly, he has formulated the progression of three levels or six stages of moral development.

  In Kohlberg's research design, each individual is given a standardized interview which consists of several hypothetical moral dilemmas. The individual's stage is then ascertained by a complex scoring system applied to the responses. Kohlberg's longitudinal study indicates that an individual's level of moral development at age 13 is highly predictive of his or her moral maturity as an adult.

In subsequent studies, Kohlberg and Elliot Turiel investigated the process by which people move from one level of moral development to another. The investigators found that movement from one stage to another occurs in a prescribed sequence, that change occurs only in small increments, and that no single stage can ever be bypassed or skipped. They also concluded that moral growth is not a simple matter of the internalization of environmental norms. The most effective way of producing change is to introduce what the authors call "cognitive conflict" by providing reasoning at the stage directly above the child's original stage, by providing an environment which would expose the child to conflicts in moral values, and by providing the child with opportunities to take the roles of others in moral dilemmas.

Kohlberg further states than an individual's stage of moral development is predictive of his or her actual behavior. His studies have shown that a high percentage of American and English delinquent boys are actually operating on the two lowest stages of moral development, while only a small percentage of nondelinquent controls are operating at the same low stages. While Kohlberg is optimistic about the possibility of raising an individual's level of moral development, he offers the pessimistic observation that less than 25 percent of the adult population of the United States or other cultures in the study are operating at the highest level.

Pamela Cantor

How can one study morality? Current trends in the fields of ethics, linguistics, anthropology, and cognitive psychology have suggested a new approach that seems to avoid the morass of semantical confusions, value bias and cultural relativity in which the psychoanalytic and semantic approaches to morality have foundered. New scholarship in all these fields is now focusing upon structures, forms, and relationships that seem to be common to all societies and all languages rather than upon the features that make particular languages or cultures different.

For twelve years, my colleagues and I studied the same group of seventy-five boys, following their development at three-year intervals from early adolescence through young manhood. At the start of the study, the boys were aged ten to sixteen. We have now followed them through to ages twenty-two to twenty-eight. In addition, I have explored moral development in other cultures—Great Britain, Canada, Taiwan, Mexico, and Turkey.

Inspired by Jean Piaget's pioneering effort to apply a structural approach to moral development, I have gradually elaborated over the years of my study a typological scheme describing general structures and forms of moral thought that can be defined independently of the specific content of particular moral decisions or actions.

The typology contains three distinct levels of moral thinking, and within each of these levels distinguishes two related stages. These levels and stages may be considered separate moral philosophies, distinct views of the sociomoral world.

We can speak of the child as having his own morality or series of moralities. Adults seldom listen to children's moralizing. If a child throws back a few adult chichés and behaves himself, most parents—and many anthropologists and psychologists as well—think that the child has adopted or internalized the appropriate parental standards.

Actually, as soon as we talk with children about morality, we find that they have many ways of making judgments that are not "internalized" from the outside, and that do not come in any direct and obvious way from parents, teachers, or even peers.

MORAL LEVELS

The *preconventional* level is the first of three levels of moral thinking; the second level is *conventional*, and the third *postconventional*, or autonomous. While the preconventional child is often "well behaved" and is responsive to cultural labels of good and bad, he interprets these labels in terms of their physical consequences (punishment, reward, exchange of favors) or in terms of the physical power of those who enunciate the rules and labels of good and bad.

This level is usually occupied by children aged four to ten, a fact long known to sensitive observers of children. The capacity of "properly behaved" children of this age to engage in cruel behavior when there are holes in the power structure is sometimes noted as tragic (*Lord of the Flies*, *High Wind in Jamaica*), sometimes as comic (Lucy in *Peanuts*).

The second, or conventional, level also can be described as conformist, but that is perhaps too smug a term. Maintaining the expectations and rules of the individual's family, group, or nation is perceived as valuable in its own right. There is a concern not only with *conforming* to the individual's social order but in *maintaining*, supporting, and justifying this order.

The postconventional level is characterized by a major thrust toward autonomous moral principles that have validity and application apart from authority of the groups or persons who hold them and apart from the individual's identification with those persons or groups.

MORAL STAGES

Within each of these three levels there are two discernible stages. At the preconvention level we have:

Stage 1: Orientation toward punishment and unquestioning deference to superior power. The physical consequences of action, regardless of their human meaning or value, determine its goodness or badness.

Stage 2: Right action consists of that which instrumentally satisfies one's own needs and occasionally the needs of others. Human relations are viewed in terms like those of the marketplace. Elements of fairness, of reciprocity, and equal sharing are present, but they are always interpreted in a physical, pragmatic way. Reciprocity is a matter of "you scratch my back and I'll scratch yours" not of loyalty, gratitude, or justice.

And at the conventional level we have:

Stage 3: Good-boy—good-girl orientation. Good behavior is that which pleases or helps others and is approved by them. There is much conformity to stereotypical images of what is majority or "natural" behavior. Behavior is often judged by intention; "he means well" becomes important for the first time, and is overused, as by Charlie Brown in *Peanuts*. One seeks approval by being "nice."

Stage 4: Orientation toward authority, fixed rules, and the maintenance of the social order. Right behavior consists of doing one's duty, showing respect for authority, and maintaining the given social order for its own sake. One earns respect by performing dutifully.

At the postconventional level, we have:

Stage 5: A social-contract orientation, generally with legalistic and utilitarian overtones. Right action tends to be defined in terms of general rights and in terms of standards that have been critically examined and agreed upon by the whole society. There is a clear awareness of the relativism of personal values and opinions and a corresponding emphasis upon procedural rules for reaching consensus. Aside from what is constitutionally and democratically agreed upon, right or wrong is a matter of personal "values" and "opinion." The result is an emphasis upon the "legal point of view," but with an emphasis upon the possibility of *changing* law in terms of rational considerations of social utility, rather than freezing it in the terms of Stage 4 "law and order." Outside the legal realm, free agreement and contract are the binding elements of obligation. This is the "official" morality of American government and finds its ground in the thought of the writers of the Constitution.

Stage 6: Orientation toward the decisions of conscience and toward self-chosen *ethical principles* appealing to logical comprehensiveness, universality, and consistency. These principles are abstract and ethical (the Golden Rule, the categorical imperative); they are not concrete moral rules like the Ten Commandments. Instead, they are universal principles of justice, of the reciprocity and equality of human rights, and of respect for the dignity of human beings as individual persons.

UP TO NOW

In the past, when psychologists tried to answer the question asked of Socrates by Meno, "Is virtue something that can be taught (by rational discussion), or does it come by practice, or is it a natural inborn attitude?" their answers usually have been dictated not by research findings on children's moral character but by their general theoretical convictions.

Behavior theorists have said that virtue is behavior acquired according to their favorite general principles of learning. Freudians have claimed that virtue is superego identification with parents, generated by a proper balance of love and authority in family relations.

The American psychologists who have actually studied children's morality have tried to start with a set of labels—the "virtues" and "vices," the "traits" of good and bad character found in ordinary language. The earliest major psychological study of moral character, that of Hugh Hartshorne, and Mark May in 1928-1939, focused on a bag of virtues including honesty, service (altruism or generosity), and self-control. To their dismay, they found that there were *no* character traits, psychological dispositions, or entities that corresponded to words like honesty, service, or self-control.

Regarding honesty, for instance, they found that almost everyone cheats some of the time, and that if a person cheats in one situation, it does not mean that he *will* or *won't* in another. In other words, it is not an identifiable character trait, *dis*honesty, that makes a child cheat in a given situation. These early researchers also found that people who cheat express as much or even more moral disapproval of cheating as those who do not cheat.

What Hartshorne and May found out about their bag of virtues is equally upsetting to the somewhat more psychological-sounding names introduced by psychoanalytic psychology: "superego strength," "resistance to temptation," "strength of conscience," and the like. When contemporary researchers have attempted to measure such traits in individuals, they have been forced to use Hartshorne and May's old tests of honesty and self-control, and they get exactly the same results—"superego strength" in one situation predicts little about "superego strength" in another. That is, virtue words like honesty (or superego strength) point to certain behaviors with approval but give us no guide to understanding them.

So far as one can extract some generalized personality factor from children's performance on tests of honesty or resistance to temptation, it is a factor of ego strength or ego control, which always involves nonmoral capacities like the capacity to maintain attention, intelligent-task performance, and the ability to delay response. "Ego strength" (called "will" in earlier days) has something to do with moral action, but it does not take us to the core of morality or to the definition of virtue. Obviously enough, many of the greatest evil-doers in history have been men of strong wills, men strongly pursuing immoral goals.

MORAL REASONS

In our research, we have found definite and universal levels of development in moral thought. In our study of seventy-five American boys from early adolescence on, these youths were presented with hypothetical moral dilemmas, all deliberately philosophical, some of them found in medieval works of casuistry.

On the basis of their reasoning about these dilemmas at a given age, each boy's stage of thought could be determined for each twenty-five basic moral concepts or aspects. One such aspect, for instance, is "motive given for rule obedience or moral action." In this instance, the six stages look like this:

1 Obey rules to avoid punishment.
2 Conform to obtain rewards, have favors returned, and so on.
3 Conform to avoid disapproval, dislike by others.
4 Conform to avoid censure by legitimate authorities and resultant guilt.
5 Conform to maintain the respect of the impartial spectator judging in terms of community welfare.
6 Conform to avoid self-condemnation.

In another of these twenth-five moral aspects, "the value of human life," the six stages can be defined thus:

1 The value of a human life is confused with the value of physical objects and is based on the social status or physical attributes of its possessor.
2 The value of a human life is seen as instrumental to the satisfaction of the needs of its possessor or of other persons.
3 The value of a human life is based on the empathy and affection of family members and others toward its possessor.
4 Life is conceived as sacred in terms of its place in a categorical mold or religious order of rights and duties.
5 Life is valued both in terms of its relation to community welfare and in terms of life being a universal human right.
6 Belief in the sacredness of human life as representing a universal human value of respect for the individual.

I have called this scheme a typology. This is because about 50 percent of most people's thinking will be at a single stage, regardless of the moral dilemma involved. We call our types stages because they seem to represent an *invariant developmental sequence.* "True" stages come one at a time and always in the same order.

All movement is forward in sequence, and does not skip steps. Children may move through these stages at varying speeds, of course, and may be found half in and half out of a particular stage. An individual may stop at any given stage and at any age, but if he continues to move, he must move in accord with these steps. Moral reasoning of the conventional, or Stage 3-4, kind never occurs before the preconventional Stage 1 and Stage 2 thought has taken place. No adult in Stage 4 has gone through Stage 6, but all Stage 6 adults have gone at least through 4.

While the evidence is not complete, my study strongly suggests that moral change fits the stage pattern just described. (The major uncertainty is whether all people at Stage 6 go through Stage 5 or whether these are two alternate mature orientations.)

HOW VALUES CHANGE

As a single example of our findings of stage sequence, take the progress of two boys on the aspect "the value of human life." The first boy, Tommy, is asked "Is it better to save the life of one important person or a lot of unimportant people?" At age ten, he answers "all the people that aren't important because one man just has one house, maybe a lot of furniture, but a whole bunch of people have an awful lot of furniture and some of these poor people might have a lot of money and it doesn't look it."

Clearly Tommy is Stage 1: he confuses the value of a human being with the value of the property he possesses. Three years later (age thirteen) Tommy's conceptions of life's values are most clearly elicited by the question, "Should the doctor 'mercy kill' a fatally ill woman requesting death because of her pain?" He answers, "Maybe it would be good to put her out of her pain, she'd be better off that way. But the husband wouldn't want it, it's not like an animal. If a pet dies you can get along without it—it isn't something you really need. Well, you can get a new wife, but it's not really the same."

Here his answer is Stage 2: the value of the woman's life is partly contingent on its hedonistic value to the wife herself but even more contingent on its instrumental value to her husband, who can't replace her as easily as he can a pet.

Three years later (age sixteen) Tommy's conception of life's value is elicited by the same question, to which he replies: "It might be best for her, but her husband—it's a human life—not like an animal; it just doesn't have the same relationship that a human being does to a family. You can become attached to a dog, but nothing like a human you know."

Now Tommy has moved from a Stage 2 instrumental view of the woman's value to a Stage 3 view based on the husband's distinctively human empathy and love for someone in his family. Equally clearly, it lacks any basis for a universal human value of the woman's life, which would hold if she had no husband or if her husband didn't love her.

Tommy, then, has moved step by step through three stages during the ages ten through sixteen. Tommy, though bright (IQ 120), is a slow developer in moral judgment. Let us take another boy, Richard, to show us sequential movement through the remaining three steps.

At age thirteen, Richard said about the mercy killing, "If she requests it, it's really up to her. She is in such terrible pain, just the same as people are always putting animals out of their pain," and in general showed a mixture of Stage 2 and Stage 3 responses concerning the value of life. At sixteen, he said:

I don't know. In one way, it's murder, it's not a right or privilege of man to decide who shall live and who should die. God put life into everybody on earth and you're taking away something from that person that came directly from God, and you're destroying something that is very sacred, it's in a way part of God and it's almost destroying a part of God when you kill a person. There's something of God in everyone.

Here Richard clearly displays a Stage 4 concept of life as sacred in terms of its place in a categorical moral or religious order. The value of human life is universal, it is true for all humans. It is still, however, dependent on something else, upon respect for God and God's authority; it is not an autonomous human value. Presumably if God told Richard to murder, as God commanded Abraham to murder Isaac, he would do so.

At age twenty Richard said to the same question:

There are more and more people in the medical profession who think it is a hardship on everyone, the person, the family, when you know they are going to die. When a person is kept alive by an artificial lung or kidney it's more like being a vegetable than being a human. If it's her own choice, I think there are certain rights and privileges that go along with being a human being. I am a human being and have certain desires for life and I think everybody else does too. You have a world of which you are the center, and everybody else does too and in that sense we're all equal.

Richard's response is clearly Stage 5, in that the value of life is defined in terms of equal and universal human rights in a context of relativity ("You have a world of which you are the center and in that sense we're all equal"), and of concern for utility or welfare consequences.

THE FINAL STEP

At twenty-four, Richard says:

> A human life takes precedence over any other moral or legal value, whoever it is. A human life has inherent value whether or not it is valued by a particular individual. The worth of the individual human being is central where the principles of justice and love are normative for all human relationships.

This young man is at Stage 6 in seeing the value of human life as absolute in representing a universal and equal respect for the human as an individual. He has moved step by step through a sequence culminating in a definition of human life as centrally valuable rather than derived from or dependent on social or divine authority.

In a genuine and culturally universal sense, these steps lead toward an increased *morality* of value judgment, where morality is considered as a form of judging, as it has been in a philosophic tradition running from the analyses of Kant to those of the modern analytic or "ordinary language" philosophers. The person at Stage 6 has disentangled his judgments of—or language about—human life from status and property values (Stage 1), from its uses to others (Stage 2), from interpersonal affection (Stage 3), and so on; he has a means of moral judgment that is universal and impersonal. The Stage 6 person's answers use moral words like "duty" or "morally right," and he uses them in a way implying universality, ideals, impersonality. He thinks and speaks in phrases like "regardless of who it was," or "I would do it in spite of punishment."

ACROSS CULTURES

When I first decided to explore moral development in other cultures, I was told by anthropologist friends that I would have to throw away my culture-bound moral concepts and stories and start from scratch learning a whole new set of values for each culture. My first try consisted of a brace of villages, one Atayal (Malaysian aboriginal) and the other Taiwanese.

My guide was a young Chinese ethnographer who had written an account of the moral and religious patterns of the Atayal and Taiwanese villages. Taiwanese boys in the ten to thirteen age group were asked about a story involving theft of food. A man's wife is starving to death, but the store owner won't give the man any food unless he can pay, which he can't. Should he break in and steal some food? Why? Many of the boys said, "He should steal the food for his wife because if she dies he'll have to pay for her funeral and that costs a lot."

My guide was amused by these responses, but I was relieved: they were, of course "classic" Stage 2 responses. In the Atayal village, funerals weren't such a big thing, so the Stage 2 boys would say, "He should steal the food because he needs his wife to cook for him."

This means that we need to consult our anthropologists to know what content a Stage 2 child will include in his instrumental exchange calculations, or what a Stage 4 adult will identify as the proper social order. But one certainly does not have to start from scratch. What made my guide laugh was the difference in form between the children's

Stage 2 thought and his own, a difference definable independently of particular cultures.

Figure 11-1 indicates the cultural universality of the sequence of stages that we have found. Figure 11-1(a) presents the age trends for middle class urban boys in the United States, Taiwan, and Mexico. At age ten in each country, the order of use of each stage is the same as the order of its difficulty or maturity.

In the United States, by age sixteen the order is the reverse, from the highest to the lowest, except that Stage 6 is still little-used. At age thirteen, the good-boy, middle stage (Stage 3) is not used.

The results in Mexico and Taiwan are the same, except that development is a little slower. The most conspicuous feature is that at the age of sixteen, Stage 5 thinking is much more salient in the United States than in Mexico or Taiwan. Nevertheless, it *is* present in the other countries, so we know that this is not purely an American democratic construct.

Figure 11-1(b) shows strikingly similar results from two isolated villages, one in Yucatan, one in Turkey. While conventional moral thought increases steadily from ages ten to sixteen, it still has not achieved a clear ascendancy over preconventional thought.

Trends for lower-class urban groups are intermediate in the rate of development between those for the middle-class and those for the village boys. In the three divergent cultures that I studied, middle-class children were found to be more advanced in moral judgment than matched lower-class children. This was not due to the fact that the middle-class children heavily favored some one type of thought that could be seen as corresponding to the prevailing middle-class pattern. Instead, middle-class and working-class children move through the same sequences, but the middle-class children move faster and further.

This sequence is not dependent upon a particular religion, or any religion at all in the usual sense. I found no important differences in the development of moral thinking among Catholics, Protestants, Jews, Buddhists, Moslems, or atheists. Religious values seem to go through the same stages as all other values.

TRADING UP

In summary, the nature of our sequence is not significantly affected by widely varying social, cultural, or religious conditions. The only thing that is affected is the *rate* at which individuals progress through this sequence.

Why should there be such a universal invariant sequence of development? In answering this question, we need first to analyze these developing social concepts in terms of their internal logical structure. At each stage, the same basic moral concept or aspect is defined, but at each higher stage this definition is more differentiated, more integrated, and more general or universal. When one's concept of human life moves from Stage 1 to Stage 2, the value of life becomes more differentiated from the value of property, more integrated (the value of life enters an organizational hierarchy where it is "higher" than property so that one steals property in order to save life), and more universalized (the life of any sentient being is valuable regardless of status or property). The same advance is true at each stage in the hierarchy. Each step of development, then, is a better cognitive organization than the one before it, one that takes account of everything present in the previous stage but makes new distinctions and organizes them into a more comprehensive or more equilibrated structure. The fact that this is the case has been demonstrated by a series of studies indicating that children and adolescents comprehend all stages up to their own, but not more than one stage beyond their own. And importantly, *they prefer this next stage.*

We have conducted experimental moral dis-

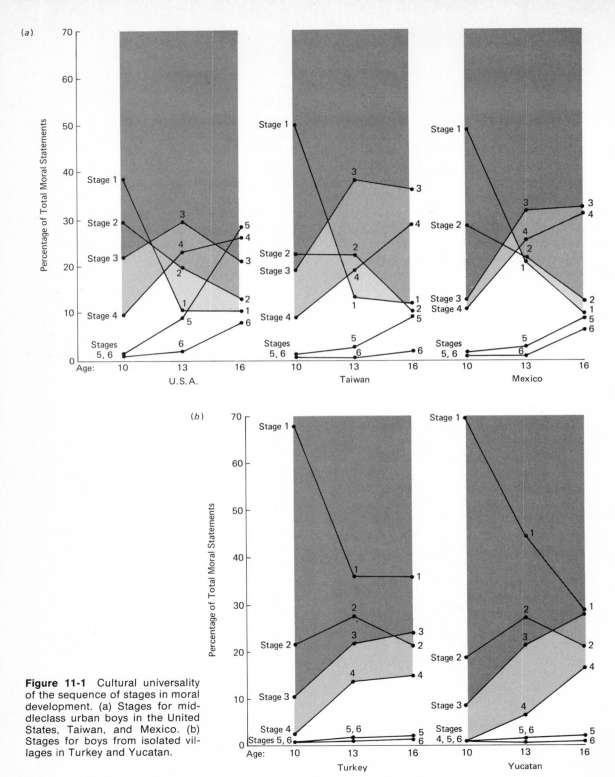

Figure 11-1 Cultural universality of the sequence of stages in moral development. (a) Stages for middleclass urban boys in the United States, Taiwan, and Mexico. (b) Stages for boys from isolated villages in Turkey and Yucatan.

cussion classes that show that the child at an earlier stage of development tends to move forward when confronted by the views of a child one stage further along. In an argument between a Stage 3 and a Stage 4 child, the child in the third stage tends to move toward or into Stage 4, while the Stage 4 child understands but does not accept the arguments of the Stage 3 child.

Moral thought, then, seems to behave like all other kinds of thought. Progress through the moral levels and stages is characterized by increasing differentiation and increasing integration, and hence is the same kind of progress that scientific theory represents. Like acceptable scientific theory—or like *any* theory or structure of knowledge—moral thought may be considered to partially generate its own data as it goes along, or at least to expand so as to contain in a balanced, self-consistent way a wider and wider experiential field. The raw data in the case of our ethical philosophies may be considered as conflicts between roles, or values, or as the social order in which men live.

THE ROLE OF SOCIETY

The social worlds of all men seem to contain the same basic structures. All the societies we have studied have the same basic institutions—family, economy, law, government. In addition, however, all societies are alike because they *are* societies—systems of defined complementary roles. In order to play a social role in the family, school, or society, the child must implicitly take the role of others toward himself and toward others in the group. These role-taking tendencies form the basis of all social institutions. They represent various patternings of shared or complementary expectations.

In the preconventional and conventional levels (Stages 1-4), moral content or value is largely accidental or culture bound. Anything from "honesty" to "courage in battle" can be the central value. But in the higher postconventional levels, Socrates, Lincoln, Thoreau, and Martin Luther King tend to speak without confusion of tongues, as it were. This is because the ideal principles of any social structure are basically alike, if only because there simply are not that many principles that are articulate, comprehensive, and integrated enough to be satisfying to the human intellect. And most of these principles have gone by the name of justice.

Behavioristic psychology and psychoanalysis have always upheld the Philistine view that fine moral words are one thing and moral deeds another. Morally mature reasoning is quite a different matter, and does not really depend on "fine words." The man who understands justice is more likely to practice it.

In our studies, we have found that youths who understand justice act more justly, and the man who understands justice helps create a moral climate that goes far beyond his immediate and personal acts. The universal society is the beneficiary.

THE CHILD IN SCHOOL

The Present Moment in Education

Paul Goodman

My own thinking is that
(1) Incidental education . . . should be the chief means of learning.
(2) Most high schools should be eliminated. . . .
(3) College training should generally follow, not precede entry into the professions.
(4) The chief task of educators is to see to it that the activities of society provide incidental education. . . .
(5) The purpose of elementary pedagogy . . . is to protect children's free growth. . . .

Editor's Introduction

There are many questions of concern to educators today. While there is much to be admired in the educational systems in operation in the United States, there is also much to be criticized. Paul Goodman is one of the most outspoken critics of the American educational systems.

The questions that concern most educators appear to revolve around issues such as the type of school which would be most advantageous to children (open classrooms, traditional classrooms, authoritarian or democratic methods of teaching), the age at which school should begin (at a few months of age, preschool, or not until kindergarten or first grade), and the age at which different subject matters can be effectively assimilated by youngsters (whether any subject can be taught at any age in some intellectually honest form or whether there is a period of readiness in which a subject matter can be most effectively taught). The issues are many and certainly of wide range, and the potential remedies are far more numerous than the problems. There are critics, however, who believe that the American schools are so pitiful that the only constructive remedy would be to dissolve them entirely and begin again. Goodman believes that the formalized instruction which most children receive is not only useless but also harmful, as it stifles the child's natural curiosity and disposition to explore and learn. The best approach to education, according to Goodman, is through the children themselves. Children are active learners and will learn best when they have the opportunity to participate in their environment, not when they are made to sit in a classroom and act as receptacles of knowledge. Goodman has said

Up to age twelve, there is no point in formal subjects or a prearranged curriculum. With guidance, whatever a child experiences is educational. . . . Teachers for this age are those who like children, pay attention to them, answer their questions, enjoy taking them around the city and helping them to explore, imitate, try out, and who sing songs with them and teach them games. Any benevolent grown-up—literate or illiterate—has plenty to teach an eight year old, . . . the only profitable training for teachers is group therapy and, perhaps, a course in child development.

While some readers may not be able to agree completely with Goodman's approach to education, his words, although written almost ten years ago, continue to present opportunity for concern.

Pamela Cantor

1. INCIDENTAL EDUCATION AND PEDAGOGY

To be educated well or badly, to learn by a long process how to cope with the physical environment and the culture of one's society, is part of the human condition. In every society the education of the children is of the first importance. But in all societies, both primitive and highly civilized, until quite recently most education of most children has occurred incidentally. Adults do their work and other social tasks; children are not excluded, are paid attention to, and learn to be included. The children are not "taught." In many adult institutions, incidental education is taken for granted as part of the function: families and age-statuses, community labor, master-apprentice arrangements, games and plays, prostitution and other sexual initiation, religious rites and churches. In Greek *paideia*, the entire network of institutions, the *polis*, was thought of as importantly an educator.

Generally speaking, this incidental process suits the nature of learning better than direct teaching. The young see real causes and effects, rather than pedagogic exercises. Reality is often complex, but the young can take it by their own handle, at their own times, according to their own interest and initiative. Most important, they can imitate, identify, be approved or disapproved, cooperate and compete, without the anxiety of being the center of attention; there is socialization with less resentment, fear, or submission. The archetype of successful education is infants learning to speak, a formidable intellectual achievement that is universally accomplished. We do not know how it is done, but the main conditions seem to be what we have been describing: adult activity is going on, involving speak-

ing; the infants are only incidental yet they participate, are attended to and spoken to; they play freely with their speech sounds; it is advantageous to them to make themselves understood. Finally, according to Jespersen, children pick up their accent and style from the gang of other children; it is their uniform, the way they appoint themselves.

Along with incidental education, however, most societies also have institutions specifically devoted to teaching the young. Such are identity rites, catechism, nurses and pedagogues, youth houses, formal schooling. I think there is a peculiar aspect to what is learned by such means rather than picked up incidentally. But let me emphasize strongly and repeatedly that it is only in the last century in industrialized countries that the majority of children have gotten much direct teaching at all, and it is only in the past few decades that formal schooling has been extended into adolescence and further. E.g., in the United States in 1900 only 6 percent went through high school and $1/4$ percent through college. Yet now formal schooling has taken over, well or badly, very much of the more natural incidental education of most other institutions.

This may or may not be necessary, but it has consequences: these institutions, and the adults in them, have correspondingly lost touch with the young, and the young do not know the adults in their chief activities. Like the jails and insane asylums, schools isolate society from its problems, whether preventing crime, curing mental disease, or bringing up the young. And to a remarkable degree vital functions of growing up have become hermetically re-defined in school terms: community service means doing homework, apprenticeship is passing tests for jobs in the distant future, sexual initation is high school dating, and rites of passage are getting diplomas. Crime is breaking school windows, and rebellion is sitting-in on the Dean. In the absence of adult culture, there develops a youth subculture.

Usually there has been a rough distinction in content, in what is learned, between incidental education and direct pedagogy. Ordinary social activities that do not exclude children tend to be matter-of-fact, and children taking part without anxiety can be objective, if not critical. But pedagogy, whether directed by elders, priests, or academics, deals with what is not evident in ordinary affairs; it aims to teach what is more abstract, intangible, or mysterious, and the learner, as the center of attention, is under personal pressure. All social activity socializes its participants, but pedagogy socializes deliberately, according to principles, instilling the morals and habits which are the social bonds.

There are, of course, two opposite interpretations of why pedagogy wants to indoctrinate, and in my opinion both are correct. On the one hand, the elders, priests, and schoolteachers are instilling an ideology to support their system of exploitation, including the domination of the old over the young, and they have to make a special effort to confuse and mystify because the system does not recommend itself to common sense. At present, when formal education swallows up so much time of life and pretends to be practical preparation for every activity, ideological processing is especially deadly. Those who succumb to it have no wits of their own left and are robots.

On the other hand, there perhaps *are* vague but important wisdom and abstractions that must be passed on, which do not appear on the surface in ordinary occasions and which require personal attention, special pointing, repetition, and cloistered reflection. Thus, champions of liberal arts colleges say that, one way or other, the young will pick up contemporary know-how and mores, but the greatness of Mankind—Hippocrates and Beethoven, Enlightenment, Civil Liberties, the Sense of the Tragic—will lapse without a trace unless the scholars work at it. I sympathize with the problem as they state it and I will return to it; but in fact I have not heard of any method whatever, scholastic or otherwise, to *teach* the humanities without killing them. Myself, I remember how at age twelve, browsing in the library, I read *Macbeth* with excitement, but in class I could not understand a word of *Julius Caesar* and hated it; and I think this was the usual experience of people who read and write well. The survival of the humanities has seemed to depend on random miracles, which are becoming less frequent.

Finally, unlike incidental learning, which is natural and inevitable, formal schooling is a deliberate intervention and must justify itself. We must ask not only is it well done, but is it worth doing and *can* it be well done? Is teaching possible at all? There is a line of critics from Lao-tse and Socrates to Carl Rogers who assert that there is no such thing as teaching, or either science or virtue; and there is strong empirical evidence that schooling has little effect on either vocational ability or citizenship—e.g., Donald Hoyt, for American College Testing, 1965, found that college grades have no "correlation" with life achievement in any profession. At the other extreme, Dr. Skinner and the operant-conditioners claim that they can "instruct" for every kind of performance, they can control and shape human behavior, as they can do with animals sealed off from the ordinary environment; but they are careful to say they do not "educate" in the sense of developing persons (whatever that might mean). It is disputable whether human children are good subjects for this kind of instruction in any society we like to envisage.

In the middle, the main line of educators, from Confucius and Aristotle to John Dewey, held that, starting from the natural motives of the young, one can teach them good habits of morals, arts, and sciences by practice; the learners take on a "second nature" which they can then use by themselves, they are not simply programmed. And on various theories, Froebel, Herbart, Steiner, or Piaget have held that such teaching is possible if it addresses the child's powers in the right order at the right moments. But sociologists like Comte or Marx seem to say that the background social institutions and their vicissitudes overwhelmingly determine what is learned, so it is not worthwhile to think about pedagogy, at least as yet. I will not pursue this discussion here—my bias is that "teaching" is largely a delusion—but we must bear in mind that such fundamental disagreements exist.

2. THE SCHOLASTIC

Turn now to actual formal schooling in the United States, the country most technologically advanced (but the story is not very different in other developed and developing countries, including China and Cuba). The school system, expanding and increasingly tightly integrated, has taken over a vast part of the educational functions of society, designing school-preparatory toys from age two and training for every occupation as well as citizenship, sexuality, and the humanities. Yet with trivial exceptions, what we mean by School—namely, curriculum generalized from the activities of life, and divided into departments, texts, lessons, scheduled periods marked by bells, specialist teachers, examinations, and graded promotion to the next step—is a sociological invention of some Irish monks in the seventh century to bring a bit of Rome to wild shepherds. It is an amazing success-story, probably more important than the Industrial Revolution.

At first, no doubt it was a good thing for wild shepherds to have to sit still for a couple of hours and pay strict attention to penmanship and spelling. And mostly it was only aspiring clerics who were schooled. By an historical accident, the same academic method later became the way of teaching the bookish part of a couple of learned professions. There is no essential reason why law and medicine are not better learned by apprenticeship, but the bookish was clerical and therefore scholastic, and (perhaps) any special education containing abstract principles was part of the system of mysteries, therefore clerical, and therefore scholastic.

This monkish rule of scheduled hours, texts, and lessons is also not an implausible method for giving a quick background briefing to large numbers, who then embark on their real business. Thus Jefferson insisted on universal compulsory schooling, for short terms in predominately rural communities, so children could read the newspapers and be catechized in libertarian political history, in order to be citizens in a democracy. Later, in compulsory urban schools, the children of polyglot immigrants were socialized and taught standard English, a peculiar dialect, so they could then try to make good in an ecomony which indeed proved to be fairly open to them in the long run. The curriculum was the penmanship, spelling, and arithmetic needed for the business world. Naturally, forced soclialization involved drastic cultural disruption and family fragmentation, but perhaps it was a good solution—we have yet to see how it works out.

The context of schooling at present, however, is entirely different. The monkish invention is now used as universal social engineering. Society is conceived as a controlled system of personnel and transactions—with various national goals, depending on the nation—and the schools are the teaching machine for all personnel. There is no other way of entry for the young. And teaching tries to give psychological preparation in depth. Schooling for one's role, in graded steps, takes up to twenty years and more and is the chief activity of growing up; any other interest may be interrupted. The real motivation for a five-year-old's behavior, thus, is geared fifteen years in the future.

In highly productive technologies like ours, of course, which do not need manpower, a more realistic interpretation is that the social function of long schooling is to keep the useless and obstreperous young *away* from the delicate social machine, to baby-sit and police them. Yet it comes to the same thing. Whether by accident or design, the schools are not like playgrounds or reservations; rather, the texture of school experience is similar to adult experience. There is little break between playing with educational toys and watching ETV, being in grade school and the Little League, being in high school and dating, being in college and drafted, being personnel of a corporation and watching NBC. It is a curious historical question whether the schools have been transformed to the model of business organization, or the adult world has become scholastic, with corresponding arrested maturation. The evidence is that up to about 1920, business methods had a preponderant influence; but since 1945 the school monks have increasingly determined the social style and adults have become puerile.

Since the trend has been to eliminate incidental education and prepare the young deliberately for every aspect of ordinary life, we would expect pedagogy to become secularized and functional. Yet radical students complain that the schooling is ideological through and through. The simplest, and not altogether superficial, explanation of this paradox is that scholastic mystery has transformed ordinary adult business. Society is run by mandarins, the New Class.

Even on its own terms, this is not working well. Schooling costs more than armaments. It does not in fact prepare for jobs and professions—e.g., evidence compiled by Ivar Berg of Columbia shows that dropouts do as well as high-school graduates on that level of jobs.[1] It does not provide peaceful baby-sitting and policing. Instead of an efficient gearing between the teaching machine and the rest of the social machine, the schools seem to run for their own sakes, accumulating bluebooks; there is a generation gap; many of the young fail or drop out and others picket. Predictably, the response of school administrators is to refine the processing, to make the curriculum still more relevant, to enrich the curriculum, to add remedial steps, to study developmental psychology for points of manipulation, to start earlier, to use new teaching technology, to eliminate friction by admitting students to administrative functions.

But social engineering is uneducational in principle. It pre-structures behavior and can become discriminating, graceful, and energetic only if the organism creates its own structures as it goes along.

In the long run, human powers are the chief resources. In the short run, unused powers assert themselves anyway and make trouble, and cramped powers produce distorted or labile effects. If we set up a structure that strictly channels energy, directs attention, and regulates movement (which are "good things"), we may temporarily inhibit impulse, wishing, daydreaming, and randomness (which are "bad things"); but we also thereby jeopardize initiative, intrinsic motivation, imagination, invention, self-reliance, freedom from inhibition, and finally even health and common sense. It is frequently said that human beings use only a small part—"2 percent"—of their abilities; so some educators propose much more demanding and intellectual tasks at a much earlier age. And there is no doubt that most children can think and learn far more than they are challenged to. Yet

---

[1]Reported in *New Generation*, Winter, 1968.

it is likely that by far the greatest waste of ability, including intellectual and creative ability, occurs because a playful, hunting, sexy, dreamy, combative, passionate, artistic, manipulative and destructive, jealous and magnanimous, selfish and disinterested animal is continually thwarted by social organization and perhaps especially by schooling. If so, *the main purpose of pedagogy at present is to counter-act and delay socialization as long as possible.* Our situation is the opposite of the seventh century; since the world has become scholastic, we must protect the wild shepherds.

The personal attitude of schoolteachers toward the young is problematic. I can understand that adults are protective and helpful to small children, and that professionals, in graduate schools, want apprentices to carry on; but why would grown-ups spend whole days hanging around adolescents and callow collegians? Sexual interest makes sense and must be common, but it is strongly disapproved and its inhibition makes a bad situation. Traditional motives have been to domineer and be a big fish in a small pond. The present preferred posture seems to me to be extremely dishonest: to take a warm interest in the young as persons while yet getting them to perform according to an impersonal schedule. Since from the teacher's (or supervisor's) point of view the performance is the essence, with failure the relation can quickly degenerate to being harsh for their own good or hating them as incorrigible animals. *I do not see any functional way to recruit a large corps of high school teachers.* With incidental education there is no problem. Most people like the young to be around and to watch them develop, and their presence often makes a job more honest and less routine, for they are honest and not routine.

Current high thought among schoolmen, for instance the National Science Foundation and the Harvard School of Education, is to criticize the syllabus as indeed wasteful and depressing, but to expand the schools and make the programming more psychological. Since the frontier of knowledge is changing so rapidly, there is no use in burdening children with knowledge that will be outdated in ten years, and with skills that will soon be better performed by ubiquitous machines. Rather, they must learn to learn; their cognitive faculties must be developed; they must be taught the big Ideas, like the Conservation of energy. (This is exactly what Robert Hutchins was saying forty years ago.) Or more daringly, the children must not be taught but allowed to discover; they must be encouraged to guess and brainstorm rather than be tested on .the right answers. But are these suggestions *bona fide*? Perhaps, as Gregory Bateson has speculated about dolphins and trainers, and as John Holt has illustrated in middle-class schools, learning to learn means picking up the structure of behavior of the teachers. The young discoverers are bound to discover what will get them past the College Boards, and the guessers and dreamers are not free to balk and drop out for a semester to brood, as proper geniuses do. And what if precisely the big Ideas are not true?—Einstein said that it was preferable to have a stupid pedant for a teacher, so a smart child could fight him all the way.

I think the pedagogic reasoning of Harvard and the N.S.F. is something like this: though knowledge changes, the function and the style of science are fixed. But this is an ideology of a political structure that, hopefully, is even more in flux than knowledge is—at least let us hope that 80 percent of Federal money for Research and Development will not continue to be used for military science. We can survive with our present science, but not with our present Science. Unless the "cognitive faculties" become more magnanimous, philosophical, and prudent than they are at present, it is a waste of money and effort to plan for ten years from now at all. But the only pedagogy that I have ever heard to teach magnanimity and feeling is Wordsworth's: the beauty of the world and simple human affections. So we are back to the wild shepherds.

But of course there is an underlying problem that earnest teachers, also at Harvard and in the N.S.F., are concerned about: how are the young to learn to cope with the complicated technological environment? Perhaps it is a mistake to look for a scholastic solution; I think this was the mistake of Dewey's earlier attempt to domesticate industrialism by learning by doing *in school.* In the first place, we older people must notice that the environment is not nearly so arcane to the young as it is to us. I have been astonished at how some of my hippie friends, inveterate dropouts, can design computer circuits. One learned it in the Army, another in an insane asylum, another just picked it up. What else *would* the young experience, and learn, except the actual environment? A child who can't count can always make change for a dollar. There is a poignant dilemma specific to a child, but in order to make it clear to himself the teacher makes it incomprehensible to the child.

New topics require new symbols and may even, though I have yet to be convinced, require new patterns of thinking. But schoolteachers inevitably decide that these must be taught in graded steps from "the" elements that they were brought up on, and theorists of cognition exhibit the same wooden attitude in adding new levels of abstraction. (Sometimes there is a flurry of simplification like New Math.) If we start from actual experience, however, we find that it determines its own elements. And long ago, Kropotkin beautifully solved the cognitive problem of levels of abstraction when he said: you can explain any scientific proposition to an intelligent unlettered peasant *if you yourself understand it concretely.* I could add, if you don't understand it concretely, are you sure it's relevant to teach?

Let me put this another way. Two hundred years ago, Immanuel Kant exhaustively and accurately mapped the territory that our new cognitive theorists are exploring in fragments and with occasional blunders.[2]

But Kant showed that our intellectual structures come into play spontaneously, by the "synthetic unity of apperception," if we are attentive in real situations. They certainly seem to do so when infants learn to speak. The problem of knowing is to have attentive experience, to get people to *pay* attention, without cramping the unifying play of free intellectual powers. Schools are bad at this; interesting reality is good. On the other hand, according to Kant, to exercise the cognitive faculties abstractly, in themselves, is precisely superstition, presumptuous theology. He wrote all this in *The Critique of Pure Reason,* which I would strongly recommend to the Harvard School of Education.

3. PROGRESSIVE EDUCATION

Progressive education is best defined as a series of reactions to schooling that has become rigid, in order to include what has been repressed in growing up. It aims to right the balance. It is a political movement, for the exclusion of a human power or style of life is always the sign of a social injustice; and

[2]E.g., J. S. Bruner: "We organize experience to represent not only the particulars that have been experienced, but the classes of events of which the particulars are exemplars. We go not only from part to whole, but irresistibly, from the particular to the general." I should think that primarily we organize experience as part of the experience, and not to represent anything. By and large we start from the confused general and global, and specify it; as Aristotle said, a baby first calls every man Daddy and then distinguishes Tom and Dick. And no animal normally goes from part to whole unless totally baffled by mazes, obsessional neurosis, or schoolteachers. What Bruner means to say, I think, is that to program a computer according to current symbolic logic, we organize "experience" in this way; but this is rather a special function to saddle all children with.

progressive education emerges when the social problem is breaking out. Put more positively, an old regime is not adequate to new conditions, and new energy and character are needed in order to cope. What the progressive educator discovers as the nature of the child is what he intuits will work best in the world, and the form that progressive education takes at each time is prophetic of the next social revolution. Thus, a rosy history of progressive education would look like this:

Rousseau was reacting to the artificiality and insincerity of the court, the parasitism of the courtiers, the callous formalism, and the pervasive superstition. Apart from its moral defects, this way of life had become simply incompetent to govern, and a generation later it abdicated. The French Revolution was confused by the invasions and the Terror, not implicit in Rousseau, but Rousseau's vision was really achieved in the first decades of the American republic, where the ideal of education and character, to be frank and simple, empirical, self-reliant, and proudly independent, could have been drawn from *Emile*. In fact, *Emile* was also drawn *from* the Americans.

John Dewey was reacting to the genteel culture irrelevant to industrialized society, rococo decoration, puritanism that denied animal nature, self-censored literature, individualism of the tycoons, rote performance imposed on common people and children. And again, after a generation, by the end of the New Deal, this moral vision had largely come to be: most of the program of the Populists and the Labor movement was law; education and culture (among whites) had become utilitarian and fairly classless; the revolution of Freud and Spock was well advanced; censorship was on its way out; there was no more *appliqué* decoration; and there was all manner of social organization rather than individualism.

A. S. Neill's Summerhill, our recent form of progressive education, has been a reaction to social-engineering, the trend to 1984, as Orwell came to call it: obedience to authoritarian rules, organizational role-playing instead of being, destruction of community by competition and grade-getting, objective knowledge without personal meaning. Since, for children, getting to class is the immutable nature of things, to make this a matter of choice was to transform reality. And to the extent that there was authentic self-government at Summerhill and small children indeed had power, the charisma of all institutions was challenged. And again progressive education has been prescient: the evidence is that we may yet have a universal shambles, but we will not see the society of 1984. The slogans and style of dissident youth around the world are like a caricature of Summerhill—naturally a caricature because they have not yet been assimilated into social change: participatory democracy, do your thing, don't trust anybody over thirty, drop out of the system. Summerhill's affectionate family of autonomous persons is a model for all pads, communities, and tribes. The sexual freedom exists that Neill approved but could not legally sanction. Careless dress has become a common uniform.

Before I discuss what is wrong with this history let me mention the criticism that *contemporary* progressive education is a middle-class gimmick (though Pestalozzi did his work and Montessori her best work with the outcast). The black community, especially, resents being used for "experiments." Poor children, it is claimed, need to learn the conventional ropes so they can compete for power in the established system, or even can con the system like hipsters. Therefore black parents demand "quality education" and expect their children to wear ties.

In my opinion, this criticism is wrongheaded. The scholastic evidence, for instance the *Eight Years Study*, shows that the more experimental the high school, the more successfully the graduates compete in conventional colleges when it is necessary. And more important is that, since black children do not get the same reward as whites for equal conventional achievement—for instance, a white high school graduate averages the same salary as a black college graduate—it is better for the blacks not to be caught in an unprofitable groove, but to have more emotional freedom, initiative, and flexibility, to be able to find and make opportunities. That is, black communities should run their own schools, and they should run them on the model of Summerhill. This has indeed been the case with the sporadic Freedom Schools, north and south, which have a dose of Neill by direct or indirect influence. But of course freedom is incalculable. My guess is that children, if free to choose, at least up to the age when they are muddled by the anxieties of puberty, will choose black and white together, quite different from their parents' politics and prejudices. (To be sure, it has not been the doing of black parents that the schools are not integrated.)

I don't agree with the theory of Head Start either, that disadvantaged children need special training of their intellectual faculties to prepare them for learning. There seems to be nothing wrong with the development of their intellectual faculties; they have learned to speak and they can make practical syllogisms very nicely if they need to and are not thwarted. If they have not learned the patterns to succeed in school, the plausible move is to change the school, not the children. But the trouble might be just the opposite, as Elliott Shapiro has suggested, that these children have been pushed too early, to take responsibility for themselves and little brothers and sisters, and their real problems have been too insoluble to reason about. They can reason but there's no use to it; it's psychically more economic to be stupid. What they need is freedom from pressure to perform, and of course better food, more quiet, and a less depoverished environment to grow in at their own pace. These are what the First Street School on the Lower East Side in New York tried to provide—modeled on Summerhill.

What is really wrong with our history is that, in their own terms, the successes of progressive education have been rather total failures. The societies that emerged in the following generation, fulfilling their programs, were not what the visionaries hoped for. Jacksonian democracy, as described by Tocqueville, was very different from the Old Regime, but it was hardly the natural nobility of *Emile* (or the vision of Jefferson). It lacked especially the good taste, the fraternity, and the general will that Rousseau hankered after. Dewey's pragmatic and social-minded conceptions have ended up as the service university, technocracy, labor bureaucracy, and suburban conformity. But Dewey was thinking of workers' management and education for workers' management; and like Frank Lloyd Wright, he wanted a functional culture of materials and processes, not glossy Industrial Design and the consumer standard of living.

The likelihood is that A. S. Neill's hope too will be badly realized. It is not hard to envisage a society in the near future in which self-reliant and happy people will be attendants of a technological apparatus over which they have no control whatever, and whose purposes do not seem to them to be any of their business. Indeed, Neill describes with near satisfaction such success-stories among his own graudates. Alternately, it is conceivable that an affluent society will compound with its hippies by supporting them like Indians on a reservation. Their Zen philosophy of *satori* was grounded originally in a violent feudalism, of which it was the spiritual solace, and it could prove so again.

How to prevent these outcomes? Perhaps, protecting his free affectionate community, Neill protects it a few years too long, both from the oppressive mechanistic world and from adolescent solitude (it is hard to be alone in Summerhill). And it seems to me that there is something inauthentic in Neill's latitudinarian lack of standards—e.g., Beethoven and rock 'n roll are equivalent, though he himself prefers Beethoven—for we are not only free organisms but parts of mankind that has historically made itself with great inspirations and terrible conflicts. We cannot slough off that accumulation, however burdensome, without becoming trivial and therefore servile. It seems clear by now that the noisy youth sub-culture is not only not grown-up, which is to the good, but prevents ever being grown-up.

4. THE PRESENT MOMENT IN PROGRESSIVE EDUCATION

It is possible that the chief problem in the coming generation will be survival, whether from nuclear bombs, genocide, ecological disaster, or mass starvation and endless wars. If so, this is the present task of pedagogy. There already exist wilderness schools for self-reliance and it has been proposed to train guerrillas in schools in Harlem. The delicately interlocking technologies of the world indeed seem to be over-extended and terribly vulnerable, and the breakdown could be pretty total. But let us fantasize that this view is not realistic.

My own thinking is that

(1) Incidental education, taking part in the on-going activities of society, should be the chief means of learning.

(2) Most high schools should be eliminated, with other kinds of communities of youth taking over their social functions.

(3) College training should generally follow, not precede, entry into the professions.

(4) The chief task of educators is to see to it that the activities of society provide incidental education, if necessary inventing new useful activities offering new education opportunities.

(5) The purpose of elementary pedagogy, through age twelve, is to protect children's free growth, since our community and families both pressure them too much and do not attend to them enough.

Let me review the arguments for this program. We must drastically cut back the schooling because the present extended tutelage is against nature and arrests growth. The effort to channel growing up according to a preconceived curriculum and method discourages and wastes many of the best human powers to learn and cope. Schooling does not prepare for real performance; it is largely carried on for its own sake. Only a small fraction, the "academically talented"—between 10 and 15 percent according to Conant—thrive in this useless activity without being bored or harmed by it. It isolates the young from the older generation and alienates them.

On the other hand, it makes no sense for many of the brightest and most sensitive young simply to drop out or confront society with hostility. This cannot lead to social reconstruction. The complicated and confusing conditions of modern times need knowledge and fresh thought, and therefore long acquaintance and participation precisely by the young. Young radicals seem to think that mere political change will solve the chief problems, or that they will solve themselves after political change, but this is a delusion. The problems of urbanization, technology, and ecology have not been faced by any political group. The educational systems of other advanced countries are no better than ours, and the young are equally dissenting. Finally, it has been my Calvinistic, and Aristotelian, experience that most people cannot organize their lives without productive activity (though, of course, not necessarily paid activity); and the actual professions, services, industries, arts and sciences are the arena in which they should be working. Radical politics and doing one's thing are careers for very few.

As it is, however, the actual activities of American society either exclude the young, or corrupt them, or exploit them. Here is the task for educators. We must make the rules of licensing and hiring realistic to the actual work and get rid of mandarin requirements. We must design apprenticeships that are not exploitative. Society desperately needs much work that is not now done, both intellectual and manual, in urban renewal, ecology, communications, and the arts, and all these could make use of young people. Many such enterprises are best organized by young people themselves, like most of the community development and community action Vocations for Social Change. Little think tanks, like the Oceanic Institute at Makapuu Point or the Institute for Policy Studies in Washington, which are not fussy about diplomas, have provided excellent spots for the young. Our aim should be to multiply the path of growing up, with opportunity to start again, cross over, take a moratorium, travel, work on one's own. To insure freedom of option and that the young can maintain and express their critical attitude, all adolescents should be guaranteed a living. (The present cost of high schooling would almost provide this.)

The advantage of making education less academic has, of course, occurred to many school people. There are a myriad of programs to open the school to the world by (1) importing outside professionals, artists in residence, gurus, mothers, dropouts as teacher's aides; and (2) giving academic credit for work-study, community action, writing novels, service in mental hospitals, junior year abroad, and other kinds of released time. Naturally I am enthusiastic for this development and only want it to go the small further step of abolishing the present school establishment instead of aggrandizing it.

Conversely, there is a movement in the United States, as in China and Cuba, for adolescent years to be devoted to public service, and this is fine if the service is not compulsory and regimenting.

It is possible for every education to be tailor-made according to each youth's developing interest and choice. Choices along the way will be very often ill-conceived and wasteful; but they will express desire and immediately meet reality, and therefore they should converge to finding the right vocation more quickly than by any other course. Vocation is what one is good at and can do, what uses a reasonable amount of one's powers, and gives one a useful occupation in a community that is one's own. The right use of the majority of people would make a stable society far more efficient than our own. And those who have peculiar excellences are more likely to find their own further way when they have entry by doing something they can do and being accepted.

Academic schooling can be chosen by those with academic talents, and such schools are better off unencumbered by sullen uninterested bodies. But the main use of academic teaching is for those already busy in sciences and professions, who need academic courses along the way. Cooper Union in New York City used to fulfill this function very well. And in this context of need, there can finally be the proper use of new pedagogic technology, as a means of learning at one's own time, whereas at present this technology makes the school experience still more rigid and impersonal.

Of course, in this set-up employers would themselves provide ancillary academic training, especially if they had to pay for it anyway, instead of using parents' and taxpayers' money. In my opinion, this ancillary rather than prior schooling would do more than any other single thing to give black, rural, and other "culturally deprived" youth a fairer entry and chance for advancement, since what is to be learned is objective and functional and does not depend on the abstract school style. As we have seen, *on the job* there is no correlation between competence and years of prior schooling.

But this leads to another problem. Educationally, schooling on the job is usually superior, but the political and moral consequences of such a system are ambiguous and need more analysis than I can give them here. At present, a youth is hired for actual credentials, if not actual skill; this is alienating to him as a person, but it also allows a measure of free-marked democracy. If he is to be schooled on the job, however, he must be hired for his promise and attended to as a person; this is less alienating, but it can lead to company paternalism, like Japanese capitalism, or like Fidel Castro's Marxist vision of farm and factory-based schools (recently reported in *New Left Notes*). On the other hand, *if the young have options and can organize and criticize*, on-the-job education is the quickest way to workers' management which, in my opinion, is the only effective democracy.

University education—liberal arts and the principles of the professions—is for adults who already know something, who have something to philosophize. Otherwise, as Plato pointed out, it is just verbalizing.

To provide a protective and life-nourishing environment for children up through twelve, Summerhill is an adequate model. I think it can be easily adapted to urban conditions if we include houses of refuge for children to resort to, when necessary, to escape parental and neighborhood tyranny or terror. Probably an even better model would be the Athenian pedagogue, touring the city with his charges; but for this the streets and working-places of the city must be made safer and more available than is likely. (The pre-requisite of city-planning is for the children to be able to use the city, for no city is governable if it does not grow citizens who feel it is theirs.) The goal of elementary pedagogy is a very modest one: it is for a small child, under his own steam, to poke interestedly into whatever goes on and to be able, by observation, questions, and practical imitation, to get something out of it in his own terms. In our society this happens pretty well at home up to age four, but after that it becomes forbiddingly difficult.

I have often spelled out this program of incidental education, and found no takers. Curiously, I get the most respectful if wistful attention at teachers' colleges, even though what I propose is quite impossible under present administration. Teachers know how much they are wasting the children's time of life, and they understand that my proposals are fairly conservative, whereas our present schooling is a new mushroom. In general audiences, the response is incredulity. Against all evidence, people are convinced that what we do must make sense, or is inevitable. It does not help if I point out that in dollars and cents it might be cheaper, and it would certainly be more productive in tangible goods and services, to eliminate most schools and make the community and the work that goes in it more educational. Yet the majority in a general audience are willing to say that they themselves got very little out of *their* school years. Occasionally an old reactionary businessman agrees with me enthusiastically, that booklearning isn't worth a penny; or an old socialist agrees, because he thinks you have to get your books the hard way.

Among radical students, I am met by a sullen silence. They want Student Power and are unwilling to answer whether they are authentically students at all. That's not where it's at. (I think they're brainwashed.) Instead of "Student Power," however, what they should be demanding is a more open entry into society, spending the education money more usefully, licensing and hiring without irrelevant diplomas, and so forth. And there *is* an authentic demand for Young People's Power, their right to take part in initiating and deciding the functions of society that concern them—as well, of course, as governing their own lives, which are nobody else's business. Bear in mind that we are speaking of ages seventeen to twenty-five, when at all other times the young would already have been launched in the real world. The young have the right to power because they are numerous and are directly affected by what goes on, but especially because their new point of view is indispensable to cope with changing conditions, they themselves being part of the changing conditions. This is why Jefferson urged us to adopt a new constitution every generation.

Perhaps the chief advantage of incidental education rather than schooling is that the young can then carry on their movement informed and programmatic, grounded in experience and competence, whereas "Student Power," grounded in a phony situation, is usually symbolic and often mere spite.

5. MANKIND AND THE HUMANITIES

Finally, let me go back to a very old-fashioned topic of educational theory, how to transmit Culture with a big C, the greatness of Man. This is no longer discussed by conventional educators and it was never much discussed by progressive educators, though Dewey took it increasingly seriously in his later years. In our generation, it is a critical problem, yet I cannot think of a way to solve it. Perhaps it is useful to try to define it.

The physical environment and social culture force themselves on us, and the young are bound to grow up to them well or badly. They always fundamentally determine the curriculum in formal schooling; but even if there is no schooling at all, they are the focus of children's attention and interest; they are what is there. Dewey's maxim is a good one: there is no need to bother about curriculum, for whatever a child turns to is potentially educative and, with good management, one thing leads to another. Even skills that are considered essential prerequisites, like reading, will be learned spontaneously in normal urban and suburban conditions.

But humane culture is not what is obviously there for a child, and in our times it is less and less so. In the environment there is little spirit of a long proud tradition, with heroes and martyrs. For instance, though there is a plethora of concerts and records, art museums, planetariums, and child-encyclopedias, the disinterested ideals of science and art are hardly mentioned and do not seem to operate publicly at all, and the sacredness of these ideals no longer exists even on college campuses. Almost no young person of college age believes that there are autonomous professionals or has even heard of such a thing. Great souls of the past do not speak to a young person as persons like himself, once he learns their language, nor does he bother to learn their language. The old conflicts of history do not seem to have been human conflicts, nor are they of any interest.

The young have strong feelings for honesty, frankness, loyalty, fairness, affection, freedom, and other virtues of generous natures. They quickly resent the hypocrisy of politicians, adminstrators, and parents who mouth big abstractions and act badly or pettily. But in fact, they themselves—like most politicians and administrators and many parents—seem to have forgotten the concrete reality of ideals like magnanimity, compassion, honor, consistency, civil liberty, integrity, justice—*ruat coelum*, and unpalatable truth, all of which are not gut feelings and are often not pragmatic, but are maintained to create and re-create Mankind. Naturally, without these ideals and their always possible and often actual conflict, there is no tragedy. Most young persons seem to disbelieve that tragedy exists; they always interpret impasse as timidity, and casuistry as finding out. I am often astonished by their physical courage, but I am only rarely moved by their moral courage.

Their ignorance has advantages. The bother with transmitting humane culture is that it must be re-created in spirit, or it is a dead weight upon present spirit, and it does produce timidity and hypocrisy. Then it is better forgotten. Certainly the attempt to teach it by courses in school or by sermons like this, is a disaster. Presumably it was kept going by the living example of a large number of people who took it seriously and leavened society, but now there seems to be a discontinuity. It has been said that the thread really snapped during the First World War, during the Spanish War, with the gas-chambers and Atom-bombs, etc., etc. I have often suggested that the logical way to teach the humanities, for instance, would be for some of us to picket the TV stations in despair; but we are tired, and anyway, when we have done similar things, students put their own rather different interpretation on it. We try to purge the university of military projects, but students attack the physical research itself that could be abused (and is even bound to be abused), as if science were not necessarily a risky adventure. They don't see that this is a tragic dilemma. They seem quite willing—though battening on them in the United States—to write off Western science and civil law.

Yet apart from the spirit congealed in them, we do not really have our sciences and arts, professions and civic institutions. It is inauthentic merely to use the products and survivals, and I don't think we can in fact work Western civilization without its vivifying tradition. The simplest reason that cities are ungovernable is that there aren't enough citizens; this happened during the Roman Empire too. It is conceivable that the so-called Third World can adapt our technology and reinterpret it according to other ideals, as was supposed to be the theme of the conference in Havana against Cultural Imperialism; but I read dozens of papers and did not find a single new proposition. Anyway, this does nothing for us. Here at home it is poignant what marvels some people expect from the revival of African masks.

A young fellow is singing a song attacking the technological way of life, but he is accompanying it on an electric guitar plugged into the infra-structure; and the rhythm and harmony are phony mountain-music popularized by Stalinists in the Thirties to give themselves an American image, and which cannot cohere with a contemporary poem. But I can't make him see why this won't do. I can't make clear to a young lady at the Antioch-Putney School of Education that a child has an historical human right to know that there is a tie between Venus and the Sun and thanks to Newton we know its equation, which is even more beautiful than the Evening Star; it is *not* a matter of taste whether he knows this or not. Yet she's right, for if it's not his thing, it's pointless to show it to him, as it is to her.

It seems to me that, ignorant of the inspiration and grandeur of our civilization, though somewhat aware of its brutality and terror, the young are patsies for the "inevitabilities" of modern times. If they cannot take on our only world appreciatively and very critically, they can only confront her or be servile to her and then she is too powerful for any of us.

Margaret Mead says, truly, that young people are in modern times like native sons, whereas we others use the technology gingerly and talk like foreign-born. I am often pleased at how competent my young friend proves to be; my apprehension for him is usually groundless. But he is swamped by present-ness. Since there is no background or structure, everything is equivalent and superficial. He can repair the TV but he thinks the picture is real. (Marshall McLuhan doesn't help.) He says my lecture blew his mind and I am flattered till he tells me that L. Ron Hubbard's metempsychosis in Hellenistic Sardinia blew his mind; I wonder if he has any mind to blow.

I sometimes have the eerie feeling that there are around the world, a few dozen of Plato's guardians, ecologists and psychosomatic physicians, who with worried brows are trying to save mankind from destroying itself. This is a sorry situation for Jeffersonian anarchists like myself who think we ought to fend for ourselves. The young are quick to point out the mess that we have made, but I don't see that they really care about that, as if it were not their mankind. Rather, I see them with the Christmas astronauts flying toward the moon and seeing the Earth shining below: it is as if they are about to abandon an old house and therefore it makes no difference if they litter it with beer cans. These are bad thoughts.

But I have occasionally had a good educational experience in the Draft Resistance movement. The resisters are exceptionally virtuous young men and they are earnest about the fix they are in, that makes them liable to two to five years in jail. Then it is remarkable how, guided by a few Socratic questions, they come to remember the ideas of Allegiance, Sovereignty, Legitimacy, Exile, and bitter Patriotism, which cannot be taught in college courses in political science. It is a model of incidental learning of the humanities, but I am uneasy to generalize from it.

The Idea of Summerhill

A. S. Neill

Summerhill is perhaps the happiest school in the world. We have no truants and seldom a case of homesickness. We very rarely have fights. . . . Hate breeds hate and love breeds love. Love means approving of children, and that is essential at any school. You can't be on the side of children if you punish them and storm at them. Summerhill is a school in which the child knows that he is approved of.

Editor's Introduction

When I first read Neill's book *Summerhill: A Radical Approach to Child Rearing,* I fell in love with the man. At each subsequent reading, I am more and more convinced of my own good taste. A. S. Neill is a believer in children, in their innate goodness, and in dealing with children in an honest and truthful manner, without denying emotions. Neill believes that a restrictive, uncreative, dishonest school will create children with the same unfortunate characteristics. A school which fosters an avoidance of real-life issues will create students who will do the same. A school which teaches blind adherence to authority, authority based on age or power without respect to the worth of the individual, will create children, and later adults, who will respond with blind acceptance of any leader, no matter how corrupt, simply because that leader is powerful and in a position of authority. Neill believes that for the child to be truly free, he or she must be in an environment which is humane and honest. According to Neill, many traditional schools foster hatred and distrust and therefore make the child hostile and difficult. A school which fosters respect and affection for children will create children who will respect themselves and who will have the capacity to respect and love others. In other words, Neill believes in children's liberation: that there are no problem children, only problem schools, problem parents, and as a result, problem societies.

Neill believes that the aim of education is to allow the individual to find happiness in life, both an intellectual and an emotional joy. He does not aim to educate children to fit into existing society but to utilize their capacities; to value what they become, not what they acquire; to be personally genuine, not monetarily successful.

While the reader is not expected to embrace Neill's philosophy in totality and without question (I think Neill would be disappointed if one did not question and evaluate), the following selection will undoubtedly give the reader insight into the warmth and candor of Neill's approach to childhood education.

Pamela Cantor

This is a story of a modern school—Summerhill.

Summerhill was founded in the year 1921. The school is situated within the village of Leiston, in Suffolk, England, and is about one hundred miles from London.

Just a word about Summerhill pupils. Some children come to Summerhill at the age of five years, and others as late as fifteen. The children generally remain at the school until they are sixteen years old. We generally have about twenty-five boys and twenty girls.

The children are divided into three age groups: The youngest range from five to seven, the intermediates from eight to ten, and the oldest from eleven to fifteen.

Generally we have a fairly large sprinkling of children from foreign countries. At the present time (1960) we have five Scandinavians, one Hollander, one German and one American.

The children are housed by age groups with a house mother for each group. The intermediates sleep in a stone building, the seniors sleep in huts. Only one or two older pupils have rooms for themselves. The boys live two or three or four to a room, and so do the girls. The pupils do not have to stand room inspection and no one picks up after them. They are left free. No one tells them what to wear: they put on any kind of costume they want to at any time.

Newspapers call it a *Go-as-you-please*

School and imply that it is a gathering of wild primitives who know no law and have no manners.

It seems necessary, therefore, for me to write the story of Summerhill as honestly as I can. That I write with a bias is natural; yet I shall try to show the demerits of Summerhill as well as its merits. Its merits will be the merits of healthy, free children whose lives are unspoiled by fear and hate.

Obviously, a school that makes active children sit at desks studying mostly useless subjects is a bad school. It is a good school only for those who believe in *such* a school, for those uncreative citizens who want docile, uncreative children who will fit into a civilization whose standard of success is money.

Summerhill began as an experimental school. It is no longer such; it is now a demonstration school, for it demonstrates that freedom works.

When my first wife and I began the school, we had one main idea: *to make the school fit the child*—instead of making the child fit the school.

I had taught in ordinary schools for many years. I knew the other way well. I knew it was all wrong. It was wrong because it was based on an adult conception of what a child should be and of how a child should learn. The other way dated from the days when psychology was still an unknown science.

Well, we set out to make a school in which

we should allow children freedom to be themselves. In order to do this, we had to renounce all discipline, all direction, all suggestion, all moral training, all religious instruction. We have been called brave, but it did not require courage. All it required was what we had—a complete belief in the child as a good, not an evil, being. For almost forty years, this belief in the goodness of the child has never wavered; it rather has become a final faith.

My view is that a child is innately wise and realistic. If left to himself without adult suggestion of any kind, he will develop as far as he is capable of developing. Logically, Summerhill is a place in which people who have the innate ability and wish to be scholars will be scholars; while those who are only fit to sweep the streets will sweep the streets. But we have not produced a street cleaner so far. Nor do I write this snobbishly, for I would rather see a school produce a happy street cleaner than a neurotic scholar.

What is Summerhill like? Well, for one thing, lessons are optional. Children can go to them or stay away from them—for years if they want to. There *is* a timetable—but only for the teachers.

The children have classes usually according to their age, but sometimes according to their interests. We have no new methods of teaching, because we do not consider that teaching in itself matters very much. Whether a school has or has not a special method for teaching long division is of no significance, for long division is of no importance except to those who *want* to learn it. And the child who *wants* to learn long division *will* learn it no matter how it is taught.

Children who come to Summerhill as kindergarteners attend lessons from the beginning of their stay; but pupils from other schools vow that they will never attend any beastly lessons again at any time. They play and cycle and get in people's way, but they fight shy of lessons. This sometimes goes on for months.

The recovery time is proportionate to the hatred their last school gave them. Our record case was a girl from a convent. She loafed for three years. The average period of recovery from lesson aversion is three months.

Strangers to this idea of freedom will be wondering what sort of madhouse it is where children play all day if they want to. Many an adult says, "If I had been sent to a school like that, I'd never have done a thing." Others say, "Such children will feel themselves heavily handicapped when they have to compete against children who have been made to learn."

I think of Jack who left us at the age of seventeen to go into an engineering factory. One day, the managing director sent for him.

"You are the lad from Summerhill," he said. "I'm curious to know how such an education appears to you now that you are mixing with lads from the old schools. Suppose you had to choose again, would you go to Eton or Summerhill?"

"Oh, Summerhill, of course," replied Jack.

"But what does it offer that the other schools don't offer?"

Jack scratched his head. "I dunno," he said slowly; "I think it gives you a feeling of complete self-confidence."

"Yes," said the manager dryly, "I noticed it when you came into the room."

"Lord," laughed Jack, "I'm sorry if I gave you that impression."

"I liked it," said the director. "Most men when I call them into the office fidget about and look uncomfortable. You came in as my equal. By the way, what department did you say you would like to transfer to?"

This story shows that learning in itself is not as important as personality and character. Jack failed in his university exams because he hated book learning. But his lack of knowledge about *Lamb's Essays* or the French language did not handicap him in life. He is now a successful engineer.

All the same, there is a lot of learning in Summerhill. Perhaps a group of our twelve-year-olds could not compete with a class of equal age in handwriting or spelling or fractions. But in an examination requiring originality, our lot would beat the others hollow.

We have no class examinations in the school, but sometimes I set an exam for fun. The following questions appeared in one such paper:

Where are the following:—Madrid, Thursday Island, yesterday, love, democracy, hate, my pocket screwdriver (alas, there was no helpful answer to that one).

Give meanings for the following: (the number shows how many are expected for each)—Hand (3) . . . only two got the third right—the standard of measure for a horse. Brass(4) . . . metal, cheek, top army officers, department of an orchestra. Translate Hamlet's To-be-or-not-to-be speech into Summerhillese.

These questions are obviously not intended to be serious, and the children enjoy them thoroughly. Newcomers, on the whole, do not rise to the answering standard of pupils who have become acclimatized to the school. Not that they have less brain power, but rather because they have become so accustomed to work in a serious groove that any light touch puzzles them.

This is the play side of our teaching. In all classes much work is done. If, for some reason, a teacher cannot take his class on the appointed day, there is usually much disappointment for the pupils.

David, aged nine, had to be isolated for whooping cough. He cried bitterly. "I'll miss Roger's lesson in geography," he protested. David had been in the school practically from birth, and he had definite and final ideas about the necessity of having his lessons given to him. David is now a lecturer in mathematics at London University.

A few years ago someone at a General School Meeting (at which all school rules are voted by the entire school, each pupil and each staff member having one vote) proposed that a certain culprit should be punished by being banished from lessons for a week. The other children protested on the ground that the punishment was too severe.

My staff and I have a hearty hatred of all examinations. To us, the university exams are anathema. But we cannot refuse to teach children the required subjects. Obviously, as long as the exams are in existence, they are our master. Hence, the Summerhill staff is always qualified to teach to the set standard.

Not that many children want to take these exams; only those going to the university do so. And such children do not seem to find it especially hard to tackle these exams. They generally begin to work for them seriously at the age of fourteen, and they do the work in about three years. Of course they don't always pass at the first try. The more important fact is that they try again.

Summerhill is possibly the happiest school in the world. We have no truants and seldom a case of homesickness. We very rarely have fights—quarrels, of course, but seldom have I seen a stand-up fight like the ones we used to have as boys. I seldom hear a child cry, because children when free have much less hate to express than children who are downtrodden. Hate breeds hate, and love breeds love. Love means approving of children, and that is essential in any school. You can't be on the side of children if you punish them and storm at them. Summerhill is a school in which the child knows that he is approved of.

Mind you, we are not above and beyond human foibles. I spent weeks planting potatoes one spring, and when I found eight plants pulled up in June, I made a big fuss. Yet there was a difference between my fuss and that of an authoritarian. My fuss was about potatoes, but the fuss an authoritarian would have made would have dragged in the question of morality—right and wrong. I did not say that it was wrong to steal my spuds; I did not make it a matter of good and evil—I made it a matter of *my spuds*. They were *my* spuds and they should have been left alone. I hope I am making the distinction clear.

Let me put it another way. To the children, I am no authority to be feared. I am their equal, and the row I kick up about my spuds has no more significance to them than the row a boy may kick up about his punctured bicycle tire. It is quite safe to have a row with a child when you are equals.

Now some will say: "That's all bunk. There can't be equality. Neill is the boss; he is bigger and wiser." That is indeed true. I am the boss, and if the house caught fire the children would run to me. They know that I am bigger and more knowledgeable, but that does not matter when I meet them on their own ground, the potato patch, so to speak.

When Billy, aged five, told me to get out of his birthday party because I hadn't been invited, I went at once without hesitation—just as Billy gets out of my room when I don't want his company. It is not easy to describe this relationship between teacher and child, but every visitor to Summerhill knows what I mean when I say that the relationship is ideal. One sees it in the attitude to the staff in general. Rudd, the chemistry man, is Derek. Other members of the staff are known as Harry, and Ulla, and Pam. I am Neill, and the cook is Esther.

In Summerhill, everyone has equal rights. No one is allowed to walk on my grand piano, and I am not allowed to borrow a boy's cycle without his permission. At a General School Meeting, the vote of a child of six counts for as much as my vote does.

But, says the knowing one, in practice of course the voices of the grownups count. Doesn't the child of six wait to see how you vote before he raises his hand? I wish he

sometimes would, for too many of my proposals are beaten. Free children are not easily influenced; the absence of fear accounts for this phenomenon. Indeed, the absence of fear is the finest thing that can happen to a child.

Our children do not fear our staff. One of the school rules is that after ten o'clock at night there shall be quietness on the upper corridor. One night, about eleven, a pillow fight was going on, and I left my desk, where I was writing, to protest against the row. As I got upstairs, there was a scurrying of feet and the corridor was empty and quiet. Suddenly I heard a disappointed voice say, "Humph, it's only Neill," and the fun began again at once. When I explained that I was trying to write a book downstairs, they showed concern and at once agreed to chuck the noise. Their scurrying came from the suspicion that their bedtime officer (one of their own age) was on their track.

I emphasize the importance of this absence of fear of adults. A child of nine will come and tell me he has broken a window with a ball. He tells me, because he isn't afraid of arousing wrath or moral indignation. He may have to pay for the window, but he doesn't have to fear being lectured or being punished.

There was a time some years back when the School Government resigned, and no one would stand for election. I seized the opportunity of putting up a notice: "In the absence of a government, I herewith declare myself Dictator. Heil Neill!" Soon there were mutterings. In the afternoon Vivien, aged six, came to me and said, "Neill, I've broken a window in the gym."

I waved him away. "Don't bother me with little things like that," I said, and he went.

A little later he came back and said he had broken two windows. By this time I was curious, and asked him what the great idea was.

"I don't like dictators," he said, "and I don't like going without my grub." (I discovered later that the opposition to dictatorship had tried to take itself out on the cook, who promptly shut up the kitchen and went home.)

"Well," I asked, "what are you going to do about it?"

"Break more windows," he said doggedly.

"Carry on," I said, and he carried on.

When he returned, he announced that he had broken seventeen windows. "But mind," he said earnestly, "I'm going to pay for them."

"How?"

"Out of my pocket money. How long will it take me?"

I did a rapid calculation. "About ten years," I said.

He looked glum for a minute; then I saw his face light up. "Gee," he cried, "I don't have to pay for them at all."

"But what about the private property rule?" I asked. "The windows are my private property."

"I know that but there isn't any private property rule now. There isn't any government, and the government makes the rules."

It may have been my expression that made him add, "But all the same I'll pay for them."

But he didn't have to pay for them. Lecturing in London shortly afterward, I told the story; and at the end of my talk, a young man came up and handed me a pound note "to pay for the young devil's windows." Two years later, Vivien was still telling people of his windows and of the man who paid for them. "He must have been a terrible fool, because he never even saw me."

Children make contact with strangers more easily when fear is unknown to them. English reserve is, at bottom, really fear; and that is why the most reserved are those who have the most wealth. The fact that Summerhill children are so exceptionally friendly to visitors and strangers is a source of pride to me and my staff.

We must confess, however, that many of our visitors are people of interest to the chil-

dren. The kind of visitor most unwelcome to them is the teacher, especially the earnest teacher, who wants to see their drawing and written work. The most welcome visitor is the one who has good tales to tell—of adventure and travel or, best of all, aviation. A boxer or a good tennis player is surrounded at once, but visitors who spout theory are left severely alone.

The most frequent remark that visitors make is that they cannot tell who is staff and who is pupil. It is true: the feeling of unity is that strong when children are approved of. There is no deference to a teacher as a teacher. Staff and pupils have the same food and have to obey the same community laws. The children would resent any special privileges given to the staff.

When I used to give the staff a talk on psychology every week, there was a muttering that it wasn't fair. I changed the plan and made the talks open to everyone over twelve. Every Tuesday night, my room is filled with eager youngsters who not only listen but give their opinions freely. Among the subjects the children have asked me to talk about have been these: The Inferiority Complex, The Psychology of Stealing, The Psychology of the Gangster, The Psychology of Humor, Why Did Man Become a Moralist?, Masturbation, Crowd Psychology. It is obvious that such children will go out into life with a broad clear knowledge of themselves and others.

The most frequent question asked by Summerhill visitors is, "Won't the child turn round and blame the school for not making him learn arithmetic or music?" The answer is that young Freddy Beethoven and young Tommy Einstein will refuse to be kept away from their respective spheres.

The function of the child is to live his own life—not the life that his anxious parents think he should live, nor a life according to the purpose of the educator who thinks he knows what is best. All this interference and guidance on the part of adults only produces a generation of robots.

You cannot *make* children learn music or anything else without to some degree converting them into will-less adults. You fashion them into accepters of the *status quo*—a good thing for a society that needs obedient sitters at dreary desks, standers in shops, mechanical catchers of the 8:30 suburban train—a society, in short, that is carried on the shabby shoulders of the scared little man—the scared-to-death conformist.

Chapter 12

Personality Development

THEORETICAL PERSPECTIVES ON PERSONALITY DEVELOPMENT

Seven Years Old

Arnold Gesell and Francis Ilg

SEVEN *may himself become involved in an elementary love affair. Boy-girl pairs are fairly common, especially at school. . . . One 7-year-old who did not have a boy-friend wailed to her parents, 'What is the matter with me? I'm not in love.'*

Editor's Introduction

A discussion of major theoretical perspectives on personality development will include Freud or Erikson as representative of the psychoanalytic approach to development, Skinner as representative of the learning theory approach to behavior, and perhaps Kurt Lewin as representative of the field-theory approach or Heinz Werner of the organismic approach. The maturational approach as represented by the work of Gesell and Ilg has too often been overlooked by professionals, probably due to the fact that Gesell and Ilg wrote for parents and the lay public. The year-by-year descriptions of developmental changes and the detailed and voluminous observations which the authors have recorded are, I believe, of great value to those who work with children or who are engaged in formal training in child psychology or in education. The work of Gesell and Ilg represents a description of the physical, emotional, cognitive, and social development of children presented in nontechnical terms.

Gesell and Ilg, in their now classic volumes *The First Five Years of Life*, *The Child from Five to Ten*, and *The Child from Ten to Sixteen*, have outlined a developmental study of children throughout the first sixteen years of life. The approach the authors take is longitudinal, biographical, clinical, and essentially maturational. The descriptions are not to be taken as rigid norms but rather are intended to illustrate the kinds of behavior which typically occur during a period of a year. The descriptions are to be used to assess the developmental sequence of mental, physical, and emotional growth unique to each child.

I first became acquainted with Gesell and Ilg when my parents purchased their copy of *The Child from Ten to Sixteen*. My mother kept the book within easy reach on the desk in her bedroom. Periodically I would stealthily remove the book while my parents were out of the house and read a few chapters just to see how I was doing. I would approach this book the way many teen-agers would approach a forbidden sex novel. (Perhaps that was the major incentive for my continued interest in psychology.) I was particularly curious to see where I was a bit behind schedule and where I was exhibiting precocious behavior. In sum, it was comforting to know that someone else knew what I was experiencing or was about to experience and would reassure me that when I was feeling a bit of a brat that it was "normal" for my age. While this is not the use that Gesell and Ilg intended, I thought I might use these pages to express my gratitude and at the same time to provide an example of the maturational approach to development which is representative of a major theoretical orientation for studying children.

The following selection is a relatively informal discussion of the 7-year-old child in the context of the social relationships which affect the child's life. The middle years of childhood, 6 through 12, are clearly of great importance, yet they have received little attention from psychologists, perhaps because it is so common to think of these years as simply a period of marking time until adolescence. It is true that there is a slowing of the rapid pace of growth which occurred during the preschool years, but much is happening to make the experience of the middle childhood years crucial to child development. These are the critical elementary school years, the years in which the child acquires the basic academic skills. It is also the time during which the child's self-concept as a good student (and therefore a success) or a poor student (and therefore a failure) emerges. The years from 6 to 16 also mark the period of acceptance or rejection of peer values and the cultural ethos of society as well as of learning appropriate sex behaviors and attitudes. The selection which follows, the discussion of the "model" 7-year-old, is but one example of the work of Gesell and Ilg and of the complexities of development during the middle years.

Pamela Cantor

FEARS AND DREAMS

Fears

SEVEN's fears focalize upon himself,—his inner self,—and his self acting on its own. He has his behavior equipment so much better in hand that he can protect himself as the 6-year-old cannot. SIX jumps right in and finds himself over his depth; SEVEN hesitates before acting. His fears and worries are to some extent useful in that they are self-protective.

Although SEVEN has some left-over fears which were not resolved at six, he now handles them differently. He may still want his parents to stay at home in the evening, but he can resign himself to their departure, once he has gotten over the first hurdle.

SEVEN is spoken of both as cowardly and brave. These words refer to the lack of or presence of an inner control. SEVEN is an age when the environment can capitalize on the child's bravery, but bravery also needs environmental support and cannot be left on its own until the child is off to a good start.

Many previously unresolved fears now resolve,—the fear of the dentist's chair, the fear of swimming with face under water, or the fear of having hair washed. The 7-year-old has all of these situations under better control. He knows what the dentist does and that he can lift his hand if being hurt. He can now hold his breath under water and no longer "breathes in" as he used to do. He may be able to wash his own hair and can control soap in his eyes and the temperature of the water on his scalp.

But there are a number of situations that SEVEN does not have under his control. He does not want to experience new situations by himself. Even his summer may have been miserable because he was afraid to start second grade. He is afraid of his school work because he doesn't know how to start. He is afraid of being shy, or of being laughed at. He is afraid of physical punishment. And he may even be afraid that his mother will "get down on him" as his teacher has.

Space and time are taking on new meaning for him. He may fear high places and unfamiliar visual impressions. Cellars become inhabited by strange creatures and attics by ghosts. Even his own closet may have a German spy in it. Shadows gather form and take on meaning. His clothes on the back of a chair may suddenly appear as a frightening ghost in a half light after he is in bed. He may be timid of his own shadow in his inability to interpret it and its sudden movements. Though he loves hut-play with his gang, he may be scared to death of the trap door in the hut.

SEVEN can, however, help to control his fears. He gets his sister to go down into the cellar with him and politely says, "Ladies first." He flashes his flashlight on the German spy in his closet and dissolves him. He calls to his mother to analyze the ghost in his room and enjoys the realization that it was only his clothes on a chair.

The very child who is most fearful of being late for school at seven may actually never have had the experience of being late. He is usually the type of child who has his inner timing mechanism under poor control. He not only has difficulty in stopping—he goes on endlessly—but he also has difficulty in starting. It is an unsettling experience to be with a 7-year-old who is extremely afraid of being late for school. He may awake at 6 A.M. and shout to his parents, "Is it time to get up yet?" This phrase recurs at intervals. The setting of an alarm may help him temporarily to control his anxiety.

Once he is up he hurries into his clothes, rushes through breakfast and then waits. Again he plagues his parents with another oft-repeated phrase: "Is it time to go yet?" Even the assurance that his father will drive him to school may not allay his anxiety. During the last ten minutes before departure his whole body is aquiver with anxiety, he has to go to the bathroom at least three times and may even have a bowel movement. Finally he rushes off in the car, rushes across the playground and at last crosses the threshold of his room and experiences immediate calm. He gives his teacher no inkling of what he has gone through in the last two and a half hours.

This type of child under the best of handling may still express some anxiety, but he can be helped to better control. In the first place he should not be held to coming to school exactly on time, for his sense of time is still only relative and his coming to school should also include a certain relativeness. If the school cannot provide this type of handling, he should be helped to bridge the gap from home to school by one of his interests. Reading a book on electricity may turn the trick, especially during the last ten minutes before starting off for school. Then he might take the book to school, show it to his teacher, and it may be hoped that the teacher will respond with interest.

As with SIX, certain stimuli in funny books or movies may bring on fears,—such tales as opening drawers and finding skulls. This is why the child still needs considerable supervision, especially if he is the type of child who is not too self-protective and who gets into situations from which he cannot get out by himself.

Dreams

Dreams are diminishing at seven or at least are not reported as much as earlier. Nightmares and dreams about animals are also declining. Only a few children have unpleasant dreams about being chased by persons or beasts.

SEVEN dreams mostly about himself. He has wonderful dreams when he flies and floats through the air, or dives into the depths of the ocean. He may dream of embarrassing situations such as wetting the bed (which may coincide with an unusual episode of wetting), or losing his pants on the way to the school bus. A clearly defined shift to the opposite sex

may be experienced in a dream. A boy may dream that he is going upstairs without any clothes on and that his nipples have become extraordinarily large.

SEVEN carries on long conversations in his dreams, with spies, pilots and unfamiliar people. As he talks out loud one gathers bits of conversation which disclose that he feels himself to be definitely involved. He may say: "It's me," or "I don't think you need a bodyguard."

Certain movies and radio programs give him bad dreams. He still needs considerable supervision in making his choices of radio and movies.

SELF AND SEX

Self

SEVEN is becoming more aware of himself. By absorbing impressions from what he sees, hears, reads, and by working things over in his own thoughts and feelings, he seems to be strengthening and building up his sense of self. At EIGHT he may take his equipment out into the outside world and try it against the environment, but at seven—for all his noisy slapdash exterior, his running through the house slamming doors and shouting—he most characteristically sits quietly by himself, reading, listening to the radio, planning about what he is going to do.

With some SEVENS, self-awareness relates strongly to the physical self. SEVEN is aware of his body and is sensitive about exposing it, especially to the opposite sex. He may refuse to go to the toilet at school if there is no door on it. He does not like to be touched. Girls are especially aware of the style in which their hair is worn, and actually may fear that their identity would be lost or at least that they might not be recognized if their braids were cut off.

Most SEVENS are concerned about their actions. They are ashamed of their mistakes and their fears, and very much ashamed to be seen crying. They are very much aware of what others might think, and are careful not to expose themselves to criticism. They cringe when they are laughed at or made fun of.

One of the ways in which SEVEN protects himself best is to withdraw from any scene of action which does not please him. His withdrawal may be combined with a distaste for physical combat. This is not the age to teach the child to "defend himself" by means of boxing lessons. By eight he may spontaneously defend himself. At seven he needs to be helped to withdraw and needs to be protected.

SEVEN is serious about himself, and about any responsibilities which may be given to him—especially if they are school or other responsibilities outside his home. He thinks and speaks seriously of such concepts as government, civilization and the like. SEVEN is not only serious but he also is cautious,—in physical activities, in social situations and in his approach to a new task. There are beginnings of slight skepticism about Santa Claus, about religion and other matters of which he has been told but which he has not experienced at first hand.

Though he withdraws successfully, he is apt to voice many complaints. He feels that people are mean and unfair. And as he thinks situations over he worries about what people think of him and fears that they do not like him, or do not think he has done well. He is particularly interested in what his mother and his friends think of him. "Of course the kids will make fun of me," he says. There is a definite minor strain in the feelings of the 7-year-old.

Boys especially may be breaking away from their mother's domination. They may refuse to wear coats, hats, rubbers. They may ask, "Why should I?" if given a command, and may counter a direction with the response, "I don't feel like it."

SEVEN wants to make a place for himself.

This place may be a physical one—his place at the table, in the family car, or a room of his own. But SEVEN is also interested in his place in the social world. He usually has strong family feelings and at the same time he may fear that he does not really belong to his family, that he has been adopted. SEVEN mulls all these things over in his mind, for even in his thoughts he withdraws. Then he may discuss the fruit of his thoughts with the adult in relation to such topics as: "The disadvantages of being over five and under sixteen." The particular 7-year-old in question advanced the following reasoning. "Under five people give you plenty of money, and over sixteen you have plenty of your own. But between those ages they make you work for your money and give you very little for what you do. And between those ages you are changing the fastest, so you need a great many things."

Sex

SEVEN is less likely than SIX to be involved in overt sex play. In fact, he may even withdraw from any possible exposure when he is undressing or going to the bathroom if a younger sibling of the opposite sex is near. If two girls expose themselves, one to the other, they may become interested in the details of the organs and even try to draw what they have seen. A few SEVENS, especially boys, may think that they can magically change themselves into girls by taping up their genitals. These same boys may enjoy playing dolls with a girl.

SEVEN's real interest is *thinking about* all these things. He shows an intense longing to have a new baby in his family, and almost always he desires a baby of his own sex. One such child, reminded a year later of her 7-year-old desire which was about to be fulfilled, exclaimed, "Now whatever made me say that!" SEVEN realizes that having babies can be repeated. He may ask his mother how many more babies she has in her stomach. He is aware that older women do not still have babies. He may even draw up a plan for his mother to have a baby every five years (because this is the easiest for him to calculate) until she is sixty when he feels she won't be able to have any more.

Pregnancy is now something that he is beginning to understand. He may be the first to notice that his mother is different. He may ask, "What's the matter with you? You don't act the same." If a baby is coming in his house he is very much excited about it. If permitted the experience, he is thrilled to feel the kicking of the baby against the mother's abdominal wall. He wants to know how big the baby is, how it is fed, will it get sick if the mother becomes ill, and how long it takes before it is ready to be born.

He does not quite understand how the mother knows that the baby has started growing. He is satisfied when he learns that two seeds (or two eggs), one from the father and one from the mother, come together to start the baby. He is not yet concerned about how the seed from the father got into the mother.

He is more concerned about the details of birth. In his own mind he may more or less vaguely figure out that you have to "split the mother open to take the baby out." He readily accepts the simplified statement that the baby is born between the mother's legs. He wonders whether this takes place with the mother on the floor or on a table, and whether the baby might fall to the floor. He may even ask to be there so that he can catch the baby when it comes out. It is no wonder that he cannot understand why a baby should cost so much when it grows inside of a person.

SEVEN may himself become involved in an elementary love affair. Boy-girl pairs are fairly common, especially at school. The boys who can write and spell may even write simple notes, "Do you like me? Yes or no." With X's for kisses. If the relationship progresses to a specific "engagement" and even to a planned marriage, the boy usually adds that he plans to return to his mother's house after the marriage. The loss of a boy-friend or girl-friend is usually taken as a matter of course, but some SEVENS are more deeply affected. One 7-year-old who did not have a boy-friend wailed to her parents, "What is the matter with me? I'm not in love."

SCHOOL LIFE

On the whole SEVEN accepts his return to school without protest but he may anticipate that second grade will be too hard. A few advance visits of the first grade group to the second grade room (i.e. a play or picnic at the end of the year) help to forestall and to alleviate such fear. SEVEN may fatigue in spells and this is noticeable at school as well as at home. He has fewer illnesses but an illness may be of longer duration.

The teacher plays an important part in SEVEN's adjustment. She becomes involved in a more personal relationship with each of her pupils and may be both liked and disliked. Boys are more apt to like their teacher and may form a close attachment to her. Girls may dislike and complain about her. SEVEN continues to bring things to the teacher but not as much as at six, nor does he bring things for the group. However, he enjoys an opportunity to display a new possession.

Home and school are more separated spheres at seven. The child may not like his mother to walk to school with him, or to visit school unless it is for a group performance when other mothers also are present. While he is with the group he may ignore her presence.

SEVEN likes to accumulate his papers in his school desk rather than take them home. If they are kept in a notebook he may wish to take this home on occasion. It would then be left at home if his mother did not remind him or put it in his hand as he leaves for school. He is apt also to leave sweaters and belongings at school unless the teacher helps him to remember them. SEVEN is not a good messenger either for teacher or for parent. . . .

As SEVEN enters the classroom he does not always refer to his teacher; he may be noisy and talkative as he makes his entrance, manipulating objects about the room. However, he is interested in a schedule and finally settles into classroom work with absorption. He is quieter while he works than he was at six, talks more to himself. He refers to the work of his nearby neighbor, or makes an impatient demand for the teacher's assistance, often by going directly to her. He is frequently seen with head resting on his forearm while he writes and also while classroom discussions are in progress. He shows temporary fatigue with some tasks by shoving his desk, opening and closing his desk top or getting up from his chair. These signs indicate that he is ready to change to a different activity. . . .

SEVEN likes to manipulate objects, so he picks up pencils, erasers, sticks and stones and accumulates them in his desk. He may attempt to insert one object into another, and manipulates them so forcibly as to break them. It may be helpful to have an emptying of pockets at the end of a morning session, and an occasional desk cleaning day. . . .

There is less interruption for toileting, as SEVEN has a longer retention span. The majority toilet before and after lunch and after rest period in the afternoon. A few very active boys may have a shorter span. SEVEN prefers the privacy provided by an enclosed toilet and may refuse to use the school toilet if it is without a door.

Classroom work requires the teacher nearby as she is in almost constant demand. There are many individual differences at seven. Some prefer work at their desks to work presented by the teacher on the blackboard and vice versa. (SEVEN does not combine the two easily; he cannot copy from the blackboard.) Boys like oral better than written arithmetic and girls may prefer concrete to oral or written arithmetic. Some wish widely spaced ruled paper, others prefer narrow. Some respond immediately, others need to be allowed extra time. By eight there will be more uniformity within the group, but such differences need to be respected at seven.

In reading, SEVEN recognizes familiar words accurately and rapidly. He is more mechanical in his approach to reading; he reads without stopping for the end of a sentence or a paragraph though in his efforts he is apt to repeat a phrase. He may omit or add familiar simple words (*and, he, had, but*) or a final *s* or *y*. He hesitates on new words and prefers to have them supplied so that he can maintain his speed; or he may simply guess, using a word of similar appearance, often one with the beginning and ending letter the same, though the length of the word may now be shortened (*green* for *garden*, *betful* for *beautiful*). Substitutions of meaning (*the* for *a*, *was* for *lived*) are prevalent. Vowel errors (*pass* for *puss*, *some* for *same*) are common. Speed of reading, like other behaviors, shows individual variations.

SEVEN likes to know how far to read; he likes to know how many pages in the book. If he has left a story unfinished he may want to go back to the beginning.

As he improves in the mechanics of reading he may temporarily be less concerned about meaning. He is, however, critical of his reading material and may refuse to re-read certain stories. Some SEVENS become inveterate readers with a special liking for comics. (A favorite time for such reading is in the early morning before breakfast.) . . . .

Pencils and erasers are almost a passion at seven. SEVEN writes to erase. He manipulates, fingers, drops his pencil and jabs it into his desk or into an object. He still reverses some letters and numbers but he usually recognizes his reversal and prefers to erase it. He may say, "Don't be surprised if you find one of my capital J's backward." His pencil grasp is tight with the index caved in and as a rule he exerts much pressure though this is variable. Several children ask to "write" rather than print; maintaining the pencil in contact with the paper may give them more security of motor control.

Pencil and paper work, although a strong interest, makes problems at this age. SEVEN may worry if he cannot finish his written work and even fears being kept after school if his paper is incomplete.

SEVEN has a new awareness of ends. "How far shall I go, Miss L?" "I can't finish," are typical remarks. He likes to complete but he wants the teacher to set his end for him, otherwise he is apt to continue too long. He likes to have his paper corrected immediately. "Did I get 100?" "Is this right?" He does not compare this with others, but in drawing he may ask the teacher to evaluate who drew the best tree or the best horse.

The thoughtful, memory-rumination of the 7-year-old is shown in the following responses to a teacher's question: *What do you see in your mind when you think of autumn?"*

"I see the leaves going zig-zag."
"I see them going down gently."
"I see pumpkins turning yellow."
"I see milk weeds turning brown."
"I see chestnuts falling down."
"I see the birds going south."
"I see the trees with pretty near all the leaves off."

SEVEN makes a characteristic "explosive" transition from schoolroom to playground at recess time; but on the playground he may be either more, or less, active than he is in the classroom. Entanglements with classmates occur even with the teacher nearby. One child may interfere with another's block structure, one child may want to remain on the swing for the entire period, or monopolize a ball or a jump rope. When several children attempt group play they may become excited and

hilarious. —his usually ends with destruction of material, or personal altercations. SEVEN needs a variety of outdoor equipment and even though he is not ready for any directed group play, adult supervision is essential. During the year some become interested in group play set up by the teacher as long as they are free to join and leave the group at will.

SEVEN wants a place in the group and may be concerned that the other children or the teacher do not like him. He can be separated from the group for special help or to work or play by himself but he does not like to be singled out for reprimand or praise while he is a part of the group. Group praise, however, is a real spur. The group is slow to include a new member and may even make fun of him.

In play, four or five children may attempt to play together; to build, to shoot airplanes, to play commandoes, or simply to talk or wander about together. But there are usually several children who prefer solitary play on swing and jungle gym or play with jump-rope or ball.

ETHICAL SENSE

SEVEN is becoming more responsive to the demands of his environment. For the most part he responds well to directions, especially if he has heard what was said to him. He does, however, forget readily and needs to be reminded. He often needs two chances. He may respond slowly or under protest, but this is reminiscent of the 6-year-old. If he is caught in a net of rigid perseveration he must be helped out of it to break its hold upon him.

SEVEN rarely needs punishment because he is a reasoning and by nature a responsible being. You can plan with him and thus avert disaster. Although he may still have some difficulty in making up his mind, especially when a demand is made of him, he is showing greater skill in making a decision. He now reasons with his parent, can compromise, and though he may still not wish to change his mind, he may change it when reasoned with. This reasoning with parents is often quite personal, and all of his sentences may begin with, "But mommy—."

SEVEN definitely wants to be good; although he wants to be himself, too. With some SEVENS it is not so much that they are concerned about being good as that they *just are* good. They are proud of a good day and concerned about bad days. They feel sorry for younger children who spoil things by being bad, and they instruct their younger siblings about the disadvantages of being bad. Some SEVENS have good and bad spells which seem to come in cycles. They are good for a period, and then impossible. Unfortunately this type of child may suddenly turn "bad," even when he means to be "good."

SEVEN's idea of good and bad is beginning to be slightly abstract. It is no longer concerned solely with specific actions allowed or forbidden by his parent, but involves the beginnings of a generalized notion of goodness and badness. One 7-year-old reviewed her day and asked to have listed all the things she had done *Thinking About Myself* and all that she had done *Thinking About Others*.

Thinking About Others:

1. Telling Margie about a gun for Johnny.
2. Obeying my mother—picking up the living room.
3. Went to bed willingly—fell asleep quickly.
4. Remembered to close the door to keep the bathroom warm.
5. I didn't shout in the library.
6. Came off the ice very quickly when Anne came for me.
7. Put my glasses away in their case.
8. Put my glasses on when I'm reading.
9. Dressing quickly without dawdling.
10. I look before I cross the street.
11. I don't tip my chair as much as I used to.

Thinking About Myself:

1. Eating omelette with my fingers.
2. Saying "Wah!"
3. Speaking rudely to my mother: "Yes you will!"
4. Contradicting.
5. Not washing hands before playing the piano.

SEVEN is less likely than SIX to blame others. He may even act with heroism, when no punishment is involved. Rather than blaming, he may alibi in order to cover up any of his mistakes. He says, "Well, that was what I meant," "I was just going to." He is now aware of a force outside of his own control which is influencing him and which he calls "fairness" and "luck." Whenever he gets into trouble, he is likely to say, "That's not fair." Although he may still be a poor loser, he is improving because he realizes that losing along the way does not always mean that you will lose in the end. Winning is often a question of luck to him, not too much under his control. Sometimes he thinks he has "all the bad luck." One SEVEN expressed it this way: "Why do I always have the bad luck? Why do things so often happen to me? I might as well be dead." The bad luck in question was that it was time to go to bed.

SEVEN may be very conscientious about taking things. He may have no use for a stealer or a cheater. But when he is in the schoolroom, he seems to be in the midst of so many things he wants and can add easily to his desk's store of belongings. He sometimes acquires new things by the more orthodox method of exchanging his possessions with friends. This is usually conducted on the basis of an "even swap" and does not involve real trading.

SEVEN has an increasing sense of possession and of the care of his possessions. He is better about putting things away, he helps his mother pick up his room, or he makes a mad scramble to put it in order the last minute before it is time to go off to school. The 7-year-old is becoming very much interested in making collections—of such objects as postcards or boxtops. The goal at this age seems to be mere quantity, with slight regard for formal arrangement or classification. He also likes to have a school-pouch or school-bag, and in this pouch he carries a veritable collection of pencils, erasers and rulers.

There is an increasing interest in money. He may be more anxious to earn money than to have an allowance. He is interested in buying specific things like a school magazine, a funny book, or war stamps. Sometimes he puts his money in the bank, which may be a means to saving part of the money for some specific object such as a bicycle or a typewriter. He is especially enchanted by the appearance of money in the toe of his slipper when he has left a tooth there. The money seems to him to be the proof that fairies do exist.

There is often considerably less lying at seven than in the years which precede and follow. However, SEVEN, with his rather strong ethical sense, may be very much concerned about the wrongness of lying and cheating. He is particularly concerned if this lying and cheating is done by his friends. . . .

THE SOCIETY OF CHILDHOOD
The Sound of the Shell
William Golding

Piggy's glasses were misted again—this time with humiliation.
"You told 'em. After what I said."
His face flushed, his mouth trembled.
"After what I said I didn't want—"
"What on earth are you talking about?"
"About being called Piggy. I said I didn't care as long as they didn't call me Piggy; an' I said not to tell and you went and said straight out—"

Editor's Introduction

Childhood is often portrayed as a joyous time and children as good, corrupted only by society. But children can be as cruel as they can be kind. The society of children is often as much one of gangs and cliques as is the society of adolescents or of adults. Children are apt to label themselves and each other, and often not in the fondest terms. Children are searching to belong, to belong to a group and to belong to themselves. Any title, no matter how negative, gives the child some assurance of belonging. However, this belonging can be painful.

William Golding introduces us to a society of children ranging in age from 6 to 12. The children are truly a society unto themselves as they find themselves stranded on an island without adults. Their reaction to this sudden freedom from authority is at first exultation, followed by fear. Within short order they move to establishing their own system of authority with a leader chosen on the basis of appearance and a symbol of power. Ritual becomes important, as does anything which will offer a semblance of order in their chaos. In the microcosm of society we can see the children as both sensitive and callous, independent and dependent, and anything but innocent.

Pamela Cantor

The boy with fair hair lowered himself down the last few feet of rock and began to pick his way toward the lagoon. Though he had taken off his school sweater and trailed it now from one hand, his grey shirt stuck to him and his hair was plastered to his forehead. All round him the long scar smashed into the jungle was a bath of heat. He was clambering heavily among the creppers and broken trunks when a bird, a vision of red and yellow, flashed upwards with a witch-like cry; and this cry was echoed by another.

"Hi!" it said. "Wait a minute!"

The undergrowth at the side of the scar was shaken and a multitude of raindrops fell pattering.

"Wait a minute," the voice said. "I got caught up."

The fair boy stopped and jerked his stockings with an automatic gesture that made the jungle seem for a moment like the Home Counties.

The voice spoke again.

"I can't hardly move with all these creeper things."

The owner of the voice came backing out of the undergrowth so that twigs scratched on a greasy wind-breaker. The naked crooks of his knees were plump, caught and scratched by thorns. He bent down, removed the thorns carefully, and turned around. He was shorter than the fair boy and very fat. He came forward, searching out safe lodgments for his feet, and then looked up through thick spectacles.

"Where's the man with the megaphone?"

The fair boy shook his head.

"This is an island. At least I think it's an island. That's a reef out in the sea. Perhaps there aren't any grownups anywhere."

The fat boy looked startled.

"There was that pilot. But he wasn't in the passenger cabin, he was up in front."

The fair boy was peering at the reef through screwed-up eyes.

"All them other kids," the fat boy went on. "Some of them must have got out. They must have, mustn't they?"

The fair boy began to pick his way as casually as possible toward the water. He tried to be offhand and not too obviously uninterested, but the fat boy hurried after him.

"Aren't there any grownups at all?"

"I don't think so."

The fair boy said this solemnly; but then the delight of a realized ambition overcame him. In the middle of the scar he stood on his head and grinned at the reversed fat boy.

"No grownups!"

The fat boy thought for a moment.

"That pilot."

The fair boy allowed his feet to come down and sat on the steamy earth.

"He must have flown off after he dropped us. He couldn't land here. Not in a plane with wheels."

"We was attacked!"

"He'll be back all right."

The fat boy shook his head.

"When we was coming down I looked through one of them windows. I saw the other part of the plane. There were flames coming out of it."

He looked up and down the scar.

"And this is what the cabin done."

The fair boy reached out and touched the

jagged end of a trunk. For a moment he looked interested.

"What happened to it?" he asked. "Where's it got to now?"

"That storm dragged it out to sea. It wasn't half dangerous with all them tree trunks falling. There must have been some kids still in it."

He hesitated for a moment, then spoke again.

"What's your name?"

"Ralph."

The fat boy waited to be asked his name in turn but this proffer of acquaintance was not made; the fair boy called Ralph smiled vaguely, stood up, and began to make his way once more toward the lagoon. The fat boy hung steadily at his shoulder.

"I expect there's a lot more of us scattered about. You haven't seen any others, have you?"

Ralph shook his head and increased his speed. Then he tripped over a branch and came down with a crash.

The fat boy stood by him, breathing hard.

"My auntie told me not to run," he explained, "on account of my asthma."

"Ass-mar?"

"That's right. Can't catch me breath. I was the only boy in our school what had asthma," said the fat boy with a touch of pride. "And I've been wearing specs since I was three."

He took off his glasses and held them out to Ralph, blinking and smiling, and then started to wipe them against his grubby wind-breaker. An expression of pain and inward concentration altered the pale contours of his face. He smeared the sweat from his cheeks and quickly adjusted the spectacles on his nose.

"Them fruit."

He glanced round the scar.

"Them fruit," he said, "I expect—"

He put on his glasses, waded away from Ralph, and crouched down among the tangled foliage.

"I'll be out again in just a minute—"

Ralph disentangled himself cautiously and stole away through the branches. In a few seconds the fat boy's grunts were behind him and he was hurrying toward the screen that still lay between him and the lagoon. He climbed over a broken trunk and was out of the jungle.

The shore was fledged with palm trees. These stood or leaned or reclined against the light and their green feathers were a hundred feet up in the air. The ground beneath them was a bank covered with coarse grass, torn everywhere by the upheavals of fallen trees, scattered with decaying coconuts and palm saplings. Behind this was the darkness of the forest proper and the open space of the scar. Ralph stood, one hand against a grey trunk, and screwed up his eyes against the shimmering water. Out there, perhaps a mile away, the white surf flinked on a coral reef, and beyond that the open sea was dark blue. Within the irregular arc of coral the lagoon was still as a mountain lake—blue of all shades and shadowy green and purple. The beach between the palm terrace and the water was a thin stick, endless apparently, for to Ralph's left the perspectives of palm and beach and water drew to a point at infinity; and always, almost visible, was the heat.

He jumped down from the terrace. The sand was thick over his black shoes and the heat hit him. He became conscious of the weight of clothes, kicked his shoes off fiercely and ripped off each stocking with its elastic garter in a single movement. Then he leapt back on the terrace, pulled off his shirt, and stood there among the skull-like coconuts with green shadows from the palms and the forest sliding over his skin. He undid the snake-clasp of his belt, lugged off his shorts and pants, and stood there naked, looking at the dazzling beach and the water.

He was old enough, twelve years and a few months, to have lost the prominent tummy of childhood; and not yet old enough for adolescence to have made him awkward. You could see now that he might make a boxer, as far as width and heaviness of shoulders went, but there was a mildness about his mouth and eyes that proclaimed no devil. He patted the palm trunk softly, and, forced at last to believe in the reality of the island, laughed delightedly again and stood on his head. He turned neatly on to his feet, jumped down to the beach, knelt and swept a double armful of sand into a pile against his chest. Then he sat back and looked at the water with bright, excited eyes.

"Ralph—"

The fat boy lowered himself over the terrace and sat down carefully, using the edge as a seat.

"I'm sorry I been such a time. Them fruit—"

He wiped his glasses and adjusted them on his button nose. The frame had made a deep, pink "V" on the bridge. He looked critically at Ralph's golden body and then down at his own clothes. He laid a hand on the end of a zipper that extended down his chest.

"My auntie—"

Then he opened the zipper with decision and pulled the whole wind-breaker over his head.

"There!"

Ralph looked at him sidelong and said nothing.

"I expect we'll want to know all their names," said the fat boy, "and make a list. We ought to have a meeting."

Ralph did not take the hint so the fat boy was forced to continue.

"I don't care what they call me," he said confidentially, "so long as they don't call me what they used to call me at school."

Ralph was faintly interested.

"What was that?"

The fat boy glanced over his shoulder, then leaned toward Ralph.

He whispered.

"They used to call me 'Piggy.'"

Ralph shrieked with laughter. He jumped up.

"Piggy! Piggy!"

"Ralph—please!"

Piggy clasped his hands in apprehension.

"I said I didn't want—"

"Piggy! Piggy!"

Ralph danced out into the hot air of the beach and then returned as a fighter-plane, with wings swept back, and machine-gunned Piggy.

"Sche-aa-ow!"

He dived in the sand at Piggy's feet and lay there laughing.

"Piggy!"

Piggy grinned reluctantly, pleased despite himself at even this much recognition.

"So long as you don't tell the others—"

Ralph giggled into the sand. The expression of pain and concentration returned to Piggy's face.

"Half a sec'."

He hastened back into the forest. Ralph stood up and trotted along to the right.

Here the beach was interrupted abruptly by the square motif of the landscape; a great platform of pink granite thrust up uncompromisingly through forest and terrace and sand and lagoon to make a raised jetty four feet high. The top of this was covered with a thin layer of soil and coarse grass and shaded with young palm trees. There was not enough soil for them to grow to any height and when they reached perhaps twenty feet they fell and dried, forming a criss-cross pattern of trunks, very convenient to sit on. The palms that still stood made a green roof, covered on the underside with a quivering tangle of reflections from the lagoon. Ralph hauled himself onto this platform, noted the coolness and shade, shut one eye, and decided that the shadows on his body were really green. He picked his way to the seaward edge of the platform and stood looking down into the water. It was clear to the bottom and bright with the efflorescence of tropical weed and coral. A school of tiny, glittering fish flicked hither and thither. Ralph spoke to himself, soulding the bass strings of delight.

"Whizzoh!"

Beyond the platform there was more enchantment. Some act of God—a typhoon perhaps, or the storm that had accompanied his own arrival—had banked sand inside the lagoon so that there was a long, deep pool in the beach with a high ledge of pink granite at the further end. Ralph had been deceived before now by the specious appearance of depth in a beach pool and he approached this one preparing to be disappointed. But the island ran true to form and the incredible pool, which clearly was only invaded by the sea at high tide, was so deep at one end as to be dark green. Ralph inspected the whole thirty yards carefully and then plunged in. The water was warmer than his blood and he might have been swimming in a huge bath.

Piggy appeared again, sat on the rocky ledge, and watched Ralph's green and white body enviously.

"You can't half swim."

"Piggy."

Piggy took off his shoes and socks, ranged them carefully on the ledge, and tested the water with one toe.

"It's hot!"

"What did you expect?"

"I didn't expect nothing. My auntie—"

"Sucks to your auntie!"

Ralph did a surface dive and swam under water with his eyes open; the sandy edge of the pool loomed up like a hillside. He turned over, holding his nose, and a golden light danced and shattered just over his face. Piggy was looking determined and began to take off his shorts. Presently he was palely and fatly naked. He tiptoed down the sandy side of the pool, and sat there up to his neck in water smiling proudly at Ralph.

"Aren't you going to swim?"

Piggy shook his head.

"I can't swim. I wasn't allowed. My asthma—"

"Sucks to your ass-mar!"

Piggy bore this with a sort of humble patience.

"You can't half swim well."

Ralph paddled backwards down the slope, immersed his mouth and blew a jet of water into the air. Then he lifted his chin and spoke.

"I could swim when I was five. Daddy taught me. He's a commander in the Navy. When he gets leave he'll come and rescue us. What's your father?"

Piggy flushed suddenly.

"My dad's dead," he said quickly, "and my mum—"

He took off his glasses and looked vainly for something with which to clean them.

"I used to live with my auntie. She kept a candy store. I used to get ever so many candies. As many as I liked. When'll your dad rescue us?"

"Soon as he can."

Piggy rose dripping from the water and stood naked, cleaning his glasses with a sock. The only sound that reached them now through the heat of the morning was the long, grinding roar of the breakers on the reef.

"How does he know we're here?"

Ralph lolled in the water. Sleep enveloped him like the swathing mirages that were wrestling with the brilliance of the lagoon.

Because, thought Ralph, because, because. "How does he know we're here?"

The roar from the reef became very distant.

"They'd tell him at the airport."

Piggy shook his head, put on his flashing glasses and looked down at Ralph.

"Not them. Didn't you hear what the pilot said? About the atom bomb? They're all dead."

Ralph pulled himself out of the water, stood facing Piggy, and considered this unusual problem.

Piggy persisted.

"This is an island, isn't it?"

"I climbed a rock," said Ralph slowly, "and I think this is an island."

"They're all dead," said Piggy, "an' this is an island. Nobody don't know we're here. Your dad don't know, nobody don't know—"

His lips quivered and the spectacles were dimmed with mist.

"We may stay here till we die."

With that word the heat seemed to increase till it became a threatening weight and the lagoon attacked them with a blinding effulgence.

"Get my clothes," muttered Ralph. "Along there."

He trotted through the sand, enduring the sun's enmity, crossed the platform and found his scattered clothes. To put on a grey shirt once more was strangely pleasing. Then he climbed the edge of the platform and sat in the green shade on a convenient trunk. Piggy hauled himself up, carrying most of his clothes under his arms. Then he sat carefully on a fallen trunk near the little cliff that fronted the lagoon; and the tangled reflections quivered over him.

Presently he spoke.

"We got to find the others. We got to do something."

Ralph said nothing. Here was a coral island. Protected from the sun, ignoring Piggy's ill-omened talk, he dreamed pleasantly.

Piggy insisted.

"How many of us are there?"

Ralph came forward and stood by Piggy.

"I don't know."

Here and there, little breezes crept over the polished waters beneath the haze of heat. When these breezes reached the platform the palm fronds would whisper, so that spots of blurred sunlight slid over their bodies or moved like bright, winged things in the shade.

Piggy looked up at Ralph. All the shadows on Ralph's face were reversed; green above, bright below from the lagoon. A blur of sunlight was crawling across his hair.

"We got to do something."

Ralph looked through him. Here at last was the imagined but never fully realized place leaping into real life. Ralph's lips parted in a delighted smile and Piggy, taking this smile to himself as a mark of recognition, laughed with pleasure.

"If it really is an island—"

"What's that?"

Ralph had stopped smiling and was pointing into the lagoon. Something creamy lay among the ferny weeds.

"A stone."

"No. A shell."

Suddenly Piggy was a-bubble with decorous excitement.

"S'right. It's a shell! I seen one like that before. On someone's back wall. A conch he called it. He used to blow it and then his mum would come. It's ever so valuable—"

Near to Ralph's elbow a palm sapling leaned out over the lagoon. Indeed, the weight was already pulling a lump from the poor soil and soon it would fall. He tore out the stem and began to poke about in the water, while the brilliant fish flicked away on this side and that. Piggy leaned dangerously.

"Careful! You'll break it—"

"Shut up."

Ralph spoke absently. The shell was interesting and pretty and a worthy plaything; but the vivid phantoms of his day-dream still interposed between him and Piggy, who in this context was an irrelevance. The palm sapling, bending, pushed the shell across the weeds. Ralph used one hand as a fulcrum and pressed down with the other till the shell rose, dripping, and Piggy could make a grab.

Now the shell was no longer a thing seen but not to be touched, Ralph too became excited. Piggy babbled:

"—a conch; ever so expensive. I bet if you wanted to buy one, you'd have to pay pounds and pounds and pounds—he had it on his garden wall, and my auntie—"

Ralph took the shell from Piggy and a little water ran down his arm. In color the shell was deep cream, touched here and there with fading pink. Between the point, worn away into a little hole, and the pink lips of the mouth, lay eighteen inches of shell with a slight spiral twist and covered with a delicate, embossed pattern. Ralph shook sand out of the deep tube.

"—mooed like a cow," he said. "He had some white stones too, an' a bird cage with a green parrot. He didn't blow the white stones, of course, an' he said—"

Piggy paused for breath and stroked the glistening thing that lay in Ralph's hands.

"Ralph!"

Ralph looked up.

"We can use this to call the others. Have a meeting. They'll come when they hear us—"

He beamed at Ralph.

"That was what you meant, didn't you? That's why you got the conch out of the water?"

Ralph pushed back his fair hair.

"How did your friend blow the conch?"

"He kind of spat," said Piggy. "My auntie wouldn't let me blow on account of my asthma. He said you blew from down here." Piggy laid a hand on his jutting abdomen. "You try, Ralph. You'll call the others."

Doubtfully, Ralph laid the small end of the shell against his mouth and blew. There came a rushing sound from its mouth but nothing more. Ralph wiped the salt water off his lips and tried again, but the shell remained silent.

"He kind of spat."

Ralph pursed his lips and squirted air into the shell, which emitted a low, farting noise. This amused both boys so much that Ralph went on squirting for some minutes, between bouts of laughter.

"He blew from down here."

Ralph grasped the idea and hit the shell with air from his diaphragm. Immediately the thing sounded. A deep, harsh note boomed under the palms, spread through the intricacies of the forest and echoed back from the pink granite of the mountain. Clouds of birds rose from the treetops, and something squealed and ran in the undergrowth.

Ralph took the shell away from his lips.

"Gosh!"

His ordinary voice sounded like a whisper after the harsh note of the conch. He laid the conch against his lips, took a deep breath and blew once more. The note boomed again: and then at his firmer pressure, the note, fluking up an octave, became a strident blare more penetrating than before. Piggy was shouting something, his face pleased, his glasses flashing. The birds cried, small animals scuttered. Ralph's breath failed; the note dropped the octave, became a low wubber, was a rush of air.

The conch was silent, a gleaming tusk; Ralph's face was dark with breathlessness and the air over the island was full of bird-clamor and echoes ringing.

"I bet you can hear that for miles."

Ralph found his breath and blew a series of short blasts.

Piggy exclaimed: "There's one!"

A child had appeared among the palms, about a hundred yards along the beach. He was a boy of perhaps six years, sturdy and fair, his clothes torn, his face covered with a sticky mess of fruit. His trousers had been lowered for an obvious purpose and had only been pulled back half-way. He jumped off the palm terrace into the sand and his trousers fell about his ankles; he stepped out of them and trotted to the platform. Piggy helped him up. Meanwhile Ralph continued to blow till voices shouted in the forest. The small boy squatted in front of Ralph, looking up brightly and vertically. As he received the reassurance of something purposeful being done he began to look satisfied, and his only clean digit, a pink thumb, slid into his mouth.

Piggy leaned down to him.

"What's yer name?"

"Johnny."

Piggy muttered the name to himself and then shouted it to Ralph, who was not interested because he was still blowing. His face was dark with the violent pleasure of making this stupendous noise, and his heart was making the stretched shirt shake. The shouting in the forest was nearer.

Signs of life were visible now on the beach. The sand, trembling beneath the heat haze, concealed many figures in its miles of length; boys were making their way toward the platform through the hot, dumb sand. Three small children, no older than Johnny, appeared from startlingly close at hand where they had been gorging fruit in the forest. A dark little boy, not much younger than Piggy, parted a tangle of undergrowth, walked on to the platform, and smiled cheerfully at everybody. More and more of them came. Taking their cue from the innocent Johnny, they sat down on the fallen palm trunks and waited. Ralph continued to blow short, penetrating blasts. Piggy moved among the crowd, asking names and frowning to remember them. The children gave him the same simple obedience that they had given to the men with megaphones. Some were naked and carrying their clothes; others half-naked, or more or less dressed, in school uniforms, grey, blue, fawn, jacketed or jerseyed. There were badges, mottoes even, stripes of color in stockings and pullovers. Their heads clustered above the trunks in the green shade; heads brown, fair, black, chestnut, sandy, mouse-colored; heads muttering, whispering, heads full of eyes that watched Ralph and speculated. Something was being done.

The children who came along the beach, singly or in twos, leapt into visibility when they crossed the line from heat haze to nearer sand. Here, the eye was first attracted to a black, bat-like creature that danced on the sand, and only later perceived the body above it. The bat was the child's shadow, shrunk by the vertical sun to a patch between the hurrying feet. Even while he blew, Ralph noticed the last pair of bodies that reached the platform above a fluttering patch of black. The two boys, bullet-headed and with hair like tow, flung themselves down and lay grinning and panting at Ralph like dogs. They were twins, and the eye was shocked and incredulous at such cheery duplication. They breathed together, they grinned together, they were chunky and vital. They raised wet lips at Ralph, for they seemed provided with not quite enough skin, so that their profiles were blurred and their mouths pulled open. Piggy bent his flashing glasses to them and could be heard between the blasts, repeating their names.

"Sam, Eric, Sam, Eric."

Then he got muddled; the twins shook their heads and pointed at each other and the crowd laughed.

At last Ralph ceased to blow and sat there, the conch trailing from one hand, his head bowed on his knees. As the echoes died away so did the laughter, and there was silence.

Within the diamond haze of the beach something dark was fumbling alone. Ralph saw it first, and watched till the intentness of his gaze drew all eyes that way. Then the creature stepped from mirage on to clear sand, and they saw that the darkness was not all shadows but mostly clothing. The creature was a party of boys, marching approximately in step in two parallel lines and dressed in strangely eccentric clothing. Shorts, shirts, and different garments they carried in their hands; but each boy wore a square black cap with a silver badge on it. Their bodies, from throat to ankle, were hidden by black cloaks which bore a long silver cross on the left breast and each neck was finished off with a hambone frill. The heat of the tropics, the descent, the search for food, and now this sweaty march along the blazing beach had given them the complexions of newly washed plums. The boy who controlled them was dressed in the same way though his cap badge was golden. When his party was about ten yards from the platform he shouted an order and they halted, gasping, sweating, swaying in the fierce light. The boy himself came forward, vaulted on to the platform with his cloak flying, and peered into what to him was almost complete darkness.

"Where's the man with the trumpet?"

Ralph, sensing his sun-blindness, answered him.

"There's no man with a trumpet. Only me."

The boy came close and peered down at Ralph, screwing up his face as he did so. What he saw of the fair-haired boy with the creamy shell on his knees did not seem to satisfy him. He turned quickly, his black cloak circling.

"Isn't there a ship, then?"

Inside the floating cloak he was tall, thin, and bony: and his hair was red beneath the black cap. His face was crumpled and freckled, and ugly without silliness. Out of this face stared two light blue eyes, frustrated now, and turning, or ready to turn, to anger.

"Isn't there a man here?"

Ralph spoke to his back.

"No. We're having a meeting. Come and join in."

The group of cloaked boys began to scatter from close line. The tall boy shouted at them.

"Choir! Stand still!"

Wearily obedient, the choir huddled into line and stood there swaying in the sun. None the less, some began to protest faintly.

"But, Merridew. Please, Merridew . . . can't we?"

Then one of the boys flopped on his face in the sand and the line broke up. They heaved the fallen boy to the platform and let him lie. Merridew, his eyes staring, made the best of a bad job.

"All right then. Sit down. Let him alone."

"But Merridew."

"He's always throwing a faint," said Merridew. "He did in Gib.; and Addis; and at matins over the precentor."

This last piece of shop brought sniggers from the choir, who perched like black birds on the criss-cross trunks and examined Ralph with interest. Piggy asked no names. He was intimidated by this uniformed superiority and the offhand authority in Merridew's voice. He shrank to the other side of Ralph and busied himself with his glasses.

Merridew turned to Ralph.

"Aren't there any grownups?"

"No."

Merridew sat down on a trunk and looked round the circle.

"Then we'll have to look after ourselves."

Secure on the other side of Ralph, Piggy spoke timidly.

"That's why Ralph made a meeting. So as we can decide what to do. We've heard names. That's Johnny. Those two—they're twins, Sam 'n' Eric. Which is Eric—? You? No— you're Sam—"

"I'm Sam—"

"'n' I'm Eric."

"We'd better all have names," said Ralph, "so I'm Ralph."

"We got most names," said Piggy. "Got 'em just now."

"Kids' names," said Merridew. "Why should I be Jack? I'm Merridew."

Ralph turned to him quickly. This was the voice of one who knew his own mind.

"Then," went on Piggy, "that boy—I forget—"

"You're talking too much," said Jack Merridew. "Shut up, Fatty."

Laughter arose.

"He's not Fatty," cried Ralph, "his real name's Piggy!"

"Piggy!"

"Piggy!"

"Oh, Piggy!"

A storm of laughter arose and even the tiniest child joined in. For the moment the boys were a closed circuit of sympathy with Piggy outside: he went very pink, bowed his head and cleaned his glasses again.

Finally the laughter died away and the naming continued. There was Maurice, next in size among the choir boys to Jack, but broad and grinning all the time. There was a slight, furtive boy whom no one knew, who kept to himself with an inner intensity of avoidance and secrecy. He muttered that his name was Roger and was silent again. Bill, Robert, Harold, Henry; the choir boy who had fainted sat up against a palm trunk, smiled pallidly at Ralph and said that his name was Simon.

Jack spoke.

"We've got to decide about being rescued."

There was a buzz. One of the small boys, Henry, said that he wanted to go home.

"Shut up," said Ralph absently. He lifted the conch. "Seems to me we ought to have a chief to decide things."

"A chief! A chief!"

"I ought to be chief," said Jack with simple arrogance, "because I'm chapter chorister and head boy. I can sing C sharp."

Another buzz.

"Well then," said Jack, "I—"

He hesitated. The dark boy, Roger, stirred at last and spoke up.

"Let's have a vote."

"Yes!"

"Vote for chief!"

"Let's vote—"

This toy of voting was almost as pleasing as the conch. Jack started to protest but the clamor changed from the general wish for a chief to an election by acclaim of Ralph himself. None of the boys could have found good reason for this; what intelligence had been shown was traceable to Piggy while the most obvious leader was Jack. But there was a stillness about Ralph as he sat that marked him out: there was his size, and attractive appearance; and most obscurely, yet most powerfully, there was the conch. The being

that had blown that, had sat waiting for them on the platform with the delicate thing balanced on his knees, was set apart.

"Him with the shell."

"Ralph! Ralph!"

"Let him be chief with the trumpet-thing."

Ralph raised a hand for silence.

"All right. Who wants Jack for chief?"

With dreary obedience the choir raised their hands.

"Who wants me?"

Every hand outside the choir except Piggy's was raised immediately. Then Piggy too, raised his hand grudgingly into the air.

Ralph counted.

"I'm chief then."

The circle of boys broke into applause. Even the choir applauded: and the freckles on Jack's face disappeared under a blush of mortification. He started up, then changed his mind and sat down again while the air rang. Ralph looked at him, eager to offer something.

"The choir belongs to you, of course."

"They could be the army—"

"Or hunters—"

"They could be—"

The suffusion drained away from Jack's face. Ralph waved again for silence.

"Jack's in charge of the choir. They can be—what do you want them to be?"

"Hunters."

Jack and Ralph smiled at each other with shy liking. The rest began to talk eagerly.

Jack stood up.

"All right, choir. Take off your togs."

As if released from class, the choir boys stood up, chattered, piled their black cloaks on the grass. Jack laid his on the trunk by Ralph. His grey shorts were sticking to him with sweat. Ralph glanced at them admiringly, and when Jack saw his glance he explained.

"I tried to get over that hill to see if there was water all round. But your shell called us."

Ralph smiled and held up the conch for silence.

"Listen, everybody. I've got to have time to think things out. I can't decide what to do straight off. If this isn't an island we might be rescued straight away. So we've got to decide if this is an island. Everybody must stay round here and wait and not go away. Three of us—if we take more we'd get all mixed, and lose each other—three of us will go on an expedition and find out. I'll go, and Jack, and, and. . . ."

He looked round the circle of eager faces. There was no lack of boys to choose from.

"And Simon."

The boys round Simon giggled, and he stood up, laughing a little. Now that the pallor of his faint was over, he was a skinny, vivid little boy, with a glance coming up from under a hut of straight hair that hung down, black and coarse.

He nodded at Ralph.

"I'll come."

"And I—"

Jack snatched from behind him a sizable sheath-knife and clouted it into a trunk. The buzz rose and died away.

Piggy stirred.

"I'll come."

Ralph turned to him.

"You're no good on a job like this."

"All the same—"

"We don't want you," said Jack, flatly. "Three's enough."

Piggy's glasses flashed.

"I was with him when he found the conch. I was with him before anyone else was."

Jack and the others paid no attention. There was a general dispersal. Ralph, Jack and Simon jumped off the platform and walked along the sand past the bathing pool. Piggy hung bumbling behind them.

"If Simon walks in the middle of us," said Ralph, "then we could talk over his head."

The three of them fell into step. This meant that every now and then Simon had to do a double shuffle to catch up with the others. Presently Ralph stopped and turned back to Piggy.

"Look."

Jack and Simon pretended to notice nothing. They walked on.

"You can't come."

Piggy's glasses were misted again—this time with humiliation.

"You told 'em. After what I said."

His face flushed, his mouth trembled.

"After I said I didn't want—"

"What on earth are you talking about?"

"About being called Piggy. I said I didn't care as long as they didn't call me Piggy; an' I said not to tell and then you went an' said straight out—"

Stillness descended on them. Ralph, looking with more understanding at Piggy, saw that he was hurt and crushed. He hovered between the two courses of apology or further insult.

"Better Piggy than Fatty," he said at last, with the directness of genuine leadership, "and anyway, I'm sorry if you feel like that. Now go back, Piggy, and take names. That's your job. So long."

He turned and raced after the other two. Piggy stood and the rose of indignation faded slowly from his cheeks. He went back to the platform.

The three boys walked briskly on the sand. The tide was low and there was a strip of weed-strewn beach that was almost as firm as a road. A kind of glamour was spread over them and the scene and they were conscious of the glamour and made happy by it. They turned to each other, laughing excitedly, talking, not listening. The air was bright. Ralph, faced by the task of translating all this into an explanation, stood on his head and fell over. When they had done laughing, Simon stroked Ralph's arm shyly; and they had to laugh again.

"Come on," said Jack presently, "we're explorers."

"We'll go to the end of the island," said Ralph, "and look round the corner."

"If it is an island—"

Now, toward the end of the afternoon, the

mirages were settling a little. They found the end of the island, quite distinct, and not mag-icked out of shape or sense. There was a jumble of the usual squareness, with one great block sitting out in the lagoon. Sea birds were nesting there.

"Like icing," said Ralph, "on a pink cake."

"We shan't see round this corner," said Jack, "because there isn't one. Only a slow curve—and you can see, the rocks get worse—"

Ralph shaded his eyes and followed the jagged outline of the crags up toward the mountain. This part of the beach was nearer the mountain than any other that they had seen.

"We'll try climbing the mountain from here," he said. "I should think this is the easiest way. There's less of that jungly stuff; and more pink rock. Come on."

The three boys began to scramble up. Some unknown force had wrenched and shattered these cubes so that they lay askew, often piled diminishingly on each other. The most usual feature of the rock was a pink cliff surmount-ed by a skewed block; and that again sur-mounted, and that again, till the pinkness be-came a stack of balanced rock projecting through the looped fantasy of the forest creepers. Where the pink cliffs rose out of the ground there were often narrow tracks wind-ing upwards. They could edge along them, deep in the plant world, their faces to the rock.

"What made this track?"

Jack paused, wiping the sweat from his face. Ralph stood by him, breathless.

"Men?"

Jack shook his head.

"Animals."

Ralph peered into the darkness under the trees. The forest minutely vibrated.

"Come on."

The difficulty was not the steep ascent round the shoulders of rock, but the occasion-al plunges through the undergrowth to get to the next path. Here the roots and stems of creepers were in such tangles that the boys had to thread through them like pliant needles. Their only guide, apart from the brown ground and occasional flashes of light through the foliage, was the tendency of slope: whether this hole, laced as it was with the cables of creeper, stood higher than that.

Somehow, they moved up.

Immured in these tangles, at perhaps their most difficult moment, Ralph turned with shin-ing eyes to the others.

"Wacco."

"Wizard."

"Smashing."

The cause of their pleasure was not obvious. All three were hot, dirty and exhaust-ed. Ralph was badly scratched. The creepers were as thick as their thighs and left little but tunnels for further penetration. Ralph shouted experimentally and they listened to the muted echoes.

"This is real exploring," said Jack. "I bet nobody's been here before."

"We ought to draw a map," said Ralph, "only we haven't any paper."

"We could make scratches on bark," said Simon, "and rub black stuff in."

Again came the solemn communion of shin-ing eyes in the gloom.

"Wacco."

"Wizard."

There was no place for standing on one's head. This time Ralph expressed the intensity of his emotion by pretending to knock Simon down; and soon they were a happy, heaving pile in the under-dusk.

When they had fallen apart Ralph spoke first.

"Got to get on."

The pink granite of the next cliff was further back from the creepers and trees so that they could trot up the path. This again led into more open forest so that they had a glimpse of the spread sea. With openness came the sun; it dried the sweat that had soaked their clothes in the dark, damp heat. At last the way to the top looked like a scramble over pink rock, with no more plunging through darkness. The boys chose their way through defiles and over heaps of sharp stone.

"Look! Look!"

High over this end of the island, the shattered rocks lifted up their stacks and chimneys. This one, against which Jack leaned, moved with a grating sound when they pushed.

"Come on—"

But not "Come on" to the top. The assault on the summit must wait while the three boys accepted this challenge. The rock was as large as a small motor car.

"Heave!"

Sway back and forth, catch the rhythm.

"Heave!"

Increase the swing of the pendulum, increase, increase, come up and bear against that point of furthest balance—increase—increase—

"Heave!"

The great rock loitered, poised on one toe, decided not to return, moved through the air, fell, struck, turned over, leapt droning through the air and smashed a deep hole in the canopy of the forest. Echoes and birds flew, white and pink dust floated, the forest further down shook as with the passage of an enraged monster: and then the island was still.

"Wacco!"

"Like a bomb!"

"Whee-aa-oo!"

Not for five minutes could they drag themselves away from this triumph. But they left at last.

The way to the top was easy after that. As they reached the last stretch Ralph stopped.

"Golly!"

They were on the lip of a circular hollow in the side of the mountain. This was filled with a blue flower, a rock plant of some sort, and the overflow hung down the vent and spilled lavishly among the canopy of the forest. The

air was thick with butterflies, lifting, fluttering, settling.

Beyond the hollow was the square top of the mountain and soon they were standing on it.

They had guessed before that this was an island: clambering among the pink rocks, with the sea on either side, and the crystal heights of air, they had known by some instinct that the sea lay on every side. But there seemed something more fitting in leaving the last word till they stood on the top, and could see a circular horizon of water.

Ralph turned to the others.

"This belongs to us."

It was roughly boat-shaped: humped near this end with behind them the jumbled descent to the shore. On either side rocks, cliffs, treetops and a steep slope: forward there, the length of the boat, a tamer descent, tree-clad, with hints of pink: and then the jungly flat of the island, dense green, but drawn at the end to a pink tail. There, where the island petered out in water, was another island; a rock, almost detached, standing like a fort, facing them across the green with one bold, pink bastion.

The boys surveyed all this, then looked out to sea. They were high up and the afternoon had advanced; the view was not robbed of sharpness by mirage.

"That's a reef. A coral reef. I've seen pictures like that."

The reef enclosed more than one side of the island, lying perhaps a mile out and parallel to what they now thought of as their beach. The coral was scribbled in the sea as though a giant had bent down to reproduce the shape of the island in a flowing chalk line but tired before he had finished. Inside was peacock water, rocks and weed showing as in an aquarium; outside was the dark blue of the sea. The tide was running so that long streaks of foam tailed away from the reef and for a moment they felt that the boat was moving steadily astern.

Jack pointed down.

"That's where we landed."

Beyond falls and cliffs there was a gash visible in the trees; there were the splintered trunks and then the drag, leaving only a fringe of palm between the scar and the sea. There, too, jutting into the lagoon, was the platform, with insect-like figures moving near it.

Ralph sketched a twining line from the bald spot on which they stood down a slope, a gully, through flowers, round and down to the rock where the scar started.

"That's the quickest way back."

Eyes shining, mouths open, triumphant, they savored the right of domination. They were lifted up: were friends.

"There's no village smoke, and no boats," said Ralph wisely. "We'll make sure later; but I think it's uninhabited."

"We'll get food," cried Jack. "Hunt. Catch things . . . until they fetch us."

Simon looked at them both, saying nothing but nodding till his black hair flopped backwards and forwards: his face was glowing.

Ralph looked down the other way where there was no reef.

"Steeper," said Jack.

Ralph made a cupping gesture.

"That bit of forest down there . . . the mountain holds it up."

Every point of the mountain held up trees—flowers and trees. Now the forest stirred, roared, flailed. The nearer acres of rock flowers fluttered and for half a minute the breeze blew cold on their faces.

Ralph spread his arms.

"All ours."

They laughed and tumbled and shouted on the mountain.

"I'm hungry."

When Simon mentioned his hunger the others became aware of theirs.

"Come on," said Ralph. "We've found out what we wanted to know."

They scrambled down a rock slope, dropped among flowers and made their way under the trees. Here they paused and examined the bushes round them curiously.

Simon spoke first.

"Like candles. Candle bushes. Candle buds."

The bushes were dark evergreen and aromatic and the many buds were waxen green and folded up against the light. Jack slashed at one with his knife and the scent spilled over them.

"Candle buds."

"You couldn't light them," said Ralph. "They just look like candles."

"Green candles," said Jack contemptuously. "We can't eat them. Come on."

They were in the beginnings of the thick forest, plonking with weary feet on a track, when they heard the noises—squeakings—and the hard strike of hoofs on a path. As they pushed forward the squeaking increased till it became a frenzy. They found a piglet caught in a curtain of creepers, throwing itself at the elastic traces in all the madness of extreme terror. Its voice was thin, needle-sharp and insistent. The three boys rushed forward and Jack drew his knife again with a flourish. He raised his arm in the air. There came a pause, a hiatus, the pig continued to scream and the creepers to jerk, and the blade continued to flash at the end of a bony arm. The pause was only long enough for them to understand what an enormity the downward stroke would be. Then the piglet tore loose from the creepers and scurried into the undergrowth. They were left looking at each other and the place of terror. Jack's face was white under the freckles. He noticed that he still held the knife aloft and brought his arm down replacing the blade in the sheath. Then they all three·laughed ashamedly and began to climb back to the track.

"I was choosing a place," said Jack. "I was just waiting for a moment to decide where to stab him."

"You should stick a pig," said Ralph fierce-ly. "They always talk about sticking a pig."

"You cut a pig's throat to let the blood out," said Jack, "otherwise you can't eat the meat."

"Why didn't you—?"

They knew very well why he hadn't: because of the enormity of the knife descending and cutting into living flesh; because of the unbearable blood.

"I was going to," said Jack. He was ahead of them and they could not see his face. "I was choosing a place. Next time—!"

He snatched his knife out of the sheath and slammed it into a tree trunk. Next time there would be no mercy. He looked round fiercely, daring them to contradict. Then they broke out into the sunlight and for a while they were busy finding and devouring food as they moved down the scar toward the platform and the meeting.

THE CHILD IN THE FAMILY
When Children Experience Divorce

J. Louise Despert

The effort to clarify emotional confusion, to find one's way through the tangle of human reactions to a deeply felt crisis, is never wasted. So much pain, so much error, so much waste and even tragedy can be avoided for parents and children if men and women can restrain the hasty action, if they take time to consider not only what is to be done, but in what manner it can be done for the good of everyone.

Editor's Introduction

Due to divorce, two out of every five children born in the United States in the 1970s can expect to reside for five years or more with a single parent. Recent Census Bureau figures show that of the 66 million children under 18, more than 11 million currently reside in one-parent families. There are presently about 1½ million families broken by divorce, and there are probably an equal number of families in which one parent is absent as a result of separation or desertion.

It would be unwise to make any statement about the effects of divorce on a child. Almost all marriages involve conflict and children always sense it. Often disturbed children belong to families in which there is severe parental conflict, and it is always best to try to remedy the situation whenever possible. Divorce is not the only solution. When divorce does occur, disaster need not follow. Divorce is not necessarily a good experience or a bad one, it is only what the individuals involved make of it.

Young children are upset, at least temporarily, when their parents separate. Most children protest against the separation unless one parent is intolerable, as most children want a family of both a mother and a father. Divorce is not easy; it changes life for the parents and for the child. Divorce usually means a more stringent budget, less social contact with married friends, the problems of arranging child care, lessened opportunity to share the satisfactions and pride of parenthood and the anxieties of child rearing, increased pressure to serve the child's needs for both male and female models, and less opportunity for a life of adult companionship. The outcome depends partly on the parents' ability to find satisfaction in a life outside the home and in the ability to maintain quality care and affection toward the child despite natural feelings of resentment, guilt, loneliness, permissiveness, and possessiveness.

Divorce need not be a destructive experience, though we cannot pretend that either children or their parents emerge from it without cost. Yet life within a continuously unhappy marriage can be far more destructive than divorce. Despert states that the same patterns of emotional disturbance exist in children of parents who do not divorce even though they have failed at marriage as in children of parents who have divorced but who have not made their peace with the divorce. In a family where the situation is covert, children cannot ask to have their fears explained. The unidentified situation between parents is far more threatening to a child than a realistic situation which can be faced together with parents. Despert feels that parents can make a success out of divorce even if they have been unable to do so with marriage, especially for their children.

The selection which follows offers a discussion of the manner in which divorce was handled in the lives of Donnie, Janie, and Peggy. These are but three examples of the 400,000 children who must deal with divorce each year. No two situations are exactly alike. Yet certain patterns occur again and again and certain guidelines can be offered for parents. The most serious danger to children lies in depriving them of the emotional support they need to thrive. Parents can be counseled to try to reassure children that they are not the cause of the marital breakup and to try to avoid making exaggerated demands on children to satisfy their own needs. Disappointed parents often turn to their children to provide satisfaction of their needs to belong and to be cared for. A special problem may arise when a parent is divorced or separated while the child is at the young age when boys or girls develop a strong attachment to the parent of the opposite sex. If a son remains with his mother or a daughter with her father, it may appear as if the secret hope of having mother or father all to himself or herself may have come true. In fantasy the child may have imagined that the parent has abandoned the spouse in order to live with the child, and that the little girl has taken her mother's place or the little boy his father's. The child may, therefore, feel as if his or her wishes had been responsible for the divorce. While this fantasy may have seemed desirable, the reality is often frightening to the child. The parent must be careful not to let the child feel that the child is the parent's sole hope for happiness.

Divorce, by its very nature, threatens the security most vital to a child—that gained from the love of a family. But Despert states that divorce can be managed with small emotional cost if parents can take the time to understand their own emotional needs and those of their children.

Pamela Cantor

Sometimes, when parents have come to me in grieved or angry bafflement at a child's difficult behavior, I have let my fancy wander, and conjured up some device by which the parent—for a day, even for an hour—could change places with the child. What a timesaver, labor-saver, painsaver—and child saver—such a magic wand would be!

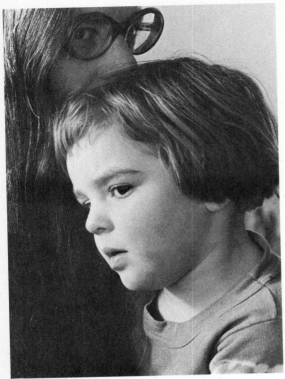

By permission of Sissy Krook, photographer.

If parents could stand in the child's place just once, could dwell in imagination within his body and mind, could know intimately his limitations—of comprehension, of capabilities, of physical size and strength—they would be able to *feel with him* the experience of divorce.

What makes it hard for us to project ourselves into the child's inner life is that we have been busy all our adult years blotting out much of our own childhood. This is how painful memories are rendered harmless.

How much anxiety, how many false starts would be spared parents if they could fully comprehend divorce in the child's terms! How differently, for example, would Donnie's father and mother have managed if they had known how Donnie first became aware of the idea of divorce.

Let us try to put ourselves in Donnie's place one night when he is awakened by loud voices in his parents' bedroom, next to his. He is lying very still in his bed. It is late, an hour when a boy of four should be sleeping. But Donnie has not been sleeping well lately, so it is not surprising that the angry argument in the next room has awakened him.

In the first moment of waking and hearing his father's voice Donnie squirmed out of his covers, ready to run and greet his father. It was a long time, as little children measure time, since his father had been home. Donnie knew that a newspaper man had to go away on "stories," but lately it seemed as though his father was never home. Presents came, big boxes which were fun to open. But it was not the same as when his father used to come home from a trip, bringing a present which they would open together. Donnie's mother kept saying that Daddy "would be home in just a few days," but her voice and face did not match the words, and Donnie, uneasy, had stopped asking.

So at first, hearing his father home again, Donnie was glad. But then the voice itself checked him. It was his father, no doubt about that, but he was speaking in the voice which Donnie did not like to hear.

Now he heard his mother. "If it weren't for Donnie I would have left you long ago!"

"Leave Donnie out of this!" his father shouted. And then he said that new word again: "divorce." Donnie did not know the meaning of the word, but from the way his father said it he knew it was something bad. And when, a few minutes later, the door of his room opened softly and his mother looked in, Donnie was in such panic that he shrank together under his covers and pretended to be asleep.

Thus, coupled with the word divorce, Donnie has already experienced fear, experienced guilt ("If it weren't for Donnie . . ." and "Leave Donnie out of this!"). With it he has already associated the unfocused but swelling uncertainties of the weeks when his father was away and his mother was anxious and worried. And in the morning, when Donnie wakes up, his father has already gone again, neglecting in his anger and distraction to think that Donnie might need just then to see him, to speak with him, to be reassured by him. And so there is included in Donnie's feelings about divorce one more feeling, that of being rejected, of having lost his father's love.

Even if the strange word had not been mentioned, Donnie would already have been inwardly shaken by the events transpiring between his parents, though he might have given no sign of it. This will be the emotional setting of Donnie's experience of divorce— unless his parents can stop in their headlong flight from each other to give heed to Donnie. In Donnie's case, as it happened, this was not to be until after several unhappy years had passed.

300,000 DONNIES A YEAR

Your child, and Donnie, and between three and four hundred thousand American children each year must deal somehow with the experience of divorce. No two of them can have precisely the same experience, not even two children of the same family, as we shall see. Yet certain patterns, in broad outline, recur again and again.

There is the child who has been bruised by a rough experience, but has come through in good order, borne up on the love which one or the other of his parents has given him. Throughout a stormy time, this mother, for instance, has been able to maintain a strong and supporting relationship, spontaneously and without design, often without even an awareness of its importance to the child. Despite the turbulence of her own emotions, she has managed never to lose the thread of communication with her child, has somehow brought comfort and serenity into the hours spent together. And this solid, supporting love has been enough.

Another child may be spared many bruises because his parents, having decided on divorce, make conscious and efficient plans for his defense. They take pains to understand his needs and to meet them. Though the home is broken up and the changes may be drastic, they give thought to making the future setting of his life warm and secure, and they preserve their own relationship to him individually, though no longer together. If either or both parents should remarry, the child will be considered in this new relationship as well.

With such a child the changes in his life may appear more revolutionary than they really are. The important core, his emotional state, is not profoundly shaken, though it is revised. He must still accept the fact that his parents no longer live together, but the acceptance is less difficult because his parents have been foresighted. By their careful and timely explanations, by their continuously loving behavior, by their wise plans for him, they have forestalled anxiety and given him security in their love.

Still another child seems to have been completely forgotten by his parents during the time of their greatest personal disturbance. Obviously parents can "forget" a child only if their own emotional difficulties are such that they have little to spare for another's. Sometimes a child who has had to go through the experience of divorce without emotional support from his parents finds it in another adult, a grandmother or other relative, a teacher, a friend of the family, or he must build his own defenses. These may enable him to function somehow, but he may also carry into his adult life some permanent scars.

Or the child may show by his behavior that he is distressed, and his parents eventually come to realize that he needs help. An awareness has been steadily growing in the public mind that a child who has suffered a serious emotional experience may need help from outside his family to set him again on a healthy path. Perhaps of their own volition, perhaps at the urging of relatives, friends, or school authorities, parents who have been unable to help the child through the divorce itself not infrequently turn to a social agency, clinic, or psychiatrist to get help for him later.

In this chapter we shall examine the experiences of divorce in the lives of several children, illustrating these several patterns. Donnie, with whom we are already acquainted, is one of those children whose parents come later to an awareness that their child is in trouble and needs help.

THE ABSENT FATHER

The explosive quarrel which precipitated the divorce of Donnie's parents brought to a climax Donnie's long though unexpressed anxiety. He was born into a home in which anxiety was already insidiously working.

Donnie's father worked in a profession which required his frequent and sometimes extended absence from home. Journalism is only one of a number of professions which separate a man from his family for long or short periods: salesmen, buyers, some merchants, many kinds of technicians and industrial specialists; musicians, actors, and most members of the entertainment world; men in the armed services and in other branches of government service; all of these must travel to some extent. Wartime of course exaggerates the problem of the absent father.

A father's absence can be accepted by his children if their mother, out of her own inner security, accepts it. But Donnie's mother did not have this inner security. A girl from a modest small-town background, she was at first dazzled by her husband's glamorous life, and only later realized that for her it had grave disadvantages. When he was at home, she found herself out of depth among his friends. When he was away, she was lonely and without resources to fill the emptiness of her days.

Any marriage requires adjustment, but this kind of marriage demands a good deal more than the average, and Donnie's mother was unprepared. Carried away by romantic love, she had not anticipated the loneliness, the frustrations of such a life. She felt inadequate, and was unable to share the part of her husband's world which was open to her. Inevitably she felt rejected, hence resentful. She turned to her baby for solace, with the consequence that she gave him an overdose of motherly devotion, keeping him in her own room, watching anxiously over him.

Donnie was aware of the gradually widening breach between his parents although he was unable to ask about it. His father's returns were more and more often marred by quarrels, until the final explosion which confirmed this feeling that he was somehow to blame for his father's absence and his mother's unhappiness.

After the separation Donnie and his mother moved to a smaller apartment. Donnie went to nursery school; his mother took a business course, and through her former husband's affiliations found a secretarial job in a newspaper office.

For the first year after the divorce Donnie still groped for a reunion of his parents. He built a fantasy around the vacation he would spend with his father at his grandparents' home. He dreamed that his mother would come too, that they would all be together again.

His mother of course did not come, and the vacation was bound to be a disappointment for other reasons as well. Donnie had built up his anticipation to impossible heights; at best his father could not satisfy his hopes. His father too had difficulties. It was hard to pick up the threads with the little boy who had grown and changed so much in the intervening months, and whom he had not known too well even before they were parted.

By the second year Donnie's mother began to bring friends home to cocktails and dinner, men from the newspaper where she worked, men not unlike his father. He regarded them with conflicting emotions, hoping he would get a new daddy, fearful that he might. A new daddy would close the door on his dream that his own daddy might someday come back. At the same time, though he liked these men who were rather like his father, he mistrusted them. They too might leave him as his father had done.

Toward his mother Donnie was increasingly hostile and difficult. Needing to be close to her, he also blamed her for the separation from his father. And he had the guilty fears of a boy who is too close to his mother, who has been kept in the mother-baby relationship past the time when he should have outgrown it.

Outside the home Donnie failed to make friends in his new neighborhood. To his schoolmates he boasted that his father was an important man—"he's on the radio"—and explained that his father was always away on a story; he could not admit that his parents were divorced. He did badly in school, and finally his disturbing, destructive behavior prompted the principal to call the mother in and insist that the boy could not stay unless he was given psychiatric treatment. His mother took him at last to a clinic.

Now for the first time Donnie had the opportunity to ventilate all those hostilities which he could not afford to express openly to his parents for fear he would lose their love entirely. Now for the first time, too, he could begin to understand that what had happened between his parents was not his fault, that though they had not been able to get along with each other, each still loved him as much as ever.

From a sympathetic neutral person with whom there were no emotional involvements, the realistic explanation came clearly and objectively. Little by little the differences between his parents, which until now had turned all against himself, took their proper place as a series of events in a relationship of which he

was not the core. His guilt for his parents' discord gradually fell away.

His guilt for his excessive closeness to and dependence on his mother had tormented him in nightmares; he was now able to tell his dreams for the first time. He had dreamed of being with his mother, and suddenly she was not there. He had dreamed of being in a boat with her, and she drowned. Children normally have dreams like these, but a happier child awakens to familiar, comforting reality. Donnie's real world had not been reassuring because of the conflict which confronted him there.

Donnie became able in time to accept his mother's love without guilt, and to accept the reality that two people can marry with a hope of happiness and can fail to find happiness together. He became able to manage the division of his allegiance.

During Donnie's treatment, which lasted several months, his mother too was strengthened and relieved of her anxiety. His father learned something of what had been going on inside his boy, and learned what he could do to make the time which he spent with Donnie more satisfactory to both of them.

Donnie's father and mother have made new marriages, and Donnie gets along well with both his step-parents. What has happened to Donnie is that he no longer rebels at the real world, to retreat into fantasy. The reality which was unbearable to him before because of his emotional confusion, his anxieties and unrealistic fears, is now more acceptable.

In a sense it was fortunate for Donnie that his delinquency at school revealed his trouble and brought him help. Until then his mother had been too involved in her own confusion and unhappiness to see his need, much less to help him. A child's behavior does not always call attention to his needs so obviously. He may only become quieter, eat poorly, sleep badly, or do inadequate work at school. A child who retreats into himself and is docile and obedient at home and at school may not get the help he needs.

We have learned from experience that too much obedience can be a distress warning. The repressed child too is signaling to us by his behavior—"Somebody, please, do something!"

Such a child was Sidney, for example, whose parents' violent quarreling about money and about him drove him cowering into a corner both literally and emotionally. Sidney made no trouble to distract his parents from their intense conflict with each other. Sidney was a "good" boy, so good that his parents were not aware of the deep trouble he was in until, when he was eleven, he made an attempt at suicide. Only then, shocked by such an extreme gesture of despair in a child, did they realize that Sidney had been pushed beyond his strength and must have help. Sidney's story is extreme, but it reminds us that the too quiet child is also in need of help.

THE CHILD'S SELF-DEFENSE

Janie on the other hand has had no help at all. She has been left to build her own defenses, for better or worse. Janie's mother went to a guidance counselor, but not for guidance. What she sought was professional support in winning custody of the child. Bitterly resentful at the failure of her marriage, this headstrong young mother fought for Janie less for Janie's sake than to take vengeance on her husband for not measuring up to her unrealistic standards.

The story of Janie and her parents is so common and yet so frequently misinterpreted that it bears telling. Like so many divorces, the divorce of Janie's parents was the climax of a multitude of small but cumulative frustrations which, if they could have been dealt with separately and in time, might have been resolved.

These two young people married on the crest of an ardent love affair, and continued the carefree pleasure-seeking of an attractive young couple until Janie was born. Then at one stroke they were confronted with a different facet of marriage, its mature responsibilities.

Janie's father tried to fit himself into his new, oversize role. He tried to give up the round of parties, tried to be home for the baby's bath and supper, tried to get to bed early to make up for the sleep he lost giving Janie her night bottle and attending to her when she cried. He took a new interest in his job; the father of a family had to get ahead.

But Janie's mother was shocked to discover that a baby was not a doll to be put away when she was tired of playing with it, that she could no longer sleep till noon and be out for lunch, cocktails, dinner, She longed for her lost freedom. She was unready for the satisfactions of motherhood which compensate a more mature personality for the lighter pleasures she had surrendered. This maturity is not a matter of birthdays but of emotional growth, and Janie's mother had simply not yet achieved it.

Unconsciously seeking a way out, with the plea of higher family expenses, she soon began renewing her contacts as a fashion model, Gradually she slipped back into her old patterns, leaving Janie to the care of a succession of part-time maids.

By the time she was six, Janie hardly knew her mother, the lovely scented creature who dropped her a kiss in passing, but who unaccountably became a sharp-voiced enemy on the maid's day off. Janie was closer to her father, who had perforce taken over many of a mother's duties. But he too was becoming sharp and irritable as his lack of sleep affected both his work and his temper, and their scale of living kept him constantly pressed for money. He was anxious, tired, and inclined to blame his wife, and she for her part felt resentful and guilty. The infrequent dinners at home began to be accompanied by quarreling

and tears. He rebuked his wife for the sloven-
ly management of the household, for her
neglect of Janie, for the thousand little irrita-
tions which daily built up the growing barrier
between them.

"If you made enough money I wouldn't
have to work!" she retorted, forgetting that
her earnings barely paid for the indifferent
maid, who took her place at home, for the
extensive wardrobe she needed in her work,
for the social activities which were part of her
"contacts."

One final quarrel, and the young wife made
good her threat. She took Janie and went
home to Mother, to "bring him to terms." In
fact she was retreating still farther from her
responsibilities, as she had retreated from
them into her modeling. Home to her was still
the protective shell where she never had unpleasant chores to do, where her every wish
was granted.

This pattern has become so familiar that we
make a joke of "going home to Mother." In an
older society, in which a girl was married
much as a cow was sold, the troubled young
wife also went to her mother or aunt, and
found there an outlet for her dissatisfactions,
but she did not also find fuel to feed the fires
of her discontent. Unless her husband had
failed in some serious obligation—and his
obligations, like hers, were clearly delineated—she was rebuked as often as she was
comforted, was reminded of her duty, and
was sent back to fulfill it.

A girl in those days, moreover, had been
taught her duty since childhood. "Love will
come later," she had been told. Her husband
was chosen, her future laid out for her, and
she knew that she could make her own happiness only by fitting herself successfully into
the role to which she had been reared.

Today the concept of marriage is very much
changed. The words *duty* and *responsibility*
are spoken softly, if at all, and *obey* is usually
omitted from the marriage vow. The girl is no

longer given passively in marriage. She makes
her own choice of whom to marry and when.
She is more responsible for her own future,
and less prepared for it. As a child, she has
had far more freedom than her sister of another day, and possibly more happiness as well,
and this is good. But somewhere between the
ages of six and eighteen the family pattern
which should enable her to take her first taste
of responsibility is not there.

Parents are apprised of sexual development
in adolescence and what to do about it, but not
of the development of personality which
should enable a girl to manage her own life. In
freeing the child from the real work of the
family we are depriving her of the necessary
emotional foundation for doing the work of
her own family when she is a woman. How
should she know that there are deep satisfactions in creating comfort and happiness for
those she loves, when she has never experienced them, when up to the day of her marriage she has been always the recipient of care
and never the giver of it?

So Janie's mother fled from the mature role
she was not prepared to play, back to her own
mother, back to the past and the longed-for
state of a dependent child. In effect she was
trying to be no longer a wife and mother, but
once more a daughter. Yet the fantasy could
not replace reality. She could not be a happy
daughter, either, since she brought with her
her conflict and its attendant guilt, resentment,
and defeat. And there was Janie, a constant,
troublesome reminder.

With the sure intuition of a child Janie
slipped into her new place, becoming her own
mother's little sister, competing for the love of
Grandma, who was the only real mother in the
house. So fierce was this competition, so
desperate Janie's need for love, that the peace
of Grandma's house was continually shattered
by the child's screaming rages, the mother's
furious discipline. Meanwhile Janie longed for
her father, and tried her mother's already

short temper still further with the monotonous question, "When is Daddy coming?"

Daddy came at last, not to set Janie's world right again by behaving like a father, but to plead with her mother to come back. He had not even unpacked his bag when Janie realized that he was saying good-by. She clung to his legs, aware even in her distress that her mother did not ask him to stay. (Janie's mother held firmly to "her terms," but what she really meant was that she could not go back and face again the realities of marriage and family.)

Janie's father, rejected and helpless, put Janie severely aside and departed. Janie thrashed about in frustrated rage, pounding with her fists against her mother, her grandmother, until her mother dragged her upstairs and locked her in her room to learn "to behave herself."

So there was a divorce. We know part of its aftermath and can project more. Janie's mother goes out with other young divorcées and unmarried friends, trying to enjoy herself, trying to expunge the seven or eight years of her marriage, but confronted always with the living symbol of them in Janie. She has defeated her husband and won custody of Janie, but it is a dubious victory. She will probably marry again; whether she will bring more wisdom to her second marriage we cannot know. The prospects at this time are not promising.

Janie meanwhile is building her defenses. She is learning to "behave herself" in sheer self-protection, but her somewhat better manners can only mask the stormy emotions underneath. In a child's terms she has had unmistakable proof that she is unloved, first by her mother, then by her grandmother, who has withdrawn from her out of pure inability to cope with such a difficult child. Finally she has lost the love of her father, whose leaving she could interpret only as a rejection of herself.

Janie is a fighter. Not knowing love, she can deal with life henceforth only by aggressive-

ness and hostility. Her native intelligence, her determination to reach a goal, especially in opposition to parents and parent figures, her toughness in the face of challenge—all this suggests a familiar pattern. She may one day become a successful career woman, an aggressive business executive. But she is not likely to make a life yielding emotional satisfactions to herself or to others around her.

THE PLANNED DEFENSE OF THE CHILD

Stories like Donnie's, to whom help came, though late, fill the clinical records, and Janie's is a story which may come out years afterward on the psychoanalyst's couch.

But there are happier stories, which do not appear in the clinical records, of those children whose parents planned in advance for their defense from the possible ill effects of divorce.

Peggy's parents, for example, carefully and thoughtfully arranged for her future before they considered the arrangements for their own legal separation. Peggy needs and will need no help outside her parents. The stories of children like Peggy come to the attention of psychiatrists and social workers only when their parents ask for advice in planning for the children.

Peggy's parents knew before she was born that their marriage was not an unqualified success. A bluff, hearty, outgoing man, fond of merry company; a gentle young woman with rather serious tastes and a need for peace and order in her home—it is not too unusual for such opposites to marry. It was not so farfetched an attraction. Both were warmhearted and affectionate. During their courtship he enjoyed the dependence of this demurely loving girl, while she appreciated, though she could not actively participate in, his exuberance and high spirits.

Once they were married the differences in their tastes became troubling to both. The get-togethers she had enjoyed in his company were now in her own house, and she took her management of them too conscientiously. The frequent and unexpected arrival of friends now became a strain. Try as she would, she could not help being upset when in the midst of preparing a simple dinner for two she was all at once called upon to serve cocktails and snacks to the half-dozen friends her husband had impulsively brought home.

Seeing her distress, he began to stay out with his companions instead of bringing them home. He realized that this was equally destructive to their marriage, but he was too much of an adolescent to see the charms of a quiet home life. Meanwhile the example of other young, carefree couples—the couple next door, for instance—impressed her with the realization that other women could manage a gay social life, and she felt inadequate and unworthy.

When she became pregnant, both hoped that the coming of a child would solidify their marriage. Each tried to change so that the other would be more comfortable. As a result he felt constrained; his zest for living was paralyzed. She was fatigued, depressed after each effort to join him and his gay cronies. Once the baby came, he enjoyed and welcomed the satisfactions of fatherhood, but the sound of the baby crying at night was not his dish. He admired his wife's willingness to take over the whole task of child care and homemaking, but could not participate in it.

Fortunately these two people cared genuinely for each other. As individuals, they were emotionally mature enough so that feelings of rejection and inadequacy did not poison their affection for each other. As he confided a developing interest in an attractive divorcée, she, on her part, told him of the renewal of her friendships in the church group to which she had belonged before her marriage, and in particular with a man of quiet tastes whom she met there.

As each began to develop a life apart from the other, together they considered a legal separation. Intuitively he grasped her need of continuing emotional support from him until the baby was out of the diaper-and-formula stage and there would be more leisure for the mother to pursue other interests. He saw too that it would be better not to interrupt the continuity of life for her and the baby, that it would be better if he were the one who went to another state to get the divorce.

All was done as planned, without haste. When little Peggy was past her second birthday she was entered in the church nursery school where her mother had already made a place for herself as an assistant. Thus the child had the opportunity to spread her affections among several mother persons—the teachers, the nurse—while having the reassurance that her mother was there with her. Going to school did not take the aspect of being thrust out of the home, rejected by her mother, as in similar circumstances it often does for a young child. Peggy was thus able to develop a good measure of independence.

Peggy's father took an extended vacation to get the divorce. His absence was comfortably explained to Peggy by her mother, who had no difficulty explaining, since she had long before accepted the plan and had no anxiety about it. When her father did not come back to live with them, but only to visit, Peggy was ready for a further explanation, and was given one:

Daddy and Mommy liked different things, and found it hard to be happy together. Daddy liked to laugh and play and be noisy; this Peggy understood very well, since this was the way Daddy played with her. Mommy liked to be quieter, to read and talk and play music, to keep house and sew for Peggy. This Peggy also understood, since it was apparent in their serene life at home. But Mommy and Daddy cared for each other, as Peggy plainly observed in their affectionate, considerate behavior when they were together.

Above all, Mommy and Daddy loved their little girl—and this Peggy had never had occasion to doubt. In her mother it was steadily demonstrated. And her father, in his exuberant warmth, made his visits an uncomplicated delight to the child.

Peggy cried at first when her father left. But she accepted his reassurance that, although he must go now, he would come again next Saturday. She accepted it because he did unfailingly come when he said he would; he was careful not to make a promise he was not sure of keeping.

As the weeks went by, Peggy asked more questions. What would happen to her? She and Mommy would stay here together as they had before, and Daddy would continue to come to see them. When she was older, Daddy would take her out sometimes to interesting places.

Then, as her father's remarriage approached, that too was explained. Daddy was getting a new wife. She would go to visit him in his new home and be friends with his new wife. Someday she might have a new sister or brother in Daddy's home.

Would Mommy get a new husband? Mommy's friend was a frequent visitor. He brought books for Peggy and read them to her. Peggy went walking with him and her mother on Sunday afternoons. He was very different from her father—this was reassuring; if he were too much like her father he might also go away. But he was familiar and kind, and incidentally he was careful to temper his courtship so as not to disturb the child by displaying ardor toward her mother in her presence.

When Peggy asked, "Is Mr. Rogers going to be my new daddy?" her mother's answer was mild.

"We want to be sure. We want to know each other very well so that we can all be happy together."

Now Peggy began pressing her mother to marry Mr. Rogers. She liked him, enjoyed his stories and the quiet games he played with her, and she wanted a man in the house. With this evidence that all promised well, when Peggy was four and a half her mother and Mr. Rogers were married.

Peggy's mother and new father love their quiet orderly life. Peggy has thrived in the serene family setting, in which she feels she belongs. She bears no resentment toward her father, who has shown in his bluff way that he loves her, and who, with the satisfactory new life he has made for himself, brings no resentments of his own into his relationship with Peggy.

Peggy may expect new brothers and sisters, and we are safe in assuming that she will continue to feel that she belongs in her new family even as it expands.

No two divorces are alike. But in all divorces in which children are involved the children need to be defended. Whatever the dynamics, whatever the relationships, the defense of the child is important to the child's future, and to the parent's peace of mind. . . .

The effort to clarify emotional confusion, to find one's way through the tangle of human reactions to a deeply felt crisis, is never wasted. So much pain, so much error, so much waste and even tragedy can be avoided for parents and children if men and women can restrain the hasty action, if they can take time to consider not only what is to be done, but in what manner it can be done for the good of everyone.

This is not to say, in the words of the fairy tales, that they will all live happily ever after. These stories of some children's experience of divorce show how the crisis of divorce itself has been surmounted with more or less success. We cannot promise that all these children and their parents will dwell henceforth in a paradise of mutual love and happiness.

We can be reasonably sure, however, that for Peggy, and to some extent for Donnie, divorce has done a minimum of damage. It may even have been a maturing and clarifying experience. And we can feel confident that a child who has been thus successfully defend-ed through divorce will be no less able than other children to meet the situations and ride out the storms which are part of every human life.

The Effects of Maternal Employment on the Child—A Review of the Research
Lois Wladis Hoffman

The most persistent concern about maternal employment has to do with the sheer absence of the mother from the home while she is working and the fear that this represents a loss to the child in terms of supervision, love or cognitive enrichment.

Editor's Introduction

The number of children in the United States who have working mothers has continued to rise in recent years, despite the fact that the total child population has substantially declined since 1970. More than 26 million mothers of 64 million children under 18 are in the work force. While the fact that maternal employment will continue to rise is hardly debatable, the effects of maternal employment on the psychological and social development of the children of working mothers is the subject of much controversy.

The controversy might be exemplified by the opinions of two popular theorists in child development, each of whom currently writes a monthly column in a magazine for women. Lee Salk, in an article entitled "Should Mothers Work?" (1974), states that women who are employed outside the home cannot possibly devote enough time to their children to meet the children's emotional needs. In fact, he suggests that women should consider not having children at all if they are not willing to remain at home during the first three or more years.

Salk bases his opinion on the fact that the child's early experiences are critical for future personality development; thus the total or near total investment of the mother's time during the first few years is essential. Salk assumes that the mother's absence from the home for an extended daily period will cause the child to feel neglected and rejected. He implies that the mother who works may be an ineffective parent, since she spends very little time with her child and comes home both physically and mentally exhausted.

Salk does not consider that the mother who works may compensate for the amount of time she spends with her child by the quality of her interactions with the child. He also assumes that the child whose mother works is likely to be shifted from one person to another during the day or that the child will come home to an

Reprinted from *Developmental Psychology*, 1974, *10*, pp. 204–228. Copyright © 1974 by the American Psychological Association. Reprinted by permission.

empty house each day after school. While it is unfortunately true that such environments do exist, Salk is not allowing for the possibility of adequate or optimal care for a child in the mother's absence. Furthermore, Salk does not describe what an exhausting and demanding task it is to spend every day and night with a child. This can be extremely wearing on even the most patient and loving mother. Her total confinement with a small child could easily lead to strain, which would then be reflected in the mother's behavior and attitude toward her child.

Bruno Bettelheim addresses the benefits of maternal employment on the child in his article, ''Why Working Mothers Have Happier Children'' (1970). Bettelheim fully agrees that the early years are critical for the child. He feels, however, that when the mother is solely responsible for her child, her efforts have to be largely directed toward supervisory activities and the minutiae of child-rearing, and that her function as provider of nurturing love is diluted. Most full-time mothers, he feels, cannot wait for their child's bedtime so that they can have a little time of their own. But then they are too tired to enjoy it. In addition, he feels that it is detrimental to the child if all the limitations and criticisms emanate from the one person who is most important to him or her. If this is the case, then even the smallest reprimand may provoke anxiety and fear in the child. He feels that it is beneficial for the child to have the opportunity to be cared for by another consistent, loving person in addition to the mother.

Bettelheim states, however, that no matter how good working may be for the mother, neither she nor her child will benefit if she sees her absence as harmful. In other words, it is the ambivalent or guilty feelings that working mothers harbor which are harmful, not the condition of maternal employment. Mothers need to accept the view that their working may be of benefit to the children; they need to become less ambivalent. According to Bettelheim, what matters most is the mother's attitude toward working. If she dislikes and resents her work, her child will suffer. If she likes it, her child will pick up her enthusiasm and view life optimistically.

Neither Bettelheim, Salk, nor Hoffman, however, have dealt realistically with the central difficulty facing women who are planning careers: Who is going to take care of the children? I think that it would help if women could restate the problem. Instead of considering who is going to take care of the children while women work, they should be asking how the nature of work can be changed so that women can maintain an active role in their careers, provide their children with other models, be with adults in a professional or work capacity, maintain their roles outside the home, and *still* mother their children.

What would be a practical solution? Employers could be pressured to allow men and women to work part-time. Jobs could be broken down into smaller components that would replace the forty-hour work week. Thus, a mother who wished to spend time with her small children could work at two or three components and add more time as her children came to need her less. The same procedure would have to operate for men as well. Men need to be given respect for working part-time in their careers in order to offer nurturance and care to their children, rather than being accorded a loss of status for this choice. The answer is not to abdicate child care but to share child care. To share child care we must change work to help mothers and fathers. Women cannot decrease the guilt or concern that may accompany their professional success without finding ways to integrate child care into a workable life-style. According to Bettelheim, what is needed first is a more rational attitude about what is best for the child and for the mother. I feel that a more rational attitude among women is impossible unless there is a more rational attitude in society.

Most women are not challenging the statement that the family must come first. They are simply asking why it should not come first for fathers as well. Feminists have argued that fathers should take equal turns in caring for children — and I am in complete agreement — but they have ignored ways of making this possible. Women's liberation has helped to remove some of the barriers to full participation in the work force, but full participation is still prevented by the inequality of child-rearing responsibilities.

The sharing of responsibilities does not have to mean a reversal of responsibilities, where the mother takes over the provider role and the father assumes the child-care role. Nor does sharing mean helping. Helping aids the mother with a task such as diapering or laundering, but it does not relieve the mother of responsibility. Shared responsibility would mean that the working father was equally responsible for assessing what needs to be done and seeing that it gets done. The sharing of responsibility might help women to deal with the guilt they feel over the missed opportunities to spend time with their children.

Hoffman's concerns are with the empirical evidence on the effects of maternal employment on the child. According to her review, research has yielded no evidence for the theory that the school-age child suffers deprivation when the mother is employed. Information on the effects of maternal employment on the infant, although perhaps more critical in light of the expanding work involvement among women, yields scant data. The effects of maternal employment on the family unit have as yet been barely researched.

REFERENCES

Bettelheim, B. Why working mothers have happier children. *Ladies Home Journal*, June 1970, pp. 24 & 87.

Salk, L. Should mothers work? *Harper's Bazaar*, August 1974, pp. 44 & 126.

Pamela Cantor

In a previous review of the literature on the effects of maternal employment on the child, we pointed out that the earlier view that maternal employment had a great many effects on the child, all of them bad, had been replaced by a new outlook—that maternal employment had no effects at all (Hoffman, 1963a). We assumed that maternal employment did have an effect. What the effect was might depend on the nature of the employment, the attitude of the working mother, her family circumstances, the social class, whether employment is full or part time, the age and sex of the child, the kinds of child care arrangements that are set up, and a whole host of other conditions, but until the research questions had been properly defined and explored, we were not prepared to concede that there was no effect. While studies of maternal employment as a general concept yielded little, it was suggested that examining the effects under specified conditions might prove more fruitful. To demonstrate, we tried to show that when the relationships between maternal employment and a child characteristic were examined separately for various subgroups, interesting patterns were revealed. Thus, juvenile delinquency did seem to relate to maternal employment in the middle class, although it did not in the lower class. Part-time maternal employment seemed to have a positive effect on adolescent children, although this was not equally true for full-time employment or for younger children. The lack of consistent findings with respect to the effects on the child's independence or academic achievement was tied to the failure to examine these relationships separately for each sex. And the mother's attitude toward employment was seen as an important aspect of the situation that would affect her child-rearing behavior and thus mediate the impact of her employment on the child.

It was our hope that such speculations would give rise to new empirical investigations, but the intervening years have produced few studies of maternal employment. About the same time our review was published three others appeared: Stolz, 1960; Siegel and Haas, 1963; and Yudkin and Holme, 1963. Perhaps the overall impression given was not that maternal employment required more careful study, but that it should not be studied at all. Most of the more recent studies reviewed here were only incidentally interested in the effects of maternal employment on the child, and the few that focused on this variable were modest in scope.

On the other hand, it was previously noted that segments of the American population that contributed more than an equal share of the working mothers—blacks and single-parent families in particular—were not studied at all. A few investigators have begun to fill this gap (Kreisberg, 1970; Rieber & Womack, 1968; Smith, 1969; Woods, 1972).

Moreover, there have been some methodological improvements. Few studies today would lump boys and girls together, and most consider relationships separately for each social class. Several studies have, in fact, focused only on one class—the professional mother being a particularly popular subject

currently (Birnbaum, 1971; Garland, 1972; Hoffman, 1973; Holmstrom, 1972; Jones, Lundsteen, & Michael, 1967; Poloma, 1972; Rapoport & Rapoport, 1972). These studies have, in turn, revealed the need to consider both the education of the parents and the nature of the mother's job. The new studies indicate that the mother who works as a professional has a very different influence than one who works in a less intellectually demanding and less prestigious position. Since women's jobs often underuse their talents and training, education and the nature of the job are important singly and also in interaction.

Even methodologically, however, the studies leave much to be desired. Very few controlled on family size or ordinal position, although these variables relate to both maternal employment and most of the child characteristics studied. Failure to match on these may give an advantage to the working mother, since her family is smaller, and small family size contributes positively to cognitive abilities, particularly in the lower class (Clausen & Clausen, 1973). The need to control on more than one variable simultaneously is apparent in a number of reports, while the crudeness of the social class control is a problem in others.

But the most distressing aspect of the current research situation is the lack of theory. The typical study uses the sniper approach—maternal employment is run against whatever other variables are at hand, usually scores on intelligence tests or personality inventories. Even when a study indicates a complex pattern of findings or results counter to the accumulated research, no attempt is made to explain the pattern or reconcile the discrepancy.

Furthermore, the typical study deals only with two levels—the mother's employment status and a child characteristic. The many steps in between—family roles and interaction patterns, the child's perceptions, the mother's feelings about her employment, the child-rearing practices—are rarely measured. As previously noted (Hoffman & Lippitt, 1960), the distance between an antecedent condition like maternal employment and a child characteristic is too great to be covered in a single leap. Several levels should be examined in any single study to obtain adequate insight into the process involved.

To help counteract the generally atheoretical aspect of so much of the maternal employment research, the present review tries to organize the data around five basic approaches.

HYPOTHESES ABOUT THE EFFECTS OF MATERNAL EMPLOYMENT ON THE CHILD

What is the process by which maternal employment might affect the child? The ideas, whether implicit or explicit, that seem to guide the research and discussion can be classified into five general forms:

1. Because the mother is employed, she, and possibly her husband, provide a different model of behavior for the children in the family. Children learn sex role behavior largely from their parents. To the extent that a different role is carried out by the working mother than the nonworking mother, the child has a different conception of what the female role is. The self-concept of girls is particularly affected.

2. The mother's emotional state is influenced by whether or not she is employed, and this affects her interaction with her children.

3. Employed and nonemployed mothers probably use different child-rearing practices, not only because the mother's emotional state is different but also because the situational demands are different.

4. Because of her regular absences from the home, the working mother provides less personal supervision of her child than does the nonworking mother; and it is usually assumed that the supervision is less adequate.

5. Again, because of the working mother's regular absences from the home, the child is deprived, either emotionally or cognitively, or perceives her absence as rejection.

In the sections that follow we examine each of these hypotheses and report the relevant research.

The ultimate dependent variables that have been studied—that is, the child characteristics that are the focus of attention—can be classified as follows: (*a*) the child's social attitudes and values; (*b*) the child's general mental health and social adjustment and independence or dependence specifically; and (*c*) the child's cognitive abilities, achievement motivation, and intellectual performance. . . .

THE WORKING MOTHER AS ROLE MODEL

Hartley (1961) has observed that one experience common to all children of working mothers is that they "are exposed to a female parent who implements a social role not implemented by the female parents of other children [p. 42]." Since the child learns sex roles from observations of his parents, maternal employment influences his concept of the female role. More importantly, since one of the earliest statuses assigned to the child is that of gender, maternal employment presumably affects the female child's concept of herself and the behavior expected of her.

There is an impressive array of data to support this theory. Hartley (1961) found that elementary-school-age daughters of working mothers, in comparison to daughters of nonworking mothers, are more likely to say that both men and women typically engage in a wide variety of specified adult activities, ranging from using a sewing machine to using a gun and from selecting home furnishings to climbing mountains. That is, the daughters of working mothers indicated more similarity in the participation of men and women. They saw women as less restricted to their homes and more active in the world outside.[1]

That the division of labor between husband and wife is affected by maternal employment is well established. Husbands of employed women help more in household tasks including child care. While considerable traditionalism remains and working women engage in more domestic tasks than do their husbands, the division of household tasks is nonetheless more egalitarian when the mother is employed. (Blood & Hamblin, 1958; Hall & Schroeder, 1970; Holmstrom, 1972; Kligler, 1954; Szolai, 1966; Walker, 1970b; Weil, 1961). Furthermore, this difference is reflected in the children's perceptions, as seen in Hoffman's (1963b) study of children in the third through sixth grades and Finkelman's (1966) more recent study of fifth and sixth graders. Children five years of age and older whose mothers work are more likely to approve of maternal employment (Duvall, 1955; Mathews, 1933), and King, McIntyre, and Axelson (1968) reported that ninth graders whose mothers worked viewed maternal employment as less threatening to the marital relationship. These investigators also found that the greater the father's participation in household tasks, the more accepting of maternal employment were the adolescent boys and girls.

Furthermore, daughters of working mothers view work as something they will want to do when they are mothers. This was reported by Hartley (1960) in her study of elementary school children and in four studies of adolescent girls (Banducci, 1967; Below, 1969; Peterson, 1958; Smith, 1969). It was also found in college women (Almquist & Angrist, 1971; Zissis, 1964) and as a background factor among working professional women (Astin,

1969; Birnbaum, 1971).[2] Douvan (1963) and Roy (1963) found that adolescent daughters of working mothers were, in fact, more likely to be already employed.

Another closely related group of findings dealt with the attitudes toward women's roles in general. Are working mothers' children less likely to endorse a traditional or stereotypic view of women? Douvan (1963) found that the daughters of working mothers scored low on an index of traditional femininity.[3] Vogel, Broverman, Broverman, Clarkson, and Rosenkrantz (1970) studied the relationship between the sex role perceptions held by male and by female college students and their mothers' employment. Sex role perceptions were measured by having subjects describe the typical adult male and the typical adult female by checking a point along a continuum between two bipolar descriptions. Previous work with this scale had indicated which descriptions were more typically assigned to each sex and also which traits were seen as positive or negative. In general the positively valued stereotypes about males included items that reflected effectiveness and competence; the highly valued female-associated items described warmth and expressiveness. Both male students and female students with employed mothers perceived significantly smaller differences between men and women, with the women being more affected by maternal em-

---

[1]When asked to indicate which activities women liked and disliked, the daughters of working mothers reported more liking and less disliking of all activities—household, work, and recreation.

[2]Studies of children usually deal with maternal employment at the time of the study. Adult subjects, on the other hand, typically report past employment, for example, "when you were growing up," and one does not know how old the child was at the time of the employment. The age of the child is also ambiguous in studies in which samples have been selected in terms of a characteristic of the mothers, since the ages of the children may vary.

[3]The fact that daughters of working mothers are lower on traditional femininity should be kept in mind in evaluating studies like Nelson's (1971) that use pencil-and-paper personality inventories. Many of these inventories are biased toward the very questionable assumption that traditional femininity is the healthy pattern for girls (Constantinople, 1973; Henshel, 1971; Lunneborg, 1968).

ployment than were the men. Furthermore, the effect of maternal employment was to raise the estimation of one's own sex; that is, each sex added positive traits usually associated with the opposite sex—daughters of working mothers saw women as competent and effective, while sons of working mothers saw men as warm and expresssive.

This result is consistent with that of an interesting study by Baruch (1972a). College women were administered a measure developed by Goldberg (1967) in which subjects are presented with a number of journal articles and asked to judge the quality of the article and of the author. Half of the articles are given female names as authors, and half are given male names. Previous research by Goldberg had indicated that college women tend to attach a lower value to the articles attributed to women authors. Baruch found that the daughters of employed women were significantly different from the daughters of full-time housewives in that they did not downgrade the articles attributed to women. Thus, the daughters of working mothers were less likely to assume lower competence on the part of women authors: "it is women whose mothers have not worked who devalue feminine competence [Baruch, 1972a, p. 37]." Meier (1972) also found among college students that maternal employment was positively related to favoring social equality for women. The most equalitarian ideology was held by daughters of women in high-status occupations.

The relationship between maternal employment and sex role ideology is not perfectly clear, however, particularly when a multidimensional sex role ideology scale is used. For example, Baruch, in the above study, developed a 26-item Likert-type scale to measure attitudes toward careers for women. Scores on this scale, which dealt with the desirability of a career orientation in women, the compatibility of the career and family roles, the femininity of the career woman, and women's

ability to achieve intellectual excellence, were not related to maternal employment per se. Rather, a positive attitude toward the dual role resulted when the respondent's mother worked and also had successfully integrated the two roles. . . .

Not only is the role represented by the working mother different in content from the role represented by the nonworking mother, but the motivation to model the working mother appears to be stronger. Thus, Douvan (1963) found that adolescent daughters of working mothers were more likely to name their mothers as the person they most admired; and Baruch (1972b) found that college women with working mothers were more likely to name their mothers as the parent they most resembled, and the one they would most want to be like.

It is clear that the effects of maternal employment considered in this light must be different for males and females. For one thing, although maternal employment might affect all children's concepts of the woman's role, it should affect only the girls' self-concept, unless the mother's working also reflects something about the father. Douvan found that lower-class adolescent boys whose mothers work full time are less likely than those whose mothers do not work to name their father as the person they most admire. In the lower class, the mother's employment may communicate to the child that the father is an economic failure. . . . In any case, maternal employment more clearly defines the mother's role change than the father's, and thus the effect on the daughter may be more pronounced.

Nevertheless, there have been few studies of the effect of maternal employment on the daughter's self-esteem, and they have not always found the expected results. Thus, Baruch (1972b) found no relationship between maternal employment and the self-esteem of college women as measured by the Coopersmith Self-Esteem Inventory. She reported that the daughters of working mothers with positive career attitudes tended to have higher self-esteem, but this relationship was not statistically significant. Kappel and Lambert (1972), using a semantic-differential-style self-esteem measure with 3,315 9- to 16-year-old Canadian children, found that the daughters of non-working mothers were lower in self-esteem than were the daughters of part-time working mothers but higher than were the daughters of full-time working mothers. The daughters of full-time working mothers did have higher self-esteem than did those of the nonworking group, however, when any one of the following conditions existed: The mother worked for self-oriented reasons, was very satisfied with work, or was a professional.

Despite the inconclusive findings on self-esteem, for girls maternal employment seems to contribute to a greater admiration of the mother, a concept of the female role that includes less restriction and a wider range of activities, and a self-concept that incorporates these aspects of the female role. Douvan (1963) found that the adolescent daughters of working mothers to be relatively independent, autonomous, and active, and there are suggestions from other studies that this may be true for younger girls as well (Hoffman, 1963a). For boys, maternal employment might influence their concept of the female role, but what the effects are on their attitudes toward their father and themselves depends very much on the circumstances surrounding the mother's employment. . . .

Nevertheless, it does seem clear that when a mother works she provides a different model of behavior for the children in the family, particularly for the girls. Further, the hypothesis that this difference is important for the daughter's concept of sex roles, and thus presumably her self-concept, makes sense. Traditional sex role stereotypes in America assign a lower status to women than to men and in-

clude the view that women are less competent. Maslow, Rand, and Newman (1960) described as one effect, "the woman in order to be a good female may feel it necessary to give up her strength, intelligence or talent, fearing them as somehow masculine and defeminizing [p. 208]." Another effect has been empirically documented by Horner (1972)—that women who dare to achieve do so with anxiety and ambivalence about their success. The role of working mother is less likely to lead to traditional sex role stereotypes and more likely to communicate competence and the value of the woman's contribution to the family. She may have higher status in the family and represent to her daughter a person who is capable in areas that are, in some respects, more salient to a growing girl than are household skills.

To summarize: Considering the four major dependent variables from the standpoint of the role-model theory, the data indicate that maternal employment is associated with less traditional sex role concepts, more approval of maternal employment, and a higher evaluation of female competence. This in turn should imply a more positive self-concept for the daughters of working mothers and better social adjustment, but there are only indirect data on this. There is some support for the idea that daughters of working mothers are more independent because of modeling their more independent mothers. Evidence also suggests that the daughters of working mothers have higher achievement aspirations, but it has not yet been demonstrated that the actual abilities of the child are affected by the different role model provided by the working mother.

THE MOTHER'S EMOTIONAL STATE

Morale

The assumption that the mother's emotional state is influenced by whether or not she is employed and that this affects her adequacy as a mother underlies several different approaches. One type of hypothesis, for example, relies on the commonly accepted belief that good morale improves job performance. Since this theory has validity in the industrial setting (Roethlisberger & Dickson, 1939), why not in the home? In fact, there is some support for it. Yarrow, Scott, deLeeuw, and Heinig (1962) examined, by means of interviews with mothers of elementary school children, the child-rearing patterns of four groups of mothers: (a) mothers who worked and preferred to work, (b) mothers who worked and preferred not to work, (c) nonworking mothers who preferred to work, and (d) nonworking mothers who preferred not to work. Among the nonworking mothers, satisfaction with their lot made a significant difference: The satisfied nonworking mothers obtained higher scores on a measure of adequacy of mothering. However, satisfaction did not differentiate the working mothers. One should keep in mind that when this study was conducted it was more socially acceptable to say, "Yes, I am working, but I wish I could be home all the time with my children" than it was to say, "Yes, I am home all day with my children, but I wish I were out working." Thus, some of the dissatisfied workers may not have been as dissatisfied as they indicated. By the same token, the dissatisfaction of the homemaker may have been more extreme, and her dissatisfaction more closely linked to the mothering role itself; that is, the very role with which she was indicating dissatisfaction included mothering. Indeed, of all four groups, the lowest scores on adequacy of mothering were obtained by the dissatisfied homemaker. (The highest, by the satisfied homemaker.) Furthermore, the investigators considered the motives for choosing full-time homemaking: Those women who stressed duty as the basis for the choice had the lowest scores of all.

The question of the dissatisfied nonworking mother is interesting. Would the working mother who enjoys her work be dissatisfied as a full-time homemaker? In the practical sense, this may be the real issue; and the Yarrow et al. (1962) data suggest that the satisfied working mother may not be as adequate a parent as the satisfied nonworking mother but she is more adequate than the dissatisfied nonworking mother. Birnbaum (1971) is an interesting study compared professionally employed mothers with mothers who had graduated from college "with distinction" but had become full-time homemakers, that is, women who had the ability to pursue professional careers had they so chosen. Both groups were about 15 to 25 years past their bachelor's degree at the time they were interviewed. With respect to morale, the professional women were clearly higher. The nonworking mothers had lower self-esteem, a lower sense of personal competence—even with respect to child care skills, felt less attractive, expressed more concern over identity issues, and indicated greater feelings of loneliness. The nonworking mothers were even more insecure and unhappy in these respects than was a third sample of professional women who had never married. Asked what they felt was missing from their lives, the predominant answer from the two groups of professional women was time, but for the housewives it was challenge and creative involvement.

The mothers were also compared with respect to orientation toward their children. In response to the question, "How does having children change a woman's life," the full-time homemakers stressed the sacrifice that motherhood entailed significantly more often than did the professional women. The professional women answered more often in terms of enrichment and self-fulfillment. Although both groups mentioned the work involved and the demanding aspects of motherhood, the homemakers stressed duty and responsibility to a greater extent. The homemakers indicated more anxiety about their children, especially with regard to the child's achievements, and they stressed their own inadequacies as mothers. In response to a projective picture showing a boy and his parents with a crutch in the background, the homemakers told more dramatic, depressed, and anxious stories. With respect to the growing independence of their children, the professional women responded positively, while the homemakers indicated ambivalence and regret. They seemed to be concerned about the loss of familiar patterns or their own importance.

There are no direct data in the Birnbaum (1971) study on the children themselves, but the pattern of the able, educated, full-time homemakers suggests that they would have shortcomings as mothers, particularly as their children approached adolescence. At that time, when the child needs a parent who can encourage independence and instill self-confidence, the anxieties and concerns of these women and their own frustrations would seem to operate as a handicap.

There are additional studies suggesting that when work is a source of personal satisfaction for the mother, her role as mother is positively affected. Kligler (1954) found that women who worked because of interest in the job were more likely than were those who worked for financial reasons to feel that there was improvement in the child's behavior as a result of employment. Kappel and Lambert (1972) found that the 9- to 16-year-old daughters of full-time working mothers who indicated they were working for self-oriented reasons had higher self-esteem and evaluated both parents more highly than did either the daughters of full-time working mothers who were working for family-oriented reasons or the daughters of nonworking mothers. In this study the measures of the mother's motives for working and the child data were obtained independently. In the studies by Yarrow et al. (1962), Birnbaum (1971), and Kligler, the mother was

the source of all the data. Woods (1972) found that in a study of fifth graders in a lower-class, predominantly black urban area where almost all of the mothers were employed, mothers who reported a positive attitude toward employment had children who obtained scores on the California Test of Personality indicating good social and personal adjustment.

Role Strain

Another dimension of morale that has been studied focuses on the strain of handling the dual roles of worker and mother. The general idea is that whatever the effect of maternal employment under conflict-free circumstances, the sheer pressure of trying to fill these two very demanding roles can result in a state of stress that in turn has a negative effect on the child. Thus, the main thrust of Kappel and Lambert's (1972) argument is that part-time employment, and full-time employment when it involves minimal conflict, have a positive effect; full-time employment under most conditions, however, involves strain and therefore has adverse effects. In Douvan's (1963) study of adolescent children in intact families, the only group of working-mother children who indicated adjustment problems were the children of full-time working mothers in the lower class. This group of working mothers was the one for whom the strain of the dual role seemed to be the greatest.

In contrast, Woods (1972) found the children of full-time workers to be the best adjusted. Her sample, however, was all lower class from a population in which most mothers were employed and included many single-parent families. Under these circumstances, the full-time employed mothers may have been financially better off than were the others and may have had more stable household arrangements to facilitate their employment. The mother's positive attitude toward employment related to the child's adjustment, as noted above, but also her satisfaction with child care arrangements contributed to a positive attitude toward employment. In a sense then, although full-time employment of lower-class mothers did not seem to have adverse effects on the child as suggested in the other two studies, strain as manifested in dissatisfaction with child care arrangements may have exerted such an influence.[4] To some extent the attitude toward employment generally may reflect the mother's feeling of role strain.

Guilt

Still another possible emotional response to employment is that the working mother feels guilty about her work because of the prevailing admonishments against maternal employment. While this may result in some appropriate compensation for her absence from home, it may also be overdone.

There is evidence that working mothers are very concerned about whether or not their employment is "bad" for their children, and they often feel guilty. Even Birnbaum's (1971) happy professional mothers indicated frequent guilt feeling. Kligler (1954) also noted that the working mothers experienced anxiety and guilt and tried to compensate in their behavior toward their children. Some evidence for guilt on the part of the working mother and the effects of this on the child is provided in a study by Hoffman (1963b). Third- through sixth-grade children of working mothers were studied, with each working-mother family matched to a nonworking-mother family on father's occupation, sex of child, and ordinal position of the child. The data included questionnaires filled out by the children, personal interviews with the mothers, teacher ratings, and classroom sociometrics. The working mothers were divided into those who indicated that they liked working and those who disliked it. Working mothers who like work, compared to the nonworking matched sample, had more positive interaction with the child, felt more sympathy and less anger toward the child in discipline situations, and used less severe discipline techniques. However, the children of these working mothers appeared to be less assertive and less effective in their peer interactions. Their intellectual performance was rated lower by teachers, and their scores on the school intelligence tests were lower. Also, these children helped somewhat less in household tasks than did the children of nonworking mothers. Thus, the overall pattern seemed to indicate that the working mother who like work not only tried to compensate for her employment but may have actually overcompensated. These data were collected in 1957 when popular sentiment was opposed to maternal employment. As a result the women may have felt guilty about working. In trying to be good mothers, they may have gone too far, since the children's behavior suggested a pattern of overprotection or "smother love."

The mothers who did not like work, on the other hand, showed a very different pattern. They seemed less involved with the child; for example, they indicated less frequent disciplining and somewhat fewer positive interactions, as compared to nonworking mothers. The children helped with household tasks to a greater extent than did the children of nonworking mothers. They were also more assertive and hostile toward their peers. Their school performance as rated by their teachers was lower, although they did not perform more poorly on the school intelligence tests. The total pattern suggested that these children were somewhat neglected in comparison to the nonworking matched sample. The working

---

[4]The study does not indicate whether the woman's satisfaction reflected the objective conditions or not; the mother's perceptions and the child's report of the situation were significantly but not highly related.

mothers who disliked work had less reason to feel guilty, since they were working for other than self-oriented reasons.

Effects on the Child

A complicated picture is presented if the data on the working mother's emotional state are considered in relation to the child characteristics cited earlier as most often linked to maternal employment: (*a*) the child's attitudes, (*b*) mental health and social adjustment and independence-dependence specifically, and (*c*) cognitive abilities and orientations. First, with respect to the attitude toward maternal employment itself, there are some indications that the tendency of working mothers' children to have a positive attitude is enhanced when the employment is accompanied by a minimum of conflict and strain for the mother (Baruch, 1972a; King et al., 1968).

Moving on to the more complex dependent variables, it appears that when maternal employment is satisfying to the mother, either because it is more easily incorporated into her activities or because it is intrinsically gratifying, the effects on the child may be positive. The effects are more clearly positive—as indicated by various measures such as an "adequacy of mothering" score, the child's self-esteem, the child's adjustment score on the California Test of Personality, and attitudes toward parents—when this situation is compared either to that of the full-time housewife who would really prefer to work (Yarrow et al., 1962) or to maternal employment when it is accompanied by strain and harassment (Douvan, 1963; Kappel & Lambert, 1972; Woods, 1972). There are even indications that in some situations, as when the children are approaching adolescence and older or when the mother is particularly educated and able, the working-mother role may be more satisfying than is the role of full-time housewife and that this may make the working mother less anxious and more encouraging of independence in

her children (Birnbaum, 1971). On the other hand, there is also evidence that the working mother with younger children who likes work might feel guilty and thus overcompensate, with adverse effects for the child in the form of passivity, ineffectiveness with peers, and low academic performance (Hoffman, 1963b). Thus the data about the mother's emotional state suggest that the working mother who obtains satisfaction from her work, who has adequate arrangements so that her dual role does not involve undue strain, and who does not feel so guilty that she overcompensates is likely to do quite well and, under certain conditions, better than does the nonworking mother.

CHILD-REARING PRACTICES

Concern here is with whether the child of a working mother is subject to different child-rearing practices and how these in turn affect his development. To some extent this topic is covered in other sections. In discussing the different role models presented in the working-mother families, for example, we indicated that the child-rearing functions are more likely to be shared by both parents. The fact that the child then has a more balanced relationship with both parents has generally been viewed with favor. The active involvement of the father has been seen as conducive to high achievement in women, particularly when he is supportive of independence and performance (Ginzberg, 1971; Hoffman, 1973), and to the social adjustment of boys (Hoffman, 1961) as well as to the general adjustment of both boys and girls (Dizard, 1968).

Data also indicate that the working mother's family is more likely to include someone outside the conjugal family who participates in child care (Hoffman, 1958; U.S. Department of Labor, 1972). This situation undoubtedly operates as a selective factor, since the presence of, for example, the grandmother makes it easier for the mother to go to work; but the effects of this pattern have not been widely examined. The specific issue of multiple mothering and frequent turnover in babysitters is discussed later in the article, primarily in terms of effects on the infant and the young child when these issues are most meaningful.

In discussing the guilt sometimes felt by the working mothers, it was suggested that they sometimes try to compensate for their employment, in some cases overdoing it. There is considerable evidence that working mothers particularly in the middle class do try to compensate. In some studies, this is made explicit by the respondents (Jones et al., 1967; Kligler, 1954; Rapoport & Rapoport, 1972), while in others it is revealed in the pattern of working-nonworking differences obtained. As examples of the latter, Yarrow and her colleagues (1962) found that the college-educated working mothers compensated by having more planned activities with children, and the professional mothers in Fisher's (1939) early study spent as many hours with their children as did the full-time homemakers. Finally, Jones et al. found that the mothers employed as professionals spent more time reading with their sixth-grade children than did nonworking mothers, though this was part of a generally greater stress on educational goals, not just compensation for employment.

When the working mother tries to make up for her employment, she often makes certain implicit judgments about what the nonworking situation is like. These may be quite inaccurate. The working mothers in Hoffman's (1963b) study who required less household help from their children than did the nonworking mothers are a case in point. And, in general, the nonworking mother is not necessarily interacting with her child as much as is imagined or as pleasantly. There is a great deal of pluralistic ignorance about the mothering role, and many mothers may be measuring themselves against, and trying to match, an overidealized image. It is possible that the nonworking mother spends relatively little time in direct positive interaction with her child, and thus the working mother's deliberate efforts might end up as more total positive interaction time. With respect to the amount of time spent in total child care, comparisons indicate that the nonworking women spend more time (Robinson, 1971; Walker & Woods, 1972). These reports, however, are geared toward other purposes and are not helpful in providing information about parent-child interaction. In most cases, working and nonworking women are compared without regard to whether or not they are mothers. Obviously the nonworking women include more mothers, and thus they do, as a group, spend more time in child care. Even when only mothers are compared, the number of children in the family and the children's ages are not considered, and the kind of child care is often not specified. Just how much of the day does the nonworking mother spend interacting with the child? This is an unfortunate gap in our knowledge.

Independence Training

Several studies have focused on whether the working mother encourages independence and maturity in her children more than does the nonworking mother. The answer seems to depend on the age of the child and the social class or education of the mother. In the work of Yarrow and her colleagues (1962), the working mothers who had not gone to college were more likely to indicate a stress on independence training and to assign the children a greater share of the household responsibilities. The college-educated working mothers did not show this pattern and in fact showed a nonsignificant tendency in the opposite direction. The subjects in this study were similar to Hoffman's (1963b) respondents in that the children were of elementary school age; thus it is interesting that the college-educated working mothers in the former study exhibit a pattern similar to the working women who liked work in the latter study. Burchinal and Lovell (1959) reported for somewhat older children that working mothers were more likely to stress independence, and a stress on independence and responsibility can be inferred as more characteristic of the working mothers in the national sample study of adolescent girls reported by Douvan (1963), although the data rely more on what the girl is like than on parental child-rearing practices. Birnbaum's (1971) study of professionally employed mothers also suggests an encouragement of independence. The age of these children varied. The study by Von Mering (1955) is often cited as evidence that professional mothers stress independence training in elementary-school-age children, but since there were only eight mothers in the sample, such conclusions do not seem justified.[5] . . .

The data are quite sketchy, but the general picture is that except for the working mothers of younger children (elementary school age) who are educated or enjoy work and possibly the working mothers in unstable families, working mothers stress independence training more than do nonworking mothers. This is consistent with what one would expect. It has already been indicated that the more educated working mothers try to compensate for their employment. Thus they would be expected to avoid pushing the younger children into maturity, stressing the nurturant aspects of their role to make up for their absence at work. As the child grows older, independence is called

for. To the nonworking mother the move from protector and nurturer to independence trainer is often very difficult. For the working mother, on the other hand, the child's growing independence eases her role strain. Furthermore, the psychological threat of becoming less essential to the child is lessened by the presence of alternative roles and sources of self-worth.

The evidence for the effect of this pattern on the child is not definitely established. Two of the studies, Hoffman's (1963b) and McCord et al.'s (1963), examined data at each of the three levels: employment status, child-rearing behavior, and child characteristics; but the findings are ambiguous. Hoffman did not directly examine the relationship between maternal behavior and the child characteristics; McCord and her colleagues did and failed to find a significant association between independence training and independence. None of the other relevant maternal employment studies obtained separate data on the child-rearing pattern and the child characteristics. On the other hand, several child development studies that have no data on maternal employment have found that parental encouragement of independence relates to high achievement motivation, competence, and achievement behavior in both males and females (Baumrind & Black, 1967; Hoffman, 1972; Winterbottom, 1958).

Household Responsibilities

Most of the data indicate that the child of the working mother has more household responsibilities (Douvan, 1963; Johnson, 1969; Propper, 1972; Roy, 1963; Walker, 1970a). The exception to this generalization is again the mothers of younger children who are more educated or who enjoy work. Although working mothers may sometimes deliberately avoid giving the child household responsibilities, such participation by children has generally been found to have a positive, not a negative,

[5]Propper (1972) found that the adolescent children of working mothers were more likely to report disagreements with parents but were not different from the children of nonworking mothers with respect to feelings of closeness of parents, parental interest, or support. The overall pattern may indicate more tolerance of disagreement by the working mothers rather than a more strained relationship. This interpretation fits well with the general picture of working mothers encouraging independence and autonomy in adolescent children.

effect (Clausen, 1966; Johnson, 1969; Woods, 1972). Obviously, this does not mean overburdening the child, but expecting the child to be one of the effectively contributing members of the family seems conducive to the development of social adjustment and responsibility.

Parental Control

What other effects of maternal employment on child-rearing practices might be expected? One hypothesis might be that the working mother leaves her child more often without care or supervision. This is the focus of the next section, but by and large, there is little evidence that this is the case. On the other hand, because of the demands imposed by the dual role of worker and mother, the working mother might be stricter and impose more conformity to a specified standard. That is, just as reality adaptation might lead her to encourage the child in independence and to take on household responsibilities, she might also be expected to demand more conformity to rules so that the household can function smoothly in her absence. There is some evidence for this pattern among the less educated groups. Yarrow et al. (1962) found that the children of working mothers in their noncollege group were generally under firmer parental control than were the children of nonworking mothers. Woods (1972) found more consistency between principles and practice in the discipline used by the full-time working mothers in her lower-class, predominantly black sample. However, Yarrow et al. found greater inconsistency in their college-educated working mothers.

Still another possibility is that the working mother is milder in discipline because of conscious efforts to compensate the child or because of higher morale. Hoffman's (1963b) working mothers, especially those who liked work, used less severe discipline and indicated less hostility in the discipline situation than did the nonworking mothers. It should be noted that the focus in this study was not on the content of the discipline but on its severity. Thus the data do not indicate whether the children were under more or less firm control but only that the discipline used was milder.

There are a few studies, such as those that compared the child-rearing views of working and nonworking mothers and found no meaningful differences (Kligler, 1954; Powell, 1963), that are not reviewed here, but we have included most of the available data on maternal employment and child-rearing practices. It is surprising how few investigations of maternal employment have obtained data about actual child-rearing behavior. Most of the studies have simply related employment to a child characteristic and then later speculated about any relationship that might be found. If the daughters of working mothers are found to be more independent or higher achievers, one cannot tell if this is a product of the working mother as model, the fact that the father is more likely to have had an active part in the girl's upbringing, the result of the fathers in working-mother families being more likely to approve of and encourage competence in females, or whether it is because these girls were more likely to have been encouraged by their mothers to achieve independence and assume responsibilities. All of these intervening variables have been linked to female independence and achievement (Hoffman, 1972, 1973).

MATERNAL ABSENCE AND SUPERVISION

The most persistent concern about maternal employment has to do with the sheer absence of the mother from the home while she is working and the fear that this represents a loss to the child in terms of supervision, love, or cognitive enrichment. Much of the earlier research on maternal employment and juvenile delinquency was based on this hypothesis: The mother was working, the child was unsupervised, and thus he was a delinquent. There is some support for this theory, despite the fact that maternal employment and delinquency do not relate as expected. In the study of lower-class boys carried out by Glueck and Glueck (1957), regularly employed mothers were no more likely to have delinquent sons than were nonemployed mothers. However, inadequate supervision seemed to lead to delinquency whatever the mother's employment status, and employed mothers, whether employed regularly or occasionally, were more likely to provide inadequate supervision. McCord and McCord (1959) also found a tie between supervision and delinquency in their longitudinal study of lower-class boys (which, unlike the Gluecks', included only intact families), but there was little difference between the working and nonworking mothers with respect to adequacy of supervision (McCord et al., 1963). Furthermore, the tie between the adequacy of supervision and social adjustment conceptualized more generally is not conclusively established. In the study by Woods (1972) of lower-class fifth-grade children, inadequate supervision did not have a statistically demonstrable adverse effect on boys, although unsupervised girls clearly showed lower school adjustment scores on tests of social relations and cognitive abilities.[6] Delinquency per se was too rare in this sample for any comparison, and the relation-

ship between maternal employment and the adequacy of supervision was not examined. . . .

Ignoring now the issue of supervision, what is the relatioship between maternal employment and delinquency? In our previous review, we suggested that there did seem to be a relationship between maternal employment and delinquency in the middle class. This relationship was found by Nye (1963) using a self-report measure of delinquent behavior and Gold (1961) who used police contact as the measure; in both studies the relationship was obtained for the middle class and not for the lower class.[7] Glueck and Glueck (1957), studying only lower-class subjects, found no tendency for the sons of regularly employed women to be delinquent despite the fact that their sample included broken homes, a variable that relates to both delinquency and maternal employment. They did find the sons of the "occasionally" employed women to be delinquent, but the occasionally employed group was clearly more unstable than were those in which the mother worked regularly or not at all. They were more likely to have husbands with poor work habits and emotional disturbances, poor marriages, or to be widowed or divorced. The Gluecks saw the occasionally employed mother as working "to escape household drudgery and parental responsibility," but, in another view, the question is not why they went to work, since their employment was obviously needed by the circumstances of their lives, but why they resisted regular employment. The delinquency of their sons seemed more a function of family instability, the inadequacies of the father, or something about the mothers not being employed

[6]The sex differences in the Woods study are both intriguing and difficult to interpret. In most child development studies, the girls show ill effects from too much supervision or control, while the boys typically suffer from too little (Becker, 1964; Bronfenbrenner, 1961; Hoffman, 1972). This may reflect the higher level of control generally exercised over girls, so that the low end of the scale for girls is not as low as for boys, either objectively or subjectively. However, there have been very few child development studies of the lower class, and it is possible that the lack of supervision is more extreme than in the typical child development sample. Thus the middle-class girl who is unsupervised relative to other middle-class girls may not represent the level of neglect encountered by Woods.

[7]There are two other recent studies (Brown, 1970; Riege, 1972) in which no relationship was found between maternal employment and juvenile delinquency. Since there was no separate examination by social class or attention to relevant mediating variables, these studies are not illuminating in this discussion.

more regularly, rather than a function of maternal employment per se. . . .

To summarize, the hypothesis that maternal employment means inadequate supervision has been primarily invoked to predict higher delinquency rates for the children of working mothers. There are data, although not very solid, that in the lower class, working mothers provide less adequate supervision for their children and that adequacy of supervision is linked to delinquency and social adjustment, but there is no evidence that the children of working mothers are more likely to be delinquent. The data suggest instead that full-time maternal employment in the very low social class groups represents a realistic response to economic stress and thus, because of selective factors or effects, may be correlated with more socially desirable characteristics in the child. Adequacy of supervision has rarely been studied in the middle class, although here there is some evidence for a higher delinquency rate among working mothers' children.

MATERNAL DEPRIVATION

The School-Age Child

For school-age children, there is very little empirically to link maternal employment to maternal deprivation. Although Woods (1972) suggests that full-time employment may represent rejection to the middle-class child, there is no evidence of this. While it has been commonly assumed that maternal employment is interpreted by the child as rejection, the evidence, as indicated above, suggests that the children of working mothers tend to support the idea of mothers working. Furthermore, as maternal employment becomes the norm in the middle, as well as in the lower, class it seems even less likely that the sheer fact that a mother is working would lead to a sense of being rejected.

The evidence as to whether the working mother actually does reject the school-age child has already been covered in earlier sections of this review. The general pattern is that the working mother, particularly in the middle class, makes a deliberate effort to compensate the child for her employment (Hoffman, 1963b; Jones et al., 1967; Kligler, 1954; Poloma, 1972; Rapoport & Rapoport, 1972; Yarrow et al., 1962) and that the dissatisfied mother, whether employed or not and whether lower class or middle class, is less likely to be an adequate mother (Birnbaum, 1971; Woods, 1972; Yarrow et al., 1962). The idea that maternal employment brings emotional deprivation to the school-age child has not been supported (Hoffman, 1963a; Peterson, 1958; Propper, 1972; Siegel & Haas, 1973; Yudkin & Holme, 1963). In part this may be because the working mother is often away from home only when the child is in school; and if her work is gratifying in some measure, if she does not feel unduly hassled, or if she deliberately sets about to do so, she may even spend more time in positive interaction with the child than does the nonworking mother. While this can sometimes be overdone and compensation can turn into overcompensation (Hoffman, 1963b), it may also be one of the important reasons why maternal employment has not been experienced by the school-age child as deprivation. In drawing action conclusions from the research, it is important to keep this in mind. The absence of negative effects does not mean that the mother's employment is an irrelevant variable; it may mean that mothers have been sufficiently concerned to counterbalance such effects effectively.

Infancy

More recently attention has focused on the possible adverse effects of maternal employment on the infant and the very young child. The importance of attachment and a one-to-one relationship in the early years has been stressed by Spitz (1945), Bowlby (1958, 1969), and others (Yarrow, 1964). Although most of this research has been carried out on children in institutions with the most dramatic effects demonstrated among children whose infancy was spent in grossly deprived circumstances, it nevertheless seems clear that something important is happening during these early years and that there are critical periods when cognitive and affective inputs may have important ramifications throughout the individual's life. Concern has been generated about this issue because of the recent increase in maternal employment among mothers of infants and young children and also because of the new interest in day care centers as a means of caring for the pre-school children of working mothers. As these two patterns emerge, the effects of maternal employment must be reevaluated. In this section we review the evidence that has been cited on one side or the other of these issues. As we shall see, however, we really know very little.

The research on maternal deprivation suggests that the infant needs a one-to-one relationship with an adult or else he may suffer cognitive and affective loss that may, in extreme conditions, never be regained. The importance of interactions in which the adult responds to the child and the child to the adult in a reciprocal relationship has been particularly stressed (Bronfenbrenner, 1973). There is some evidence of a need for cuddling (Harlow & Harlow, 1966) and a need for environmental stimulation (Dennis & Narjarian, 1957; Hunt, 1961). These studies are often cited as evidence for the importance of the mother's full-time presence in the home when the infant is young.

Extending these findings to the maternal employment situation may be inappropriate, however. Not only were the early Bowlby (1953, 1958) and Spitz (1945) data obtained from studies of extremely barren, understaffed institutions, but later research suggested that the drastic effects they had observed might be avoided by increasing the staff-child ratio, by providing nurses who attended and responded to the infants' cries, smiles and vocalizations, and by providing a more stimulating visual environment. Further, the age of the child, the duration of the institutionalization, and the previous and subsequent experiences of the child all affect the outcome (Rheingold, 1956; Rheingold & Bayley, 1959; Rheingold, Gewirtz, & Ross, 1959; Tizard, Cooperman, Joseph, & Tizard, 1972; Yarrow, 1964). Most important, however, institutionalization is not the same as day care, and day care is not the same as maternal employment. The inappropriateness of the studies of institutionalized infants to maternal employment has also been noted by Yudkin and Holme (1963), by Yarrow (1964), and by Wortis (1971).

In addition, there is no evidence that the caretaker has to be the mother or that this role is better filled by a male or a female. There is some evidence that the baby benefits from predictability in handling, but whether this is true throughout infancy or only during certain periods is not clear, nor is it clear whether the different handling has any long-lasting effects. Studies of multiple mothering have produced conflicting results (Caldwell, 1964). Child psychologists generally believe that there must be at least one stable figure to whom the infant forms an attachment, but this is not definitely established, and we do not know whether the periodic absence from the infant that is likely to go along with the mother's employment is sufficient to undermine her potential as the object of the infant's attachment.

Nevertheless, a number of child development studies suggest that within the normal range of parent-child interaction, the amount of expressive and vocal stimulation and response the mother gives to the infant affects his development (Emerson & Schaffer, 1964; Kagan, 1969; Lewis & Goldberg, 1969; Moss, 1967). Furthermore, although the attempts to increase cognitive performance through day care programs have not been very successful, attempts to increase the mother-infant interaction in the home appear to have more enduring effects (Bronfenbrenner, 1973; Levenstein, 1970, 1971). While there is no evidence that employment actually affects the quantity or quality of the mother-infant interaction, the voluntary employment of mothers of infants and young children has not heretofore been common, and it has rarely been studied. It is therefore important to find out whether the mother's employment results in less (or more) personal stimulation and interaction for the infant.

In addition to the importance of stimulation and interaction and the issue of emotional attachment for the infant, there are less fully explored questions about the effects on the mother. Bowlby (1958) and others (Hess, 1970) believe that the mother-child interaction is important for the development of the mother's "attachment," that an important source of maternal feeling is the experience of caring for the infant. Yudkin and Holme (1963), who generally approve of maternal employment in their review, stress this as one of the real dangers of full-time maternal employment when the child is young:

We would consider this need for a mother to develop a close and mutually satisfying relationship with her young infant one of the fundamental reasons why we oppose full-time work for mothers of children under 3 years. We do not say that it would not be possible to combine the two if children were cared for near their mothers so that they could see and be with each other during the day for parts of the day, and by such changes in households as will reduce the amount of time and energy needed for household chores. We are only stating that this occurs very rarely in our present society and is unlikely to be general in the foreseeable future and that the separation of children from their mothers for eight or nine hours a day, while the effects on the children may be counteracted by good substitute care, must

have profound effects on the mother's own relationship with her young children and therefore on their relationship in the family as they grow older. [pp. 131-132].

The issue of day care centers is not discussed in this review in any detail; however, our ignorance is almost as great here. While the cognitive advances expected from the Head Start day care programs were not adequately demonstrated (Bronfenbrenner, 1973), neither were there negative effects of these programs (Caldwell, Wright, Honig, & Tannenbaum, 1970). Obviously, the effects of day care centers for working mothers' children depend on the quality of the program, the time the child spends there, what happens to the child when he is not at the day care center, and what the alternatives are.

Arguments on either side of the issue of working mothers and day care often use data from studies on the kibbutzim in Israel, since all kibbutzim mothers work and from infancy on the child lives most of the time in the child centers. Some investigators have been favorably impressed with the development of these children (Kohn-Raz, 1968; Rabkin & Rabkin, 1969), while others have noted at least some deleterious consequences (Bettelheim, 1969; Spiro, 1965). In fact, however, these data are probably quite irrelevant. According to Bronfenbrenner (1973), these children spend more time each day interacting with their parents than do children in the more conventional nuclear family arrangement, and the time they spend together is less subject to distractions. The whole living arrangement is parents' work and the social context within which interaction takes place. The mother participates a great deal in the infant care, breast feeding is the norm, and both parents play daily with the child for long periods and without other diversions even as he matures. Thus, the Israeli kibbutz does not provide an example of maternal deprivation, American day care, or maternal employment as it is experienced in the United States. . . .

Obviously the effects of maternal employment on the infant depend on the extent of the mother's absence and the nature of the substitute care—whether it is warm, stimulating, and stable. However, while studies of maternal employment and the school-age child by and large offer reassurance to the working mother, we have very little solid evidence concerning the effect on the younger child.

REFERENCES

Almquist, E. M., & Angrist, S. S. Role model influences on college women's career aspirations. *Merrill-Palmer Quarterly*, 1971, **17**, 263–279.

Astin, H. S. *The woman doctorate in America.* New York: Russell Sage Foundation, 1969.

Atkinson, J. W. (Ed.) *Motives in fantasy, action, and society.* Princeton, N. J.: Van Nostrand, 1958.

Banducci, R. The effect of mother's employment on the achievement, aspirations, and expectations of the child. *Personnel and Guidance Journal*, 1967, **46**, 263–267.

Baruch, G. K. Maternal influences upon college women's attitudes toward women and work. *Developmental Psychology*, 1972, **6**, 32–37. (a)

Baruch, G. K. Maternal role pattern as related to self-esteem and parental identification in college women. Paper presented at the meeting of the Eastern Psychological Association, Boston, April 1972. (b)

Baumrind, D., & Black, A. E. Socialization practices associated with dimensions of competence in preschool boys and girls. *Child Development*, 1967, **38**, 291–327.

Becker, W. C. Consequences of different kinds of parental discipline. In M. L. Hoffman & L. W. Hoffman (Eds.), *Review of child development research.* New York: Russell Sage Foundation, 1964.

Below, H. I. Life styles and roles of women as perceived by high-school girls. Unpublished doctoral dissertation, Indiana University, 1969. •

Bettelheim, B. *The children of the dream.* London: Macmillan, 1969.

Birnbaum, J. A. Life patterns, personality style and self esteem in gifted family oriented and career committed women. Unpublished doctoral dissertation, University of Michigan, 1971.

Blood, R. O., & Hamblin, R. L. The effect of the wife's employment on the family power structure. *Social Forces*, 1958, **36**, 347–352.

Bowlby, J. A. Some pathological processes engendered by early mother-child separation. In M. J. E. Senn (Ed.), *Infancy and childhood.* New York: Josiah Macy, Jr. Foundation, 1953.

Bowlby, J. A. The nature of the child's tie to his mother. *International Journal of Psychoanalysis*, 1958, **39**, 350–373.

Bowlby, J. A. *Attachment.* New York: Basic Books, 1969.

Bronfenbrenner, U. Some familial antecedents of responsibility and leadership on adolescents. In L. Petrullo & B. M. Bass (Eds.), *Leadership and interpersonal behavior.* New York: Holt, Rinehart & Winston, 1961.

Bronfenbrenner, U. Is early intervention effective? Paper presented at the biennial meeting of the Society for Research in Child Development, Philadelphia, March 1973.

Brown, S. W. *A comparative study of maternal employment and nonemployment.* (Doctoral dissertation, Mississippi State University) Ann Arbor, Mich.: University Microfilms, 1970, No. 70–8610.

Burchinal, L. G. Personality characteristics of children. In F. I. Nye & L. W. Hoffman (Eds.), *The employed mother in America.* Chicago: Rand McNally, 1963.

Burchinal, L. G., & Lovell, L. Relation of employment status of mothers to children's anxiety, parental personality and PARI scores. Unpublished manuscript (1425), Iowa State University, 1959.

Caldwell, B. M. The effects of infant care. In M. L. Hoffman & L. W. Hoffman (Eds.), *Review of child development research.* New York: Russell Sage Foundation, 1964.

Caldwell, B. M., Wright, C. M., Honig, A. S., & Tannenbaum, J. Infant day care and attachment. *American Journal of Orthopsychiatry*, 1970, **40**, 397–412.

Clausen, J. A. Family structure, socialization, and personality. In L. W. Hoffman & M. L. Hoffman (Eds.), *Review of child development research.* Vol. 2, New York: Russell Sage Foundation, 1966.

Clausen, J. A., & Clausen, S. R. The effects of family size on parents and children. In J. Fawcett (Ed.), *Psychological perspectives on fertility.* New York: Basic Books, 1973.

Constantinople, A. Masculinity-femininity: An exception to a famous dictum? *Psychological Bulletin*, 1973, **80**, 389–407.

Dennis, W., & Najarian, P. Infant development under environmental handicap. *Psychological Monographs*, 1957, **71**, (7, Whole No. 436).

Dizard, J. *Social change in the family.* Chicago: University of Chicago, Community and Family Study Center, 1968.

Douvan, E. Employment and the adolescent. In F. I. Nye & L. W. Hoffman (Eds.), *The employed mother in America.* Chicago: Rand McNally, 1963.

Duvall, E. B. Conceptions of mother roles by five and six year old children of working and non-working mothers. Unpublished doctoral dissertation, Florida State University, 1955.

Emerson, P. E., & Schaffer, H. R. The development of social attachments in infancy. *Monographs of the Society for Research in Child Development*, 1964, **29**(3, serial No. 94).

Farley, J. Maternal employment and child behavior. *Cornell Journal of Social Relations*, 1968, **3**, 58–70.

Finkelman, J. J. Maternal employment, family relationships, and parental role perception. Unpublished doctoral dissertation, Yeshiva University, 1966.

Fisher, M. S. Marriage and work for college women. *Vassar Alumnae Magazine*, 1939, **24**, 7–10.

Frankel, E. Characteristics of working and non-working mothers among intellectually gifted high and low achievers. *Personnel and Guidance Journal*, 1964, **42**, 776–780.

Garland, T. N. The better half? The male in the dual profession family. In C. Safilios-Rothschild (Ed.), *Toward a sociology of women.* Lexington, Mass.: Xerox College Publishing, 1972.

Ginzberg, E. *Educated American women: Life styles and self-portraits.* New York: Columbia University Press, 1971.

Glueck, S., & Glueck, E. Working mothers and delinquency. *Mental Hygiene*, 1957, **41**, 327–352.

Gold, M. *A social-psychology of delinquent boys.* Ann Arbor, Mich.: Institute for Social Research, 1961.

Goldberg, P. Misogyny and the college girl. Paper presented at the meeting of the Eastern Psychological Association, Boston, April 1967.

Hall, F. T., & Schroeder, M. P. Time spent on household tasks. *Journal of Home Economics*, 1970, **62**, 23–29.

Harlow, H., & Harlow, M. H. Learning to love. *American Scientist*, 1966, **54**, 244–272.

Hartley, R. E. Children's concepts of male and female roles. *Merrill-Palmer Quarterly*, 1960, **6**, 83–91.

Hartley, R. E. What aspects of child behavior should be studied in relation to maternal employment? In A. E. Siegel (Ed.), *Research issues related to the effects of maternal employment on children.* University Park, Penn.: Social Science Research Center, 1961.

Henshel, A. Anti-feminist bias in traditional measurements of masculinity-femininity. Paper presented at the meeting of the National Council on Family Relations, Estes Park, Colorado, August 1971.

Hess, H. Ethology and developmental psychology. In P. Mussen (Ed.), *Carmichael's manual of child psychology.* New York: Wiley, 1970.

Hoffman, L. W. *Effects of the employment of mothers on parental power relations and the division of household tasks.* Unpublished doctoral dissertation, University of Michigan, 1958.

Hoffman, L. W. Effects on children: Summary and discussion. In F. I. Nye & L. W. Hoffman (Eds.), *The employed mother in America.* Chicago: Rand McNally, 1963. (a)

Hoffman, L. W. Mother's enjoyment of work and effects on the child. In F. I. Nye & L. W. Hoffman (Eds.), *The employed mother in America.* Chicago: Rand McNally, 1963. (b)

Hoffman, L. W. Parental power relations and the division of household tasks. In F. I. Nye & L. W. Hoffman (Eds.), *The employed mother in America.* Chicago: Rand McNally, 1963. (c)

Hoffman, L. W. Early childhood experiences and women's achievement motives. *Journal of Social Issues*, 1972, **28**(2), 129–155.

Hoffman, L. W. The professional woman as mother. In R. B. Kundsin (Ed.), *A conference on successful women in the sciences*. New York: New York Academy of Sciences, 1973.

Hoffman, L. W., & Lippitt, R. The measurement of family life variables. In P. Mussen (Ed.), *Handbook of research methods in child development*. New York: Wiley, 1960.

Holmstrom, L. L. The two-career family. Paper presented at the conference of Women: Resource for a Changing World, Radcliffe Institute, Radcliffe College, Cambridge, April 1972.

Horner, M. S. Femininity and successful achievement: A basic inconsistency. In J. M. Bardwick, E. Douvan, M. S. Horner, & D. Gutman, *Feminine personality and conflict*. Belmont, Calif.: Brooks/Cole, 1972.

Hunt, J. McV. *Intelligence and experience*. New York: Ronald Press, 1961.

Johnson, C. L. *Leadership patterns in working and non-working mother middle class families*. (Doctoral dissertation, University of Kansas) Ann Arbor, Mich.: University Microfilms, 1969, No. 69–11, 224.

Jones, J. B., Lundsteen, S. W., & Michael, W. B. The relationship of the professional employment status of mothers to reading achievement of sixth-grade children. *California Journal of Educational Research*, 1967, **43**, 102–108.

Kagan, J. Continuity of cognitive development during the first year. *Merrill-Palmer Quarterly*, 1969, **15**, 101–119.

Kappel, B. E., & Lambert, R. D. Self worth among the children of working mothers. Unpublished manuscript, University of Waterloo, 1972.

Keidel, K. C. Maternal employment and ninth grade achievement in Bismarck, North Dakota. *Family Coordinator*, 1970, **19**, 95–97.

King, K., McIntyre, J., & Axelson, L. J. Adolescents' views of maternal employment as a threat to the marital relationship. *Journal of Marriage and the Family*, 1968, **30**, 633–637.

Kligler, D. The effects of employment of married women on husband and wife roles: A study in culture change. Unpublished doctoral dissertation, Yale University, 1954.

Kohn-Raz, R. Mental and motor development of kibbutz, institutionalized, and home-reared infants in Israel. *Child Development*, 1968, **39**, 489–504.

Kreisberg, L. *Mothers in poverty: A study of fatherless families*. Chicago: Aldine, 1970.

Lipman-Blumen, J. How ideology shapes women's lives. *Scientific American*, 1972, **226**(1), 34–42.

Levenstein, P. Cognitive growth in preschoolers through verbal interaction with mothers. *American Journal of Orthopsychiatry*, 1970, **40**, 426–432.

Levenstein, P. Verbal interaction project: Aiding cognitive growth in disadvantaged preschoolers through the Mother-Child Home Program July 1, 1967—August 31, 1970. Final report to Children's Bureau, Office of Child Development, U. S. Department of Health, Education, and Welfare, 1971. (Mimeo)

Levine, A. G. Marital and occupational plans of women in professional schools: Law, medicine, nursing, teaching. Unpublished doctoral dissertation, Yale University, 1968.

Lewis, M., & Goldberg, S. Perceptual-cognitive development in infancy: A generalized expectancy model as a function of the mother-infant interaction. *Merrill-Palmer Quarterly*, 1969, **15**, 81–100.

Low, S., & Spindler, P. *Child care arrangements of working mothers in the United States*. (Children's Bureau Publication 461) Washington, D.C.: U.S. Government Printing Office, 1968.

Lunneborg, P. W. Stereotypic aspect in masculinity-femininity measurement. Paper presented at the meeting of the American Psychological Association, San Francisco, September 1968.

Maccoby, E. E. Sex differences in intellectual functioning. In E. E. Maccoby (Ed.), *The development of sex differences*. Stanford, Calif.: Stanford University Press, 1966.

Maslow, A. H., Rand, H., & Newman, S. Some parallels between sexual and dominance behavior of infra-human primates and the fantasies of patients in psychotherapy. *Journal of Nervous and Mental Disease*, 1960, **131**, 202–212.

Mathews, S. M. The development of children's attitudes concerning mothers' out-of-home employment. *Journal of Educational Sociology*, 1933, **6**, 259–271.

McCord, W., & McCord, J. *Origins of crime.* New York: Columbia University Press, 1959.

McCord, J., McCord, W., & Thurber, E. Effects of maternal employment on lower-class boys. *Journal of Abnormal Social Psychology*, 1963, **67**, 177–182.

Meier, H. C. Mother-centeredness and college youths' attitudes toward social equality for women: Some empirical findings. *Journal of Marriage and the Family*, 1972, **34**, 115–121.

Moore, T. Children of working mothers. In S. Yudkin & H. Holme (Eds.), *Working mothers and their children.* London: Michael Joseph, 1963.

Moss, H. A. Sex, age, and state as determinants of mother-infant interaction. *Merrill-Palmer Quarterly*, 1967, **13**, 19–36.

Nelson, D. D. A study of school achievement among adolescent children with working and nonworking mothers. *Journal of Educational Research*, 1969, **62**, 456–457.

Nelson, D. D. A study of personality adjustment among adolescent children with working and nonworking mothers. *Journal of Educational Research*, 1971, **64**, 1328–1330.

Nolan, F. L. Effects on rural children. In F. I. Nye & L. W. Hoffman (Eds.), *The employed mother in America.* Chicago: Rand McNally, 1963.

Nye, F. I. *Family relationships and delinquent behavior.* New York: Wiley, 1958.

Nye, F. I. The adjustment of adolescent children. In F. I. Nye & L. W. Hoffman (Eds.), *The employed mother in America.* Chicago: Rand McNally, 1963.

Peterson, E. T. The impact of maternal employment on the mother-daughter relationship and on the daughter's role-orientation. Unpublished doctoral dissertation, University of Michigan, 1958.

Poloma, M. M. Role conflict and the married professional woman. In C. Safilios-Rothschild (Ed.), *Toward a sociology of women.* Lexington, Mass.: Xerox College Publishing, 1972.

Powell, K. Personalities of children and child-rearing attitudes of mothers. In F. I. Nye & L.W. Hoffman (Eds.), *The employed mother in America.* Chicago: Rand McNally, 1963.

Propper, A. M. The relationship of maternal employment to adolescent roles, activities, and parental relationships. *Journal of Marriage and the Family*, 1972, **34**, 417–421.

Rabkin, L. Y., & Rabkin, K. Children of the kibbutz. *Psychology Today*, 1969, **3**(4), 40.

Rapoport, R., & Rapoport, R. The dual-career family: A variant pattern and social change. In C. Safilios-Rothschild (Ed.), *Toward a sociology of women.* Lexington, Mass.: Xerox College Publishing, 1972.

Rees, A. N., & Palmer, F. H., Factors related to change in mental test performance. *Developmental Psychology Monograph*, 1970, **3**(2, Pt. 2).

Rheingold, H. The modification of social responsiveness in institutional babies. *Monographs of the Society for Research in Child Development*, 1956, **21**(2, Serial No. 63).

Rheingold, H., & Bayley, N. The later effects of an experimental modification of mothering. *Child Development*, 1959, **52**, 68–73.

Rheingold, H., Gewirtz, J. L., & Ross, H. W. Social conditioning of vocalizations in the infant. *Journal of Comparative and Physiological Psychology*, 1959, **52**, 68–73.

Rieber, M., & Womack, M. The intelligence of preschool children as related to ethnic and demographic variables. *Exceptional Children*, 1968, **34**, 609–614.

Riege, M. G. Parental affection and juvenile delinquency in girls. *The British Journal of Criminology*, 1972, **12**, 55–73.

Robinson, J. B. Historical changes in how people spend their time. In A. Michel (Ed.), *Family issues of employed women in Europe and America.* Leiden, Netherlands: E. J. Brill, 1971.

Roethlisberger, F. J., & Dickson, W. J. *Business Research Studies.* Cambridge, Mass.: Harvard Business School, Division of Research, 1939.

Roy, P. Adolescent roles: Rural-urban differentials. In F. I. Nye & L. W. Hoffman (Eds.), *The employed mother in America.* Chicago: Rand McNally, 1963.

Siegel, A. E., & Haas, M. B. The working mother: A review of research. *Child Development*, 1963, **34**, 513–542.

Smith. H. C. *An investigation of the attitudes of adolescent girls toward combining marriage, motherhood and a career.* (Doctoral dissertation, Columbia University) Ann Arbor, Mich.: University Microfilms, 1969, No. 69–8089.

Spiro, M. E. *Children of the kibbutz.* New York: Schocken Books, 1965.

Spitz, R. A. Hospitalism: An inquiry into the genesis of psychiatric conditions in early childhood. *Psychoanalytic Studies of the Child.* 1945, **1**, 53–74.

Stolz, L. M. Effects of maternal employment on children: Evidence from research. *Child Development*, 1960, **31**, 749–782.

Szolai, A. The multinational comparative time budget: A venture in international research cooperation. *American Behavioral Scientist*, 1966, **10**, 1–31.

Tangri, S. S. Role innovation in occupational choice. Unpublished doctoral dissertation, University of Michigan, 1969.

Tizard, B., Cooperman, O., Joseph, A., & Tizard, J. Environmental effects on language development: A study of young children in long-stay residential nurseries. *Child Development*, 1972, **43**, 337–358.

U. S. Department of Labor, Women's Bureau. *Who are the working mothers?* (Leaflet 37) Washington, D. C.: U.S. Government Printing Office, 1972.

Vogel, S. R., Broverman, I. K., Broverman, D. M., Clarkson, F. E., & Rosenkrantz, P. S. Maternal employment and perception of sex roles among college students. *Developmental Psychology*, 1970, **3** 384–391.

Von Mering, F. H. Professional and non-professional women as mothers. *Journal of Social Psychology*, 1955, **42**, 21–34.

Walker, K. E. How much help for working mothers?: The children's role. *Human Ecology Forum*, 1970, **1**(2), 13–15. (a)

Walker, K. E. Time-use patterns for household work related to homemakers' employment. Paper presented at the meeting of the Agricultural Outlook Conference, Washington, D. C., February 1970. (b)

Walker, K. E., & Woods, M. E. Time use for care of family members. (Use-of-time Research Project, working paper 1) Unpublished manuscript, Cornell University, 1972.

Weil, M. W. An analysis of the factors influencing married women's actual or planned work participation. *American Sociological Review*, 1961, **26**, 91–96.

Winterbottom, M. R. The relation of need for achievement to learning experiences in independence and mastery. In J. W. Atkinson (Ed.), *Motives in fantasy, action, and society.* Princeton: Van Nostrand, 1958.

Woods, M. B. The unsupervised child of the working mother. *Developmental Psychology*, 1972, **6**, 14–25.

Wortis, R. P. The acceptance of the concept of the maternal role by behavioral scientists: Its effects on women. *American Journal of Orthopsychiatry*, 1971, **41**, 733–746.

Yarrow, L. J. Separation from parents during early childhood. In M. L. Hoffman & L. W. Hoffman (Eds), *Review of child development research.* New York: Russell Sage Foundation, 1964.

Yarrow, M. R., Scott, P., DeLeeuw, L., & Heinig, C. Child-rearing in families of working and non-working mothers. *Sociometry*, 1962, **25**, 122–140.

Yudkin, S., & Holme, A. *Working mothers and their children.* London: Michael Joseph, 1963.

Zissis, C. A study of the life planning of 550 freshman women at Purdue University. *Journal of the National Association of Women Deans and Counselors*, 1964, **28**, 153–159.

Part Five

Adolescence

Chapter 13

Physical and Mental Development

WHAT IS ADOLESCENCE?

Cultural Factors in Adolescence

Committee on Adolescence, Group for the Advancement of Psychiatry

It has been suggested that in Samoa adolescence is relatively free of stress and turmoil because Samoan culture allows its young people considerable freedom in their sexual behavior.

Editor's Introduction

There are three major factors which influence human development: biological, cultural, and psychological. The selection which follows discusses the social forces which influence adolescent development in various cultures throughout the world as well as in subcultural groups within our own society. In addition, the selection discusses the influence of adolescents on their own culture.

The authors of this selection would argue that psychological adolescence does not necessarily parallel the physical development of adolescence but is a cultural phenomenon produced by a delay in the assumption of adult roles.

Adolescence in the United States is becoming more and more prolonged. We now see children beginning the social functions of adolescence while still chronologically and biologically in childhood. We also see, at the other end of the continuum, individuals who are chronologically and biologically adults still functioning as adolescents, unable to make a commitment to career or to family. Not by their own shortcomings but by the impositions of prolonged education, career preparation, and economic sanctions, they are unable to join the work force and to make a commitment to other human beings. These young people certainly have the capacity for committing themselves but are kept from doing so by what are primarily cultural influences. Our society has a very prolonged period of subadult status. The psychiatric definition of adolescence includes the ages of 11 to 21. In our culture, however, if adolescence is to be defined by cultural roles, it actually may cover a period from approximately age 9 or 10 through age 30.

The fact that cultures differ to a great degree in the way that they facilitate or inhibit adolescent development and the attainment of adult status is the topic of the following article. The discussion includes cultures as diverse as those of the Dobuans of Melanesia and the middle class of America. While the differences are enormous, the similarities should not be overlooked. All adolescents, regardless of cultural background, seem to share certain universals: all adolescents appear to function under the incest taboo, all have the task of separating from the family of origin and moving toward a family of procreation, and all adolescents are expected to learn how to work and to love rather than being taken care of as they were as children.

Pamela Cantor

CULTURE AS "ENVIRONMENT" IN ADOLESCENCE

In considering adolescence, one tends to have implicit preconceptions derived from his own adolescence in his own culture. But the categories of culture cannot be taken as absolute or inevitable. Cultural "environments" differ enormously and in startling ways, and they produce discernibly different standard adults. National temperament—for example, British reserve or French vivacity—is much more the result of different cultural expectancies and procedures toward children and adolescents than it is of racial heredity. Furthermore, because a society can apply pressure and produce stress in many areas of human development, different cultures can produce different character types and can even cause their own characteristic range and incidence of psychopathologic individuals or standardized deviants.

Basically, however, the cultural forms of each society must take their origin from the physiological differences between child and adult; they are shaped to deal with the contrasting biological tasks of childhood and of adulthood—being nurtured and providing nurture. But societies differ widely in their handling of both biological and status change. Physical maturity and status maturity are by no means the same. Self and society often appear to be antagonists, because society does require and attempt to enforce upon the individual varying kinds and degrees of suppression and control of the sexual and aggressive drives. Because of their different value systems, human societies seem almost to be unwitting experiments in the possibilities of "human nature," much as the nuclear family is the laboratory of individual personality.

To illustrate the wide divergence of adult functioning in a biological and psychological sense, and of adult-status "maturity," a striking example is given by the Mentawei of western Indonesia. Among the Mentawei a man may procreate a biological family, but only when his children are grown enough to support him can he formally adopt the children, marry their mother, and retire to the workless, semireligious status of father of a family. Here there is a spectacular lag of decades between functioning physiological maturity and a fully adult status accorded by society—far more of a lag, even, than in our own society. The system works well to gain Mentawei economic ends, for the man is motivated to produce and serve a family and to be faithful to one woman lest he lose the opportunity to finally get married and thus achieve full adult status.

Again, as far as the status of social fatherhood is concerned, biological fathers among the Nayar of Malabar never achieve this in a family of procreation; they remain lifelong unmarried *ciscisbei* (the male counterpart of concubines) of the mother. Instead, "fatherly" economic and social responsibilities come to a male by virtue of his uterine brotherhood to a mother from the same family of origin—i.e., to his sister. The biologic responsibilities of adult males and females to children are the same, since these are universal to the species, but they are redistributed from the family of procreation (which is our norm) to the family of origin. This economic and status displacement of the father by the maternal uncle, which is widespread in Oceania and elsewhere, derives from differing cultural emphases upon family of origin versus family of procreation. By way of contrast, our society nowadays minimizes the extended or kinship family but maximizes the marital family or family of procreation.

Sexual-functioning maturity and adult-status maturity are also widely disparate in the Polynesian cultures. Here social status and authority accrue to the first-born of first-born lineage, the eldest son of the senior lineage being the living embodiment of the ancestor god and repository of the *mana* of divine kingship, a status hedged about by taboos. Younger sons in successive lineages make up the pyramid of society, the youngest sons of the most junior lineages being at the bottom of the heap. Along with this social structure, many Polynesian societies have an institutionalized youth group, the *kahioi*, who provide feasts, entertainment, and sexual hospitality to tribal vistors. Sexual functioning is by no means prohibited to the youth group, but they must remain unmarried and childless to stay in it. Nor is membership in the youth group a function of chronological age. Thus there may be a younger son in a junior lineage who had tentatively married, later divorced his wife, killed his children, and rejoined the youth group—a *kahioi* 40 or 50 years old who never made the grade to social-status adulthood. The sop of irresponsible and promiscuous sexuality is thrown to the *kahioi*, of whatever age, but he never achieves the social status of founder of a lineage. Sexual-functioning maturity and social-status maturity thus are quite different from each other in societies with *kahioi*. Sexual potential is biologically given, but status must be socially achieved and accorded—as, indeed, in all societies. *Kahioi* may be remotely related culturally to the custom of the Nambutiri Brahmans of Malabar, among whom strict primogeniture (granting a special status to the first-born son) allows only the eldest son to marry, the younger sons becoming the statusless *ciscisbei* of Nayar women.

Throughout Oceania the emphasis, in general, is on status, not on sexual functioning, as the criterion of adulthood. In much of Oceania, pubescent boys can no longer sleep in their parents' house but must creep into the houses of eligible girls and sleep with them, and creep out again before dawn. Premarital "sleep-crawling" is also found among the Dobuans of Melanesia, where the line of descent is via the maternal side of the family. The boy continues this practice until he is "captured" in marriage by the girl's family, whereupon economic responsibilities are thrust upon him. In parts of Borneo even a husband must "sleep-crawl" to his wife, under pain of ridicule and embarrassment if caught. Here his sexual prerogative is officially discountenanced, but not his status as socio-economic husband; and here, as among the Mentawei, it is the man who is struggling for the status of marriage, not the woman, as in Western societies.

Nevertheless, universals do remain in the contrast of children and adults. Regardless of how the tasks of child-rearing are redistributed among various status and function categories, the tasks must still be carried out. Socio-economic responsibility for children, rather than sexual reproduction per se, would seem perhaps the ultimate criterion of adult status in most of the world.

WESTERN CULTURE AS ENVIRONMENT IN ADOLESCENCE

In our culture, there exist a profusion and a confusion of different function definitions and status definitions of adulthood. In the category of status criteria, there is a whole range of different ages at which one becomes officially an adult in one manner but not necessarily in others. The first is the age of 12, after which one is an "adult" as regards theaters, movie houses, airlines, and so on. This first change of status confers no privileges whatsoever, only the penalty of having to pay more. The next general age post is 16. At this age, in most states, a person can obtain a driver's license; and he is released from many of the restrictions of the child labor laws. Both of these changes of status essentially do permit increased adult privileges. The young person does not have to work but may do so under certain conditions if he wishes. His legal right to drive is generally as unrestricted as that of his elders, but equivalent legal adult responsi-

bility for his driving is seldom expected or enforced by the courts.

An even greater status change occurs at age 18. Males are then adults by decree of Congress for purposes of war and are subject to the draft. This is also the age after which, in many but not all states, young people may marry without parental consent. Often, however, they may legally toast their marriage only with beer—not with stronger alcoholic beverages. Thus we have the status paradox of the married soldier who may not enter a bar and drink, and who cannot vote, but who can procreate and kill. A girl at this age, again in most but not all states, may now consent to sexual intercourse, from the standpoint of law. If she were to have intercourse while younger than age 18, she would be considered to have been raped, regardless of the circumstances.

The final status change comes at age 21, when all the privileges and responsibilities of adulthood are legally invested in the young man or woman. The right to vote, the right to drink, eligibility for most public offices, the ability to enter into a binding financial contract, and full penalties for criminal transgressions—all are attendant upon reaching one's majority. Formal adult legal status should not be confused with the various levels of adult function or of respect status, which may continue to mount throughout life. The dean of a law school or the president of a mammoth corporation has no more legally conferred privileges and responsibilities because of age alone than does the 21-year-old undergraduate or café waitress.

In the category of function criteria, the definitions of adulthood in our culture are infinitely more complex and confused. Very few 12-year-old airline passengers who pay an adult's fare fulfill any adult role. Many 14-year-old girls are capable of bearing children and thus of functioning sexually as adults, yet there are no status categories to make this meaningful. Indeed, this functional capacity carries only potential penalty. The previously cited late-teenager soldier is a perfect example of an individual functioning as an adult in many roles without actually having full adult status. Conversely, the automatic investiture of full adult status at age 21 in no way guarantees that all such individuals will function as adults, emotionally or otherwise.

Earlier we defined functional adulthood as the assumption of one or more of the responsibilities for self, mate, offspring, and society. From this point of view, adult function after the mid-teens is quite unrelated to age, which is the basis for our definition of adult status. Many an 18-year-old is self-sufficient, yet many 23-year-olds are still in school and partly or totally dependent. These same 23-year-old graduate students may have wives and children and may admirably fulfill many family responsibilities even while unable to support themselves. In the more highly specialized professions, a man may not be fully self-sufficient—that is, as an economically functioning adult—until his middle or late 30s, in spite of his having otherwise functioned as an adult quite well for as long as 15 years.

Adult function and adult status appear to find definition in a series of stages, and the two are integrated but little or not at all. The social definition of a functioning adult would seem to be achieved in Western civilization when he first assumes full responsibility for himself. This generally follows the attainment of a relatively stable mental and emotional equilibrium, a characteristic of the psychological offset of adolescence. Ordinarily, responsibilities are assumed for self, mate, offspring, and society in that order. For purposes of cross-cultural comparisons of adolescence and its psychological resolution, definitions of adult function would appear to be more basic and useful than formal definitions of adult status. The nature, quality, and timing of an individual's function are much more dependent upon

his inner conflicts and his solutions of them than is his status, which may, as in our culture, be awarded or withheld despite function.

UNIVERSAL TASKS OF ADOLESCENCE

Are there any universals in the tasks of adolescence that transcend cultural differences and thus apply to all individuals? It has already been noted that man is a learning animal, and all adolescents therefore must learn, though what they learn differs from one culture to another. Also, the incest taboo is universal and, in general, relates to all parents and their children; in its basic form—the taboo on mother-son incest—there is no known exception. Thus, the adolescent has enforced upon him the invariable task of moving from his family of origin to a different (his own) family of procreation; to assume adult procreative function, he must sever close ties with the nuclear family and establish them with blood strangers. Another common denominator is the change from being nurtured to providing nurture. Finally, regardless of the surrounding culture, each adolescent normally is expected to learn how to work and how to love, both of these abilities being necessary to his functioning as an adult.

Biologically, the same needs and drives exist throughout the species; culturally, alternative modes are offered for their satisfaction; and psychologically, in the effort to reconcile his drives with cultural decrees, the adolescent in any culture employs previously developed, identical defense mechanisms such as repression, denial, and projection.

CULTURAL FACILITATION AND INHIBITION AT ADOLESCENCE

Each society has cultural commitments it regards as good. These commitments may not, in truth, be appropriate to the current world of reality, and certainly adolescents may not always regard them as immediately desirable. Nevertheless, the problem for society persists: how to fit new organisms into the older cultural context, how to make individuals achieve the kinds of discipline over their sexual and aggressive drives which are prescribed, preferred, or adaptive in a specific society and culture.

But it is just here that adult cultural judgment is so diverse and variable. Christian culture, for example, requires a relatively heavy repression and denial of direct aggressive drives. The individual is expected to cope with his aggressive drives only through a variety of defensive maneuvers. Among them are projection of his own inner self onto external forces such as "bad" teachers or officers of the law; self-disapproval for harboring sinful, destructive thoughts; sublimation into competitive endeavor such as dancing or sports; or identification with cultural heroes. By contrast, however, in some head-hunting and cannibalistic Indonesian and Melanesian groups, the direct expression of aggression is demanded and enforced to such a degree as to arouse anxieties in the individual which require containment through ritual, or expression in bizarre but (for the society) standardized, psychotic (insane) behavior. Similarly, the cultural demands for stylized aggression in Plains Indian warfare were often enough such an intolerable psychic burden for the individual as to create a standardized social deviant, the berdache: the "not-man," who may hunt, marry, and even procreate children but who wears women's clothes and who can never go on the warpath to take scalps—or to risk his own. If the critical definition of a man in the Plains is a male person who goes on the warpath and takes scalps, then the berdache is a "not-man" and must be socially so signalized in his clothing, no matter what his activities as a male. Similarly, if head-taking is the criterion of ritual manhood or the requirement for marriage in

the Wa States, Borneo, or New Guinea, then of course many males will attempt this cultural hurdle, at whatever individual psychic cost. Perhaps it is well that an adolescent now and again questions the goals proffered him by the adults in his society.

Cultures differ considerably in the way they facilitate or inhibit the attainment of full maturity. Many primitive societies appear to begrudge adult status and to demand that the individual prove his manhood in various ways from scalp-collecting or head-hunting to undergoing a painful and threatening puberty ordeal, with various bodily, significantly often genital, mutilations. And it may be that the least stressful and psychologically most secure way of achieving adult status is to be made a man, magically, by the puberty ordeal or initiation. If the skin, teeth, or genitals are altered in the process, one at least has, so to speak, a documented bodily proof of his adult status, and if the puberty ordeal contains threatening elements, they are at least circumscribed and delimited in time. A similar but more refined example from Jewish culture is the bar mitzvah ceremony.

Adolescence may be stressful, then, not solely for biological reasons but because of the pressures and demands that culture exerts upon the developing child. It has been suggested that in Samoa adolescence is relatively free of stress and turmoil because the Samoan culture allows its young people considerable freedom in their sexual behavior. Here, the physiological and the functional aspects of sexuality tend to coincide in the individual's life cycle, and his psychological problems are not focused around sexuality. If the function of eating, instead of sexual functioning, were the focus of massive cultural repressions and prohibitions, then eating might become a greater focus than sex for the development of emotional disturbance.

It is conceivable that cultural values for which there was a valid reason at one time—

for example, sanctions for virginity associated with the custom of wife purchase, or the complete prohibition of premarital sexual relations at a time when conception and venereal diseases could not be controlled—may warrant re-evaluation when social, economic, and technological conditions have changed.

Again in Samoa, the gap between adult and child functions is minimized by the custom of having slightly elder siblings rather than adults provide the most immediate care for younger brothers and sisters. Consequently there is no great disparity in age and power between socializer and socialized, and this may help explain why Samoans have less anguish over power struggles than do Americans, in whose childhood the parents, comparatively, are omnipresent and seemingly omnipotent.

In much of Negro Africa, life membership in the same successively promoted "age group" achieves transition to adult status for the individual not only with the reassuring mutual example of peers but also with the powerful support of the adult culture. This system may suffer, however, for lack of individual freedom, spontaneity, variety, and adaptive social change. Initiation, a painful and threatening ordeal, may successfully achieve only the "authoritarian personality" of tribal orthodoxy and a compulsive, unreflecting loyalty to tradition.

For adolescents, *rites de passage* undoubtedly ease status transitions psychologically, and, in effect, such "rites" are provided in our culture. Qualifying for a driver's license at age 16 is essentially a *rite de passage*, certainly so in the mind of the adolescent. Again, the bar mitzvah is a socially useful and psychologically meaningful ritual in a tradition that emphasizes patriarchal leadership and responsibility. Similarly, in societies that emphasize the importance of virginity, a young woman may need a church wedding with all of its accoutrements in order to dramatize psychologically her marked change of status. The male, some-

what less burdened with sexual repression, may well be content with a marriage before a civil magistrate. Perhaps job and fatherhood represent more critical areas for the young male adult than does sexuality, for it is in job and fatherhood that his important status tests lie. It is of interest to note that adolescents often invent their own *rites de passage*, such as "joining the crowd" in drinking to the point of nausea or stupefaction, or submitting to the primitive hazing practices associated with achieving membership in a college fraternity.

It is in relative terms, then, that one must consider adolescence in contemporary Judaeo-Christian culture and attempt to understand its manifestations and significance. This cannot be accomplished with any degree of completeness or finality. Not only is the magnitude of the task overwhelming, but the conditions of our culture and of our reality are constantly changing, and today's observations and conclusions soon belong to yesterday. Nevertheless, we may be able to sketch the matrix of our culture in relation to adolescence as it currently exists.

ADOLESCENCE IN THE AMERICAN MIDDLE CLASS

There are a number of reasons for choosing to focus discussion on the American middle-class culture and the adolescent of that culture: the middle class embraces the greatest proportion of our population; middle-class cultural attitudes are more widespread and affect more people than do those of any firmly delineated subcultural groups; and more reliable information is available about middle-class adolescence. Other class and regional, subcultural differences, of course, need to be taken into account. For example, southern Appalachian personality, bred in isolated, homogeneous rural culture, has a fundamentalist stolidity which, by comparison, makes urban middle-class excitability and restlessness appear as something antic; and, conversely, these Southern rural whites seem to be appallingly lacking in the motivations and goals of urban, middle-class culture. In urban Negro ghettos, individual "success," in middle-class terms, depends far more upon accidental emotional factors, relationship to authority, and opportunities for identification than upon a given family of origin. Siblings in the same family may therefore very widely in their career trajectories.

Subcultural mores always somewhat overlap the main body of any culture, just as minority attitudes inject themselves into, and complicate, any generalizations about majority opinions. This discussion, therefore, will have some application outside of the middle-class majority. At the same time we are fully cognizant of the unavoidable oversimplification and overgeneralization attendant upon any brief discussion of so immense a phenomenon as the American middle class.

Certain qualities and distinguishing features help define and characterize adolescence in the American middle class. Of major importance are the facts that adolescence is a well-delineated stage of development and that adolescents form a special, self-conscious status group. This is by no means true in all cultures. Perhaps at no other time in history and in no other culture could one find so much attention being focused upon the adolescents. Products, advertising, entertainment, books, and newspaper columns are often designed for and aimed at this particular age group, and today they offer a special market and wield tremendous purchasing power. At one time a 15-year-old would have been referred to as a child or a youngster, but now he is known as a teenager—a term that denotes a large, influential, and important status group. The teenager has become very conscious of his special status. He is eager for the accompanying privileges, impatient or downright defiant of the restrictions, and not a little cocky about the vaguely defined power his group wields.

Closely related to the status of adolescents as a separate group is their intense and almost exclusive allegiance to the peer group. The adolescent peer group has its own forms and standards for fashions, fads, dancing, music, recreation, dating practices, vocabulary, etc., and all of this appears to be quite impervious to adult influence. This description is not limited only to the overtly rebellious adolescents. It portrays a frame of mind which is more or less characteristic of all adolescents, even those who are outwardly compliant.

The peer group is particularly important as a strong support to teenagers, both individually and collectively, in their characteristic questioning and challenging of adult values and cultural institutions. Younger children may protest and rebel, but their dependency and immaturity keep them much more closely tied to their parents than to their peers. Adolescents are able, then, to subject the cultural values learned in earlier childhood to a careful and sometimes devastating scrutiny and criticism to determine their applicability to the world of today, as it seen by adolescents. Some adolescents appear not to accept any adult values, even superficially; some pass through a phase of experimentation with many different value systems, as a part of their search for identity; some feel the necessity of accepting adult values so as to survive in an adult-defined world; some achieve a close, positive identification with adults and their values but then fear loss of their newly developing independence and autonomy through absorption by the adult.

Another distinguishing feature of middle-class adolescence is what might be called its "hiatus status." Adolescents are no longer considered to be children, and yet they are not really expected to take their position in the adult world. They have some adult privileges (status) but are not expected to take on full adult responsibilities (functions). Though this hiatus status has many frustrating aspects, it also has some tempting gratifications. The transgressions of adolescents, even those which occur within such categories of adult status as driving, are often looked upon with tolerance. Adolescents are not usually required to assume full financial responsibility for themselves. Even though a boy may be earning enough money to meet his own expenses, most middle-class parents still expect to continue paying some of the bills. Of those adolescents who achieve the adult status of being married, thereby becoming legally emancipated, many still will receive a large degree of economic support from their parents, because the young husband or wife or both are in school. Adolescents may even succumb to the seductive and persuasive temptation to remain adolescent, enjoying a large measure of adult status and privilege while avoiding the responsibilities implied in acceptance of the adult role. Such over-aged, "professional" adolescents are a unique by-product of this particular aspect of our culture, and they contrast sharply with those ambitious adolescents who are impatient to enter the adult world and assume all of the adult responsibilities.

The hiatus status of adolescence with the granting of many adult privileges to those still technically adolescent leads to a paradoxically reversed situation. The acceleration of the granting of privileges to young people has the effect of telescoping the generations and obscuring adult-child differences. Examples may be seen in the earlier dating, increased buying power, and greater mobility of adolescents today. This quasi-adulthood does not make adults of adolescents, nor does it negate adolescent status. But it does strip adulthood of many of its traditionally distinguishing prerogatives.

Middle-class attitudes toward individuality versus conformity also may provide the basis for conflict. Traditionally, American society has stressed freedom of the individual, including choice of career. Self-fulfillment in an open society which provides "vertical mobil-

ity" means "finding oneself" in one of many fully accessible roles suitable to the special capacities of the individual. This frequently requires repudiation and leaving behind one's group of origin. Our history books inculcate in the child an admiration for the self-determined, often rebellious individuals who indeed greatly shaped our world through their very individuality. Today, however, our society also places a considerable emphasis on adaptive conformity, whether mediated unconsciously in training or even as an overtly stated goal: in order to "get ahead" one must "fit in" and not be too different. Adolescents are aware of the contradictory nature of these parental and cultural attitudes and tend to see them as an example of adult hypocrisy. They often feel that the pursuit of either one of these goals, individuality or conformity, incurs disapproval, and they find it difficult to embrace both at once. The implied freedom of choice necessary to the unique individuation which our culture so much desires appears to the adolescent to be countermanded by the emphasis on conformity. The result is frustration and conflict, or an avoidance of conflict by "choosing" to go in one direction or the other.

A primary determinant to middle-class adolescence is the fact that middle-class society is organized so exclusively around the nuclear family as opposed to the extended family. The biological mother and father and their offspring live together in a home which usually is not shared with others, and nearly all of the discipline and the culturally determined attitudes about child-rearing are conveyed to the child by his parents, at least during the preschool years. While our culture is still officially patrilineal (line of descent via the male side of the family), kinship ties tend nowadays to be important only legally. Paternal and maternal roles may be delegated (usually quite temporarily), but are not routinely distributed beyond the biological mother and father to other relatives. The increasing tendency for married couples to move away from their place of birth and to live separately from their elders and relatives further reduces the significance of relatives to the children. Elder siblings are required to carry little or no responsibility for the care of the younger children, and parents tend to regard the children as being equal to each other regardless of age. This family configuration means that children grow up in a society of competitive siblings or playmates, a kind of status group distinctly separate from the mother and father. And it also means that the children direct most of their conflict and aggression toward the biological parents rather than toward a multiplicity of parent surrogates. This early childhood period, in which culture and authority are mediated primarily by the parents, sets the stage for later childhood and adolescence. So, when other persons of authority come into a child's life, he perceives them more as extensions or copies of the parents than as new and different individuals, and cultural values and institutions also tend to be seen only as they were interpreted by the parents.

Another of the major cultural influences on adolescence is our "middle-class morality." This term includes morals in their usual sense, their derivatives in child-rearing techniques and attitudes, and, most particularly, the shifting of values so clearly observable in contemporary middle-class society. Some moral issues have intensified in significance, others have declined. Many attitudes that used to be bulwarks of society, such as the unquestioning belief in a traditional religion, have diminished as truly shaping forces.

The weakening of conviction and belief in the established value systems also contributes to the inconsistency between proclaimed attitudes and observable behavior. For better or worse the "official" standards always change more slowly than actual behavior. Whereas attitudes favoring greater sexual freedom can be discerned among some of the clergy as well as others who seriously appraise the morality of our culture, the long-established, prohibitive standards continue to be vigorously defended. The virtue of virginity, the ideal of sexual abstinence and "purity" until marriage, the concepts of carnal sin and "dirty" sex still are a part of the proclaimed ethic in a large proportion of our society. The same is true of the strong taboo against the direct expression of aggression, although aggression does not carry the same degree of reproach as does sexuality.

Middle-class culture, of course, is not monolithic in sexual attitudes. There are sizable segments of the population, particularly the more sophisticated adults in the larger urban areas, that openly disagree with the prohibitive morality of their parents and grandparents and that try to rear their children accordingly. But most observers would regard these elements as exponents of change rather than as arbiters of current majority attitudes. Middle-class culture, for the most part, does not provide for a guilt-free orgastic sexual outlet between puberty and marriage.

One result of this kind of morality is that the adolescent has both the tremendous task of controlling his sexual feelings and urges, and the heavy burden of guilt arising from the almost inevitable failure to do so. Referring again to the emphasis middle-class culture places on the nuclear family, it seems likely that this plays an important role in intensifying the adolescent sexual conflict by focusing virtually all of the developing child's sexual feelings on his biological parents.

Adolescents find it very difficult to live by the culturally prescribed sexual morality, and they often pay a high price emotionally in attempting to do so. Many have just about given up making the effort, for no one whose childhood was lived in the context of a prohibitive morality can be really free of its legacy of sexual guilt. The nature of the dilemma determines the standard variations of adolescent efforts at solution of the problem: rebellion against sexual ethics and denial of conscience;

early dependent marriage; early marriage with withdrawal from the socio-economic struggle; repudiation of sexual prohibitions in good faith and sincerity but with unavoidable unconscious guilt; subordination of sex to, and contamination of sex with, competitive goals; or strong repression of sexuality, with the likelihood of subsequent mental or emotional disorder. The attitudes of middle-class culture make it very nearly impossible for adolescents to employ, in a healthy way, the alternatives to such modes of behavior, namely, masturbation or sexual intimacies with the opposite sex, appropriate to the individual's age and degree of emotional maturity.

This generalized view of middle-class morality as being prohibitive and inhibitive may seem to be contradicted by the obvious current emphasis upon sex in our culture. Note the content of much of what is expressed through the media of mass communication and the child-rearing practices of many parents who condone and sometimes foster such things as dating and the wearing of make-up and sexually provocative clothing at a very early age. These attitudes usually are more sexually stimulating than truly permissive, however, and they tend only to add to the sexual conflict. In most families, particularly in some subcultural groups, the line is firmly drawn at sexual intercourse, or even at masturbation. The degree of sexual behavior which is permitted also differs for boys as against girls. For the girl it is competitive "sexiness," not functional sexuality, that is fostered. The attitude of many adults is paraphrased in the expression, "Hang your clothes on a hickory limb but don't go near the water."

DISCONTINUITY OF ROLE FROM CHILDHOOD TO ADULTHOOD

While there are obvious biological and functional differences between child and adult, cultures may polarize these distinctions to the detriment of individual growth. This can happen if the child and adult roles are defined in such a rigid and sharply contrasting way that one role does not lead naturally and logically into the other. Similarly, contradictory training may interfere with normal role maturation. As adulthood approaches, difficulties in adjustment are likely to confront the adolescent who has been too stringently inculcated with attitudes of dependency, obedience, and abstinence from sexual behavior; particularly so when the criteria of success in adulthood are independence, self-direction, assumption of responsibility, and sexual performance. Thus an adolescent who has adapted too well in his role as a child and has become too comfortable with it finds it difficult to assume his new role as an adult.

It is possible, then, that our social forms are not as well-suited for training children to become adults as for training them to be successful children. For the adolescent, these contrastively defined roles tend to place him in the position of being damned if he tries to act like an adult and damned if he doesn't. As a result, adolescents become "problems" to adults as well as to themselves.

The Papago Indians, among others, achieve a more successful continuity of role training; even the small child is rewarded for economic and other behavior befitting the future adult, and thus he begins in childhood to be trained for successful adulthood. This does not mean that the adult must abdicate the responsibilities of adulthood, or cease to be a model for the child, or pretend to a spurious and seductive siblinghood with the child (as in wanting to be regarded as a pal rather than a parent). It does mean that whatever training is imposed upon a child will be carried by him into adulthood, and that he and his society will suffer if the training ill fits the child for the adult world.

These brief comments indicate in part the degree of interaction of definitive cultural attitudes and adolescence. A further dimension is added when some cultural institutions have in fact begun to lose meaning and force for the adults who continue to uphold them. The adolescent is a particularly sharp observer of adult culture, and even the most casual observation reveals a decreasing adherence to the Judaeo-Christian ethic, which is still the "official" ethic of our culture. The adolescent perceives that such things as financial success, respectability, and the holding of public office often seem to bear little relationship to the individual's ethical behavior, and that failure to live by traditional values is not necessarily followed by unpleasant consequences.

It has been suggested that it is not frustration alone that makes children neurotic, but also the lack of ultimate cultural rewards for the frustration the child must endure. Clearly, middle-class adolescents are often caught in this trap. There was once a time (though this could sound like a fairy tale to today's young people) when a person could plan his future on the basis of commitments made during and at the end of adolescence. Certain things in the community happened to those who accepted and at least tried to live by the cultural values. If these things were important to the young person, he knew how to get them. The approved modes of harnessing one's instinctual drives had practical and demonstrable meaning. Quite other life paths lay open to those who repudiated middle-class morality, and quite other consequences, too, which were edifyingly visible and sure. The two types of life commitment were mutually exclusive.

This description perhaps is overgeneralized but, nonetheless, there is an important difference between an adult society that as a whole believes in and tries to live by its own moral values and one that does not. There is often little consonance between the expressed middle-class values and actual adult behavior. Caught in their own confusion, adults may be at a loss to demonstrate to adolescents any consistent rewards in their own lives which derive from accepting the "official" ethic. The

adult world therefore often appears to adolescent eyes to operate upon principles contrary to honesty and other espoused cultural values.

Ours is a competitive technological society, and this fact also shapes the adolescent stage of development. The adult world places emphasis upon winning the struggle for status and position, and since the outcome rather than the means is emphasized, ability is often subordinated to agility. A society in which vertical social mobility is not only possible but applauded, automatically makes such advancement a high-priority goal. Children very early are initiated into this mêlée through the competitive sibling structure of our nuclear family unit, and are kept aware of this orientation throughout their school and playground activities. Grading systems also maintain this emphasis, and thoughtful teachers of adolescents complain that the real goal of many of their pupils is "second-guessing" the teacher and getting the grades, rather than learning for the sake of its lasting benefits.

Increasing technology, with its demand for more and more education, before one is eligible to compete, meanwhile adds to the real tasks of adolescence. There are fewer and fewer jobs for the unskilled and semiskilled, and those young people who cannot or do not accept the challenge of gaining an adequate education generally are doomed to a substandard socio-economic existence. On the other hand, the demand for more and more education and the resulting longer period of dependency exist alongside the relatively unchanging prohibitions against adolescent sexuality. Thus the gap between physical sexual maturity and the socio-economic readiness for self-sufficiency and marriage becomes still wider.

Some adolescent problems that are insignificant or invisible in more primitive societies loom quite large, and understandably so, in our society. One of these is the problem of identity. In simple societies that offer only two sex-defined role models there is little problem.

The quest for identity is a problem, however, in the more complex cultures which are characterized by rapid social change, so that the father may become outmoded as a model for his son; by geographic mobility, so that cultural models are constantly changing; by emphasis on individuality with great freedom of choice; by a high degree of complexity, in which there are many models from which to choose; and by "classlessness," wherein everyone strives to upgrade his social status. The fact that these conditions pose problems for the adolescent in his quest for identity is counterbalanced, however, by the fact that they also offer a richness of choice which our culture certainly would not wish to forego.

All of these factors complicating the adolescents' search for identity exist in our middle-class culture, and simultaneously increase both the rewards and the burdens of the task. Such a multiplicity of possible future selves has probably seldom before been available to eager, healthy youngsters. The adolescent clearly knows of these relatively limitless choices that have been constantly in evidence throughout his childhood years. But identity by no means automatically accrues to the individual as he grows older. Thus there arises not only the time-consuming necessity to experiment and choose, but also the possibility for neurotic conflict and inappropriate choice.

A further complication to the task of establishing identity lies in the increasing diffusion of male and female parental roles and the blurring of the traditional lines of distinction between the sexes. The mother and father both may be working, and in many cases the mother handles the finances. "Togetherness" means that the father shares in the housework and baby care after he comes home from work. There also has been a great increase in the role possibilities for females so that, today, few fields remain closed to women. There are, for example, many female policewomen

and business executives—counterparts, so to speak, of the male hairdressers and dress designers. In such a society, sex-defined roles become ambiguous, and the developing child may receive few clear clues, other than anatomical, to sex differentiation. Since the fact remains that "anatomy is destiny," at least as regards the male and female roles in procreation, the adolescent is left to struggle with his most momentous identity task, sexual identity, in the absence of clearly sex-defined roles. Thus the richly varied, changing, and individually fulfilling legacy of unlimited identity alternatives is a bequest with strings attached, and one sees many adolescents who have become tangled in the strings as well as many who have benefited from the gift.

RAPID SOCIAL CHANGE AS A PROBLEM OF ADOLESCENCE

Our times have been called the Age of Anxiety, and certainly the quality of mounting uncertainty has immeasurable consequences for the adolescent. It is difficult to be certain, however, that this attribute is peculiar to our culture and time. Surely the future has never been truly certain for any society at any time, and there have been other historical instances of cultural despair. But if one may take evidence from the recorded attitudes of earlier periods in our own culture, there usually has been a prevailing, generally accepted fantasy that the future was predictable and secure. Even if dangers lay ahead, specific measures formulated by the mentors of society would surely avert them.

Today there is no such preponderance of widely accepted prophets of security. Instead, much of current literature conveys prophecies of doom, retrospective analyses of what has gone wrong with humanity, exposés of the neurotic substructure of contemporary values and behavior, and a philosophy of "live for today for tomorrow you may be vaporized."

Existential philosophy emphasizes that the only reality is the present moment of existence. Scientists engage repeatedly in public debates about whether mankind will or will not survive the next war, or the next bomb tests, or the next fifty years of population growth. The general attitude is that no one really knows what to do to keep *homo sapiens* from joining the dinosaurs, and anyone who believes that there is a solution to this problem is likely to be regarded with condescending skepticism.

Whether or not it is unique to our time and culture, the fact remains that adolescents are hardly ever given, and would find it hard to accept, the reassuring myth of a predictable future. When most adults have belief in the future, it provides a basis for youth to believe similarly, and to seek culturally continuous identities similar to those of the adults. When adults confess that they are lost, confused, and lack direction, it is not surprising that adolescents, driven as they are by the thrust of puberty, often repudiate adult values and at times give way to "orgies" of seemingly meaningless and sometimes destructive behavior. We should note, too, that adolescent culture itself changes with breathtaking rapidity. To today's college student, the "Joe College" of a few years ago is terribly outdated, and to a Peace Corps generation the stylized social dropout, the beatnik, is rapidly becoming passé. Thus, whatever the identity the adolescent is striving to achieve, he may find the rug pulled out from under him by a succeeding adolescent generation.

It should now be clear that some of the manifestations of adolescence are not only specific to, but are partially caused by, the culture. Comparative anthropological considerations are useful to give perspective, to alert us to the arbitrariness and contingency of much of our cultural handling of adolescence, and even to offer possible alternatives and modifications. The biology of puberty is universal, but human reactions to puberty always occur within a particular culture, and adolescence becomes fully intelligible only through an awareness and understanding of the culture which surrounds it.

PHYSIOLOGICAL CHANGES OF ADOLESCENCE

Psychological Conflict and the Reproductive System

Judith M. Bardwick

I am going to suggest that in our middle class culture the best that can be hoped for, in psychologically healthy girls, is an ambivalent attitude toward sex and reproduction. The psychological model of equal sexuality for boys and girls is not valid.

Editor's Introduction

Most discussions of physiological changes during adolescence focus on biological processes such as the growth spurt and the menarche. Judith Bardwick's research concerns the psychological implications of biological and sexual functions for the

From "Psychological Conflict and the Reproductive System," by J. M. Bardwick. In J. M. Bardwick, E. Douvan, M. S. Horner, and D. Gutmann, *Feminine Personality and Conflict*. Copyright © 1970 by Wadsworth Publishing Company, Inc. Reprinted by permission of the publisher, Brooks/Cole Publishing Company, Monterey, California.

female personality. She focuses on the ambivalence that women in Western culture feel toward their reproductive systems, on the psychosomatic defenses which manifest themselves in the female reproductive system, and on the mood changes which are a result of the monthly cycles.

Bardwick maintains that a woman's self-esteem and self-concept are more closely linked to the appearance and the functioning of her body than is true for a man, that young women are more dependent on others for self-esteem than are men, and that this dependency is increased at puberty due to a woman's definition of self as sexual partner and mother. She concludes that women experience conflict regarding the use of their bodies, and that this conflict is often somaticised in complaints involving the reproductive system. Further, she states that the female personality is in constant flux—subject to hormonal alterations due to the menstrual cycle—and that these mood shifts are extreme enough to affect behavior. Women have a higher incidence of suicide, homicide, and other violent acts; car accidents; and psychiatric, medical, and surgical illness during the immediate premenstrual and menstrual days. Yet it is true that the percentage of women who commit suicide or violent crimes or who have car accidents is much lower than the corresponding percentage of men.

Female monthly cycles are obvious. Only females have the ability to bleed profusely and to heal themselves each month. Throughout history, bleeding has been associated with injury and death; the healing aspect has been neglected. Women are often considered incapable of consistently calm behavior because they suffer from extreme cyclical fluctuations imposed by sex-hormone rhythms. Men, unlike women, are thought to be endowed with a biological stability which is unfailing. Thus, the acceptance of a monthly cycle has been made difficult for women because of the association with blood and gore and with emotional instability. The acceptance of a monthly cycle for men has been made difficult by the lack of obvious visibility and by the theory that the presence of a monthly cycle might seem to go against the theory of male stability.

There is, however, extensive research to support the evidence of a monthly cycle for men. Over forty years ago, Dr. Rex Hersey conducted a study which showed a predictable monthly period for men, with lows characterized by apathy and a tendency to magnify minor problems out of proportion to reality. High periods were often marked by a feeling of well-being, energy, high self-esteem, and a decreased need for sleep. These results parallel Bardwick's findings for women.

If we recognized the presence of cycles—monthly and daily—in both men and women, we might be able to make practical use of their rhythms in the treatment and prevention of disease, both mental and physical. For instance, resistance to disease might be different at different points in the monthly cycle. Japanese researchers have discovered that certain psychoses in adolescent and adult men appear to occur in monthly cycles. Daily or "circadian" cycles have been shown to affect changes in the adrenal hormones and in the secretion of testosterone. There is also evidence to show that the timing of the administration of a drug is critical in determining its effects. Amphetamines which were administered to rats at the daily peak of their temperature cycles proved lethal to almost 78 percent of them, while the same dose given to litter mates of these rats at the lowest points in their daily activity cycle resulted in the death of only 6 percent. Thus, overdoses in human beings may be as much an error in timing as in dosage (Ramey, 1973, pp. 174–181).

It is clear that all human beings are subject to daily and monthly cycles, many of which we are just beginning to understand. Bardwick's work helps to clarify the impact of the female's cycle on the feminine personality. It is my hope that we may be able to study the less obvious cycles, both monthly and daily, that affect all living things. Such research might prove useful in such practical ways as determining the maximum effectiveness of anticancer chemicals; then treatment might be administered at a time when the cancer cells are most sensitive to the destructive agents and the normal cells are most resistant to them. The study of biological cycles might also help to determine how emotional problems are affected by alterations in an individual's time clock.

REFERENCE

Ramey, E. Men's monthly cycles (They have them too you know). In Ms. Editors (Eds.), *The first ms. reader*. New York: Warner Paperback Library, 1973.

Pamela Cantor

To a very large extent women *are* their bodies. In this essay I discuss three ideas: (1) the ambivalence that women in modern Western culture commonly feel toward the reproductive system, (2) psychosomatic changes in the reproductive system that act as psychological defenses, and (3) mood changes that are a direct result of the menstrual cycle. I conclude that women experience conflict about the sexual use of their body. They express that conflict in somatic symptoms in the reproductive system. They also experience conflict with different aspects of their personality in premenstrual feelings of anxiety, hostility, depression, and inadequacy.

AMBIVALENCE TOWARD THE REPRODUCTIVE SYSTEM

It is fairly obvious that a woman's self-esteem and self-concept are more closely linked to the appearance and functioning of her body than is true for the man. Whereas masculinity is at least partially defined by success in marketplace achievements, femininity is largely defined by success in establishing and maintaining love relationships and by maternity. A woman's attractiveness is clearly instrumental in attracting men, and her self-evaluation as a woman will largely depend on her sexual and maternal success.

The menstrual cycle and pregnancy reinforce an awareness of internal reproductive functions. The obstetric and gynecological literature strongly supports the idea that women have a close psychological relationship to their reproductive system, which is a frequent site for the acting out of impulses, especially aggression and its derivatives, sex anxiety, and maternity-pregnancy fears. When we examine the dynamics of these psychosomatic behaviors, we find that they are closely linked to the level of the woman's self-esteem. There is, in women, a common psychological vulnerability that comes from low feelings of self-esteem, a strong and persistent need for respect from others in order to support self-esteem, and the fear of loss of love that could destroy self-esteem. A vulnerable sense of self-esteem—one that is dependent on appraisals from others—implies that there is no independent sense of self.

How can we understand this apparently curtailed development of independence in the female? I believe that the tendency of little girls to be less motorically impulsive, less physically aggressive, and less sexually active than little boys means that girls tend generally to get into less trouble than boys, tend not to engage in physical fighting, and tend not to masturbate. They are as a result less likely to perceive parents as people who thwart impulses. To the extent that girls are not separated from their parents as sources of support and nurturance, they are not forced to develop internal controls and an independent sense of self. In addition, girls can remain dependent and infantile longer than boys because the dependency, fears, and affection-seeking that are normal in early childhood for both sexes are defined as feminine in older children. Girls are, then, not pressed, by virtue of intense impulses, and by the culture's definition of "sissy" after the age of $2^{1}/_{2}$, to become independent as early as boys. When the boy can no longer depend on continuous, nondemanding approval from his parents, he is pushed to develop internal, independent sources for good feelings about his self.

Unlike the boy, girls tend to continue in the affectionate, dependent relationships that are characteristic of all young children. More than boys, they will continue for an extended period of their lives to value the self as a function of reflected appraisals. This means, in a very pervasive and significant way, that unless something intervenes, the girl and then the woman will continue to have a great need for approval from others and that her behavior will be guided by a fear of rejection, or the fear of a loss of love. Although the prepubertal girl had a bisexual rearing in the sense that individual achievements, especially academic, were important resources for feelings of self-esteem, the emphasis changes at puberty. Our societal definition of successful femininity requires interpersonal success, especially with males; and at puberty the pressure on the girl increases to be successful in heterosexual relations. For the boy there is a parallel pressure to achieve esteem through individual academic or occupational successes.

What I am suggesting is that young girls are more dependent on others for feelings of self-esteem than boys are and that this dependency is increased at puberty because of our definition of femininity and successful role performance. The heterosexual relationship at puberty is clearly a sexual one, and anxiety and uncertainty about sex will increase the girl's vulnerability. The emotionally healthy daughter will tend to transfer her feelings of dependency, trust, and intimacy from her father to her boyfriend and then to her husband. But dependency implies vulnerability; although girls may become more sure of themselves and more independent, new relationships, especially with males, are likely to resurrect old needs, old fears, and a pressing search for reassurance. Even the healthy girl will be selectively dependent, especially in important emotional relationships and when she is not certain of her status within that relationship. Women perceive the world in interpersonal terms—that is, they personalize the objective world in a way that men do not. Notwithstanding occupational achievements, they regard themselves with esteem insofar as they are esteemed by those they love. Women remain dependent on the affectionate responses of their lovers, husbands, and children for good feelings about the self.

I think that young children preceive their sex as a verbal given or a label—one of the few things that they do not have to earn and that does not change as they grow older, as they succeed or fail, or as they are good or bad. Their sex identity remains a given until external demands make it something that has to be earned. At that time anxiety about one's sex, and therefore one's identity, begins. The pressure to become masculine, to grow up, to give up the femininity of childish behavior begins much earlier for boys than for girls, and sex identity may well be a crucial issue in the self-identity of the boy as early as the age of 5. Although the prepubertal girl anticipates her future role, I think that the crucial issues of feminine self-identity are postponed until the physical changes of puberty. At that time she will experience pressure to become really feminine and to inhibit masculine behaviors and personality traits. She will simultaneously experience pressure to succeed in heterosexual relationships and suffer restrictions on her freedom. Her sex identity, which now has to be proven, will fuse interpersonal success and adolescent perceptions of sex and reproduction.

Prepubertal girls are obviously aware of their sex: they practice certain housekeeping roles, they sometimes babysit, they mimic pregnancy with pillows, and they can tell you what their future responsibilities as women will be. But this is all just anticipatory play. When pubertal development results in the extraordinary physical changes of the menstrual cycle and the secondary sex characteristics, the girl's status will depend on her feminine desirability, and her psyche will depend on her acceptance of these happy and threatening changes. Now the source of her anxiety about her self-identity comes both from external pressures and from the radical changes within her own body. In adolescence and early adulthood, girls as well as boys are preoccupied with questions about their identity: their relations with others, their worth, their abilities, their goals, and their morality. For boys achievement is primary and affiliation is secondary; for girls the order of importance is reversed. Feminine sexual identity depends on heterosexual affiliative success. Affiliation is realistically perceived as the critical achievement for self-esteem, which, for a woman, depends on loving and being loved and respected by a man and then by one's children. Attitudes about the self and about the sexual self are critical.

I am going to suggest that in our middle-class culture the best that can be hoped for, in psychologically healthy girls, is an ambivalent attitude toward sex and reproduction. The psychological model of equal sexuality for boys and girls is not valid. The minimal masturbation observed in girls is not the result of massive repression but of the physiology of the female reproductive system. The girl has an insensitive vagina, no breasts, and a small and relatively inaccessible clitoris. Whereas male sexuality is always penile-genital and is a relatively linear development from childhood to adulthood, genital sexuality for girls occurs after puberty. Although prepubertal girls may be tactilely sensitive, affectionate, and even sensual, they do not perceive the genitals as an important source of pleasure. This idea is important because it means that girls evolve their original concepts of sex and reproduction at a time when the genitals are not erotic or pleasurable.

It is strange but true that apparently negative feelings about menstruation and the menstruating woman are expressed in all cultures. The menstruating woman is labeled dirty, unclean, taboo. Advertisements for sanitary napkins and tampons assure the woman that, if she uses these products, she will be able to carry on as if she were "normal." The same negative affect surrounds the idea of pregnancy. We design maternity clothes to maximize the illusion of slenderness as long as possible, and we tell the pregnant woman that she, too, ought to carry on as though she were "normal." This situation implies that we view menstruating and pregnant women as abnormal. As a culture we deny the crisis qualities of menstruation, pregnancy, childbirth, and lactation; girls swiftly learn that these topics are not to be discussed (except, if they are lucky, in scientific terms in school) and that there is something "not normal" involved. As a result, they are given little opportunity to express their fears and gain reassurance.

For prepubertal girls, sex and sensuality—especially genital sex—are not highly salient topics. Girls anticipate having babies and being mothers, and they are curious; but I suspect that at best prepubertal girls view reproduction with ambivalence. While the child's tolerance for blood and pain is minimal, menstruation brings bleeding, the "curse," and the pain of cramps. Intercourse is intrusion into the most embarrassingly private part of the self. Pregnancy is awkward and distorted and culminates with the terror of labor. Lactation is something done by animals, especially cows. I sometimes think that penis envy or a general envy of males by adolescent girls stems from the fact that men do not menstruate or get pregnant.

Girls who have had no preparation for menstruation commonly express fears of having been ripped (or raped?) in their vulnerable body interior. Shainess (1961) found that even the 75% of the girls in her study group who did have advance information anticipated menstruation with anxiety, fear, and dread. Benedek (1959) writes that menstruation is the forerunner of the pain and defloration and of childbirth. Thus the girl's awareness of the uterus and the rest of the internal reproductive system emerges from pain and fear. Benedek continues by saying that the girl faces the enormous task of accepting the uterus and motherhood as part of her self; if she does so, she will be able to accept menstruation "without undue protest." This attitude is really very negative.

Menstruation is a critical event that arouses powerful and negative feelings about blood and pain as well as a narcissistic concern for the welfare of the body. The menstruating girl experiences periodic increases in sexual arousability and an increased anxiety about sex and mutilation. There is now a cycle of emotional changeability that also includes positive feelings of being normal and female. The girl feels grown up but is disappointed that her role in the world changes so little. She feels pleasure from the appearance of her body and from the sensuality of masturbation, but anxiety and guilt accompany that sensuality. In short, she is ambivalent.

With only one exception, every woman I have ever interviewed could recall the circumstances of her first menstrual period and how she felt about it. This fact alone attests to the enormous importance of the event in their lives. In a few rare cases young women I have interviewed considered menstruation a profound pleasure because it reassures their femininity. Most psychologically healthy American women whom I see simply report that menstruation is "just there," "all right," or "OK." What they mean is that it is not too intrusive in their lives.

I find it very interesting that in this culture emphasis and rewards are reserved for the cosmetic *exterior* of the sexual body—as though breasts and hips were created specifically for purposes of seduction. Adolescent girls can verbalize their concern about their competitive appearance but not their fears about internal reproductive functions. Defensively, fantasies about being torn or dismembered internally and ideas about blood, pain, and cruelty are submerged deeply into the unconscious. What we observe is a general irritation about having to menstruate that is only a dilute derivative of the original negative affect.

The healthy adolescent girl accepts her femininity, anticipates her sexual functions, takes pleasure in being desired and courted, and is acutely aware of the changes in her appearance. Because she is still responding to others, she values these physical changes primarily because they are a means of securing love. Her sexuality, emerging from pubertal changes, is confounded by fear and by her anticipation of love from the chosen. The adolescent crush is a very sexy relationship, but for the girl the sexuality involved is not vaginal. Although adolescent girls enjoy flirting, kissing, and petting, they are not motivated by strong genital urges. The adolescent girl fuses genital sexuality with maternity, she is not vaginally aroused, and she is afraid of becoming pregnant (although she is equally afraid of providing a contraceptive). Her primary motive for engaging in coitus is not the gratification of her own genital sexuality but the gratification of the needs of the male and the securing of his love.

The sexuality of the adolescent girl is combined with the rewards of dating. Dating is the testing ground for desirability as a woman, and the girl is ready to fall in love again and again because each relationship assures her of that desirability. She is much less aware of the sexual character of her feelings than is the boy; she enjoys the power of flirting but is very frightened that the boy will pressure her to intercourse. Characteristically she is ambivalent toward her genitals, simultaneously regarding them as something precious and as something dirty. The genitals are also a source of danger in our double-standard culture because participation in premarital coitus will lower her self-esteem in her own eyes and, even more dangerously, in the eyes of her lover. The girl's sexual inhibition has several origins: she is afraid of personal and social rejection; she has no intense, independent sex drive and thus has difficulty in perceiving vaginal sex as pleasurable; and she relates coitus to blood, mutilation, pain, penetration, and pregnancy. This combination of minimal vaginal eroticism, a frightened, masochistic view, and an internalized concept of a "good girl" will reinforce minimal sexuality. Girls are eager to grow up and enjoy the privileges of maturity, but they are frightened by the reality and responsibilities of their new body. Ambivalence toward the sexual body is likely to be a part of the psyche of most women. In addition, the girl, who is still evolving feelings of self-esteem, must be seductive enough to ensure dates and popularity but responsible enough to maintain control of sexual impulses.

The Need for Achievement in Sex

The infrequency of vaginal masturbation in young girls is probably not the result of massive repression so much as a derivative of the neural innervations of the vaginal barrel that make it relatively insensitive. Eroticism of the vagina does not normally occur until coitus. Moreover, because of the small size and inaccessibility of the clitoris, girls engage in relatively little clitoral masturbation. Neverthe-

less, the periodic increase in sexual tension during the secretory or postovulation phase of the menstrual cycle, the increased erogeneity of the breasts, and the psychological concept of vaginal-penile fusion in coitus will combine in adolescence to create a demand for a metamorphosis from an asexual girl to a sexual woman.

I think that an improtant error has been made in much of the theory about female development. We have assumed that the vagina is like the penis and that the female hormone estrogen is like the male's testosterone—in effect, that female sexuality is the same as that of the male. We have made the achievement of an orgasm, preferably a "vaginal orgasm," a viable goal. What the data suggest is that girls are relatively asexual, that their sexual arousal not only takes more time but is more fragile or easily disturbed, and that there is a range of orgasmic reaction in females that is very different from the all-or-none phenomenon in males. We have viewed vaginal orgasm as identical to penile orgasm and as a necessary goal for both sexual partners. Yet the girl's sexual ambivalence, as well as her physiology, make this achievement difficult. The slower arousabilily of the female (despite the clitoris and skin erogenicity) and her infrequency of orgasm remind us that there is a difference in the imperativeness of sexual impulses in men and women. Sexual orgasm is a highly touted goal for women; but, in truth, I believe that love and maternity are far more crucial than sex in the woman's self-definition and self-esteem.

The orgasmic reaction of women includes a range of responses and is not limited to the single large response of men. Thus, although the reported frequency of orgasm in women includes lesser responses, it is still far lower than for men. Kinsey, Pomeroy, Martin, and Gebhard (1953) found that in their sample almost 100% of the boys but only 35% of the girls had achieved orgasm by the age of 17.

Kinsey added that only 30% of the females reporting had achieved orgasm before marriage, and the maximum frequency after marriage was reached by age 35. (Experience and increased pelvic vascularity after pregnancy probably contribute to this rise in frequency.) Of interest is the work of Wallin (1960), who interviewed 540 wives. Some described themselves as rarely or never reaching orgasm but also reported that they usually experienced complete relief from sexual desires. This finding has two implications: (1) that intercourse as an affirmation of being loved is critical, and (2) that these women never reached high levels of sexual arousal in the first place. The orgasmic response depends on the level of sexual arousal; similarly, sexual frustration is a function of nongratification of a high level of arousal. Arousability is slower to develop in women than in men, and momentary levels of arousal tend to be lower. As a result, the excitement phase in women must be significantly longer than in men if they are to achieve a high enough plateau phase to reach orgasm (Masters & Johnson, 1966). The psychosomatic combination of infrequent masturbation, an insensitive vagina, an inaccessible clitoris, the absence of significant genital stimulation until middle or late adolescence, and the inhibitions resulting from ambivalence toward sex and the "good-girl" syndrome make arousal harder and customary levels of arousability lower. It is pathological when the male, having achieved an erection, is unable to achieve an orgasm. I think it is relatively uncommon when the female achieves sufficiently high arousal level that she experiences either frustration or a satisfying orgasm.

Many women whom I interview say that their sexual life is satisfactory although they never achieve an orgasm. And I believe them. They probably have never reached a sufficiently high level of arousal for the lack of an orgasm to result in discomfort or pain. Their only regret is the feeling that they are missing something that is supposed to be wonderful, and they feel rather cheated. Their disappointment is not a crucial problem. Another common response that I hear, especially with college-aged women, is that they do achieve orgasm and it is "pleasant." "Pleasant" does not describe a major orgasm.

I think it is fairly common for young and relatively inexperienced women to achieve a plateau state of arousal with relatively small and minor surges toward the orgasmic level. This kind of sensation is probably well described as pleasant or tingly. Maximal sexual arousal is not reached, a maximal orgasm is not achieved, resolution (the return to the prearousal state) occurs slowly, and there is a "nice" feeling without frustration. For these women the primary source of gratification is the feeling of loving someone and being loved. This kind of physical gratification can probably be achieved as well through petting as through coitus. Sex as the gratification of physical demands is subordinate to sex as an affectionate gratification. With some regrets but not deep grief, many women never leave this level of arousability.

That sex can be primarily a psychological rather than physical act and therefore enjoyable without orgasm (even a minor one) clearly implies to me a lack of strong sexual arousal in the first place; the female who has reached a high plateau level of sexual arousal would need release from the physical tension created by that arousal or the experience would not be pleasant. Schaefer (1964) also found in her studies with women that orgasm is not always a factor in sexual contentment, that the orgasmic reaction appears to be learned rather than automatic, and that orgasm is experienced in an individual and subjective way.

The male model of a strong sexual drive is not generalizable to women. When physical impulses are not so powerful, the possibility for emotional contributions is stronger. Sexuality has a greater experiential component for women than for men, and it is more closely linked with emotional ties. The sexuality of the woman seems to me to be a developed ability. Through experience and experimentation, and in the trust of a stable, loving relationship some women learn to maximize physical sensation and pleasure. They learn to forget the self, to discard old inhibitions, and to respond to the physical sensations of sexual arousal. The female who is sexually arousable has to be disinhibited, tactilely sensitive, psychologically able to give of herself, and capable of enjoying the awareness of body penetration. Women can be—and some are—spontaneously and honestly sensual; this capacity is just more uncommon in females than in males. The infrequency of high levels of arousal and orgasm contributes to the lack of strong sexual longings in women. Yet the expectation of high sexual responsivity as evidence of psychological health creates a physical and psychological need for successful sexual performance. The absence of a powerful sex motive in women is a logical extension of the anatomy of the female body and of the girl's relationship to her sexual body. The idea that women are motivated by strong sex drives has led to an overestimation of sex as a significant variable in their lives, an assumption of equal orgasmic responses, a failure to recognize the periodicity of desire as a function of menstrual endocrine changes, and an underestimation of the strength of maternity-nurturance needs. A large part of feminine sexuality has its origin in the need to feel loved, to feel reassured in that love, and to create love.

Sexual conflict arises from the assumption that the female must have an orgasm, which is the sign of successful sexual performance. Because she can participate in sex without being sexually aroused, she may feel debased, used, or prostituted. She may also feel anxious about her inability to become aroused and reach a vaginal orgasm. Masters and Johnson

(1966) found that the vaginal orgasm is a fiction—the orgasm is a response of the entire pelvis area and the clitoris is always stimulated in any coital position. Sherfey (1966) has commented that women have difficulty in describing their sexual sensations, probably because they think they should experience something (that is, a vaginal orgasm) that they know they do not. Women are afraid that what they are feeling is not what healthy women should feel. This problem parallels the expectation that women respond simultaneously and similarly to men and the belief that the vagina is the site of important erogenous sensations. Coitus is the physical and psychological fusion with the loved man, but the site of sensations is not predominantly vaginal.

It is not surprising that, with few exceptions, the sexual life of women remains more inhibited than that of men. Simultaneously we have created a goal of fantastic sexual freedom and responsivity in women. In reality, women subordinate sexuality to maternity, deny the importance of orgasm and sexual arousal and wonder whether what they feel is normal. Sex and pregnancy are intrusions into the self. The conditions for sexuality for girls are love and trust. Only in the romantic circumstances of mutual love and mutual commitment can the girl feel that she is not being used and that she is not desecrating her bodily integrity.

The Psychology of Sex and Unmarried Women

Mores about sex are evolving—they have not yet changed. Thus, although the incidence of premarital sexuality may be increasing, the older, internalized value judgments are still salient in the minds of the young, even if their behavior is at variance with those judgments. The cultural resexualization of the female body began only at the turn of the 20th century; yet already there has been a radical shift from the anticipated frigidity of the Victorian to the desired spontaneous sexuality of the Scandinavian. Despite the availability of inexpensive contraceptives with almost 100% effectiveness, we see premarital sex but not promiscuity. The responsibility for participating in sex still rests primarily with the girl. Whereas she may find it difficult to deliberately engage in premarital relationships (preferring a heady sweep of passion to override her inhibitions and defenses) because she is "good," she also feels pressure to engage in relationships to prove that she is not pathologically frigid or inhibited or square. The condition for sexual participation is the girl's perception of a mutual respect and commitment by both partners. But there is no certainty of commitment prior to the legalities of marriage, and participation in sex acts increases the girl's feeling of psychological vulnerability in the relationship. The "justification" for the sexual behavior is love, but ambivalence remains acute. In addition to the girl's ambivalence toward sex and her sexual body, she is also frightened by the idea that, by participating in premarital relationships, she has depreciated herself and will lose the male's respect and love. On the other hand, if she agrees to engage in premarital sex, the male is very likely to leave her. This possibility is not simply part of the mythology. Ehrmann (1959, p. 269) found that "males are more conservative and the females are more liberal in expressed personal codes of sex conduct and in actual behavior with lovers than with nonlovers. In other words, the degree of physical intimacy actually experienced or considered permissible is among males *inversely* related and among females *directly* related to the intensity of familiarity and affection in the male-female relation. . . . "

I think that, instead of proving to be the great liberator, absolute contraception has increased many girls' difficulties because it has removed the main realistic reason for virginity. Participating in sex and assuming the re-

sponsibility for contraception are important and conflict-ridden behaviors for most unmarried girls. . . .

PSYCHOSOMATIC CHANGE IN THE REPRODUCTIVE SYSTEM

The woman's reproductive system can provide critically important feelings of self-esteem, and psychosomatic change in this salient system is often used as a psychological defense—that is, as a technique for keeping the personality intact. This system is an obvious and logical means by which women can express conflicts about aggression, anxiety, sexual feelings, maternity, and their relationships with themselves and other people. It is not accidental that certain women "choose" to wordlessly act out anxieties, fears, and hopes not only in general somatic symptoms but specifically and repetitively in the reproductive system. These symptoms express a strong conflict, which these women are unable to express more directly or resolve more efficiently.

Women who are very passive, dependent, sexually anxious, and prone to use the defense mechanism of denial are likely to express their conflicts through changes in the functioning of the reproductive system. Since the system is both psychologically salient and internal, it lends itself to such motivated dysfunctions. The working or not-working of this internal system seems automatic or nonvoluntary. Dysfunctions of this system are not guilt producing, and these women do not feel responsible for their symptoms.

The passive, dependent, and conformist woman assesses the self by others' reactions to it. She is likely to tell an interviewer that she is independent and prides herself on that independence. This description not only is untrue but reflects her pervasive use of denial. The effects of denial are generalized: such women deny that their sex life is inadequate or unsatisfactory, they deny their general inadequacy, they deny their dependence, and they sometimes deny their femininity through a conversion symptom like amenorrhea. Because their behavior is motivated to fulfill others' expectations of what is normal, they express a conscious desire for sex, pregnancy, and maternity. However, these women often unconsciously reject their roles.

The psychological defense functions of psychosomatic symptoms are often very clear. For example, amenorrhea represents a denial of the menstrual flow and thus a regression to prepuberty, when dependency was normal and responsibility was minimal. This is also a regression to an asexual time and expresses sex anxiety. Amenorrhea symbolizes a denial of being an adult female and in reality prohibits conception. Sometimes the amenorrheic suppression of menstruation is a defense against sexuality and pregnancy, and sometimes it seems to be the denial of not being pregnant. The temporary amenorrhea of the unmarried girl may be a masochistic punishment for premarital sex or a sadomasochistic threat to force the male into marriage. Masochistic punishment may also appear as dysmenorrhea or traumatic vomiting in pregnancy. Other clinical syndromes affect the uterus and vagina, and they include habitual spontaneous abortion, premature labor, incoordinate uterine contractions, menstrual and menopausal tension, vaginismus, premature dilation of the cervix, premature rupture of the membranes, and pseudocyesis (false pregnancy) (Javert, 1957; Kelly, 1962). . . .

AFFECT CHANGE AND THE MENSTRUAL CYCLE

Another kind of conflict in women that is also related to the reproductive system derives directly from the physiology of that system. Psychologists have traditionally studied body change or disease *resulting* from psychological

states or motives, but now there is evidence that body change may also directly *affect* psychological states. Studies of the menstrual cycle reveal an extraordinary affect change in normal girls that correlates with menstrual-cycle phase. That is, at different cycle phases the personality is actually in conflict with itself. I am suggesting that there are regular and predictable changes in the personality of sexually mature women that correlate with changes in the menstrual cycle. These personality changes are extreme, they occur in spite of individual personality differences, and they are the result of the endocrine or other physical changes that occur during the cycle. The content of the change will be a function of the personality and real world of the individual, but the direction of the change will be a function of the physical state.

Reports of premenstrual depression, irritability, anxiety, and low self-esteem have varied in frequency from 25%-100% of the population, depending on definitions and types of measurement. Sutherland and Stewart (1965) studied 150 women and found that 69% of them experienced premenstrual irritability, 63% experienced depresssion, and 45% experienced both negative affects. Coppen and Kessel (1963), in their sample of 465 women, found that the levels of depression and irritability were more severe premenstrually than during menstruation. Although they felt that neurotic women may react more severely during the cycle phases, populations of normal, neurotic, and psychotic women show similar affect cycles. Similarly, Moos (1968) found that approximately 30%-50% of his sample of 839 women indicated, on a recall questionnaire, cyclic symptoms in irritability, mood swings, tension, or depression. (I strongly suspect that this result is an underestimate, because many women are unaware of these mood shifts. Affect change must be measured behaviorally—not through a questionnaire.)

These mood shifts are severe enough to

affect behavior, and Dalton (1964) has found that a large proportion of the women who commit suicide or engage in criminal acts of violence do so during the premenstrual and menstrual phases of the cycle. She also found that, during the four premenstrual and four menstrual days, 45% of industrial employees reported sick, 46% of the psychiatric admissions occurred, 49% of the acute medical and surgical admissions occurred, 49% of prisoners committed their crimes, and 52% of the emergency admissions occurred. These data, along with the high frequency of symptoms in normal women, clearly suggest that this syndrome often has important consequences.

During the high-estrogen phase of ovulation, women experience high levels of self-esteem and low levels of negative affects. During the premenstrual phase, when the levels of the hormones estrogen and progesterone are low, there are strong feelings of helplessness, anxiety, hostility, and a yearning for love. Shainess (1961) found that the premenstrual phase was usually associated with these negative affects. Housman (1955) found an increasing need for affection and approval, a high sensitivity to interpersonal slight, and a high anxiety level during menstruation. Benedek (1959) has described the premenstrual phase as characterized by anxiety and depression, fears of mutilation and death, and sexual fantasies. She found that during ovulation there is almost a total absence of anxiety-related themes. Benedek and Rubenstein (1942) reported that, at the beginning of the menstrual cycle, when estrogen production is gradually increasing, there are good feelings of well-being and alertness; at ovulation the highest feeling of relaxation and well-being occurs; when the estrogen and progesterone levels swiftly decline during the premenstrual phase, there is a regression in the psychosexual integration. With some individual differences, premenstruation characteristically brings anger, excitability, fatigue, crankiness, crying

spells, and a fear of mutilation. More than at any other time of the cycle, all emotions are less controlled, frustrations are perceived as unbearable, and the gratification of needs seems imperative. Benedek and Rubenstein found that the onset of menstruation was usually accompanied by a relaxation of the tension and irritability, although this relief was often mixed with a feeling of depression that continued until estrogen production increased.

I would like to illustrate the enormity of the psychological changes that occur even in normal subjects. Ivey and I (Ivey & Bardwick, 1968) studied a group of 26 normal college students over two menstrual cycles. Twice at ovulation and twice at premenstruation they were asked to tell us about some experience they had had. These verbal samples were tape-recorded and were later scored using Gottschalk's Verbal Anxiety Scale (Gottschalk, Spring, & Gleser, 1961). We scored Death, Mutilation, Separation, Guilt, Shame, and Diffuse Anxiety. The premenstrual anxiety scores were significantly higher (at the 0.0005 level)* than the anxiety scores at ovulation.

When we combined the scores for all the subjects, we found that the Death Anxiety score at premenstruation was significantly higher than that at ovulation ($p < 0.02$), as was the Diffuse Anxiety score ($p < 0.01$). Separation Anxiety, Mutilation Anxiety, and Shame Anxiety were also higher premenstrually (at approximately 0.13 levels), whereas Guilt Anxiety remained fairly constant.

Because the instructions were nonexplicit and simply asked the subject to talk about some experience, the shifts in content become important. When we examined the verbal samples for consistent topics, we found recurring themes that were unique to a menstrual-cycle phase. A constant theme at ovulation

---

*That is, the odds that this effect could occur by chance are 5 in 10,000.

was self-satisfaction over success or the ability to cope:

> . . . so I was elected chairman. I had to establish
> with them the fact that I knew what I was doing. I
> remember one particularly problematic meeting
> and afterward L. came up to me and said, "you
> really handled the meeting well." In the end it
> came out the sort of thing that really bolstered
> my confidence in myself.

The following sample came from the same girl
premenstrually during the same cycle:

> They had to teach me how to water-ski. I was so
> clumsy it was really embarrassing, 'cause it was
> kind of like saying to yourself you can't do it and
> the people were about to lose patience with me.

Another theme that occured often was hostility. The following response was recorded at
premenstruation:

> . . . talk about my brother and his wife. I hated
> her. I just couldn't stand her. I couldn't stand her
> mother. I used to do terrible things to separate
> them.

This angry and incestuous verbal sample is in
striking contrast to the same girl's sample
from the ovulatory phase of the same cycle.

> Talk about my trip to Europe! It was just the
> greatest summer of my life. We met all kinds of
> terrific people everywhere we went and just the
> most terrific things happened.

The theme of Death Anxiety was evident at
premenstruation:

> I'll tell you about the death of my poor dog. . . .
> Oh, another memorable event—my grandparents
> died in a plane crash. That was my first contact
> with death, and it was very traumatic for me. . . .
> Then my other grandfather died.

In contrast, the sample at ovulation for the
same girl was as follows:

> Well, we just went to Jamaica and it was fantas-
> tic. The island is so lush and green and the water
> is so blue. . . . The place is so fertile and the
> natives are just so friendly.

My last example is an illustration of premenstrual Mutilation Anxiety, which was in strong
contrast to the contented ovulation narrative
for the same girl during one cycle:

> . . . we came around a curve and did a double
> flip and landed upside down. I remember the car
> coming down on my hand and slicing it right
> open, and all this blood was all over the place.
> Later they thought it was broken because every
> time I touched the finger it felt like a nail was
> going through my hand.

At ovulation she told of the following experience:

> We took our skis and packed them on top of the
> car, and then we took off for up North. We used
> to go for long walks in the snow and it was just
> really great—really quiet and peaceful. . . .

Thus these physical (especially endocrine)
changes so influence psychological behavior
that, despite personality differences, and even
in normal women, psychological behavior becomes predictable on the basis of menstrual-
cycle phase. These data suggest that physical
states, as well as core psychological characteristics, will determine whether women will
cope or not cope; will be anxious, hostile, or
depressed when tested; or will appear healthy
or neurotic on psychological tests.

The reproductive system of women is the
most salient physical system for the gratification of needs for self-esteem and for the
expression of needs, affects, and conflicts. It is
also a system that directly affects these psy-

chological variables. Menstruation, pregnancy, childbirth, lactation, and menopause are all periods of normal crisis for women and should be understood as such.

REFERENCES

Bardwick, J. M., & Behrman, S. J. Investigation into the effects of anxiety, sexual arousal, and menstrual cycle phase on uterine contractions. *Psychosomatic Medicine*, 1967, 29(5), 468–482.

Bardwick, J. M., & Zweben, J. E. A predictive study of psychological and psychosomatic changes associated with oral contraceptives. In preparation.

Benedek, T. Sexual functions in women and their disturbance. In S. Aricti (Ed.), *American handbook of psychiatry*. New York: Basic Books, 1959, P. 726.

Benedek, T., & Rubenstein, B. *The sexual cycle in women: The relation between ovarian function and psychodynamic processes*. Washington, D. C.: National Research Council, 1942.

Coppen, A., & Kessel, N. Menstruation and personality. *British Journal of Psychiatry*, 1963, 109, 711–721.

Dalton, K. *The premenstrual syndrome*. Springfield, Ill.: Thomas, 1964.

Ehrmann, W. *Premarital dating behavior*. New York: Holt, 1959.

Gottschalk, L. A., Springer, K. J., & Gleser, G. C. Experiments with a method of assessing the variations in intensity of certain psychological states occurring during two psychotherapeutic interviews. In L. A. Gottschalk (Ed.), *Comparative psycholinguistic analysis of two psychotherapeutic interviews*. New York: International Universities Press, 1961. Chap. 7.

Housman, H. A psychological study of menstruation. Unpublished doctoral dissertation, University of Michigan, 1955.

Ivey, M. E., & Bardwick, J. M. Patterns of affective fluctuation in the menstrual cycle. *Psychosomatic Medicine*, 1968, 30(3), 336–345.

Javert, C. *Spontaneous and habitual abortion*. New York: McGraw-Hill, 1957. Chap. 12.

Kelly, J. V. Effects of fear upon uterine motility. *American Journal of Obstetrics and Gynecology*, 1962, 83(5), 576–581.

Kinsey, A. C., Pomeroy, W. B., Martin, C. E., & Gebhard, P. H. *Sexual behavior in the human female*. Philadelphia: Saunders, 1953.

Masters, W. H., & Johnson, V. E. *Human sexual response*. Boston: Little, Brown, 1966.

Moos, R. H. The development of a menstrual distress questionnaire, *Psychosomatic Medicine*, 1968, 6, 853–867.

Paige, K. E. The effects of oral contraceptives on affective fluctuations associated with the menstrual cycle. Unpublished doctoral dissertation, University of Michigan, 1969.

Schaefer, L. Sexual experiences and reactions of 30 women. Unpublished doctoral dissertation, Columbia University, 1964.

Shainess, N. A re-evaluation of some aspects of femininity through a study of menstruation: A preliminary report. *Comprehensive Psychiatry*, 1961, 2, 20–26.

Sherfey, M. J. The evolution and nature of female sexuality in relation to psychoanalytic theory. *Journal of the American Psychoanalytic Association*, 1966, 14(1), 28–128.

Sutherland, H., & Stewart, I. A critical analysis of the premenstrual syndrome. *Lancet*, 1965, 1, 1180–1183.

Wallin, P. A study of orgasm as a condition of woman's enjoyment of intercourse. *Journal of Social Psychology*, 1960, 51, 191–198.

A Few Words about Breasts

Nora Ephron

I suppose that for most girls, breasts, brassieres, that entire thing, has more trauma, more to do with the coming of adolescence, of becoming a woman, than anything else. Certainly more than getting your period, although that too was traumatic, symbolic. But you could see *breasts; they were there; they were visible. Whereas a girl could claim to have her period for months before she actually got it and nobody would know the difference.*

Editor's Introduction

I have read this article at least fifteen times and each time I laugh harder than the last. Clearly, this is because I identify with Nora Ephron. I remember my summer at camp when I was 12 years old. My best friend (who will remain anonymous for fear that she would be mortally embarrassed by this) and I concocted the F.F.F.A. club, of which we were the only two members. The club, "Flat-Chested Frustrated Females of America," had a theme song: "F.F.F.A. club, F.F.F.A. club, forever shall we hold your banner high. F.F.F.A. club, F.F.F.A. club, we shall always be a member till we die." That was the era of Marilyn Monroe, Anita Ekberg, and Gina Lollobrigida. What chance did a 12-year-old with a flat chest have for success in life and love? Not much. So we bought bras with great, bouyant padding, carefully chose bathing suits which would allow us to sew in rubber cups and prayed that no one would notice the seams. We would check our suits after each swim and our clothing each time we dressed to make sure that everything was in place. No one counseled consistency, so that our breasts changed size with each change of attire. In the morning I might be the economy size, in the afternoon I was average, and by evening I was the superdeluxe model. Sexual intimacy was an impossibility because, heaven forbid, some boy would find out. The efforts we expended in order to be chesty were incredible. The highest compliment someone could pay my lithe frame was to say I was voluptuous. I look back at this stage in utter disbelief and thank my lucky stars for the advent of Twiggy, the braless look, and the elimination of cinched waists, girdles, and total constriction from the fashion scene. The memories of the embarrassing times my padded breasts caused—the time when I couldn't do the cha-cha because I was strapped into a waist-cinching bra and was too mortified to explain to my date, the times when I would refuse to "pet" and feigned prudishness rather than confess—could fill the pages of this book. I only hope my own daughter will be spared these ludicrous experiences.

But for every woman, no matter what her age, her feelings toward her own body are intimately involved with her self-concept and her sexuality. For both males and females, practically every feature of the adolescent body—the nose, ears, hair, legs, breasts, muscles, penis, or beard—becomes the focus of favorable or unfavorable opinion. But most adolescents' feelings about their physical characteristics rarely correspond to the views that others have of them.

Breast development, including size and contour, plays an important role in the adolescent female's view of herself. (I actually recall reading, as a teen-ager, a *Vogue* article which discussed the shape of the breast—conical, like an ice-cream cone; spherical, like a ball; etc.—and being concerned as to whether I belonged to the "best" category.) Judging from the advertisements for bras and no bras and the dimensions of the Playmate of the Month, breasts are of great importance in the United States. The unusual anxiety of adolescent girls as to the size of their breasts relates to their concepts of sexually appropriate development and of the ideal woman which are often unrealistic.

Boys are concerned about the size of the penis. Often boys who have small penises are vulnerable to two misconceptions: that the penis is a measure of manly physique and that a man's ability to satisfy a woman depends upon the size of his genitals. Masters and Johnson (1966) found that the size of the penis was less consistently related to general physical development than that of any other organ of the body and that the increase in the size of a small penis during intercourse was relatively larger than that of a large penis. They found that the ability to give satisfaction is not dependent upon the size of the penis because the vagina is both distensible and contractible and rapidly accommodates to the size of the penis. These myths, however, continue to trouble adolescents.

Obesity is another great worry of the adolescent population. About 10 percent of the child population is judged to be obese, but the incidence is greater during adolescence. Many adolescent boys have what appear to be inappropriate fat deposits. They express great relief when these fat deposits in the breasts, thighs, and trunk prove to be only temporary. Worries about obesity also plague even the thinnest of adolescents. I recall living on cottage cheese and peaches week after week during my high school years, claiming that my 110-pound 5-foot-5 frame was disgraceful and I would not be content until I weighed 105 (which, when reached, made me look concentration-camp thin).

Early or late maturing also has an effect on psychological development. A study by Mussen and Jones (1957) has shown that boys who mature late are likely to have negative self-conceptions, feelings of inadequacy, and rebellious attitudes toward parents. In contrast, early maturing boys present a much more favorable psychological picture during adolescence.

Many observations have been made which show that early or late maturing has an impact on adolescent girls. While the early maturing girls may feel somewhat conspicuous, their precocious development more often appears to be a source of satisfaction and popularity. Early maturing girls appear to have a more favorable view of themselves during adolescence. But what lasting importance does early or delayed maturing have for adult women? Shipman (1964) studied 82 women with a mean age of 39 and found that the women who reached menarche at ages 10 or 11 tended to be

more conservative and unthinking in their thinking, more lax and inexact, more trusting of others, and more group dependent. The middle menarche group, ages 12 to 13, tended to be more feminine. They also tended to have a higher average number of children. . . . The late menarche group, age 14+, were more dominant and aggressive, more critical thinking and ready to experiment. They were more suspecting and more self-controlled.

Shipman explains these findings in terms of the increased sublimation and intellectual mastery which was possible for the women who matured later, which he feels accounted for their greater independence and self-direction. Shipman's study is one of the few which addresses benefits associated with delayed maturation in women.

Nora Ephron discusses the tribulations of delayed sexual maturation and the emotional difficulties which she encountered. For that section of the female population which can identify with Nora Ephron, the article is sheer pleasure. For those women who found their adolescent shape more than ample, the article might provide an insight into the private thoughts and agonies of friends who are less well endowed. Perhaps, also, it will allow all women to reflect on the tribulations of defining and living with adolescent sexuality.

REFERENCES

Masters, V. E., & Johnson, W. H. *Human sexual response*. Boston: Little, Brown, 1966.

Mussen, P. H., & Jones, M. C. Self-conceptions, motivations and attitudes of late and early-maturing boys. *Child Development*, 1957, **28**, 243–256.

Shipman, W. Age of menarche and adult personality. *Archives of General Psychiatry*, 1964, **10**, 155.

Pamela Cantor

I have to begin with a few words about androgyny. In grammar school, in the fifth and sixth grades, we were all tyrannized by a rigid set of rules that supposedly determined whether we were boys or girls. The episode in *Huckleberry Finn* where Huck is disguised as a girl and gives himself away by the way he threads a needle and catches a ball—that kind of thing. We learned that the way you sat, crossed your legs, held a cigarette and looked at your nails, your wristwatch, the way you did these things instinctively was absolute proof of your sex. Now obviously most children did not take this literally, but I did. I thought that just one slip, just one incorrect cross of my legs or flick of an imaginary cigarette ash would turn me from whatever I was into the other thing; that would be all it took, really. Even though I was outwardly a girl and had many of the trappings generally associated with girldom—a girl's name, for example, and dresses, my own telephone, an autograph book—I spent the early years of my adolescence absolutely certain that I might at any point gum it up. I did not feel at all like a girl. I was boyish. I was athletic, ambitious, outspoken, competitive, noisy, rambunctious. I had scabs on my knees and my socks slid into my loafers and I could throw a football. I wanted desperately not to be that way, not to be a mixture of both things but instead just one, a girl, a definite indisputable girl. As soft and pink as a nursery. And nothing would do that for me, I felt, but breasts.

I was about six months younger than everyone in my class, and so for about six months after it began, for six months after my friends had begun to develop—that was the word we used, develop—I was not particularly worried. I would sit in the bathtub and look down at my breasts and know that any day now, any second now, they would start growing like everyone else's. They didn't. "I want to buy a bra," I said to my mother one night. "What for?" she said. My mother was really hateful about bras, and by the time my third sister had gotten to the point where she was ready to want one, my mother had worked the whole business into a comedy routine. "Why not use a Band-Aid instead?" she would say. It was a source of great pride to my mother that she had never even had to wear a brassiere until she had her fourth child, and then only because her gynecologist made her. It was incomprehensible to me that anyone could ever be proud of something like that. It was the 1950's, for God's sake. Jane Russell. Cashmere sweaters. Couldn't my mother see that? *"I am too old to wear an undershirt."* Screaming. Weeping. Shouting. "Then don't wear an undershirt," said my mother. "But I want to buy a bra." "What for?"

I suppose that for most girls, breasts, brassieres, that entire thing, has more trauma, more to do with the coming of adolescence, of becoming a woman, than anything else. Certainly more than getting your period, although that too was traumatic, symbolic. But you could *see* breasts; they were there; they were visible. Whereas a girl could claim to have her period for months before she actually got it and nobody would ever know the difference. Which is exactly what I did. All you had to do was make a great fuss over having enough nickels for the Kotex machine and walk around clutching your stomach and moaning for three to five days a month about The Curse and you could convince anybody. There is a school of thought somewhere in the women's lib/women's mag/gynecology establishment that claims that menstrual cramps are purely psychological, and I lean toward it. Not that I didn't have them finally. Agonizing cramps, heating-pad cramps, go-down-to-the-school-nurse-and-lie-on-the-cot cramps. But unlike

any pain I had ever suffered, I adored the pain of cramps, welcomed it, wallowed in it, bragged about it. "I can't go, I have cramps." "I can't do that. I have cramps." And most of all, gigglingly, blushingly: "I can't swim. I have cramps." Nobody ever used the hard-core word. Menstruation. God, what an awful word. Never that. "I have cramps."

The morning I first got my period, I went into my mother's bedroom to tell her. And my mother, my utterly-hateful-about-bras mother, burst into tears. It was really a lovely moment, and I remember it so clearly not just because it was one of the two times I ever saw my mother cry on my account (the other was when I was caught being a six-year-old kleptomaniac), but also because the incident did not mean to me what it meant to her. Her little girl, her first-born, had finally become a woman. That was what she was crying about. My reaction to the event, however, was that I might well be a woman in some scientific, textbook sense (and could at least stop faking every month and stop wasting all those nickels). But in another sense—in a visible sense—I was as androgynous and as liable to tip over into boyhood as ever.

I started with a 28AA bra. I don't think they made them any smaller in those days, although I gather that now you can buy bras for five year olds that don't have any cups whatsoever in them; trainer bras they are called. My first brassiere came from Robinson's Department Store in Beverly Hills. I went there alone, shaking, positive they would look me over and smile and tell me to come back next year. An actual fitter took me into the dressing room and stood over me while I took off my blouse and tried the first one on. The little puffs stood out on my chest "Lean over," said the fitter (to this day I am not sure what fitters in bra departments do except to tell you to lean over). I leaned over, with the fleeting hope that my breasts would miraculously fall out of my body and into the puffs. Nothing.

"Don't worry about it," said my friend Libby some months later, when things had not improved. "You'll get them after you're married."

"What are you talking about?" I said.

"When you get married," Libby explained, "your husband will touch your breasts and rub them and kiss them and they'll grow."

That was the killer. Necking I could deal with. Intercourse I could deal with. But it had never crossed my mind that a man was going to touch my breasts, that breasts had something to do with all that, petting, my God they never mentioned petting in my little sex manual about the fertilization of the ovum. I became dizzy. For I knew instantly—as naïve as I had been only a moment before—that only part of what she was saying was true: the touching, rubbing, kissing part, not the growing part. And I knew that no one would ever want to marry me. I had no breasts. I would never have breasts.

My best friend in school was Diana Raskob. She lived a block from me in a house full of wonders. English muffins, for instance. The Raskobs were the first people in Beverly Hills to have English muffins for breakfast. They also had an apricot tree in the back, and a badminton court, and a subscription to *Seventeen* magazine, and hundreds of games like Sorry and Parcheesi and Treasure Hunt and Anagrams. Diana and I spent three or four afternoons a week in their den reading and playing and eating. Diana's mother's kitchen was full of the most colossal assortment of junk food I have ever been exposed to. My house was full of apples and peaches and milk and homemade chocolate-chip cookies—which were nice, and good for you, but-not-right - before - dinner - or - you'll - spoil - your - appetite. Diana's house had nothing in it that was good for you, and what's more, you could stuff it in right up until dinner and nobody cared. Bar-B-Q potato chips (they were the first in them too), giant bottles of ginger ale, fresh popcorn with melted butter, hot fudge sauce on Baskin-Robbins jamoca ice cream, powdered-sugar doughnuts from Van de Kamps. Diana and I had been best friends since we were seven; we were about equally popular in school (which is to say, not particularly), we had about the same success with boys (extremely intermittent) and we looked much the same. Dark. Tall. Gangly.

It is September, just before school begins. I am eleven years old, about to enter the seventh grade, and Diana and I have not seen each other all summer. I have been to camp and she has been somewhere like Banff with her parents. We are meeting, as we often do, on the street midway between our two houses and we will walk back to Diana's and eat junk and talk about what has happened to each of us that summer. I am walking down Walden Drive in my jeans and my father's shirt hanging out and my old red loafers with the socks falling into them and coming toward me is . . . I take a deep breath . . . a young woman. Diana. Her hair is curled and she has a waist and hips and a bust and she is wearing a straight skirt, an article of clothing I have been repeatedly told I will be unable to wear until I have the hips to hold it up. My jaw drops, and suddenly I am crying, crying hysterically, can't catch my breath sobbing. My best friend has betrayed me. She has gone ahead without me and done it. She has shaped up.

Here are some things I did to help:

Bought a Mark Eden Bust Developer.

Slept on my back for four years.

Splashed cold water on them every night because some French actress said in *Life* magazine that that was what *she* did for her perfect bustline.

Ultimately, I resigned myself to a bad toss and began to wear padded bras. I think about them now, think about all those years in high school I went around in them, my three padded bras, every single one of them with different sized breasts. Each time I changed bras I changed sizes: one week nice perky but not too obtrusive breasts, the next medium-sized slightly pointy ones, the next week knockers, true knockers; all the time, whatever size I was, carrying around this rubberized appendage on my chest that occasionally crashed into a wall and was poked inward and had to be poked outward—I think about all that and wonder how anyone kept a straight face through it. My parents, who normally had no restraints about needling me—why did they say nothing as they watched my chest go up and down? My friends, who would periodically inspect my breasts for signs for growth and reassure me—why didn't they at least counsel consistency?

And the bathing suits. I die when I think about the bathing suits. That was the era when you could lay an uninhabited bathing suit on the beach and someone would make a pass at it. I would put one on, an absurd swimsuit with its enormous bust built into it, the bones from the suit stabbing me in the rib cage and leaving little red welts on my body, and there I would be, my chest plunging straight downward absolutely vertically from my collarbone to the top of my suit and then suddenly, wham, out came all that padding and material and wiring absolutely horizontally.

Buster Klepper was the first boy who ever touched them. He was my boyfriend my senior year of high school. There is a picture of him in my high-school yearbook that makes him look quite attractive in a Jewish, horn-rimmed glasses sort of way, but the picture does not show the pimples, which were air-brushed out, or the dumbness. Well, that isn't really fair. He wasn't dumb. He just wasn't terribly bright. His mother refused to accept it, refused to accept the relentlessly average report cards, refused to deal with her son's inevitable destiny in some junior college or other. "He was tested," she would say to me, apropos of nothing, "and it came out 145. That's near-genius." Had the word undera-

chiever been coined, she probably would have lobbed that one at me, too. Anyway, Buster was really very sweet—which is, I know damning with faint praise, but there it is. I was the editor of the front page of the high-school newspaper and he was editor of the back page; we had to work together, side by side, in the print shop, and that was how it started. On our first date, we went to see *April Love* starring Pat Boone. Then we started going together. Buster had a green coupe, a 1950 Ford with an engine he had hand-chromed until it shone, dazzled, reflected the image of anyone who looked into it, anyone usually being Buster polishing it or the gas-station attendants he constantly asked to check the oil in order for them to be overwhelmed by the sparkle on the valves. The car also had a boot stretched over the back seat for reasons I never understood; hanging from the rearview mirror, as was the custom, was a pair of angora dice. A previous girl friend named Solange who was famous throughout Beverly Hills High School for having no pigment in her right eyebrow had knitted them for him. Buster and I would ride around town, the two of us seated to the left of the steering wheel. I would shift gears. It was nice.

There was necking. Terrific necking. First in the car, overlooking Los Angeles from what is now the Trousdale Estates. Then on the bed of his parents' cabana at Ocean House. Incredibly wonderful, frustrating necking, I loved it, really, but no further than necking, please don't, please, because there I was absolutely terrified of the general implications of going-a-step-further with a near-dummy and also terrified of his finding out there was next to nothing there (which he knew, of course; he wasn't that dumb).

I broke up with him at one point. I think we were apart for about two weeks. At the end of that time I drove down to see a friend at a boarding school in Palos Verdes Estates and a disc jockey played *April Love* on the radio four times during the trip. I took it as a sign. I drove straight back to Griffith Park to a golf tournament Buster was playing in (he was the sixth-seeded teen-age golf player in Southern California) and presented myself back to him on the green of the 18th hole. It was all very dramatic. That night we went to a drive-in and I let him get his hand under my protuberances and onto my breasts. He really didn't seem to mind at all.

"Do you want to marry my son?" the woman asked me.

"Yes," I said.

I was nineteen years old, a virgin, going with this woman's son, this big strange woman who was married to a Lutheran minister in New Hampshire and pretended she was Gentile and had this son, by her first husband, this total fool of a son who ran the hero-sandwich concession at Harvard Business School and whom for one moment one December in New Hampshire I said—as much out of politeness as anything else—that I wanted to marry.

"Fine," she said. "Now, here's what you do. Always make sure you're on top of him so you won't seem so small. My bust is very large, you see, so I always lie on my back to make it look smaller, but you'll have to be on top of the time.

I nodded. "Thank you," I said.

"I have a book for you to read," she went on. "Take it with you when you leave. Keep it." She went to the bookshelf, found it, and gave it to me. It was a book on frigidity.

"Thank you," I said.

That is a true story. Everything in this article is a true story, but I feel I have to point out that that story in particular is true. It happened on December 30, 1960. I think about it often. When it first happened, I naturally assumed that the woman's son, my boyfriend,

was responsible. I invented a scenario where he had had a little heart-to-heart with his mother and had confessed that his only objection to me was that my breasts were small; his mother then took it upon herself to help out. Now I think I was wrong about the incident. The mother was acting on her own, I think: that was her way of being cruel and competitive under the guise of being helpful and maternal. You have small breasts, she was saying; therefore you will never make him as happy as I have. Or you have small breasts; therefore you will doubtless have sexual problems. Or you have small breasts; therefore you are less woman than I am. She was, as it happens, only the first of what seems to me to be a never-ending string of women who have made competitive remarks to me about breast size. "I would love to wear a dress like that," my friend Emily says to me, "but my bust is too big." Like that. Why do women say these things to me? Do I attract these remarks the way other women attract married men or alcoholics or homosexuals? This summer, for example. I am at a party in East Hampton and I am introduced to a woman from Washington. She is a minor celebrity, very pretty and Southern and blonde and outspoken and I am flattered because she has read something I have written. We are talking animatedly, we have been talking no more than five minutes, when a man comes up to join us. "Look at the two of us," the woman says to the man, indicating me and her. "The two of us together couldn't fill an A cup." Why does she say that? It isn't even true, dammit, so why? Is she even more addled than I am on this subject? Does she honestly believe there is something wrong with her size breasts, which, it seems to me, now that I look hard at them, are just right. Do I unconsciously bring out competitiveness in women? In that form? What did I do to deserve it?

As for men.

There were men who minded and let me know they minded. There were men who did not mind. In any case, I always minded.

And even now, now that I have been countlessly reassured that my figure is a good one, now that I am grown up enough to understand that most of my feelings have very little to do with the reality of my shape, I am nonetheless obsessed by breasts. I cannot help it. I grew up in the terrible Fifties—with rigid stereotypical sex roles, the insistence that men be men and dress like men and women be women and dress like women, the intolerance of androgyny—and I cannot shake it, cannot shake my feelings of inadequacy. Well, that time is gone, right? All those exaggerated examples of breast worship are gone, right? Those women were freaks, right? I know all that. And yet, here I am, stuck with the psychological remains of it all, stuck with my own peculiar version of breast worship. You probably think I am crazy to go on like this: here I have set out to write a confession that is meant to hit you with the shock of recognition and instead you are sitting there thinking I am thoroughly warped. Well, what can I tell you? If I had had them, I would have been a completely different person. I honestly believe that.

After I went into therapy, a process that made it possible for me to tell total strangers at cocktail parties that breasts were the hangup of my life, I was often told that I was insane to have been bothered by my condition. I was also frequently told, by close friends, that I was extremely boring on the subject. And my girl friends, the ones with nice big breasts, would go on endlessly about how their lives had been far more miserable than mine. Their bra straps were snapped in class. They couldn't sleep on their stomachs. They were stared at whenever the word "mountain" cropped up in geography. And *Evangeline*, good God what they went through every time someone had to stand up and recite the Prologue to Longfellow's *Evangeline:* "... *stard like druids of eld* .../ *With beards that rest on their bosoms."* It was much worse for them, they tell me. They had a terrible time of it, they assure me. I don't know how lucky I was, they say.

I have thought about their remarks, tried to put myself in their place, considered their point of view. I think they are full of shit.

Chapter 14

Personality Development

THE SEARCH FOR IDENTITY

Womanhood and the Inner Space

Erik Erikson

Am I saying that "anatomy is destiny"? Yes, it is destiny, insofar as it determines not only the range and configuration of physiological functioning and its limitation, but also, to an extent, personality configurations. The basic modalities of woman's commitment and involvement naturally also reflect the ground plan of her body.

Editor's Introduction

The stage between youth and maturity is the stage of identity formation. Is there something different or special about female identity which deserves consideration apart from the identity formation of the adolescent male? Erikson (pp. 365-387) believes that there is and that this difference is largely determined by female anatomy: the fact that a woman harbors an "inner space" and that she is aware of this from her very earliest years. Erikson, however, sees the formation of identity among women in terms of their relations to men. Female identity formation is achieved, according to Erikson, when "the young woman, whatever her work career, relinquishes the care received from the paternal family in order to commit herself to the love of a stranger and to the care to be given to his and her offspring." Thus, identity is achieved when the woman commits herself to the future father of their children and transfers her emotional and economic dependency from her family of origin to her family of procreation. This theory stimulates anger from a large number of women because it reflects the idea of being possessed by one's own body and because it reflects a definition of self totally based upon others. It seems to me that there is something disquieting about inferring social roles entirely from physiological functioning.

Another aspect of Erikson's essay which arouses concern is his pessimistic view of the future for young girls. If men unconsciously perceive women as castrated men, and if the dominant cultural identity is male, how can a young girl grow up without incorporating the negative view that she is a second-class citizen who needs to be mindful of her place?

To this Erikson replies that we must also evaluate the positive aspects of feminine sexual identity. Erikson does feel that the capacity for commitment to care for human life, whether or not it is ever actualized in motherhood, is the central issue in the formation of female identity. Erikson states that due to her innate capacities to care for others, a woman has the unique ability to bring a voice of reason and compassion to a world badly in need of both these qualities. Women, Erikson states in *Women and Analysis* (1974), should not try to become "one of the boys." Equal opportunity for women should not mean the same jobs but can only mean the right to give "new meaning and a new kind of competence to (so far) 'male' occupations." Only when women are seen in this capacity can our society project changes in social custom which can liberate both men and women from the roles that have exploited them both.

Thus, Erikson concludes that women have an identity that depends upon others for its realization and one that is at least partially formulated on negative evaluation by the dominant cultural models. What is hopeful about Erikson's theories, however, is the statement that "as women take their share in the over-all economic and political planning of affairs so far monopolized by men, they cannot fail to cultivate a concerted attention to the whole earth as an inner space, no matter how far out any of the outer spaces may reach."

REFERENCE

Erikson, E. H. Once more the inner space: Letter to a former student. In Jean Strouse (Ed.), *Women and analysis*. New York: Dell, 1974

Pamela Cantor

If the "inner space" is so pervasive a configuration, it should be found to have its place in the evolutionary beginnings of social organization. Here, too, we can call on visual data.

Recent motion pictures taken in Africa by

[1]Three films taken in Kenya, 1959: *Baboon Behavior, Baboon Social Organization*, and *Baboon Ecology*.

Washburn and deVore[1] demonstrate vividly the morphology of basic baboon organization. The whole wandering troop in search of food over a certain territory is so organized as to keep within a safe inner space the females who bear future offspring within their bodies or carry their growing young. They are protectively surrounded by powerful males who, in turn, keep their eyes on the horizon, guiding the troop toward available food and guarding it from potential danger. In peacetime the strong males also protect the "inner circle" of pregnant and nursing females against the encroachments of the relatively weaker and definitely more importunate males. Once danger is spotted, the whole wandering configuration stops and consolidates into an inner space of safety and an outer space of combat. In the center sit the pregnant females and mothers with their newborns. At the periphery are the males best equipped to fight or scare off predators.

I was impressed with these movies not only for their beauty and ingenuity, but because here I could see in the bush configurations analogous to those in the Berkeley play constructions. The baboon pictures, however, can lead us one step further. Whatever the morphological differences between the female and male baboons' bony structures, postures, and behaviors, they are adapted to their respective tasks of harboring and defending the concentric circles, from the procreative womb to the limits of the defensible territory. Thus morphological trends "fit" given necessities and are therefore elaborated by basic social organization. And it deserves emphasis that even among the baboons the greatest warriors display a chivalry which permits the female baboons, for example, to have weaker shoulders and lesser fighting equipment. In both prehuman and human existence, then, the formula holds that whether, when, and in what respects a female anywhere can be said to be "weaker" is a matter to be decided not on the basis of comparative tests of isolated muscles, capacities, or traits but on that of the functional fitness of each item for an organism which, in turn, fits into an ecology of divided function.

Human society and technology has, of course, transcended evolutionary arrangement, making room for cultural triumphs of adaptation as well as for physical and mental maladaptation on a large scale. But when we speak of biologically given strengths and weaknesses in the human female, we may yet have to accept as one measure of all difference the biological rock-bottom of sexual differentiation. In this, the woman's productive inner space may well remain an inescapable criterion, whether conditions permit her to build her life partially or wholly around it or not. At any rate, many of the testable items on the long list of "inborn" differences between human males and females can be shown to have a meaningful function within an ecology which is built, as any mammalian ecology must be, around the fact that the human fetus must be carried inside the womb for a given number of months, and that the infant must be suckled or, at any rate, raised within a maternal world best staffed at first by the mother (and this for the sake of her own awakened motherliness, as well) with a gradual addition of other women. Here years of specialized womanhours of work are involved. It makes sense, then, that the little girl, the future bearer of ova and of maternal powers, tends to survive her birth more surely and turns out to be a tougher creature, to be plagued, to be sure, by many small ailments, but more resistant to some man-killing diseases (for example, of the heart) and with a longer life expectancy. It also makes sense that she is able earlier than boys to concentrate on details immediate in time and space, and has throughout a finer discrimination for things seen, touched, and heard. To these she reacts more vividly, more personally, and with greater compassion. More easily touched and touchable. However, she is said also to recover faster, ready to react again and elsewhere. That all of this is essential to the "biological" task of reacting to the differential needs of others, especially weaker ones, is not an unreasonable interpretation; nor should it, in this context, seem a deplorable inequality that in the employment of larger muscles woman shows less vigor, speed, and co-ordination. The little girl also learns to be more easily content within a limited circle of activities and shows less resistance to control and less impulsiveness of the kind that later leads boys and men to "delinquency." All of these and more certified "differences" could be shown to have corollaries in our play constructions.

Now it is clear that much of the basic schema suggested here as female also exists in some form in all men and decisively so in men of special giftedness—or weakness. The inner life which characterizes some artistic and creative men certainly also compensates for their being biologically men by helping them to specialize in that inwardness and sensitive indwelling (the German *Innigkeit*) usually ascribed to women. They are prone to cyclic swings of mood while they carry conceived ideas to fruition and toward the act of disciplined creation. The point is that in women the basic schema exists within an over-all optimum configuration such as cultures have every reason to nurture in the *majority of women*, for the sake of collective survival as well as individual fulfillment. It makes little sense, then, when discussing basic sex differences to quote the deviations and accomplishments (or both) of exceptional men or women without an inclusive account of their many-sided personalities, their special conflicts, and their complex life histories. On the other hand, one should also emphasize (and especially so in a post-Puritan civilization which continues to decree predestination by mercilessly typing individuals) that successive stages of life offer growing and maturing individuals ample leeway for free variation in essential sameness.

For example, woman's life too contains an adolescent stage which I have come to call a psychosocial moratorium, a sanctioned period of delay of adult functioning. The maturing girl and the young woman, in contrast to the little girl and the mature woman, can thus be relatively freer from the tyranny of the inner space. In fact, she may venture into "outer space" with a bearing and a curiosity which often appears hermaphroditic or not outright "masculine." A special ambulatory dimension is thus added to the inventory of the spatial behavior, which many societies counteract with special rules of virginal restraint. Where the mores permit, however, the young girl tries out a variety of possible identifications with the phallic-ambulatory male even as she experiments with the experience of being his counterpart and principal attraction—a seeming contradiction which will eventually be transformed into a polarity and a sexual and personal style. In all this, the inner space remains central to subjective experience but is overtly manifested only in persistent and selective attractiveness, for whether the young woman draws others to herself with magnetic inwardness, with challenging outwardness, or with a dramatic alternation of both, she selectively invites what seeks her.

Young women often ask whether they can "have an identity" before they know whom they will marry and for whom they will make a home. Granted that something in the young woman's identity must keep itself open for the peculiarities of the man to be joined and of the children to be brought up, I think that much of a young woman's identity is already defined in her kind of attractiveness and in the selective nature of her search for the man (or men) by whom she wishes to be sought. This, of course, is only the psychosexual aspect of her identity, and she may go far in postponing its closure while training herself as a worker and a citizen and while developing as a person within the role possibilities of her time. The singular loveliness and brilliance which young women display in an array of activities obviously removed from the future function of childbearing is one of those esthetic phenomena which almost seem to transcend all goals and purposes and therefore come to symbolize the self-containment of pure being—wherefore young women, in the arts of the ages, have served as the visible representation of ideals and ideas and as the creative man's muse, anima, and enigma. One is somewhat reluctant, therefore, to assign an ulterior meaning to what seems so meaningful in itself, and to suggest that the inner space is tacitly present in it all. A true moratorium must have a term and a conclusion: womanhood arrives when attractiveness and experiences have succeeded in selecting what is to be admitted to the welcome of the inner space "for keeps."

Thus only a total configurational approach—somatic, historical, individual—can help us to see the differences of functioning and experiencing in context, rather than in isolated and senseless comparison. Woman, then, is not "more passive" than man simply because her central biological function forces her or permits her to be active in a manner tuned to inner-bodily processes, or because she may be gifted with a certain intimacy and contained intensity of feeling, or because she may choose to dwell in the protected inner circle within which maternal care can flourish. Nor is she "more masochistic" because she must accept inner periodicities in addition to the pain of childbirth, which is explained in the Bible as the eternal penalty for Eve's delinquent behavior and interpreted by writers as recent as de Beauvoir as "a hostile element within her own body." Taken together with the phenomena of sexual life and motherhood, it is obvious that woman's knowledge of pain makes her a "dolorosa" in a deeper sense than one who is addicted to small pains. She is, rather, one who "takes pains" to understand and alleviate suffering and can train others in the forebearance necessary to stand unavoidable pain. She is a "masochist," then, only when she exploits pain perversely or vindictively, which means that she steps out of, rather than deeper into, her female function.

By the same token, a woman is pathologically passive only when she becomes too passive within a sphere of efficacy and personal integration which includes her disposition for female activity.

One argument, however, is hard to counter. Woman, through the ages (at any rate, the patriarchal ones), has lent herself to a variety of roles conducive to an exploitation of masochistic potentials; she has let herself be confined and immobilized, enslaved and infantilized, prostituted and exploited, deriving from it at best what in psychopathology we call "secondary gains" of devious dominance. This fact, however, could be satisfactorily explained only within a new kind of biocultural history which (and this is one of my main points) would first have to overcome the prejudiced opinion that woman must be, or will be, what she is or has been under particular historical conditions.

Am I saying, then, that "anatomy is destiny"? Yes, it is destiny, insofar as it determines not only the range and configuration of physiological functioning and its limitation but also, to an extent, personality configurations. The basic modalities of woman's commitment and involvement naturally also reflect the ground plan of her body. I have in another context identified "inception" as a dominant modality already in the early lives and in the play of children.[2] We may mention in passing woman's capacity on many levels of existence to actively *include*, to accept, *"to have and to hold"*—but also to *hold on*, and *hold in*. She may be protective with high selectivity and overprotective without discrimination. That she must protect means that she must rely on protection—and she may demand overprotection. To be sure, she also has an organ of intrusion, the nipple which nurses, and her wish to succor can, indeed, become intrusive

[2]Erik H. Erikson, *Childhood and Society*, Second Edition. New York: W. W. Norton, 1963, p. 88.

and oppressive. It is, in fact, of such exaggerations and deviations that many men—and also women—think when the unique potentials of womanhood are discussed.

As pointed out, however, it makes little sense to ask whether in any of these respects a woman is "more so" than a man, but how much she varies within womanhood and what she makes of it within the leeway of her stage of life and of her historical and economic opportunities. So far I have only reiterated the physiological rock-bottom which must neither be denied nor given exclusive emphasis. For a human being, in addition to having a body, is *somebody*, which means an indivisible personality and a defined member of a group. In this sense, Napoleon's dictum that history is destiny, which Freud, I believe, meant to counterpoint with his dictum that destiny lies in anatomy (and one often must know what dicta a man tried to counterpoint with *his* most one-sided dicta), is equally valid. In other words: anatomy, history, and personality are our combined destiny.

Men, of course, have shared and taken care of some of the concerns for which women stand: each sex can transcend itself to feel and to represent the concerns of the other. For even as real women harbor a legitimate as well as a compensatory masculinity, so real men can partake of motherliness—if permitted to do so by powerful mores. . . .

IN THE HOME

The Roots of Radicalism

Bruno Bettelheim

Hardly a culture in the world does not provide in some way for distinct male and female roles; only in the affluent sector of our own society does the blurring of distinction make it difficult for the son to identify with his father.

Editor's Introduction

In recent years there have been striking changes in the foundations of the American family. The family unit has moved from an extended kinship structure of aunts, uncles, grandparents, parents, and children all living within close proximity of each other to a nuclear family structure which, at best, includes two parents and often only one.

Not only the structure of the family is changing but, according to Bettelheim, so are the characteristic roles of the family members. Bettelheim sees the father as becoming emasculated and distant from his children, increasingly unable to serve as an effective role model for his sons. He sees women changing and cautions that women must increase their usefulness by developing roles which allow them to find themselves as women, not roles which allow them to emulate men. He views the rebelliousness of today's youth as the destructive result of the dissolution of the clear-cut and distinctive roles which have existed for men and women. He sees the unisex culture as a reflection of the diminishing distinction between the roles of men and women, mothers and fathers.

Bettelheim states, "to understand why authority is under such vehement attack, one must look to American fathers." Bettelheim looks to American fathers, mothers, and society for the causes of the destruction of the family and the origins of radicalism.

While Bettelheim's views are provocative, it is my hope that everyone will not agree with his position on the negative value of youthful rebellion or with his views on the necessary distinctions between the roles of men and women.

Bettelheim believes that to blur the distinctions between the roles of men and women can only be harmful to the child. I oppose the rigid adherence to sexual stereotypes which insists that each sex specialize in a particular set of virtues. Rather, I would prefer to aspire toward complete, nonsegregated personalities and to reject the assigning of one set of characteristics to the male and another to the female. I believe that it can be highly beneficial if not essential to a child to have a mother who can be both strong and tender and a father who can be both gentle and stern, as the situation demands. To imply that the maternal and paternal functions and characteristics must be separate and opposite is to deny the laws of nature—the fact that each of us embodies genetic characteristics of both sexes.

Pamela Cantor

To understand why authority in this country is under such vehement attack, one must look to American fathers. Just as the ineptitude, moral collapse and failure of nerve of the French aristocracy paved the way for the great Revolution of 1789, so the loss of a distinct role for the fathers has much to do with today's rebellion of the young. Freud found the roots of Victorian emotional problems in the excesses of stern, authoritarian patriarchs. Conversely, if some modern boys engage in rampages, I believe we can trace it to the virtual abdication of their dads from any sort of clear-cut position in the family.

The present situation is the logical result of developments that began in the 19th Century. In the past 70 years, women have achieved biological and technological liberation. The advent of contraception, while it did not greatly reduce the actual number of children reared to maturity (which was formerly decreased by miscarriage, stillbirth and childhood diseases), did put an end to the incessant pregnancies that had drained the women's time and energy. And with the general economic prosperity resulting from technological progress, women in the upper classes of the Western nations became able, as economist Thorstein Veblen saw it, to lead lives of ceremonial futility. Thus, in the early years of the 20th Century, the popular notion of normal life was that of man doing the productive work, while woman was an ornamental consumer.

This notion never quite matched reality, certainly not among the working classes, but it dominated the imagination of the well-to-do European and American *bourgeoisie* until World War Two. Eventually, though, women became dissatisfied with their empty existences. The War presented an opportunity to become more active. Many wives and mothers went to work. Others became socially concerned, vigorously involving themselves in reformist and humane acitivities—the P. T. A., the League of Women Voters, Planned Parenthood, local women's clubs, charities and the like. The socially active housewife was able to be as busy as her husband, but her activity sprang from interest rather than necessity. As a result, her commitment was exciting, dramatic, but not necessarily enduring. If politics palled, she might turn to gardening.

As for the father, at the opening of this era he usually believed that his work was vitally important, because without him the family could not survive. "I have to take care of them," the middle-class father proudly told himself. "I am responsible. They are weak. Without me, they would perish."

Sometimes, after a husband died, a woman might go to work and be more of a financial success than her man had been. In fact, wealth has slowly been accumulating in the hands of women so that today, as a class, they possess more riches than ever before (though, unquestionably, economic power is still a male province). But the fiction of the indispensable father continued to be generally believed. Again, World War Two marked the watershed for this notion. The women who stayed at home had proved their self-sufficiency. The men who had gone forth to conquer fascism came back with a great longing for peace and comfort and were bemused by the increasing complexity of the American corporate economy. Novels of the Forties and Fifties such as *The Hucksters* and *The Man in the Gray Flannel Suit*, popular works of sociology such as *The Organization Man* and *The Lonely Crowd* tell the story. The American man, having lived through the Depression and the War, having to live now through the Cold War, settled with a sigh into the barrackslike suburban developments that mushroomed around the big cities. Since prosperity and personal affluence with its pension plans seemed to assure survival and security, his life was no longer ruled by necessity but by the wish for ever greater comfort. Its purpose seemed directed toward acquiring superfluous adornments, rather than essentials. It's easy to achieve self-respect—and with it the respect of others, which comes from the inner security they feel one possesses—if one's work

provides his wife and children with the necessities of life. But when men were not working for survival and were not after real, intrinsic achievements (such as are inherent, for example, in scientific discovery), or at least after power, but merely after luxury, only their busyness prevented them from realizing how devoid of true meaning their lives had become. Today, the children of such fathers are in their late teens and early 20s.

In these affluent families, the father often describes his work as a rat-race. Indeed, the successful businessman scurries through a maze of corporate politics, spurred on by a yearning for such rewards as profit sharing, pension plans, stock options, bonuses, annuities. He is often a minor functionary in a bureaucracy whose purpose, other than to grow larger, tends to be ill-defined. His work often seems pointless to him, as he is shifted from one position to another with little say about his destiny. And if he listens to social critics inveighing against environmental pollution, cultivation of artificial needs, dollar imperialism, war profiteering and related evils, he may begin to suspect the worth of his activities and, with it, his own value.

The effect of these changes in parental attitudes on the children has been drastic. The small child recognizes only what he sees. What he is told has much less of an impact on him. He sees his mother working around the house, for him. He is told only that his father also works for his well-being; he does not see it. In the suburban family, when the father commutes to work, he has to leave early and he comes home when the child is about to be put to bed. More often than not, he sees his father watching TV, hiding behind his paper, maybe taking what to the father is a well-deserved nap but to the boy seems like sheer idleness. Even if the middle-class father takes his son to his place of work some 20 or 30 miles away, it's such a different world from the child's life at home that he cannot bring the two together. And what he sees there of the father's work he cannot comprehend. How can talking on the telephone—which from his experience at home he knows is done mainly to order goodies or for fun—or into a machine secure the family's well-being? Thus, the boy's experience can hardly dispel the notion that his father is not up to much. The father's work remains unseen and seems unreal, while the mother's activities are very visible, hence real. Since he does not see him do important things, the child comes to doubt the legitimacy of the father's authority and may grow up to doubt the legitimacy of all authority.

For ages, the father, as a farmer, as a craftsman working in his shop, had been very visible to his sons and, because of his physical prowess and know-how in doing real things in the real world, was an object of envious adulation. Now, the mother, who traditionally is the one who nurtures the child, becomes ever more the carrier of authority. If for no other reason than that she is with the child during the father's waking hours, the mother becomes the disciplinarian, the value giver, who tells the child all day long what goes and what does not. In short, mother knows best, and father next to nothing. As one boy put it—and there is some truth in the words of the most naive child—"What is my fat-her? Just a fat-her."

Even though the father doesn't think much of his work, he expects the son to follow in his dreary footsteps. The child is sent to the best grammar school, not to satisfy his intellectual curiosity, not to develop his mind, not to understand himself better but to make good marks and to pass examinations so that he can get into the best high school. There he is pushed to compete for the highest grades, so that he can go to a famous college, often not because he can get a better education there but because going to a school with a big name adds to the prestige of the parents. And college is merely a means to an end—admission

to graduate school. Graduate work in turn furnishes the "union card," enabling him to get a good job with a big corporation, where he can work until he finally retires on a good pension and then waits to die. Given this distorted, purgatorial picture of the world of education and work, is it any wonder that many young people scornfully reject it?

The American social and economic system, despite its obvious shortcomings, is much more than a gigantic staircase that leads nowhere. American society is creative and progressive and offers unprecedented opportunities for individual fulfillment and achievement. But that's not the way it has been presented to many young Americans born in the Forties and Fifties. The people who taught these youngsters to despise American society were their own parents.

Psychoanalysis asserts that each child, growing up in a family, must choose a parent to emulate. But a son cannot emulate his father's great abilities as a worker if that father seems a little man at home, meekly taking out the garbage or mowing the lawn according to a schedule devised by his wife. The process of becoming a person by emulation is enormously important, because the child doesn't copy just external mannerisms; he tries—as far as his understanding will let him—to think and feel like the chosen parent. For boys in today's suburban society, many fathers offer little with which to identify. The problem is not created by the father's absence due to commuting and the long executive workday—sailors and men at war have been good objects for identification though absent from the home for months and years. The problem arises because the image of the father, in the eyes of the mother and others, has been downgraded.

In order not to have to identify with a superfluous father, many boys in the more affluent reaches of our society try to solve the problem by identifying with their mothers.

But, while this solves one problem, it creates another, not for the boys' self-respect as human beings but for their self-respect as males. This emulation of the mother is not, by the way, manifested only in long hair or unisex clothing, which are merely matters of fashion. Boys tend to adopt the consumer mentality, like their mothers, rather than their fathers' producer mentality. A mother's role is also more attractive—at least in England and America—because she is often the more cultured member of the household. She is apt to be more liberally educated, more aware of the arts than her practical husband. This attitude is typified by the couple portrayed in Sinclair Lewis's *Main Street*. On the Continent, culture is a male prerogative, and this at least has slowed down the attrition of the father's dominance in the European household.

In the reformist and revolutionary activities of middle-class American college men, I see a repetition of the behavior patterns of their socially conscious mothers. These boys work for a cause with emotional fervor, rather than with the approach that business or technical activities require. Accomplishment in business—indeed, in politics—demands devotion to logic, long-range planning, practicality, willingness to compromise, acceptance of routine and drudgery. These qualities, indispensable to productive work, are repellent to many young radicals. They engage passionately in a controversy but are ready to withdraw from it the moment it becomes boring or tedious. Ralph Nader has commented bitterly on the waning of student enthusiasm for the ecology movement after the initial hoopla of Earth Day 1970. During the student strike after the Kent State calamity, it was only *work* that stopped in many colleges, while fun—in the form of movies, rock concerts and the like— went right on. And, of course, immediately after Cambodia and Kent State thousands of young men and women vowed that they would be out the following November to work for

peace candidates. A little over six months later, however, the number of students actively working during the 1970 elections was insignificant when compared with those who had claimed they would.

Marx never said that revolution would be fun. The New Left speaks of "revolution for the hell of it" and its values are theatrical. The melodrama becomes tragedy when some young people begin to see themselves as romantic bomb throwers. They shirk the task of educating the people and building a mass movement, those long-established practical strategies of the left. They think they can do their teaching by breaking plate-glass windows, by setting fire to buildings that could be used to educate the people.

The student revolutionary's lack of realism is an important reason for which he is frequently rejected by members of the working class. Typically, he tries to get close to the workers through his dress; he wears blue jeans and a work shirt. Trying to get to people by dressing in a certain way is a feminine, consumer approach, focusing on external attire rather than on basic function. It is the mother who tells a boy he can't go to church without a jacket and tie; he learns the lesson so well that ten years later, he still feels that there is a correct uniform for every occasion and he wouldn't be caught dead in the streets without blue jeans and a work shirt. I remember that in the early days of the Communist Party in Austria, members were taught that you couldn't reach the workers merely by dressing like them; you had to live like them and work like them; you had to learn from them long before you dared to try to teach them. Today, a left-wing student thinks he can walk into a factory wearing the appropriate garb and start lecturing the workers on the way our fascist-pig establishment oppresses the struggling third-world peoples. This is exactly the attitude of the Victorian Lady Bountiful, who feels herself above the men who do dirty work and who don't know about the really important things in life. American workingmen sense that they are being patronized and want to kick the snobbish young sermonizer right out the plant gate.

Such aberrant behavior as this feminized approach to politics does not take place when children are able to identify with the parent of the same sex and to love the parent of the opposite sex. To make such healthy identification possible, it is not important whether the father has all the authority or whether the mother and the father share it; it is important simply that there be specific male authority and specific female authority. It is the attractiveness of each role that makes the child want to identify with it and decide which parent he will want to choose for the object of his love. Hardly a culture in the world does not provide in some way for distinct male and female roles; only in the affluent sector of our own society does the blurring of distinctions make it difficult for the son to identify with his father.

Psychoanalysis has derived its notions of the proper role a male parent should play in his children's lives from the observations Freud made in Vienna in the late 19th Century. His studies, of course, were limited to authoritarian, Victorian families. He learned that psychological problems stemmed from the faults of this type of family. But when the Victorian family worked well, mental health, as Freud understood it, resulted. Today, we are so used to hearing about the oppressive horrors of Victorian life that we forget that many of these families were happy and produced healthy children. The popular idea that the family in the 19th Century was a dreadful institution and the psychoanalytical idea that all families resemble it are both wrong.

In Freud's day, the male personality still developed as Goethe, both statesman and poet, had described his own: "From father is my stately gait, / My sober way of conduct, /

From mother is my sunny mind, / My zeal for spinning tales." As Freud saw it, the paternal influence created the superego—that element in a person's character that laymen call the conscience. The mother, on the other hand, gave the child unconditional love and satisfied his needs, thus teaching him how to gratify those bodily drives and emotional needs that psychoanalysts describe as belonging to the id. A child carries images of his parents in his mind, or, as psychoanalysts say, he internalizes them. If all goes well, the boy acts as he thinks his father would want him to and he tries to be the kind of person his mother would love. The ego, which is the conscious self, is formed, according to Freud, to mediate between the conflicting images of the judging father and the loving mother.

For a child to form his personality out of interacting masculine and feminine images, the two must be truly different. Today, the mother is both nurturing and demanding, while the father often is neither. The child is not offered the example of one person representing the principle of pleasure and the other person the principle of duty. Out of this confusion, the child develops a conscience, which tells him, "You have a *duty* to enjoy life." Thus, there are young people who feel that work ought to be all fun and who look on nine-to-five drudgery as somehow immoral. They often try to drop out of the world of work and careers. Other people turn the fun of life into grueling labor: zealous tourists, dogged golf-swing improvers, fanatic car buffs, people who worry that they're not getting as much pleasure as they ought to out of sex. How impossible the pursuit of pleasure becomes, even in sex, when it assumes the character of a moral duty!

In old Vienna, the male parent unquestionably represented the principle of duty, and sons felt respect, awe, even fear, toward their fathers. And the boys had something to look forward to: the idea of having similar authority and commanding similar respect when they grew up. In adolescence, through revolt against paternal authority, one gained further strength and masculine pride. But how can one revolt against the weak fathers of today? They often do not seem worth the trouble. Instead, the children revolt against the establishment. But this does not work out for them, either. After a successful adolescent revolt, the boy may reidentify with the best in the father. But how can our student revolutionaries reidentify with a distant and anonymous establishment? Either they get stuck in their adolescent revolt or the establishment defeats them. In either case, they can't reach maturity and deep down they despise themselves for a failure that is not of their own making.

Freud's teachings have generally been taken as the last word on psychodynamics, but he made scientific observations, he did not formulate laws. Freud would never have made the mistake of declaring that people in a different society, such as our own, could follow the Victorian pattern for effective child rearing without appropriate modifications. Families can take many forms as long as they serve the needs of children. A few years ago, I studied the Israeli *kibbutzim*, the collective communities, for a short time. Here children do not live with their parents; they are raised in groups. One of the most important factors in the lives of the children, though, is that they constantly visit both parents at work. And when the children come, everybody stops working and explains to the children what they're doing and why it is important to them and to the community. Through that experience, the child gains respect for the work of the parents. People have wondered how *kibbutz* children grow up so well when their parents are distant figures. The answer is that, while there are only a few basic needs, there are many ways to satisfy them.

A child need not be raised by his biological parents. Freud made so much of the Oedipus complex or Oedipal situation that many people believe a male child *must* have a jealous desire for his mother and an envious hatred for his father in order to grow up normally. But there has been much argument among anthropologists about whether or not this Oedipal relationship really exists in all societies. As I see it, the chief thing is to understand the basic principle underlying the Oedipus phenomenon, which is applicable to any family structure: The human infant for many years is entirely dependent upon and in the power of some individual or individuals. If you're in someone's power, for better or worse you have to come to terms with that person. If the person doesn't abuse his power, you come to love him. But in whose power the child is, and with whom he has to come to terms, can vary greatly.

Consider my own history. Today, I teach psychoanalysis at the University of Chicago and, of course, my students read Freud on the subject of how all-important a child's mother is. After I've let them expound on the subject, I try to open their minds a bit more by telling them some of my personal story. During my early childhood, the person who fed me, took care of me and was with me most of the time was not my mother but a wet nurse. This was a custom among the upper-middle classes in Vienna at the time. The nurse was a peasant girl in her late teens, who had just had a baby out of wedlock. She left the baby with relatives and hired herself out to suckle the child of a well-to-do family. To make sure she gave a lot of milk, she followed the folklore formula of drinking a lot of beer. So my entire care as an infant was entrusted to a girl who had little education, was by our standards a sex delinquent, was a little high on beer most of the time and was so devoid of maternal instinct that she left her own child. I am the deplorable result.

The reasons why a relationship that, according to theory, should have been unpromising worked so well were that the girl had no interest other than me; she took good physical care of me and, being a peasant, was without undue fastidiousness about diapering and toilet training; the beer kept her relaxed and happy, she didn't discipline me excessively and didn't overawe me intellectually. It was not an idyllic upbringing but it certainly was adequate. And because my nurse was awed by my father, I learned to look up to him by observing her. Thus, I acquired respect for him without his having to discipline me directly. My father was a gentle man, very secure in himself, so convinced of his inner authority that he never needed to make a show of it. I didn't have continual fights with my parents, because the dos and don'ts came from the nurse, somebody who wasn't much of an authority. An infant learns very early what the power relations are in his family and these hold the key to his development.

My father was a good model for me. As a child, I visited him at his place of work. I spent many hours there, watching him, more often just playing. The pace of life was still leisurely enough to permit my father to drop what he was doing and explain things to me. I saw other strong men work hard. Their respect for my father and his for them, without my being aware of it, made a deep impression on me. Such experiences make identifications with his father seem worth while for a boy.

Besides respecting the roles of the two sexes, people should be able to clearly differentiate between them. Dichotomy, duality, is one of the most fundamental characteristics of both nature and philosophy. As Buckminster Fuller says, "Unity is plural and at minimum two." The oracular Chinese book, the *I Ching*, presents 64 figures made up of six lines. This large number of figures is made of different combinations of just two kinds of lines, solid and broken. The solid lines represent the masculine yang principle and the broken lines, the feminine yin principle. The child selects the characteristics he prefers, inventing his own individual mix. There are many more than six characteristics in the human personality, each of which has its feminine or masculine version; thus, the possible kinds of human personality are infinite.

The trend I've described in today's middle-class family is that the loss of attractiveness and distinctness in the father's role impedes the satisfactory working out of this process. What can be done about this situation? Obviously, we can't turn back the economic or technological clocks. But ideas as much as tangible necessities have caused the decline of the father. We must renew our appreciation of the popularity of the sexes and be enriched by the inner tensions it creates. While I do sympathize with liberated women to a degree, I don't think they should make it their goal to become as much like men as possible or to change the image of men. They should concentrate on finding themselves as women.

We males cannot expect women to find roles for us that are suitably masculine; we have to do this ourselves. The new masculine, heroic ideal may possibly focus on discovery. All through recorded history, the discoverer has been a man, even the discoverer of the pill, which may solve the most pressing problem of mankind: overpopulation. The astronauts who set foot on the moon, and also those who managed to return their crippled spaceship, fired the imagination of the entire world. A new masculine pride can come from discoveries of the mind, from the brain, not from brawn. Our cities need to be rethought and rebuilt, the very pattern of our lives will have to be reshaped so that men will again be able to derive pride from what they are doing on this earth, maybe even beyond it. The problems and possibilities are immense.

The task is not one that can be mastered in comfortable leisure. But leisure, the absence of struggle, order, harmony were the ideals the GIs of World War Two adopted, a natural but mistaken reaction to a horribly destructive conflict. The absence of tension is just as deadly as too much of it. This is one meaning of the Zen question "What is the sound of one hand clapping?" One hand alone strikes empty air and makes no sound at all. This is why the young crave confrontations. The college administrators who face student dissenters are too often men who are lacking in masculine security and have based their careers on the principle of harmony at all costs. So, instead of meeting questions and openly recognizing that unavoidable conflict exists, they try to evade it. One reason Dr. Hayakawa has succeeded in restoring some order at San Francisco State College is that he was not afraid of real confrontation in place of academic soothing syrup. He stood up to the demonstrators in a manly way, instead of pretending to be on their side while actually trying to undermine them. One of the most compelling testimonies to the life-giving properties of conflict is Sartre's description of how it felt to be in the French Resistance from 1940 to 1945:

We were never more free than during the German occupation. . . . Because the Nazi venom seeped even into our thoughts, every accurate thought was a conquest. Because an all-powerful police tried to force us to hold our tongues, every word took on the value of a declaration of principles. Because we were hunted down, every one of our gestures had the weight of a solemn commitment.

Freud said that life results from an imbalance and the effort to re-establish balance. If a new imbalance is not created, however, there will be death. Hegel and Marx both summed up life as the conflict between thesis and antithesis, which is resolved in synthesis, which in turn generates a new antithesis for a new conflict. Without this process, life would come to a stop.

Next to sexual pleasure, one of the great experiences of life is climbing a mountain and growing hot and sweaty in the process, then coming upon a cold lake and jumping in. You may be shivering and have to jump out again in a minute, but what delight there is in the sudden change from hot to cool! Compare this with swimming in a tepid pool. Where there is no tension created, none is relieved. The affluent middle-class American wants life to run smoothly, doesn't want any difficulties. He wants the mountain to be level and the pool to be tepid. And then he wonders why his children reject him.

Kant said that aesthetic pleasure of the highest order comes from the fact that the artist creates a unity out of a variety of elements. One of the oldest images of the human soul is this metaphor from Plato's *Phaedrus*:

Let the figure be composite—a pair of winged horses and a charioteer. Now the winged horse and the charioteers of the gods are all of them noble and of noble descent, but those of other races are mixed; the human charioteer drives his in a pair; and one of them is noble and of noble breed, and the other is ignoble and of ignoble breed; and the driving of them of necessity gives a great deal of trouble to him.

At this point, the naïve utopian asks, "If both horses were alike, wouldn't they pull together better?"

Yes, they might. But how empty, how boring!

TEEN CULTURE: RELATIONS WITH PEERS

The Adolescent

Anonymous

Since I have been thirteen, I have sought to improve my personality, but with every shock, minor or otherwise, and with every change of mood, I have discarded an old personality and embarked on a new one. The inner struggle, I am certain, is not confined to me alone—many others, especially among adolescents, must be experiencing a similar turmoil.

Editor's Introduction

Erik Erikson writes "The study of identity, then, becomes as strategic in our time as the study of sexuality was in Freud's time" (1950, pp. 282–283). Erikson hypothesizes that the identity crisis in adolescence as well as other developmental crises are universal phenomena, although different cultures accentuate different phases. Erikson stresses the seemingly inherent wisdom of each culture in dealing with its inevitable developmental problems. He feels that Americans handle most areas wisely—with the notable exception of the adolescent period. As his concern is primarily social, he poses the question: How does society hinder or help the crisis? In applying this question to adolescence, Erikson observes that Americans force the adolescent to delay gratification to an impossible degree in order to reach goals which no longer have any meaning. He is further critical of the fact that we give our adolescents little or no opportunities to participate in society. Our culture makes the task of the adolescent—that of forming ego identity—harder, or it helps minimally.

According to Erikson, identity is achieved after the developmental phases of infancy and childhood are completed and the individual has come to terms with the "identity crisis" of adolescence. But how can "identity" be defined? It is more than simply the answer to the question, "Who am I?" Identity also encompasses finding a role in society that is both acceptable and attainable. Essentially it is determining the answers to the questions "Who am I?" "Where do I fit in?" and "Do I like myself?"

There are many factors which influence the formation of one's "identity"—factors which are both personal and social. The rapid physical changes of adolescent development, parents' expectations, and parental difficulties in handling the young person's needs for independence while remaining within the family are a few areas in which turmoil is likely to arise—turmoil that influences an individual's self-concept and satisfaction with that concept.

The following selection is an account written by an adult in the process of exploring his own youth—with the distinct advantage of hindsight. The author, who remains anonymous, shares some of the turmoil he experienced while trying to survive his own identity crisis.

Reprinted by permission of the Editor of the *American Journal of Psychoanalysis*, 1971, Vol. XXXI, No. 1, pp. 29–32.

REFERENCE

Erikson, E. H. *Childhood and society*. New York: W. W. Norton, 1950.

Pamela Cantor

If my adolescence began with a vague awareness that I was experiencing change, it ended with the recognition that the world is not an easy place to live in, that I need to accept the person that I am and continue to try to comprehend my own inconsistencies and anxieties.

My adolescence was not very different from that of my friends in that period of my life. We happened all to be first-born sons of middle-class Jewish families who had moved from New York City to suburban Long Island. Until I was eight years old, I was raised in Bedford-Stuyvesant (a district in Brooklyn) when it was still a predominantly Jewish neighborhood, until . . . my parents moved to the suburbs. My father's business continued to prosper and we moved again, when I was thirteen, even further out from the city. My adolescent period thus took place in a sparsely populated area, in comparison to the previous neighborhoods where we had lived. Our house was in a development where all the homes were on one acre of land, and there was a small tract of woods behind our house. There were several boys of my own age and background living nearby who constituted the circle of my closest friends.

My friends' parents were friends of my own parents. All of them had high expectations for their sons. Eventually we all fulfilled our parents' ambitions, if not our own. My mother was devoted to her family. She tended, however, to be demanding and rigid in her concept of "the straight and narrow" for a Jewish boy, approving only when she perceived signs of my attaining the goals that she had ordained. Her concerns about scholastic achievement and "culture" set the pattern that I was required to deal with throughout my adolescence and into adulthood. She was modest in her dress and general appearance, and not physically affectionate. She demanded a good-night kiss only because it was "the proper thing to do"—and I hated the nightly courtesy because it placed affection on the level of a propriety. Nonetheless, she did respect my privacy and I soon learned to evade her interminable interrogations about my personal affairs. My father had similar expectations for me. Proper use of time in order to excel, or at least to be constructive, was his standing order. Anything less than straight A's was reason for him to scrutinize where my time had been spent. He had built up his own business and, in my opinion, it occupied an inordinate amount of his time. When he was not at work, he used to be puttering around the house, finishing attics, basements, and porches of each of our suburban homes. This was his only hobby. I was always the reluctant assistant. My reluctance was dealt with by his comments about what he used to do when he was a boy.

My father never seemed able to deal with my questions about sex—but he was a warm and jovial man who made me feel comfortable enough to ask them, at least. We respected each other and it was clear that so long as I demonstrated that I was excelling I was free to do what I pleased. Both my parents focused most of their attention on me—they were not as friendly with the parents of my sisters' friends, and they invested more time and money in helping me with my needs (as they perceived them). My sisters, four and eight years younger than I, respectively, I considered irrelevant to the adolescent changes that were beginning to occur in this family setting. They esteemed my accomplishments and occasionally looked to me for advice and help, subtly reinforcing the role already established for me by my parents.

It seems to me that there was a time in my life when I began having questions to which no one could be relied on to give answers. Perhaps because I had already developed an obsessive style, I needed to understand the strange new feelings that I had begun to experience and I turned them into questions that could be verbalized. Who am I? Whom do I want to be like? These were representative of the questions I asked. The answers that I wanted were answers which would gain for me superiority over all; I needed tangible evidence that this is what I would expect if I persevered. I needed some sort of sounding board for my questions—and to that end, I began sporadically keeping notes. As I progressed, platitudes about self-recognition became increasingly complex as I realized that perseverance, which had become my style, was only an inadequate answer to the questions about my identity. When I was thirteen, I decided to emulate Albert Schweitzer, whom I imagined to be a quiet, unsmiling, dedicated man. But I found I couldn't stick to it—I enjoyed laughing, and playing gin and poker with my friends. One couldn't conceive of Albert Schweitzer doing things like that. He would be listening to his parents, not gambling—and he would certainly not laugh. Well, if I didn't know enough about him, how about the president of the Student Council? So I tried copying him for a little while until I found I was not doing a very good job of it, and it didn't seem to be working out—after all, I was not captain of the football team. Perhaps John—he was the next possibility. I could be more like John, the Italian kid who was always getting into some sort of trouble. But he seemed to like to get into trouble. I thought maybe I should team up with John and like getting into trouble, too. So, we shoplifted together at the local Woolworth's and gloated over the snitched yo-yo and mousetrap. And I tried to let my hair grow into the then-fashionable "duck's ass" style; my collar was turned up at the back, my chest was left a little more exposed, and the sleeves of my T-shirt got hiked up to the shoulders. We "burglarized" a nearby estate—that is, we stole a cheap wristwatch from a windowsill where the window was left open. Then I went home to face my father whom I had sneered about as "de old man." I walked in sporting my tough new style, and my father's large, round face became an enraged scarlet. My old lady whimpered. The thunderous anger: "*What the goddamn do you think you're doing, you lousy. . . .*" With my new, cool facade: "You mean, 'Who the goddam . . . ?'" Their response: "*Get the hell out of this house.*"

The walls seem to rip apart, the earth shudders under my feet, as my father's wrath casts me out into utter darkness—my pride makes me leave the house, but there is nowhere to go. So, why not just give up being like John? Later that evening, I sneak back into the house, go over to the piano, sit down, and play a Paderewski minuet so that my sister can dance to it.

The episode is forgotten, and I don't know where I am. A few days later, I write:

Since I have been thirteen, I have sought to improve my personality, but with every shock, minor or otherwise, and with every change of mood, I have discarded an old personality and embarked on a new one. This inner struggle, I am certain, is not confined to me alone—many others, especially among adolescents, must be experiencing a similar turmoil.

The sage generalization: "Be Thyself," I have also applied. But the question arises, what is the myself that I should be? I must first learn who I am; only then can I know myself. Very well. But how can I know myself? It seems to me as though the two statements go round and round in a circle.

Unable to settle the problem, I retreat back to the piano, to my books, to my self-righteous pursuit of obsessive unemotionality.

The racking despair after each unsuccessful wrestling match, after failing to be elected president of the National Honor Society, after coming in last of the team in the mile run, after not getting "pussy" at the movies—how will I ever survive? I am just an unremarkable, ordinary guy who will end up going to the local college—and that is as far as I am able to see at the moment.

"Ruth likes you," says Paul, the other trombonist in the school band.

"Who, the flute player?"

"Yes. Why don't you see what you can get?"

"Oh, shit," I think to myself. All I know is that I better start to do something. Some of the others are fucking, and I have had so little "experience." I'm scared, that's what I am, and I don't know what to do. Then, after several sessions of peering at each other over Mr. Small's music stands, the flutist and I manage to get off alone into a practice room, and I feel her up. For once I am triumphant, and decide that I am indeed remarkable. I decide that I am attractive and cool, and that it's time for me to make passes. On Saturday afternoons Paul and I ride around our neighborhood picking up chicks. Nothing ever really happens, and once again I am thrown back into doubt about my being a man. When will I get laid? Am I perhaps sexually impotent? Finally, one of the girls with a "reputation" comes on strong. We go and park in one of the deserted parking lots and I am making progress, but still trying to wriggle into a convenient position, until a cop shines his flashlight into our half-clothed bodies. Chased away,

embarrassed, cowed and angry, we try again—but as soon as I put on my "protection," I wilt. She feigns annoyance, and we "forget it."

"Well, how did things go with Beth?" ask two of the fellows who were in on the whole thing. I look at their expectant faces and decide that they are close enough friends for me to say: "Not too well, I'm afraid I'm impotent."

"You mean im-potent."

"You mean impotent."

And that goes on for a while. I become furious at their insensitivity, and learn that friends are not always so consoling, that I'd better not expect reassurance from them, but keep my mouth shut, so I wrote:

> I don't know whether I'm potent or impotent—fuck the pronunciation! Rather, I sit on, fattening buttocks, tickling a dull, flopping penis. Stand up, I say! What a worm you are. Ugly, with a hole in your head and a fat, upper lip. Wherefore draggeth thou thy wrinkled sack through the black grass of the Kingdom of Croth, over which thou rulest?

Paul and I finally decide that we could probably get more sex if we became beatniks—and then I could write verse without capitals and punctuation. Paul was popular, he knew more people than I did. So I decide that becoming a beatnik would at least win me notoriety—perhaps some of Paul's popularity would rub off on me, or, at least, people would realize that I was really a kind and decent and likeable person. I had read Durant's *Story of Philosophy* and I thought I knew a lot. What did my father know of Spinoza? Or Russell? Or Plato? Or Dostoyevsky? Nothing, nothing at all. All he knows is his lousy business and how to finish porches. So I let my hair grow again, I started to wear sandals and dungarees that I shredded at the cuffs. I carried around a paperback copy of Camus. The change was rather gradual. As the demands to get a haircut, to shave, to buy some decent clothes grew louder, I received an admission to Columbia—and my folks were satisfied. Now that I had proven what they wanted me to prove, there was nothing left for them, except to bemoan my beat ways, and to warn me about college. My mother was far more affected than my father, but I could deal with that by being what they considered "good," which continued to consist of that goodnight kiss. My new identity did not fulfill any of the promises it was supposed to, but it kept my parents at a distance. They were proud of my going to Columbia, and I was able to come and go without having to give too many explanations.

There were still a good many episodes of self-doubt—depression about my inability to compete quite as successfully as I had at high school, but my turmoil became less. I rejected my parents' values, but less and less with each passing year. And by my third year of college, I was able to sit through a Passover Seder in the bosom of the family, and without a single sarcastic remark about the pointlessness of ritual or of religion.

PROBLEMS OF ADOLESCENCE

Drug Use and Abuse among Youth

Alvin E. Strack

Marijuana does not cause physical dependence or an abstinence syndrome. Tolerance does not appear to develop; in short, it causes little physical damage in the user.

No one, of course, wants to restrict rights or freedom or to have to argue against them. We must recognize, though, that the "right" that these drug abusers claim is the right to be immature and uncaring about themselves and society to the point of stupidity.

Editor's Introduction

In the following article Strack discusses the use and abuse of opiates, depressants, stimulants, hallucinogens, and solvents. He is primarily concerned with the physical and psychological effects of the drugs described, although he also mentions an approach to treatment, prevention, and drug education.

Before we can deal with the question of drug abuse, it is necessary to define the terms surrounding drug usage. Traditionally, drug abuse has been described as "drug addiction." In 1963 the World Health Organization defined drug addiction as "a state of periodic or chronic intoxication detrimental to the individual and to society." In 1965 the same organization revised its definition and recommended that the term "drug dependence" be used to replace both "drug addiction" and the less frequently used "drug habituation." This recommendation reflected the increasing awareness that the drugs that do not cause physical dependency can nevertheless be the agents involved in problems which are as serious as those caused by the addictive drugs. "Drug dependence" has been defined as "a state

From *Journal of Health, Physical Education and Recreation*, 1968, *39*, pp. 26–28, 55–57. Reprinted by permission.

arising from repeated administration of a drug on a periodic or continual basis. Its characteristics may vary with the agent involved, and this must be made clear by designating 'drug dependence' of a particular type." The definition which the Consumers Union (*Licit and Illicit Drugs*) adopted in 1974 perhaps more closely reflects the impression the general public holds of drug abuse.

An addicting drug is one that most users continue to take even though they want to stop, try to stop, and actually succeed in stopping for days, weeks, months, or even years. It is a drug for which men and women will prostitute themselves. It is a drug to which most users return after treatment at Lexington, at the California Rehabilitation Center, at the New York State and City centers, and at Synanon, Daytop, Phoenix House, or Liberty Park Village. It is a drug which most users continue to use despite the threat of long-term imprisonment and to which they promptly return after experiencing long-term imprisonment. (p. 89)

This emotionally charged definition was felt to be necessary due to the misleading information which was circulating at the time regarding the curability of addiction. Thus, the authors stressed the enslaving capabilities of the opiates and other addictive drugs.

The following article focuses primarily on drugs such as morphine, heroin, cocaine, depressants, amphetamines, LSD, DMT, glues, and marijuana, since views of these drugs are presently clouded by a mass of contradictory and confusing information as well as by fear and arguments regarding law enforcement and morality. However, the drugs which are most widely used among youth besides marijuana—caffeine, nicotine, and alcohol—are not mentioned. Adolescents and adults in our culture take caffeine to wake up in the morning, nicotine to complete a meal, alcohol to complement a meal or to be sociable. Adults buy their drugs at the supermarket, the pharmacy, or the liquor store. Young adults buy these drugs at the same locations and might add to the list marijuana bought from suppliers—friends, or other contacts. We are clearly a drug-oriented society, opting for chemical solutions to nonorganic problems. The danger lies in choosing drugs which offer permanent solutions to temporary problems. Because alcohol, tobacco, and caffeine are legal, few people think of the harmful effects they can have. Alcohol acts as a nervous-system depressant and is strongly addictive. There are 6 million alcoholics in the United States today. It is becoming increasingly clear that there is a strong relationship between smoking and lung cancer, heart disease, emphysema, and other respiratory and circulatory conditions. There is evidence for the relationship between alcohol abuse and cirrhosis of the liver; this disease is among the leading causes of death in America. The relationship between drunken driving and over half our traffic fatalities needs no elaboration. Caffeine may contribute to hypertension and heart disease. Despite the common classification of marijuana as a "dangerous drug," and in spite of the fact that all the evidence is not in, it may be that marijuana is among the "safest" of the commonly used drugs. It is possible, however, that consistent marijuana usage may lead to the same damaging respiratory effects as those of tobacco.

In 1969 *Time* magazine listed the most common drugs according to the degree of damage they are likely to cause. The list was headed by heroin due to the fact that addiction demands frequent and increasing doses, and large doses can result in death. Barbiturates were second. They also have strong habituating properties, and overdoses can also be fatal. Amphetamines were third. Amphetamines can produce physiological dependency, psychiatric disorders, and damage to the brain. Lysergic acid diethylamide (LSD) was fourth. LSD does not produce physical dependence and doses are rarely fatal. The psychotic effects of the drug can be dangerous, however, as perceptions are affected. Its psychological and physical effects can be long-lasting. Marijuana was fifth. Marijuana is not physically addictive. Tetrahydrocannabinol (TCH), a chemical component of marijuana, can, however, cause hallucinations. Marijuana usage has stimulated the most controversy, as some experts maintain that the drug is completely harmless while others contend that marijuana usage is the first step in the progression toward narcotic addiction. The danger that Strack points out lies in the possibility that a psychological dependence may develop. The National Institute of Mental Health has recently estimated that the majority of marijuana users quit after a brief period, while 10 percent become habitual users.

It seems sad to me that somewhere near 100 million prescriptions for tranquilizers are sold each year, that most adults "need" at least three cups of coffee or tea to get through the day, and that many adults use barbiturates to enable them to sleep at night. That young people follow these same patterns is not surprising.

REFERENCES

Brecher, E., & the editors of Consumer Reports. *Licit and illicit drugs*. Mount Vernon, N. Y.: Consumers Union, 1972.

Eddy, N. B., et al. Drug dependence: Its significance and characteristics. *Bulletin of the World Health Organization*. 1965, **32**, 721–733.

Pop drugs: The high as a way of life. *Time*, 1969, **94**, 13, 68–78.

Pamela Cantor

To start, let us consider the following proposition: Any substance capable of altering man's mood has abuse capability. What is implied in this statement, of course, is that the specific substance abused is of less direct importance to the user than the end result, and indeed, this is frequently the case. With this as a general premise, let me cite some specific drugs and substances frequently abused in our society.

We need to define three terms about which there is considerable confusion: addiction, habituation, and dependence. Through the years "addiction" and "habituation" have been used interchangeably to describe forms or results of drug use and abuse. The resulting confusion has led to decisions by the World Health Organization to replace these terms with the more general one of "dependence."

Dependence is described as "a state arising from repeated administration of a drug on a periodic or continuous basis." The use of the term dependence necessitates delineating the *exact* drug which one is discussing. Therefore, we have drug dependence of the barbiturate type, drug dependence on the opiate type, etc.

OPIATES

The opiates are among the oldest drugs known to man. They have no equal, to this day, in relieving pain. They are medically irreplaceable at the present time. When properly used in medical practice, there is little or no danger of development of dependence. When abused, they produce very serious physical and psychological dependence. Drugs in this class include morphine, codeine, and other natural opium derivatives, and also heroin, which is synthetically produced from morphine. It is heroin, of course, which is the drug of choice among opiate addicts. Given intravenously, it produces a "kick" or "high" of an almost orgasmic nature, followed by the "nod" or period of oblivion which the addict also prizes. It is perhaps this double effect which makes the opiates so attractive to individuals seeking the escape from reality.

The manufacture, distribution, possession, and use of the opiates or narcotics are subject to stringent international, federal, and state regulation and control. Penalties for illicit sale are severe, and rightly so. Opiate addiction, per se, is not a crime, and yet opiate addicts have constructed a surer prison for themselves and their minds than any jailer could hope to build.

Narcotic withdrawal makes a familiar tale. Usually somewhat overdramatized, it has been portrayed on many occasions in movies, television, and other media. Withdrawal from a heavy heroin habit is indeed a painful and agonizing process. In practice today, however, and thanks to vigilant police efforts, there are few so-called "heavy" habits around, because heroin is too scarce and because the heroin bought by most addicts has been highly diluted by the seller. Hence, "cold turkey" withdrawal for most narcotic addicts is today much less formidable than it is often described.

The most prevalent form of narcotic use among young people limits itself to exempt narcotics marketed in cough syrups. The practice seems to be confined to localized areas, and the exact extent of the problem is extremely difficult to determine.

The effects of narcotic use include drowsiness and sleep; the side effects are nausea, vomiting, constipation, itching, flushing, constriction of pupils, and respiratory depression.

DEPRESSANTS: BARBITURATES AND TRANQUILIZERS

The barbiturate drugs have been used in medicine for half a century. They are used as sedatives, sleep producers, for epilepsy, high blood pressure, gastrointestinal disorders, and many other disease states. Used as directed, and in the doses prescribed, they are quite safe. Abused at high doses for long periods of time, they produce severe psychological dependence and a type of physical dependence which in at least one respect is more severe than that seen with narcotics. To be specific, abrupt withdrawal of barbiturates from a dependent individual can cause convulsions which can be fatal if untreated. It is this fact which has caused some investigators to say that the barbiturates are more toxic when abused than narcotics. Symptoms of barbiturate abuse include slurred speech, staggering gait, and sluggish reactions. The user is erratic and may easily be moved to tears or to laughter. Perhaps the best description of the barbiturate intoxicated individual is a reeling drunk who does not smell of alcohol.

Certain tranquilizers, notably those usually designated as minor tranquilizers and employed for the less severe mental and emotional disorders, have occasionally been abused, with the development of psychological and physical dependence. Symptoms in dependent individuals during withdrawal of these drugs closely resemble those seen with barbiturates.

STIMULANTS: COCAINE AND AMPHETAMINES

Cocaine is derived from the leaves of the coca tree. Although a stimulant, and not a narcotic, it is treated as a narcotic for legal control purposes. Once widely used as a local anesthetic, cocaine has disappeared from the medical scene. It is a very potent stimulant. It produces excitability, talkativeness, and a reduction in the feeling of fatigue. Cocaine may produce a sense of euphoria, increased muscular strength, and hallucinations. Its use has been associated with violent behavior.

The amphetamine derivatives have been used in medicine for about 35 years. They are very useful in the treatment of obesity, depression, hyperactivity, behavior disorders in children, and narcolepsy (a disorder characterized by excessive and sudden periods of sleep). Amphetamines increase alertness, dispel depression, mask fatigue, elevate mood, and produce a feeling of well-being. It is generally agreed that amphetamines do not produce physical dependence with abuse, but psychological dependence is common with excessive use. With abuse of amphetamines the body becomes tolerant to it, and abusers frequently use doses many times those usually employed for medical purposes. Symptoms of abuse include talkativeness, excitability, and restlessness. The abuser will suffer from insomnia, perspire profusely, have increased urinary frequency, and often exhibit tremor. Acute psychotic episodes may occur with intravenous use, or may develop with the chronic use of large doses.

Manufacturer, distribution, and sale of the depressants and stimulants (except cocaine as previously mentioned) are controlled by a variety of federal and state laws, most notable of which is the recently enacted federal legislation which requires manufacturers and distributors of these drugs to register with the government and to maintain for inspection complete inventory and sales records. These laws restrict the number of times a prescription may be refilled, and place a six-month time limit on refills.

HALLUCINOGENS

The hallucinogens which include LSD, DMT, peyote, psilocybin, mescaline, and also marijuana, have received an inordinate amount of publicity through the news media. Only one of these agents is currently considered to have any possible medical use, and that one is LSD. When used under very carefully controlled conditions, LSD has been found to be of some value in the treatment of alcoholism and certain psychosexual disorders.

If one can judge from the publicity generated by certain enthusiastic proponents of the hallucinogens, their use is increasing by leaps and bounds. A somewhat less biased view would be that abuse of these substances has increased to worrisome proportions, especially among young people of college age.

As their name suggests, the hallucinogens produce a variety of hallucinatory effects, primarily in visual perception. When abused, these substances produce a psychological dependence which, in some individuals, amounts to an almost religious fervor. The drugs do not produce physical dependence and no physical symptoms occur on withdrawal.

LSD was synthesized in the late 1930's, but its hallucinogenic effect was not discovered for several years. Abuse of this substance has become a problem only in recent years, in part because of the articulate and persuasive devotees of "expansion of consciousness." The LSD experience is certainly memorable. It involves visual, auditory, and tactile hallucinations, changes in perception, thought, mood and activity, time sense, and comprehension. All too frequently, the LSD "trip" is a shattering psychic experience which leaves the user disoriented, in panic, or even frankly psychotic. Psychosis has developed after use of LSD in individuals who previously exhibited no signs of emotional instability. Moreover, this psychotic state may persist or recur for weeks after the drug was taken. Mescaline, psilocybin, and DMT all produce effects similar to those of LSD, differing only quantitatively in their effects and duration of action. DMT is interestingly enough called the "businessman's trip," since its effect lasts only about as long as the ordinary business lunch. Manufacture, distribution, and sale of LSD is now restricted under the same federal laws governing stimulants and depressants.

The popular weed marijuana is also known as cannabis, pot, ghang, hashish, charas, and a variety of other names. Marijuana is an irregular stimulant of the central nervous system, and is a hallucinogen. It has no established medical use. It is used—usually smoked or eaten—for its ability to produce euphoria, a feeling of exaltation and dreaming, and hallucinations. Use of marijuana is associated with a distorted sense of time and distance. Panic and fear sometimes result, but the user is usually talkative and in good humor, or conversely sometimes drowsy and quiet.

Marijuana does not cause physical dependence or an abstinence syndrome. Tolerance does not appear to develop; in short, it causes little physical damage in the user. However, reports from areas of the world where the more potent forms of cannabis and marijuana are used indicate an association between continued intake of this substance and the development of psychosis. Psychological dependence, which is moderate to strong, can develop readily, especially in susceptible individuals.

The most serious problem associated with marijuana is pointed out in the *Bulletin of the World Health Organization*:

> Abuse of cannabis (marijuana) facilitates the association with social groups and subcultures involved with more dangerous drugs, such as opiates and barbiturates. Transition to the use of such drugs would be a consequence of this association rather than an inherent effect of cannabis. The harm to society derived from abuse of cannabis rests in the economic consequences of the impairment of the individual's social functions and his enhanced proneness to asocial and antisocial behavior (Eddy et al., 1965).

SOLVENTS

The abuse of solvents is commonly but somewhat inaccurately labeled "glue sniffing." Inhalation of solvents contained in glues, gasoline, paint thinners, lighter fluids, and the like produces a state of excitation, exhilaration, and excitement resembling alcohol intoxication. Eventually blurred vision, slurred speech, loss of balance, and hallucinations result. Tolerance develops, but physical dependence does not occur. A strong psychological dependence develops. Reports of actual physical damage resulting from solvent abuse are rare, although the toxicity of these solvents for man is widely recognized in industry. One of the very real dangers is that of suffocation in habitues who use plastic bags to hold the glue or solvents up to the face. It is an unfortunate fact that abuse of these substances occurs to the largest extent in young adolescents.

METHODS OF TREATMENT

We are really just beginning to realize and act on the idea that abuse of drugs and other substances will require as many different methods of treatment as it has causes. Certainly, habilitation and rehabilitation will not be easy, but we must try. The comprehensive programs of California, Maryland, and New York, and the coordinated program in New York City headed by Efren Ramirez, must be given the opportunity to function effectively in this problem area. Such organizations as Daytop and Synanon must also have their chance to show what can be done. We have too few answers to turn aside any reasonable approach to cure and rehabilitation.

Legal facets of drug and substance abuse have been mentioned briefly before. I would like here to defend the role of law enforcement in preventing drug abuse. Law enforcement is primarily charged with removing one of the proximate causes of drug and substance abuse, namely, availability. There is a social need to stamp out the illicit trade in drugs and substances, and for this we are dependent in large measure on good law enforcement. They have done very well. No greater testimonial to this fact exists than the real scarcity of heroin in this country.

I would like to emphasize that it is *not* the province of law enforcement officers to be philosophical about drug addiction and abuse. They are sworn to enforce the law. It is our business to assist them whenever possible.

There are many social aspects of drug and substance abuse, but I wish to offer only a few for consideration. First, society must accept the existence of, and differentiate between, the spree or occasional drug abuser and the chronic abuser for whom abuse has become a way of life. Second, the chronic abuser is a sick individual, and however society chooses to provide care and custody for him, he should be treated as a sick man. Third, drug abuse is a symptom of some deeper, underlying disorder. It may range on the one hand from adolescent rebellion to deep-seated character disorders on the other. In all of these, loneliness and alienation play a large role.

We are left with what might be called the morality of the situation, but perhaps more precisely, the realities of the situation. One hears these days a refrain that goes something like this: "I have the right and should have the freedom to use drugs if I wish to, especially if they don't physically harm me. And even if they do harm me, they hurt only me and nobody else." This argument is frequently put forth by those who, for one reason or another, claim the right to use drugs occasionally for other than their intended medical purposes.

It is interesting that, lacking an adequate logical reason for drug abuse, these people fall back on the argument for rights and freedoms. No one, of course, wants to restrict rights or freedoms or to have to argue against them. We

must recognize, though, that the "right" that these drug abusers claim is the right to be immature and uncaring about themselves and society to the point of stupidity. Society, any society, has always had the privilege of limiting individual rights and freedoms to the extent necessary to preserve the common good. This function of society extends even to protecting the individual from himself if this is necessary.

From the earliest times, man and his societies have restricted the distribution and the use of certain substances. Many early recognized the medical usefulness of certain plants and chemicals—but also their antisocial potential in terms of poisonous or intoxicant effects. Social and legal control of such substances has been accepted as a necessary limitation on individual freedom for centuries. Even the primitive societies of today have such controls in the form of a witch doctor or medicine man.

Legal controls of these substances then is not really an unnecessary, and certainly not a recent, intrusion on man's inalienable rights. They are a very real social necessity.

The delicate balance between the individual's rights, duties, and responsibilities in a society certainly enters into this picture.

Another aspect is the physical harm, or the lack of it, caused by the abuse of drugs and other substances. In this sense, physical harm means physical dependence and a withdrawal syndrome, or the toxic effect of long-term use. There is little doubt that there are substances that do *not* cause such physical harm when abused. As has already been pointed out, the real harm in these substances is their asocial or antisocial effect; their leading the abuser to association with substances which are harmful and dangerous; and the general economic impairment which they produce.

The suggestion that if drugs do harm me but no one else, then there is no reason why I should not use them, is patently ridiculous.

Has the young adult gone psychotic after taking LSD harmed only himself? Who must care for him, keep him from further harming himself or others? Who has to try to put his shattered mind back together?

If you inquire of a drug abuser what he expects to get from drugs, you can expect a variety of answers:

I want to get high.
I want to get away.
I want to stay awake.
I want to go to sleep.
I want a new thrill.
I want to expand my consciousness.
I want a mystic experience.
I want to enhance my creativity.

Many users have no real reason except that "everyone was doing it," or the seldom expressed but often present need to rebel, somehow.

Many, of course, are very serious about using drugs for insight, for a mystic experience, or to enhance creativity. In the latter group one finds many of the hippies of Haight-Ashbury or Greenwich Village. They regard ingestion of drugs and other substances for these purposes as *use*, not abuse. They regard drugs as functional in this respect. They are optimistic to the point of being naive about the ability of drugs to enhance creativity or promote insights into life, love, and the things which really matter to them. They do not see abuse of drugs as dysfunctional in their lives.

Like many rebel and avant-garde groups before them, these young people have a real message to and about our society and our way of life. It is sad that most of their message is blurred and confused by being bound up with the problem of drug abuse.

Prevention is the real answer to drug abuse; the key to prevention is education. But who should educate, and what should be told about drug abuse?

The family remains of primary importance in influencing child development, and it is within the family and the home that most can be accomplished in preventing the abuse of drugs and other substances. A caring, loving, and directing home atmosphere is, and will remain, the best means of guiding youth through the difficult adolescent years. The alienation and loneliness which characterize so many abusers are much less likely to develop in a good home atmosphere. A willing ear, a kind word when needed, gentle direction, and a loving heart may be the only way to explain that most young people who are exposed to drugs do *not* abuse drugs. Most young people have no need for this kind of crutch or escape. But too many, unfortunately, must look for crutches and escapes.

To professional educators, however, will fall the role of telling young people about drugs and drug abuse. In doing this they must provide factual, clear-cut information—no horror stories, no finger-wagging. In short, they must "tell it like it is." Today's youth is quite knowledgeable concerning drugs and other substances and will quickly turn off anyone who doesn't tell a straight story about the problem. The educator, too, will often find himself in a strategic position to influence youth, either as an example setter or even in a surrogate parent role.

So what do we do for our young people? First, we listen to them as hard as we have ever listened in our lives. This shows them we care. Then tell all the facts, and in the manual for educators, *Drug Abuse: Escape to Nowhere*, I think we have the facts. It is a good starting point. But the most important message to convey to our young people is that abuse of drugs and other substances is one of the biggest "cop-outs" of all time. It is a "cop-out" on oneself.

Today's young people stress physical, material, intellectual, psychological, and spiritual self-fulfillment. I can think of very few actions that an individual can take that are more damaging to this self-fulfillment than drug abuse. Society has nothing to do with it, morality has nothing to do with it, rights and freedoms have nothing to do with it. Young people must be told: This is you—emphasis *you*. At almost any level of function you, emphasis *you*, will find yourself hung-up if you abuse drugs or substances.You will have "copped-out" on yourself. It matters little what you use—alcohol, marijuana, LSD, opiates, or whatever—it is still your "cop-out."

The total answer to the drug abuse problem lies in a judicious blend of education, legal control, more research on drugs and other substances now available, and, most important, the establishment of a dialogue across the generation gap. The latter, of course, has meaning for many social problems other than drug abuse.

Life in a Children's Detention Center: Strategies of Survival

Susan M. Fisher

I learned from one therapy group of a sixteen-year-old boy drinking his own urine, burning his forehead with cigarettes, and calling himself "black Jesus." He was not noticed by the staff. . . .

A female counselor stood and impassively watched a girl bite out a piece of another girl's cheek and told me later, "Nice girls don't fight."

Editor's Introduction

Juvenile delinquency, which is defined as a violation of legal codes of conduct, may range from a minor infringement of the law (drinking in public, shoplifting a comic book) to major crimes against persons or property (vandalism, assault, theft), or may include behavior which is illegal only because of the subject's youthful age (such as school truancy or purchasing liquor). Thus, the behaviors of delinquency do not fit into one clearly defined mold. The outcomes of delinquency are as variable as the acts which define it. The delinquent youth may be brought before a judge, may come to the attention of a public agency, may be detected and not brought to the attention of any agency or court, or may go completely undetected.

Evidence cited by Wirt and Briggs (1965, pp. 1–26) indicates that a delinquent's prospect of being detected, arrested, referred to a social agency, or let go depends upon sex, social status, family income level, and the availability of social agencies and judicial sources in a given community. Males and lower-class youth are more likely to be arrested than girls and middle- or upper-class youth who commit the same crime. The availability of treatment centers tends to decrease the number of

From *American Journal of Orthopsychiatry*, *42*, 1972, pp. 368–374. Copyright © 1972 by the American Orthopsychiatric Association, Inc. Reproduced by permission.

arrests but, conversely, the availability of a juvenile court in a particular neighborhood increases the likelihood of arrest.

The variability of the definition of a delinquent act, and the vast latitude in the consequences of a delinquent act, make it difficult to assess the extent of delinquency in the United States. There is, however, little doubt that the number of adolescents who come to the attention of authorities falls far below the actual number who commit delinquent acts, since only a small proportion of these acts are recorded or punished by legal authorities. A study by Offer, Sabshin, and Marcus (1965) reported delinquent acts among 75 percent of "normal" adolescents who exhibited no other forms of problem behavior. These young people were from suburban, middle-class homes. Similar reports of undetected delinquency have led some researchers to conclude that almost all adolescents engage in acts which would be labeled delinquent if brought to the attention of public officials and that this may be an important part of balancing ethical and moral issues in normal psychosocial development.

My own experience leads me to a similar conclusion. When I was 10 and in sixth grade, my friend and I spent a Saturday afternoon trying to steal comic books from a local stationery store. We got caught, since we were not especially skillful in disguising our prizes in our large shopping bag. The owner of the store said that he was going to call our parents and report our behavior. We gave him our names, addresses, and phone numbers and returned to our homes. I closed myself in the bathroom and cried—partly from shame, partly from fear, and partly by way of a deliberate effort to obtain parental sympathy in view of my obvious remorse. My mother and father showed concern and questioned me. I confessed my transgression, to which my father replied "That's perfectly normal. I did the same thing when I was your age. I stole [I have forgotten what he stole] from Woolworth's in Syracuse. It's just a stage and you will get over it." I was immensely grateful for his wisdom, with which my mother concurred. I never did confess that my friend and I had stolen a few small china figurines of rabbits from Woolworth's ourselves the previous weekend and hadn't gotten caught. But I never did it again. If I had been black, if I had been from a lower-class neighborhood, if I had been poor, if I had been male, if I did not have such understanding parents, my essentially innocent act might have elicited quite different consequences. Susan Fisher's description of the way society allows lower-class delinquent black children to be treated is a horror story. This form of treatment ensures that the young people who are unfortunate enough to find their way into a detention center will learn to behave like pathological adults and will be trapped by the system which seeks to help them.

Several states are considering the abolition of detention centers for children and adolescents. The statistics of repeated offenses and incarcerations among delinquents attests to the ineffectuality of these institutions. Apparently the only lesson that the young, inexperienced residents of such institutions learn is to model themselves after older, more experienced delinquents.

One viable alternative to the institution, considered recently by the state of Massachusetts, is the group home in which young people can obtain treatment and vocational training while living within the community. After reading Susan Fisher's account of life in the detention centers, it should become clear that this departure from traditional practice can be nothing but an improvement.

REFERENCES

Offer, D., Sabshin, M., & Marcus, D. Clinical evaluation of normal adolescents. *American Journal of Psychiatry*, 1965, **121,** 864–872.

Wirt, R. D. & Briggs, P. F. The meaning of delinquency. In H. C. Quay (Ed.), *Juvenile delinquency: Research and theory.* Princeton, N. J.: Van Nostrand, 1965.

Pamela Cantor

The children come out of vans, handcuffed to policemen. Their belongings are taken, except a comb. They wait in the lobby from ten minutes to half a day. No one looks at them. From the start, no one wants to know them. They are there awaiting trial. Some for ten days, some for three hundred, they never know when they will go to court, when they will see their probation officer, when they will be visited. If convicted, the time spent waiting does not count in their sentence; time in the detention center is not related to time before or time that will come. A twelve-year-old waits from October to June to be screened. He has been forgotten. The children are issued clothes, stripped, and searched for drugs. Sometimes drugs are in balloons, swallowed, to be vomited up later. No rules are explained to them. They are put onto the units without introductions. Girls are separated. The boys are grouped by age, except the armed offenders, and a special unit for homosexuals, transvestites, and the rare white boy. Segregation by race, poverty, education, capacity to adapt, has occurred already. One counselor watches thirty children in space meant for fifteen. Eight hours. Brick walls, naked light bulbs, loud music; no solitude is permitted voluntarily. They must stay together in the main room of the unit, yet for any alleged infraction—smoking outside the allotted smoking period, cursing back to a counselor—or for no specific violation at all, they can be put into isolation. Officially all isolation detentions are to be reported; reports are often not made, and any child can be locked up within the eight hours of a shift, and no one will know. And with

other such institutions it shares: one hundred degrees in summer, smells of urine and unwashed bodies. Twenty-three beds in a sleeping room; some isolation rooms have only a toilet bowl, and the counselor can turn off the water supply. To fight roaches, the rooms are heavily sprayed. Physical abuse with no redress; the word of a child is never accepted against that of a staff member.

These children are innocent before the law. Some are accused of major crimes—assaults, armed robbery, rape, murder. Others are not held for crimes at all but for being unmanageable and intractable in homes and schools where rebellion may be a measure of vigorous health; such children are designated "beyond control." Some are detained because mental hospitals refuse them and they are caught in a circuit between detention center, foster home, and hospital. They have the same needs for "rules of the game" as any incarcerated person, the same needs to create an internal social structure in which to participate, but it is hard to establish one when the formal roles and relationships of the institution are undefined, illusive, even contradictory. They are innocent but treated as guilty. Counselors are to maintain safety, watch, and protect them but often abuse and threaten them. Held within a legal system designed to insulate them from depersonalized adult bureaucracies, they have no civil rights and are isolated from the world of their origins. The atmosphere within the detention center is chaotic for the children and the staff. The chaos mirrors the inner state of the children and the social existence they came from.

The children are almost all black, between seven and eighteen. White children are not so quickly picked up for similar offenses. Frequently, black parents are not called from the station house and their children are detained before the parents know where they are, whereas white parents are usually located and the children released into their custody.

Some common perceptions of the world unite these children before they reach the detention center. They have learned to view social authorities as persecutory and punishing, coming at them with prejudged expectations of their responses and performances—guilty, stubborn, irresponsible, unlovable. They have been faceless objects to be manipulated, as others are to them; and manipulation is effected through behavior, not language. The establishment figures of their world—teachers, police, welfare workers, storekeepers, bus drivers—are to them arbitrary and rejecting; while their sources of food and shelter, the intimate associates to count on, are precarious. Psychiatrists might call these children paranoid, except that their perceptions are accurate most of the time; and the model for dealing with outer danger and uncertainty perpetuates a style of projection of internal distress.

On the units they are passive. They lie on the floor, near or on each other, sometimes playing games. Occasionally they riot, fight, or gang bang. Sudden swings from immobility to violence are part of accepted and expected behavior, for staff and children alike. They pass in lines from unit to school to meals to recreation. Unexplained shifts in schedule for work, school, and play occur almost daily; rules vary according to the counselor on duty.

One's fate is sealed on arrival day. Each new boy is physically challenged. If he doesn't defend himself, he will be beaten up or threatened sexually. If he fights but loses he will still be accepted. He must not back off or cry. Group homosexual assaults are common among the older boys. Younger boys are simply taken sexually; sometimes they offer themselves. A shrewd newcomer can ally himself with tougher kids by being a good "cracker," a style of speech to be discussed later. The genuinely innocent kid—the eight- or nine-year-old who is not street-wise and is physically weak—gets it in every way and learns fast.

Throughout the system, anger is vented on weaker members, and weakness is defined in physical struggles. A tough counselor can alter the threats of violence on a unit by being the strong man himself. Often a less punitive counselor will ally himself with the toughest boy to maintain order and survive. A rare counselor interrupts this pecking order by engaging children in group activities and loyalties and presenting different values of strength. Such counselors, though respected by the children, usually do not last long.

Once a child has entered the unit, what are his strategies for survival? The only method with positive rewards is to con the system. This means being deliberately friendly with counselors and administrators, thereby getting jobs in the kitchen, the offices, school, and laundry. This gives extra privileges—more food, smoking, new contacts, and, most important, movement off the unit. All conning activities are safe as long as they are perceived by the other kids as tongue-in-cheek, as long as a child is not thought a "patsy" or a "ratter."

The second major tack to survive, by far the most prevalent, is to disappear into the woodwork, to be utterly passive, faceless, nonexistent. Even bizarre behavior is not seen. I learned from one therapy group of a sixteen-year-old boy drinking his own urine, burning his forehead with cigarettes, and calling himself "black Jesus." He was not noticed by the staff. From another, I met a group member who used different names each time he came to the detention center without anyone ever recognizing it was the same child.

Only rarely will a child beat down the system. These are big kids who are good "crackers" and physically overbearing. They are the brightest boys, who supersede whatever alliance a counselor makes with other tough kids and become a kind of spokesman. They are feared by the staff because of their cunning, their power to disrupt. The hostility toward them is intense but they are left alone. The system often expels them and, for some, the penalty is high. Sammy was a master at this, and intimidated the staff to its limit. Having traveled between hospital and detention center, he was released to his home, where he was stabbed to death by his father.

Closely tied to survival is the informer system. The administration corrals, bribes, and frightens certain children into informing on their peers. The rules are strict. If discovered, informing is tolerated by the other children if suffering would have been the penalty for silence—if you would have gotten more time, or been severely punished. But one can never inform to gain something. The penalty for this is physical abuse, rape, or ostracism.

An important aspect of survival is called "cracking." It is a mocking, jeering, joking use of language that establishes with words the same pecking order as physical strength does initially. You crack *on* someone, you don't crack *with* him. "Ass-kissers," boys who con about going straight when they get out, are particular targets. This is vicious humor and in therapy groups it is important to cut through it but not threaten its effectiveness on the units. It is the major non-physical cohesive force that allies them. Cracking represents an implied ability to fight and to withstand and dish out verbal abuse. You put people down, put feelings down, always mocking tenderness and sentiment. Feelings are hidden. Language is not a neutral circle for contact or communication. When not cracking, the boys sit silently on the floor. It is the only conversation.

When is there tenderness? When is there protection? Only under extreme circumstances. Most of the time, extreme physical helplessness is protected. A severe stutterer on a very tough unit cannot be teased. I learned of a boy in isolation for twenty-four hours in severe drug withdrawal. The administration had refused to send him and several others to the hospital, accusing them of malingering; some were, but some weren't. He lay with his head on a roll of toilet paper, his face in his vomitus, shaking under blankets. Outside the door, keeping check, was a boy from the unit who had watched him throughout the day, keeping him warm.

Psychological helplessness is not so protected, and the disturbed are good subjects for cracking. Out of fear, the extremely bizarre are left alone; sometimes boys will point out to a mental health consultant sick kids, ignored by the staff. Vince had been in isolation for six days and had not been visited except for food put in his room. He was locked up to finish an isolation punishment meted out a year before in a previous period at the detention center, unfinished because he had gone to court and been released. When I saw him, he was incoherent, babbling, drooling, terrified; his ravings soon became comprehensible to me. He wanted a particular doctor every day—a man who had been kind to him four years before. He had held the gun during an armed robbery because he wanted "those guys" to like him and he couldn't say no. He was afraid to go back to the unit because he would be raped.

The primary defense mechanisms operating on every level in the detention center are projection, denial, and dissociation. One's internal wretchedness, when experienced at all, is "because of them." Children are tormented by counselors, counselors are threatened by administrators, administrators are endangered by "downtown," and "downtown" is harassed by the legislators. Too often, they are right; the concrete realities of these people's lives makes interruption and examination of these defenses almost impossible. Few people within the detention center distinguish external and internal sources of misery or notice any personal difficulty in tolerating painful feelings.

Who are the counselors and administrators, and how do they function? Like the children, they have no options. Their supervisors and senior administrators offer them no intimacy, no range of techniques to handle problems; only authoritarian strength or deflection of responsibility to a vague "other." As the counselors fail the children, so the senior administrators permit no identifications or sharing, acknowledge no conflictual feelings. Like the children, counselors receive no positive rewards, only negative reinforcement. If they fly through a window to prevent an escape, that is expected behavior. If they are five minutes late, it is written into their record. They are frequently spied upon and lied to.

Like the children, they wait—for promotions, commendations, course certificates that don't ever come or are delayed without explanation. They too have no privacy. Personnel files lie open, rumors abound and threaten everyone. Counselors rarely protect each other, and children are pawns in staff rivalries. Three boys were left naked in one isolation room in a struggle over which counselor would get them clothes.

The relationship between counselors and children is a deadly game, and the main rule is "beat them or they'll beat you." A drug user is caught by a counselor. In the morning statistical report, without intended irony, is printed, "Congratulations, Mr. X. You are the biggest drug catcher of them all." Counselors try to outguess and outfox the children, as in a ruthless sport. Understanding, empathizing, helping is emasculating. Fundamentally, the

children must never be seen as like themselves; they cannot imagine their own children in such a setting.

Respectful intimacy is non-existent in the detention center and the counselors use the children in different ways. Like objects of pornography, they are erotically used. Some stimulate the kids by teasing them and egging them on. One counselor has the boys talk about homosexual exploits into a tape recorder. Some female counselors are visibly titillated by illegitimate pregnancies and stories of prostitution. Occasionally, a counselor rapes a child, with or without consent. One senses that the children are discharging the forbidden aggressive and sexual impulses of the staff, who reestablish their self-image, distance, and self-control by massively suppressing the children.

Most counselors cannot tolerate any physical and verbal show of aggression in the children, and some hit and even beat them at the first sign. Once, a counselor called a psychologist for himself because he was putting a child into isolation for no apparent reason, yet he knew he was going to hit him unless he got rid of him. That amount of self-observation is rare. Encouraging and watching violence is irresistible for some, and their fascination is not acknowledged. A female counselor stood and impassively watched a girl bite out a piece of another girl's cheek and told me later, "Nice girls don't fight."

Always there is the reality of actual danger working with severe overcrowding. This too is used, and counselors often flirt with danger, provoking avoidable situations that excite them, and provide an opportunity to watch, experience unacceptable behavior, and then divorce themselves from it entirely. When overcrowding occasionally diminishes, there is no change in staff behavior.

The counselors use language as the children

do—bitter cracking with each other; they rarely have shared, matter-of-fact exchanges. With their senior authorities, they retreat into sullen silence. Meetings between them reveal similarities with the children on the units. Counselors are impassive, talked at, immobile, and then break into fits of temper, screaming, physically threatening, banging chairs. These outbursts by counselors are dealt with by their bosses as tangentially and immaterially as the fires and riots of the children. I once dared a senior administrator to risk telling the counselors at such a meeting that he was sometimes depressed working there. They fell into an astonished calm.

Occasionally more flexible persons are hired. Senior administrators don't want to hear their complaints and suggestions, and will harass them until they quit. Often such men cannot tolerate the frustration and depression. A powerful clique of authoritarian counselors makes life miserable for a more flexible person, and very few remain. The detention center is a place to get out of—for everyone who can. What remains is a group of people who feed on the chaos within the center to avoid facing their own doubts and fears, and issues of their own competence. Tactics to improve working conditions are never gripped and applied vigirously; they hide behind the system's inadequacies and extrude more effective people. What is rewarded is security, passivity, immobility, no overt conflict. And the staff lives with a sense of impending destruction—each television interview, meeting, call from a judge is potentially the loss of safety, job, promotion, status, perhaps reflecting deep projected guilts.

Although of different backgrounds, staff, like the children, are locked within constricted character structures with little internal mobility. Almost all black, with some higher education, the staff struggles to maintain a middle-class identity in jobs that have little social status. Significantly, a large number come from the rural South, farms or small towns, where angry outbursts were often forcibly suppressed, and the need for control was related to the dangers of white society "out there." Rarely, a counselor will admit his outrage at seeing these urban boys doing what they never could; sometimes senior administrators, who spend far less time with the children, connect their dislike of the new music, new haircuts, new freedoms to the compromises they made to "make it" in a white bureaucracy. Their hatred of the children, which is felt after a few hours in the detention center, is a necessary piece of the delicate equilibrium required to maintain their self-esteem.

Cracking, the only language effective on every hierarchical level of the detention center, is also a metaphor for the cracks, the split, the dissociation that mark this institution. Everywhere one meets the illusion of infinite distance and difference. These children are a different species, not human. Top administrators are unreachable, unknowable bosses. Distance between castes is experienced as a non-crossable space. Yet each level is partially identified with and living through the other, dependent on the other; the illusion of infinite separation masks an unconscious fusion between the groups based on mutual projection—a partial symbiosis. Fusion versus infinity—on every level the same image is reflected, like facing mirrors.

No one trusts here, and everybody is hungry. In therapy groups, in consultations with senior administrators, in talks with counselors, the imagery is oral. Beneath the hatred, the backbiting, the projections, the chaos, lie enormous reservoirs of depression. Ultimately, the maintenance of the chaos may itself be defending against the hopelessness and lack of mobility in their lives, which get perpetuated throughout the institution.

At the core of several decisions by the United States Supreme Court has been its recognition that the juvenile court system, established to protect the special interests of children before the law, has violated not only their civil rights under the Constitution, but has perpetrated those very abuses of human growth the special systems were created to avoid.

This detention center represents the failure of all structures in urban society—family life, schools, courts, welfare systems, organized medicine, hospitals. It is a final common pathway to wretchedness. Occasionally a scandal in the newspaper, an outraged lawyer, an interested humanitarian judge makes a ripple. The surface smooths rapidly over again, because, locked away in a distant part of town, society forgets the children it does not want or need.

Suicide and Attempted Suicide among Students: Problem, Prediction, and Prevention

Pamela C. Cantor

Aside from the fact that a suicide attempt is not an uncommon behavior, such an attempt may not even be self-destructive in intent. It may, in fact, be seen by the attempter as the most constructive action under the circumstances. The suicide attempt might be the only means by which a young person can get sorely needed attention and help.

Editor's Introduction

Although the college years are supposed to be among life's happiest, the suicide rate among youth has risen steadily during the last decade and suicide now ranks as second only to accidents as a major cause of death on America's campuses. The suicide rate for college students is considerably higher than the rate for men and women of college age who do not attend college. While it is possible that certain problems of campus life may contribute to the youthful suicide rate, research has indicated that suicide and attempted suicide are not primarily the result of excessive academic pressures or involvement with drugs. Rather, loneliness, isolation, alienation, and a feeling of being unloved by parents and peers are the important determinants of suicide potential. The suicide, or the suicide attempt, may be a desperate effort to communicate with significant individuals in an unresponsive environment.

The one optimistic note among these pessimistic statistics is that the life of almost every suicidal young person can be saved, provided that the right kind of help is offered in time, preferably even before an attempt takes place. In order to give help, we must know to whom it is to be offered. The aim of the research discussed in the following article is to determine which individuals are likely to attempt suicide and what the psychological factors are which predispose a young person toward attempted suicide. It is surprising that these areas have received such limited attention, since attempted suicide may be as much as a hundred times as common as suicide itself among the college population. The lack of interest is even more surprising in view of the fact that the youthful attempter probably offers the greatest hope for positive intervention.

Pamela Cantor

PROBLEM

Suicide and attempted suicide disturbs us all because self-destruction rejects the deeply held belief that life must be worth living. Otherwise why would we keep struggling to survive, often under conditions which appear intolerable? Yet in the United States alone it is conservatively estimated that 20,000 persons choose to die by their own hands each year. Of these deaths the most tragic and disturbing are the deaths of young people. Most of us can comprehend the suicide of old people or perhaps the incurably ill. But the thought that a young person, just beginning life, should be devoid of any hope for the future is anathema to us (Seiden, 1969).

The question of youthful suicide and attempted suicide has received a good deal of attention. Yet the results are inconclusive, as most of the research has focused on issues of a demographic nature. This paper attempts to review the available information regarding the questions (1) What is known about student suicide? (2) What is known about attempted suicide among students? (3) What is known about those individuals who attempt suicide? (4) What has research shown which might facilitate prediction? (5) What can an individual offer to another in an effort to prevent a suicide or a suicide attempt?

What is known about the subject of student suicide? The first thorough study of student suicide in the United States was conducted in 1937 (Raphael, Power, & Berridge). This and subsequent studies conducted at Harvard (Temby, 1961), Yale (Parrish, 1957) and Cornell (Braaten & Darling, 1962) indicated that the risk of suicide was greater for students than for their nonstudent peers. Temby reported a rate of 15 suicides per 100,000 at Harvard, and Parrish reported a suicide rate of 14 per 100,000 at Yale. The expected rate for the general population in this age range was 7 to 10 per 100,000. Research conducted at Oxford and Cambridge supported these conclusions. Parnell (1951) found that the suicide rate for Oxford students was twelve times as great as that of the nonstudent population, and Carpenter (1959) concluded that the rate of male suicides among Cambridge students was higher than that of a nonacademic comparison group. Lyman (1961) found that the suicide rate for the general population of England and Wales, ages 20 to 24, was approximately 4 per 100,000; while the rate for Oxford University was 26 per 100,000; for Cambridge University, 21 per 100,000; for the University of London, 16 per 100,000; and for other, less prestigious British universities, 6 per 100,000. Bruyn and Seiden (1965) investigated the incidence of suicide at the University of California and found that the suicide rate among students was significantly greater than for comparable groups of nonstudents. To make these conclusions even more startling, Bruyn and Seiden found that the general mortality rate for students due to all causes was significantly lower than that for their nonstudent peers.

While there is no evidence which directly answers the question of which colleges have the highest suicide rates, Lyman's research clearly shows that Oxford and Cambridge had a substantially higher suicide rate than the less prestigious British universities. It might therefore be reasonable to expect the suicide rates of the more prestigious American colleges and universities to be higher than those of less prestigious schools.

If this hypothesis proved to be correct, we would then need to ask whether the more prestigious schools contributed to the suicide rate by creating greater academic pressures than the institutions of lesser academic reputation or whether the students brought previously internalized pressures with them. Thus the higher suicide rate might be due to the criteria by which these students were selected.

This question might be applied to students in general. Are students at a greater risk for suicide than nonstudents because the college environment subjects them to pressures which make them more susceptible to suicide or because students have more difficulties coping with stress? We do not have the answers.

In fact, there is even disagreement about the effect of school success or failure on the incidence of suicide. One study (Reese, 1967) showed a relationship between low IQ, school failure, and suicide. However, the research has indicated that suicidal college students have displayed greater intellectual competence than nonsuicidal classmates. Seiden (1966) found that students who committed suicide had higher grade-point averages and had won more scholastic awards than the nonsuicidal students. These students, however, were never secure in their academic success. They were generally despondent over their academic adequacy and dissatisfied with their achievements. They did not see their academic success as a measure of their self-worth. Munter (1966) speculated that these students felt that they did not deserve the grades they received. He called this the "fraud complex," implying that the students felt unworthy of their accomplishments. He stated that this was a frequent cause of depression among students. We might hypothesize that these students needed to achieve in order to feel worthwhile, and when they actually did achieve, they found that the victory was hollow, the self-worth did not necessarily evolve from good grades.

Research aimed at differentiating students who had committed suicide from those who were not suicidal was conducted by Seiden (1966) at the University of California. Seiden found that the suicidal students tended to be older, were more likely to be language majors and foreign students, and in general displayed more signs of emotional disturbance. He also found higher grades among the suicidal students. Paffenbarger and Asnes (1966) studied the records of 40,000 students at Harvard and the University of Pennsylvania and found early father absence or loss to be a major distinguishing characteristic of those male students who had committed suicide.

This summary of research shows how little is known about the factors which contribute to the incidence of suicide among students. It is surprising that so little is known, as suicide is the second cause of death among adolescents and youth. Approximately 4,000 young people between the ages of 15 and 24 kill themselves each year.

While 4,000 unnecessary deaths is an alarming figure, the increase in the rates of suicide during the most recent ten-year period is even more disturbing than the actual numbers. Among males aged 20 to 29, the rates have doubled between 1960 and 1970 (18 to 41 per 100,000). Among females in the same age range, the rates have quadrupled (from 6.3 to 26.2 per 100,000); and the rates for teen-agers, 14 to 19, of both sexes have gone up 200 times (from 0.04 to 8.0 per 100,000) (Binzen, 1973); we have no reason to believe that this trend toward increasing suicide rates will decline.

While little is known about the incidence or causes of completed suicide among youth, even less is known about the incidence or etiology of attempted suicide. According to a recent issue of *The New York Times* (Nemy, 1973), estimates of attempted suicide among young people ran as high as 70,000 to 80,000 each year. A study I have recently completed at Boston University has indicated that the actual number of attempted suicides might be significantly higher (Cantor, 1976a). In a study of female college students between the ages of 18 and 25, 10 percent of the sample was found to have attempted suicide. If this figure could be generalized directly to the 40 million young people in the same age range in the United States—and it cannot for reasons which I will elaborate—an annual rate of 400,000 suicide attempts among individuals between the ages of 15 and 25 would be anticipated.

The figure cannot be generalized, because—as is well known among suicide researchers—more females attempt suicide than males, more college students attempt suicide than individuals who are not attending college, and more individuals who are between the ages of 18 and 25 attempt suicide than individuals between the ages of 15 and 17. Yet it still appears that the alarming figure of 70,000 to 80,000 youthful suicide attempts annually might be greatly underestimated.

In addition to those who actually complete or attempt suicide, there are many young people who are seriously considering suicide or who have done so at one time or another in their lives.

In my study (Cantor, 1976a) the frequency of suicidal thought among the student population was assessed by asking 199 females the following: "During periods of extreme stress, have you ever *seriously* thought about killing yourself as an alternative to problems or as a means of coping with stress?" Twenty of the students were found to have a history of one or more suicide attempts, while 179 had no previous history of attempted suicide. Of these 179 students, 70 indicated that, when under extreme stress, they thought about suicide at least once a month; many thought about it daily. Thus, including the students who indicated that they had attempted suicide, approximately half the sample said that they thought about suicide at least once a month.

Therefore, out of a roomful of 100 students, it might be expected that 10 would have attempted suicide by the time they reached age 25 and 50 would have had suicidal thoughts on a frequent basis.

If suicidal thoughts and attempted suicide are as common as these figures would indicate, is it appropriate to consider attempted suicide or suicidal thinking as abnormal? The definition of "abnormal" which is most frequently applied is "that which is statistically unusual." Since suicidal thoughts and behavior appear to be fairly common, it is probably ill advised to consider suicidal thought or behavior as abnormal. Aside from the fact that a suicide attempt is not an uncommon behavior, such an attempt may not even be self-destructive in intent. It may, in fact, be seen by the attempter as the most constructive action under the circumstances. The suicide attempt might be the only means by which a young person can get sorely needed attention and help. If a young person's resources are so limited as to necessitate a suicide attempt as a means of calling for help, then one should respond with the help and attention which is asked for and not with a label of maladjustment or pathological behavior.

PREDICTION

Having briefly reviewed what is known about suicide and attempted suicide among students, let us turn now to the question of how to facilitate prediction and thus, possibly, prevention of suicidal behavior.

Studies by Balser and Masterson (1959) and Cantor (1972b) have indicated that 90 percent of all youthful suicide attempters are female. Is there any way by which we can recognize young women who are in trouble before they resort to a suicide attempt, so that they may be helped to meet their needs in a constructive rather than a potentially destructive manner?

The object of my research has been to determine the prominent personality and status characteristics of these young women and to provide a configuration of the psychological complex which might predispose a young woman toward attempted suicide. The following discussion is a summary statement of some of the more significant aspects of my findings.

With regard to personality characteristics, the young women who had attempted suicide were found to prefer to be with others rather than to be alone, to want others to provide help when they felt they were in trouble, and to want to offer help to others whenever possible. While they wished to be with others, they felt uncomfortable in approaching others. While they strongly wanted help, they found it extemely difficult to ask for that help. They experienced no apparent conflict, however, with regard to the desire to help others (Cantor, 1976b).

The combined presence of the desire to help others, the wish to receive help from others, and the inability to fulfill these needs would support the view of researchers that a suicide attempt is frequently a "cry for help" (Shneidman & Farberow, 1961), a way of moving toward other people (Stengel, 1964), and that young suicidal females resort to this dramatic means of communication because they have so few other resources available (Gould, 1965). In addition, there appeared to be a considerable degree of conflict between suicidal young women and their parent or parents. These women were unable to call upon their parent or parents for support, and it was virtually impossible for them to communicate with or count on their fathers (Cantor, 1976c). This conflict may have led to an inability to ask for parental help.

The women who had attempted suicide appeared to be more impulsive than the nonsuicidal subjects and to have a lower tolerance for frustration and psychological stress. The results of my research have also shown these young women to be characterized by a tendency to express aggression directly against the source of frustration rather than thwarting aggression or turning it inward, as was originally hypothesized by Freud (1917, 1957).

Two of the more important aspects of the lives of the young women who had attempted suicide appeared to focus on family relationships, particularly on sibling position and family disorganization. A disproportionate number of the women who had attempted suicide were found to be firstborn and to have experienced father absence (Cantor, 1972a, 1976b, 1976c). These two areas warrant further discussion.

Studies of ordinal position indicate that mothers interact with their firstborn children much more frequently than they do with their succeeding children (Cushna, 1966; Rothbart, 1967; Gerwitz & Gerwitz, 1965; Bayley, 1965), and that firstborn children suffer a sudden decrease in attention at age 4 or 5 (Lasko, 1954). As a result of this decrease in attention, there is a discrepancy between the treatment the firstborn receives in early childhood and the treatment received after early childhood. As the firstborn progresses through childhood and into adolescence, he or she appears to be most in need of adult reassurance, most in need of attention, and least willing to express antagonism toward parents in any direct way (Sears, 1951). Thus, the firstborn's early treatment may result in expectations for attention and help which are far in excess of what may realistically be obtained during adolescence.

As young girls, firstborns learn to expect help from others. As they grow older, however, it is likely that their requests for help will be rebuked, especially since the older female is generally expected to become a mothering person herself rather than asking to be mothered far beyond her own childhood. As an adolescent, she might want help from others; yet she may experience conflict about asking for this help since she is not encouraged to ask for it at home. Her special needs for others interacting with her inability to reach significant others in her environment, specifically her parents, could lead to a more drastic expression of these needs, perhaps through a suicide attempt.

The discrepancy between childhood, when help was so readily given, and adolescence, when it is so reluctantly offered, might be further pronounced if the household does not contain a father. While father absence is not peculiar to any one sibling position, it may be that it will negatively affect firstborn females to a greater extent than females in other sibling positions. In families where there is no father, the girl may turn to her mother for help. The mother, however, may not be willing or able to offer this help. Further, she may expect her oldest daughter to share the burden of caring for the younger children and expect her to give care rather than to receive it. Caring for others allows the firstborn the opportunity to express and to be rewarded for helping behavior. But caring for others does not afford her much opportunity to be cared for by others or to be rewarded for asking for help from others. The longer her needs for help are neglected, the greater her needs may become. Reaching-out behavior, being unreinforced, may therefore decrease.

Regardless of a young woman's place with regard to birth order, there is evidence that a female will be affected negatively by the loss of her father. While the importance of paternal deprivation is mentioned by very few investigators (Brigas, Gauthier, Bouchard, & Tasse, 1966; Gorceix, 1963; Toolan, 1962; Zimbacca, 1965), the results of my research have led me to believe that father absence may be a crucial precursor of eventual suicide attempts among young females.

According to Gorceix (1963), it is during adolescence that a female will feel father loss most acutely. If the mother is missing, the adolescent is able to learn the maternal role elsewhere, perhaps from a substitute such as an aunt or a grandmother, and it is in childhood that a young female has most need of a mother. Zimbacca (1965) notes that the father serves an irreplaceable function for the female, especially in adolescence. Deprived of a father at that age, the young woman "lacks reference, authority, support, aid, advice, a model and a source of identification. The father is indispensable to this time period; the adolescent needs her father both as a refer-

ence for emancipation and as a source of ego strength."

An example from my own life might make this point more clearly. I remember a time when I was in ninth grade, dating a young man named John. I wore Johnny's ring around my neck and, of course, was considered his steady. One night as I was getting ready for bed my "girlfriend" Wendy called to tell me that Johnny had asked her for a date for the coming Saturday night and she wanted to go; did I mind? Of course I minded, I minded a week's worth of tears, but what could I do? I cried. My mother came into my room to find out what was the matter and I told her. She tried to comfort me by telling me that Johnny was foolish, he didn't know what he was missing, that I would find someone better, that I was pretty and that I shouldn't worry. I kept crying. After all, what could she know, she was only my mother. My father came in. He asked the same question and got the same answer. In response he told me the same thing. But he was my father, he was a man, he would know what men felt, he would know if I really was pretty and what my chances were for the future. I stopped crying. Thus, as Zimbacca states, fathers may serve a special and critical role in the formation of a young woman's self-esteem.

Gorceix (1963) makes the additional point that females who have experienced actual father loss or who have ineffectual fathers are unable to tolerate frustration. These girls want everything, cannot delay gratification, and blame their fathers for their discontent.

Other researchers indicate that the lack of a secure relationship with a father may have lasting consequences for the female's ability to establish interpersonal relationships (Toolan, 1962; Gould, 1965). Such young women are likely to find themselves socially isolated, and social isolation is one of the most important causal factors in suicide attempts (Stengel, 1964). Not having a father, the adolescent may expect her boyfriend to serve as a substitute father. A fight with a boyfriend frequently is the final precipitating factor in the suicide attempt.

Thus, father absence or perhaps even severe conflict, indifference, or meekness may have a profound effect on the adolescent female. It can influence ego development, reduce tolerance for frustration, and leave her without her most important source of support.

In addition to the fact of father absence, the cause of father absence and the time of father absence appeared to be of significance. The reports of previous investigators (Leonard, 1967; Dorpat, Jackson, & Ripley, 1965) indicate that the death of a parent was the major precursor of an eventual suicide attempt. The results of my investigations have shown that death was not the major cause of father absence among the attempters. Rather, loss was attributed to separation, divorce, or prolonged business trips. It might be hypothesized that loss for reasons other than death might be viewed by a young woman as a voluntary desertion, one in which her father had purposely chosen to live without her. Death is irreparable and usually not the result of choice. The adolescent may resent the father who appears to abandon her of his own accord, while she may not resent a loss which is involuntary and therefore somewhat comprehensible (Cantor, 1976c).

Perhaps because of the early childhood emphasis of most developmental studies, parent absence has been thought to be most severe in its consequence if it occurs during the first few years of life (Leonard, 1967). The effects of inflicted crises during the critical developmental phases after the first few years of life have been underestimated (Blinder, 1972). The results of my research have led me to speculate that father absence may be more traumatic for a female if it occurs during adolescence and may, in fact, be of even greater consequence if it occurs only during

adolescence rather than consistently since birth. The abrupt disappearance of a father who has heretofore been present and even somewhat rewarding may be more destructive for the adolescent female than conditions where the father has been consistently absent.

Thus, both firstborn and father-absent females present a similar but modified pattern of personality traits. Females who are both firstborn and father-absent appear to have strong needs to be with others and to receive help from others, but they appear to be conflicted with regard to their abilities to fulfill their needs. Neither sibling position nor father absence alone appears to be a sufficient determinant of attempted suicide. The two factors interacting with each other, however, may be more adequate predictors of personality development and of attempted suicide.

PREVENTION: IMPLICATIONS FOR PSYCHOLOGICAL THEORY AND FOR INTERVENTION

My research has shown that the combination of firstborn female sibling status and a father-absent home may affect a young woman's propensity for attempted suicide.

Sibling position and father absence are not conditions which can be altered at will. Perhaps in greatest measure, however, there is hope for primary prevention in childhood by altering the manner in which a firstborn child is reared. Assuming that the inconsistent treatment the firstborn receives (Lasko, 1954; Sears, Maccoby, & Levin, 1957; Sutton-Smith & Rosenberg, 1970) is productive of increased needs to be with others and increased needs for help from others, it may be advisable to advocate optimal spacing of children so that it would be possible to decrease the discrepancy in the treatment which the young child receives as she makes the transition from early to late childhood. Perhaps one alternative would be to advocate closer age spacing between siblings in order to reduce the period in which the child receives the sole attention of her parents and to make the eventual adjustment to the birth of a sibling less traumatic. A second alternative would be large age spacing between children, making each one in effect an "only" child. The goal of this method would depend upon the future determination of optimal periods of affection and attention which would result in a complete feeling of security for each child. A third alternative is to offer the firstborn child less attention during early childhood. Thus, the attention the first child receives throughout her early years would be reduced but consistent. The reduction of initial affection in favor of consistent patterns of mothering would result in an approximation of the patterns of mothering which the later-born child receives.

Regardless of the sibling position of the child, parents have the major responsibility for teaching their children alternative methods for coping with stress early in life so that they do not resort to suicidal behavior as a "solution" for problems. Children must be taught not to avoid crises but to meet them intelligently, to live with them, and to seek help from others when necessary.

Conditions of father absence offer one feasible alternative. It is often possible to provide a father substitute for an adolescent female.

A possible solution to the problems of the effects of sibling position and father absence is a return to the extended kinship family system in lieu of the nuclear family which is presently most visible in Western culture. At its best, the nuclear family offers the child two adult sources of support. At its worst, the system offers the child one or no sources of support. The extended kinship family may offer the child aunts, uncles, grandparents, and peers as sources of affection, attention, and solace in times of need. In the extended family, the role models are numerous and the child's options are increased. It may be possible that Western culture has sacrificed a great deal in the stability of the life of the developing child for the sake of independence and mobility, which are so highly prized in the new American tradition.

The previously discussed implications for psychological theory deal with the antecedents of suicidal behavior. From a clinical standpoint, my suggestions for prevention are naturally more practical than theoretical.

Often individuals who are not professionals are in the best position to help the suicidal young person. While a suicide attempt is the result of diverse factors and it is difficult to generalize, there are some guidelines which can be suggested when it appears that a young person is suicidal.

The most emphatic guideline is this: anyone trying to help a person who is suicidal needs to *pay attention* and to *listen*. The attempter or potential attempter is trying to communicate his or her needs to someone. If these requests are not heard or are ignored as they have been in the past, the suicide attempt may well be carried out. Paying attention implies both concern and respect for the individual rather than a dismissal of the act as a gesture for attention. Attention may, in fact, be just what the individual wants; but if it is necessary to go to these lengths to achieve it, then it is the desperation and the inability to cope with stress which must be noticed rather than the manipulative aspects of the act (Gould, 1965).

It is generally not wise to reassure the individual without understanding the problem. Words such as "everything will be all right, don't worry" should be avoided. They offer empty reassurance, are superficial, and may even be deadly. All that will result is that the person will feel a lowered sense of self-esteem and perhaps anger at not having been understood. The thinking might be as follows: "If I am so lucky to be alive and I don't realize it, then I must really be in a bad way. And if things are so rosy and I am so miserable, then why bother to stay alive? If *you* don't understand me, then nobody can help me."

It is worth noting that although many young people do not succeed in killing themselves when they really want to, many miscalculate and die when all they really wanted was to get help in order to live. It is important to make your limitations known to the person you are trying to help. If someone is truly determined to kill himself, you are powerless to stop him. In most suicide attempts, the young person really wants and expects to be saved. It is easy for a young person to feel that he or she can be saved by the "omnipotent" friend, parent, teacher, or therapist—and this is not always possible.

Suicide and suicide attempts are most likely to occur at precisely the time when it appears that depression is lifting. There are two theories which try to account for this apparently contradictory event. The first states that it is only when a person is no longer depressed that he or she will have the psychic energy available to carry out the planning necessary to put an end to life. The second states that the decision to end one's own life is the very factor which causes the lifting of the depression. In either case it is difficult to remember this, particularly when you are relieved to see someone you care about beginning to come out of a depression.

An example might serve to emphasize this point. A few years ago a friend of mine called me because she was depressed. I talked with her frequently. I recall telling her one evening how delighted I was because she appeared to be so much better. The next morning she took seventy-five phenobarbital, fifteen Sominex, and a bottle of bourbon. Fortunately, she felt sick, vomited, called for help, and lived. But I have not forgotten the hard learned lesson that the end of a depression may signal an attempt to end life.

If someone is depressed, it is best to avoid any procedure which will further diminish the person's self-esteem, such as the use of ridicule or criticism. It is probably best to make yourself as available as possible even to the point of allowing yourself to be manipulated, to try to give prompt attention, and to make an appointment with someone who can help. It may be necessary for you to make the appointment, as the person may have used up all his or her available energies in asking for your help.

Whenever possible, I would suggest ending a conversation with someone who is considering suicide with a date for the following day at a definite time and place. This gives the individual something to look forward to and to count on to help fill the void that is being experienced.

If you think that someone you know may be contemplating suicide, I would ask directly "Are you thinking about suicide?" If you do not appear shocked by the subject, the person will probably be able to respond. If he or she says "yes," discuss it and ask about the plans. Anyone who has made careful plans to end his or her life is likely to be serious about it. While impulsive suicide attempts certainly do occur, they are often less lethal. In either case, talk about it.

It is important to try not to appear shocked or astonished over someone's self-destructive thoughts. You can do much more damage by not talking about suicide than can ever be done by talking about it. You will not give someone the idea of suicide by mentioning the word, but you might be able to keep someone from carrying through with suicide by listening to his or her words and questions. Your understanding, acceptance and concern may constitute immediate lifesaving answers.

One issue which remains is the question which is basic to the issue of prevention. Should you or I try to prevent someone from taking his or her own life? Should the individual have control over his or her own life? I would answer both of these questions affirmatively and thus appear to be taking both sides of the issue at once. I do feel that people should have control over the time at which they die. But I also know that most young people who attempt suicide and live, live to tell us that they are glad that they did not succeed. Most young people who attempt suicide are profoundly unhappy and want to change their lives. But they do not want to die. They want to change their lives enough to make it possible to continue to live. As a therapist, I would try to help these young people to change their lives so that they no longer want to die, to help them through the period of depression. When someone is depressed they have what I call "tunnel vision." They see in one direction only—straight ahead through a bleak, long, dark tunnel. They cannot see the light at the end of the tunnel and they are unaware of the fact that there is daylight on either side. I would want to help them to realize that most depressions are self-limiting and that most tunnels do end. I say this with the realization that it is always most difficult to help those we care most about.

REFERENCES

Balser, B. H. & Masterson, J. H. Suicide in adolescents. *American Journal of Psychiatry*, 1959, **116**, 400–404.

Bayley, N. Comparison of mental and motor test scores for ages 1–15 months by sex, birth order, race, geographical location, and education of parents. *Child Development*, 1965, **36**, 379–411.

Binzen, P. When a youth takes his life. *The Boston Globe* (Living Section), January 6, 1973, 9.

Blinder, B. J. Sibling death in childhood. *Child Psychiatry and Human Development*, 1972, **2**(4), 169–175.

Braaten, L. J. & Darling, C. D. Suicidal tendencies among college students. *Psychiatric Quarterly*, 1962, **36**, 665–692.

Brigas, J., Gauthier, Y., Bouchard, C., & Tasse, Y. Suicidal attempts in adolescent girls: A preliminary study. *Canadian Psychiatric Association Journal*, 1966 (Suppl.), 275–282.

Bruyn, H. & Seiden, R. H. Student suicide: Fact or fancy? *Journal of the American College Health Association*, 1965, **14**(2): 69–77.

Cantor, P. C. The adolescent attempter: Sex, sibling position and family constellation. *Life-Threatening Behavior*, 1972a, **2**, 252–261.

Cantor, P. C. Adolescent suicide. *Time*, Jan. 3, 1972b, 57.

Cantor, P. C. Frequency of suicidal thought and self-destructive behavior among females. *Suicide and Life-Threatening Behavior*, 1976a, **6**(2), 92–100.

Cantor, P. C. Personality characteristics found among youthful female suicide attempters. *Journal of Abnormal Psychology*, 1976b, **85**, 324–329.

Cantor, P. C. Birth order and paternal absence as predisposing factors in suicide attempts among youthful females. Address presented to the American Association of Suicidology, Los Angeles, April 1, 1976c.

Carpenter, R. G. Statistical analysis of suicide and other mortality rates of students. *British Journal of Preventive and Social Medicine*, 1959, **13**(4), 163–174.

Cushna, B. Agency and birth order differences in very early childhood. Address presented to the American Psychological Association, New York, September, 1966.

Dorpat, T. L., Jackson, J. K., & Ripley, H. S. Broken homes and attempted and committed suicide. *Archives of General Psychiatry*, 1965, **12**, 213–216.

Freud, S. [Contributions to a discussion on suicide] In J. Strachey (Ed. and Trans.), *The standard edition of the complete psychological works of Sigmund Freud* (Vol. 2). London: Hogarth, 1957 (Originally published in 1917).

Gerwitz, J. L. & Gerwitz, H. B. Stimulus conditions, infant behaviors, and social earnings in four Israeli child-rearing environments: A preliminary report illustrating differences in environment and behavior between "only" and the "youngest" child. In B. M. Foss (Ed.), *Determinants of infant behavior* III. London: Metheun; New York: Wiley, 1965.

Gorceix, A. Le suicide, l'adolescence et le poison. *Semaine des Hôpitaux de Paris*, 1963, **39**, 2371–2374.

Gould, R. Suicide problems in children and adolescents. *American Journal of Psychotherapy*, 1965, **19**, 228–246.

Lasko, J. K. Parent behavior toward first and second children. *Genetic Psychological Monographs*, 1954, **49**, 96–137.

Leonard, C. *Understanding and preventing suicide.* Springfield, Ill.: Charles C Thomas, 1967.

Lyman, J. L. Student suicide at Oxford University, *Student Medicine*, 1961, **10**, 218–234.

Munter, P. K. Depression and suicide in college students. In Lenore McNeer (Ed.), *Proceedings of Conference on Depression and Suicide in Adolescents and Young Adults.* Fairlee, Vt: June, 1966, 20–25.

Nemy, E. Suicide now no. 2 cause of death among young. *The New York Times*, April 16, 1973, 1.

Paffenbarger, R. S. & Asnes, D. P. Chronic disease in former college students: III. Precursors of suicide in early and middle life. *American Journal of Public Health*, 1966, **56**, 1026–1036.

Parnell, R. W. Mortality and prolonged illness among Oxford undergraduates. *Journal-Lancet*, March 31, 1951, **260**, 731–733.

Parrish, H. M. Epidemiology of suicide among college students. *Yale Journal of Biology and Medicine*, 1957, **29**, 585–595.

Raphael, T., Power, S. H., & Berridge, W. L. The question of suicide as a problem in college mental hygiene. *American Journal of Orthopsychiatry*, 1937, **7**, 1–14.

Reese, F. D. School-age suicide: The educational

parameters. *Dissertation Abstracts*, 1967, **27**(9-A), 2895–2896.

Rothbart, M. K. L. Birth order and mother child interaction. (Doctoral dissertation: Stanford University). Ann Arbor, Mich. University Microfilms, 1967, No. 67–7961.

Sears, P. S. Doll play aggression in normal young children: Influence of sex and sibling status, father's absence. *Psychological Monographs*, 1951, **65** (No. 323).

Sears, R. R., Maccoby, E., & Levin, H. *Patterns in child rearing*, Evanston, Ill.: Row Peterson, 1957.

Seiden, R. H. Campus Tragedy: A study of student suicide. *Journal of Abnormal Psychology*, 1966, **71**, 389–399.

Seiden, R. H. *Suicide among youth.* Chevy Chase, Md.: U.S. Dept. of Health, Education, and Welfare, 1969.

Schneidman, E. & Farberow, N. Statistical comparisons between attempted and committed suicides. In Norman Farberow and Edwin Shneidman (Eds.) *The cry for help.* New York: McGraw-Hill, 1961.

Stengel, E. *Suicide and attempted suicide.* Baltimore, Md: Penguin Books, 1964.

Sutton-Smith, B. & Rosenberg, B. G. *The sibling*, New York: Holt, 1970.

Temby, W. D. Suicide. In G. B. Blaire and C. C. McArthur (Eds.), *Emotional problems of the student.* New York: Appleton-Century-Crofts, 1961.

Toolan, J. M. Suicide and suicide attempts in children and adolescents. *American Journal of Psychiatry*, 1962, **118**, 719–724.

Zimbacca, N. Suicide in adolescents. *Concours Médical*, 1965, **87**, 4991–4997.

EGO STRENGTHS OF ADOLESCENCE
Youth: A "New" Stage of Life
Kenneth Keniston

Today it seems clear that most youths are considered nuisances or worse by the established order, to which they have not fully pledged their allegiance. Indeed, many of the major stresses in contemporary American society spring from or are aggravated by those in this stage of life. . . . The answer of the majority of the public seems clear; we already have too many "youths" in our society; youth as a developmental stage should be stamped out.

Editor's Introduction

According to Keniston, our society is now experiencing the emergence of another stage of life. After infancy, childhood, and adolescence we must add the stage of youth before progressing to adulthood. Keniston is careful to state that this stage is not new but is assuming a new importance in our society. The central issue during this transition stage is the "tension between self and society." The tension arises in the youth who senses who he is and yet is not certain that he fits or wants to fit into the existing order. It is a period of the delicate balance between a personal definition and a commitment to society. Keniston states that while an individual youth may have the capacity for commitment to society, he may not have made that commitment.

  While many in society view American and world youth with dismay, Keniston takes the position that the emergence of this stage of life is of great positive value to society. Keniston points to the enormous discontinuities and instabilities in our society and indicates that the emergence of this stage in life will allow individuals the opportunity for new and more appropriate forms of social cooperation and organization. The passive acceptance of the status quo appears to Keniston to be a far less favorable outcome of development than a more autonomous attitude toward society.

Pamela Cantor

Before the twentieth century, adolescence was rarely included as a stage in the life cycle. Early life began with infancy and was followed by a period of childhood that lasted until around puberty, which occurred several years later than it does today. After puberty, most young men and women simply entered some form of apprenticeship for the adult world. Not until 1904, when G. Stanley Hall published his monumental work, *Adolescence: Its Psychology and Its Relations to Physiology, Anthropology, Sociology, Sex, Crime, Religion, and Education*, was this further pre-adult stage widely recognized. Hall's work went through many editions and was much popularlized; "adolescence" became a household word. Hall's classic description of the *sturm und drang*, turbulence, ambivalence,

From *The American Scholar*, Autumn 1970. Reprinted by permission of the author.

dangers and possibilities of adolescence has since been echoed in almost every discussion of this stage of life.

But it would be incorrect to say that Hall "discovered" adolescence On the contrary, from the start of the nineteenth century, there was increasing discussion of the "problem" of those past puberty but not yet adult. They were the street gang members and delinquents who made up what one nineteenth-century writer termed the new "dangerous classes"; they were also the recruits to the new public secondary schools being opened by the thousands in the late nineteenth century. And once Hall had clearly defined adolescence, it was possible to look back in history and discover men and women who had shown the hallmarks of this stage long before it was identified and named.

Nonetheless, Hall was clearly reflecting a gradual change in the nature of human development, brought about by the massive transformations of American society in the decades after the Civil War. During these decades, the "working family," where children labored alongside parents in fields and factories, began to disappear; rising industrial productivity created new economic surpluses that allowed millions of teenagers to remain outside the labor force. America changed from a rural agrarian society to an urban industrial society, and this new industrial society demanded on a mass scale not only the rudimentary literacy taught in elementary schools, but higher skills that could only be guaranteed through secondary education. What Hall's concept of adolescence reflected, then, was a real change in the human experience, a change intimately tied to the new kind of industrial society that was emerging in America and Europe.

Today, Hall's concept of adolescence is unshakably enshrined in our view of human life. To be sure, the precise nature of adolescence still remains controversial. Some ob-

servers believe that Hall, like most psychoanalytic observers, vastly overestimated the inevitability of turbulence, rebellion and upheaval in this stage of life. But whatever the exact definition of adolescence, no one today doubts its existence. A stage of life that barely existed a century ago is now universally accepted as an inherent part of the human condition.

In the seven decades since Hall made adolescence a household word, American society has once again transformed itself. From the industrial era of the turn of the century, we have moved into a new era without an agreed-upon name—it has been called postindustrial, technological, postmodern, the age of mass consumption, the technetronic age. And a new generation, the first born in this new era of postwar affluence, television and the Bomb, raised in the cities and suburbs of America, socially and economically secure, is now coming to maturity. Since 1900, the average amount of education received by children has increased by more than six years. In 1900, only 6.4 percent of young Americans completed high school, while today almost eighty percent do, and more than half of them begin college. In 1900, there were only 238,000 college students: in 1970, there are more than seven million, with ten million projected for 1980.

These social transformations are reflected in new public anxieties. The "problem of youth," "the now generation," "troubled youth," "student dissent" and "the youth revolt" are topics of extraordinary concern to most Americans. No longer is our anxiety focused primarily upon the teenager, upon the adolescent of Hall's day. Today we are nervous about new "dangerous classes"—those young men and women of college and graduate school age who can't seem to "settle down" the way their parents did, who refuse to consider themselves adult, and who often vehemently challenge the existing social or-

By permission of Sissy Krook, photographer.

der. "Campus unrest," according to a June, 1970, Gallup Poll, was considered the nation's *main* problem.

The factors that have brought this new group into existence parallel in many ways the factors that produced adolescence: rising prosperity, the further prolongation of education, the enormously high educational demands of a postindustrial society. And behind these measurable changes lie other trends less quantitative but even more important: a rate of social change so rapid that it threatens to make obsolete all institutions, values, methodologies and technologies within the lifetime of each generation; a technology that has created not only prosperity and longevity, but power to destroy the planet, whether through war-

fare or violation of nature's balance; a world of extraordinarily complex social organization, instantaneous communication and constant revolution. The "new" young men and young women emerging today both reflect and react against these trends.

But if we search among the concepts of psychology for a word to describe these young men and women, we find none that is adequate. Characteristically, they are referred to as "late-adolescents-and-young-adults"—a phrase whose very mouth-filling awkwardness attests to its inadequacy. Those who see in youthful behavior the remnants of childhood immaturity naturally incline toward the concept of "adolescence" in describing the unsettled twenty-four-year-old, for this word makes it easier to interpret his objections to war, racism, pollution or imperialism as "nothing but" delayed adolescent rebellion. To those who are more hopeful about today's youth, "young adulthood" seems a more flattering phrase, for it suggests that maturity, responsibility and rationality lie behind the unease and unrest of many contemporary youths.

But in the end, neither label seems fully adequate. The twenty-four-year-old seeker, political activist or graduate student often turns out to have been *through* a period of adolescent rebellion ten years before, to be all too formed in his views, to have a stable sense of himself, and to be much farther along in his psychological development than his fourteen-year-old high school brother. Yet he differs just as sharply from "young adults" of age twenty-four whose place in society is settled, who are married and perhaps parents, and who are fully committed to an occupation. What characterizes a growing minority of postadolescents today is that they have not settled the questions whose answers once defined adulthood: questions of relationship to the existing society, questions of vocation, questions of social role and life-style.

Faced with this dilemma, some writers have fallen back on the concept of "protracted" or "stretched" adolescence—a concept with psychoanalytic origins that suggests that those who find it hard to "settle down" have "failed" the adolescent developmental task of abandoning narcissistic fantasies and juvenile dreams of glory. Thus, one remedy for "protracted adolescence" might be some form of therapy that would enable the young to reconcile themselves to abilities and a world that are rather less than they had hoped. Another interpretation of youthful unease blames society, not the individual, for the "prolongation of adolescence." It argues that youthful unrest springs from the unwillingness of contemporary society to allow young men and women,

especially students, to exercise the adult powers of which they are biologically and intellectually capable. According to this view, the solution would be to allow young people to "enter adulthood" and do "real work in the real world" at an earlier age.

Yet neither of these interpretations seems quite to the point. For while some young men and women are indeed victims of the psychological malady of "stretched adolescence," many others are less impelled by juvenile grandiosity than by a rather accurate analysis of the perils and injustices of the world in which they live. And plunging youth into the "adult world" at an earlier age would run directly counter to the wishes of most youths, who view adulthood with all the enthusiasm of a condemned man for the guillotine. Far from seeking the adult prerogatives of their parents, they vehemently demand a virtually indefinite prolongation of their nonadult state.

If neither "adolescence" nor "early adulthood" quite describes the young men and women who so disturb American society today, what can we call them? My answer is to propose that *we are witnessing today the emergence on a mass scale of a previously unrecognized stage of life*, a stage that intervenes between adolescence and adulthood. I propose to call this stage of life the stage of *youth*, assigning to this venerable but vague term a new and specific meaning. Like Hall's "adolescence," "youth" is in no absolute sense new: indeed, once having defined this stage of life, we can study its historical emergence, locating individuals and groups who have had a "youth" in the past. But what is "new" is that this stage of life is today being entered not by tiny minorities of unusually creative or unusually disturbed young men and women, but by millions of young people in the advanced nations of the world.

To explain how it is possible for "new" stages of life to emerge under changed historical conditions would require a lengthy excursion into the theory of psychological development. It should suffice here to emphasize that the direction and extent of human development—indeed the entire nature of the human life cycle—is by no means predetermined by man's biological constitution. Instead, psychological development results from a complex interplay of constitutional givens (including the rates and phases of biological maturation) and the changing familial, social, educational, economic and political conditions that constitute the matrix in which children develop. Human development can be obstructed by the absence of the necessary matrix, just as it can be stimulated by other kinds of environments. Some social and historical conditions demonstrably slow, retard or block development, while others stimulate, speed and encourage it. A prolongation and extension of development, then, including the emergence of "new" stages of life, can result from altered social, economic and historical conditions.

Like all stages, youth is a stage of transition rather than of completion or accomplishment. To begin to define youth involves three related tasks. First, we need to describe the major *themes* or issues that dominate consciousness, development and behavior during this stage. But human development rarely if ever proceeds on all fronts simultaneously: instead, we must think of development as consisting of a series of sectors of "developmental lines," each of which may be in or out of phase with the others. Thus we must also describe the more specific *transformations* or changes in thought and behavior that can be observed in each of several "lines" of development (moral, sexual, intellectual, interpersonal, and so on) during youth. Finally, we can try to make clear what youth is *not*. What follows is a preliminary sketch of some of the themes and transformations that seem crucial to defining youth as a stage of life.

MAJOR THEMES IN YOUTH

Perhaps the central conscious issue during youth is the *tension between self and society*. In adolescence, young men and women tend to accept their society's definitions of them as rebels, truants, conformists, athletes or achievers. But in youth, the relationship between socially assigned labels and the "real self" becomes more problematic, and constitutes a focus of central concern. The awareness of actual or potential conflict, disparity, lack of congruence between what one is (one's identity, values, integrity) and the resources and demands of the existing society increases. The adolescent is struggling to define who he is; the youth begins to sense who he is and thus to recognize the possibility of conflict and disparity between his emerging selfhood and his social order.

In youth, *pervasive ambivalence* toward both self and society is the rule: the question of how the two can be made more congruent is often experienced as a central problem of youth. This ambivalence is not the same as definitive rejection of society, nor does it necessarily lead to political activism. For ambivalence may also entail intense self-rejection, including major efforts at self-transformation employing the methodologies of personal transformation that are culturally available in any historical era: monasticism, meditation, psychoanalysis, prayer, hallucinogenic drugs, hard work, religious conversion, introspection, and so forth. In youth, then, the potential and ambivalent conflicts between autonomous selfhood and social involvement—between the maintenance of personal integrity and the achievement of effectiveness in society—are fully experienced for the first time.

The effort to reconcile and accommodate these two poles involves a characteristic stance vis-à-vis both self and world, perhaps best described by the concept of the *wary probe.* For the youthful relationship to the social order consists not merely in the experimentation more characteristic of adolescence, but with now more serious forays into the adult world, through which its vulnerability, strength, integrity and possibilities are assayed. Adolescent experimentation is more concerned with self-definition than are the probes of youth, which may lead to more lasting commitments. This testing, exacting, challenging attitude may be applied to all representatives and aspects of the existing social order, sometimes in anger and expectation of disappointment, sometimes in the urgent hope of finding honor, fidelity and decency in society, and often in both anger and hope. With regard to the self, too, there is constant self-probing in search of strength, weakness, vulnerability and resiliency, constant self-scrutiny designed to test the individual's capacity to withstand or use what his society would make of him, ask of him, and allow him.

Phenomenologically, youth is a time of alternating *estrangement and omnipotentiality.* The estrangement of youth entails feelings of isolation, unreality, absurdity, and disconnectedness from the interpersonal, social and phenomenological world. Such feelings are probably more intense during youth than in any other period of life. In part they spring from the actual disengagement of youth from society; in part they grow out of the psychological sense of incongruence between self and world. Much of the psychopathology of youth involves such feelings, experienced as the depersonalization of the self or the derealization of the world.

Omnipotentiality is the opposite but secretly related pole of estrangement. It is the feeling of absolute freedom, of living in a world of pure possibilities, of being able to change or achieve anything. There may be times when complete self-transformation seems possible, when the self is experienced

as putty in one's own hands. At other times, or for other youths, it is the nonself that becomes totally malleable; then one feels capable of totally transforming another's life, or creating a new society with no roots whatsoever in the mire of the past. Omnipotentiality and estrangement are obviously related: the same sense of freedom and possiblity that may come from casting off old inhibitions, values and constraints may also lead directly to a feeling of absurdity, disconnectedness and estrangement.

Another characteristic of youth is the *refusal of socialization* and acculturation. In keeping with the intense and wary probing of youth, the individual characteristically begins to become aware of the deep effects upon his personality of his society and his culture. At times he may attempt to break out of his prescribed roles, out of his culture, out of history, and even out of his own skin. Youth is a time, then, when earlier socialization and acculturation is self-critically analyzed, and massive efforts may be made to uproot the now alien traces of historicity, social membership and culture. Needless to say, these efforts are invariably accomplished within a social, cultural and historical context, using historically available methods. Youth's relationship to history is therefore paradoxical. Although it may try to reject history altogether, youth does so in a way defined by its historical era, and these rejections may even come to define that era.

In youth we also observe the emergence of *youth-specific identities* and roles. These contrast both with the more ephemeral enthusiasms of the adolescent and with the more established commitments of the adult. They may last for months, years or a decade, and they inspire deep commitment in those who adopt them. Yet they are inherently temporary and specific to youth: today's youthful hippies, radicals and seekers recognize full well that, however reluctantly, they will eventually become older; and that aging itself will change their status. Some such youth-specific identities may provide the foundation for later commitments; but others must be viewed in retrospect as experiments that failed or as probes of the existing society that achieved their purpose, which was to permit the individual to move on in other directions.

Another special issue during youth is the enormous value placed upon change, transformation and *movement*, and the consequent abhorrence of *stasis*. To change, to stay on the road, to retain a sense of inner development and/or outer momentum is essential to many youths' sense of active vitality. The psychological problems of youth are experienced as most overwhelming when they seem to block change: thus, youth grows panicky when confronted with the feeling of "getting nowhere," of "being stuck in a rut," or of "not moving."

At times the focus of change may be upon the self, and the goal is then to *be moved*. Thus, during youth we see the most strenuous, self-conscious and even frenzied efforts at self-transformation, using whatever religious, cultural, therapeutic or chemical means are available. At other times, the goal may be to create movement in the outer world, to *move others:* then we may see efforts at social and political change that in other stages of life rarely possess the same single-minded determination. And on other occasions, the goal is to *move through* the world, and we witness a frantic geographic restlessness, wild swings of upward or downward social mobility, or a compelling psychological need to identify with the highest and the lowest, the most distant and apparently alien.

The need for movement and terror of stasis often are a part of a heightened *valuation of development* itself, however development may be defined by the individual and his culture. In all stages of life, of course, all individuals often wish to change in specific ways: to become more witty, more attractive, more sociable or wealthier. But in youth, specific changes are often subsumed in the devotion to change itself—to "keep putting myself through the changes," "not to bail out," "to keep moving." This valuation of change need not be fully conscious. Indeed it often surfaces only in its inverse form, as the panic or depression that accompanies a sense of "being caught in a rut," "getting nowhere," "not being able to change." But for other youths, change becomes a conscious goal in itself, and elaborate ideologies of the techniques of transformation and the *telos* of human life may be developed.

In youth, as in all other stages of life, *the fear of death* takes a special form. For the infant, to be deprived of maternal support, responsiveness and care is not to exist; for the four-year-old, non-being means loss of body intactness (dismemberment, mutilation, castration); for the adolescent, to cease to be is to fall apart, to fragment, splinter, or diffuse into nothingness. For the youth, however, to lose one's essential vitality is merely *to stop*. For some, even self-inflicted death or psychosis may seem preferable to loss of movement; and suicidal attempts in youth often spring from the failure of efforts to change and the resulting sense of being forever trapped in an unmoving present.

The youthful *view of adulthood* is strongly affected by these feelings. Compared to youth, adulthood has traditionally been a stage of slower transformation, when, as Erik H. Erikson has noted, the relative developmental stability of parents enables them to nurture the rapid growth of their children. This adult deceleration of personal change is often seen from a youthful vantage point as concretely embodied in apparently unchanging parents. It leads frequently to the conscious identification of adulthood with stasis, and to its unconscious equation with death or nonbeing. Although greatly magnified today by the specific political disillusionments of many youths with the "older generation," the adulthood = stasis

(= death) equation is inherent in the youthful situation itself. The desire to prolong youth indefinitely springs not only from an accurate perception of the real disadvantages of adult status in any historical era, but from the less conscious and less accurate assumption that to "grow up" is in some ultimate sense to cease to be really alive.

Finally, youths tend to band together with other youths in *youthful counter-cultures*, characterized by their deliberate cultural distance from the existing social order, but *not* always by active political or other opposition to it. It is a mistake to identify youth as a developmental stage with any one social group, role or organization. But youth *is* a time when solidarity with other youths is especially important, whether the solidarity be achieved in pairs, small groups, or formal organizations. And the groups dominated by those in this stage of life reflect not only the special configurations of each historical era, but also the shared developmental positions and problems of youth. Much of what has traditionally been referred to as "youth culture" is, in the terms here used, adolescent culture; but there are also groups, societies and associations that are truly youthful. In our own time, with the enormous increase in the number of those who are entering youth as a stage of life, the variety and importance of these youthful counter-cultures is steadily growing.

This compressed summary of themes in youth is schematic and interpretive. It omits many of the qualifications necessary to a fuller discussion, and it neglects the enormous complexity of development in any one person in favor of a highly schematic account. Specifically, for example, I do not discuss the ways the infantile, the childish, the adolescent and the truly youthful interact in all real lives. And perhaps most important, my account is highly interpretative, in that it points to themes that underlie diverse acts and feelings, to issues and tensions that unite the often scattered experiences of real individuals. The themes, issues and conflicts here discussed are rarely conscious as such; indeed, if they all were fully conscious, there would probably be something seriously awry. Different youths experience each of the issues here considered with different intensity. What is a central conflict for one may be peripheral or unimportant for another. These remarks, then, should be taken as a first effort to summarize some of the underlying issues that characterize youth as an ideal type.

TRANSFORMATIONS OF YOUTH

A second way of describing youth is by attempting to trace out the various psychological and interpersonal transformations that may occur during this stage. Once again, only the most preliminary sketch of youthful development can be attempted here. Somewhat arbitrarily, I will distinguish between development in several sectors or areas of life, here noting only that, in fact, changes in one sector invariably interact with those in other sectors.

In pointing to the *self-society relationship* as a central issue in youth, I also mean to suggest its importance as an area of potential change. The late adolescent is only beginning to challenge his society's definition of him, only starting to compare his emerging sense of himself with his culture's possibilities and with the temptations and opportunities offered by his environment. Adolescent struggles for emancipation from external familial control and internal dependency on the family take a variety of forms, including displacement of the conflict onto other "authority figures." But in adolescence itself, the "real" focus of conflict is on the family and all of its internal psychic residues. In youth, however, the "real" focus begins to shift: increasingly, the family becomes more paradigmatic of society than vice versa. As relatively greater emancipation from the family is achieved, the tension between self and society, with ambivalent probing of both, comes to constitute a major area of developmental "work" and change. Through this work, young people can sometimes arrive at a synthesis whereby both self and society are affirmed, in the sense that the autonomous reality, relatedness yet separateness of both, is firmly established.

There is no adequate term to describe this "resolution" of the tension between self and society, but C. G. Jung's concept of *"individuation"* comes close. For Jung, the individuated man is a man who acknowledges and can cope with social reality, whether accepting it or opposing it with revolutionary fervor. But he can do this without feeling his central selfhood overwhelmed. Even when most fully engaged in social role and societal action, he can preserve a sense of himself as intact, whole, and distinct from society. Thus the "resolution" of the self-society tension in no way necessarily entails "adjusting" to the society, much less "selling out"—although many youths see it this way. On the contrary, individuation refers partly to a psychological process whereby self and society are differentiated internally. But the actual conflicts between men and women and their societies remain, and indeed may become even more intense.

The meaning of individuation may be clarified by considering the special dangers of youth, which can be defined as extremes of *alienation, whether from self or from society.* At one extreme is that total alienation from self that involves abject submission to society, "joining the rat race," "selling out." Here, society is affirmed but selfhood denied. The other extreme is a total alienation from society that leads not so much to the rejection of society, as to its existence being ignored, denied and blocked out. The result is a kind of self-absorption, an enforced interiority and subjectivity, in which only the self and its extensions are granted live reality, while all the rest is relegated to a limbo of insignificance. Here the integrity of the self is purchased at the price of a determined denial of social reality, and the loss of social effectiveness. In youth both forms of alienation are often assayed, sometimes for lengthy periods. And for some whose further development is blocked, they become the basis for life-long adaptations—the self-alienation of the marketing personality, the social alienation of the perpetual drop-out. In terms of the polarities of Erikson, we can define the central developmental possibilities of youth as individuation vs. alienation.

Sexual development continues in important ways during youth. In modern Western societies, as in many others, the commencement of actual sexual relationships is generally deferred by middle-class adolescents until their late teens or early twenties: the modal age of first intercourse for American college males today is around twenty, for females about twenty-one. Thus, despite the enormous importance of adolescent sexuality and sexual development, actual sexual intercourse often awaits youth. In youth, there may occur a major shift from masturbation and sexual fantasy to interpersonal sexual behavior, including the gradual integration of sexual feelings with intimacy with a real person. And as sexual behavior with real people commences, one sees a further working through, now in behavior, of vestigial fears and prohibitions whose origin lies in earlier childhood—specifically, of Oedipal feelings of sexual inferiority and of Oedipal prohibitions against sex with one's closest intimates. During youth, when these fears and prohibitions can be gradually worked through, they yield a capacity for genitality, that is, for mutually satisfying sexual relationships with another whom one loves.

The transition to genitality is closely related to a more general pattern of *interpersonal development*. I will term this the shift from *identicality* to mutuality. This development begins with adolescence* and continues through youth: it involves a progressive expansion of the early-adolescent assumption that the interpersonal world is divided into only two categories: first, me-and-those-who-are-identical-to-me (potential soulmates, doubles and hypothetical people who "automatically understand everything"), and second, all others. This conceptualization gradually yields to a capacity for close relationships with those on an approximate level of *parity* or similarity with the individual.

The phase of parity in turn gives way to a phase of *complementarity*, in which the individual can relate warmly to others who are different from him, valuing them for their dissimilarities from himself. Finally, the phase of complementarity may yield in youth to a phase of *mutuality*, in which issues of identicality, parity and complementarity are subsumed in an overriding concern with the other *as other*. Mutuality entails a simultaneous awareness of the ways in which others are identical to oneself, the ways in which they are similar and dissimilar, and the ways in which they are absolutely unique. Only in the stage of mutuality can the individual begin to conceive of others as separate and unique selves, and relate to them as such. And only with this stage can the concept of mankind assume a concrete significance as pointing to a human universe of unique and irreplaceable selves.

Relationships with elders may also undergo

characteristic youthful changes. By the end of adolescence, the hero worship or demonology of the middle adolescent has generally given way to an attitude of more selective emulation and rejection of admired or disliked older persons. In youth, new kinds of relationships with elders become possible: psychological apprenticeships, then a more complex relationship with mentorship, then sponsorship, and eventually peership. Without attempting to describe each of these substages in detail, the overall transition can be described as one in which the older person becomes progressively more real and three-dimensional to the younger one, whose individuality is appreciated, validated and confirmed by the elder. The sponsor, for example, is one who supports and confirms in the youth that which is best in the youth, without exacting an excessive price in terms of submission, imitation, emulation or even gratitude.

Comparable changes continue to occur during youth with regard to *parents*. Adolescents commonly discover that their parents have feet of clay, and recognize their flaws with great acuity. Childish hero worship of parents gives way to a more complex and often negative view of them. But it is generally not until youth that the individual discovers his parents as themselves complex, three-dimensional historical personages whose destinies are partly formed by their own wishes, conscious and unconscious, and by their historical situations. Similarly, it is only during youth that the questions of family tradition, family destiny, family fate, family culture and family curse arise with full force. In youth, the question of whether to live one's parents' life, or to what extent to do so, becomes a real and active question. In youth, one often sees what Ernst Prelinger has called a "telescoped re-enactment" of the life of a parent—a compulsive need to live out for oneself the destiny of a parent, as if to test its possibilities and limits, experience it from the inside, and (perhaps)

*Obviously, interpersonal development, and specifically the development of relationships with peers, begins long before adolescence, starting with the "parallel play" observed at ages two to four and continuing through many stages to the preadolescent same-sex "chumship" described by Harry Stack Sullivan. But puberty in middle-class Western societies is accompanied by major cognitive changes that permit the early adolescent for the first time to develop hypothetical ideals of the possibilities of friendship and intimacy. The "search for a soulmate" of early adolescence is the first interpersonal stage built upon these new cognitive abilities.

free oneself of it. In the end, the youth may learn to see himself and his parents as multidimensional persons, to view them with compassion and understanding, to feel less threatened by their fate and failings and to be able, if he chooses, to move beyond them.

In beginning by discussing affective and interpersonal changes in youth, I begin where our accounts of development are least precise and most tentative. Turning to more cognitive matters, we stand on somewhat firmer ground. Lawrence Kohlberg's work on *moral development*, especially on the attainment of the highest levels of moral reasoning, provides a paradigmatic description of developments that occur only in youth, if they occur at all.

Summarized over-simply, Kohlberg's theory distinguishes three general stages in the development of moral reasoning. The earliest or *pre-moral* stage involves relatively egocentric concepts of right and wrong as that which one can do without getting caught, or as that which leads to the greatest personal gratification. This stage is followed, usually during later childhood, by a stage of *conventional* morality, during which good and evil are identified with the concept of a "good boy" or "good girl," or with standards of the community and the concept of law and order. In this stage, morality is perceived as objective, as existing "out there."

The third and final major stage of moral development is *post-conventional*. It involves more abstract moral reasoning that may lead the individual into conflict with conventional morality. The first of two levels within the postconventional stage basically involves the assumption that concepts of right and wrong result from a *social contract*—an implicit agreement entered into by the members of the society for their own welfare, and therefore subject to amendment, change or revocation. The highest postconventional level is that in which the individual becomes devoted to *personal principles* that may transcend not only

conventional morality but even the social contract. In this stage, certain general principles are now seen as personally binding although not necessarily "objectively" true. Such principles are apt to be stated at a very high level of generality: for example, the Golden Rule, the sanctity of life, the categorical imperative, the concept of justice, the promotion of human development. The individual at this stage may find himself in conflict with existing concepts of law and order, or even with the notion of an amendable social contract. He may, for example, consider even democratically-arrived-at laws unacceptable because they lead to consequences or enjoin behaviors that violate his own personal principles.

Kohlberg's research suggests that most contemporary Americans, young or old, do not pass beyond the conventional stage of moral reasoning. But some do, and they are most likely to be found today among those who are young and educated. Such young men and women may develop moral principles that can lead them to challenge the existing moral order and the existing society. And Kohlberg finds that the achievement of his highest level, the stage of personal principles, occurs in the twenties, if it occurs at all. Moral development of this type can thus be identified with youth, as can the special moral "regressions" that Kohlberg finds a frequent concomitant of moral development. Here the arbitrariness of distinguishing between sectors of development becomes clear, for the individual can begin to experience the tension between self and society only as he begins to question the absolutism of conventional moral judgments. Unless he has begun such questioning, it is doubtful whether we can correctly term him "a youth."

In no other sector of development do we have so complete, accurate and convincing a description of a "development line" that demonstrably characterizes youth. But in the area of *intellectual development*, William

Perry has provided an invaluable description of the stages through which college students may pass. Perry's work emphasizes the complex transition from epistemological dualism to an awareness of multiplicty and to the realization of relativism. Relativism in turn gives way to a more "existential" sense of truth, culminating in what Perry terms "commitment within relativism." Thus, in youth we expect to see a passage beyond simple views of Right and Wrong, Truth and Falsehood, Good and Evil to a more complex and relativistic view; and as youth proceeds, we look for the development of commitments within a universe that remains epistemologically relativistic. Once again, intellectual development is only analytically separable from a variety of other sectors—moral, self-society and interpersonal, to mention only three.

In his work on *cognitive development*, Jean Piaget has emphasized the importance of the transition from concrete to formal operations, which in middle-class Western children usually occurs at about the age of puberty. For Piaget the attainment of formal operations (whereby the concrete world of the real becomes a subset of the hypothetical world of the possible) is the highest cognitive stage possible. But in some youths, there seem to occur further stages of cognitive development that are not understandable with the concept of formal operations. Jerome Bruner has suggested that beyond the formal stage of thought there lies a further stage of "thinking about thinking." This ability to think about thinking involves a new level of consciousness—consciousness of consciousness, awareness of awareness, and a breaking-away of the phenomenological "I" from the contents of consciousness. This breaking-away of the phenomenological ego during youth permits phenomenological games, intellectual tricks, and kinds of creativity that are rarely possible in adolescence itself. It provides the cognitive underpinning for many of the characteristics

and special disturbances of youth, for example, youth's hyperawareness of inner processes, the focus upon states of consciousness as objects to be controlled and altered, and the frightening disappearance of the phenomenological ego in an endless regress of awarenesses of awarenesses.

Having emphasized that these analytically separated "lines" of development are in fact linked in the individual's experience, it is equally important to add that they are never linked in perfect synchronicity. If we could precisely label one specific level within each developmental line as distinctively youthful, we would find that few people were "youthful" in all lines at the same time. In general, human development proceeds unevenly, with lags in some areas and precocities in others. One young woman may be at a truly adolescent level in her relationship with her parents, but at a much later level in moral development; a young man may be capable of extraordinary mutuality with his peers, but still be struggling intellectually with the dim awareness of relativism. Analysis of any one person in terms of specific sectors of development will generally show a simultaneous mixture of adolescent, youthful and adult features. The point, once again, is that the concept of youth here proposed is an ideal type, a model that may help understand real experience but can never fully describe or capture it.

WHAT YOUTH IS NOT

A final way to clarify the meaning of youth as a stage of life is to make clear what it is not. For one thing, youth is not the end of development. I have described the belief that it is—the conviction that beyond youth lie only stasis, decline, foreclosure, and death—as a characteristically youthful way of viewing development, consistent with the observation that it is impossible truly to understand stages of development beyond one's own. On the con-

trary, youth is but a preface for further transformations that may (or may not) occur in
later life. Many of these center around such
issues as the relationship to work and to the
next generation. In youth, the question of
vocation is crucial, but the issue of work—of
productivity, creativity, and the more general
sense of fruitfulness that Erikson calls
generativity—awaits adulthood. The youthful
attainment of mutuality with peers and of
peerhood with elders can lead on to further
adult interpersonal developments by which
one comes to be able to accept the dependency of others, as in parenthood. In later life,
too, the relations between the generations are
reversed, with the younger now assuming
responsibility for the elder. Like all stages of
life, youth is transitional. And although some
lines of development, such as moral development, may be "completed" during youth,
many others continue throughout adulthood.

It is also a mistake to identify youth with
any one social group, role, class, organization,
or position in society. Youth is a *psychological* stage; and those who are in this stage do
not necessarily join together in identifiable
groups, nor do they share a common social
position. Not all college students, for example,
are in this stage of life: some students are
psychological adolescents, while others are
young adults—essentially apprentices to the
existing society. Nor can the experience of
youth as a stage of life be identified with any
one class, nation or other social grouping.
Affluence and education can provide a freedom from economic need and an intellectual
stimulation that may underlie and promote the
transformations of youth. But there are poor
and uneducated young men and women, from
Abraham Lincoln to Malcolm X, who have
had a youth, and rich, educated ones who have
moved straightaway from adolescence to
adulthood. And although the experience of
youth is probably more likely to occur in the
economically advanced nations, some of the
factors that facilitate youth also exist in
the less advanced nations, where comparable
youthful issues and transformations are expressed in different cultural idioms.

Nor should youth be identified with the
rejection of the status quo, or specifically with
student radicalism. Indeed, anyone who has
more or less definitively defined himself as a
misanthrope or a revolutionary has moved
beyond youthful probing into an "adult" commitment to a position vis-à-vis society. To
repeat: what characterizes youth is not a
definitive rejection of the existing "system,"
but an ambivalent tension over the relationship between self and society. This tension
may take the form of avid efforts at self-
reform that spring from acceptance of the
status quo, coupled with a sense of one's own
inadequacy vis-à-vis it. In youth the relationship between self and society is indeed proble-
matical, but rejection of the existing society is
not a necessary characteristic of youth.

Youth obviously cannot be equated with
any particular age-range. In practice, most
young Americans who enter this stage of life
tend to be between the ages of eighteen and
thirty. But they constitute a minority of the
whole age-grade. Youth as a developmental
stage is emergent; it is an "optional" stage, not
a universal one. If we take Kohlberg's studies
of the development of postconventional moral
reasoning as a rough index of the "incidence"
of youth, less than forty percent of middle-
class (college-educated) men, and a smaller
proportion of working-class men have developed beyond the conventional level by the age
of twenty-four. Thus, "youths" constitute but
a minority of their age group. But those who
are in this stage of life today largely determine
the public image of their generation.

Admirers and romanticizers of youth tend
to identify youth with virtue, morality and
mental health. But to do so is to overlook the
special youthful possibilities for viciousness,
immorality and psychopathology. Every time

of human life, each level of development, has its characteristic vices and weaknesses, and youth is no exception. Youth is a stage, for example, when the potentials for zealotry and fanaticism, for reckless action in the name of the highest principles, for self-absorption, and for special arrogance are all at a peak. Furthermore, the fact that youth is a time of psychological change also inevitably means that it is a stage of constant recapitulation, reenactment and reworking of the past. This reworking can rarely occur with real regression, whereby the buried past is reexperienced as present and, one hopes, incorporated into it. Most youthful transformation occurs *through* brief or prolonged regression, which, however benignly it may eventually be resolved, constitutes part of the psychopathology of youth. And the special compulsions and inner states of youth—the euphoria of omnipotentiality and the dysphoria of estrangement, the hyperconsciousness of consciousness, the need for constant motion and the terror of stasis—may generate youthful pathologies with a special virulence and obstinacy. In one sense those who have the luxury of a youth may be said to be "more developed" than those who do not have (or do not take) this opportunity. But no level of development and no stage of life should be identified either with virtue or with health.

Finally, youth is not the same as the adoption of youthful causes, fashions, rhetoric or postures. Especially in a time like our own, when youthful behavior is watched with ambivalent fascination by adults, the positions of youth become part of the cultural stock-in-trade. There thus develops the phenomenon of *pseudoyouth*—preadolescents, adolescents and frustrated adults masquerade as youths, adopt youthful manners and disguise (even to themselves) their real concerns by the use of youthful rhetoric. Many a contemporary adolescent, whether of college or high school age, finds it convenient to displace and express his

battles with his parents in a pseudo-youthful railing at the injustices, oppression and hypocrisy of the Establishment. And many an adult, unable to accept his years, may adopt pseudo-youthful postures to express the despairs of his adulthood.

To differentiate between "real" and pseudo youth is a tricky, subtle and unrewarding enterprise. For, as I have earlier emphasized, the concept of youth as here defined is an ideal type, an abstraction from the concrete experience of many different individuals. Furthermore, given the unevenness of human development and the persistence throughout life of active remnants of earlier developmental levels, conflicts and stages, no one can ever be said to be completely "in" one stage of life in all areas of behavior and at all times. No issue can ever be said to be finally "resolved"; no earlier conflict is completely "overcome." Any real person, even though on balance we may consider him a "youth," will also contain some persistent childishness, some not-outgrown adolescence, and some precocious adulthood in his makeup. All we can say is that, for some, adolescent themes and levels of development are *relatively* outgrown, while adult concerns have not yet assumed full prominence. It is such people whom one might term "youths."

THE IMPLICATIONS OF YOUTH

I have sketched with broad and careless strokes the rough outlines of a stage of life I believe to characterize a growing, although still small, set of young men and women. This sketch, although presented dogmatically, is clearly preliminary; it will doubtless require revision and correction after further study. Yet let us for the moment assume that, whatever the limitations of this outline, the concept of a postadolescent stage of life has some merit. What might be the implications of the emergence of youth?

To most Americans, the chief anxieties raised by youth are over social stability and historical continuity. In every past and present society, including our own, the great majority of men and women seem to be, in Kohlberg's terms, "conventional" in moral judgment, and, in Perry's terms, "dualistic" in their intellectual outlook. Such men and women accept with little question the existing moral codes of the community, just as they endorse their culture's traditional view of the world. It is arguable that both cultural continuity and social stability have traditionally rested on the moral and epistemological conventionality of most men and women, and on the secure transmission of these conventional views to the next generation.

What, then, would it mean if our particular era were producing millions of postconventional, nondualistic, postrelativistic youth? What would happen if millions of young men and women developed to the point that they "made up their own minds" about most value, ideological, social and philosophical questions, often rejecting the conventional and traditional answers? Would they not threaten the stability of their societies?

Today it seems clear that most youths are considered nuisances or worse by the established order, to which they have not finally pledged their allegiance. Indeed, many of the major stresses in contemporary American society spring from or are aggravated by those in this stage of life. One aspect of the deep polarization in our society may be characterized psychologically as a struggle between conventionals and postconventionals, between those who have not had a youth and those who have. The answer of the majority of the public seems clear: we already have too many "youths" in our society; youth as a developmental stage should be stamped out.

A more moderate answer to the questions I am raising is also possible. We might recognize the importance of having a *few* postconventional individuals (an occasional Socrates, Christ, Luther or Gandhi to provide society with new ideas and moral inspiration), but nonetheless establish a firm top limit on the proportion of postconventional, youth-scarred adults our society could tolerate. If social stability requires human inertia—that is, unreflective acceptance of most social, cultural and political norms—perhaps we should discourage "youth as a stage of life" in any but a select minority.

A third response, toward which I incline, seems to me more radical. To the argument from social stability and cultural continuity, one might reply by pointing to the enormous *in*stabilities and gross cultural *dis*continuities that characterize the modern world. Older forms of stability and continuity have *already* been lost in the postindustrial era. Today, it is simply impossible to return to a bygone age when massive inertia guaranteed social stability (if there really was such an age). The cake of custom crumbled long ago. The only hope is to learn to live without it.

In searching for a way to do this, we might harken back to certain strands in socialist thought that see new forms of social organization possible for men and women who are more "evolved." I do not wish to equate my views on development with revolutionary socialism or anarchism, much less with a Rousseauistic faith in the goodness of the essential man. But if there is anything to the hypothesis that different historical conditions alter the nature of the life cycle, then men with different kinds of development may require or be capable of living in different kinds of social institutions. On the one hand, this means that merely throwing off institutional shackles, as envisioned by some socialist and anarchist thinkers, would not automatically change the nature of men, although it may be desirable on other grounds. "New men" cannot be created by institutional transformations alone, although institutional changes may, over the long run, affect the possibilities for continuing development by changing the matrix in which development occurs.

But on the other hand, men and women who have attained higher developmental levels may be capable of different kinds of association and cooperation from those at lower levels. Relativism, for example, brings not only skepticism but also tolerance of the viewpoints of others, and a probable reduction in moralistic self-righteousness. Attaining the stage of personal principles in moral development in no way prevents the individual from conforming to a just social order, or even for that matter from obeying unreasonable traffic laws. Men and women who are capable of interpersonal mutuality are not for that reason worse citizens; on the contrary, their capacity to be concerned with others as unique individuals might even make them better citizens. Examples could be multiplied, but the general point is obvious: higher levels of development, including the emergence on a mass scale of "new" stages of life, may permit new forms of human cooperation and social organization.

It may be true that all past societies have been built upon the unquestioning inertia of the vast majority of their citizens. And this inertia may have provided the psychological ballast that prevented most revolutions from doing more than reinstating the *ancien régime* in new guise. But it does not follow that this need always continue to be true. If new developmental stages are emerging that lead growing minorities to more autonomous positions vis-à-vis their societies, the result need not be anarchy or social chaos. The result might instead be the possibility of new forms of social organization based less upon unreflective acceptance of the status quo than upon thoughtful and self-conscious loyalty and cooperation. But whether or not these new forms can emerge depends not only upon the psychological factors I have discussed here, but even more upon political, social, economic and international conditions.

Part Six

Disturbances in a Child's World

Chapter 15

Personality Development

THE PRESCHOOL YEARS

The Theory of Infantile Sexuality

Erik H. Erikson

I had been told that Peter had been retaining his bowel movements, first for a few days at a time, but more recently up to a week. I was urged to hurry when, in addition to a week's supply of fecal matter, Peter had incorporated and retained a large enema in his small, four-year-old body. He looked miserable, and when he thought nobody watched him he leaned his bloated abdomen against a wall for support.

Editor's Introduction

Erik Erikson has criticized, clarified, and expanded much of Freudian theory. His influence on psychoanalysis has been mixed. Many feel that he has made a real contribution to developmental and psychoanalytic theory. Others feel that he is tangential. It is the author's opinion that Erikson has penetrated and enriched this field of thought.

Erikson's main contribution is that of extending the matrix in which Freud was embedded. Freud's main concern was for the family. Erikson has expanded this

Reprinted from *Childhood and Society*, Second Edition, revised by Erik H. Erikson. By permission of W. W. Norton & Company, Inc. Copyright © 1950, 1963 by W. W. Norton & Company, Inc.

concern to society and culture: the family as viewed through historical, social, religious, and cultural perspectives. Erikson's is a clinical approach to the total picture of human and cultural history.

In examining the differences between the two theorists, one must remember that the missions of these two men were necessarily different. Freud sought to prove the existence and the importance of the unconscious. His main concern was that of altering intrapsychic development. The psychoanalytic method is largely a historical method: it interprets present symptoms and conflicts in terms of past experience. Erikson's concern is for the present rather than for a reworking of infancy problems. Erikson accounts for the different approaches as follows: "Different periods thus permit us to see in temporary exaggeration different aspects of essentially inseparable aspects of personality." Erikson rebuilds Freud's theories of psychosexual development and expands them into psychosocial theory. He underplays the concept of defense mechanisms, since he is more concerned with adaptation. Like Freud, he believes that anatomy is destiny, and he stresses the importance of constitutional factors. He accepts the theory of the unconscious. He acknowledges the "libido" as "sexual energy" and expands it to encompass all "life energy." He shifts the emphasis in personality structure from the id to the ego and its synthesizing functions.

Erikson, one of the most famous child analysts in the world today, presents the cases of Peter and of Ann in light of Freud's theories of infantile sexuality and his own insights into the events and thoughts which shape the emotional life of a child. While the psychoanalytic method is primarily historical and Erikson's theoretical perspective emphasizes the present, Erikson acknowledges that we are all products of our past experiences and most of us harbor irrational fears which have their origins in childhood events. Erikson takes us step by step through the process of his analyses of Peter and of Ann, exposing the conflicts the children feel and bringing us to the resolution of each child's difficulties.

Pamela Cantor

As an introduction to a review of Freud's theories concerning the infantile organism as a powerhouse of sexual and aggressive energies, let me now present observations on two children who seemed strangely deadlocked in combat with their own bowels. As we try to understand the social implications of the eliminative and other body apertures, it will be necessary to reserve judgment regarding the children studied and the symptoms observed. The symptoms seem odd; the children are not. For good physiological reasons the bowels are farthest away from the zone which is our prime interpersonal mediator, namely the face. Well-trained adults dismiss the bowels, if they function well, as the non-social backside of things. Yet for this very reason bowel dysfunction lends itself to confused reflection and to secret response. In adults this problem is hidden behind somatic complaints; in children it appears in what seem to be merely willful habits.

Ann, a girl of four, enters the office, half gently pulled, half firmly pushed by her worried mother. While she does not resist or object, her face is pale and sullen, her eyes have a blank and inward look, and she sucks vigorously on her thumb.

I have been informed of Ann's trouble. She seems to be losing her usual resilience; in one way she is much too babyish, in another much too serious, too unchildlike. When she does express exuberance, it is of an explosive kind which soon turns to silliness. But her most annoying habit is that of holding on to her bowel movements when requested to relinquish them, and then of stubbornly depositing them in her bed during the night, or rather in the early morning just before her sleepy mother can catch her. Reprimands are borne silently and in reverie behind which lurks obvious despair. This despair seems recently to have increased following an accident in which she was knocked down by an automobile. The damage to her body is only superficial, but she has withdrawn even further from the reach of parental communication and control.

Once inside the office the child lets go of the mother's hand and walks into my room with the automatic obedience of a prisoner who no longer has a will of his own. In my playroom she stands in a corner, sucking tensely on her thumb and paying only a very reserved kind of attention to me.

The child indicates clearly that I will not get anything out of her. To her growing surprise and relief, however, I do not ask her any questions; I do not even tell her that I am her friend and that she should trust me. Instead I start to build a simple block house on the floor. There is a living room; a kitchen; a bedroom with a little girl in a bed and a woman standing close by her; a bathroom with the door open; and a garage with a man standing next to a car. This arrangement suggests, of course, the regular morning hour when the mother tries to pick the little girl up "on time," while the father gets ready to leave the house.

Our patient, increasingly fascinated with this wordless statement of a problem, suddenly goes into action. She relinquishes her thumb to make space for a broad and toothy grin. Her face flushes and she runs over to the toy scene. With a mighty kick she disposes of the woman doll; she bangs the bathroom door shut, and she hurries to the toy shelf to get three shiny cars, which she puts into the garage beside the man. She has answered my

"question": she, indeed, does not wish the toy girl to give to her mother what is her mother's, and she is eager to give to her father more than he could ask for.

I am still pondering over the power of her aggressive exuberance when she, in turn, seems suddenly overpowered by an entirely different set of emotions. She bursts into tears and into a desperate whimper, "Where is my mummy?" In panicky haste she takes a handful of pencils from my desk and runs out into the waiting room. Pressing the pencils into her mother's hand, she sits down close to her. The thumb goes back into the mouth, the child's face becomes uncommunicative, and I can see the game is over. The mother wants to give the pencils back to me, but I indicate that I do not need them today. Mother and child leave.

Half an hour later the telephone rings. They have hardly reached home when the little girl asks her mother whether she may see me again that same day. Tomorrow is not early enough. She insists with signs of despair that the mother call me immediately for an appointment the same day so that she may return the pencils. I must assure the child over the phone that I appreciate her intentions but that she is quite welcome to keep the pencils until the next day.

The next day, at the appointed time, Ann sits beside her mother in the waiting room. In one hand she holds the pencils, unable to give them to me. In the other she clutches a small object. She shows no inclination to come with me. It suddenly becomes quite noticeable that she has soiled herself. As she is picked up to be taken to the bathroom, the pencils fall to the floor and with them the object from the other hand. It is a tiny dog, one of whose legs has been broken off.

I must add here the information that at this time a neighbor's dog plays a significant role in the child's life. This dog soils too; but he is beaten for it, and the child is not. And the dog, too, has recently been knocked down by a car;

but he has lost a leg. Her friend in the animal world, then, is much like herself, only more so; and he is much worse off. Does she expect (or maybe even wish) to be punished likewise?

I have now described the circumstances of a play episode and of an infantile symptom. I shall not go further here into the relativities and relevances which led up to the described situation; nor shall I relate how the deadlock was finally resolved in work with parents and child. I appreciate and share the regret of many a reader that we are not able here to pursue the therapeutic process and, in fact, the passing of this infantile crisis. Instead I must ask the reader to accept this story as a "specimen" and to analyze it with me.

The little girl had not come of her own free will. She had merely let herself be brought by the very mother against whom, as everything indicated, her sullenness was directed. Once in my room, my quiet play apparently had made her forget for a moment that her mother was outside. What she would not have been able to say in words in many hours she could express in a few minutes of non-verbal communication: she "hated" her mother and she "loved" her father. Having expressed this, however, she must have experienced what Adam did when he heard God's voice: "Adam, where art thou?" She was compelled to atone for her deed, for she loved her mother too and needed her. In her very panic, however, she did compulsively what ambivalent people always do: in turning to make amends to one person they "inadvertently" do harm to another. So she took my pencils to appease the mother, and then wanted to force the mother to help her make restitution.

The next day her eagerness to conciliate me is paralyzed. I think I had become the tempter who makes children confess in unguarded moments what nobody should know or say. Children often have such a reaction after an initial admission of secret thoughts. What if I told her mother? What if her mother refused to bring her back to me so she could modify and qualify her unguarded acts? So she refused to act altogether, and let her symptom speak.

Soiling represents a sphincter conflict, an anal and urethral problem. This aspect of the matter we shall call the zonal aspect, because it concerns a *body zone*. On closer review, however, it becomes clear that this child's behavior, even where it is not anal in a zonal sense, has the quality of a sphincter problem. One may almost say that the whole little girl acts like a multiple sphincter. In her facial expression, as well as in her emotional communication, she closes up most of the time, to open up rarely and spasmodically. As we offer her a toy situation so that she may reveal and commit herself in its "unreality," she performs two acts: she closes, in vigorous defiance, the bathroom door of the toy house, and she gives in manic glee three shiny cars to the father doll. More and more deeply involved in the opposition of the simple modalities of taking and giving, she gives to the mother what she took from me and then wants desperately to return to me what she has given to her mother. Back again, her tense little hands hold pencils and toy tight, yet drop them abruptly, as equally suddenly the sphincters proper release their contents.

Obviously then, this little girl, unable to master the problem of how to give without taking (maybe how to love her father without robbing her mother), falls back on an automatic alternation of retentive and eliminative acts. This alternation of holding on and letting go, of withholding and giving, of opening up and closing up, we shall call the *mode* aspect of the matter. The anal-urethral sphincters, then, are the anatomic models for the *retentive* and *eliminative* modes, which, in turn, can characterize a great variety of behaviors, all of which according to a now widespread clinical habit (and I mean bad habit), would be referred to as "anal."

A similar relationship between a zone and a mode can be seen in this child's moments of most pronounced babyishness. She becomes all mouth and thumb, as if a milk of consolation were flowing through this contact of her very own body parts. She is now "oral." But upon uncoiling from this withdrawal into herself, the young lady can become quite animated indeed, kicking the doll and grasping the cars with a flushed face and a throaty laugh. From the retentive-eliminative position then, an avenue of regression seems to lead further inward (isolation) and backward (regression), while a progressive and aggressive avenue leads outward and forward, toward an initiative which, however, immediately causes guilt. This, then, circumscribes the kind of aggravated crisis in which a child and a family may need help.

The pathways of such regression and progression are the subject-matter of this chapter. In order to demonstrate further the systematic relationship between zones and modes, I shall describe a second episode, concerning a little boy.

I had been told that Peter was retaining his bowel movements, first for a few days at a time, but more recently up to a week. I was urged to hurry when, in addition to a week's supply of fecal matter, Peter had incorporated and retained a large enema in his small, four-year-old body. He looked miserable, and when he thought nobody watched him he leaned his bloated abdomen against a wall for support.

His pediatrician had come to the conclusion that this feat could not have been accomplished without energetic support from the emotional side, although he suspected what was later revealed by X-ray, namely that the boy indeed had by then an enlarged colon. While a tendency toward colonic expansion may initially have contributed to the creation of the symptom, the child was now undoubtedly paralyzed by a conflict which he was unable to verbalize. The local physiological condition was to be taken care of later by diet and exercise. First it seemed necessary to

understand the conflict and to establish communication with the boy as quickly as possible so that his co-operation might be obtained.

It has been my custom before deciding to take on a family problem to have a meal with the family in their home. I was introduced to my prospective little patient as an acquaintance of the parents who wanted to come and meet the whole family. The little boy was one of those children who make me question the wisdom of any effort at disguise. "Aren't dreams wonderful?" he said to me in a decidedly artificial tone as we sat down to lunch. While his older brothers ate heartily and quickly and then took to the woods behind the house, he improvised almost feverishly a series of playful statements which, as will be clear presently, revealed his dominant and disturbing fantasy. It is characteristic of the ambivalent aspect of sphincter problems that the patients surrender almost obsessively the very secret which is so strenuously retained in their bowels. I shall list here some of Peter's dreamy statements and my silent reflections upon them.

"I wish I had a little elephant right here in my house. But then it would grow and grow and burst the house."—The boy is eating at the moment. His intestinal bulk is growing to the bursting point.

"Look at that bee—it wants to get at the sugar in my stomach." —"Sugar" sound euphemistic, but it does transmit the thought that he has something valuable in his stomach and that somebody wants to get at it.

"I had a bad dream. Some monkeys climbed up and down the house and tried to get in to me."—The bees wanted to get at the sugar in his stomach; now the monkeys want to get at him in his house. Increasing food in his stomach—growing baby elephant in the house—bees after sugar in his stomach—monkeys after him in the house.

After lunch coffee was served in the garden. Peter sat down underneath a garden table, pulled the chairs in toward himself as if barricading himself, and said, "Now I am in my tent and the bees can't get at me."—Again he is inside an enclosure, endangered by intrusive animals.

He then climbed out and showed me to his room. I admired his books and said, "Show me the picture you like the best in the book you like best." Without hesitation he produced an illustration showing a gingerbread man floating in water toward the open mouth of a swimming wolf. Excitedly he said, "The wolf is going to eat the gingerbread man, but it won't hurt the gingerbread man because [loudly] *he's not alive*, and food can't feel it when you eat it!" I thoroughly agreed with him, reflecting in the meantime that the boy's playful sayings converged on the idea that whatever he had accumulated in his stomach was alive and in danger of either "bursting" him or of being hurt. I asked him to show me the picture he liked next best in any of the other books. He immediately went after a book called "The Little Engine That Could" and looked for a page which showed a smoke-puffing train going into a tunnel, while on the next page it comes out of it—its funnel *not smoking*. "You see," he said, "the train went into the tunnel and in the dark tunnel it *went dead*!"—Something alive went into a dark passage and came out dead. I no longer doubted that this little boy had a fantasy that he was filled with something precious and alive; that if he kept it, it would burst him and that if he released it, it might come out hurt or dead. In other words, he was pregnant.

The patient needed immediate help, by interpretation. I want to make it clear that I do not approve of imposing sexual enlightenment on unsuspecting children before a reliable relationship has been established. Here, however, I felt "surgical" action was called for. I came back to his love for little elephants and suggested that we draw elephants. After we had reached a certain proficiency in drawing all the outer appointments and appendages of an elephant lady and of a couple of elephant babies, I asked whether he knew where the elephant babies came from. Tensely he said he did not, although I had the impression that he merely wanted to lead me on. So I drew as well as I could a cross section of the elephant lady and of her inner compartments, making it quite clear that there were two exits, one for the bowels and one for the babies. "This," I said, "some children do not know. They think that the bowel movements and the babies come out of the same opening in animals and in women." Before I could expand on the dangers which one could infer from such misunderstood conditions, he very excitedly told me that when his mother had carried him she had had to wear a belt which kept him from falling out of her when she sat on the toilet; and that he had proved too big for her opening so she had to have a cut made in her stomach to let him out. I had not known that he had been born by cesarean section, but I drew him a diagram of a woman, setting him straight on what he remembered of his mother's explanations. I added that it seemed to me that he thought he, too, could have babies, that while this was impossible in reality it was important to understand the reason for his fantasy; that, as he might have heard, I made it my business to understand children's thoughts and that, if he wished, I would come back the next day to continue our conversation. He did wish; and he had a superhuman bowel movement after I left.

There was no doubt, then, that once having bloated his abdomen with retained fecal matter this boy thought he might be pregnant and was afraid to let go lest he hurt himself or "the baby." But what had made him retain in the first place? What had caused in him an emotional conflict at this time which found its expression in bowel retention and a pregnancy fantasy?

The boy's father gave me a key to one

immediate "cause" of the deadlock. "You know," he said, "the boy begins to look just like Myrtle." "Who is Myrtle?" "She was his nurse for two years; she left three months ago." "Shortly before his symptoms became so much worse?" "Yes."

Peter, then, has lost an important person in his life: his nurse. A soft-spoken Oriental girl with a gentle touch, she had been his main comfort for years because his parents were out often, both pursuing professional careers. In recent months he had taken to attacking the nurse in a roughhousing way, and the girl had seemed to accept and quietly enjoy his decidedly "male" approach. In the nurse's homeland such behavior is not only not unusual, it is the rule. But there it makes sense, as part of the whole culture. Peter's mother, so she admitted, could not quite suppress a feeling that there was something essentially wrong about the boy's sudden maleness and about the way it was permitted to manifest itself; and, indeed, it did not quite fit *her* culture. She became alerted to the problem of having her boy brought up by a foreigner, and she decided to take over herself.

Thus it was during a period of budding, provoked, and disapproved masculinity that the nurse left. Whether she left or was sent away hardly mattered to the child. What mattered was that he lived in a social class which provides paid mother substitutes from a different race or class. Seen from the children's point of view this poses a number of problems. If you like your ersatz mother, your mother will leave you more often and with a better conscience. If you mildly dislike her, your mother will leave you with mild regret. If you dislike her very much and can provoke convincing incidents, your mother will send her away—only to hire somebody like her or worse. And if you happen to like her very much in your own way or in her own way, your mother will surely send her away sooner or later.

In Peter's case, insult was added to injury by a letter from the nurse, who had heard of his condition and who was now trying her best to explain to him why she had left. She had originally told him that she was leaving in order to marry and was going to have a baby of her own. This had been bad enough in view of the boy's feelings for her. Now she informed him that she had taken another job instead. "You see," she explained, "I always move on to another family when the child in my care becomes too big. I like best to tend babies." It was then that something happened to the boy. He had tried to be a big boy. His father had been of little help because he was frequently absent, preoccupied with a business which was too complicated to explain to his son. His mother had indicated that male behavior in the form provoked or condoned by the nurse was unacceptable behavior. The nurse liked babies better.

So he "regressed." He became babyish and dependent, and in desperation, lest he lose more, *he held on*. This he had done before. Long ago, as a baby, he had demonstrated his first stubbornness by holding food in his mouth. Later, put on the toilet and told not to get up until he had finished, he did not finish and he did not get up until his mother gave up. Now he held on to his bowels—and to much more, for he also became tight-lipped, expressionless, and rigid. All of this, of course, was one symptom with a variety of related meanings. The simplest meaning was: I am holding on to what I have got and I am not going to move, either forward or backward. But as we saw from his play, the object of his holding on could be interpreted in a variety of ways. Apparently at first, still believing the nurse to be pregnant, he tried to hold on to her by becoming the nurse and by pretending that he was pregnant too. His general regression, at the same time, demonstrated that he too, was a baby and thus as small as any child the nurse might have turned to. Freud called this the *overdetermination* of the meaning of a symptom. The overdetermining items, however, are always systematically related: the boy identifies with *both partners of a lost relationship*; he is the nurse who is now with child and he is the baby whom she likes to tend. Identifications which result from losses are like that. In mourning, we become the lost person *and* we become again the person we were when the relationship was at its prime. This makes for much seemingly contradictory symptomatology.

Yet, we can see that here *retention* is the mode and the eliminative tract the model zone used to dramatize holding back, holding on, and holding in. But once it looked and felt as if he did indeed have the equivalent of a baby in him, he remembered what his mother had said about birth and about the danger of birth to mother and child. He could not let go.

The interpretation of this fear to him resulted in a dramatic improvement which released the immediate discomfort and danger and brought out the boy's inhibited autonomy and boyish initiative. But only a combination of dietetic and gymnastic work as well as interviews with mother and child could finally overcome a number of milder setbacks.

THE MIDDLE YEARS
Dibs in Search of Self
Virginia Axline

He clasped his hands together tightly against his chest and said over and over again, "no lock doors. No lock doors. No lock doors." His voice took on a note of desperate urgency. "Dibs no like locked doors," he said. There was a sob in his voice.

Editor's Introduction

It is difficult to give an accurate account of the incidence of maladjustment in childhood. A variety of sources have reached an estimate of approximately 10 percent as the proportion of maladjusted school-age children in America. There is a large discrepancy, however, between the number of children who are reported to be maladjusted and the number who are actually receiving help, which is consistently reported to be less than 1 percent of the child population. Frequently it is the child's difficulties in school which bring help, as was the case with Dibs. Difficulty in school is the reason for referral of approximately three-fourths of the children between the ages of 7 and 14 who come to the attention of psychologists and psychiatrists. In America, education is seen as the key to success, and learning difficulties are therefore seen as very serious.

In view of what is known about the importance of the early years of a child's life, it is paradoxical that referrals for psychological difficulties are so scarce before the age of 6. The problems which are recognized in the early years are those which are quite disruptive or quite dramatic or which are relatively serious, such as infantile autism or mental retardation. Those which are more subtle, although perhaps more easily treated and cured, will go unnoticed. Because young children grow and change so rapidly, parents often hope that the problem will disappear in time; they will therefore fail to seek help. With the increase in day care and early education programs, perhaps the more subtle and earlier problems will be detected, diagnosed, and treated and referrals will increase because those young children who need help will be recognized.

When we are first introduced to Dibs, he has been in school for almost two years, almost two years of nearly total silence and withdrawal broken only by violent temper tantrums, for which no one knew the cause. Virginia Axline gives a detailed account of Dibs and his history while also outlining the dynamics of play therapy with young children. She makes the point that human psychological growth is a complex and fragile process which cannot be achieved by the simple repetition of patterns and responses but only through patient understanding and skilled intervention.

Pamela Cantor

It was lunch time, going-home time, and the children were milling around in their usual noisy, dawdling way getting into their coats and hats. But not Dibs. He had backed into a corner of the room and crouched there, head down, arms folded tightly across his chest, ignoring the fact that it was time to go home. The teachers waited. He always behaved this way when it was time to go home. Miss Jane and Hedda gave a helping hand to the other children when it was needed. They watched Dibs surreptitiously.

The other children left the school when their mothers called for them. When the teachers were alone with Dibs they exchanged glances and looked at Dibs huddled against the wall, "Your turn," Miss Jane said and walked quietly out of the room.

"Come on, Dibs. It's time to go home now. It's time for lunch," Hedda spoke patiently. Dibs did not move. His resistance was tense and unwavering. "I'll help you with your coat," Hedda said, approaching him slowly, taking his coat to him. He did not look up. He pressed back against the wall, his head buried in his arm.

"Please, Dibs. Your mother will be here soon." She always came late, probably hoping the battle of hat and coat would be over by the time she arrived and that Dibs would go with her quietly.

Hedda was close to Dibs now. She reached down and patted his shoulder. "Come, Dibs," she said, gently. "You know it's time to go."

Like a small fury Dibs was at her, his small fists striking out at her, scratching, trying to bite, screaming. "No go home! No go home! No go home!" It was the same cry every day.

"I know," Hedda said. "But you have to go home for lunch. You want to be big and strong, don't you?"

Suddenly Dibs went limp. He stopped fighting Hedda. He let her push his arms into his coat sleeves and button his coat.

"You'll come back tomorrow," Hedda said.

When his mother called for him, Dibs went with her, his expression blank, his face tear-stained.

Sometimes the battle lasted longer and was not over when his mother arrived. When that happened, his mother would send the chauffeur in to get Dibs. The man was very tall and strong. He would walk in, scoop Dibs up in his arms, and carry him out to the car without a word to anyone. Sometimes Dibs screamed all the way out to the car and beat his fists against the driver. Other times, he would suddenly become silent—limp and defeated. The man never spoke to Dibs. It seemed not to matter to him whether Dibs fought and screamed or was suddenly passive and quiet.

Dibs had been in this private school for almost two years. The teachers had tried their best to establish a relationship with him, to get a response from him. But it had been touch and go. Dibs seemed determined to keep all people at bay. At least, that's what Hedda thought. He had made some progress in the school. When he started school, he did not talk and he never ventured off his chair. He sat there mute and unmoving all morning. After many weeks he began to leave his chair and to crawl around the room, seeming to look at some of the things about him. When anyone approached him, he would huddle up in a ball on the floor and not move. He never looked directly into anyone's eyes. He never answered when anyone spoke to him.

Dibs' attendance record was perfect. Every day his mother brought him to school in the car. Either she led him in, grim and silent, or the chauffeur carried him in and put him down just inside the door. He never screamed or cried on his way into the school. Left just inside the door, Dibs would stand there, whimpering, waiting until someone came to him and led him into his classroom. When he wore a coat he made no move to take it off. One of the teachers would greet him, take off his coat, and then he was on his own. The other children would soon be busily occupied with some group activity or an individual task. Dibs spent his time crawling around the edge of the room, hiding under tables, or in back of the piano, looking at books by the hour.

There was something about Dibs' behavior that defied the teachers to categorize him, glibly and routinely, and send him on his way. His behavior was so uneven. At one time, he seemed to be extremely retarded mentally. Another time he would quickly and quietly do something that indicated he might even have superior intelligence. If he thought anyone

was watching him, he quickly withdrew into his shell. Most of the time he crawled around the edge of the room, lurking under tables, rocking back and forth, chewing on the side of his hand, sucking his thumb, lying prone and rigid on the floor when any of the teachers or children tried to involve him in some activity. He was a lone child in what must have seemed to him to be a cold, unfriendly world.

He had temper tantrums sometimes when it was time to go home, or when someone tried to force him to do something he did not want to do. The teachers had long ago decided that they would always invite him to join the group, but never try to force him to do anything unless it was absolutely necessary. They offered him books, toys, puzzles, all kinds of materials that might interest him. He would never take anything directly from anyone. If the object was placed on a table or on the floor near him, later he would pick it up and examine it carefully. He never failed to accept a book. He pored over the printed pages "as though he could read," as Hedda so often said.

Sometimes a teacher would sit near him and read a story or talk about something while Dibs lay face down on the floor, never moving away—but never looking up or showing any overt interest. Miss Jane had often spent time with Dibs in this way. She talked about many things as she held the materials in her hand, demonstrating what she was explaining. Once her subject was magnets and the principles of magnetic attraction. Another time it was an interesting rock she held. She talked about anything she hoped might spark an interest. She said she often felt like a fool—as though she were sitting there talking to herself, but something about his prone position gave her the impression that he was listening. Besides, she often asked, what did she have to lose?

The teachers were completely baffled by Dibs. The school psychologist had observed him and tried several times to test him, but Dibs was not ready to be tested. The school pediatrician had looked in on him several times and later threw up his hands in despair. Dibs was wary of the white-coated physician and would not let him come near. He would back up against the wall and put his hands up "ready to scratch," ready to fight if anyone came too close.

"He's a strange one," the pediatrician had said. "Who knows? Mentally retarded? Psychotic? Brain-damaged? Who can get close enough to find out what makes him tick?"

This was not a school for mentally retarded or emotionally disturbed children. It was a very exclusive private school for children aged three to seven, in a beautiful old mansion on the upper East Side. It had a tradition that appealed to parents of very bright, sociable children.

Dibs' mother had prevailed upon the headmistress to accept him. She had used influence through the board of trustees to have him admitted. Dibs' great-aunt contributed generously to the support of the school. Because of these pressures he had been admitted to the nursery school group.

The teachers had suggested several times that Dibs needed professional help. His mother's response had been repetitive: "Give him more time!"

Almost two years had gone by and even though he had made some progress, the teachers felt that it was not enough. They thought it was unfair to Dibs to let the situation drag on and on. They could only hope that he might come out of his shell. When they discussed Dibs—and not a day went by that they did not—they always ended up just as baffled and challenged by the child. After all, he was only five years old. Could he really be aware of everything around him and keep everything locked inside? He seemed to read the books he pored over. This, they told themselves, was ridiculous. How could a child read if he could not express himself verbally? Could such a complex child be mentally retarded? His be-

havior did not seem to be that of a mentally retarded child. Was he living in a world of his own creation? Was he autistic? Was he out of contact with reality? More often it seemed that his world was a bruising reality—a torment of unhappiness.

Dibs' father was a well-known scientist— brilliant, everyone said, but no one at the school had ever met him. Dibs had a younger sister. Her mother claimed that Dorothy was "very bright" and a "perfect child." She did not attend this school. Hedda had met Dorothy once with her mother in Central Park. Dibs was not with them. Hedda told the other teachers that she thought "perfect Dorothy" was "a spoiled brat." Hedda was sympathetically interested in Dibs and admitted she was prejudiced in her evaluation of Dorothy. She had faith in Dibs and believed that someday, somehow, Dibs would come out of his prison of fear and anger.

The staff had finally decided that something must be done about Dibs. Some of the other parents were complaining about his presence in the school—especially after he had scratched or bitten some other child.

It was at this point that I was invited to attend a case conference devoted to Dibs' problems. I am a clinical psychologist, and have specialized in working with children and parents. I first heard about Dibs at this conference, and what I have written here was related by the teachers, the school psychologist, and the pediatrician. Thy asked me if I would see Dibs and his mother and then give the staff my opinion before they decided to dismiss him from school and write him off as one of their failures.

The meeting was held in the school. I listened with interest to all the remarks. I was impressed by the impact of Dib's personality on these people. They felt frustrated and continually challenged by his uneven behavior. He was consistent only in his antagonistic, hostile rejection of all who would come too close to him. His obvious unhappiness troubled these sensitive people who felt its desolate chill.

"I had a conference with his mother last week," Miss Jane said to me. "I told her that in all probability we might have to drop him from school because we feel we have done all we can to help him and our best is not enough. She was very upset. But she is such a difficult person to figure out. She agreed to let us call in a consultant and try one more time to evaluate him. I told her about you. She agreed to have a talk with you about Dibs, and to let you observe him here. Then she said if we couldn't keep him here she would like us to give her the name of a private boarding school for mentally retarded children. She said that she and her husband have accepted the fact that he is probably mentally retarded or brain-damaged."

This remark brought forth an explosion from Hedda. "She'd rather believe he is mentally retarded than admit that maybe he is emotionally disturbed and maybe she is responsible for it!" she exclaimed.

"We don't seem to be able to be very objective about him," Miss Jane said. "I think that's why we have kept him as long as we have and made so much of the little progress he *has* made. We couldn't bear to turn him away and not have some hand in defending him. We've never been able to discuss Dibs without getting involved in emotional reactions of our own about him and the attitudes of his parents. And we're not even sure that our attitudes about his parents are justified."

"I'm convinced he's on the verge of coming through," Hedda said. "I don't think he can bear to keep his defenses up much longer."

There was obviously something about this child that captivated their interests and feelings. I could feel their compassion for this child. I could feel the impact of his personality. I could sense the overwhelming awareness of our limitations to understand in clear, concise, immutable terms the complexities of a personality. I could appreciate the respect for this child that permeated the conference.

It was decided that I would see Dibs for a series of play therapy sessions—if his parents agreed to the idea. We had no way of knowing what this might add to Dibs' story. . . .

I will go to the school tomorrow morning, I decided. I'll telephone Dibs's mother and arrange to have a conference with her at their home as soon as possible. I'll see Dibs next Thursday in the play therapy room at the Child Guidance Center. And where will it all end? If he doesn't manage to break through that wall he has built so sturdily around himself—and it is quite possible that he won't—I'll have to think of some other kind of referral. Sometimes one thing works out very well with one child, but not at all with another child. We don't give up easily. We don't write off a case as "hopeless" without trying just one more thing. Some people think this is very bad—to keep hope alive when there is no basis for hope. But we are not looking for a miracle. We are seeking understanding, believing that understanding will lead us to the threshold of more effective ways of helping the person to develop and utilize his capacities more constructively. The inquiry goes on and on and we will continue to seek a way out of the wilderness of our ignorance.

The next morning I arrived at the school before the children came. The rooms occupied by the kindergarten were bright and cheerful, with appropriate, attractive equipment.

"The children will be here soon," Miss Jane said. "I shall be very interested in your opinion of Dibs. I hope he can be helped. That child worries me to death. You know, when a child is really mentally retarded there's an overall consistent pattern of behavior that shows up in his interests and actions. But Dibs? We never know what kind of mood he'll be in, except that we *do* know there won't be any smiles. None of us has ever seen him smile. Or look even remotely happy. That's one reason we've felt that his problem goes far beyond just mental retardation. He is too emotional. Here come some of the children, now."

The children began to arrive. Most of them came in with looks of happy expectancy on their faces. They certainly seemed relaxed and comfortable in this school. They called out cheery greetings to one another and to the teachers. Some of them spoke to me, asked my name, asked why I was there. They took off their hats and coats and hung them up in their lockers. The first period was a free choice period. The children sought out the toys and activities in which they were interested and played and talked together in a very spontaneous way.

Then Dibs arrived. His mother led him into the room. I had only a quick glimpse of her because she spoke briefly to Miss Jane, said goodbye, and left Dibs. He was wearing a grey tweed coat and a cap. He stood where she left him. Miss Jane spoke to him, asked him if he would like to hang up his coat and hat. He did not answer.

He was large for his age. His face was very pale. When Miss Jane took off his cap I noticed he had black, curly hair. His arms hung limply at his sides. Miss Jane helped him off with his coat. He seemed to be uncooperative. She hung up his hat and coat in his locker.

As she came up to me she said quietly, "Well, there is Dibs. He would never take off his coat and hat by himself, so now we do it routinely. Sometimes we try to get him to join one of the other children in some activity—or give him something specific to do. But he rejects all our offers. This morning we'll just let him alone and you can see for yourself what he will do. He may stand there for a long, long time. Or he may start to move from one thing to another. Sometimes, he flits from one thing to another as though he had no attention

span at all. Then, again, he'll focus on something for an hour. It all depends on how he feels."

Miss Jane went over to some of the other children. I observed Dibs, trying not to seem to be focusing my attention upon him.

He stood there. Then he turned, very slowly and deliberately. He raised his hands in an almost futile gesture of despair, then dropped them down to his sides. He turned again. Now I was in his range of vision—if he cared to look at me. He sighed, bit his lip, stood there.

One little boy ran up to Dibs. "Hi, Dibs!" he said. "Come play!"

Dibs struck out at the boy. He would have scratched him but the little boy jumped back quickly.

"Cat! Cat! Cat!" teased the boy.

Miss Jane came over and told the boy to go to the other part of the room and play.

Dibs moved over to the wall, near a small table on which were some stones, shells, pieces of coal, and other minerals. Dibs stood beside the table. Slowly, he picked up first one object and then another. He ran his fingers around them, touched his cheek with them, smelled them, tasted them. Then he replaced them carefully. He glanced in my direction. It was a fleeting look toward me, then quickly down. He got down, crawled under the table and sat there, almost completely out of sight.

Then I noticed the other children were bringing their chairs up in a small circle around one of the teachers. It was time for the children to show the others what they had brought to school and to tell some bit of news that was important to them. The teacher told them a story. They sang a few songs.

Dibs, under the table, was not too far away. From his vantage point he could hear what they were saying and see what they were showing—if he wanted to. Had he anticipated this activity of the group when he crawled under the table? It was difficult to say. He stayed under the table until the morning circle broke up and the children went to other activities. Then he, too, moved on to something else.

He crawled around the room, staying close to the wall, stopping to examine many things he came upon. When he came to the wide windowsill where the terrarium and aquarium were, he climbed up beside them and gazed steadily into the big, square, glass containers. Occasionally, he would reach in and touch something in the terrarium. Then, his touch seemed deft and light. He stayed there for half an hour, seemingly absorbed in his observation. Then he crawled on, completing his trip around the room. Some things he touched, quickly and carefully, then passed on to something else.

When he came to the book corner, he fingered the books on the table, selected one, took a chair, dragged it across the room to a corner, and sat down on it, facing the wall. He opened the book at the beginning and slowly examined every page, turning the leaves carefully. Was he reading? Was he even looking at the pictures? One of the teachers went over to him.

"Oh, I see," she said. "You're looking at the bird book. Do you want to tell me about it, Dibs?" she inquired in a gentle, kindly voice.

Dibs hurled the book away from him. He threw himself down on the floor and lay stiff and rigid, face down, immobilized.

"I'm sorry," the teacher said. "I didn't mean to bother you, Dibs." She picked up the book, put it back on the table, walked over to me. "Now that was typical," she said. "We've learned not to bother him. But I wanted you to see."

Dibs, in his prone position, had turned his head so that he could watch the teacher. We pretended not to be observing him. Finally, he got up and walked slowly around the edge of the room. He touched the paints, crayons, clay, nails, hammer, wood, drum, cymbals. He picked them up and put them down again. The other children went about their business with-

out too much concern for Dibs. He avoided any physical contact with them, and they let him alone.

Then, it was time to go out and play. One of the teachers told me, "Maybe he will. Maybe he won't. I wouldn't bet a nickel either way." She announced that it was time to go out and play. She asked Dibs if he wanted to go out.

He said, "No go out," in a flat, heavy tone.

I said I thought that I would go out, it was such a nice day. I put on my coat.

Suddenly Dibs said, "Dibs go out!" The teacher put his coat on for him. He walked clumsily out into the play yard. His coordination was very poor. It was as though he was all tied up in knots, physically as well as emotionally.

The other children played in the sandbox, on the swings, on the jungle gym, on the bicycles. They played ball, catch, hide and seek. They ran, skipped, climbed, jumped. But not Dibs. He walked off to a remote corner, picked up a little stick, squatted down and scratched it back and forth in the dirt. Back and forth. Back and forth. Making little grooves in the dirt. Not looking at anyone. Staring down at the stick and the ground. Hunched over this lonely activity. Silent. Withdrawn. Remote.

We decided that when the children came back into the room and after their rest period, I would take Dibs down to the playroom at the end of the hall. If he would go with me.

When the teacher rang the bell the children all came in. Even Dibs. Miss Jane helped him off with his coat. He handed her his cap this time. The teacher put a record of soft, relaxing music on the phonograph. Each child got out his mat, stretched out on the floor for the rest period. Dibs got out his mat and unrolled it. He put his mat under the library table, a distance away from the other children. He lay face down on his mat, put his thumb in his mouth, rested with the other children. What was he thinking about in his lonely little world? What were his feelings? Why did he behave in this manner? What had happened to the child to cause this kind of withdrawal from people? Could we manage to get through to him?

After rest period the children put away their mats. Dibs rolled his mat up and put it away in the correct space on the shelf. The children were dividing into smaller groups. One group would have a work period and build things out of lumber. Another group would paint or play with clay.

Dibs stood by the door. I went over and asked him if he would come down the hall to the little playroom with me for a while. I held out my hand to him. He hesitated for a moment, then took my hand without a word and walked to the playroom with me. As we passed the doors of some of the other rooms he muttered something I could not understand. I did not ask him to repeat what he had said. I remarked that the playroom was at the end of the hall. I was interested in this initial response from him. He had left the room with a stranger without a backward look. But as he held my hand I noticed the hard grip. He was tense. But, surprisingly enough, willing to go.

At the end of the hall, under the back stairs, there was a small room designated as the play therapy room. It was not attractive—there was a cold drabness about its lack of color or decoration. It had a narrow window that let some sunlight filter in, but the total effect was gloomy, even though the lights were turned on. The walls were a dingy, buff color with uneven smears of washed spots here and there. Some of the spots were ringed with stains of the paint that clung to the rough surface of the plaster. The floor was covered with dull brown linoleum that was streaked by a quickly swung, not too clean mop. There was a pungent smell of moist clay, wet sand, and stale watercolor paints.

Toys were on the table, on the floor, and on some shelves around the room. There was a

doll house on the floor. Each room in the doll house was furnished sparingly with sturdy block furniture. A family of small dolls lay on the floor in front of the doll house. They were heaped there—mother, father, boy, girl, and baby dolls, with an open box containing other miniature dolls nearby. There were a few rubber animals—a horse, a lion, a dog, a cat, an elephant, a rabbit. There were some toy cars and airplanes. A box of building blocks was on the floor. In the sandbox were some pans, spoons, a few tin dishes. There was a jar of clay on the table, some paints and drawing paper on the easel. A nursing bottle filled with water was on the shelf. A large rag doll sat on a chair. In the corner stood a tall, inflated rubber figure weighted on the bottom so that it would resume an upright position after being knocked over. The toys were sturdily made, but they looked worn and roughly used.

There was nothing about the room or the materials in it that would tend to restrain the activities of a child. Nothing seemed to be either too fragile or too good to touch or knock about. The room provided space and some materials that might lend themselves to the emergence of the personalities of the children who might spend some time there. The ingredients of experience would make the room uniquely different for each child. Here a child might search the silence for old sounds, shout out his discoveries of a self momentarily captured, and so escape from the prison of his uncertainties, anxieties, and fears. He brings into this room the impact of all the shapes and sounds and colors and movements, and rebuilds his world, reduced to a size he can handle.

As we entered the room I said, "We'll spend an hour together here in the playroom. You can see the toys and the materials we have. You decide what you would like to do."

I sat down on a little chair just inside the door. Dibs stood in the middle of the room, his back toward me, twisting his hands together. I waited. We had an hour to spend in this room. There was no urgency to get anything done. To play or not to play. To talk, or to be silent. In here, it would make no difference. The room was very small. No matter where he went in here, he couldn't get too far away. There was a table under which he could crawl, if he felt like hiding. There was a little chair beside the table if he felt like sitting down. There were the toys to play with, if he so desired.

But Dibs just stood in the middle of the room. He sighed. Then he slowly turned and walked haltingly across the room, then around the walls. He went from one toy to another, tentatively touching them. He did not look directly at me. Occasionally he would glance in my direction but would quickly avert his eyes if our glances met. It was a tedious trip around the room. His step was heavy. There seemed to be no laughter or happiness in this child. Life, for him, was a grim business.

He walked over to the doll house, ran his hand along the roof, knelt down beside it, and peered inside at the furniture. Slowly, one by one, he picked up each piece of furniture. As he did, he muttered the name of the objects with a questioning, halting inflection. His voice was flat and low.

"Bed? Chair? Table?" he said. "Crib? Dresser? Radio? Bathtub? Toilet?" Every item in the doll house he picked up, named, carefully replaced. He turned to the pile of dolls, and sorted slowly through them. He selected a man, a woman, a boy, a girl, a baby. It was as though he tentatively identified them as he said, "Mamma? Papa? Sister? Baby?" Then he sorted out the little animals. "Dog? Cat? Rabbit?" He sighed deeply and repeatedly. It seemed to be a very difficult and painful task he had set himself.

Each time he named an object I made an attempt to communicate my recognition of his spoken word. I would say, "Yes. That is a bed," or, "I think it is a dresser," or "It does look like a rabbit." I tried to keep my response brief, in line with what he said, and with enough variation to avoid monotony. When he picked up the father doll and said "Papa?" I replied, "It could be papa." And that is the way our conversation went with every item that he picked up and named. I thought that this was his way to begin verbal communication. Naming the objects seemed a safe enough beginning.

Then he sat down on the floor facing the doll house. He stared at it in silence for a long time. I didn't prod him on. If he wanted to sit there in silence, then we would have silence. There must have been some reason for what he was doing. I wanted him to take the initiative in building up this relationship. Too often, this is done for a child by some eager adult.

He clasped his hands tightly together against his chest and said over and over again, "No lock doors. No lock doors. No lock doors." His voice took on a note of desperate urgency. "Dibs no like locked doors," he said. There was a sob in his voice.

I said to him, "You don't like the doors to be locked."

Dibs seemed to crumple. His voice became a husky whisper. "Dibs no like closed doors. No like closed and locked doors. Dibs no like walls around him."

Obviously, he had had some unhappy experiences with closed and locked doors. I recognized the feelings he expressed. Then he began to take the dolls out of the house where he had placed them. He took out the mother and father dolls. "Go store! Go store!" he said. "Go away to the store. Go away!"

"Oh, is mother going to go away to the store?" I commented. "And papa, too? And sister?" He quickly moved them out and away from the house.

Then he discovered that the walls of the rooms in the doll house could be removed. He took each wall out, saying as he did, "No like walls, Dibs no like walls. Take away all walls, Dibs!" And in this playroom Dibs took away a little of the walls he had built around himself.

In this manner he slowly, almost painfully played. When the hour was up I told him that the play time here was almost over and we would go back to his classroom.

"There are five more minutes," I said. "Then we will have to go."

He sat on the floor in front of the doll house. He neither moved nor spoke. Neither did I. When the five minutes were up, we would go back to his room.

I didn't ask him if he wanted to go. There was no real choice for him to make. I didn't ask him if he would like to come back again. He might not want to commit himself. Besides, that decision was not up to him to make. I didn't say that I would see him next week, because I had not yet completed the plans with his mother. This child had been hurt enough without my introducing promises that might not materialize. I didn't ask him if he had had a good time. Why should he be pinned down to an evaluation of the experience he had just had? If a child's play is his natural way of expressing himself, why should we cast it in a rigid mold of a stereotyped response? A child is only confused by questions that have been answered by someone else before he is asked.

When the five minutes had passed, I rose and said, "It is time to go now, Dibs." He slowly stood up, took my hand, and we left the room and started down the hall. When we were halfway down the hall and the door of his classroom was in view, I asked him if he thought he could go the rest of the way to his room alone.

"That's right," he said. He dropped his hand and walked down the hall to the door of his room by himself.

I did this because I hoped Dibs would gradually become more and more self-sufficient and responsible. I wanted to communicate to him my confidence in his ability to measure up to my expectations. I believed he could do it. If he had faltered, shown signs of it being too much for him to do this first day, I would have gone a little farther down the hall with him. I would have gone all the way to the door of his room with him, if he had seemed to need that much support. But he went by himself. I said, "Goodbye, Dibs!"

He said, "That's right!" His voice had a soft, gentle quality. He walked down the hall, opened the door of his room, then looked back. I waved. The expression on his face was interesting. He looked surprised—almost pleased. He walked into his room and closed the door firmly behind him. It was the first time Dibs had ever gone any place alone.

One of my objectives in building up this relationship with Dibs was to help him achieve emotional independence. I did not want to complicate his problem by building up a supportive relationship, to make him so dependent upon me that it would postpone the more complete development of his feelings of inner security. If Dibs was an emotionally deprived child—and indications were that he was—to attempt to develop an emotional attachment at this point might seem to be satisfying a deep need of the child, but it would create a problem that must of necessity ultimately be resolved by him.

As I left that first play session with Dibs I could understand why the teachers and the other staff members could not write him off the books as a hopeless failure. I had respect for his inner strength and capacity. He was a child of great courage.

ADOLESCENCE AND YOUTH

I Never Promised You a Rose Garden

Hannah Green

It was at camp that Yr had first come to her, but she did not tell the doctor of it, or of the Gods or the Collect with their great realms. From her absorption in the telling of events she looked out again and saw the doctor's expressive face indignant for her. She wanted to thank this earth person who was capable of being moved to anger. "I did not know that they endowed Earth-ones with insides," she said musingly, and then she was very tired.

Editor's Introduction

Schizophrenic reactions are probably the most fascinating of all psychopathology, Over 20,000 articles and books have been written on the topic. The subject of the etiology of schizophrenia—genetic, biochemical, psychological, or environmental—is one of the most lively controversies in the field of mental health. As the etiology of schizophrenia is not known, so the treatment must remain eclectic, with advocates of organic approaches (psychopharmaceuticals, electroconvulsive therapy, and lobotomy), psychological remedies (psychotherapy of various types), and environmental treatments each having their proponents. Even reports of cure vary with the clinician. Ulett and Goodrich (1969) report, "No truly satisfactory remedy exists to repair the devastating personality damage encountered in many of these individuals" (p. 143), while Cameron (1963) states, "If it has not gone too far, or lasted too long, the schizophrenic reaction can usually be much ameliorated through expert psychotherapy. Sometimes it can be recognized early and headed off. It can often be cured" (p. 578).

Thus, the origin of schizophrenia, the treatment method, and the prognosis are all in question. There appears to be less confusion, however, regarding the symptoms of schizophrenia. Speech patterns are likely to reflect a disorder in cognitive processes. Schizophrenic adolescents show disassociation or discontinuities in their thinking, blocking, condensation of two ideas into one, and paralogical thinking in which ideas are linked by grammatical form or similarity rather than by logic. There may be stereotypy or echolalia. In the area of affective relations, there may be marked difference or an oversensitivity to emotion, but without any depth of feeling. Affective expressions may be inconsistent with thoughts or actions and may be extremely labile. There is difficulty in establishing or maintaining relationships with peers. But it is the accessory symptoms which give the disease its hallmark. Hallucinations (which are most frequently auditory) and delusions (which are usually persecutory) are often present.

If therapy is the treatment involved, the therapist must overcome the adolescent schizophrenic's resistance to an intimate and trusting relationship by relying on an understanding of the patient's speech and behavior. Opinions vary as to the proper technique for dealing with the material of schizophrenic thought. Followers of

Rosen advocate active participation in the patient's delusional system, with the therapist using the symbolic or metaphorical language of schizophrenics in discussions. Frieda Fromm-Reichmann advocated a more conservative, cautious approach in which the therapist helps to understand the fluctuating meaning of the patient's behavior while maintaining a basis for the patient to test reality. Thus the patient may, for example, be able to deal with fears of abandonment by testing the therapist's constancy or to examine his or her fears by observing the therapist's reaction to them. A third approach is to view the patient's fantasies or delusions as evidence of pathology, which is to be eliminated as soon as possible. In this manner the therapist empathizes with the patient's feelings but continually encourages the patient to deal directly with the world.

I Never Promised You a Rose Garden is a fictionalized account of Frieda Fromm-Reichmann's treatment of a schizophrenic adolescent. Dr. Fried is the thinly disguised name for Dr. Frieda Fromm-Reichmann. Hannah Green is the pseudonym of the author. A pseudonym was used because the book is said to have been written by the once schizophrenic patient. The selection begins with a discussion between the patient's mother and Dr. Fried. Deborah's mother talks about how much Deborah was loved and how she wanted to protect her from every evil in the world. She talks about Deborah's solitary and withdrawn behavior and the many clues to her illness which she and her husband chose to or needed to ignore. She talks about Deborah's sense of rejection by peers and the rejection which the entire family experienced from their neighbors and community. She discusses Deborah's tumor, her surgery and the intense pain she suffered, and the lies the doctors told the 5-year-old child. She discusses the suicide attempt which immediately precipitated Deborah's hospital admission and treatment. Then we hear about the actual treatment; the bizarre schizophrenic language and thought patterns; the inadequate control of affect, ideation, and behavior; the limited capacity for relating to others and to reality. We learn of the hospital atmosphere and the skills and empathy of the therapist. From this personalized account, which is far more powerful and far more meaningful than an academic treatise on the illness could ever hope to be, we learn some of the secrets of schizophrenia, a disease which appears in approximately one person in a hundred, primarily in adolescence and young adulthood.

REFERENCES

Cameron, M. *Personality development and psychopathology: A dynamic approach*, Boston: Houghton Mifflin, 1963.

Ulett, G. A., & Goodrich, D. W. *A synopsis of contemporary psychiatry.* St. Louis: Mosby, 1969.

Pamela Cantor

Dr. Fried saw Esther Blau in the doctor's bright, cluttered office. It was important to Dr. Fried to know whether Deborah's mother would be an ally in this treatment or an adversary. Many parents said—even thought— that they wanted help for their children, only to show, subtly or directly, that their children were part of a secret scheme for their own ruin. A child's independence is too big a risk for the shaky balance of some parents. On Esther's impeccable surface Dr. Fried saw intelligence, sophistication, and straightforwardness. There was also an intensity that made her smile a little hard. How those two blunt wills must have struggled over the years!

They sat down in the comfortable chairs, the doctor breathing a little heavily and feeling somewhat dowdy as she faced Esther's formidable jewelry. She examined her again. The woman was sane: she accepted the heavy penalties of reality and enjoyed its gifts also. Her daughter did not. Where was the difference to be found?

The mother was looking about the room, "Is this—is this where Deborah comes?"

"Yes."

Relief showed on the carefully composed surface. "It's pleasant. No—bars." She got the word out, straining so hard for relaxed matter-of-factness that the doctor almost winced.

"Right now it hardly matters. I don't know if she trusts me enough to see the room as it really is."

"Can she get well? I love her so very much!"

If it is so, Dr. Fried thought, the love will meet a strong test in what they are all about to undergo. She said, "If she is going to get well, we are all going to have to be patient and to work like anything." The colloquialism sounded strange in her accent. "She will need a tremendous amount of energy to give to this, to fight her own impulses for safety . . . and so you may find her tired and not keeping herself groomed as she should. Is there something that worries you particularly about her now?"

Esther tried to frame her thoughts. It was too soon to think about Deborah's progress really; the worry was something else. "You see—all these days . . . all these days we've been thinking and thinking how and why this could have happened. She was so much loved! They tell me that these illnesses are caused by a person's past and childhood. So all these

days we've been thinking about the past. I've looked, and Jacob has looked, and the whole family has thought and wondered, and after all of it we just can't see any reason for it. It's without a cause, you see, and that's what is so frightening."

She had spoken louder than she wished, trying to convince the chairs and the tables and the doctor and the whole institution with its bars and screaming people whose reasons for being there must be different . . . must be.

"Causes are too big to see all at once, or even as they really are, but we can tell our own truths and have our own causes. Tell me what you know about Deborah and yourself in *your* own way and as you knew it."

"I suppose I should start with my own father."

Pop had come from Latvia. He had a clubfoot. Somehow these two things represented him more fully than his name or occupation. He had come to America a young man, poor and foreign and lame, and he had borne down on his new life as if it were an enemy. In anger he had educated himself; in anger he had gone into business, failed, succeeded, and made a fortune. With his fortune and his anger he had bought a great home in an old neighborhood of the inbred and anciently rich. His neighbors had every manner he admired, and in turn they despised his religion, his accent, and his style. They made the lives of his wife and children miserable, but he cursed them all, the neighbors and wife and children, in the crude, blunt words of his abhorrent past. The true conquest, he saw, would not be for him, but for his seed, educated and accentless and gently conditioned. The Latvian and Yiddish curses that they had learned at his knee he tried to temper with tutoring in genteel French.

"In 1878," Esther said, "the daughters of noblemen took harp lessons. I know because I had to take harp lessons, even though playing the instrument had gone out of fashion, even though I hated it and had no talent for it. It was one of the flags to capture, you see, and he had to try to win it, even through me. Sometimes when I played, Pop would pace the floor and mutter to his nobleman, "Look, damn you—it's me, the little cripple!"

Pop's "American" children had grown up knowing that all their worth and gentility and culture and success was only a surface. For a glimpse of their true value they had only to look into their neighbors' eyes or to hear Pop's remarks if the soup was cold or the suitor came late. As for the suitors, they were to be flags also; the proud banners of great families; the emblems of conquests in alliance, as it has been among the great in the old country. But willful Esther had chosen beneath her family's hopes. The boy was smart enough, well-spoken, and presentable; still he had put himself through accountancy school and his family was "a bunch of poor greenhorns," beneath Esther, beneath the dream in every way. They had argued and fought and at last, on the strength of Jacob's prospects for the future, Pop had given in. Natalie had married well enough for the family to afford a gamble. Soon both of the young wives were pregnant. Pop began to think of himself as the founder of a dynasty.

And Esther's daughter was blonde! a singular, thrilling, impossible fair-skinned blonde. She was Esther's redemption from secret isolation, and for Pop she was the final retort to a long-dead village nobleman and his fair-skinned daughters. This one would go in gold.

Esther recalled then the time of the depression and the cast of fear that had surrounded everything. It was fear and—Esther groped for the word that would evoke those years—unreality. Jacob had entered his working life at the very nadir of opportunity. The accounts that he had sworn to take in order to deserve Esther as a wife—the boring and routine, the scraps that others threw away—were simply not there. For every column of figures there were a hundred minds waiting, as hungry and

well-educated as his. Yet they lived in one of the best new sections of town. The daughters of the dynasty had to live well and Pop paid all their bills. When Deborah was born it was into the handmade lace—the heirloom of some great European house felled by the revolution. Capturing an old flag was better than weaving a new one, and the princely carriage caps that Deborah wore for her outings had once been fitted to the head of a prince. Though the peasant's mud-village past was already a generation removed, there was still in that peasant a peasant's dream: not simply to be free, but to be free to be titled. The New World was required to do more than obliterate the bitterness of the Old. Like the atheist saying to God, "You don't exist and I hate You!" Pop kept sounding his loud shots of denial into the deaf ear of the past. When Jacob was earning fifteen and then twenty dollars a week, Deborah had twelve hand-embroidered silk dresses and a German nurse.

Jacob could not pay for her food. After a while they moved back into the family home, surrounded by a new generation of neighborhood scorn. Even as a prisoner of her own past, Esther saw that Jacob was unhappy, that he was taking charity from a man who despised him, but her own fear made her subtly and consistently side with her father against her husband. It seemed then as if having Deborah had made her allegiance right. Jacob was consort of the dynasty, but Deborah—golden, gift-showered Deborah—always smiling and contented, was a central pin on which the dream could turn.

And then they found that their golden toy was flawed. In the perfumed and carefully tended little girl a tumor was growing. The first symptom was an embarrassing incontinence, and how righteously wrathful the rigid governess was! But the "laziness" could not be cured by shaming or whipping or threats.

"We didn't know!" Esther burst out, and the doctor looked at her and saw how passionate and intense she was under the careful, smooth façade. "In those days the schedules and the governesses and the rules were god! It was the 'scientific' approach then, with everything sterile and such a horror of germs and variation."

"And the nursery like a hospital! I remember," said the doctor laughing, and trying to comfort Esther with her laughter because it was too late for anything but remorse for the mistaken slaps and the overzealous reading of misguided experts.

At last there were examinations and a diagnosis and trips from doctor to doctor in search of proof. Deborah would have nothing but the best of course. The specialist who finally did the operation was the top man in the Midwest, and far too busy to explain anything to the little girl or stay with her after the miracles of modern surgery were over and the ancient and barbaric pain took their place. Two operations, and after the first, a merciless pain.

Esther had forced herself to stay cheerful and strong, to go to Debby's room always with a smile. She was pregnant again and worried because of the earlier stillbirth of twin sons, but to the hospital staff, the family, and Deborah, her surface never varied, and she took pride in the strength she showed. At last they learned that the operations had been successful. They were jubilant and grateful, and at Deborah's homecoming the whole house was festive and decorated, and all the relatives were present for a party. Two days later Jacob got the Sulzburger account. Esther found old names coming to mind from nowhere.

At the time the Sulzburger account had seemed to be the most important thing in their lives. It was a series of very lucrative smaller accounts and they had gone a little crazy with it. At last Jacob could be free, more than a consort in his own house. He bought a new one in a quiet and modest neighborhood not too far from the city. It was small, with a little garden and trees and lots of children close by

with lots of different last names. Deborah was cautious at first, but before long she began to open, to go out and make friends. Esther had friends, too, and flowers that she could take care of herself, and sunlight, and open windows, and no need for servants, and the beginnings of her own decisions. One year— one beautiful year. Then one evening Jacob came home and told her that the Sulzburger account was a vast chain of fraud. He had been three full months discovering how and where the money was going. He said to Esther on the evening before he went to resign it, "A fraud that's as diverse and clever as this one is has a kind of beauty in it. It's going to cost us—everything. You know that, don't you? . . . But I can't help admiring that mind. . . ."

They had to give up the house and a month later they were back in the family home once again. There was very little money, but Esther's parents decided to give the house to them; there was too much room without the whole family and the parents had rented an apartment in Chicago. But the big house *had* to stay in the family, of course. And so the hated place became the Blau house.

Deborah went to the best schools in the winter and the best camps in the summer. Friendships came hard to her, but they do to many people, Esther thought. The family had not known until years later that the first summer camp (three silent years of it), was cruelly anti-Semitic. Deborah had never told them. What Esther and Jacob saw were the laughing teams of girls at play and singing over toasted marshmallows the old camp songs about Marching on to Victory.

"Was there nothing to show you that she was ill or suffering—just reticence?" Dr. Fried asked.

"Well, yes. . . . I mentioned school—it was small and friendly and they all thought well of her. She was always very bright, but one day the psychologist called us and showed us a test that all the children had been given.

Deborah's answers seemed to show him that she was 'disturbed.'"

"How old was she then?"

"Ten," Esther said slowly. "I looked at my miracle trying to see her mind, if it were true. I saw that she didn't play with other children. She was always home, hiding herself away. She ate a lot and got fat. It had all been so gradual that I had never really seen it until then. And—and she never slept."

"A person must sleep. You mean she slept little?"

"I knew that she must sleep, but I never *saw* her asleep. Whenever we came into her room at night, she would be wide awake, saying that she heard us coming up the stairs. The steps were heavily carpeted. We used to joke about our light sleeper, but it was no joke. The school recommended that we take her to a child psychiatrist, and we did, but she only seemed to get more and more disturbed and angry, and after the third session she said, 'Am I not what you wanted? Do you have to correct my brain, too?' She had that way of speaking even at ten, a kind of bitterness that was too old for her. We stopped the visits because we never wanted her to feel that way. Somehow, even without realizing it, we got into the habit of listening, even in our sleep, for——"

"For what?"

"I don't know . . ." And she shook her head to ward off a forbidden word.

When the Second World War began it was no longer possible to maintain a fifteen-room house. Esther struggled on while they tried to get rid of it, feeling overwhelmed by its huge, musty rooms and the awful compulsion to "keep things up" in the critical eyes of Mom and Pop and the rest of the family. At last they found a buyer, dropped the weight of the past gratefully, and moved into an apartment in the city. It seemed a good thing, especially for Deborah; her little oddities, her fears, and her loneliness would seem less strange in the anonymity of a large city. She was still not really happy, but her teachers thought highly of her in the new school and the studies went well without any great effort on her part. She took music lessons and did all the ordinary things that young girls do.

Esther tried to think of something that would make Deborah's present condition believable. Well . . . she was intense. Esther remembered speaking to her about it now and then, telling her not to take things so very very seriously, but it was part of both of them, and not something to be stopped just by a decision or request. In the city Deborah discovered art. The opening of her interest was like a torrent; she spent every spare moment drawing and sketching. In those first years, when she was eleven and twelve, she must have done thousands of pictures, not to mention the little sketches and bits of drawing on scrap paper at school.

They had taken some of the drawings to art teachers and critics and were told that the girl was, indeed, talented and should be encouraged. It was a bright and easy answer to Esther's gray, vague suspicions, and she tried to pull it up over her eyes. To the whole family it suddenly seemed to explain all the sickness and sensitivity, the sleeplessness, the intensity, and the sudden looks of misery, covered quickly by a blank hardness of the face or the bitter wit's backthrust. Of course . . . she was special, a rare and gifted spirit. Allowances were made for her complaints of illness, for her vagueness. It was adolescence; the adolescence of an exceptional girl. Esther kept saying it and saying it, but she never could quite believe it. There was always this or that nagging sign that seemed to taunt her perceptions. One evening Deborah had gone to the doctor for another one of her mysterious pains. She had come home strangely blank and fearful. The next day Deborah had left early on some errand and not come home until late. At about four in the morning, Esther had awakened for some unknown and instinctive reason and she had gone to Deborah's room with a certainty that now, in the telling, brought her a strange feeling of guilt. The room was empty. When she looked in the bathroom, she had found Deborah sitting quietly on the floor, watching the blood from her wrist flow into a basin.

"I asked her why she didn't just let it go into the sink," the doctor said, "and she answered interestingly, I thought. She said that she had not wanted to let it get too far away. You see, she knew, in her own way, that she was not attempting suicide, but making the call for help, the call of a mute and confused person. You live in an apartment house; you have from your windows a death much quicker and surer at every hand and yet this—and she knew you to be light sleepers because she was."

"But did she decide to do this? Could she have planned it?"

"Not consciously, of course, but her mind chose the best way. She is, after all, here. Her call for help was successful. Let us go back a way now, to the camps and the school. Was there always trouble between Deborah and the campers and schoolmates? Did she work her own troubles out or did she call on you for help?"

"I tried to help, certainly. I remember quite a few times when she needed me and I was there. There was the time when she had just started school and was having trouble with a little clique there. I took them all out for a big day at the zoo and that broke the ice. In the summer camp sometimes people didn't understand her. I was always friendly with the counselors and that would ease the way a little. She had great trouble with one of the teachers at the public school in the city. I had the teacher in to tea and just talking a bit, explaining Deborah's fears of people and how sometimes they were misinterpreted, I helped her to understand Deborah. They were friends through the rest of school, and at the end the teacher told me that having known Deborah had been a real privilege, that she was such a fine girl."

"How did Deborah take this help?"

"Well, she was relieved, of course. These troubles loom so large at that age and I was glad to be a real mother to her, helping in things like that. My own mother never could."

"Looking back at those times—what was the feeling of them? How did you feel during them?"

"Happy, as I said. The people Deborah had trouble with were relieved and I was happy to be helping her. I worked hard to overcome my own shyness, to make it fun always to be where I was. We sang and told jokes. I had to learn how to bring people out of themselves. I was proud of her and often told her so. I told her often how much I loved her. She never felt unprotected or alone."

"I see," the doctor said.

It seemed to Esther that the doctor did not see. Somehow the wrong picture was there before them, and Esther said, "I fought for Deborah all her life. Maybe it was the tumor that started it all. It was not us—not the love that Jacob and I had for each other or for our children. It was in spite of all our love and care, this awful thing."

"You knew for a long time, didn't you, that things were not right with your daughter? It was not only the psychologist at the school. When did it seem to you that the trouble started?"

"Well, there was the summer at camp—no—it was before that. How does one sense just when the atmosphere changes? Suddenly it just seems to be, that's all."

"What about the camp?"

"Oh, it was the third year she had been going. She was alone then. We had come up to see her toward the end of the season and she seemed unhappy. I told her how I had gotten over bad spots of growing up by going in for sports. It's a good way to get recognition and friends when you are young. When we left, she seemed all right, but somehow, after that year . . . something . . . went out of her. . . . It was as if she had her head down from then on, waiting for the blows."

"Waiting for the blows . . ." the doctor said musingly. "And then there came a time, later—a time when she began to arrange for blows to fall."

Esther turned toward the doctor, her eyes full of recognition. "Is that what the sickness is?"

"Maybe it is a symptom. I once had a patient who used to practice the most horrible tortures on himself, and when I asked him why he did such things, he said, 'Why, before the world does them.' I asked him then, 'Why not wait and see what the world will do,' and he said, 'Don't you see? It always comes at last, but this way at least I am master of my own destruction.'"

"That patient . . . did he get well?"

"Yes, he got well. Then the Nazis came and they put him into Dachau and he died there. I tell you this because I am trying to tell you, Mrs. Blau, that you can never make the world over to protect the ones you love so much. But you do not have to defend your having tried."

"I had to try to make things better," Esther said, and then she sat back, thinking. "Somehow, as I see it now, there were mistakes— great mistakes—but they are more toward Jacob than Deborah." She paused, looking at the doctor incredulously. "How could I have done such things to him? All these long years . . . since that overpriced apartment, the years of Pop's charity, the years and years I let him come second, even today—if 'Pop thinks so,' or 'Pop wants it.' Why—when he was my husband and his wishes were so simple and modest?" She looked again. "It's not enough, then, just to love. My love for Jacob didn't stop me from hurting him and lowering him in his own eyes as well as my father's. And our love for Deborah didn't stop us from . . . well, from causing . . . this . . . sickness."

Dr. Fried looked at Esther and listened to the words of love and pain coming from the carefully composed mother of a girl sick to death with deception. The love was real enough and the pain also, so that she said very gently, "Let us, Deborah and I, study for the causes. Do not agonize and blame yourself or your husband or anyone else. She will need your support, not your self-recrimination."

Brought back to the present, Esther realized that she would now have to face Deborah of the present. "How—how can I know the right thing to say while I am talking to her? You know, don't you, that she won't let Jacob see her, and she had such a strange, sleepwalker's look when I last saw her?"

"There is only one thing that is really dangerous, especially now because she is so sensitive to it."

"And what is that, Doctor?"

"Why, lying, of course."

They rose because the time was over. Too short, Esther thought, to say a fraction of what needed to be said. Dr. Fried saw her to the door with a last small gesture of comfort. She was thinking that the patient's versions would be radically different from the ones her mother ascribed to both of them. The helpful parent, the grateful child. But if it were not so, the child would not be a patient. The quality of and the difference between these versions of reality would help to give depth to each of their interpretations of it.

Leaving the doctor's office, it seemed to Esther that she had not put her case correctly. Perhaps her attempt to help had been, after all, interference. The hospital had given her permission to take Deborah out by herself. The two of them would go to a movie and dinner in town, and they would talk. "I swear to you," Esther said to the Deborah in her mind, "I swear to you that I will not use you. I will not ask you what we did or didn't do."

She went to the small hotel room to tell Jacob that Deborah still refused to see him. The doctor had said that they must not force her, that perhaps what she had done was not so much a slighting of Jacob as an attempt, poor and misdirected, to make her own decisions. Esther had thought that this was only placating, but she had said nothing. Poor Jacob—and I am in the middle again—the deliverer of the blow.

And after a while Jacob stopped insisting, but Esther saw him in the back of the theater, watching Deborah instead of the film. And as they came out she saw him standing in the shadows alone, watching her, and on the corner as they went into the restaurant, he was standing in the cold path of early winter.

"Tell me about your life before this hospital," the doctor said.

"My mother told you all about it," Deborah answered bitterly from the high, cold regions of her kingdom.

"Your mother told me what she gave, not what you took; what she saw, not what you saw. She told me what she knew of that tumor of yours."

"She doesn't know much about it," Deborah said.

"Then tell me what you know."

She had been five, old enough to be ashamed when the doctors shook their heads about the wrongness inside her, in the feminine, secret part. They had gone in with their probes and needles as if the entire reality of her body were concentrated in the secret evil inside that forbidden place. On the evening that her father made the plans for her to appear at the hospital the next day, she had felt the hard anger of the willful when they are dealt with and moved about like objects. That night she had had a dream—a nightmare—about being broken into like a looted room, torn apart, scrubbed clean with scouring powder, and reassembled, dead but now acceptable. After it had come another about a broken flowerpot whose blossom seemed to be her own ruined strength. After the dreams she had

lapsed into a mute, stunned silence. But the nightmares had not taken into account the awful pain.

"Now just be quiet. This won't hurt a bit," they had said, and then had come the searing stroke of the instrument. "See, we are going to put your doll to sleep," and the mask had moved down, forcing the sick-sweet chemical of sleep.

"What is this place?" she had asked.

"Dreamland," had come the answer, and then the hardest, longest burning of that secret place she could imagine.

She had asked one of them once, an intern who had seemed to be discomfited at her suffering, "Why do you all tell such terrible lies?" He had said, "Oh, so you will not be frightened." On another afternoon, tied to that table yet again, they had said, "We are going to fix you fine now." In the language of the game-playing liars she had understood that they were going to murder her. Again the transparent lie about the doll.

What terrible scorn they had had to give that lie so often! Was it to have been worse than murder? What could they have had in their demented minds, those killers with their false "fine"? And afterward, through the brutal ache: "How is your doll?"

As she told it, she looked at Dr. Fried, wondering if the dead past could ever wake anything but boredom in the uncaring world, but the doctor's face was heavy with anger and her voice full of indignation for the five-year-old who stood before them both. "Those damn fools! When will they learn not to lie to children! Pah!" And she began to jab out her cigarette with hard impatience.

"Then you're not going to be indifferent . . ." Deborah said, walking very gingerly on the new ground.

"You're damn right I'm not!" the doctor answered.

"Then I will tell you what no one knows," Deborah said. "They never said they were sorry; not one of them. Not for going in so callously, not that they made me take all that pain and be ashamed of feeling it, not that they lied so long and so stupidly that their lies were like a laughing at me. They never asked my pardon for these things and I never gave it to them."

"How so?"

"I never lost that tumor. It's still there, still eating on the inside of me. Only it is invisible."

"That punishes you, not them."

"*Upuru* punishes us both."

"*Upu*—what?"

Yr had opened suddenly, in horror that one of its guarded secrets had slipped into the earthworld, the sunny office with the booby-trap furniture. The language of Yr was a deep secret, kept always more rigidly away from people as it crept toward great control of the inner voice. *Upuru* was Yr's word for the whole memory and emotion of that last hospital day—that day after which all things had seemed to gray to dimness.

"What did you say?" the doctor was asking, but Deborah had fled, terrified into Yr, so that it closed over her head like water and left no mark of where she had entered. The surface was smooth and she was gone.

Looking at her, drawn away from words or reasons or comforts, Dr. Fried thought: The sick are all so afraid of their own uncontrollable power! Somehow they cannot believe that they are only people, holding only a human-sized anger!

A few days later, Deborah returned to the Midworld looking out on Earth. She was sitting with Carla and some others on the corridor of the ward.

"Do you have town privileges?" Carla asked her.

"No, but they let me go out when my mother was here."

"Was it a good visit?"

"I guess so. She couldn't help trying to get me to figure out what made me sick. We were no sooner sitting down when it came out in a big rush. I knew she had to ask it, but I couldn't tell her—even if I knew."

"Sometimes I hate the people who made me sick," Carla said. "They say that you stop hating them after you've had enough therapy, but I wouldn't know about that. Besides, my enemy is beyond hating or forgiving."

"Who is it?" Deborah asked, wondering if it could only have been one.

"My mother," Carla answered matter-of-factly. "She shot me and my brother and herself. They died; I lived. My father married again, and I went crazy."

They were hard words, and stark, with no euphemisms such as one always heard outside. Starkness and crudity were two important privileges of the hospital, and everyone used them to the fullest. To those who had never dared to think of themselves, except in secret, as eccentric and strange, freedom was freedom to be crazy, bats, nuts, loony, and, more seriously, mad, insane, demented, out of one's mind. And there was a hierarchy of privilege to enjoy these freedoms. The screaming, staring ones on Ward D were called "sick" by others and "crazy" by themselves. Only they were allowed to refer to themselves by the ultimate words, like "insane" and "mad," without contradiction. The quieter wards, A and B, were lower on the upside-down scale of things and were permitted only lighter forms: nuts, cuckoo, and cracked. It was the patients' own unspoken rule, and one learned without benefit of being told. B-ward patients who called themselves crazy were putting on airs. Knowing this, Deborah now understood the scorn of the rigid, dull-eyed Kathryn when a nurse had said, "Come on now, you are getting upset," and the woman had laughed. "I'm not upset; I'm cuckoo!"

Deborah had been two months in the hospital. Other patients had come and some had gone up to "D" among the "insane," and some to other hospitals.

"We're getting to be veterans," Carla said, "old hands at the funny-farm." And perhaps it was true. Except for "D," Deborah was no longer frightened of the place. She did what she was told and apart from that wielder of horrors, Dr. Fried, in her innocent-looking white house, there was no mark of excessive caution put on anything by the Censor.

"How long is the time until we know if we're going to make it or not?" Deborah asked.

"You kids are just in the honeymoon phase," said a girl sitting near them. "That takes about three months. I know, too. I've been in six hospitals. I've been analyzed, paralyzed, shocked, jolted, revolted, given metrazol, amatyl, and whatever else they make. All I need now is a brain operation and I'll have had the whole works. Nothing does any good, not this crap or anything else." She got up in the very doomed, dramatic way she had and left them, and Lactamaeon, second in command of Yr, whispered, *If one is to be doomed, one must be beautiful, or the drama is only a comedy. And therefore, Unbeautiful . . . .*

Kill me, my lord, in the form of an eagle, Deborah said to him in the language of Yr. "How long has she been here?" she asked Carla in the language of Earth.

"More than a year, I think," Carla said.

"Is this . . . forever?"

"I don't know," Carla answered.

The winter hung around them. It was December, and outside the windows the tree limbs were black and stark. A group in the dayroom was decorating a tree for Christmas. Five staff and two patients—God, they tried so hard to make the madhouse look like home. It was all lies; their laughter hung very false among the ornaments (no sharp edges and no glass), and Deborah thought that at least they had the decency to be embarrassed. At the doctor's house the dragging forth of her history, the retreats, camouflaging, and hiding went on. Except for her contact with Carla and Marion on the ward, she was drawing away from the world even the under-voice that answered questions and stood in place of herself when she wished to be in Yr. "I can't describe the feeling," she said, thinking of the Yri metaphors which she had used to tell herself and the Yri ones what she wished. In recent years thoughts often came, and happenings also, for which there seemed no sharer on the hard earth, and so the plains, pits, and peaks of Yr began to echo a growing vocabulary to frame its strange agonies and grandeurs.

"There must be some words," the doctor said. "Try to find them, and let us share them together."

"It's a metaphor—you wouldn't understand it."

"Perhaps you could explain it then."

"There is a word—it means Locked Eyes, but it implies more."

"What more?"

"It's the word for sarcophagus." It meant that at certain times her vision reached only as far as the cover of her sarcophagus; that to herself, as to the dead, the world was the size of her own coffin.

"With the Locked Eyes—can you see me?"

"Like a picture only, a picture of something that is real."

The exchange was making her terribly frightened. Because of it the walls began to thrum a little, vibrating like a great, blood-pumping heart. Anterrabae was reciting an incantation in Yri, but she couldn't understand his words.

"I hope you are happy with your prying," she said to the fading doctor in her chair.

"I am not trying to frighten you," the doctor said, not seeing the walls writhe, "but there is still much to do. I wanted to ask you, since we had spoken about the tumor operations, how the world went gray suddenly after that, what the rest was like, the rest of those early years."

It was difficult speaking to a half-present shape in the grayness outside of Yr, but there was an aching sense of loss and misery about the past and if this doctor could give a form to it, the memory might be easier to endure. Deborah began to pick through the happenings, and wherever she looked there was failure and confusion. Even at the hospital where the tumor had been so successfully removed those years ago, she had somehow not been equal to the game they were playing. Its rules had been lies and tricks and she had seen through them but had not known how to respond to the play—to fall in with it and believe. The convalescence had also been hypocritical, since the illness itself had not passed.

When her sister Suzy had been born, Deborah's senses had told her that the intruder was a red-faced puckered bundle of squall and stink, but the relatives had all come crowding into the nursery, crowding her out in their wonderment at the beauty and delicacy of the newborn child. They had been shocked and angered at the truth she felt so naturally: that she thought the thing ugly, did not love it, and could not conceive of it as ever being beautiful or a companion.

"But she is your sister," they had said.

"That was not my doing. I wasn't even in on the consultation."

With that remark the family's discomfort about her had begun. A clever and precocious comment for a five-year-old, they had said, but cold, almost cruel. An honesty, they had said, but one which rose from anger and selfishness and not from love. As the years went by the aunts and uncles had stood off from Deborah, proud but not loving; and Suzy had come behind with a careless, bright sweet-ness, all woman-child, and had been loved without reservation.

Like a dybbuk or the voice of a possession, the curse proclaimed itself from Deborah's body and her mouth. It never left her. Because of the operation she was late starting school and stood apart from the first friendships and groups that the little schoolmates had formed in her absence. A kind and sorrowing mother, recognizing the fatal taint, took hold and played hostess to the girls of the most popular group. Deborah had been too heartsick to dissuade her. Perhaps through a lovely mother, taint or no, Deborah would be tolerated. And it was somewhat so. But in the neighborhood the codes of long-established wealth still prevailed and the little-girl "dirty Jew," who already accepted that she was dirty, made a good target for the bullies of the block. One of them lived next door. When he met her, he would curse her with the deep-rooted, hierarchical curse he loved: "Jew, Jew, dirty Jew; my grandmother hated your grandmother, my mother hates your mother *and I hate you!*" Three generations. It had a ring to it; even she could feel that. And in the summer there was camp.

They said it was nonsectarian, and it might have been so for the niceties which differentiated various sorts of middle-class Protestants, but she was the only Jew. They scrawled the hate-words on the walls and in the privy (that place where the evil girl with the tumor had screamed once at the release of burning urine).

The instincts of these hating children were shared, for Deborah heard sometimes that a man named Hitler was in Germany and was killing Jews with the same kind of evil joy. One spring day before she left for camp she had seen her father put his head on the kitchen table and cry terrible, wrenching men's tears about the "checks-and-the-poles." In the camp a riding instructor mentioned acidly that Hitler was doing one good thing at least, and that was getting rid of the "garbage people." She wondered idly if they all had tumors.

Deborah's world revolved around an inborn curse and a special, bitter-sweet belief in God and the Czechs and the Poles; it was full of mysteries and lies and changes. The understanding of the mysteries was tears; the reality behind the lies was death; and the changes were a secret combat in which the Jews, or Deborah, always lost.

It was at the camp that Yr had first come to her, but she did not tell the doctor of it, or of the Gods or the Collect with their great realms. From her absorption in the telling of events she looked out again and saw the doctor's expressive face indignant for her. She wanted to thank this Earth person who was capable of being moved to anger. "I did not know that they endowed Earth-ones with insides," she said musingly, and then she was very tired.

Yr was massed against her when she got back to the ward. Sitting on a hard chair, she listened to the cries and screams of the Collect and the roaring of the lower levels of Yr's realms. *Listen, Bird-one; listen Wild-horse-one; you are not of them!* The Yri words sounded an eternity of withdrawal. *Behold me!* Anterrabae fell and said, *You are playing with the Pit forever. You are walking around your destruction and poking a little finger at it here and there. You will break the seal. You will end.* And in the background: *You are not of us,* from the cruel-jawed Collect.

Anterrabae said, *You were never one of them, not ever. You are wholly different.*

There was a long, profound comfort in what

he said. Quietly and happily, Deborah set out to prove the distance across the yawning gap of difference. She had the top of a tin can, which she had found on one of her walks and picked up, both knowing and not knowing what she expected of it. The edges were rippled and sharp. She dragged the metal down the inside of her upper arm, watching the blood start slowly from the six or seven tracks that followed the metal down below the elbow. There was no pain, only the unpleasant sensation of the resistance of her flesh. The tin top was drawn down again, carefully and fastidiously following the original tracks. She worked hard, scraping deeper, ten times or so up and back until the inside of the arm was a gory swath. Then she fell asleep.

"Where's Blau? I don't see her name here."

"Oh, they moved her up to Disturbed. Cates went in the room this morning to wake her up and saw a real mess—blood on the sheets and on her face and an arm all cut up with a tin can. Ugh! A tetanus shot and right up in the elevator."

"It's funny . . . I never figured that kid was really sick. Everytime I saw her I thought: There goes the rich girl. She walked as if we were too low to look at. It was all beneath her; and the sarcastic way she said things—not what she said, really but the coldness. A spoiled little rich kid, that's all."

"Who knows what's inside them? The doctors say that all of them are sick enough to be in here and that the therapy is damn hard in those sessions."

"That snooty little bitch never did anything hard in all her life."

HELP FOR THE SEVERELY DISTURBED CHILD

Aversive Control of Self-injurious Behavior in a Psychotic Boy

B. G. Tate and George S. Baroff

As soon as Sam's hands were released for the 24-min. free-responding period he began hitting his face with his fists. The intensity of the SIRS (self-injurious behavior) immediately increased as a temper tantrum developed during which he screamed, flailed his arms about wildly, twisted his body about, hit his face and head with his fists, hit his shoulder with his chin, and banged his head with great force against the iron side rail of the bed.

Editor's Introduction

In recent years the use of punishment as a therapeutic tool has received a good deal of attention. Electric shock often has been used as the means of punishment to reduce the frequency of the behavior which immediately precedes the use of the electric shock. While electric shock as a method of shaping behavior has received recent attention, it has also aroused the concern of many in the mental health field. It is felt by many of the critics that the infliction of pain on one human being by another is barbaric. Such punishment, it is said, is cruel and should be avoided. However, the authors of this article and other behaviorists who utilize aversive stimuli in the treatment of maladaptive behavior, would argue otherwise. They contend that the use of pain can help people to unlearn behaviors that put them in greater pain, and that this is both justifiable and of therapeutic value.

Sam's case is an extreme example of self-injurious behavior. Therapists usually work with patients whose pain is of a psychological rather than a physical nature. In Sam's situation, the authors feel that his subjection to a number of brief painful experiences is more than offset by his future freedom from self-inflicted mutilation. Tate and Baroff state that, in fact, previous treatment, which did not include painful shocks, might have been reinforcing Sam's behavior. The staff could not have ignored Sam when he engaged in self-destructive behavior; therefore, whenever he would begin to harm himself, a nurse would intervene by restraining him or holding Sam's hand. This hand-holding and attention to Sam's self-destructive behavior, the authors believe, could only have been reinforcing to Sam. Of course, the nurses did not intend to strengthen Sam's disturbing behavior, but this may nevertheless have been the unwanted outcome. The authors therefore argue that the use of painful stimuli is both effective and warranted. Their major thesis is that punishment is justified when it relieves an individual of even greater pain and punishment.

Pamela Cantor

From *Behavior Research and Therapy*, 1966, pp. 281–287. Pergamon Press Ltd. Reprinted by permission.

There have been many attempts to explain self-injurious behavior (Cain, 1961; Dollard et al., 1939; Freud, 1954; Goldfarb, 1945; Greenacre, 1954; Hartmann et al., 1949; Sandler, 1964). It has been labeled masochism, auto-aggression, self-aggression, and self-destructive behaviors. The present authors prefer the term self-injurious behavior because it is more descriptive and less interpretive. Self-injurious behavior (SIB) does not imply an attempt to destroy, nor does it suggest aggression; it simply means behavior which produces physical injury to the individual's own body. Typically SIB is composed of a series of self-injurious responses (SIRS) that are repetitive and sometimes rhythmical, often with no obvious reinforcers, and therefore similar to stereotyped behavior. Common types of SIB are forceful head-banging, face slapping, punching the face and head, and scratching and biting one's body.

A patient who emits SIRS at high frequency and/or magnitude is particularly difficult to work with because the behavior interferes with the production of more desirable responses and there is always the risk of severe and permanent physical injury, e.g., head and eye damage. Usually such patients must be physically restrained or maintained on heavy dosages of drugs. Lovaas et al. (1964), however, successfully employed punishment in the form of painful electric shock to dramatically reduce the frequency of SIRS in several schizophrenic children. Ball (1966) used the same technique with a severely retarded girl and achieved similar results.

The present paper describes two punishment procedures used to control SIB in a psychotic boy. In Study I, punishment was withdrawal of human physical contact contingent on a SIR . In Study II, punishment was response-contingent painful electric shock. Following a description of the subject, the procedures and results of Studies I and II are presented, followed by a report on related behavioral changes and a general discussion.

SUBJECT

Sam was a nine-year-old blind male who was transferred for evaluation and treatment on a research basis from an out-of-state psychiatric hospital to Murdoch Center, a state institution for the mentally retarded. At the age of five he was diagnosed as autistic and was hospitalized. For the next four years he received group and individual psychotherapy, and drug therapy with no long-term benefit. Drugs were used in an effort to control self-injurious behavior, screaming, and hyperactivity.

The SIB began at about the age of four and consisted of face slapping. By age nine, his SIB repertoire included banging his head forcefully against floors, walls, and other hard objects, slapping his face with his hands, punching his face and head with his fists, hitting his shoulder with his chin, and kicking himself. Infrequently he would also pinch, bite, and scratch others.

At age eight, bilateral cataracts, a complete detachment of the left retina, and partial detachment of the right retina were discovered. An ophthalmologist has suggested that the cataracts were probably congenital but were not noticed until they matured and that the retinal detachments were likely caused by head-banging. The cataract in the right eye was removed soon after its discovery, leaving Sam with some light-dark vision and possibly some movement perception.

Upon arrival at Murdoch Center, Sam was assigned a room in the infirmary and drugs were immediately discontinued. Casual observations were made for the first two weeks while he was adapting to his new environment. Following the adaptation period, eighteen 30-min. daily observations periods were conducted during which a female research assistant held Sam, tried to interest him in games, and ignored all SIRS. These observations yielded a median daily average SIR rate of 2.3/min. (range: 0.9-7.9/min.). A second type of observation consisted of 5-min. periods four times a day at random intervals. Over a 26-day period the median daily average SIR rate was 1.7/min. (range: 0.3-4.1/min.). SIB, therefore, was a frequent form of behavior observed under a wide variety of situations.

Observations also revealed the following: Sam had a firm hematoma approximately 7 cm. in diameter on his forehead—a result of previous head-banging. His speech was limited to jargon and to approximately twenty words usually spoken in a high-pitched, whining manner and often inappropriately used. He was not considered autistic at this time because he obviously enjoyed and sought bodily contact with others. He would cling to people and try to wrap their arms around him, climb into their laps and mold himself to their contours. When left alone and free, he would cry, scream, flail his arms about, and hit himself or bang his head. When fully restrained in bed he was usually calm, but often engaged in head-rolling and hitting his chin against his shoulder.

STUDY I: CONTROL BY WITHDRAWAL AND REINSTATEMENT OF HUMAN PHYSICAL CONTACT

Early observations of Sam strongly indicated that physical contact with people was reinforcing to him and that being alone, particularly when he was standing or walking, was aversive. Study I was undertaken in an effort to learn if a procedure of withdrawing physical contact when a SIR occurred and reinstating the contact after a brief interval during which no SIRS occurred could be used to control Sam's SIB.

Procedure

Study I began on the fourth day following the end of the 26-day observation period mentioned. During the three weeks preceding the commencement of the study, Sam was restrained in his bed except for morning baths given by attendants and for daily walks around the campus and through the infirmary corridors with two female research assistants (Es). During the walks Es held Sam's hands and chatted to him and to each other and ignored SIRS.

Study I consisted of twenty daily 20-min. sessions run at the same time each day by the same Es. There were five control sessions (SIRS were ignored), followed by five experimental sessions (SIRS were punished), five control sessions, and five experimental sessions.

Control sessions consisted of a walk around the campus with the two Es who chatted with Sam and with each other. Sam walked between them, holding onto a hand of each. When he emitted SIRS the Es ignored them.

Experimental sessions were identical to the control sessions except that when Sam hit himself, Es jerked their hands free so that he had no physical contact with them. The time-out from physical contact lasted 3 sec. following the last SIR. At the end of 3 sec., Es allowed him to grasp their hands and the walk resumed. No comments were made to Sam when a hit occurred—the only responses to the SIR were withdrawal of contact and cessation of talk if Es were talking at the time.

All sessions began when Sam left his room and entered the corridor leading outside the building. The same route around the campus was followed each day. Each session ended while he was outside the building, but the procedure for the particular session was continued until Sam was returned to his room, undres ·d, placed in bed, and restrained—usually about 12 additional min. Records were

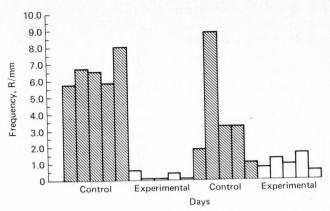

Figure 15-1   Effect of the punishment procedure of Study 1 on the daily average frequency of SIRs. On experimental days SIRs were followed by withdrawal of human physical contact and reinstatement of contact after a minimum interval of three seconds. On control days the SIRs were ignored.

kept by one E who silently marked the SIRS on a piece of paper during the walks.

Results of Study I

Virtually all of the SIRS made during the sessions were chin-to-shoulder hits. On a few occasions Sam would punch his head with his fist during punishment but he rarely withdrew his hand from an assistant and hit himself.

Figure 15-1 presents the average SIRS per min. for each day of the study. The median average rate of SIRS for the first 5 control days was 6.6 responses per min. and sharply declined to a median average of 0.1 responses per min. for the following 5 experimental days. The response rate recovered somewhat (median average = 3.3) during the second 5 control days and decreased again during the second 5 experimental days (median average = 1.0). The unusually high rate of SIRS on the second day of the second control run was associated with a temper tantrum which lasted about 15 min.

On the experimental days an interesting change in Sam's behavior occurred which was noticed by both Es and the authors. On con-

trol days Sam typically whined, cried, hesitated often in his walk, and seemed unresponsive to the environment in general. His behavior on experimental days was completely different—he appeared to attend more to environmental stimuli, including the Es; there was no crying or whining, and he often smiled. A brief discussion of this change in behavior appears at the end of the paper.

The results of this study indicate that the relatively simple procedure of controlling the contingencies of this chronic SIB produced a dramatic reduction in its frequency. Of interest also are the relative effects of punishing the SIR and ignoring it. These results do not, of course, mean that long-term effects would be the same.

STUDY II: CONTROL BY ELECTRIC SHOCK

Although the SIB could be reduced by response-contingent withdrawal of physical contact, it was decided that the risk of completely destroying the right retina by further head-banging was great enough to preclude the long-term use of this method. Parental permission was then obtained for the use of painful electric shock.

The shock apparatus was a stock prod (Sears & Roebuck Number 325971) similar to one used by Lovaas et al. (1964). The prod was a cylinder 58 cm. long and 3 cm. in diameter containing seven D cells and an induction coil. With fresh batteries approximately 130 V were available at the two 0.48 cm. diameter terminals, 1.24 cm. apart, projecting from one end of the prod. Shock was administered by turning the induction coil on and touching the terminals to the bare skin of the patient.

Study II began 46 hours after the termination of Study I.

Procedure

For 24 min. prior to the administration of electric shock, Sam was allowed a free-responding period. The authors, accompanied by a physician, entered Sam's room, talked to him pleasantly and freed his hands, leaving him lying in bed with both feet restrained. They remained close to his bed while an assistant in an adjoining room recorded each SIR. After 24 min. of observing and recording the free-responding behavior, it was explained to Sam that if he continued to hit himself he would be shocked, and the shock would hurt. A shock of approximately 0.5 seconds duration then immediately followed each SIR. No more comments were made to Sam concerning the shock which was delivered to the lower right leg.

The contingent shock period was continued for 90 min. After the first two shocks were administered, Sam's feet were untied and he was placed in a sitting position in bed. The authors talked pleasantly to him and encouraged him to play with toys. Approximately 1 hour after the first shock he was placed in a rocking chair for 30 min. Sam was then returned to his bed and left alone unrestrained, while being observed for another 90 min. over

closed-circuit television. Contingent shock was continued, but there was a delay of 30-35 sec. between the SIR and the adminstration of punishment (time required to reach Sam's room from the observation room).

Shock was continued on subsequent days and was sometimes delivered immediately and sometimes delayed 30 sec. depending on whether the therapist was with Sam or observing him on television. At night he was restrained in bed at the wrists and ankles with cloth restraints.

Results of Study II

As soon as Sam's hands were released for the 24-min. free-responding period he began hitting his face with his fists. The intensity of the SIRS immediately increased as a temper tantrum developed during which he screamed, flailed his arms about wildly, twisted his body about, hit his face and head with his fists, hit his shoulder with his chin, and banged his head with great force against the iron side rail of the bed. The head-banging was so forceful that it was necessary to cushion the blows by placing the authors' hands over the bed rail. The average rate of SIRS during the 6-min. temper tantrum was 14.0 per min. During the next 18 min. he became calmer and the average rate dropped to 2.0 responses per min.

During the first 90-min. contingent shock period a total of only five SIRS were emitted (average rate = 0.06 responses per min.). The shocks produced a startled reaction in Sam and avoidance movements, but no cries. The authors talked to him, praised virtually all non-injurious responses, and generally behaved pleasantly. When led from the bed to the rocking chair, he immediately began crying and flailing his arms. A SIR was promptly followed by a shock and he became calm. A few seconds later he was sitting in the chair and smiling with apparent pleasure. At the end of the 90-min period Sam was returned to his bed and left in it free while being observed over closed-circuit television. Throughout the second 90-min. observation period he remained quietly in bed posturing with his hands. Four SIRS were emitted and were followed by delayed shocks. The SIR rate had decreased from 2.0/min. in the last minutes of the free responding period to 0.04/min. At the end of the period a meal was offered which he refused. He was then restrained for the night.

The following day Sam was free from 9:00 A.M. until 2:30 P.M. All of this time was spent in bed with toys except for 1 hour in the afternoon during which the authors encouraged him to rock in a rocking chair and walk around his room. Twenty SIRS of light intensity occurred during the 5½-hour period (average rate = 0.06 responses per min.). Four of these were followed by immediate shock and the other sixteen by delayed shock.

On the second day following the commencement of shock Sam was free from 8:00 A.M. until 4:30 P.M. There were only fifteen SIRS during the entire day (average rate = 0.03/min.) but most of these occurred during one brief period of agitation at noon. He was out of bed about 3 hours being rocked, walked, and entertained with toys.

In the ensuing days Sam's daily activities were gradually increased until he remained out of bed 9 hours a day. He was still restrained at night because of limited personnel available to check him. He began attending physical therapy classes for the severely retarded 3 hours a day where he was encouraged to play with a variety of toys. He now apparently enjoys walks, playground equipment, and playing "games" involving following directions and making discriminations, for example, various objects (ball, book, music box, etc.) are put on a table across the room and he is asked to bring a specific one to E. He is more spontaneous in his activities than he was when he arrived and he is now capable of walking and running alone without clinging to people.

Punishment of SIRS with shock was continued and the decline in rate progressed. Since the beginning of shock 167 days have elapsed. The last observed SIR was emitted on day 147.

OTHER CHANGES IN BEHAVIOR

Sam's intake of food and liquids had undergone an over-all decrease since his admission although there were wide day-to-day fluctuations. Three months after his admission (5 days before the use of shock), his weight had decreased by 14 pounds (20 per cent). On days when he ate nothing, he usually held great quantitites of saliva in his mouth for hours—emptying his mouth only by accident or when forced to. In the 36 hours preceding the commencement of shock, Sam ate only a small portion of one meal and drank only 400 ml. of liquids. Supper was refused on the day shock was first administered. The following day he drank a small quantity of milk and ate some cereal for breakfast, but all other liquids and food were refused during the day—he had started saving saliva again. In addition he was posturing with his hands most of the day (posturing had been observed before any treatment began).

On the second day following the commencement of shock he refused all food during the morning. At 2:00 P.M., he was again offered juice which he refused. He was then told firmly to drink but he would not open his mouth. It was then discovered that a firm command followed by the buzz of the stock prod (but no shock delivered), would cause him to open his mouth and take the juice, but he then held it in his mouth without swallowing. Again, a command and a buzz produced swallowing. The sequence of "Drink," and "Swallow" was repeated until he had consumed all of the juice. Verbal praise and affectionate pats were used to reinforce each desirable response. With this procedure, command-buzz-reinforcement, he drank a glass of milk and ate some ice cream. This was the most food he had consumed in 4 days. Only one shock was actually administered—buzzing of the prod was sufficient the other times. This procedure was continued for the evening meal and the following day. On the third day he began eating spontaneously and had continued, although there are still occasions when he has to be prompted. In the following 15 days he gained 10 pounds and his weight continues to increase, but at a normal rate.

The posturing was stopped in similar fashion. When, for example, Sam held his hands up instead of down by his sides, he was told firmly to put his hands down, and if he did not, the buzzing of the prod was presented. The act of holding saliva in his mouth was stopped by telling him firmly to swallow and sounding the prod if he did not obey. The same procedure was effective in reducing his clinging to people.

DISCUSSION

Both punishment procedures effectively reduced SIB in this psychotic boy. Aversive control by withdrawal of physical contact was immediately effective both times it was used.

Aversive control by painful electric shock also reduced the SIB immediately and has remained effective over a 6-month period. In addition, it was found that eating behavior could be reinstated, posturing could be stopped, and saliva-saving and clinging could be terminated by firm commands followed by the sound of the shock apparatus if there was no compliance, and followed by social reinforcement if compliance occurred. Over the

6-month period since the inception of shock, its use has decreased. Part of the beneficial effects of punishment by shock obviously were derived from the more stimulating environment provided him following the initial treatment—an envirnoment which could not have been provided had the SIR rate not been suppressed to avoid injury. A secondary gain was probably derived from the marked positive change in behavior of attendants and nurses toward Sam. It should also be noted that punishment by electric shock prevented accidental reinforcement of SIRS. Before any treatment began it was sometimes necessary to interfere with SIRS by holding Sam's arms, a procedure which may have been reinforcing to him. No deleterious effects of the shock were observed.

An intriguing area of speculation is how to account for the complete change in behavior observed on experimental days of Study I and observed often after shock was delivered in Study II. One plausible explanation for the difference in behavior is that the whining, crying, and SIB belong to the same response class and the suppression of SIB also suppresses these other behaviors. Once the undesirable behaviors are suppressed the more desirable ones, e.g., smiling, listening, attending to the environment, and cooperating with others can occur.

Another conjecture is that both types of punishment produce a general arousal in the central nervous system which results in increased attention (Hebb, 1955). Attention to the external environment could account for the cooperative behavior, smiling and apparent listening. This idea is further supported by the immediacy of the punishment effect—not only did SIB, whining, crying, and negativistic behavior cease abruptly, but within seconds the more desirable behaviors emerged.

REFERENCES

Ball, T. S. (1965) Personal communication.

Cain, A. C. (1961) The presuperego turning inward of aggression. *Psychoanal. Q.* **30**, 171–208.

Dollard, J., Doob, L. W., Miller, N. E., Mowrer, O. H., & Sears, R. R. (1939), *Frustration and Aggression.* Yale University Press, New Haven.

Freud, A. (1954) Problems of infantile neurosis: a discussion. In *The Psychoanalytic Study of the Child*, Vol. IX. International Universities Press, New York.

Goldfarb, W. (1945) Psychological privation in infancy. *Am. J. Orthopsychiat.* **15**, 247–255.

Greenacre, P. (1954) Problems of infantile neurosis: a discussion. In *The Psychoanalytic Study of the Child*, Vol. IX. International Universities Press, New York.

Hartmann, H., Kris, E., & Loewenstein, R. M. (1949) Notes on the theory of aggression. In *The Psychoanalytic Study of the Child.* Vols. III-IV. International Universities Press, New York.

Hebb, D. O. (1955) Drives and the C.N.S. (Conceptual Nervous System). *Psychol. Rev.* **62**, 243–254.

Lovaas, O. I., Freitag, G., Kinder, M. I., Rubenstein, D. B., Schaeffer, B., & Simmons, J. B. (1964) *Experimental Studies in Childhood Schizophrenia. Developing Social Behavior Using Electric Shock.* Paper read at American Psychological Association Annual Convention, Los Angeles, California.

Sandler, J. (1964) Masochism: an empirical analysis. *Psychol. Bull.* **62**, 197–204.